Organizational Behaviour

Improving Performance and Commitment in the Workplace

CANADIAN EDITION

JASON A. COLQUITT
University of Florida

JEFFERY A. LEPINE
University of Florida

MICHAEL J. WESSON
Texas A&M University

IAN R. GELLATLY
University of Alberta

The McGraw·Hill Companies

McGraw-Hill Ryerson
Connect. Learn. Succeed.

**Organizational Behaviour: Improving Performance and Commitment in the Workplace
Canadian Edition**

ISBN-13: 978-0-07-096745-8
ISBN-10: 0-07-096745-8

1 2 3 4 5 6 7 8 9 10 TCP 1 9 8 7 6 5 4 3 2 1 0

Printed and bound in Canada

Vice-President and Editor-in-Chief: Joanna Cotton
Senior Sponsoring Editor: Kim Brewster
Managing Editor, Development: Kelly Dickson
Developmental Editor: Tracey Haggert
Marketing Manager: Cathie Lefebvre
Senior Editorial Associate: Christine Lomas
Manager, Editorial Services: Margaret Henderson
Supervising Editor: Cathy Biribauer
Copy Editor: Michael Kelly
Permissions Editor: My Editor Inc.
Team Lead, Production: Jennifer Hall
Inside Design: Michelle Losier
Composition: Heather Brunton / ArtPlus Design & Communications
Cover Design: Michelle Losier
Cover Image: © NBC/PhotoFest
Printer: Transcontinental Printing Group

Library and Archives Canada Cataloguing in Publication Data
Colquitt, Jason
Organizational behaviour : improving performance and commitment in the workplace / Jason A. Colquitt, Jeffery A. Lepine, Michael J. Wesson. — 1st Canadian ed.

Includes index.

ISBN 978-0-07-096745-8

1. Organizational behavior — Textbooks. 2. Personnel management — Textbooks. I. Lepine, Jeffery A. II. Wesson, Michael J. III. Title.

HD58.7.C6256 2010 658.3 C2009-901991-4

Dedication

To Catherine, Cameron, Riley, and Connor, and also to Mom, Dad, Alan, and Shawn. The most wonderful family I could imagine, two times over.

—J.A.C.

To my parents who made me, and to Marcie, Izzy, and Eli, who made my life complete.

—J.A.L.

To Liesl and Dylan: Their support in all I do is incomparable. They are my life and I love them both. To my parents: They provide a foundation that never wavers.

—M.J.W.

To my parents, Roy and Beverly, who taught me everything I ever needed to know about commitment, unconditional love, and achievement striving.
To my brother, Duncan, who left this life too soon.

—I.R.G.

About the Authors

JASON A. COLQUITT is a professor in the management department at the University of Florida's Warrington College of Business. He received his PhD from Michigan State University's Eli Broad Graduate School of Management and earned his BS in psychology from Indiana University. He teaches organizational behaviour and human resource management at the undergraduate, masters, and executive levels and also teaches research methods at the doctoral level. He was recognized as one of the Warrington College's Teachers of the Year due to his high marks in the classroom.

Jason's research interests include organizational justice, trust, team effectiveness, and personality influences on task and learning performance. He has published more than 20 articles on these and other topics in *Academy of Management Journal, Academy of Management Review, Journal of Applied Psychology, Organizational Behavior and Human Decision Processes,* and *Personnel Psychology.* He is currently serving as an associate editor for *Academy of Management Journal* and has served (or is serving) on a number of editorial boards, including *Academy of Management Journal, Journal of Applied Psychology, Organizational Behavior and Human Decision Processes, Personnel Psychology, Journal of Management,* and *International Journal of Conflict Management.* He is a recipient of the Society for Industrial and Organizational Psychology's Distinguished Early Career Contributions Award and the Cummings Scholar Award for early to mid-career achievement, sponsored by the Organizational Behavior division of the Academy of Management. He was also elected to be a Representative-at-Large for the Organizational Behavior division.

Jason enjoys spending time with his wife, Catherine, and three sons, Cameron, Riley, and Connor. His hobbies include playing basketball, playing the trumpet, watching movies, and rooting on (in no particular order) the Pacers, Colts, Cubs, Hoosiers, Spartans, and Gators.

JEFFERY A. LEPINE is the Darden Restaurants Diversity Management Professor at the Warrington College of Business, University of Florida. He received his PhD in organizational behaviour from the Eli Broad Graduate School of Management at Michigan State University. He also earned an MS in management from Florida State University and a BS in finance from the University of Connecticut. He teaches organizational behaviour, human resource management, and management of groups and teams at undergraduate and graduate levels.

Jeff's research interests include team functioning and effectiveness, individual and team adaptation, citizenship behaviour, voice, and occupational stress. He has published more than 20 articles on these and other topics in *Academy of Management Journal, Academy of Management Review, Journal of Applied Psychology, Organizational Behavior and Human Decision Processes,* and *Personnel Psychology.* He is currently serving or has served on the editorial boards of *Academy of Management Journal, Journal of Applied Psychology, Organizational Behavior and Human Decision Processes, Personnel Psychology, Journal of Management, Journal of Organizational Behavior,* and *Journal of Occupational and Organizational Psychology.* He is a recipient of the Society for Industrial and Organizational Psychology's Distinguished Early Career Contributions Award and the Cummings Scholar Award for early to mid-career achievement, sponsored by the Organizational Behavior division of the Academy of Management. He was also elected to the Executive Committee of the Human Resource division of the Academy of Management. Prior to earning his PhD, Jeff was an officer in the U.S. Air Force.

Jeff spends most of his free time having fun with his family. He also enjoys playing guitar, avoiding sharks, devising ways to keep mole crickets off his lawn, and watching NCAA championship games.

MICHAEL J. WESSON is an associate professor in the management department at Texas A&M University's Mays Business School. He received his PhD from Michigan State University's Eli Broad Graduate School of Management. He also holds an MS in human resource management from Texas A&M University and a BBA from Baylor University. He has taught organizational behaviour and human resource management–based classes at all levels but currently spends most of his time teaching Mays MBAs, EMBAs, and executive development at Texas A&M. He was awarded Texas A&M's Montague Center for Teaching Excellence Award.

Michael's research interests include organizational justice, goal-setting, organizational entry (employee recruitment, selection, and socialization), person–organization fit, and compensation and benefits. His articles have been published in journals such as *Journal of Applied Psychology, Personnel Psychology, Academy of Management Review,* and *Organizational Behavior and Human Decision Processes.* He currently serves on the editorial boards of the *Journal of Applied Psychology* and the *Journal of Organizational Behavior* and is an ad hoc reviewer for many others. He is active in the Academy of Management and the Society for Industrial and Organizational Psychology. Prior to returning to school, Michael worked as a human resources manager for a *Fortune* 500 firm. He has served as a consultant to the automotive supplier, health care, oil and gas, and technology industries in areas dealing with recruiting, selection, onboarding, compensation, and turnover.

Michael spends most of his time trying to keep up with his wife Liesl and son Dylan. He is a self-admitted food and wine snob, home theatre aficionado, and college sports addict (Gig 'em Aggies!).

IAN R. GELLATLY is a professor in the department of strategic management and organization at the University of Alberta's School of Business. He received his PhD in industrial and organizational psychology from the University of Western Ontario. Prior to joining the University of Alberta in 1998, Ian taught in the faculty of management at the University of Lethbridge. Ian teaches a variety of undergraduate- and graduate-level seminars. At the undergraduate level, Ian teaches courses in organizational behaviour, human resource management, staffing, and performance management and rewards. Within the MBA program, Ian has taught human resource management. Ian is active in the PhD program and teaches the doctoral seminar in organizational behaviour.

Ian's research interests include: (a) the three-component model of organizational commitment, (b) employees' motivation to engage in a variety of work behaviours (e.g., performance, citizenship), (c) the personal and social/organizational determinants of employee absenteeism, and (d) personality-behaviour relations. He has published more than 20 articles on these and other topics in *Journal of Applied Psychology, Journal of Organizational Behavior, Journal of Vocational Behavior, Human Performance,* and *Human Resource Management.* He currently serves on the editorial board of the *Journal of Applied Psychology* and is an ad hoc reviewer for many other journals.

Ian enjoys spending time with his two children, Kyle and Kaitlyn. His hobbies include squash, cycling, playing guitars, rock concerts, travel (road trips), spending time in western Canada's mountain parks, home renovations, discussing politics, watching James Bond movies, live NHL hockey (Go Oilers!), Sudoku puzzles, and visiting family, friends, and colleagues.

Brief Contents

Contents

CHAPTER 10 Team Characteristics and Processes 249

CHAPTER 11 Power and Influence 283

CHAPTER 12 Leadership Styles and Behaviours 310

CHAPTER 13 Organizational Structure 340

Preface

Why did we decide to write this textbook? Well, for starters, organizational behaviour (OB) remains a fascinating topic that everyone can relate to (because everyone either has worked or is going to work in the future). What makes people effective at their job? What makes them want to stay with their employer? What makes work enjoyable? Those are all fundamental questions that organizational behaviour research can help answer. However, our desire to write this book also grew out of our own experiences (and frustrations) teaching OB courses using other textbooks. We found that students would end the semester with a common set of questions that we felt we could answer if given the chance to write our own book. With that in mind, *Organizational Behaviour: Improving Performance and Commitment in the Workplace,* was written with the following questions in mind.

DOES ANY OF THIS STUFF REALLY MATTER?

Organizational behaviour might be the most relevant class any student ever takes, but that doesn't always shine through in OB texts. The introductory section of our book contains two chapters not included in other books: "Job Performance" and "Organizational Commitment." Being good at one's job and wanting to stay with one's employer are obviously critical concerns for employees and managers alike. After describing these topics in detail, every remaining chapter in the book links that chapter's content to performance and commitment. Students can then better appreciate the practical relevance of organizational behaviour concepts.

IF THAT THEORY DOESN'T WORK, THEN WHY IS IT IN THE BOOK?

In putting together this book, we were guided by the question, "What would OB texts look like if all of them were first written in 2010?" We found that many of the organizational behaviour texts on the market include outdated (and indeed, scientifically disproven!) models or theories, presenting them sometimes as fact, or possibly for the sake of completeness or historical context. Our students were always frustrated by the fact that they had to read about, learn, and potentially be tested on material that we would tell them in class we knew to be wrong. Although we believe that historical context can be important at times, we believe that focusing on what we really know at this point is paramount in today's fast-paced classes. Thus, this textbook includes new and emerging topics that others leave out and excludes flawed and outdated topics that some other books leave in.

HOW DOES ALL THIS STUFF FIT TOGETHER?

Organizational behaviour is a diverse and multidisciplinary field, and it's not always easy to see how all its topics fit together. Our book deals with this issue in two ways. First, all the chapters in our book are organized around an integrative model that opens each chapter (see Figure 1-1). That model provides students with a roadmap of the course, showing them where they've been and where they're going. Second, our chapters are tightly focused around specific topics and aren't "grab-baggish" in nature. Our hope is that students (and instructors) won't ever come across a topic and think, "Why is this topic being discussed in this chapter?"

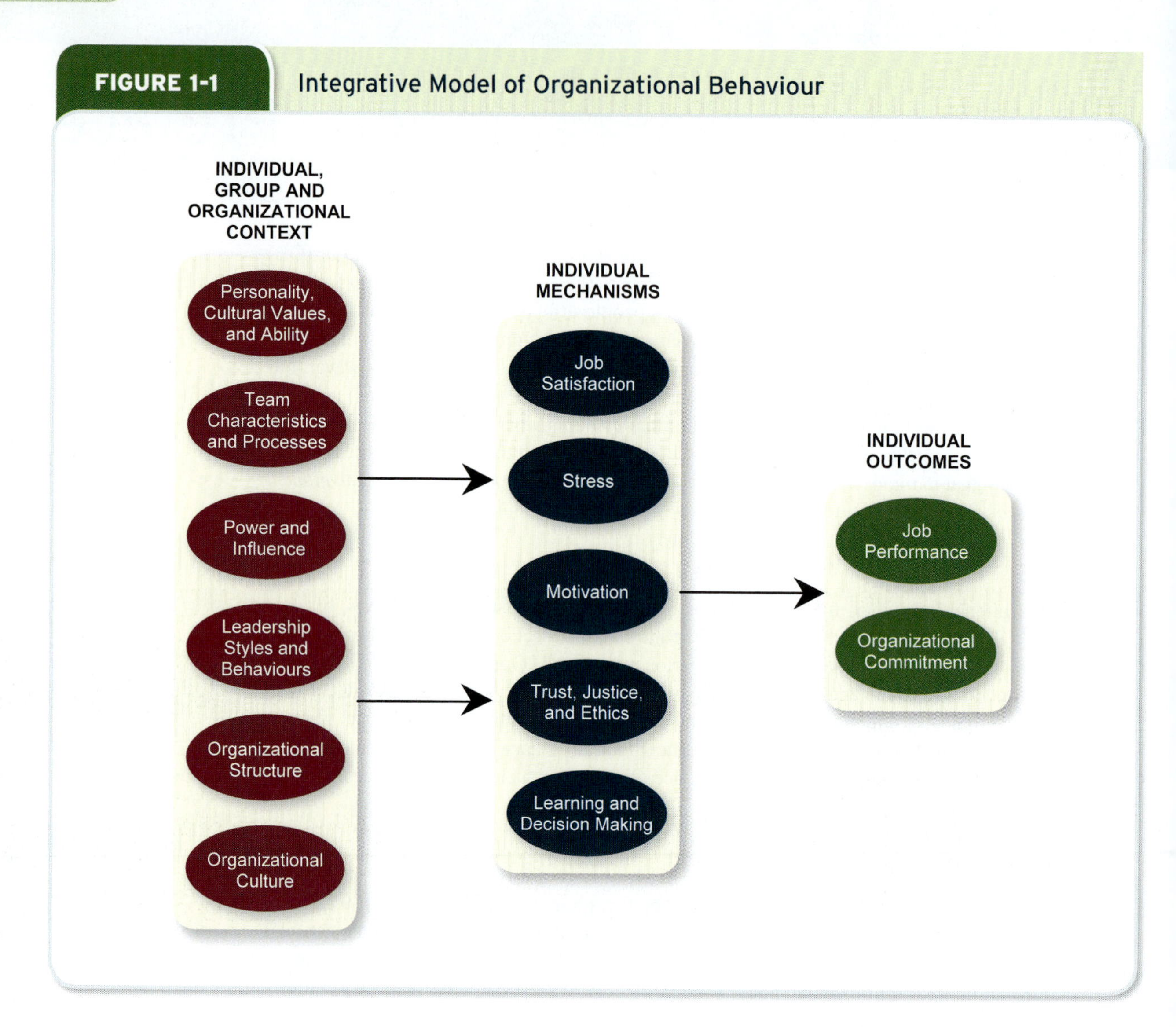

DOES THIS STUFF HAVE TO BE SO DRY?

Research on motivation to learn shows that students learn more when they have an intrinsic interest in the topic, but many organizational behaviour texts do little to stimulate that interest. Put simply, we wanted to create a book that students enjoy reading. To do that, we used a more informal, conversational style when writing the book. We also tried to use company examples that students will be familiar with and find compelling. We included insert boxes, self-assessments, and exercises that students should find engaging (and sometimes even entertaining!).

These questions come up in OB classes of all types, including undergraduate, masters, and executive courses. We therefore believe that *Organizational Behaviour: Improving Performance and Commitment in the Workplace* will be appealing to OB students of all varieties, regardless of the class level, university type, or course format.

Special Features: OB Insert Boxes

As you probably noticed from our choice of covers, we see organizational behaviour—the good, the bad, and the ugly—at work everywhere. The OB insert boxes take OB out of the classroom and show students how the OB concepts in each chapter apply to so much more than just the workplace.

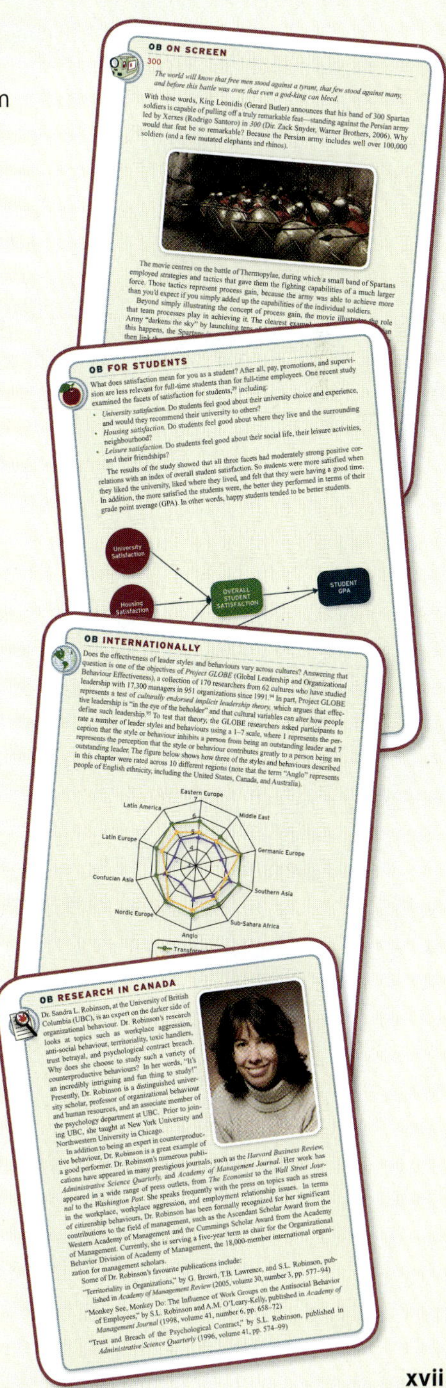

OB ON SCREEN

This feature uses movie quotes and scenes from recent and classic films to illustrate organizational behaviour concepts. From *Office Space* to *The Break-Up*, *Talledega Nights* to *The Queen*, Hollywood continues to offer rich, vivid, examples of OB in action.

OB FOR STUDENTS

Whether undergraduates, masters, or executives, everyone enrolled in an organizational behaviour class has one thing in common: They're students. This feature applies OB theories and concepts to student life. It examines questions like the following: "What makes students satisfied with their university?" "What personality traits improve performance in student groups?" and "Should student grades be kept secret from recruiters?"

OB INTERNATIONALLY

Changes in technology, communications, and economic forces have made business more global and international than ever. This feature spotlights the impact of globalization on the organizational behaviour concepts described in this book. It describes cross-cultural differences in OB theories, how to apply them in international corporations, and how to use OB to manage cultural diversity in the workplace.

OB RESEARCH IN CANADA

An important theme in this book is to present and discuss concepts, models, and theories that have been tested and validated using carefully applied scientific methods. But who are the people behind the research findings? What is it about OB that captivates their attention? Of the many scientific papers they have published, what are some of their very favourite works? In this textbook we introduce a number of Canadian-based researchers who are recognized as experts in one or more of the topic areas we will be reading about.

Special Features: In-Chapter Sections

Throughout each chapter, we have included features that we feel will help facilitate learning, clarify concepts, and keep students focused on what is important in each chapter.

LEARNING OUTCOMES

To help students identify the key concepts being explored in the chapter, we have opened each chapter with a list of questions they should be able answer at the conclusion of the chapter. These Learning Outcomes are then referenced in the page margins of the chapter discussion so that students can easily discover where each topic is being explored.

CHAPTER-OPENING VIGNETTES

We want students to be able to recognize organizational behaviour concepts at work, and the chapter-opening vignettes feature events and people in real organizations to encourage students to critically evaluate and apply each situation to the chapter content.

MARGIN TERMS

Students often find that they are bombarded by terms and concepts, and that it is difficult to keep them all straight. To mitigate this challenge, we have highlighted key terms and placed the definitions in the text margins. This way, terms appear where they are discussed and students are able get to know the language of organizational behaviour.

Special Features: End-of-Chapter Sections

Chapters conclude with a series of features that provide a tie-in to the chapter-opening features or reinforce chapter concepts through additional experiential material.

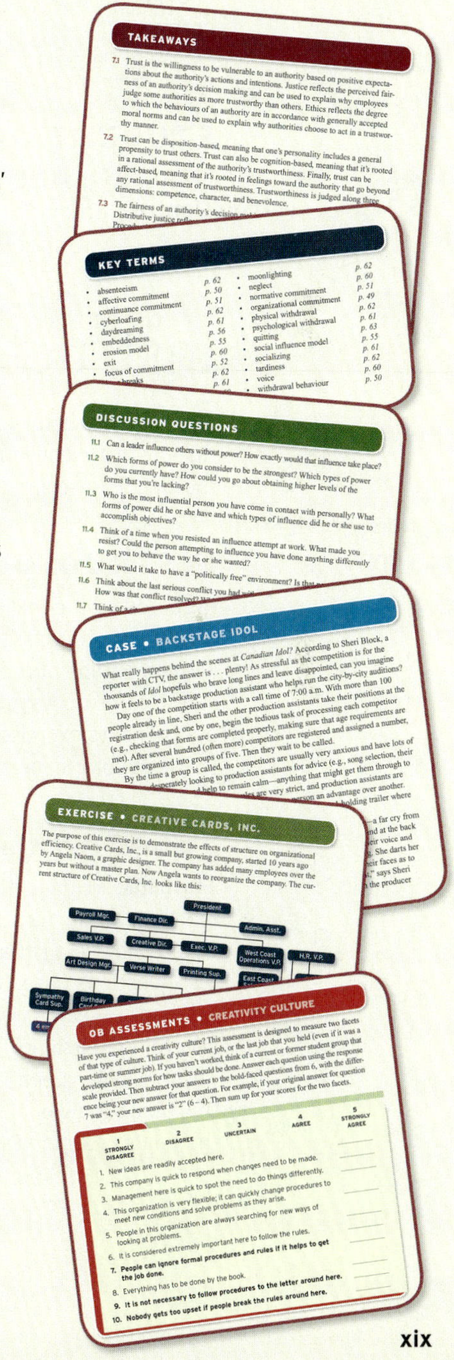

TAKEAWAYS

Students are always asking, "What are the most important 'takeaways' from this chapter?" This section gives a point-by-point review of the Learning Outcomes found at the beginning of each chapter.

KEY TERMS

This end-of-chapter list of the key terms featured in the chapter includes page numbers for quick cross-referencing. All terms and definitions are also available in the Glossary at the end of the text.

DISCUSSION QUESTIONS

Not only for review purposes, our Discussion Questions ask students to apply concepts in the chapter to their own lives and experiences.

CASES

To help bring students full circle, a case appears at the end of every chapter, providing a follow-up to the company or organization highlighted in the chapter's opening vignette.

EXERCISES

Each chapter features an OB-related exercise: Some of them we have created ourselves over the years, but we also included some "classics" that are tried and true and that nearly everyone we know uses in class.

OB ASSESSMENTS

We close each chapter with a feature designed to help students find out where they stand on key OB concepts covered in the chapter. Students gain insights into their personality, their emotional intelligence, their style of leadership, and their ability to cope with stress, which can help them understand their reactions to the working world.

Student Resources

CONNECT ORGANIZATIONAL BEHAVIOUR

Connect—Available 24/7 with instant feedback so you can study when you want, how you want, and where you want. Take advantage of the Study Plan—an innovative tool that helps students customize their own learning experience. Students can diagnose their knowledge with pre- and post-tests, identify the areas where they need help, search contents of the entire learning package for content specific to the topic they're studying, and add these resources to their study plan. Visit **www.connectob.ca** to register—take practice quizzes, run interactive scenarios, and much more. Also visit the Student Online Learning Centre for additional study tools.

STUDENT ONLINE LEARNING CENTRE (OLC)

The OLC at **www.mcgrawhill.ca/olc/colquitt** includes practice questions in a format similar to those found in the test bank, links to relevant external Web sites, and other valuable resources for students.

Instructor Resources

Allowing instructors to create a customized multimedia presentation, all our instructor resources are conveniently housed on the password-protected Instructor's section of the Online Learning Centre.

INSTRUCTOR'S MANUAL

Prepared by the text author Ian Gellatly, this manual was developed to help with organizing your classroom presentation. It contains an extensive "chapter roadmap" with an outline of the chapter, Teaching Tips (e.g., hints on how to handle difficult topics), suggestions on ways to maximize the use of in-chapter pedagogy and the usage of assessments/exercises in the text, and suggested resources for exploring topics related to the chapter content.

TESTBANK AND EZ TEST ONLINE

Testbank: Our Testbank contains a variety of true/false, multiple-choice, and short- and long-essay questions, as well as "scenario-based" questions, which are application-based and use a situation described in a narrative, with three to five multiple-choice test questions based on the situation described in the narrative. We've aligned our Testbank questions with Bloom's Taxonomy and AACSB guidelines, tagging each question according to its knowledge and skills areas. Categories include Global, Ethics and Social Responsibility, Legal and Other External Environment, Communication, Diversity, Group Dynamics, Individual Dynamics, Production, and IT. Designations aligning questions with the text's Learning Outcomes and features exist as well.

EZ Test Online: McGraw-Hill's EZ Test Online is a flexible and easy-to-use electronic testing program. The program allows instructors to create tests from book-specific items, accommodates a wide range of question types, and enables instructors to add their own questions. Multiple versions of the test can be created, and any test can be exported for use with course management systems such as WebCT, BlackBoard, or any other course management system. EZ Test Online is accessible to busy instructors virtually anywhere via the Web, and the program eliminates the need to install test software. For more information about EZ Test Online, please see the Web site at **www.eztestonline.com**.

POWERPOINT PRESENTATION SLIDES

Based on instructor feedback, the PowerPoint presentation slides consist of two types of presentations: **Outline** and **Detailed** formats that give instructors the flexibility to tailor their presentations to their class needs. The Outline format follows a "don't give them everything" philosophy, which requires students to attend class and take notes to have all the information available to them. The Outline format therefore leaves a significant amount of room on the slides for students to take notes but still maintains the use of tables and figures straight from the book. The Detailed set builds on the outline format to include full definitions and descriptions for the topics covered. This format is designed for instructors who prefer that the students be listening to them instead of taking basic, definition-oriented notes during class. Each format has advantages and disadvantages, but the provision of multiple sets of slides should make it easier for instructors to access ready-made presentations designed to fit their teaching style.

ORGANIZATIONAL BEHAVIOUR VIDEO DVD

For instructors who want to incorporate more "real-world" examples into the classroom, *Organizational Behaviour: Improving Performance and Commitment in the Workplace* offers this compilation video DVD, which features news clips on OB-related topics from NBC, PBS, and *BusinessWeek* TV. Videos are organized by topic and include such companies as Disney Imagineering, 1154 LILL, Johnson & Johnson, and Xerox, as well as topics such as Outsourcing, Work/Life Balance, Layoffs and Their Psychological Effects, Discrimination, and Employees with Passion. Instructor Notes can be found in the Instructor section of the Online Learning Centre. Quizzes on each video can also be found in the Student section of the Online Learning Centre.

ONLINE LEARNING CENTRE (www.mcgrawhill.ca/olc/colquitt)

If you're looking for a one-stop shopping area for all things OB, look no further than our Online Learning Centre. Separated into both Instructor and Student areas, each section holds a variety of material for instructors to develop and use in their course and for students to use to review. Instructors will find supplements, an image bank from the text, additional course materials, and links to the Management Asset Gallery, Group and Video Resource Manual, and Manager's HotSeat Online.

MANAGEMENT ASSET GALLERY

McGraw-Hill Ryerson, in conjunction with McGraw-Hill/Irwin Management, is excited to now provide a one-stop-shop for our wealth of assets, making it super quick and easy for instructors to locate specific materials to enhance their courses. The Asset Gallery includes our non-text-specific management resources (Self-Assessments, Test Your Knowledge exercises, videos and information, additional group and individual exercises) along with supporting PowerPoint® and Instructor Manual materials.

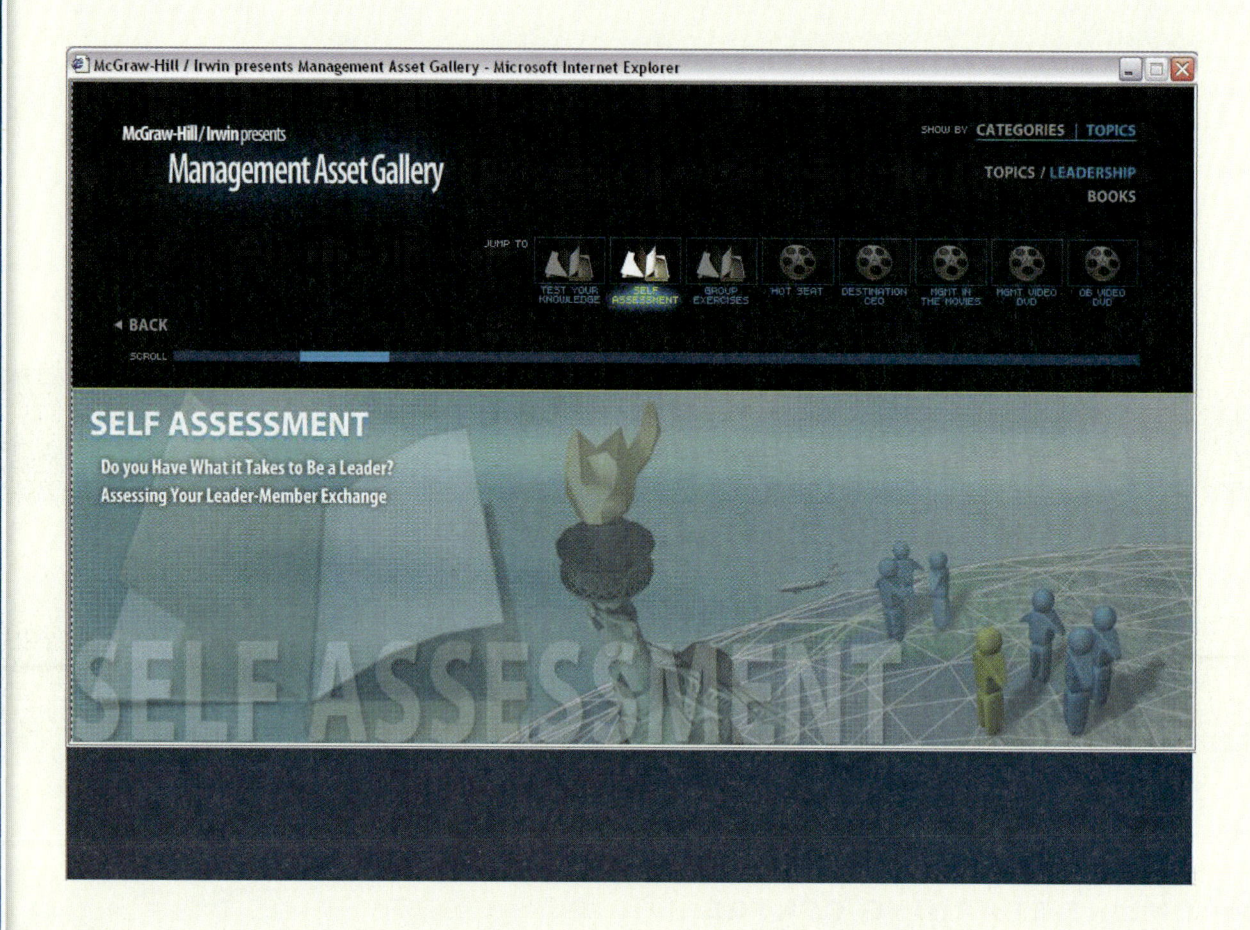

MANAGER'S HOTSEAT ONLINE (www.mhhe.com/mhs)

In today's workplace, managers are confronted daily with issues involving ethics, diversity, working in teams, and the virtual workplace. The Manager's HotSeat offers interactive software that allows students to watch as 15 real managers apply their years of experience to confront these issues. Students assume the role of the manager as they watch the video and answer multiple-choice questions that pop up, forcing them to make decisions on the spot. They learn from the manager's mistakes and successes, and then write a report critiquing the manager's approach by defending their reasoning. Reports can be e-mailed or printed out for credit. These video segments are a powerful tool for your course that truly immerses students in the learning experience. Ask your McGraw-Hill sales representative how you can obtain access.

GROUP AND VIDEO RESOURCE MANUAL: AN INSTRUCTOR'S GUIDE TO AN ACTIVE CLASSROOM (www.mhhe.com/mobmanual)

This manual, created for instructors, contains everything needed to integrate activities successfully into the classroom. It includes a menu of items to use as teaching tools in class. All of our interactive Self-Assessment exercises, Test Your Knowledge quizzes, group exercises, and Manager's HotSeat videos are located in this one manual, along with teaching notes and PowerPoint slides to use in class. Group exercises include everything you might need to use the exercise in class–handouts, figures, and so forth.

This manual is organized into 25 topics including ethics, decision making, change, and leadership for easy inclusion in your lecture. A matrix appears at the front of the manual that references each resource by topic. Students can access all the exercises and self-assessments on their textbook's Web site. The Manager's HotSeat exercises are located online at www.mhhe.com/MHS.

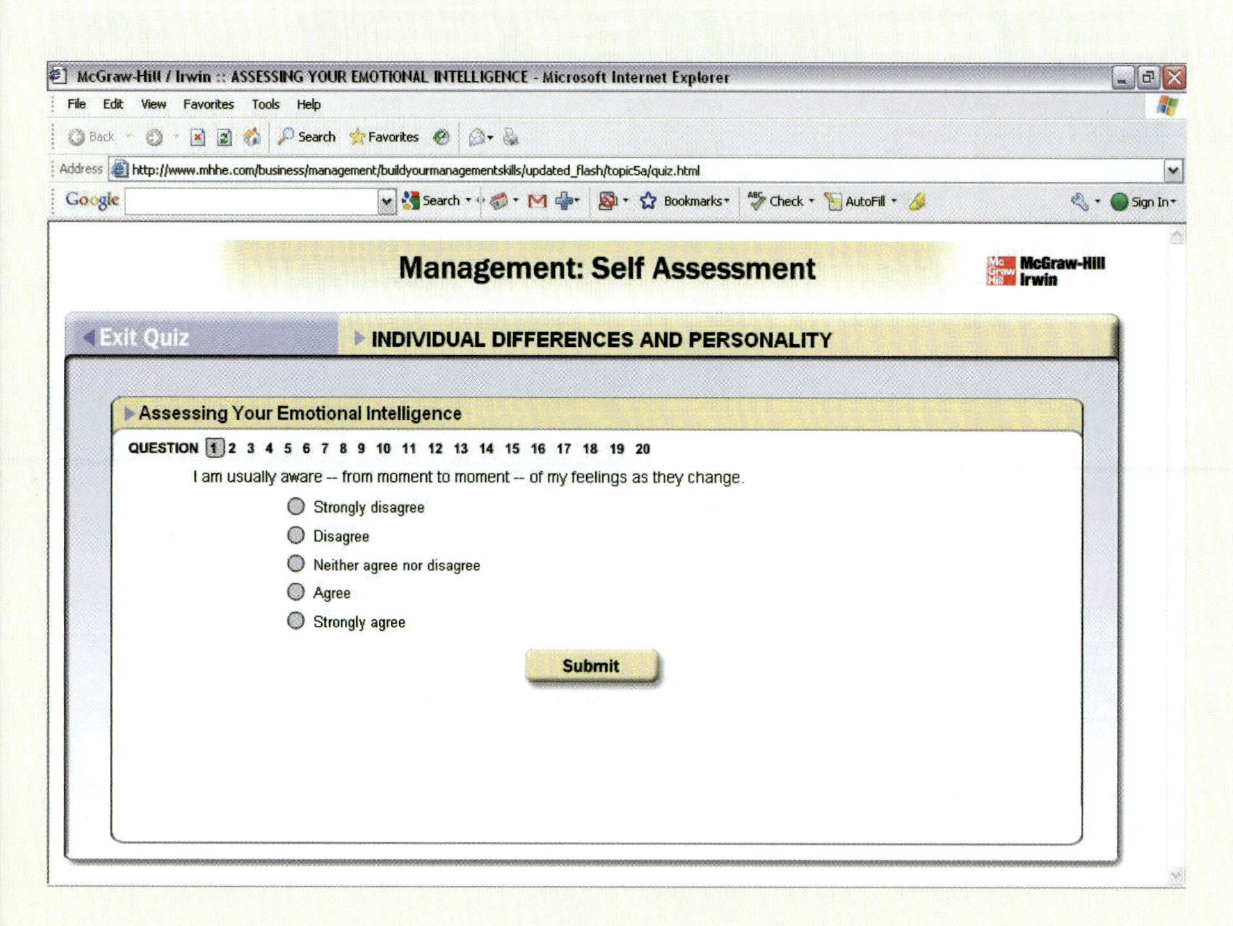

Acknowledgments

An enormous number of persons played a role in helping us put the first edition of this textbook together. Truth be told, we had no idea that we would have to rely on and put our success in the hands of so many different people! Each of them had unique and useful contributions to make toward the publication of this book, and they deserve and thus receive our sincere gratitude.

We are overly indebted to Kim Brewster, our senior sponsoring editor, for her encouragement to write the textbook and her support for our desire to write a "different kind" of textbook. Thanks also go out to Tracey Haggert, our development editor, who did her very best to keep us on track in terms of actually getting things done and who provided valuable feedback throughout the process. Special thanks to Michael Kelly and Cathy Biribauer, who helped to pull all of this together. We are particularly grateful to the following people who allowed us to showcase their work in our *OB Research In Canada* feature:

Natalie Allen, *University of Western Ontario*
Julian Barling, *Queen's University*
Ramona Bobocel, *University of Waterloo*
Stéphane Côté, *University of Toronto*
Marylène Gagné, *Concordia University*
Rick Hackett, *McMaster University*
Gary Latham, *University of Toronto*
Kibeom Lee, *University of Calgary*
Sally Maitlis, *University of British Columbia*
John Meyer, *University of Western Ontario*
Sandra Robinson, *University of British Columbia*
Kevin Tasa, *McMaster University*
Michael Withey, *Memorial University of Newfoundland*
Jia Lin Xie, *University of Toronto*

In addition to the initial feedback from the U.S. market, we have also had the great fortune of having had so many Canadian faculty members from colleges and universities around the country provide feedback on various aspects of the Canadian edition of this textbook. Their input made this book substantially better and we thank them for their time and effort:

Alfred Jaeger, *McGill University*
Andrew Fergus, *Thompson Rivers University*
Angela Davis, *University of Winnipeg*
Dan Kazakoff, *University of Lethbridge*
Diana Krause, *University of Western Ontario*
Dianne Cyr, *Simon Fraser University*
Don H. Caplan, *Royal Roads University*
Doreen MacAulay, *St. Mary's University*
Joanne Leck, *University of Ottawa*
Kelly Dye, *Acadia University*
Lissa McRae, *Bishop's University*

Lisa Keeping, *Wilfrid Laurier University*
Lynne Siemens, *University of Victoria*
Martha Reavley, *University of Windsor*
Roy L. Kirby, *Carleton University*
Scott Jeffrey, *University of Waterloo*
Stan Arnold, *Humber College Institute of Technology & Advanced Learning*
Teal McAteer, *McMaster University*

We would also like to thank our students at the undergraduate, masters, and executive levels who were taught with early versions of these chapters for their constructive feedback toward making them more effective in the classroom. Thanks also to our PhD students for allowing us to take time out from research projects to focus on this book.

Finally, we thank our families, who gave up substantial amounts of time with us and put up with the stress that necessarily comes at times during an endeavour such as this.

Jason Colquitt
Jeff LePine
Michael Wesson
Ian Gellatly

Part 1 **INTRODUCTION TO ORGANIZATIONAL BEHAVIOUR**

CHAPTER 1

What Is Organizational Behaviour?

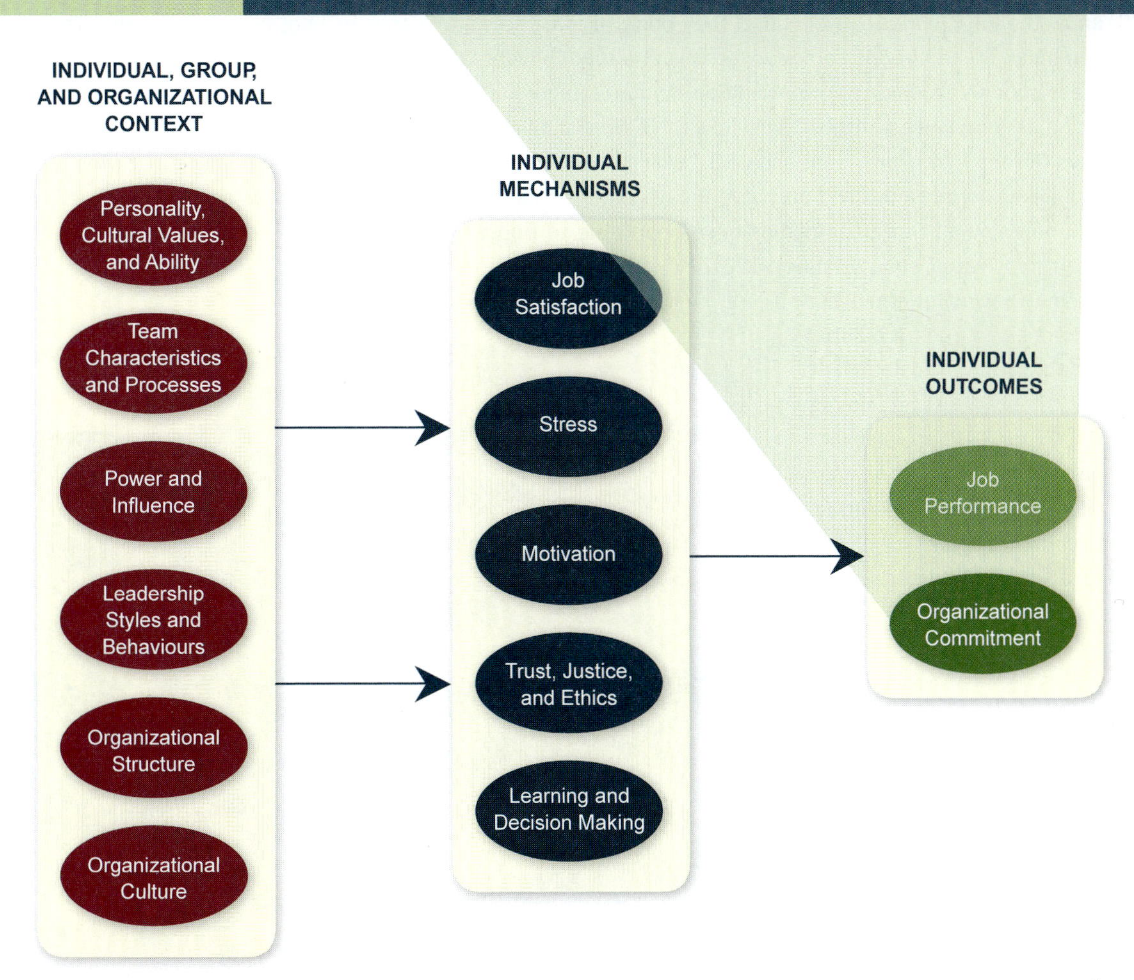

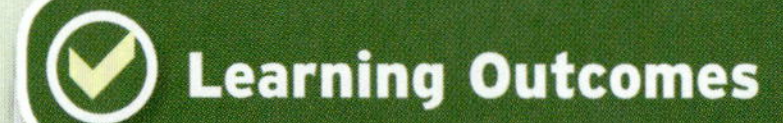

Learning Outcomes

After reading this chapter, you should be able to answer the following questions:

1.1 What is the definition of "organizational behaviour"?

1.2 What are the two primary outcomes in studies of organizational behaviour? What factors affect those two primary outcomes?

1.3 Do firms that are good at organizational behaviour tend to be more profitable? Why might that be, and is there any research evidence to support this tendency?

1.4 What is the value of theory and research?

LEADING THE WAY IN CHALLENGING TIMES

What do WestJet, Boston Pizza, and the Royal Bank of Canada (RBC) all have in common? Recently, all three organizations were recognized as among the most admired Canadian companies according to a national survey of prominent business leaders.[1] Why? All three had developed their respective corporate cultures in such a way that the talents and behaviours of employees were closely aligned with important organizational goals. The result: phenomenal performance!

According to Sean Duffy, president and CEO of WestJet, "culture is the most important element of what we do. It is supported, promoted and embraced at the top, but it really is in the 6,700 WestJetters across our networks. The culture is with each of them, encouraging them to provide the exceptional guest experience for which we are known." Regardless of one's technical role (e.g., pilots, flight attendants, baggage handlers, mechanics, salespeople, senior managers), elements of the culture include a shared understanding of core values (i.e., what is really important), fun, trust, hard work, communication, and sense of personal ownership. When hiring, Boston Pizza places an emphasis on fit over skills. According to Caroline Schein, vice president of people development, "A person may know the job technically well, but if they don't fit into the culture, they will not be as successful. The idea that you can build a team around somebody who isn't a team builder is a mistake." For RBC, a winning corporate culture has meant openly valuing teamwork and on-going learning and development, and embracing and harnessing the diversity of its employees. "At RBC, we know the power of diversity is unleashed when we respect and value differences," says Gordon Nixon, president and CEO. "We know our strength comes from the combination of what we have in common, like shared values and purpose, and what makes us different, like experiences and perspective."

Somehow all three companies have been able to find employees who are conscientious and intelligent, who seem motivated and satisfied with their jobs, who remain committed to their organizations for a longer-than-normal period of time, and who perform their job duties reliably and enthusiastically. Put simply, WestJet, Boston Pizza, and RBC are all examples of Canadian companies that seem to be doing an excellent job managing organizational behaviour!

Richmond, B.C.–based Boston Pizza International's phenomenal success is due in large part to its mastery of organizational behaviour, enabling it to hire enthusiastic and motivated employees who demonstrate a strong fit with the culture.

WHAT IS ORGANIZATIONAL BEHAVIOUR?

Before we define exactly what the field of organizational behaviour represents, take a moment to ponder the following: Who was the single *worst* co-worker you've ever had? Picture fellow students with whom you've worked on class projects; colleagues from part-time or summer jobs; or peers, subordinates, or supervisors working in your current organization. What did this co-worker do that earned him or her "worst co-worker" status? Was it some of the behaviours shown in the right column of Table 1-1 (or perhaps all of them)? Now take a moment to consider the single *best* co-worker you've ever had. Again, what did this co-worker do to earn "best co-worker" status—some or most of the behaviours shown in the left column of Table 1-1?

If you ever found yourself working alongside the two people profiled in the table, two questions probably would be foremost on your mind: "*Why* does the worst co-worker act that way?" and "*Why* does the best co-worker act that way?" Once you understand why the two co-workers act so differently, you might be able to figure out ways to interact with the worst co-worker more effectively (thereby making your working life a bit more pleasant). If you happen to be a manager, you can formulate plans for how to improve attitudes and behaviours in the unit. Such plans may include how to screen applicants, train and socialize new organizational members, manage evaluations and rewards for performance, and deal with conflicts that arise between employees. Without understanding why employees act the way they do, it is very difficult to find a way to change their attitudes and behaviours at work.

TABLE 1-1 The Best of Co-workers, the Worst of Co-workers

THE BEST	THE WORST
Have you ever had a co-worker who usually acted this way?	Have you ever had a co-worker who usually acted this way?
√ Got the job done, without having to be managed or reminded	√ Did not get the job done, even with a great deal of hand-holding
√ Adapted when something needed to be changed or done differently	√ Was resistant to any and every form of change, even when changes were beneficial
√ Always was a "good sport," even when bad things happened at work	√ Whined and complained, no matter what was happening
√ Attended optional meetings or functions to support colleagues	√ Optional meetings? Was too lazy to make it to some required meetings and functions!
√ Helped new co-workers or people who seemed to need a hand	√ Made fun of new co-workers or people who seemed to need a hand
√ Followed key rules, even when the reasons for them were not apparent	√ Broke virtually any rule that somehow made their work more difficult
√ Felt an attachment and obligation to the employer for the long haul	√ Seemed to always be looking for something else, even if it wasn't better
√ Was first to arrive, last to leave	√ Was first to leave for lunch, last to return

Million Dollar Question:
Why do these two employees act so differently?

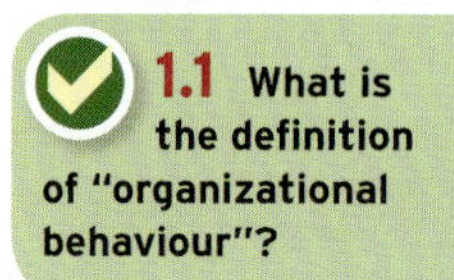

1.1 What is the definition of "organizational behaviour"?

ORGANIZATIONAL BEHAVIOUR DEFINED

Organizational behaviour (OB) is a field of study devoted to understanding, explaining, and ultimately improving the attitudes and behaviours of individuals and groups in organizations. Scholars in management departments of universities and scientists in business organizations conduct research on OB. The findings from those research studies are then applied by managers or consultants to find out whether they help meet "real-world" challenges. In addition, OB can be contrasted with two other courses commonly offered in management departments: human resource management and strategic management. **Human resource management** takes the theories and principles studied in OB and explores the "nuts-and-bolts" applications of those principles in organizations. An OB study might explore the relationship between learning and job performance, whereas a human resource management study might examine the best ways to structure training programs to promote employee learning. **Strategic management** focuses on the product choices and industry characteristics that affect an organization's profitability. For example, a strategic management study might examine the relationship between firm diversification (when a firm expands into a new product segment) and firm profitability.

organizational behaviour (ob) Field of study devoted to understanding, explaining, and ultimately improving the attitudes and behaviours of individuals and groups in organizations

human resource management Field of study that focuses on the applications of OB theories and principles in organizations

strategic management Field of study devoted to exploring the product choices and industry characteristics that affect an organization's profitability

The theories and concepts found in OB are actually drawn from a wide variety of disciplines. For example, research on job performance and individual characteristics draws primarily from studies in industrial and organizational psychology. Research on satisfaction, emotions, and team processes draws heavily from social psychology. Sociology research is vital to research on team characteristics and organizational structure, and anthropology research helps inform the study of organizational culture. Finally, models from economics are used to understand motivation, learning, and decision making. This diversity brings a unique quality to the study of OB, as most students will be able to find a particular topic that is intrinsically interesting and thought provoking to them.

THE ROLE OF MANAGEMENT THEORY

The theories and concepts found in OB have also been heavily influenced by the popular management approaches of the day. Over time our ideas about how to best organize, coordinate, and manage human work activities have changed, as have our view of cause-effect relationships. As you will see, many of the "modern" theories and concepts described in the text have their roots in one or more of these management theories or approaches.

Classical management scholars, such as Frederick Taylor (1856–1917) and Max Weber (1864–1920), placed heavy emphasis on specialization, coordination, and efficiency. A major influence on the way people viewed and thought about OB was the work of Frederick Taylor, the "father" of **scientific management**.[2] As an engineer, Taylor was focused on designing optimal and efficient work processes. Using scientific methods (e.g. careful observation, measurement, experimentation), Taylor and his colleagues would study how to optimize performance of any task (e.g., by reducing the number of hand movements exhibited by bricklayers, and thus reducing fatigue, more bricks could be laid in a given time period). Once determined, these new work procedures would be taught to workers and encouraged with financial incentives.

scientific management Using scientific methods to design optimal and efficient work processes and tasks

Another important contributor to the classical approach to management was Max Weber, most often associated with the term **bureaucracy**.[3] Rather than focus on specific work processes, Weber looked at the entire organization. For Weber, the bureaucratic form was a technically superior method of organizing, coordinating, and controlling human work activities (Chapter 13). Characteristics of bureaucracy included: (a) the division of labour with a high level of technical specialization; (b) a strict chain of command (authority hierarchy) where every member reported to someone at a higher level in the organization; (c) a system of formal rules and procedures that ensured consistency, impartiality, and imper-

bureaucracy An organizational form that emphasizes the control and coordination of its members through a strict chain of command, formal rules and procedures, high specialization, and centralized decision making.

sonality throughout the organization; and (d) decision making at the top of the organization. For the classical theorists, productivity problems, if and when they occurred, were likely viewed at the job level as the result of design flaws, failures to implement specified processes, or inadequate working conditions (e.g., illumination, not enough work breaks), and at the organizational level as the result of deficient structural characteristics.

In stark contrast to the classical approaches that stressed the importance of the formal organization and its functioning, the **human relations movement** emerged as management scholars began to recognize that the psychological attributes of individual workers (e.g., needs, attitudes) and the social forces within work groups had important effects on behaviours. A famous serious of studies, conducted between 1924 and 1933 at the Western Electric Company's Hawthorne plant, revealed the limitations with the classic approach to management and organization.[4] Originally these studies were designed to resolve the organization's productivity problems by applying popular scientific-management techniques. The irony, of course, is that a classical-approach application produced the foundation on which the human relations movement was built. The Hawthorne studies, although crude in comparison to the organizational research being conducted today, revealed the importance of many of the topics we discuss in this text, such as group values and norms, leadership, motivation, job satisfaction, and organizational culture. For the human relations theorists, productivity problems, if and when they occurred were likely viewed as the result of worker alienation from the organization, failure of the work to satisfy important personal needs or goals, low organizational commitment, or work-group norms encouraging low rather than high performance—in other words, very little causal emphasis on the characteristics of formal organization.

human relations movement Field of study that recognizes that the psychological attributes of individual workers and the social forces within work groups have important effects on work behaviours

Today, contemporary management theory recognizes the dependencies between the classical approach and the human relations approach. We see this contingency approach reflected in a number of the theories and models of OB where the consequences of situational characteristics (e.g., financial incentives, job design, assigned goals) are thought to *depend* on characteristics of the individual or visa versa. Fundamental to the contingency approach is the idea that there is no one-best, universal principles. The same is true for OB. As you will see, OB—in all its forms—is the result of many different kinds of variables coming together.

AN INTEGRATIVE MODEL OF ORGANIZATIONAL BEHAVIOUR

Because of the diversity in its topics and disciplinary roots, it is common for students in an organizational behaviour class to wonder "How does all this stuff fit together?" How does what gets covered in Chapter 3 relate to what gets covered in Chapter 12? To clarify such issues, this textbook is structured around an integrative model of OB, shown in Figure 1-1, that is designed to provide a roadmap for the field of organizational behaviour. The model shows how the topics in the next 13 chapters—represented by the 13 ovals in the model—all fit together. We should stress that there are other potential ways of combining the 13 topics, and Figure 1-1 likely oversimplifies the connections among the topics. Still, we believe the model provides a helpful guide as you move through this text. Figure 1-1 groups these topics into three categories.

INDIVIDUAL OUTCOMES The right-most portion of the model contains the two primary outcomes of interest to organizational behaviour researchers (and employees and managers in organizations): *job performance* and *organizational commitment.* Most employees have two primary goals for their working lives: to perform their jobs well and to remain members of an organization that they respect. Likewise, most managers have two primary goals for their employees: to maximize their job performance and to ensure that they stay with the firm for a significant length of time. As described in Chapter 2, there are several

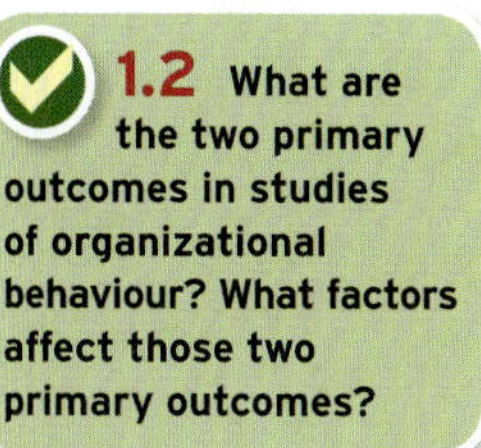
1.2 What are the two primary outcomes in studies of organizational behaviour? What factors affect those two primary outcomes?

FIGURE 1-1 Integrative Model of Organizational Behaviour

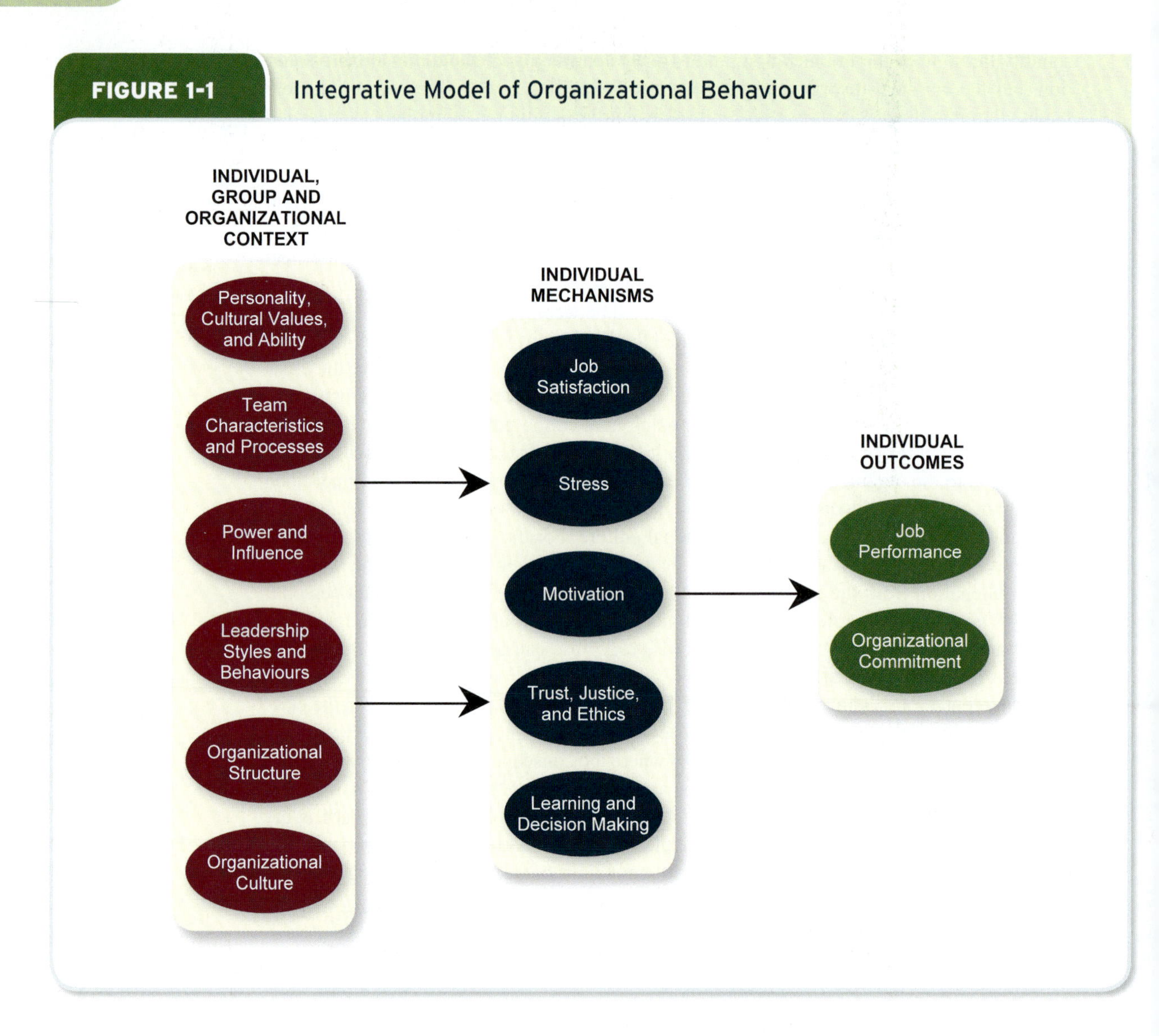

specific behaviours that, when taken together, constitute good job performance. Similarly, as described in Chapter 3, there are a number of beliefs, attitudes, and emotions that cause an employee to remain committed to an employer.[5]

This book starts by covering job performance and organizational commitment so that you can better understand the two primary organizational behaviour goals. Our hope is that by using performance and commitment as starting points, we can highlight the practical importance of OB topics. After all, what could be more important than having employees who perform well and want to stay with the company? This structure also enables us to conclude the other chapters in the book with sections that describe the relationships between each chapter's topic and performance and commitment. For example, the chapter on motivation concludes by describing the relationships between motivation and performance and motivation and commitment. In this way, you'll learn which of the topics in the model are most useful for understanding your own job performance and your own desires to stay with (or leave) your company.

INDIVIDUAL MECHANISMS Our integrative model also illustrates a number of individual mechanisms that directly affect job performance and organizational commitment. These include *job satisfaction,* which captures what employees feel when thinking about their jobs and doing their day-to-day work (Chapter 4). Another individual mechanism is *stress,* which reflects employees' psychological responses to job demands that tax or exceed their capacities (Chapter 5). The model also includes *motivation,* which captures the energetic forces that drive employees' work effort (Chapter 6). *Trust, justice, and ethics* reflect the degree to which employees feel that their company conducts business with fairness, honesty, and integrity (Chapter 7). The final individual mechanism shown in the model is *learning and decision making,* which deals with how employees gain job knowledge and how they use that knowledge to make accurate judgments on the job (Chapter 8).

INDIVIDUAL, GROUP, AND ORGANIZATIONAL CONTEXT Of course, if satisfaction, stress, motivation, and so forth are key drivers of job performance and organizational commitment, it becomes important to understand that these mechanisms are influenced by several important contexts. Each of us brings a unique set of personal attributes to our work that not only makes us unique as humans but also provides an individual context that explains behaviour. In this section we explore how personal attributes, such as *personality, cultural values, and ability,* influence how we behave at work and the kinds of tasks that interest us, and might account for our responses to events that happen on the job (Chapter 9). The integrative model in Figure 1-1 also acknowledges that employees do not work alone. Instead, they typically work in one or more groups or teams led by some formal (or sometimes informal) leader. Like the individual characteristics, these group factors shape satisfaction, stress, motivation, trust, and learning. Chapter 10 describes *team characteristics and processes.* In this chapter we explore the structure of effective work groups, such as their norms, their roles, and the way members depend on one another. We also describe the processes that summarize how groups and teams behave, including topics like cooperation, conflict, and communication. The next two chapters focus on the leaders of those teams. We first describe how individuals become leaders in the first place and consider *power and influence* to summarize the process by which individuals attain authority over others (Chapter 11). We then describe how leaders behave in their leadership roles; *leadership styles and behaviours* capture the specific actions that leaders take to influence others at work (Chapter 12). Finally, our integrative model acknowledges that individuals and groups function within an organizational context. Every company, for example, has an *organizational structure* that dictates how the units within the firm link to (and communicate with) other units (Chapter 13). Sometimes, structures are centralized around a decision-making authority; other times, structures are decentralized, affording each unit some autonomy. Every company also has an *organizational culture* that captures "the way things are" in the organization—shared knowledge about the rules, norms, and values that shape employee attitudes and behaviours (Chapter 14).

THE VALUE OF AN INTEGRATIVE MODEL Each of the chapters in this textbook will open with a depiction of this integrative model, with the subject of each chapter highlighted. We hope that this opening will serve as a guide for where you are in this book, as well as where you've been and where you're going. Some of you will be able to apply those topic areas to your current working life, whether you're working full-time or part-time and whether you occupy a managerial or non-managerial role. Of course, some of you are full-time students or between jobs at the moment. Regardless of your work status, one thing all of you have in common is that you're students. As it turns out, many of the same concepts that predict success in an organization also predict success in a classroom. We will explore some of those commonalities in our **OB for Students** feature, which appears in each chapter and illustrates how OB concepts can be applied to improve academic success.

OB FOR STUDENTS

This feature is designed to demonstrate the generalizability of many OB principles by applying them to another area of life: life as a student. Each chapter will explore how a particular topic occurs in the classroom. This inaugural edition highlights some of the things you can expect in the chapters to come:

Job satisfaction (Chapter 4): How do students judge how satisfied they are with their university life? How do they weigh things like where they live, how much they like their classmates, and how much they enjoy what they're studying?

Stress (Chapter 5): The working world doesn't corner the market on stress; juggling several classes along with life's other responsibilities can be quite stressful in its own right. We'll explore how various kinds of stressful demands affect student learning and class performance.

Team characteristics and processes (Chapter 10): Several classes use team projects. We'll explore some of the important drivers of the effectiveness of student groups, in the hope that you can use this discussion to improve your own team's functioning.

Organizational structure (Chapter 13): What kinds of organizational structures do most students find attractive when they are on the job market? Do some students have different structural preferences than others?

Organizational culture (Chapter 14): How do new students learn about the culture of a university? Are there benefits of socializing new students in the same way that organizations socialize new employees? What would such socialization efforts look like?

DOES ORGANIZATIONAL BEHAVIOUR MATTER?

Having described exactly what OB is, it is time to discuss another fundamental question: Does it really matter? Is there any value in taking a class on this subject, other than fulfilling some requirement of your program? (You might guess that we are biased in our answers to these questions, given that we wrote an entire book on this subject!) Few would disagree that organizations need to know principles of accounting and finance to be successful; it would be impossible to conduct business without such knowledge. Similarly, few would disagree that organizations need to know principles of marketing, as consumers need to know about the firm's products and what makes those products unique or noteworthy.

However, people sometimes wonder whether a firm's ability to manage OB has any bearing on its bottom-line profitability. After all, if a firm has a good-enough product, won't people buy it regardless of how happy, motivated, or committed its workforce is? Perhaps for a time, but effective OB can help keep a product good over the long term. This same argument can be made in reverse: If a firm has a bad-enough product, isn't it true that people won't buy it, regardless of how happy, motivated, or committed its workforce is? Again, perhaps for a time, but the effective management of OB can help make a product get better, incrementally, over the long term.

In 2006, J.D. Power and Associates surveyed automobile owners to determine the initial quality of their vehicles.[6] What do you think they found? Test your knowledge. Rank the following list of automobile brands with respect to quality: Honda, Toyota, Porsche, Lexus, Jaguar, and Hyundai. It shouldn't surprise you to learn that Porsche was ranked #1 and Lexus was ranked #2. Who do you think was #3? Jaguar? Honda? Toyota? Nope—the answer is Hyundai. What makes these results interesting is that in the previous year, Hyundai was ranked #11 in the same group. Hyundai's offerings were once criticized as being "cheap," with Jay Leno famously comparing a Hyundai to a bobsled ("It has no room, you have to push it to get going, and it only goes downhill!").[7] Going from #11 to #3 in one year is a remarkable accomplishment, and no doubt reflects Hyundai's increased emphasis on quality; work teams devoted to quality have been expanded eightfold, and almost all employees have enrolled in special training programs devoted to quality issues.[8] Hyundai represents a case in which OB principles are being applied to multiple cultures. Our **OB Internationally** feature spotlights such international and cross-cultural applications of OB topics in each chapter.

A recent survey of automobile owners rated Hyundai as among the very best in terms of initial quality.

BUILDING A CONCEPTUAL ARGUMENT

Of course, we shouldn't just accept it on faith that OB matters, nor should we merely look for specific companies that appear to support the premise. What we need instead is a logical conceptual argument that captures exactly why OB might affect the bottom-line profitability of an organization. One such argument is based on the **resource-based view** of organizations. This perspective describes what exactly makes resources valuable—that is, what makes them capable of creating long-term profits for the firm.[9] A firm's resources include financial (e.g., revenue, equity) and physical (e.g., buildings, machines, technology)

resource-based view A model that argues that rare and inimitable resources help firms maintain competitive advantage

OB INTERNATIONALLY

Changes in technology, communications, and economic forces have made business more global and international than ever. This feature spotlights the impact of globalization on the organizational behaviour concepts described in this book. More specifically, this feature will cover a variety of topics:

Cross-cultural differences: Research in cross-cultural organizational behaviour has illustrated that national cultures affect many of the relationships in our integrative model. Put differently, there is little that we know about OB that is "universal" or "culture free."[10]

International corporations: An increasing number of organizations are international in scope, with both foreign and domestic operations. Applying organizational behaviour concepts in these firms represents a special challenge—should policies and practices be consistent across locations or tailored to meet the needs of the culture?

Expatriation: Working as an expatriate—an employee who lives outside his or her native country—can be particularly challenging. What factors influence expatriates' job performance and organizational commitment levels?

Managing diversity: More and more work groups are composed of members of different cultural backgrounds. What are the special challenges involved in leading and working in such groups?

FIGURE 1-2 What Makes a Resource Valuable?

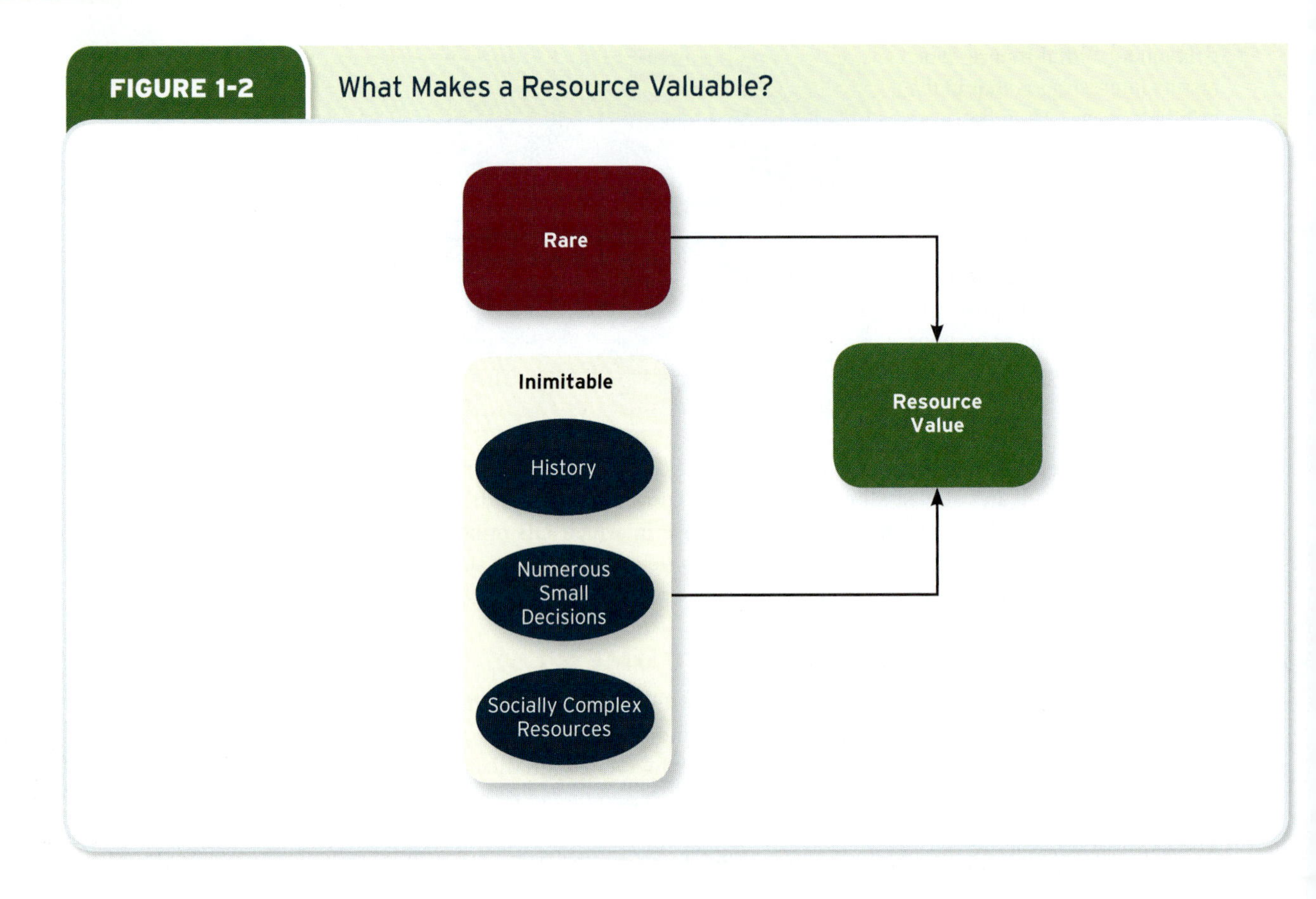

resources, but they also include resources related to organizational behaviour, such as the knowledge, decision making, ability, and wisdom of the workforce, as well as the image, culture, and goodwill of the organization.

The resource-based view suggests that the value of resources depends on several factors, shown in Figure 1-2. For example, a resource is more valuable when it is **rare**. Diamonds, oil, Howie Morenz hockey cards, and Action Comics #1 (the debut of Superman) are all expensive precisely because they are rare. Good people are also rare—witness the adage "good people are hard to find." Ask yourself what percentage of the people you have worked with have been talented, motivated, satisfied, and good team players. In many organizations, cities, or job markets, such employees are the exception rather than the rule. If good people really are rare, then the effective management of OB should prove to be a valuable resource.

rare In short supply

The resource-based view also suggests that a resource is more valuable when it is **inimitable**, meaning that it cannot be easily copied. A new form of technology can help a firm gain an advantage for a short time, but what happens when a competing firm adopts the same technology? Many of a firm's resources can be imitated, though it is sometimes expensive. Manufacturing practices can be copied, building layouts can be mimicked, equipment and tools can be approximated. Good people, in contrast, are much more difficult to imitate. As shown in Figure 1-2, there are three reasons why people are inimitable.

inimitable Incapable of being imitated or copied

HISTORY People create a **history**—a collective pool of experience, wisdom, and knowledge that benefits the organization. History cannot be bought. Consider an example from the discount airline industry. Calgary-based WestJet is the leader in this industry, profiting from more frequent point-to-point daily schedules routed into less expensive airports. In the fall of 2002, Air Canada created a new discount airline named Zip to provide Western

history A collective pool of experience, wisdom, and knowledge created by people that benefits the organization

Canadians with the same kind of service, though two years later the brand was abandoned and folded back into Air Canada's regular operations.[11] One challenge facing Zip was that it was competing, for the first time, in a market in which WestJet had existed for some time. Their respective positions on the "industry learning curve" were quite different.

NUMEROUS SMALL DECISIONS The concept of **numerous small decisions** captures the idea that people make many small decisions day in and day out, week in and week out. "So what?" you might say, "Why worry about small decisions?" Ask yourself how much time elapsed between the arrival of *Diet Coke with Lime* on grocery store shelves and the arrival of *Diet Pepsi Lime.* Answer? About two months.[12] Big decisions can be copied; they are visible to competitors and observable by industry experts and analysts. In the case of Zip, the company was able to copy one of WestJet's observable signatures—cheap, short-haul flights. However, it would prove be more difficult to copy some of the other WestJet signatures (e.g., the playful, whimsical style displayed by flight attendants and service personnel). To successfully mimic the practices of a competitor, it would be necessary to take into consideration all the little day-to-day decisions and trade-offs that employees make every day. For example, watching a flight attendant spontaneously use humour to attract inattentive passengers to the safety instructions, or observing a ticket agent use his discretion to make an anxious passenger smile. These are the kinds of small daily activities that are often invisible to competitors.

numerous small decisions People making many small decisions every day that are invisible to competitors

SOCIALLY COMPLEX RESOURCES People are the source of **socially complex resources**, like culture, teamwork, trust, and reputation. These resources are termed "socially complex" because it is not always clear how they came to develop, though it is clear which organizations do (and do not) possess them.[13] Unlike tangible resources, such as a new computer system, sleek new aircraft, or deluxe cabin features (e.g., leather seats; televisions), leadership, culture, and teamwork cannot be easily copied (otherwise, the Toronto Maple Leafs would have won another Stanley Cup by now). Culture, teamwork, trust, and reputation spring from the social dynamics within a given organization at a given time.

socially complex resources Resources created by people, such as culture, teamwork, trust, and reputation; the source of competitive advantage is known, but the method of replicating the advantage is unclear

RESEARCH EVIDENCE

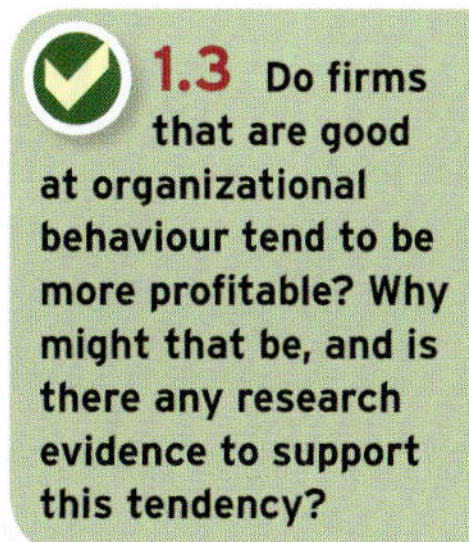
1.3 Do firms that are good at organizational behaviour tend to be more profitable? Why might that be, and is there any research evidence to support this tendency?

Thus, we can build a conceptual argument for why OB might affect an organization's profitability: Good people are both rare and inimitable and therefore create a resource that is valuable for creating competitive advantage. Conceptual arguments are helpful, of course, but it would be even better if there were hard data to back them up. Fortunately, it turns out that there is a great deal of research evidence supporting the importance of OB for company performance. Several research studies have been conducted on the topic, each employing a somewhat different approach.

One study began by surveying executives from 968 publicly held firms with 100 or more employees.[14] The survey assessed so-called "high performance work practices"—OB policies that are widely agreed to be beneficial to firm performance. The survey included 13 questions asking about a combination of hiring, information sharing, training, performance management, and incentive practices, and each question asked what proportion of the company's workforce was involved in the practice. Table 1-2 provides the questions used to assess the high performance work practices (and also shows which chapter of this textbook describes each particular practice in more detail). The study also gathered the following information for each firm: average annual rate of turnover, productivity level (defined as sales per employee), market value of the firm, and corporate profitability. The results revealed that a one-unit increase in the proportion of the workforce involved in the practices was associated with an approximately 7 percent decrease in turnover, $27,000 more in sales per employee, $18,000 more in market value, and $3,800 more in profits. Put simply, better OB practices were associated with better firm performance.

TABLE 1-2 Survey Questions Designed to Assess High Performance Work Practices

SURVEY QUESTION ABOUT OB PRACTICE	CHAPTER IN WHICH PRACTICE IS DISCUSSED
1. What is the proportion of the workforce who are included in a formal information sharing program (e.g., a newsletter)?	Chapter 7 (Trust, Justice, and Ethics)
2. What is the proportion of the workforce whose jobs have been subjected to a formal job analysis?	Chapter 2 (Job Performance)
3. What proportion of non-entry-level jobs have been filled from within in recent years?	Chapter 6 (Motivation)
4. What is the proportion of the workforce who are administered attitude surveys on a regular basis?	Chapter 4 (Job Satisfaction)
5. What is the proportion of the workforce who participate in Quality of Work Life (QWL) programs, Quality Circles (QC), and/or labour-management participation teams?	Chapter 10 (Team Characteristics and Processes)
6. What is the proportion of the workforce who have access to company incentive plans, profit-sharing plans, and/or gain-sharing plans?	Chapter 6 (Motivation)
7. What is the average number of hours of training received by a typical employee over the last 12 months?	Chapter 8 (Learning and Decision Making)
8. What is the proportion of the workforce who have access to a formal grievance procedure and/or complaint resolution system?	Chapter 7 (Trust, Justice, and Ethics)
9. What proportion of the workforce are administered an employment test prior to hiring?	Chapter 9 (Personality, Cultural Values, and Ability)
10. What is the proportion of the workforce whose performance appraisals are used to determine compensation?	Chapter 6 (Motivation)
11. What proportion of the workforce receive formal performance appraisals?	Chapter 6 (Motivation)
12. Which of the following promotion decision rules do you use most often? (a) merit or performance rating alone; (b) seniority only if merit is equal; (c) seniority among employees who meet a minimum merit requirement; (d) seniority.	Chapter 6 (Motivation)
13. For the five positions that your firm hires most frequently, how many qualified applicants do you have per position (on average)?	Chapter 9 (Personality, Cultural Values, and Ability)

Source: M.A. Huselid, "The Impact of Human Resource Management Practices on Turnover, Productivity, and Corporate Financial Performance," *Academy of Management Journal* 38 (1995), pp. 635–72.

Although there is no doubting the importance of turnover, productivity, market value, and profitability, another study examined an outcome that is even more fundamental: firm survival.[15] The study focused on 136 non-financial companies that made initial public offerings (IPOs) in 1988. Firms that undergo an IPO typically have shorter histories and need an infusion of cash to grow or introduce some new technology. Rather than conducting a survey, the authors of this study examined the prospectus filed by each firm. (Reporting rules require that prospectuses contain honest information, and firms can be liable for any inaccuracies that might mislead investors.) The authors coded each prospectus for information that might suggest OB issues were valued. Examples of valuing OB issues included describing employees as a source of competitive advantage in strategy and mission statements, emphasizing training and continuing education, having a human resources management officer, and emphasizing full-time rather than temporary or contract employees. By 1993, 81 of the 136 firms included in the study had survived (60 percent). The key question is whether the value placed on OB predicted which did (and did not) survive. The results revealed that firms that valued OB had a 19 percent higher survival rate than firms that did not value OB.

In early 2007, a study of 185 Canadian business leaders was conducted by Waterstone Human Capital Ltd., a retained executive search firm, in association with the *National Post.*[16] Study participants were interviewed and asked to evaluate a number of the nation's largest companies on the five criteria listed in Table 1-3. As you can see, participants were asked to consider financial performance as well as several critical OB issues such as leadership, culture, motivation (rewards), and ethics (social responsibility). On the basis of these criteria, a total score was computed for each company.

TABLE 1-3 Five Criteria for Determining Top 10 Corporate Cultures

RATING CRITERIA	MEASURE
Vision and leadership	The nominated company must have demonstrated vision and leadership over the years where the company's leaders inspire their people toward a new level of growth and achievement.
Cultural alignment, measurement, and sustainability	How is the culture of the organization aligned to its vision, people, and process? How is it measured and sustained to support corporate performance?
Rewards, recognition, and innovative business achievement	How does the nominated company reward and recognize its people? How is the nominee unique and innovative in its relationship with its employees, stakeholders, and customers? Why is it unique and how has it demonstrated excellence in its field?
Corporate financial performance	The Board of Governors will review key financial statistics and indicators provided by the nominated company for the close of last year.
Corporate social responsibility	An outstanding organization promotes a culture that supports organizational and individual involvement in overcoming community, social, and environmental issues.

Source: "Canada's 10 Most Admired Corporate Cultures™ 2007," Marty Parker, Managing Director, Waterstone Human Capital Ltd., Toronto.

TABLE 1-4 Canada's 10 Most Admired Corporate Cultures

TOP 10 CORPORATIONS	3-YEAR AVERAGE REVENUE GROWTH	3-YEAR AVERAGE ASSET GROWTH
1. WestJet Airlines	105.45%	84.69%
2. Four Seasons Hotels	-7.52%	52.54%
3. Boston Pizza International	69.25%	55.86%
4. Royal Bank of Canada	45.55%	9.70%
5. Yellow Pages Group	126.09%	101.74%
6. Maple Leaf Foods	52.59%	8.41%
7. Manulife Financial Corporation	107.16%	140.17%
8. Purolator Courier	24.78%	124.39%
9. Tim Hortons	9.43%	12.80%
10. Toronto Dominion Bank Financial Group	30.52%	43.64%
Average	**56.33%**	**63.38%**
S&P/TSX 60	**16.33%**	**13.09%**

Source: "Canada's 10 Most Admired Corporate Cultures™ 2007," Marty Parker, Managing Director, Waterstone Human Capital Ltd., Toronto.

The top 10 companies are listed in Table 1-4. As you see, these organizations are drawn from a range of industry sectors. More importantly, these results suggest that firms with very good OB practices also tend to be higher performers. Across the top 10 companies in Table 1-4, average revenue growth (56.33%) and asset growth (63.88%) are noticeably higher than the average performance of companies listed on the Toronto Stock Exchange (S&P/TSX 60).

SO WHAT'S SO HARD?

Clearly this research evidence seems to support the conceptual argument that good people constitute a valuable resource for companies. Good OB does seem to matter in terms of company profitability. You may wonder then, "What's so hard?" Why doesn't every company prioritize the effective management of OB, devoting as much attention to it as they do accounting, finance, marketing, technology, physical assets, and so on? Some companies do not do a good job managing their people. Why is that?

Work by Jeffrey Pfeffer provides one potential answer. Pfeffer has written extensively about the OB practices that tend to be used by successful organizations. According to Pfeffer there is no "magic bullet" OB practice—one thing that, in and of itself, can increase profitability. Instead, the effective management of OB requires a belief that several different practices are important, along with a long-term commitment to improving those practices. This premise can be summarized with what might be called the **rule of one-eighth**:

rule of one-eighth The belief that at best one-eighth, or 12 percent, of organizations will actually do what is required to build profits by putting people first

> One must bear in mind that one-half of organizations won't believe the connection between how they manage their people and the profits they earn. One-half of those who do see the connection will do what many organizations have done—try to make a single change to solve their problems, not realizing that the effective management of people requires a more comprehensive and systematic approach. Of the firms that make comprehensive changes, probably only about one-half will persist with their practices long enough to actually derive economic benefits. Since one-half times one-half times one-half equals one-eighth, at best 12 percent of organizations will actually do what is required to build profits by putting people first.[17]

The integrative model of OB used to structure this book was designed with this rule of one-eighth in mind. Figure 1-1 (page 6) suggests that high job performance depends not just on employee motivation but also on fostering high levels of satisfaction, effectively managing stress, creating a trusting climate, and committing to employee learning. Failing to do any one of those things could hinder the effectiveness of the other concepts in the model. Of course, that systemic nature reveals another reality of organizational behaviour: It is often difficult to "fix" companies that struggle with OB issues. Such companies often struggle in a number of different areas and on a number of different levels. One such (fictitious) company is spotlighted in our **OB on Screen** feature, which appears in each chapter and uses well-known movies to demonstrate OB concepts.

OB ON SCREEN

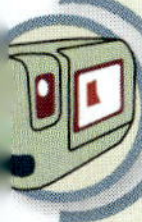

OFFICE SPACE

This feature is designed to allow you to imagine OB in action on the silver screen. After you've read about an OB topic, you'll find that you see it play out all around you, especially in movies. This inaugural edition spotlights (what else?) *Office Space* (Dir: Mike Judge. 20th Century Fox, 1999).

> *Since I started working, every single day has been worse than the day before, so that every day you see me is the worst day of my life.*

With these words, Peter Gibbons (Ron Livingston) summarizes what it is like to work at Initech, the computer programming firm where he updates bank software. Peter doesn't exhibit particularly good job performance (he works very slowly and breaks company rules), nor is he very committed to the organization (he comes in late, leaves early, and misses a lot of work).

Of course, the key question from an OB perspective is, "Why does Peter act that way?" At Initech, the better question might be, "Why doesn't everybody?" From the perspective of our integrative model of OB, the problem starts at the top and flows down. The culture of the organization is rigid and emotionless, with management seeming to delight in pointing out mistakes (like Peter's failure to use a cover sheet on his reports). The structure of the organization somehow assigns eight different bosses to Peter (providing eight opportunities to relive the cover sheet conversation). From a leadership perspective, the evil Bill Lumbergh (Gary Cole) seems to relish the power that comes with his title but does little to improve the functioning of his unit. The result is a workforce that feels little to no motivation, because performance has no impact on the money they earn. All this is worsened by the arrival of "the two Bobs," consultants whose job it is to choose which employees to fire and which to retain. The imminent layoffs combine with all the other problems to create a sense of distrust in the office.

Clearly it would take a lot of time and effort to turn Initech around. The effort would require several changes to several different practices to address several different components of our OB model. And those changes would need to be in place for a long period of time before the company could turn the corner. An uphill climb, to be sure, but Initech has one thing going for it: The Bobs are on the job!

HOW DO WE "KNOW" WHAT WE KNOW ABOUT ORGANIZATIONAL BEHAVIOUR?

1.4 What is the value of theory and research?

Now that we have described what OB is and why it is an important topic of study, we now turn to how we "know" what we know about the topic. In other words, where does the knowledge in this textbook come from? Consider the following prediction: Providing social recognition, in the form of public shows of praise and appreciation for good behaviours, will increase the performance and commitment of work units. Perhaps you feel that you "know" this claim to be true because you yourself have always responded well to praise and recognition. Or perhaps you feel that you "know" it to be true because it seems like common sense—who wouldn't work harder after a few public pats on the back? Maybe you feel that you "know" it to be true because a respected boss from your past always extolled the virtue of public praise and recognition. However, your experience or intuition also might have led you to the opposite belief—that providing social recognition has no impact on the performance and commitment of work units. It may be that public praise has always made you uncomfortable or embarrassed, to the point that you tried to hide especially effective behaviours to avoid being singled out by your boss. Or it may seem logical that social recognition will be viewed as "cheap talk," with employees longing for financial incentives rather than verbal compliments. Or perhaps the best boss you ever worked for never offered a single piece of social recognition in her life, yet her employees always worked their hardest on her behalf.

theory A collection of verbal and symbolic assertions that specify how and why variables are related, as well as the conditions in which they should (and should not) be related

From a scientist's point of view, it doesn't really matter what a person's experience or intuition suggests: The prediction must be tested with data. In other words, scientists don't simply assume that their beliefs are accurate; they acknowledge that their beliefs must be tested scientifically. Scientific studies are based on the scientific method, originated by Sir Francis Bacon in the 1600s and adapted in Figure 1-3.[18] The scientific method begins with **theory**, defined

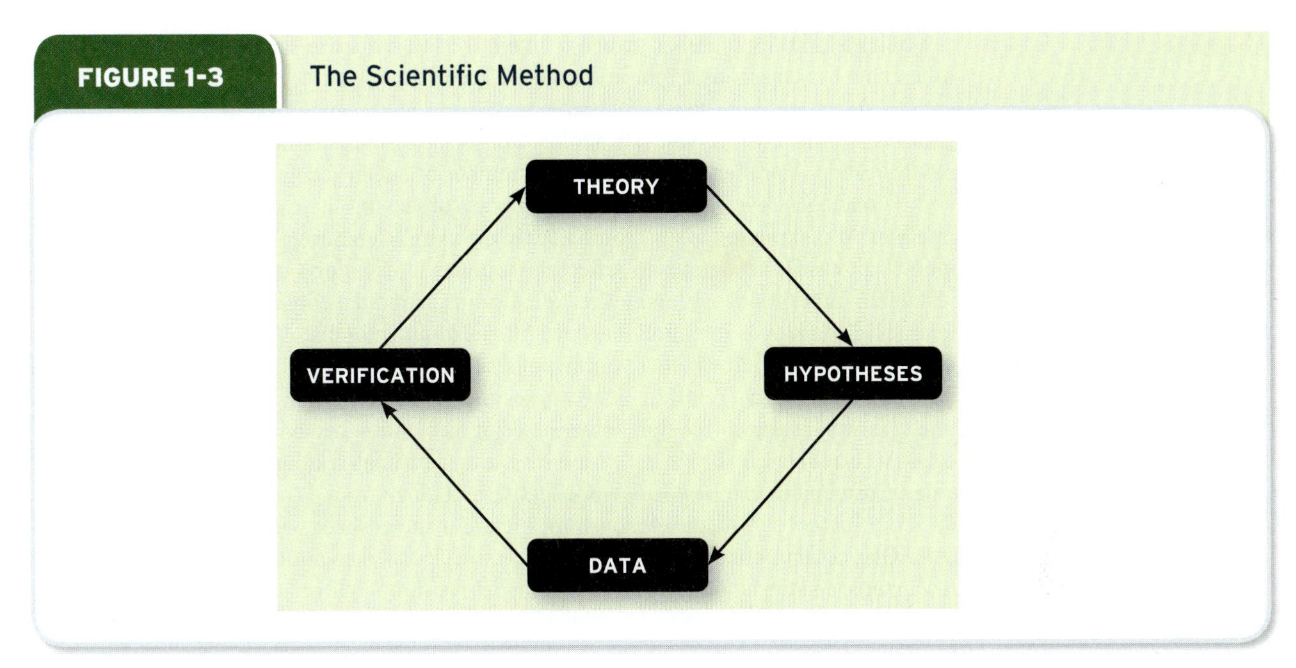

Source: Adapted from F. Bacon, M. Silverthorne, and L. Jardine, *The New Organization* (Cambridge: Cambridge University Press, 2000).

as a collection of assertions—both verbal and symbolic—that specify how and why variables are related, as well as the conditions in which they should (and should not) be related.[19] More simply, a theory tells a story and supplies the familiar who, what, where, when, and why elements found in any newspaper or magazine article.[20] Theories are often summarized with theory diagrams, the "boxes and arrows" that graphically depict relationships between variables. Our integrative model of OB in Figure 1-1 (page 6) represents one such diagram, and there will be many more to come in the remaining chapters of this textbook.

A scientist could build a theory explaining why social recognition might influence the performance and commitment of work units. From what sources would that theory be built? Theories may be built from interviews with employees in a work setting, which provide insights into their views about the strengths and weaknesses of social recognition. They also may be built from observations of people at work, in which case scientists take notes, keep diaries, and pore over company documents to find all the elements of a theory story.[21] Alternatively, theories may be built from research reviews, which examine findings of previous studies to look for general patterns or themes.[22]

Although many theories are interesting, logical, or thought provoking, many also wind up being completely wrong. After all, scientific theories once predicted that the earth was flat and the sun revolved around it. Closer to home, OB theories once argued that money was not an effective motivator and that the best way to structure jobs was to make them as simple and mundane as possible.[23] Theories must therefore be tested to verify that their predictions are accurate. As shown in Figure 1-3, the scientific method requires that theories be used to inspire **hypotheses**. Hypotheses are written predictions that specify relationships between variables. For example, a theory of social recognition could be used to inspire this hypothesis: "Social recognition behaviours on the part of managers will be positively related to the job performance and organizational commitment of their units." This hypothesis states, in black and white, the expected relationship between social recognition and unit performance.

hypotheses Written predictions that specify relationships between variables

Assume a family member owned a chain of 21 fast-food restaurants and allowed you to test this hypothesis using the restaurants. Specifically, you decided to train the managers in a subset of the restaurants about how to use social recognition as a tool to reinforce behaviours. Meanwhile, you left another subset of restaurants unchanged to represent a control group. You then tracked the total number of social recognition behaviours exhibited by managers over the next nine months by observing the managers at specific time intervals. You measured job performance by tracking drive-through times for the next nine months and used those times to reflect the minutes it takes for a customer to approach the restaurant, order food, pay, and leave. You also measured the commitment of the work unit by tracking employee retention rates over the next nine months.

correlation The statistical relationship between two variables; abbreviated *r*, it can be positive or negative and range from 0 (no statistical relationship) to ±1 (a perfect statistical relationship)

So how can you tell whether your hypothesis was supported? You could analyze the data by examining the **correlation** between social recognition behaviours and drive-through times, as well as the correlation between social recognition behaviours and employee turnover. A correlation, abbreviated *r*, describes the statistical relationship between two variables. Correlations can be positive or negative and range from 0 (no statistical relationship) to ±1 (a perfect statistical relationship). Picture a spreadsheet with two columns of numbers. One column contains the total numbers of social recognition behaviours for all 21 restaurants, and the other contains the average drive-through times for those same 21 restaurants. The best way to get a feel for the correlation is to look at a scatterplot—a graph made from those two columns of numbers. Figure 1-4 presents three scatterplots, each depicting differently sized correlations. The strength of the correlation can be inferred from the "compactness" of its scatterplot. Panel (a) shows a perfect 1.0 correlation; knowing the score for social recognition allows you to predict the score for drive-through times perfectly. Panel (b) shows a correlation of .50, so the trend in the data is less obvious than in panel (a) but still easy to see with the naked eye. Finally, panel (c) shows a correlation of .00—no statistical relationship. Understanding the correlation is important because OB questions are not "yes or no" in nature. That is, the question is not "*Does* social recognition lead to higher job performance?" but rather "*How often* does social recognition lead to higher job performance?" The correlation provides a number that expresses an answer to the "how often" question.

So what is the correlation between social recognition and job performance (and between social recognition and organizational commitment)? It turns out that a study very similar to the one described was actually conducted, using a sample of 21 Burger King restaurants with 525 total employees.[24] The correlation between social recognition and job performance was .28. The restaurants that received training in social recognition averaged 44 seconds of drive-through time nine months later versus 62 seconds for the control group locations. The correlation between social recognition and retention rates was .20. The restaurants that received training in social recognition had a 16 percent better retention rate than the control group locations nine months later. The study also instituted a financial "pay-for-performance" system in a subset of the locations and found that the social recognition effects were just as strong as the financial effects.

A study of Burger King restaurants revealed a correlation between social recognition—praise and appreciation by managers—and employees' performance and commitment. Such studies contribute to the growing body of organizational behaviour knowledge.

Of course, you might wonder whether correlations of .28 or .20 are impressive or unimpressive. To understand those numbers, let's consider some context for them. Table 1-5 (page 20)

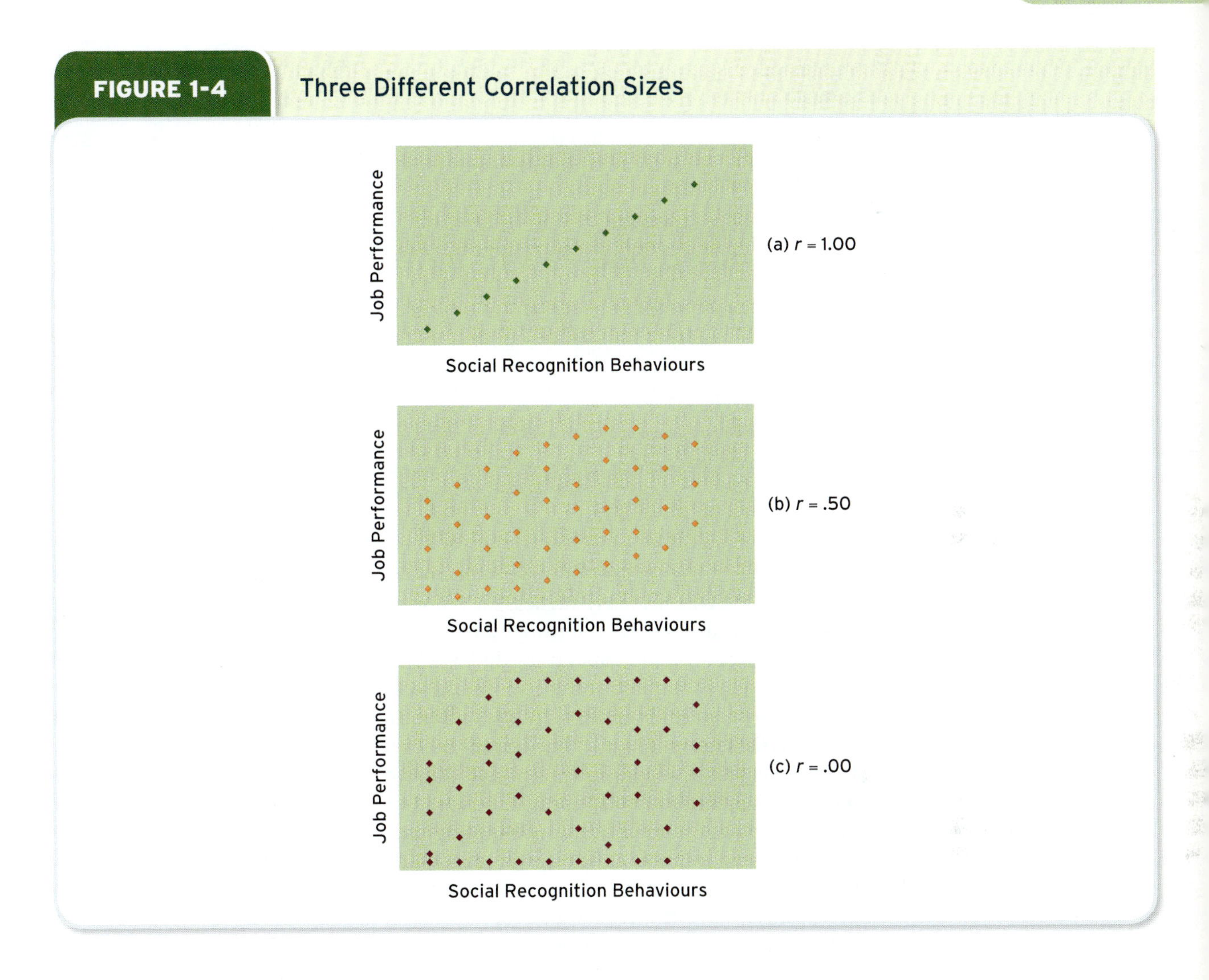

provides some notable correlations from other areas of science. If the correlation between height and weight is only .44, then a correlation of .28 between social recognition and job performance doesn't sound too bad! In fact, a correlation of .50 is considered "strong" in organizational behaviour research, given the sheer number of things that can affect how employees feel and act.[25] A .30 correlation is considered "moderate," and many studies discussed in this book will have results in this range. Finally, a .10 correlation is considered "weak" in organizational behaviour research. It should be noted, however, that even "weak" correlations can be important if they predict costly behaviours such as theft or ethical violations. The .08 correlation between smoking and lung cancer within 25 years is a good example of how important small correlations can be.

Does this one study settle the debate about the value of social recognition for job performance and organizational commitment? Not really, for a variety of reasons. First, it included only 21 restaurants with 525 employees. Maybe the results would have turned out differently if the study had included more locations. Second, maybe there is something unique about fast-food employees or restaurant employees in general that makes them particularly responsive to public praise and recognition. Third, it may be that social recognition affects drive-through times but not other forms of job performance, like customer service ratings or the accuracy of completed food orders.

TABLE 1-5 Some Notable Correlations

CORRELATION BETWEEN...	*r*	SAMPLE SIZE
Height and weight	.44	16,948
Viagra and sexual functioning	.38	779
Ibuprofen and pain reduction	.14	8,488
Antihistamines and reduced sneezing	.11	1,023
Smoking and lung cancer within 25 years	.08	3,956
Coronary bypass surgery and 5-year survival	.08	2,649

Source: R. Hogan, "In Defense of Personality Measurement: New Wine for Old Whiners," *Human Performance* 18 (2005), pp. 331–41.

The important point is that little can be learned from a single study. The best way to test a theory is to conduct many studies, each of which is as different as possible from the ones that preceded it.[26] So if you really wanted to study the effects of social recognition, you would conduct several studies using different kinds of samples and different measures. After completing all of those studies, you could look back on the results and create some sort of average correlation across all of the studies. This process is what a technique called **meta-analysis** does. It takes all of the correlations found in studies of a particular relationship and calculates a weighted average (such that correlations based on studies with large samples are weighted more than correlations based on studies with small samples). It turns out that a meta-analysis has been conducted on the effects of social recognition and job performance and indicates an average correlation of .21 across studies conducted in 96 different organizations in the service industry.[27] That meta-analysis offers more compelling support for the potential benefits of social recognition than the methods of experience, intuition, or authority could have provided.

meta-analysis A method that combines the results of multiple scientific studies by essentially calculating a weighted average correlation across studies (with larger studies receiving more weight)

MOVING FORWARD IN THIS BOOK

The chapters that follow will work through the integrative model of OB in Figure 1-1 (page 6). Each chapter begins with a case scenario for context and discussion. Theories relevant to that topic will be highlighted and discussed. The concepts in those theories will be demonstrated in the **OB on Screen** features to show how OB phenomena have "come to life" in film. You'll also get to see how those concepts can be applied to student life in the **OB for Students** feature. In addition, the **OB Internationally** features describe how those concepts operate differently in different cultures and nations. Finally, it is important to recognize that the knowledge contained in this text represents the collective efforts of a global community of researchers who carefully apply the scientific method to study specific questions within the field of organizational behaviour. The **OB Research in Canada** feature in each chapter will showcase a prominent (or promising) Canadian-based researcher who studies organizational behaviour.

Each chapter ends with three sections. The first section provides a summarizing theory diagram that explains why some employees exhibit higher levels of a given concept than others. For example, the summarizing theory diagram for Chapter 4 explains why some employees are more satisfied with their jobs than others. As we noted in the opening of this chapter, knowledge about *why* is critical to any employee who is trying to make sense of his or her working life or any manager who is trying to make his or her unit more effective. How often have you spent time trying to explain your own attitudes and behaviours to yourself? If you consider yourself to be a reflective person, you've probably thought about such questions quite a bit. Our **OB Assessments** feature will help you find out how reflective you really are. This feature also appears in each chapter of this textbook and allows you to gain valuable knowledge about your own personality, abilities, job attitudes, and leadership styles.

OB ASSESSMENTS

This feature is designed to illustrate how OB concepts actually get measured in practice. In many cases, these OB assessments will provide you with potentially valuable insights into your own attitudes, skills, and personality. The OB assessments that you will see in each chapter consist of multiple survey questions. Two concepts are critical when evaluating how good the OB assessments are: *reliability* and *validity*. Reliability is defined as the degree to which the survey questions are free from random error. If survey questions are reliable, then similar questions will yield similar answers. Validity is defined as the degree to which the survey questions seem to assess what they are meant to assess. If survey questions are valid, then experts on the subject will agree that the questions seem appropriate.

PRIVATE SELF-CONSCIOUSNESS

How reflective or introspective are you? This assessment is designed to measure private self-consciousness—the tendency to direct attention inward to better understand your attitudes and behaviours. Answer each question using the response scale provided. Then subtract your answers to the bold-faced questions from 4, with the difference being your new answers for those questions. For example, if your original answer for question 5 was "3," your new answer is 1 (4 – 3). Then sum your answers for the six questions.

0 EXTREMELY UNCHARACTERISTIC OF ME	1 SOMEWHAT UNCHARACTERISTIC OF ME	2 NEUTRAL	3 SOMEWHAT CHARACTERISTIC OF ME	4 EXTREMELY CHARACTERISTIC OF ME

1. I'm always trying to figure myself out. ________
2. Generally, I'm not very aware of myself. ________
3. I reflect about myself a lot. ________
4. I'm often the subject of my own daydreams. ________
5. I never scrutinize myself. ________
6. I'm generally attentive to my inner feelings. ________
7. I'm constantly examining my motives. ________
8. I sometimes have the feeling that I'm off somewhere watching myself. ________
9. I'm alert to changes in my mood. ________
10. I'm aware of the way my mind works when I work through a problem. ________

SCORING

If your scores sum up to 26 or above, you do a lot of self-reflection and are highly self-aware. You may find that many of the theories discussed in this textbook will help you better understand your attitudes and feelings about working life.

Source: A. Fenigstein, M.F. Scheier, and A.H. Buss, "Public and Private Self-Consciousness: Assessment and Theory," *Journal of Consulting and Clinical Psychology* 43 (1975), pp. 522–27.

The next concluding section describes the results of meta-analyses that summarize the relationships between that chapter's topic and both job performance and organizational commitment. Over time, you'll gain a feel for which of the topics in Figure 1-1 (page 6) have strong, moderate, or weak relationships with these outcomes. This knowledge will help you recognize how everything in OB fits together and what the most valuable tools are for improving performance and commitment in the workplace. As you will discover, some of the topics in OB have a greater impact on how well employees perform their jobs, whereas others have a greater impact on how long employees remain with their organizations.

Finally, the third concluding section describes how the content of that chapter can be applied, at a specific level, in an actual organization. For example, the motivation chapter concludes with a section describing how compensation practices can be used to maximize employee effort. If you're currently working, we hope that these concluding sections help you see how the concepts you're reading about actually could be used to improve your own organizations. Even if you're not working, these application sections give you a glimpse into how you will experience OB concepts once you begin your working life.

In closing, we hope you come to believe that OB is an interesting subject, because almost everyone can relate to the concepts discussed within it. Almost everyone has experienced a bad boss, instructor, or other authority figure. Almost everyone has grappled with issues of trust or had to find a way to cope with stress. You will read about how noteworthy companies have dealt with these issues, but you can also ask yourself how you would react in the same situation. In summary, happy reading—we hope you enjoy the book!

TAKEAWAYS

1.1 Organizational behaviour is a field of study devoted to understanding and explaining the attitudes and behaviours of individuals and groups in organizations. More simply, it focuses on *why* individuals and groups in organizations act the way they do.

1.2 The two primary outcomes in organizational behaviour are job performance and organizational commitment. Performance and commitment are directly influenced by several key individual mechanisms (job satisfaction; stress; motivation; trust, justice, and ethics; learning and decision making). The relations must be considered in several important contexts, such as the personal attributes of the individual (personality, cultural values, and ability), the attributes and processes that characterize the groups in which the individual works, and the structure and culture of the organization.

1.3 The effective management of organizational behaviour can help a company become more profitable—even in challenging economic times—because good people are a valuable resource. Not only are good people rare, but they are also hard to imitate.

They create a history that cannot be bought or copied, they make numerous small decisions that cannot be observed by competitors, and they create socially complex resources such as culture, teamwork, trust, and reputation. Many scientific studies support the relationship between effective organizational behaviour and company performance. Good OB policies have been linked to employee productivity, firm profitability, and even firm survival.

1.4 Theories about organizational behaviour are valuable because they help to organize and describe how concepts might relate to one another, and they help to inspire hypotheses that can be tested with data. Scientific studies collect and analyze data to test the validity of theoretical relationships, which in turn, can be the basis for further theoretical refinements and sound management practices.

KEY TERMS

- bureaucracy *p. 4*
- correlation *p. 18*
- history *p. 10*
- human relations movement *p. 5*
- human resource management *p. 4*
- hypotheses *p. 17*
- inimitable *p. 10*
- meta-analysis *p. 20*
- numerous small decisions *p. 11*
- organizational behaviour (ob) *p. 4*
- rare *p. 10*
- resource-based view *p. 9*
- rule of one-eighth *p. 14*
- scientific management *p. 4*
- socially complex resources *p. 11*
- strategic management *p. 4*
- theory *p. 16*

DISCUSSION QUESTIONS

1.1 Can you think of other service businesses that, like Boston Pizza, seem to do an effective job with customer service? Which organizational behaviour topics would be most important to maintaining that high service level?

1.2 Think again about the worst co-worker you've ever had—the one who did some of the things listed in Table 1-1 on page 3. Think about what that co-worker's boss did (or didn't do) to try to improve his or her behaviour. What did the boss do well or poorly? What would you have done differently, and which organizational behaviour topics would have been most relevant?

1.3 Which of the individual mechanisms in Figure 1-1 on page 6 (job satisfaction; stress; motivation; trust, justice, and ethics; learning and decision making) seems to drive your performance and commitment the most? Do you think you're unique in that regard, or do you think most people would answer that way?

1.4 Think of something that you "know" to be true based on the method of experience, the method of intuition, or the method of authority. Could you test your knowledge using the method of science? How would you do it?

CASE • LEADING THE WAY IN CHALLENGING TIMES: RBC

According to Zabeen Hirji, a senior vice president of human resources at the Royal Bank of Canada (RBC), only by fully leveraging the talents and potential of a diverse workforce, can companies ensure economic prosperity in the face of changing conditions and challenging economic times.

RBC is Canada's largest bank, with total assets of $605 billion, and 70,000 full- and part-time employees serving more than 15 million personal, business, public sector, and institutional clients through offices in Canada and around the world. As of October 2006, RBC employed approximately 8,000 people in management-level positions with over half (55 percent) being women and 20 percent of these position staffed with visible minorities. According to Zabeen Hirji, RBC strives to foster an organizational culture that brings out the best in everyone, provides opportunities for talented employees of all backgrounds, and contributes to the creation of innovative solutions for clients and communities. In this organization, differences in people and their talents are seen as valuable and potential assets, and a source of sustainable competitive advantage.

But how does RBC implement its diversity strategy? Several key activities include hiring people who have the technical, behavioural, and diversity requirements for the position being filled, investing heavily in training throughout the company, and by promoting internal mentoring relationships. For example, RBC recently launched its *Diversity Dialogues* program, a reciprocal mentoring program in which an RBC executive is matched with a diverse, high potential employee.

1.1 Most of you would agree that it is easy to get along and work with people who share similar values, interests, perspectives, and experiences. Is it possible to be different yet feel similar? Explain.

1.2 Do you believe that RBC's focus on diversity has given the organization a competitive advantage in the industry? Explain.

Sources: RBC website (www.rbc.com); accessed April 2008; Z. Hirji, "Growth and Innovation Rests on Diversity," *Canadian HR Reporter,* December 2006, p. 18; M. Shin, "Minority Report," *CorporateKnights: The Cleantech Issue* 2007, Volume 6.2, pp. 34–42.

EXERCISE • IS OB COMMON SENSE?

The purpose of this exercise is to take some of the topics covered in this textbook and examine whether improving them is "just common sense." This exercise uses groups of six participants, so your instructor will either assign you to a group of six or ask you to create your own group of six. The exercise has the following steps:

1. Consider the theory diagram shown below. It explains why two "independent variables" (the quality of a movie's script and the fame of its stars) affect a "dependent variable" (how much the movie makes at the box office).

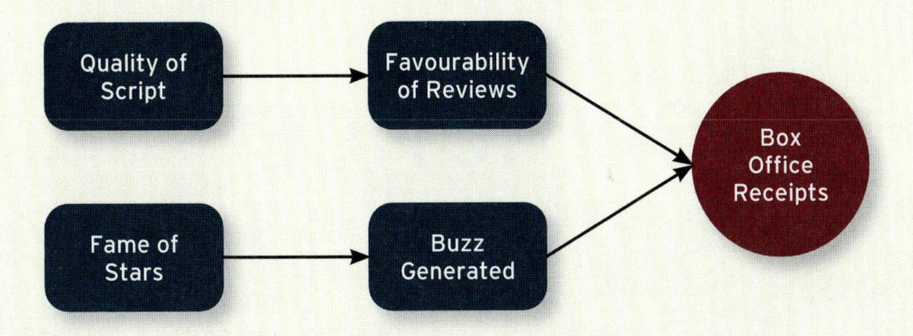

2. Now build your own theory diagram about organizational behaviour. In groups of four to six students, choose one of the following four topics to use as your dependent variable:
   - *Job satisfaction:* The pleasurable emotions felt when performing job tasks
   - *Strain:* The headaches, fatigue, or burnout resulting from workplace stress
   - *Motivation:* The intensity and persistence of job-related effort
   - *Trust in supervisor:* The willingness to allow a supervisor to have significant influence over key job issues

   Using a transparency, laptop, or chalkboard, build a theory diagram that summarizes the factors that affect your chosen dependent variable. To be as comprehensive as possible, try to include at least four independent variables. Keep your books closed! You should build your diagrams using only your own experience and intuition.
3. Each group should present its theory diagram to the class. Do the predicted relationships make sense? Should anything be dropped? Should anything be added?
4. Now compare the theory diagram you created with the diagrams in the textbook (Figure 4-7 for job satisfaction, Figure 5-4 for strain, Figure 6-7 for motivation, and Figure 7-8 for trust in supervisor). How does your diagram compare to the textbook's diagrams (search the bold-faced key terms for any jargon that you don't understand)? Did you leave out some important independent variables or suggest some variables that have not been supported by the academic research summarized in the chapters? If so, it shows that OB is more than just common sense.

CONNECT—Available 24/7 with instant feedback so you can study when you want, how you want, and where you want. Take advantage of the Study Plan—an innovative tool that helps students customize their own learning experience. Students can diagnose their knowledge with pre- and post-tests, identify the areas where they need help, search contents of the entire learning package for content specific to the topic they're studying, and add these resources to their study plan. Visit **www.connectob.ca** to register—take practice quizzes, run interactive scenarios, and much more. Also visit the Student Online Learning Centre for additional study tools.

www.mcgrawhill.ca/olc/colquitt

CHAPTER 2

Job Performance

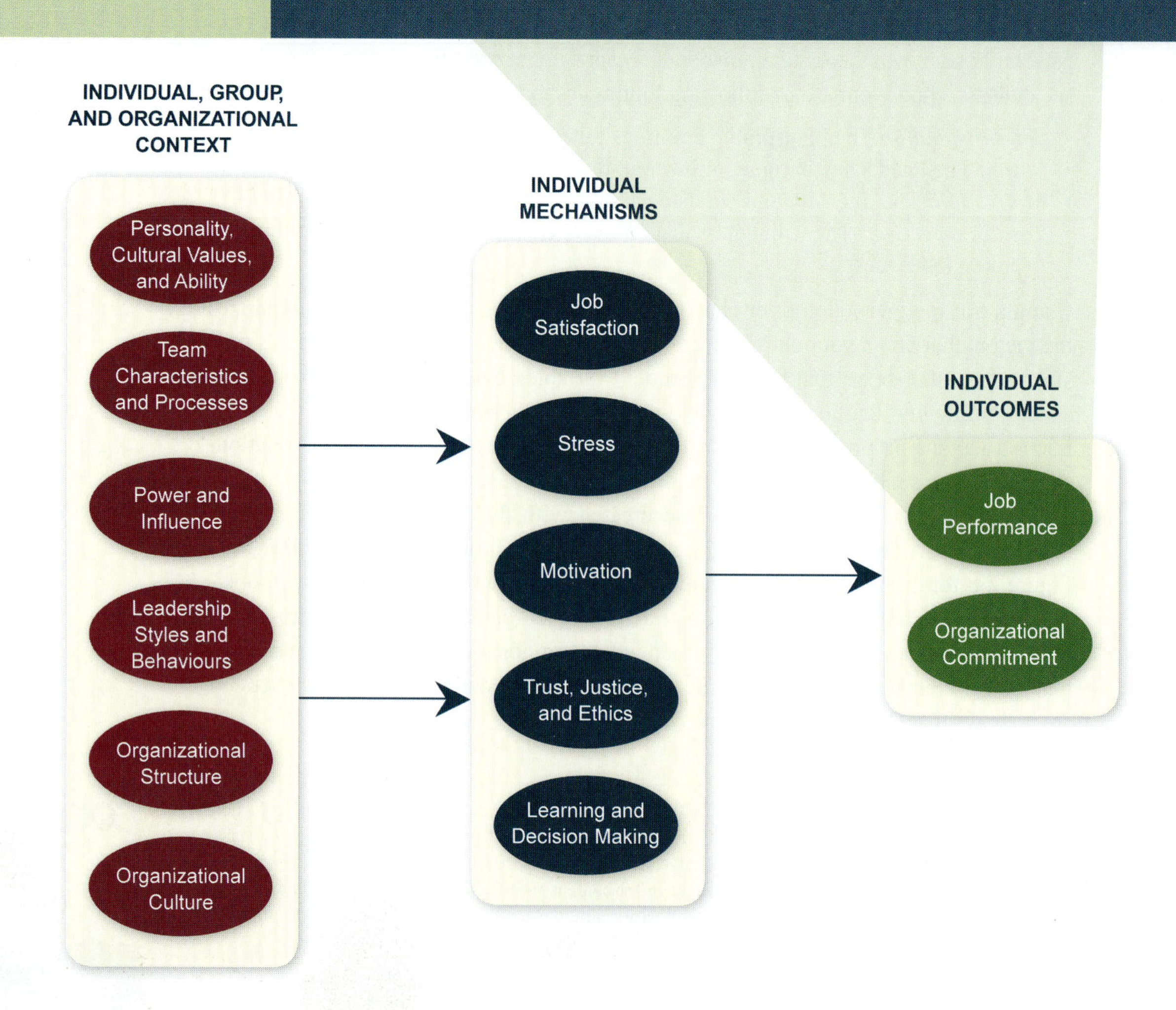

WALKERTON

The town of Walkerton is located in southwestern Ontario's rural heartland, not far from the shores of Georgian Bay. In early 2000, who could have imagined that the residents of this quiet little farming town would have experienced the most serious case of water contamination in Canadian history! In total, seven people died and almost half the town's population became seriously ill after Walkerton's water supply became contaminated with *E. coli* from cattle manure that had washed into a town well. If that wasn't bad enough, many of the people who became ill, particularly children, have had to endure ongoing health issues. "We still have hundreds of people in this community whose health has been permanently impaired," said Bruce Davidson, vice-chairman of the grassroots lobby group Concerned Walkerton Citizens. "The cost of this is just beyond belief."[1] A study released the following year concluded that the total cost to clean up and fix the Walkerton water problem would be $65 million, but this cost was closer to $155 million when human suffering from the tragedy was considered.[2] The question on everyone's mind was how could this tragedy have happened in the richest province in one of the richest countries in the world?

The Walkerton Public Utilities Commission (PUC) was responsible for the operation of the town's water and electricity resources. At the time of the incident, the PUC supplied water to the vast majority of Walkerton's residential, commercial, and public buildings. Stan Koebel, 51, was the general manager of the PUC. He worked with his younger brother Frank, who held the position of water foreman. Both had been with the PUC since the early 1970s.[3] Together, as licensed operators, Stan and Frank had primary responsibility for all day-to-day operations, including monitoring and testing water quality, and for keeping accurate records.[4] Although both brothers held a Level 3 certification, Stan and Frank had no formal training or testing of their skills before being licensed to run Walkerton's water system; both brothers were grandfathered to the status of licensed operators by virtue of two decades of on-the-job experience, which came with little technical or scientific expertise.[5]

Learning Outcomes

After reading this chapter, you should be able to answer the following questions:

2.1 What is the definition of job performance? What are the three dimensions of job performance?

2.2 What is task performance? How do organizations identify the behaviours that underlie task performance?

2.3 What is citizenship behaviour, and what are some specific examples of it?

2.4 What is counterproductive behaviour, and what are some specific examples of it?

2.5 How can organizations use job performance information to manage employee performance?

In early 2000, the quiet little farming town of Walkerton, Ontario, experienced the most serious case of water contamination in Canadian history. An inquiry revealed that this tragedy was, in part, the result of key individuals within the water utility not performing their jobs.

Dr. Murray McQuigge, the local medical officer of health, stunned the country with his revelation on CBC Radio on May 25, 2000, that the Walkerton PUC knew there was a problem with the water several days before they told the public.[6] In the fall of 2000, a public inquiry under Justice Dennis O'Connor began.[7] During the inquiry, Frank testified about drinking on the job and routine falsification of safety tests and records.[8] Stan Koebel began his testimony at the inquiry by apologizing for his role in the tragedy. He confessed that he didn't really know what *E. coli* was or its health effects.[9] On March 25, 2003, Stan Koebel and Frank Koebel were charged, under section 180 of the *Criminal Code of Canada,* with public nuisance, uttering forged documents, and breach of public duty.[10] On November 30, 2004, both brothers pleaded guilty to endangering the lives, safety, or health of the public by failing to use a chlorinator; by failing to properly monitor, sample, and test well water supplying the town of Walkerton; and by failing to accurately record the required information in the logs, and more particularly, by inaccurately completing the daily operating sheet, knowing that it would be relied on as if genuine.[11] Three weeks later, Stan was sentenced to a year in jail. Frank was sentenced to nine months of house arrest. Ontario Superior Court Justice Bruce Durno took more than two hours to read out and explain his ruling. He stressed that there was never any intent on the part of the Koebels to harm anyone, but found them negligent in performing their duties.[12]

JOB PERFORMANCE

We begin our journey through the integrative model of organizational behaviour with job performance. Why begin with performance? Because understanding one's own performance is a critical concern for any employee, and understanding the performance of one's unit is a critical concern for any manager. Consider for a moment the job performance of your university's football coach. If you were the university's athletic director, you might gauge the coach's performance by paying attention to various behaviours. How effective are the coach's practices? Are his offensive and defensive systems well designed, and is his play calling during games appropriate? Does he win? You might also gauge some other behaviours that fall outside the strict domain of football. Does the coach run a clean program? Do his players graduate on time? Does he represent the university well during interviews with the media?

This example illustrates one dilemma when examining job performance. Is performance a set of behaviours that a person does (or does not) perform, or is job performance the end result of those behaviours? You might be tempted to believe that it is more appropriate to define performance in terms of results rather than behaviours, because results seem more "objective" and are more connected to the central concern of managers or football coaches—"the bottom line." For example, the job performance of salespeople is often measured by the amount of sales revenue generated by each person over some time span (e.g., a month, a quarter, a year). For the most part, this logic makes perfect sense: Salespeople are hired by organizations to generate sales, and therefore, those who meet or exceed sales goals are worth more to the organization and should be considered higher performers.

However, as sensible as this logic seems, using results to indicate job performance creates a problem because results are often influenced by factors that are beyond the employee's control—product quality, competition, equipment, technology, budget constraints, co-workers, and supervisors, just to name a few. Even if these uncontrollable factors are less relevant in a given situation, there is another problem with a results-based view of job performance, in that results don't indicate how to reverse a "bad year." That is, performance feedback based on results does not generally provide people with enough information to learn what they need to change in their behaviour to improve. Given that OB as a field of study aims to understand, predict, and improve behaviour, we will refer to job performance as behaviour. The outcomes associated with those behaviours will therefore be termed "job performance results."

So what types of employee behaviours constitute job performance? To understand this question, consider that **job performance** is formally defined as the value of the set of employee behaviours that contribute, either positively or negatively, to organizational goal accomplishment.[13] Our definition of job performance raises a number of important questions. Specifically, you might be wondering which employee behaviours fall under the umbrella heading of "job performance." In other words, from an employee's perspective, what exactly does it mean to be a "good performer"? We could probably spend an entire chapter just listing various behaviours that are relevant to job performance. However, those behaviours generally fit into three broad categories.[14] Two categories are task performance and citizenship behaviour, both of which contribute positively to the organization. The third category is counterproductive behaviour, which contributes negatively to the organization. In our **OB on Screen** feature, you'll find an example of employees who demonstrate various levels of all three aspects of job performance. The sections that follow describe these broad categories of job performance in greater detail.

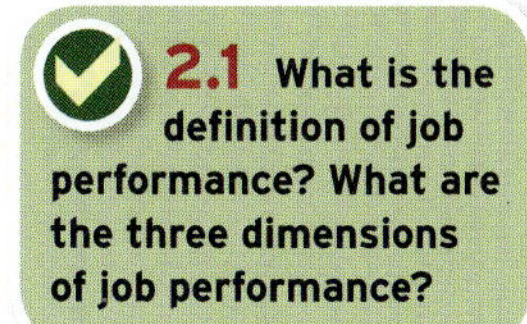

2.1 What is the definition of job performance? What are the three dimensions of job performance?

job performance Employee behaviours that contribute either positively or negatively to the accomplishment of organizational goals

TASK PERFORMANCE

Task performance includes employee behaviours that are directly involved in the transformation of organizational resources into the goods or services that the organization produces. If you read a description of a job in an employment ad online, that description will focus on task performance behaviours—the tasks, duties, and responsibilities that are a core part of the job. Put differently, task performance is the set of explicit obligations that an employee must fulfill to receive compensation and continued employment. For a flight attendant, task performance includes explaining and demonstrating safety procedures and checking the general condition of the aircraft cabin. For a firefighter, task performance includes controlling and extinguishing fires using manual and power equipment and rescuing victims from burning buildings and accident sites. For an accountant, task performance involves planning, setting up, and administering accounting systems, and preparing financial statements and reports. Finally, for operators in a water-treatment facility, task performance involves monitoring, testing, and reporting water quality.[15]

2.2 What is task performance? How do organizations identify the behaviours that underlie task performance?

task performance Employee behaviours that are directly involved in the transformation of organizational resources into the goods or services that the organization produces

Although the specific activities that constitute task performance differ widely from one job to another, task performance also can be understood in terms of more general categories. One way of categorizing task performance is to consider the extent to which the context of the job is routine or changing. **Routine task performance** involves well-known responses to demands that occur in a normal, routine, or otherwise predictable way. In these cases, employees tend to act in more or less habitual or programmed ways that vary little from one instance to another. As an example of a routine task activity, you may recall watching an expressionless flight attendant robotically demonstrate how to insert the seatbelt tongue into the seatbelt buckle before your flight takes off. Seatbelts haven't really changed since . . . oh . . . 1920, so the instructions to passengers tend to be conveyed the same way, over and over again.

routine task performance Well-known or habitual responses by employees to predictable task demands

In contrast, **adaptive task performance**, or more commonly, *adaptability*, involves employee responses to task demands that are novel, unusual, or at the very least, unpredictable.[16] For example, on August 2, 2005, Air France flight 358, carrying 297 passengers and 12 crew members from Paris, France, to Toronto, Canada, skidded off the runway on landing and into a ravine. Amid smoke and flames, the flight attendants quickly responded to the emergency and assisted three-quarters of the 297 passengers safely off the plane within 52 seconds, before the emergency response team arrived. One minute later, the remaining

adaptive task performance Thoughtful responses by an employee to unique or unusual task demands

OB ON SCREEN

MONSTERS, INC.

I'm in the zone today, Sullivan. I'm gonna do some serious scaring, putting up some big numbers.

With these words, Randall (the evil-looking purple monster) challenged Sulley (the big, blue, furry lug) to match his task performance in *Monsters, Inc.* (Pixar, 2001, released by Disney).[17] You see, the source of electricity in the monster world is the screams provoked by highly specialized monster "scarers" who enter the bedroom doors of unsuspecting human children at night.

Sulley and Randall would both score well in terms of task performance. They are the two best scarers at Monsters, Inc., and compete with each other throughout the film for the all-time "scare" record. The similarity between Sulley and Randall ends there however.

Sulley has a positive attitude about his job and is more than willing to go above and beyond to help his co-workers and the organization. For example, in one scene, Sulley offers to stay late to do some paperwork for his co-worker Mike (the green, pear-shaped guy) so that Mike can keep his date with Celia, his demanding, serpent-haired girlfriend. In another scene, Sulley offers to help train some very pathetic new scarers. Late in the film, he even comes up with a valuable suggestion that fundamentally improves the operations and profitability of Monsters, Inc. Clearly, Sulley would score high on citizenship behaviour.

In terms of counterproductive behaviour, much of the film centres on Sulley's covert attempts to return a 2-year-old girl, whom Sulley names Boo, back to her bedroom after she finds her way into the monster world. Direct contact with human children is strictly forbidden at Monsters, Inc., because the monsters believe that even the slightest touch from a child can be lethal. Although you would probably agree that Sulley's behaviour is ethical because he is acting in the best interest of Boo's safety, from Monsters, Inc.'s, perspective, the behaviour is counterproductive; the company wants Sulley to turn the girl over to the government's Child Detection Agency. However, Randall puts any of Sulley's indiscretions to shame. In conjunction with his evil boss, Randall assaults and kidnaps others to test an illegal (and potentially deadly) new method for extracting energy from children. Fortunately, Sulley (and Mike) are around to try to save the day. Do they return Boo safely to her bedroom? You'll have to watch to find out.

passengers and 12 crew members were out safely.[18] From this example, you can see that flight attendants' task performance shifted from activities such as providing safety demonstrations and handing out beverages to performing emergency procedures to save passengers' lives.

Although flight attendants receive training so that they can handle emergency situations such as this one, executing these behaviours effectively in the context of an actual emergency differs fundamentally from anything experienced previously. Because of the increasing pace of change in the workplace due to globalization, technological advances, and the greater prevalence of knowledge-intensive work, adaptability is becoming increasingly important as a type of performance in and of itself.[19] As a consequence, organizations are beginning to implement practices that promote the types of behaviours associated with adaptability. As you should be able to discern from the list in Table 2-1,[20] the behaviours involved in adaptability are diverse and may be involved in a variety of jobs in today's economy.

TABLE 2-1 Behaviours Involved in Adaptability

BEHAVIOUR TITLE	EXAMPLES OF ACTIVITIES
Handling emergencies or crisis situations	Quickly analyzing options for dealing with danger or crises and their implications; making split-second decisions based on clear and focused thinking
Handling work stress	Remaining composed and cool when faced with difficult circumstances or a highly demanding workload or schedule; acting as a calming and settling influence to whom others can look for guidance
Solving problems creatively	Turning problems upside-down and inside-out to find fresh new approaches; integrating seemingly unrelated information and developing creative solutions
Dealing with uncertain and unpredictable work situations	Readily and easily changing gears in response to unpredictable or unexpected events and circumstances; effectively adjusting plans, goals, actions, or priorities to deal with changing situations
Learning work tasks, technologies, and work situations	Quickly and proficiently learning new methods or how to perform previously unlearned tasks; anticipating change in the work demands and searching for and participating in assignments or training to prepare for these changes
Demonstrating interpersonal adaptability	Being flexible and open-minded when dealing with others; listening to and considering others' viewpoints and opinions and altering own opinion when it is appropriate to do so
Demonstrating cultural adaptability	Willingly adjusting behaviour or appearance as necessary to comply with or show respect for others' values and customs; understanding the implications of one's actions and adjusting approach to maintain positive relationships with other groups, organizations, or cultures

Source: E.D. Pulakos, S. Arad, M.A. Donovan, and K.E. Plamondon, "Adaptability in the Workplace: Development of a Taxonomy of Adaptive Performance," *Journal of Applied Psychology* 85 (2000), pp. 612–24. Copyright © 2000 by the American Psychological Association. Adapted with permission. No further reproduction or distribution is permitted without permission from the American Psychological Association.

Now that we've given you a general understanding of task performance behaviours, you might be wondering how organizations identify the sets of behaviours that represent "task performance" for different jobs. Many organizations identify task performance behaviours by conducting a **job analysis**. Although there are many different ways to conduct a job analysis, most boil down to the following three steps. First, a list of all the activities involved in a job is generated. This list generally results from data from several sources, including observations, surveys, and interviews of employees. Second, each activity on this list is rated by "subject matter experts" according to things like the importance and frequency of the activity. Subject matter experts generally have experience performing the job or managing people who perform the job and therefore are in a position to judge the degree to which specific activities contribute to the organization. Third, the activities that are rated highly in terms of their importance and frequency are retained and used to define task performance.

job analysis A process by which an organization determines requirements of specific jobs

Those retained behaviours often find their way into the measures that managers use to evaluate the task performance of employees. Consider the job of customer service representative (CSR) at your local bank. Apart from the technical activities routinely performed (e.g., processing customer cash deposits and withdrawals; obtaining and processing client information; balancing daily transactions using computer programs), many CSRs are expected to sell a variety of banking services and products and perform a wide range of face-to-face customer service behaviours.[21] A sample of the behaviours in these performance areas are listed in Table 2-2. After the behavioural information is collected for each CSR (from supervisors, co-workers, or clients), the bank manager is in a position to provide feedback and coaching to the employee about which types of behaviours he or she needs to change or improve. Put yourself in the place of a CSR for a moment. Wouldn't you rather have your task performance evaluated on the basis of the behaviours in Table 2-2 rather than some overall index of errors committed, shortages, or products sold. After all, those behaviours are completely within your control, and the feedback you receive from your boss will be more informative and helpful than the simple directive to "sell more next year."

TABLE 2-2 Performance Review Form for a Customer Service Representative at the Bank

IMPORTANT TASK BEHAVIOURS
Smiles when interacting with customers
Is attentive and considerate when communicating with customers
Demonstrates some flexibility with banking procedures to accommodate customers
Reads all available literature pertaining to new products/services
Follows the planned weekly selling "script"
Suggests potential bank services during normal counter interactions
Checks to see whether all pertinent information has been included on paperwork
Follows normal banking procedures regarding financial transactions
Processes client transactions quickly
Shares information that is relevant for others to carry out their assignments
Helps other CSRs who are experiencing difficulties
Develops and maintains effective working relationships with others in the bank

When organizations find it impractical to use job analysis to identify the set of behaviours needed to define task performance, they can turn to a database the government has created to help describe a wide variety of jobs. The **National Occupational Classification (NOC)** is the nationally accepted reference on occupations in Canada. It organizes over 30,000 job titles into 520 occupational group descriptions.[22] The NOC is used daily by thousands of people to compile, analyze, and communicate information about occupations, as well as to understand the jobs found throughout Canada's labour market. Of course, the NOC represents only a first step in figuring out the important tasks for a given job. Many organizations ask their employees to perform tasks that their competitors do not so that their workforce performance is assessed in a unique and valuable way. The NOC cannot capture those sorts of unique task requirements, the "numerous small decisions" that separate the most effective organizations from their competitors. For instance, the NOC will convey that CSRs who work in financial service organizations perform, among other things, routine banking transactions and respond to customers' needs. What the NOC is unable to do is convey the unique ways these activities are enacted. For instance, a bank with a strong customer focus may encourage its CSRs to demonstrate some flexibility with policies and procedures to accommodate customer needs. Thus, though the NOC may be a good place to start, the task information from the database should be supplemented with information regarding behaviours that support the organization's values and strategies.

National Occupational Classification (NOC) A national database of occupations in Canada, organizing over 30,000 job titles into 520 occupational group descriptions

Before concluding our section on task performance, it is important to note that task performance behaviours are not simply performed versus not performed. Although poor performers often fail to complete required behaviours, it is just as true that the best performers often exceed all expectations for those behaviours. The most valuable employees in any organization are those who "go the extra mile" by engaging in levels of task performance that previously were unheard of. For example, it is expected that hotel employees care for guests and make sure they have everything they need to enjoy their stay. However, the employees at the Hilton New Orleans Riverside Hotel "went the extra mile" as the city was ravaged by Hurricane Katrina. The 450 employees in the hotel cared for approximately 4,500 guests during the storm, guarding their safety while the hurricane blew through the city and afterward when the levees failed. One employee carried elderly guests down 16 flights of stairs because of the oppressive heat on the higher floors. Hotel executives even arranged for charter buses to make the trip to Texas to evacuate guests.[23] If you asked the hotel employees, they might be tempted to understate their actions by saying, "We were just doing our jobs." And that's true—but they were doing their jobs at an exceptionally high level that will not soon be forgotten by those hotel guests.

CITIZENSHIP BEHAVIOUR

2.3 What is citizenship behaviour, and what are some specific examples of it?

Sometimes, employees go the extra mile by actually engaging in behaviours that are not within their job description—and thus that do not fall under the broad heading of task performance. This situation brings us to the second category of job performance, called citizenship behaviour. **Citizenship behaviour** is defined as voluntary employee activities that may or may not be rewarded but that contribute to the organization by improving the overall quality of the setting in which work takes place.[24] Have you ever had a co-worker or fellow student who was always willing to help someone who was struggling? Who always attended optional meetings or social functions to support his or her colleagues? Who always maintained a good attitude, even in trying times? We tend to call those people "good citizens" or "good soldiers."[25] High levels of citizenship behaviour earn them such titles. Although there are many different types of behaviours that might seem to fit the definition of citizenship behaviour, research suggests two main categories that differ according to who benefits from the activity: co-workers or the organization (see Figure 2-1).[26]

citizenship behaviour Voluntary employee behaviours that contribute to organizational goals by improving the context in which work takes place

FIGURE 2-1 Types of Citizenship Behaviours

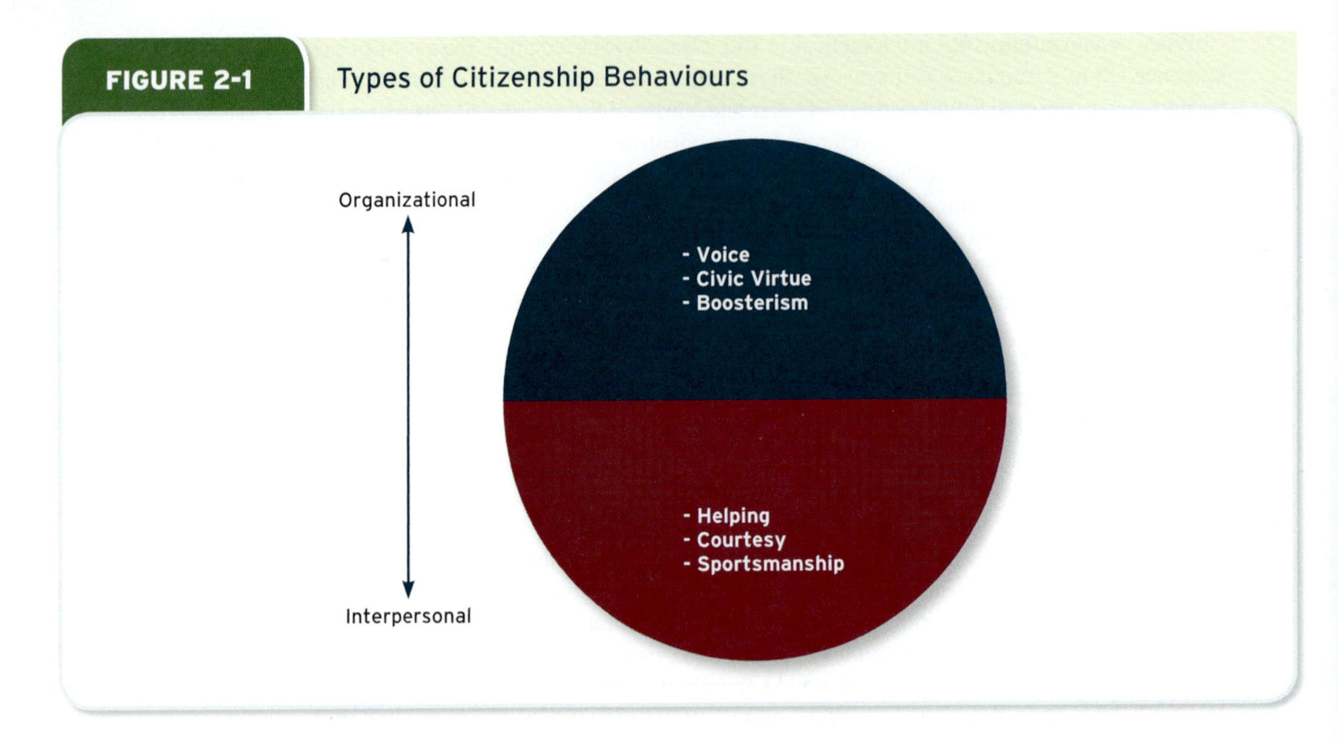

interpersonal citizenship behaviour Going beyond normal job expectations to assist, support, and develop co-workers and colleagues

helping Assisting co-workers who have heavy workloads, aiding them with personal matters, and showing new employees the ropes when they are first on the job

courtesy Sharing important information with co-workers

sportsmanship Maintaining a positive attitude with co-workers through good and bad times

organizational citizenship behaviour Going beyond normal expectations to improve operations of the organization, as well as defending the organization and being loyal to it

The first category of citizenship behaviour is the one with which you're most likely to be familiar: **interpersonal citizenship behaviour**. Such behaviours benefit co-workers and colleagues and involve assisting, supporting, and developing other organizational members in a way that goes beyond normal job expectations.[27] For example, **helping** involves assisting co-workers who have heavy workloads, aiding them with personal matters, and showing new employees the ropes when they first arrive on the job. Do you consider yourself a helpful person? At the end of this chapter, check the **OB Assessments** feature to find out how helpful you really are. **Courtesy** refers to keeping co-workers informed about matters that are relevant to them. Some employees have a tendency to keep relevant facts and events secret. Good citizens do the opposite; they keep others in the loop because they never know what information might be useful to someone else. **Sportsmanship** involves maintaining a good attitude with co-workers, even when they've done something annoying or when the unit is going through tough times. Whining and complaining are contagious; good citizens avoid being the squeaky wheel who frequently makes mountains out of molehills.

Although interpersonal citizenship behaviour is important in many different job contexts, it may be even more important in contexts in which employees work in small groups or teams. A team with members who tend to be helpful, respectful, and courteous is also likely to have a positive team atmosphere in which members trust one another. This type of situation is essential to foster the willingness of team members to work toward a common team goal rather than goals that may be more self-serving.[28] In fact, if you think about the behaviours that commonly fall under the "teamwork" heading, you'll probably agree that most are examples of interpersonal citizenship behaviour.[29]

The second category of citizenship behaviour is **organizational citizenship behaviour**. These behaviours benefit the larger organization by supporting and defending the company, working to improve its operations, and being especially loyal to it.[30] For example,

voice involves speaking up and offering constructive suggestions for change. Good citizens react to bad rules or policies by constructively trying to change them as opposed to passively complaining about them (we return to the subject of voice in Chapter 3 on organizational commitment).[31] **Civic virtue** refers to participating in the company's operations at a deeper-than-normal level by attending voluntary meetings and functions, reading and keeping up with organizational announcements, and keeping abreast of business news that affects the company. **Boosterism** means representing the organization in a positive way when out in public, away from the office, and away from work. Think of friends you've had who worked for a restaurant. Did they always say good things about the restaurant when talking to you and keep any "kitchen horror stories" to themselves? If so, they were being good citizens by engaging in high levels of boosterism.

voice When an employee speaks up to offer constructive suggestions for change, often in reaction to a negative work event

civic virtue Participation in company operations at a deeper-than-normal level through voluntary meetings, readings, and keeping up with news that affects the company

boosterism Positively representing the organization when in public

Two important points should be emphasized about citizenship behaviours. First, as you've probably realized, citizenship behaviours are relevant in virtually any job, regardless of the particular nature of its tasks,[32] and there are clear benefits of these behaviours in terms of the effectiveness of work units and organizations.[33] As examples, research conducted in a paper mill found that the quantity and quality of crew output was higher in crews that included more good citizens.[34] Research of 30 restaurants also showed that higher levels of citizenship behaviour promoted higher revenue, better operating efficiency, higher customer satisfaction, higher performance quality, less food waste, and fewer customer complaints.[35] Thus, it seems clear that citizenship behaviours have a significant influence on the bottom line.

From an employee's perspective, it may be tempting to discount the importance of citizenship behaviours—to just focus on your own job tasks and leave aside any "extra" stuff. After all, citizenship behaviours appear to be voluntary and optional, whereas task duties are not. However, discounting citizenship behaviours is a bad idea, because supervisors do not always view such actions as optional. In fact, research on computer salespeople, insurance agents, petrochemical salespeople, pharmaceutical sales managers, office furniture makers, and sewing machine operators has shown that citizenship behaviours relate strongly to supervisor evaluations of job performance, even when differences in task performance are also considered.[36] As we discuss in our **OB Internationally** feature, the tendency of supervisors to consider citizenship behaviours in evaluating overall job performance appears to hold even across countries with vastly different cultures.[37] Of course, this issue has a lot of relevance to you, given that in most organizations, supervisors' evaluations of job performance play significant roles in determining pay and promotions. Indeed, employee citizenship behaviour has been found to influence the salary and promotion recommendations people receive, over and above their task performance.[38] Put simply, it pays to be a good citizen!

2.4 What is counterproductive behaviour, and what are some specific examples of it?

COUNTERPRODUCTIVE BEHAVIOUR

Now we move from the "good soldiers" to the "bad apples." Whereas task performance and citizenship behaviour refer to employee activities that help the organization achieve its goals and objectives, other activities in which employees engage do just the opposite. The third broad category of job performance is **counterproductive behaviour,** defined as employee behaviours that intentionally hinder organizational goal accomplishment. The word *intentionally* is a key aspect of this definition; these are things that employees mean to do, not things they accidentally do. Although there are many different kinds of counterproductive behaviours, research suggests that—like task performance and citizenship behaviour—they can be grouped into more specific categories (see Figure 2-2 on page 37).[39]

counterproductive behaviour Employee behaviours that intentionally hinder organizational goal accomplishment

Property deviance refers to behaviours that harm the organization's assets and possessions. For example, **sabotage** represents the purposeful destruction of physical equipment,

property deviance Behaviours that harm the organization's assets and possessions

sabotage Purposeful destruction of equipment, organizational processes, or company products

OB INTERNATIONALLY

As we have already explained, citizenship behaviour tends to be viewed as relatively voluntary because it is not often explicitly outlined in job descriptions or directly rewarded. However, people in organizations vary in their beliefs regarding the degree to which citizenship behaviour is truly voluntary, and these differences have important implications.[40]

As an example, consider a situation in which an employee chooses not to engage in certain citizenship behaviours because of his or her belief that the behaviours are voluntary. However, this employee works for a supervisor who believes that the behaviours are part of the job. If the supervisor were to give this employee a poor performance evaluation for failing to engage in citizenship behaviours, the employee would believe that the evaluation was unfair and likely protest. As another example, consider a situation in which an employee engages in citizenship behaviours because of his or her belief that the behaviours are part of the job. However, this employee works for a supervisor who believes that citizenship behaviours are unnecessary. Assuming that the supervisor would not consider the citizenship behaviours on a performance evaluation, the employee would likely react negatively because he or she has not been recognized for putting effort into activities that help other member of the organization.

So what types of factors cause differences in beliefs regarding whether or not citizenship behaviour is discretionary? One factor that would appear to be important is national culture. It is widely believed that the culture in countries like Canada, the United States, and the Netherlands encourages behaviours that support competition and individual achievement, whereas the culture in countries like China, Colombia, and Portugal encourages behaviours that promote cooperation and group interests over self-interests.[41] On the basis of these cultural differences, it is only natural to expect that people from the former set of countries would consider citizenship performance relatively unimportant compared with people from the latter set of countries. In reality, however, the findings from one recent study comparing Canadian and Chinese managers found that this cultural stereotype was simply not true.[42] Managers in both countries not only took citizenship behaviour into account when evaluating overall job performance, but the weight they gave to citizenship behaviour in their overall evaluation of employees was the same. One explanation for this result is that the realities of running effective business organizations in a global economy have a significantly stronger impact on managerial practices than do cultural norms.

So what is the lesson here? Although employees may view citizenship behaviour as voluntary because it is not spelled out in job descriptions or explicitly rewarded, managers take these behaviours into account, and this evaluation appears to be true across countries with vastly different cultural traditions.

organizational processes, or company products. Do you know what a laser disc is? Probably not—and the reason you don't is because of sabotage. A company called DiscoVision (a subsidiary of MCA) manufactured laser discs in the late 1970s, with popular movie titles like *Smokey and the Bandit* and *Jaws* retailing for $15.95. Although this level matches the price of DVDs today, it was far less than the $50 to $100 needed to buy videocassettes (which were of inferior quality) at the time. Unfortunately, laser discs had to be manufactured in "clean rooms," because specs of dust or debris could cause the image on the TV to freeze, repeat, skip, or drop out. When MCA merged with IBM in 1979, the morale of the employees fell, and counterproductive behaviours began to occur. Specifically, employees sabotaged the devices that measured the cleanliness of the rooms and began eating in the rooms—even "popping" their potato chip bags to send food particles into the air. This sabotage eventually

FIGURE 2-2 Types of Counterproductive Behaviours

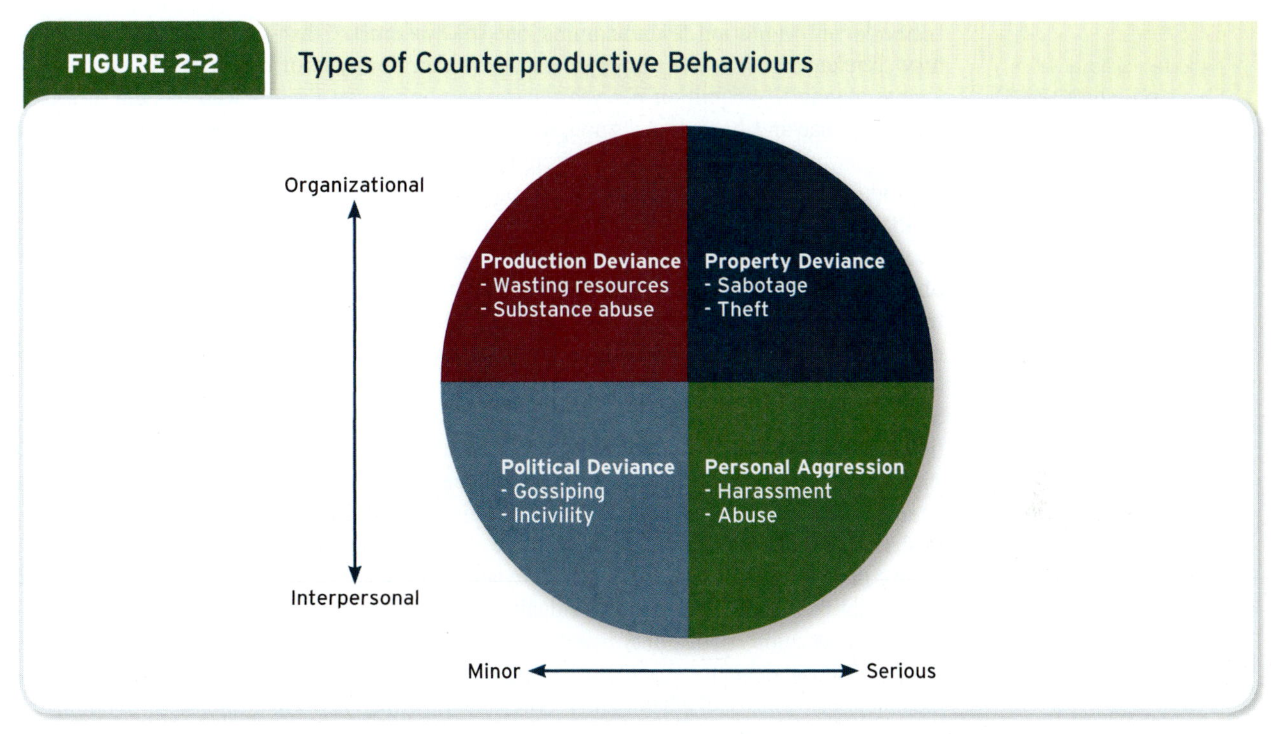

Source: Adapted from S.L. Robinson and R.J. Bennett, "A Typology of Deviant Workplace Behaviours: A Multidimensional Scaling Study," *Academy of Management Journal* 38 (1995), pp. 555–72.

created a 90 percent disc failure rate that completely alienated customers. As a result, despite its much lower production costs and higher quality picture, the laser disc disappeared, and the organizations that supported the technology suffered incredible losses.[43]

Even if you've never heard of the laser disc, you've certainly eaten in a restaurant. The cost of counterproductive behaviours in the restaurant industry is estimated to be 2 to 3 percent of revenues per year, but what may be more disconcerting is the nature of those counterproductive behaviours.[44] Thirty-one percent of employees who responded to a survey knowingly served improperly prepared food, 13 percent intentionally sabotaged the work of other employees, and 12 percent admitted to intentionally contaminating food they prepared or served to a customer (yuck!). At a minimum, such sabotage of the restaurant's product can lead to a bad meal and a customer's promise to never return to that establishment. At a maximum, such behaviours can lead to food poisoning, health code violations, and a damaging lawsuit.

Counterproductive behaviour by employees can be destructive to the organization's goals. In some settings, such as a restaurant, it can even be a problem for customers.

theft Stealing company products or equipment from the organization

Theft represents another form of property deviance and can be just as expensive as sabotage (if not more). Research has shown that up to three-quarters of all employees have engaged in counterproductive behaviours such as theft, and the cost of these

production deviance Intentionally reducing organizational efficiency of work output

wasting resources Using too many materials or too much time to do too little work

substance abuse The abuse of drugs or alcohol before coming to work or while on the job

political deviance Behaviours that intentionally disadvantage other individuals

gossiping Casual conversations about other people in which the facts are not confirmed as true

incivility Communication that is rude, impolite, discourteous, and lacking in good manners

personal aggression Hostile verbal and physical actions directed toward other employees

harassment Unwanted physical contact or verbal remarks from a colleague

abuse Employee assault or endangerment from which physical and psychological injuries may occur

behaviours is staggering.[45] For example, one study estimated that 47 percent of store inventory shrinkage was due to employee theft and that this type of theft costs organizations approximately $14.6 billion per year.[46] Maybe you've had friends who worked at a restaurant or bar and been lucky enough to get discounted (or even free) food and drinks whenever you wanted. Clearly that circumstance is productive for you, but it's quite counterproductive from the perspective of the organization.

Production deviance is also directed against the organization but focuses specifically on reducing the efficiency of work output. **Wasting resources** is the most common form of production deviance, when employees use too many materials or too much time to do too little work. Manufacturing employees who use too much wood or metal are wasting resources, as are restaurant employees who use too many ingredients when preparing the food. Workers who work too slowly or take too many breaks are also wasting resources because "time is money" (we return to this particular subject in Chapter 3 on organizational commitment). **Substance abuse** represents another form of production deviance. As we saw in the Walkerton tragedy, if employees abuse drugs or alcohol while on the job or shortly before coming to work, then the efficiency of their production will be compromised because their work will be done more slowly and less accurately.

In contrast to property and production deviance, **political deviance** refers to behaviours that intentionally disadvantage other individuals rather than the larger organization. **Gossiping**—casual conversations about other people in which the facts are not confirmed as true—is one form of political deviance. Everyone has experienced gossip at some point in time and knows the emotions people feel when they discover that other people have been talking about them. Such behaviours undermine the morale of both friendship groups and work groups. **Incivility** represents communication that is rude, impolite, discourteous, and lacking in good manners.[47] The erosion of manners seems like a society-wide phenomenon, and the workplace is no exception. Recall the classic scene from *Jerry Maguire,* in which Tom Cruise's character, after getting fired from his job, scoops the company fish out of the tank and takes them with him because "these fish have manners" (unlike everyone else in that particular company).

Taken one by one, these political forms of counterproductive behaviour may not seem particularly serious to most organizations. However, in the aggregate, acts of political deviance can create an organizational climate characterized by distrust and unhealthy competitiveness. Beyond the productivity losses that result from a lack of cooperation among employees, organizations with this type of climate likely cannot retain good employees. Moreover, there is some evidence that gossip and incivility can "spiral"—meaning that they gradually get worse and worse until some tipping point—after which more serious forms of interpersonal actions can occur.[48]

Those more serious interpersonal actions may involve **personal aggression,** defined as hostile verbal and physical actions directed toward other employees. **Harassment** falls under this heading and occurs when employees are subjected to unwanted physical contact or verbal remarks from a colleague. **Abuse** also falls under this heading; it occurs when an employee is assaulted or endangered in such a way that physical and psychological injuries may occur. Three points should be noted about counterproductive behaviour. First, there is evidence that people who engage in one form of counterproductive behaviour also engage in others.[49] In other words, such behaviours tend to represent a pattern of behaviour rather than isolated incidents. In this sense, there really are "bad apples." Second, like citizenship behaviour, counterproductive behaviour is relevant to any job. It doesn't matter what the job entails; there are going to be things to steal, resources to waste, and people to be uncivil toward. Third, it is often surprising which employees engage in counterproductive behaviour. You might be tempted to guess that poor task performers will be the ones who do these sorts of things, but there is only a weak negative correlation between task performance and counterproductive behaviour.[50] Sometimes the best task performers are the ones who can best get away with counterproductive actions, because they are less likely to be suspected or blamed.

OB RESEARCH IN CANADA

Dr. Sandra L. Robinson, at the University of British Columbia (UBC), is an expert on the darker side of organizational behaviour. Dr. Robinson's research looks at topics such as workplace aggression, anti-social behaviour, territoriality, toxic handlers, trust betrayal, and psychological contract breach. Why does she choose to study such a variety of counterproductive behaviours? In her words, "It's an incredibly intriguing and fun thing to study!" Presently, Dr. Robinson is a distinguished university scholar, professor of organizational behaviour and human resources, and an associate member of the psychology department at UBC. Prior to joining UBC, she taught at New York University and Northwestern University in Chicago.

In addition to being an expert in counterproductive behaviour, Dr. Robinson is a great example of a good performer. Dr. Robinson's numerous publications have appeared in many prestigious journals, such as the *Harvard Business Review, Administrative Science Quarterly,* and *Academy of Management Journal.* Her work has appeared in a wide range of press outlets, from *The Economist* to the *Wall Street Journal* to the *Washington Post.* She speaks frequently with the press on topics such as stress in the workplace, workplace aggression, and employment relationship issues. In terms of citizenship behaviours, Dr. Robinson has been formally recognized for her significant contributions to the field of management, such as the Ascendant Scholar Award from the Western Academy of Management and the Cummings Scholar Award from the Academy of Management. Currently, she is serving a five-year term as chair for the Organizational Behavior Division of Academy of Management, the 18,000-member international organization for management scholars.

Some of Dr. Robinson's favourite publications include:

"Territoriality in Organizations," by G. Brown, T.B. Lawrence, and S.L. Robinson, published in *Academy of Management Review* (2005, volume 30, number 3, pp. 577–94)

"Monkey See, Monkey Do: The Influence of Work Groups on the Antisocial Behavior of Employees," by S.L. Robinson and A.M. O'Leary-Kelly, published in *Academy of Management Journal* (1998, volume 41, number 6, pp. 658–72)

"Trust and Breach of the Psychological Contract," by S.L. Robinson, published in *Administrative Science Quarterly* (1996, volume 41, pp. 574–99)

WHAT DOES IT MEAN TO BE A "GOOD PERFORMER"?

So what does it mean to be a "good performer"? As shown in Figure 2-3, being a good performer means a lot of different things. It means someone is good at the particular job tasks that fall within his or her job description, whether those tasks are routine or require more adaptability. But it also means that the employee engages in citizenship behaviours directed at both co-workers and the larger organization. And it means that he or she refrains from engaging in the counterproductive behaviours that can so badly damage the climate

FIGURE 2-3 What Does It Mean to Be a "Good Performer?"

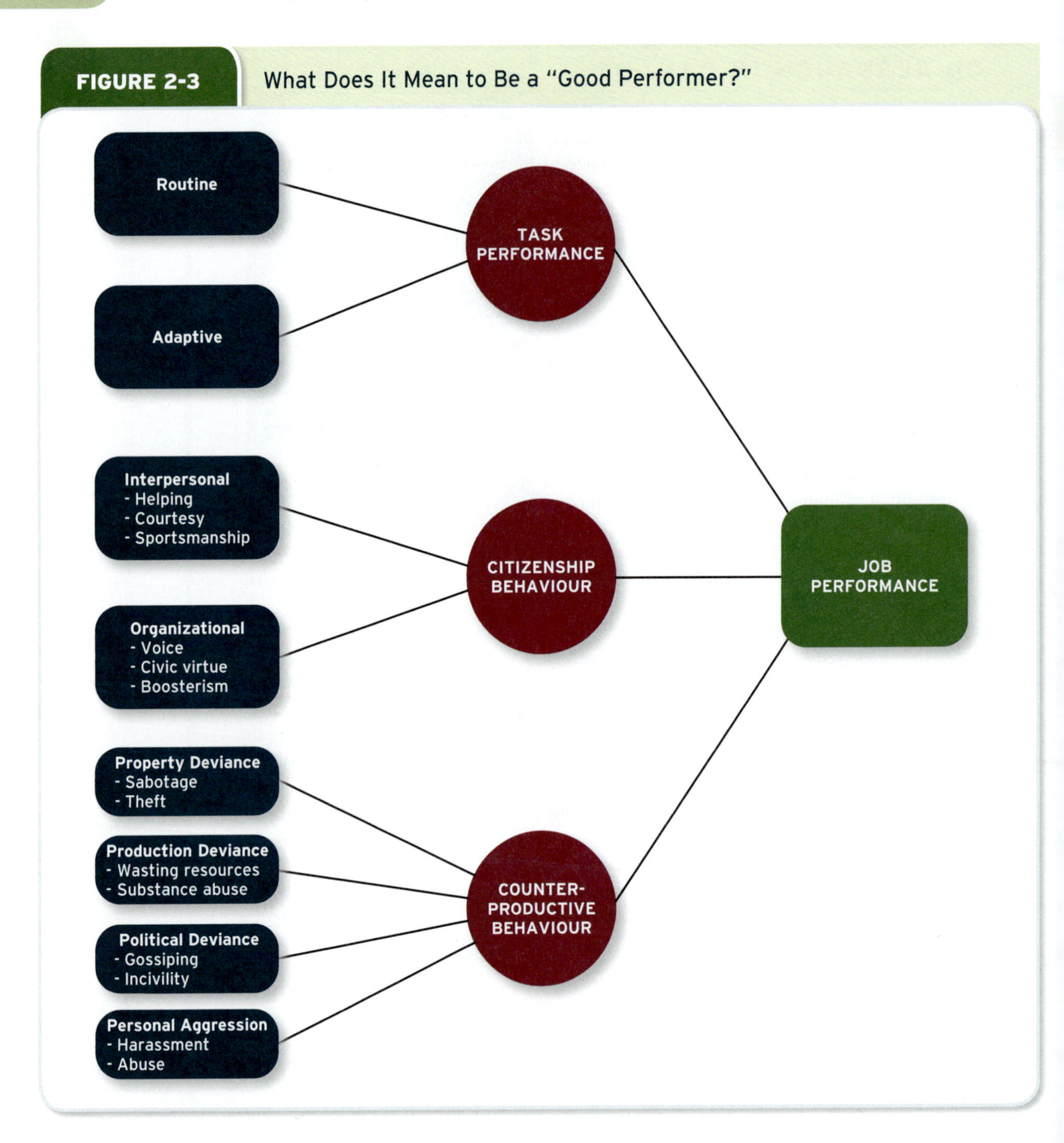

of an organization. The goal for any manager is therefore to have employees who fulfill all three pieces of this good performer description.

As you move forward in this book, you'll notice that almost every chapter includes a description of how that chapter's topic relates to job performance. For example, Chapter 4 on job satisfaction describes how employees' feelings about their jobs affect their job performance. You'll find that some chapter topics seem more strongly correlated with task performance, whereas other topics are more strongly correlated with citizenship behaviour or counterproductive behaviour. Such differences will help you understand exactly how

OB FOR STUDENTS

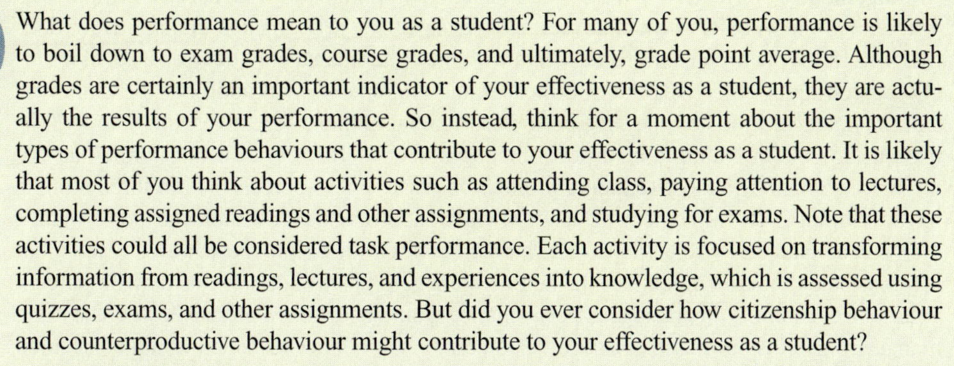

What does performance mean to you as a student? For many of you, performance is likely to boil down to exam grades, course grades, and ultimately, grade point average. Although grades are certainly an important indicator of your effectiveness as a student, they are actually the results of your performance. So instead, think for a moment about the important types of performance behaviours that contribute to your effectiveness as a student. It is likely that most of you think about activities such as attending class, paying attention to lectures, completing assigned readings and other assignments, and studying for exams. Note that these activities could all be considered task performance. Each activity is focused on transforming information from readings, lectures, and experiences into knowledge, which is assessed using quizzes, exams, and other assignments. But did you ever consider how citizenship behaviour and counterproductive behaviour might contribute to your effectiveness as a student?

- First, in classes that require teamwork, your team will likely perform at a much higher level if you and your teammates are helpful to one another, actively participate in team meetings, and suggest improvements to the team's routine. Similarly, your team will likely perform at a lower level if you and your teammates gossip about one another, refuse to share information, or blame one another for errors.
- Second, many courses devote points to participation. It may be that displays of citizenship and counterproductive behaviours can influence professors' assessments of participation points. Although we are not advocating using these behaviours as "impression management" tactics, you can probably understand why a professor might give more participation points to a student who had high attendance, participated above the norm, attended voluntary office hours, and did extra work to improve his or her class standing. Similarly, you can probably understand why a professor might give fewer participation points to a student who routinely showed up late for class, chatted with neighbours and read newspapers during lectures, and was confrontational or argumentative.
- Third, it could be argued that the ultimate indicator of your effectiveness as a student is your ability to apply what you've learned to the "real world." As we have noted elsewhere, citizenship behaviour and counterproductive behaviour will likely be considered by your employer when evaluating your overall performance. In essence, your career may depend on whether you routinely engage in the right behaviours on the job, even when the boss isn't around to watch.

and why a given topic, be it satisfaction, stress, motivation, or something else, influences job performance. By the end of the book, you'll have developed a good sense of the most powerful drivers of job performance. That knowledge will come in handy in your working life and, as described in our **OB for Students** feature, in your academic life as well.

APPLICATION: PERFORMANCE MANAGEMENT

Now that we've described what job performance is, along with some of the workplace trends that affect it, it's time to discuss how organizations use job performance information. In this section, we describe how job performance information may be used to manage employee performance. Although organizations manage employee performance in a wide variety of ways, we'll spotlight three of the most representative: management by objectives, behaviourally anchored rating scales, and 360-degree feedback.

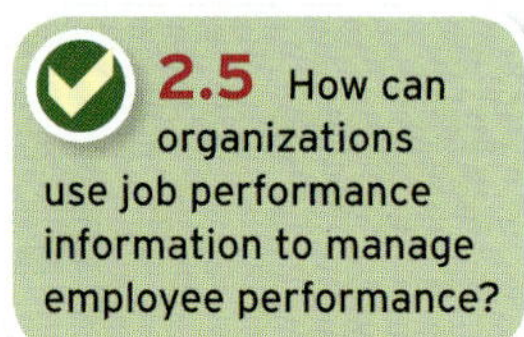

MANAGEMENT BY OBJECTIVES

management by objectives (MBO) A management philosophy that bases employee evaluations on whether specific performance goals have been met

Management by objectives (MBO) is a management philosophy that bases an employee's evaluations on whether the employee achieves specific performance goals.[51] How does MBO work? Typically, an employee meets with his or her manager to develop a set of mutually agreed-upon objectives that are measurable and specific. In addition, the employee and the manager agree on the time period for achieving those objectives and the methods used to do so. An example of a performance objective for a line manager in a factory might be something like, "Reducing production waste by 35 percent within three months by developing and implementing new production procedures." Employee performance then can be gauged by referring to the degree to which the employee achieves results that are consistent with the objectives. If the line manager cuts production waste by 37 percent within three months, the manager's performance would be deemed effective, whereas if the manager only cuts production waste by 2 percent, his or her performance would be deemed ineffective. However, MBO is best suited for managing the performance of employees who work in contexts in which objective measures of performance can be quantified.

BEHAVIOURALLY ANCHORED RATING SCALES

behaviourally anchored rating scales (BARS) Use of examples of critical incidents to evaluate an employee's job performance behaviours directly

You might have noticed that MBO emphasizes the results of job performance as much as it does the performance behaviours themselves. In contrast, **behaviourally anchored rating scales (BARS)** assess performance by directly assessing job performance behaviours. The BARS approach uses "critical incidents"—short descriptions of effective and ineffective behaviours—to create a measurement instrument that managers can use to evaluate employee performance. Consider the job of a computer programmer as an example and assume that a manager wants to measure the adaptive task performance of employees. A BARS approach might use critical incidents to create the following response anchors, ranging from excellent adaptive performance (5) to poor adaptive performance (1):

- 5 = Open-minded; learns new methods easily
- 4 = Willing to make changes without much need for persuasion or supervision
- 3 = Able to make changes with average amount of instruction
- 2 = Requires persuasion and supervision to make changes
- 1 = Unwilling to accept changes; does not adjust readily

Typically, supervisors rate several performance dimensions using BARS and score an employee's overall job performance by taking the average value across all the dimensions. In addition, because the critical incidents convey the precise kinds of behaviours that are effective and ineffective, feedback from BARS can help an employee develop and improve over time. That is, employees can develop an appreciation of the types of behaviours that would make them effective. Such information provides a nice complement to MBO, which is less capable of providing specific feedback about why an objective might have been missed.

360-DEGREE FEEDBACK

360-degree feedback A performance evaluation system that uses ratings provided by supervisors, co-workers, subordinates, customers, and the employees themselves

The **360-degree feedback** approach involves collecting performance information not just from the supervisor but from anyone else who might have firsthand knowledge about the employee's performance behaviours. These other sources of performance information typically include the employee's subordinates, peers, and customers. With the exception of the supervisor's ratings, the ratings are combined so that the raters can remain anonymous to the employee. Most 360-degree feedback systems also ask the employee to provide ratings of his or her own performance. The hope is that this 360-degree perspective will provide a more balanced and comprehensive examination of performance. By explicitly comparing self-provided ratings with the ratings obtained from others, employees can develop a better sense of how their performance may be deficient in the eyes of others and exactly where they need to focus their energies to improve.

Although the information from a 360-degree feedback system can be used to evaluate employees for administrative purposes such as raises or promotions, there are problems with that sort of application. First, because ratings vary across sources, there is the question of which source is most "correct." Even if multiple sources are taken into account in generating an overall performance score, it is often unclear how the information from the various sources should be weighted. Second, raters may give biased evaluations if they believe that the information will be used for compensation, as opposed to just skill development. Peers in particular may be unwilling to provide negative information if they believe it will harm the person being rated. As a result, 360-degree feedback is best suited to improving or developing employee talent, especially if the feedback is accompanied by coaching about how to improve the areas identified as points of concern.

TAKEAWAYS

2.1 Job performance is the set of employee behaviours that contribute to organizational goal accomplishment. Job performance has three dimensions: task performance, citizenship behaviour, and counterproductive behaviour.

2.2 Task performance includes employee behaviours that are directly involved in the transformation of organizational resources into the goods or services that the organization produces. Organizations gather information about relevant task behaviours using job analysis.

2.3 Citizenship behaviours are voluntary employee activities that may or may not be rewarded but that contribute to the organization by improving the overall quality of the setting in which work takes place. Examples of citizenship behaviour include helping, courtesy, sportsmanship, voice, civic virtue, and boosterism.

2.4 Counterproductive behaviours are employee behaviours that intentionally hinder organizational goal accomplishment. Examples of counterproductive behaviour include sabotage, theft, wasting resources, substance abuse, gossiping, incivility, harassment, and abuse.

2.5 The MBO, BARS, and 360-degree feedback practices are three ways that organizations can use job performance information to manage employee performance.

KEY TERMS

- abuse *p. 38*
- adaptive task performance *p. 29*
- behaviourally anchored rating scales (BARS) *p. 42*
- boosterism *p. 35*
- citizenship behaviour *p. 33*
- civic virtue *p. 35*
- counterproductive behaviour *p. 35*
- courtesy *p. 34*
- gossiping *p. 38*

- harassment *p. 38*
- helping *p. 34*
- incivility *p. 38*
- interpersonal citizenship behaviour *p. 34*
- job analysis *p. 32*
- job performance *p. 29*
- management by objectives (MBO) *p. 42*
- National Occupational Classification (NOC) *p. 33*
- organizational citizenship behaviour *p. 34*
- personal aggression *p. 38*
- political deviance *p. 38*
- production deviance *p. 38*
- property deviance *p. 35*
- routine task performance *p. 29*
- sabotage *p. 35*
- sportsmanship *p. 34*
- substance abuse *p. 38*
- task performance *p. 29*
- theft *p. 37*
- 360-degree feedback *p. 42*
- voice *p. 35*
- wasting resources *p. 38*

DISCUSSION QUESTIONS

2.1 Describe the job that you currently hold or hope to hold after graduation. Now look up that job in the National Occupational Classification (NOC) database (www5.hrsdc.gc.ca/NOC-CNP). Does the profile of the job fit your expectations? Are any task behaviours missing from the NOC profile?

2.2 Describe a job in which citizenship behaviours would be especially critical to an organization's functioning and one in which citizenship behaviours would be less critical. What is it about a job that makes citizenship more important?

2.3 Figure 2-2 on page 37 classifies production deviance and political deviance as more minor in nature than property deviance and personal aggression. When might those types of counterproductive behaviour prove especially costly?

2.4 Consider how you would react to 360-degree feedback. If you were the one receiving the feedback, whose views would you value most: your manager's or your peers'? If you were asked to assess a peer, would you want your opinion to affect that peer's raises or promotions?

CASE • WALKERTON

The opening case is a sober reminder of how important it is to measure and manage job performance. Clearly there was a failure of the "licensed" operators to perform critical technical tasks at minimally acceptable levels. Tasks such as monitoring and testing water quality or adjusting chlorination levels are examples of core technical activities that were either neglected or performed below acceptable standards. In addition, we see evidence of counterproductive behaviours. Drinking alcohol on the job or deliberately falsifying records to hide mistakes are examples of things employees do to put themselves and others at risk, as well as hinder organizational goal accomplishment. Although the judge in the criminal proceedings ruled that the actions of Stan and Frank Koebel were neither malicious nor intentional, the case demonstrates that technical incompetence combined with deviance is a recipe for disaster. Sadly, it is very common to hear managers talk about their ineffective or poorly performing employees. Given the complexity and cost of fixing them, most organizations knowingly choose to ignore dysfunctions within their performance management system.

2.1 As students, many of you work in small groups to complete your course assignments. Why do you tolerate team members who do not pull their fair share of the load, yet you know will receive the same grade on the assignment as you?

2.2 Why do you think it took almost 30 years for Stan and Frank Koebel to be exposed?

2.3 After carefully considering the complexity of the situation, what recommendations would you make regarding the way employees are hired and trained, and the way performance is managed at the Walkerton PUC?

EXERCISE • PERFORMANCE OF A SERVER

The purpose of this exercise is to explore what job performance means for a server in a restaurant. This exercise uses groups of six participants, so your instructor will either assign you to a group of six or ask you to create your own group of six. The exercise has the following steps:

1. Conduct a job analysis for a restaurant server. Begin by drawing a circle like the one below. Use that circle to summarize the major job dimensions of a restaurant server. For example, one job dimension might be "Taking Meal Orders." Divide the circle up with four additional job dimensions. Now get more specific by listing two behaviours per job dimension. For example, two behaviours within the "Taking Meal Orders" dimension might be "Describing the Menu" and "Making Recommendations." At the end of Step 1, you should have a list of eight specific behaviours that summarize the tasks involved in being a restaurant server. Write your group's behaviours down on a transparency, laptop, or chalkboard, leaving some space for some additional behaviours down the line.

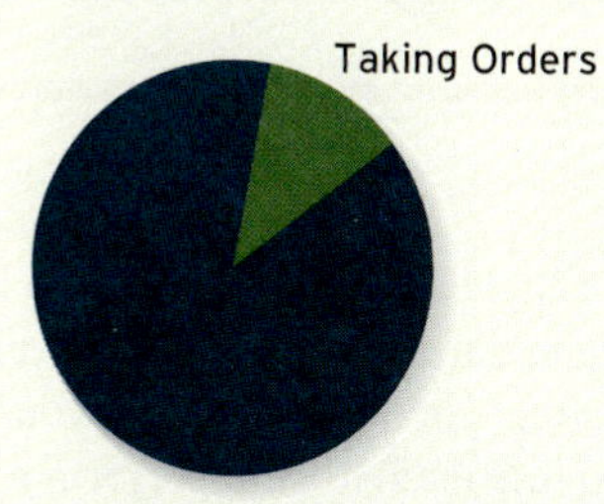

2. Take a look at the resulting list. Did you come up with any behaviours that would be described as "citizenship behaviours"? If you didn't include any in your list, does that mean that citizenship behaviour isn't important in a restaurant setting? If your group includes someone who has worked as a server, ask him or her to describe the importance of citizenship behaviour. Come up with two especially important citizenship behaviours and add those to your list.
3. Take another look at your list. Did you come up with any behaviours that would be described as "counterproductive behaviours"? If you didn't include any in your list, does that mean that counterproductive behaviour isn't an important concern in a restaurant setting? If your group includes someone who has worked as a server, ask him or her to describe the potential costs of counterproductive behaviour. Come up with two especially costly counterproductive behaviours and add those to your list.

4. Class discussion (whether in groups or as a class) should centre on how a restaurant owner or manager might use the resulting list to evaluate the performance of restaurant servers. How could this list be used to assess server performance? Would such an approach be valuable? Why or why not?

OB ASSESSMENTS • HELPING

How helpful are you? This assessment is designed to measure helping, an interpersonal form of citizenship behaviour. Think of the people you work with most frequently, either at school or at work. The questions below refer to these people as your "work group." Answer each question using the scale below, then sum up your answers.

1 STRONGLY DISAGREE	2 MODERATELY DISAGREE	3 SLIGHTLY DISAGREE	4 NEITHER DISAGREE NOR AGREE	5 SLIGHTLY AGREE	6 MODERATELY AGREE	7 STRONGLY AGREE

1. I volunteer to do things for my work group. _____
2. I help orient new members of my work group. _____
3. I attend functions that help my work group. _____
4. I assist others in my group with their work for the benefit of the group. _____
5. I get involved to benefit my work group. _____
6. I help others in this group learn about the work. _____
7. I help others in this group with their work responsibilities. _____

SCORING

If your scores sum up to 40 or higher, you perform a high level of helping behaviour, which means you frequently engage in citizenship behaviours directed at your colleagues. This is good, as long as it doesn't distract you from fulfilling your own job duties and responsibilities. If your scores sum up to less than 40, you perform a low level of helping behaviours. You might consider paying more attention to whether your colleagues need assistance while working on their task duties and pitching in when appropriate.

Source: L.V. Van Dyne and J.A. LePine, "Helping and Voice Extra-Role Behaviours: Evidence of Construct and Predictive Validity," *Academy of Management Journal* 41 (1998), pp. 108–19. Copyright © 1998 Academy of Management. Reproduced via permission from Copyright Clearance Center.

CHAPTER 3

Organizational Commitment

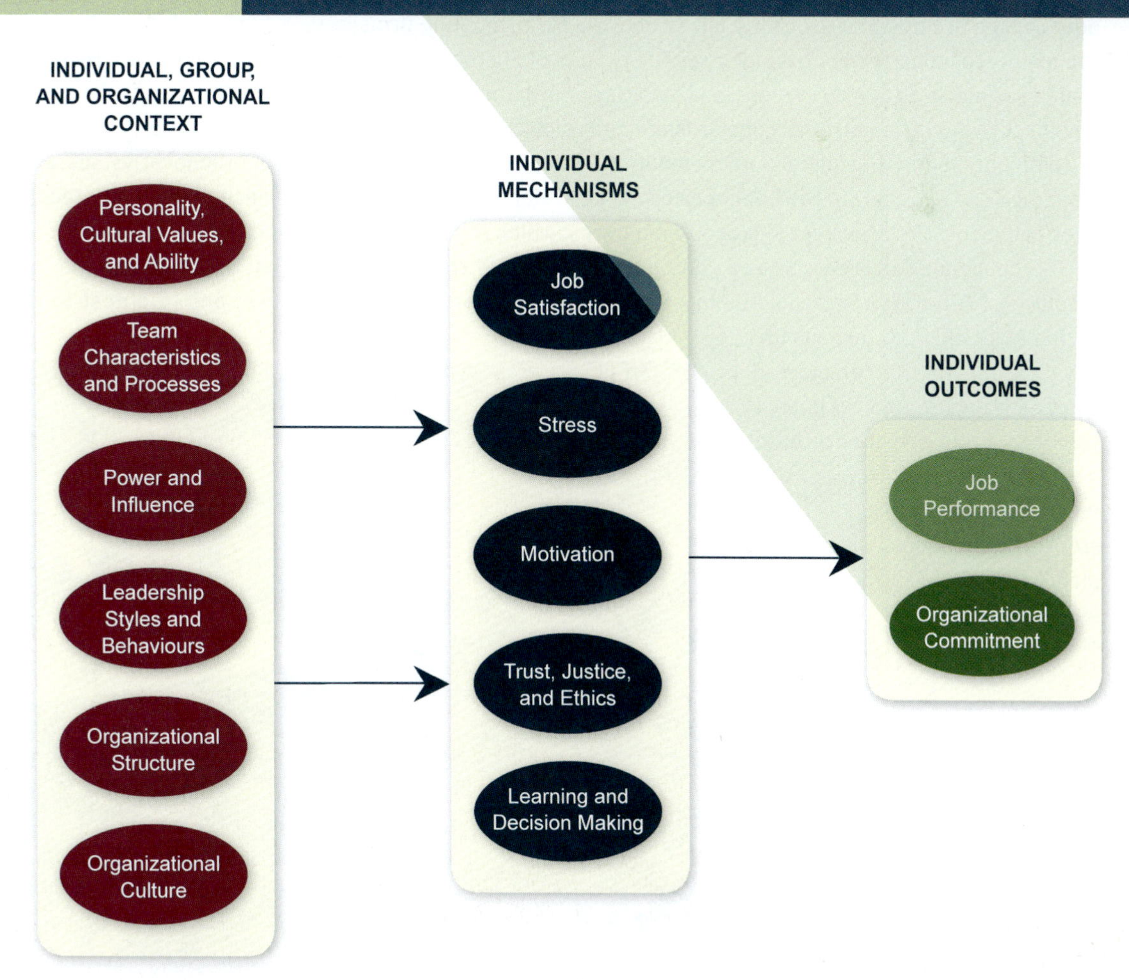

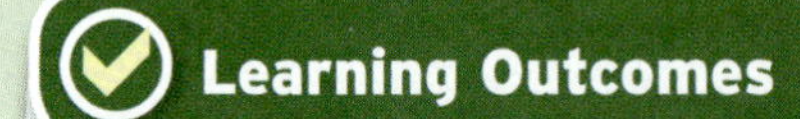

Learning Outcomes

After reading this chapter, you should be able to answer the following questions:

3.1 What is organizational commitment? What is withdrawal behaviour? How are the two connected?

3.2 What are the three forms of organizational commitment, and how do they differ?

3.3 What are the four primary responses to negative events at work?

3.4 What are some examples of psychological withdrawal? Of physical withdrawal? How do the different forms of withdrawal relate to each other?

MICROSOFT

When was the last time you used a Microsoft product? Chances are, it was within the past few hours, whether you were surfing the Web using Internet Explorer, answering e-mail using Outlook Express, writing a paper or memo using Word, using a computer running Windows, or playing a videogame on an Xbox. How did Microsoft become successful enough to attain this presence in our day-to-day lives? If you were to ask the chairman of the company, Bill Gates, or the CEO of the company, Steve Ballmer, they'd likely explain that Microsoft hires the best computer science students from the best universities, year in and year out. After all, if a company wants to have the best products in a given market, it helps to have the best people. Microsoft has been able to hire the best people in part by being known as a great place to work. For example, Microsoft placed 50 on *Fortune*'s list of the "100 Best Companies to Work For" in 2007.[1]

However, for the first time in its history, Microsoft is having trouble holding on to its best and brightest.[2] Microsoft's annual rate of voluntary turnover, which captures the percentage of the workforce that decides to quit in a given year, is just 9 percent—still below the industry average.[3] But many of Microsoft's most respected software developers, engineers, managers, and marketers have recently left to go work for competing firms in the high-tech industry.[4] For example, Kai-Fu Lee, one of Microsoft's foremost experts on speech recognition, left for Google, as did Mark Lucovsky, Joe Beda, and Gary Burd, three of the company's most distinguished engineers.[5] The employees who have quit their jobs at Microsoft voice a wide range of complaints about the company, including a swelling bureaucracy, sagging morale among the rank-and-file employees, a lack of innovative spark, cuts in compensation and benefits, and an unfair performance evaluation system.[6] Many of these complaints are echoed on Web sites and blogs run by current Microsoft employees, which reinforce a culture of criticism within the company.

The challenge for Microsoft is to find a way to reverse these trends so that it can retain the most talented employees. After all, what could be more damaging than losing one of your best and brightest to a major competitor? Not only do you no longer have access to that employee's knowledge and experience, but now your competitor can draw on his or her wisdom to find a way to beat you. Microsoft is already taking steps to combat some of the complaints raised by former employees, including a reorganization of

Microsoft has had great success with its many computer products but has recently had trouble holding on to some of its software developers.

its business units designed to make the company more nimble and innovative.[7] Of course, there isn't likely to be a "magic bullet" that will single-handedly prevent further exit of more and more talented and valuable employees.

ORGANIZATIONAL COMMITMENT

Organizational commitment sits side by side with job performance in our integrative model of organizational behaviour, reflecting one of the starting points for our journey through the concepts covered in this text. Why begin with a discussion of organizational commitment? Because as illustrated in the Microsoft example, it is simply not enough to have talented employees who perform their jobs well. You also need to be able to hang on to those employees for long periods of time so that the organization can benefit from their efforts. Put yourself in the shoes of a business owner. Let's say you spent a great deal of time recruiting a graduate from the local university, selling her on your business, and making sure that she was as qualified as you initially believed her to be. Now assume that, once hired, you took a personal interest in that employee, showing her the ropes and acting as mentor and instructor. Then, just as the company was set to improve as a result of that employee's presence, she leaves to go to work for a competitor. As an employer, can you think of many things more distressing than that scenario?

Unfortunately, that scenario, like the events at Microsoft, is not far-fetched. One recent survey by Towers Perrin showed that 68 percent of employees were looking for a new job.[8] With so many people planning to leave, it isn't surprising that the average voluntary turnover in 2007 for Canadian organizations was roughly 10 percent for full-time positions and even higher for part-time positions.[9] Making matters worse, many organizations report difficulty attracting skilled employees.[10] According to the Conference Board of Canada, organizations most likely to experience staff shortages were in the natural resources, education, health, and government sectors. Job skills in the highest demand included accounting/finance, skilled trades, engineering (all types), information technology specialists, sales and marketing, management, professionals (e.g., lawyers), physical scientists, and health care professionals. What this all means, frankly, is that talented employees in many fields are in short supply, and that the risk of turnover, among a firm's most valued employees, is becoming higher all the time. Managers should be alarmed about these findings because the cost of turnover can be very high. Estimates suggest that it costs about 0.5 times the annual salary plus benefits to replace an hourly worker, 1.5 times the annual salary plus benefits to replace a salaried employee, and as much as 5 times the annual salary plus benefits to replace an executive.[11] Why so expensive? Those estimates include various costs, including the administrative costs involved in the separation, recruitment expenses, screening costs, and training and orientation expenses for the new hire.[12] They also include "hidden costs" due to decreased morale, lost organizational knowledge, and lost productivity.

3.1 What is organizational commitment? What is withdrawal behaviour? How are the two connected?

Organizational commitment is defined as the desire on the part of an employee to remain a member of the organization.[13] Organizational commitment influences whether an employee stays a member of the organization (is retained) or leaves to pursue another job (turns over). It is important to acknowledge that turnover can be both voluntary and involuntary. Voluntary turnover occurs when employees themselves decide to quit; involuntary turnover occurs when employees are fired by the organization for some reason. Our attention in this chapter is focused primarily on reducing voluntary turnover—keeping the employees that the organization wants to keep.

organizational commitment An employee's desire to remain a member of an organization

FIGURE 3-1 Organizational Commitment and Employee Withdrawal

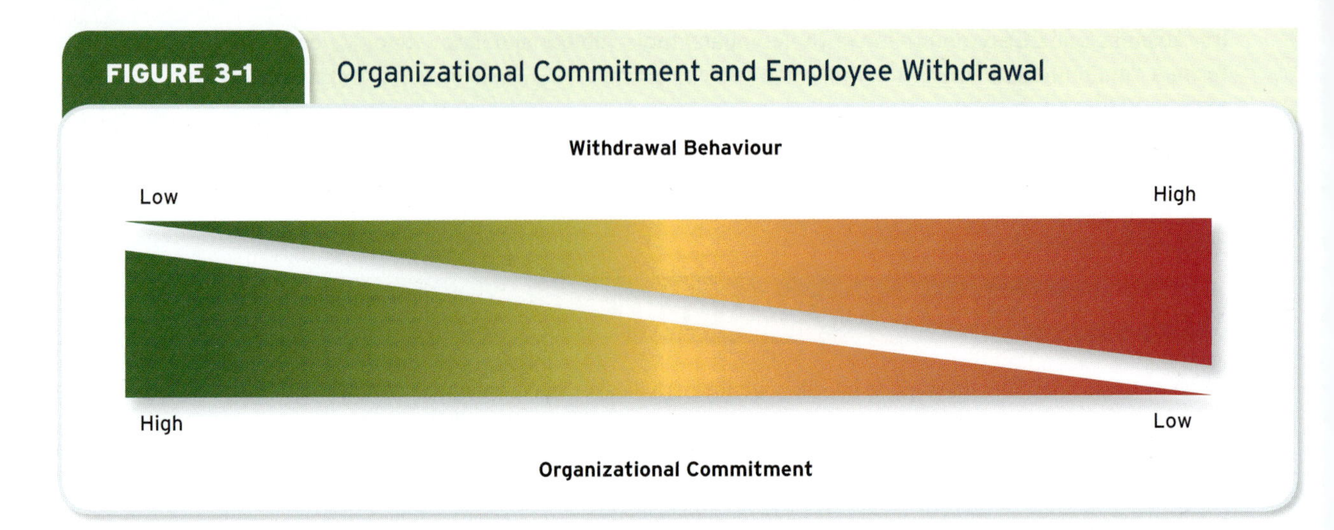

withdrawal behaviour Employee actions that are intended to avoid work situations

Employees who are not committed to their organizations engage in **withdrawal behaviour**, defined as a set of actions that employees perform to avoid the work situation—behaviours that may eventually culminate in quitting the organization.[14] The relationship between commitment and withdrawal is illustrated in Figure 3-1. Some employees may exhibit much more commitment than withdrawal, finding themselves on the green end of the continuum. Leaving aside personal or family issues, these employees are not "retention risks" for the moment. Other employees exhibit much more withdrawal than commitment, finding themselves on the red end of the continuum. These employees are retention risks—teetering on the edge of quitting their jobs. The sections that follow review both commitment and withdrawal in more detail.

WHAT DOES IT MEAN TO BE A "COMMITTED" EMPLOYEE?

3.2 What are the three forms of organizational commitment, and how do they differ?

One key to understanding organizational commitment is to understand where it comes from. In other words, what creates a desire to remain a member of an organization? To explore this question, consider the following scenario: You've been working full-time for your employer for around five years. The company gave you your start in the business, and you've enjoyed your time there. Your salary is competitive enough that you were able to purchase a new home in a family-oriented community, which is important because you have one young child and another on the way. Now assume that a competing firm contacted you while you were attending a conference and offered you a similar position in its company. What kinds of things might you think about? If you created a list to organize your thoughts, what kinds of issues would appear on that list?

THREE FORMS OF COMMITMENT

affective commitment An employee's desire to remain a member of an organization due to a feeling of emotional attachment

One potential list is shown in Table 3-1. The left-hand column reflects some emotional reasons for staying with the current organization, including feelings about friendships, the atmosphere or culture of the company, and a sense of enjoyment when completing job duties. These sorts of emotional reasons create **affective commitment**, defined as a desire to remain a member of an organization due to an emotional attachment to, and involvement with, that

TABLE 3-1 The Three Forms of Organizational Commitment

What Makes Someone Want to Stay with Their Current Organization?		
EMOTION-BASED REASONS	**COST-BASED REASONS**	**OBLIGATION-BASED REASONS**
Some of my best friends work in my office. I'd miss them if I left.	I'm due for a promotion soon. Will I advance as quickly at the new company?	My boss has invested so much time in me, mentoring me, training me, showing me the ropes.
I really like the atmosphere at my current job; it's fun and relaxed.	My salary and benefits get us a nice house in our town. The cost of living is higher in this new area.	My organization gave me my start; they hired me when others thought I wasn't qualified.
My current job duties are very rewarding. I enjoy coming to work each morning.	The school system is good here; my spouse has a good job. We've really put down roots where we are.	My employer has helped me out of a jam on a number of occasions. How could I leave now?
Affective Commitment	Continuance Commitment	Normative Commitment
Staying because you ***want*** to.	Staying because you ***have*** to.	Staying because you ***ought*** to.

organization.[15] Put simply, you stay because you *want* to. The middle column reflects some cost-based reasons for staying, including issues of salary, benefits, and promotions, as well as concerns about uprooting a family. These sorts of reasons create **continuance commitment**, defined as a desire to remain a member of an organization because of an awareness of the costs associated with leaving it.[16] In other words, you stay because you *have* to. The right-hand column reflects some obligation-based reasons for staying with the current organization, including a sense that a debt is owed to a boss, a colleague, or the larger company. These sorts of reasons create **normative commitment**, defined as a desire to remain a member of an organization due to a feeling of obligation.[17] In this case, you stay because you *ought* to.

continuance commitment An employee's desire to remain a member of an organization due to an awareness of the costs of leaving

normative commitment An employee's desire to remain a member of an organization due to a feeling of obligation

As shown in Figure 3-2, the three forms of organizational commitment combine to create an overall sense of psychological attachment to the company. Of course, people may weight these three components of commitment differently. One person may be very rational and cautious by nature, focusing primarily on continuance commitment when evaluating his or her overall desire to stay. Another person may be more emotional and intuitive by nature, going more on "feel" than a calculated assessment of costs and benefits. The importance of the three components also may vary over the course of a career. For example, you might

FIGURE 3-2 Drivers of Overall Organizational Commitment

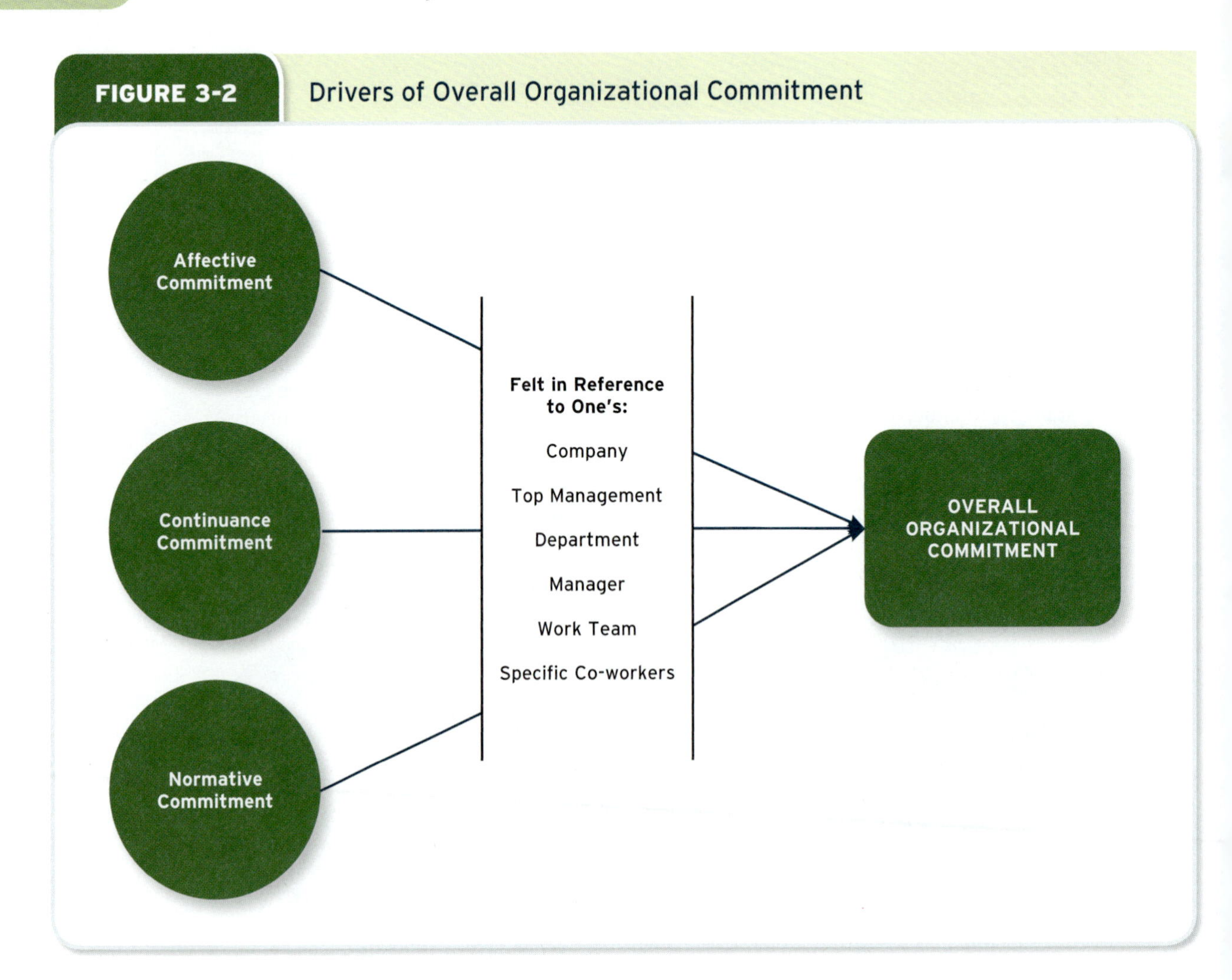

prioritize affective reasons early in your work life before shifting your attention to continuance reasons as you start a family or become more established in a community. Regardless of how the three types are prioritized, however, they offer an important insight into *why* someone might be committed and what an organization can do to make employees feel more committed.

focus of commitment The people, places, and things that inspire a desire to remain a member of an organization

Figure 3-2 also shows that organizational commitment depends on more than just "the organization." That is, people aren't always committed to companies; they're also committed to the top management that leads the firm at a given time, the department in which they work, the manager who directly supervises them, or the specific team or co-workers with whom they work most closely.[18] We use the term **focus of commitment** to refer to the various people, places, and things that can inspire a desire to remain a member of an organization. For example, you might choose to stay with your current employer because you are emotionally attached to your work team, worry about

Committed employees often have strong positive feelings about one particular aspect of their job, such as their colleagues, their manager, or the particular work they do.

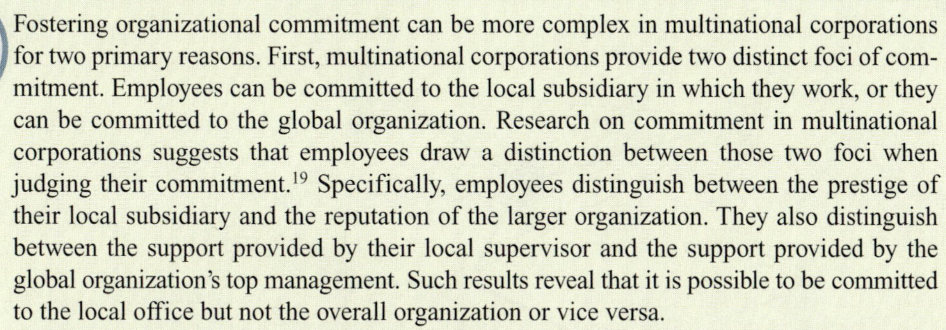

OB INTERNATIONALLY

Fostering organizational commitment can be more complex in multinational corporations for two primary reasons. First, multinational corporations provide two distinct foci of commitment. Employees can be committed to the local subsidiary in which they work, or they can be committed to the global organization. Research on commitment in multinational corporations suggests that employees draw a distinction between those two foci when judging their commitment.[19] Specifically, employees distinguish between the prestige of their local subsidiary and the reputation of the larger organization. They also distinguish between the support provided by their local supervisor and the support provided by the global organization's top management. Such results reveal that it is possible to be committed to the local office but not the overall organization or vice versa.

Second, multinational corporations require many employees to serve as expatriates for significant periods of time. Research suggests that the organizational commitment of expatriates depends, in part, on how well they adjust to their foreign assignments.[20] Research further suggests that expatriates' adjustment comes in three distinct forms:[21]

- *Work adjustment.* The degree of comfort with specific job responsibilities and performance expectations.
- *Cultural adjustment.* The degree of comfort with the general living conditions, climate, cost of living, transportation, and housing offered by the host culture.
- *Interaction adjustment.* The degree of comfort when socializing and interacting with members of the host culture.

A study of American multinational corporations in the transportation, service, manufacturing, chemical, and pharmaceutical industries showed that all three forms of adjustment relate significantly to affective commitment.[22] If expatriates cannot feel comfortable in their assignment, it's difficult for them to develop an emotional bond to their organization. Instead, they are likely to withdraw from the assignment, both psychologically and physically.

What factors contribute to an expatriate's adjustment levels? It turns out that work adjustment depends on many of the same things that drive domestic employees' job satisfaction and motivation.[23] Cultural and interactional adjustment, in contrast, are very dependent on spousal and family comfort. If an expatriate's spouse or children are unhappy in their new environment, it becomes very difficult for the expatriate to remain committed. Fortunately, research suggests that cultural and interactional adjustment can increase with time, as experiences in the host nation gradually increase expatriates' sense of comfort and, ultimately, their commitment to the work assignment.

the costs associated with losing your company's salary and benefits package, and feel a sense of obligation to your current manager. If so, your desire to remain cuts across multiple types of commitment (affective, continuance, and normative) and multiple foci (or focuses) of commitment (work team, company, manager). See our **OB Internationally** feature for a glimpse into how these different foci might affect employee commitment in multinational corporations. Now that you're familiar with the drivers of commitment in a general sense, let's go into more depth about each type.

AFFECTIVE COMMITMENT One way to understand the differences among the three types of commitment is to ask yourself what you would feel if you left the organization. Consider the reasons listed in the left-hand column of Table 3-1. What would you feel if, even after taking all those reasons into account, you decided to leave your organization to join another one? Answer: You'd feel a sense of *sadness.* Employees who feel a sense of

FIGURE 3-3 A Social Network Diagram

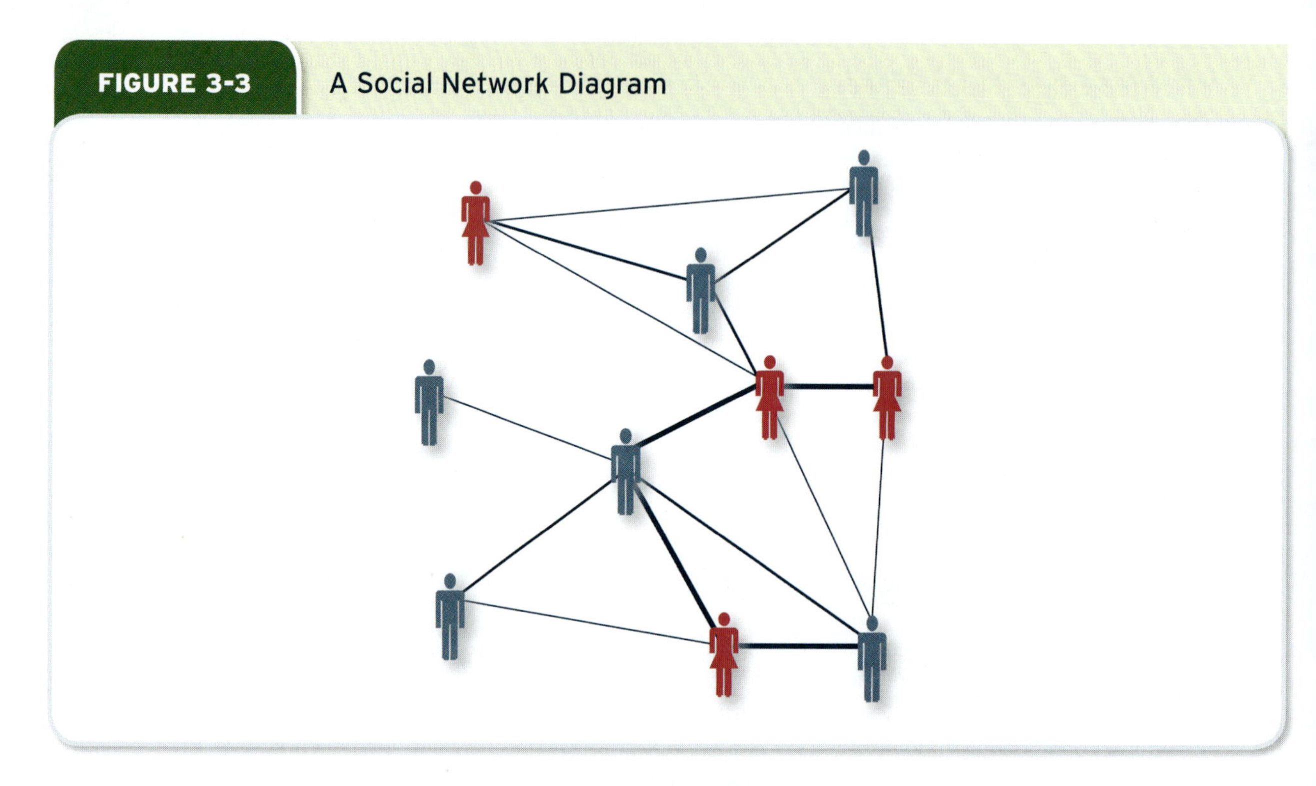

affective commitment identify with the organization, accept that organization's goals and values, and are more willing to exert extra effort on behalf of the organization.[24] Is affective commitment something that you feel for your current employer or have felt for a past employer? Check the **OB Assessments** feature at the end of this chapter to find out.

It's safe to say that if managers could choose which type of commitment they'd like to instill in their employees, they would choose affective commitment. Moreover, when a manager looks at an employee and says "She's committed" or "He's loyal," that manager usually is referring to a behavioural expression of affective commitment.[25] For example, employees who are affectively committed to their employer tend to engage in more interpersonal and organizational citizenship behaviours, such as helping, sportsmanship, and boosterism. One meta-analysis of 22 studies with more than 6,000 participants revealed a moderately strong correlation between affective commitment and citizenship behaviour.[26] (Recall that a meta-analysis averages together results from multiple studies investigating the same relationship.) Such results suggest that emotionally committed employees express that commitment by "going the extra mile" whenever they can.

Because affective commitment reflects an emotional bond to the organization, it's only natural that the emotional bonds among co-workers influence it.[27] We can therefore gain a better understanding of affective commitment if we take a closer look at the bonds that tie employees together. Assume you were given a sheet with the names of all the employees in your department or members of your class. Then assume you were asked to rate the frequency with which you communicated with each of those people, as well as the emotional depth of those communications. Those ratings could be used to create a "social network diagram" that summarizes the bonds among employees. Figure 3-3 provides a sample of such a diagram. The lines connecting the 10 members of the work unit represent the communication bonds that connect each of them, with thicker lines representing more frequent communication with more emotional depth. The diagram illustrates that some employees are "nodes," with several direct connections to other employees, whereas others remain at the fringes of the network.

The **erosion model** suggests that employees with fewer bonds will be most likely to quit the organization.[28] If you look at Figure 3-3, who's most at risk for turning over? That's right—the employee who only has one bond with someone else (and a relatively weak bond at that). From an affective commitment perspective, that employee is likely to feel less emotional attachment to work colleagues, which makes it easier to decide to leave the organization. Social network diagrams can also help us understand another explanation for turnover. The **social influence model** suggests that employees who have direct linkages with "leavers" will themselves become more likely to leave.[29] In this way, reductions in affective commitment become contagious, spreading like a disease across the work unit. Think about the damage that would be caused if the central figure in the network (the one who has linkages to five other people) became unhappy with the organization.

erosion model A model that suggests that employees with fewer bonds with co-workers are more likely to quit the organization

social influence model A model that suggests that employees with direct linkages to co-workers who leave the organization will themselves become more likely to leave

More and more Canadian companies seem to understand the importance of affective commitment, and the need to promote emotional bonding among employees and between employees and the organization.[30] For example, bitHeads, inc., a rapidly growing software development firm based in Ottawa, has an office located in a former cinema. One of the things that bitHeads does to create a fun work culture is to allow its employees to use the movie theatre to play Wii and Xbox games. Cementation Canada Inc., a successful mining development company based in North Bay, schedules weekly volleyball games with its employees to encourage positive social relations. General Dynamics Canada, a defence contractor located near Ottawa, maintains an outdoor rink so that employees can skate and enjoy afternoon shinny games. Blake, Cassels and Graydon LLP, an award-winning Toronto-based law firm, features employee-directed short films and musical performances at its Christmas parties. These sorts of activities are examples of the many ways that organizations encourage and strengthen the emotional bonds between the company and its employees. Interestingly, there appears to be regional differences in the degree of emotional attachment (personal engagement) that employees demonstrate, with Alberta is the lowest in the country (61 percent compared to the national average of 63 percent) and the highest in Quebec (71 percent).[31] No doubt chronic skill shortages over the past decade have forced many Alberta-based employers to use signing bonuses and other forms of financial incentives to attract and retain workers, which, as we turn to now, may foster a different form of commitment.

CONTINUANCE COMMITMENT Now consider the reasons for staying that are listed in the middle column of Table 3-1 (page 51). What would you feel if, even after taking all those reasons into account, you decided to leave your organization to join another one? Answer: You'd feel a sense of *anxiety*. Continuance commitment exists when there is a benefit associated with staying and a cost associated with leaving,[32] with high continuance commitment making it very difficult to change organizations because of the steep penalties associated with the switch (e.g., loss of seniority, reduction in wages or salary).[33] One factor that increases continuance commitment is the total amount of investment (in terms of time, effort, energy, etc.) that an employee has made in mastering his or her work role or fulfilling his or her organizational duties.[34] Picture a scenario in which you've worked extremely hard for a number of years to finally master the "ins and outs" of working at a particular organization, and now you're beginning to enjoy the fruits of that labour in terms of financial rewards and better work assignments. That effort might be wasted if you moved to another organization (and had to start over on the learning curve).

Another factor that increases continuance commitment is a lack of employment alternatives.[35] If an employee has nowhere else to go (e.g., suitable alternatives are not available, other organizations do not pay as well), the need to stay will be higher. Employment alternatives themselves depend on several factors, including economic conditions, the unemployment rate, and the marketability of a person's skills and abilities.[36] Of course, no one likes to feel "stuck" in a situation, so it may not be surprising that the behavioural benefits associated with affective commitment (i.e., more citizenship behaviour, higher job performance) do not really occur with continuance commitment. In fact, the correlation between continuance commitment and work outcomes, other than turnover, tends to be characterized as negligible or *weak negative* (higher continuance commitment is associated with lower job performance).[37] Perhaps the best explanation for this negative correlation is the tendency for continuance-committed employees to perform at minimally acceptable standards (enough so that their job is not at risk, but no more than necessary)—remember that they only stay because they have to. Over time, people who feel strong continuance commitment should perform, on average, lower than employees who do not experience this form of commitment or are attached for other reasons (e.g., affective commitment). Can you imagine what it must be like to have a relationship with someone who feels strong continuance commitment? This is probably how organizations feel about their employees who are committed for these reasons. On the other hand, an organization may be so desperate for employees that any form of commitment will do.

It is important to note that some of the reasons in the middle column of Table 3-1 (page 51) centre on personal or family issues. Continuance commitment focuses on personal and family issues more than the other two commitment types, because employees often need to stay for both work and non-work reasons. One concept that demonstrates the work and non-work forces that can bind us to our current employer is **embeddedness**, which summarizes a person's links to the organization and the community, his or her sense of fit with that organization and community, and what he or she would have to sacrifice for a job change.[38] As demonstrated in Table 3-2, embeddedness strengthens continuance commitment by providing more reasons why a person needs to stay in his or her current position (and more sources of anxiety if he or she were to leave).

embeddedness An employee's connection to and sense of fit in the organization and community

Think about your current situation. If you're a student who is working part-time, you likely don't feel very embedded. Your links to your job are probably only short term, and you may feel that the job is more routine than you'd like from a fit perspective. You probably also wouldn't feel you were sacrificing much if you left the job. From a community perspective, you may be going to school in a different city or province than where you grew up, again resulting in few

TABLE 3-2 Embeddedness and Continuance Commitment

"Embedded" People Feel:		
FACET	**FOR THE ORGANIZATION:**	**FOR THE COMMUNITY:**
Links	• I've worked here for such a long time. • I'm serving on so many teams and committees.	• Several close friends and family live nearby. • My family's roots are in this community.
Fit	• My job utilizes my skills and talents well. • I like the authority and responsibility I have at this company.	• The weather where I live is suitable for me. • I think of the community where I live as home.
Sacrifice	• The retirement benefits provided by the organization are excellent. • I would sacrifice a lot if I left this job.	• People respect me a lot in my community. • Leaving this community would be very hard.

Source: Adapted from T.R. Mitchell, B.C. Holtom, T.W. Lee, C.J. Sablynski, and M. Erez, "Why People Stay: Using Job Embeddedness to Predict Voluntary Turnover," *Academy of Management Journal* 44 (2001), pp. 1102–21.

links, low perceived fit, or a lack of felt sacrifice. However, if you're a full-time employee who is relatively established in your job and community, you may feel quite embedded in your current situation. To see how a law firm took advantage of the concepts of embeddedness and continuance commitment to retain its employees, see our **OB on Screen** feature.

OB ON SCREEN

THE FIRM

The firm encourages children . . . because children bring stability.

By repeating a comment made to her during a recruitment event, Mitch McDeere's wife suggests that there's something spooky about the Memphis law firm that is about to hire her husband in *The Firm* (Dir: Sydney Pollack. Paramount Pictures, 1993), based on the book by John Grisham. Mitch (Tom Cruise) is somewhat confused by the strange comment but still decides to accept the job and make the move to Memphis.

Why does the firm care so much about how stable its employees are? Because the firm's only client is the Mafia, so it needs to know that its employees will remain committed once they learn that secret. The firm therefore wants Mitch to become embedded—to have kids and develop links in the community—so that he feels he needs to stay.

The firm creates a sense of continuance commitment in a number of ways. First, it pays 10 percent more than any other law firm, meaning that an employee would sacrifice a lot of money in any job change. Second, it provides a low-interest loan to make it easier for employees to buy a house, thereby enhancing their links to the community. In addition to encouraging children, the firm hires only married couples, providing more opportunity for family-related embeddedness to develop. Most important, though, is the understanding that anyone who decides to leave the firm will likely suffer a tragic "accident." Clearly such a threat creates the sense that one needs to stay, with commitment rooted in a strong feeling of fear and anxiety.

Unfortunately for the firm, continuance commitment is the only type of commitment it can foster. As a result, Mitch never develops the kind of affective or normative commitment that might result in behaviours that benefit the firm. To the contrary, Mitch spends all his time and energy in the quest to escape from his "trap" by finding a way to expose the firm to the FBI. Lesson #1 for employers: It's important to build all three types of commitment, not just continuance. Lesson #1 for students: Stay away from the mob!

We see many examples of Canadian organizations offering generous financial compensation combined with, in many cases, innovative benefit packages that make it hard for employees to leave.[39] For instance, if you work at KPMG, a large Toronto-based professional services firm specializing in audit, tax, and corporate finance, you may think twice about leaving an organization that subsidizes your childcare and/or eldercare costs. In this era of ever-increasing gasoline prices, Shell Canada Ltd. of Calgary is confident that many of its members will find it hard to give up the discounts it offers employees on their personal fuel purchases. People with cats or dogs will find it hard to replace the pet insurance program offered by Ceridian Canada Ltd., a Winnipeg-based company that provides HR and payroll solutions for businesses across the country. TD Canada Trust offers its employees low-interest home loans, making it easier for employees to purchase a home and invest in their communities. Clearly there will be employees in all of these companies who will feel a bit anxious at the prospect of having to sacrifice these outcomes if a competitor came calling.

NORMATIVE COMMITMENT Now consider the reasons for staying listed in the right-hand column of Table 3-1 (page 51). What would you feel if, even after taking all those reasons into account, you decided to leave your organization to join another one? Answer: You'd feel a sense of *guilt.* Normative commitment exists when there is a sense that staying is the "right" or "moral" thing to do.[40] The sense that people *should* stay with their current employers may result from personal work philosophies or more general codes of right and wrong developed over the course of their lives. They may also be dictated by early experiences within the company, if employees are socialized to believe that long-term loyalty is the norm rather than the exception.[41]

In addition to personal work philosophies or organizational socialization, there seem to be two ways to build a sense of obligation-based commitment among employees. One way is to create a feeling that the employee is in the organization's debt—that he or she owes something to the organization. For example, an organization may spend a great deal of money training and developing an employee. In recognition of that investment, the employee may feel obligated to "repay" the organization with several more years of loyal service.[42] Picture a scenario in which your employer paid your tuition, allowing you to further your education, while also providing you with training and developmental job assignments that increased your skills. Wouldn't you feel a little guilty if you took the first job opportunity that came your way?

Wardrop Engineering Ltd., based in Winnipeg, is in the business of providing engineering, environmental, and information technology solutions to companies around the world, and is a company that clearly recognizes the value of normative commitment. As you might imagine, Wardrop is one of those organizations that finds itself competing globally for highly skilled employees. Recently, Wardrop Engineering was recognized as one of the Top 20 Best Employers for New Canadians.[43] According to Brent Thompson, the president of Wardrop, "We have had programs in place that welcome new Canadians to our company for many years." Apart from providing a variety of programs aimed at promoting inclusiveness and workplace integration (e.g., providing cross-cultural and language training to new recruits and existing employees; providing in-house prayer facilities if requested), the company helps these new Canadians obtain their Canadian professional designations through an extensive technical mentoring and development program. In exchange for the support provided by organization, many of these new Canadians will, in all likelihood, feel an obligation to reciprocate this goodwill.[44] It is this sense of "wanting to give something back" or "feeling like you owe the organization" that is the essence of normative commitment. Employees stay because they feel it is the right thing to do—for Wardrop Engineering, this represents another effective business solution.

OB RESEARCH IN CANADA

Drs. John P. Meyer and Natalie J. Allen are professors in industrial and organizational psychology at the University of Western Ontario. Both are recognized experts in several areas of organizational behaviour and, most notably, organizational commitment. Both are credited with the development of the three-component model of organizational commitment that we have read about in this chapter. Over the past 25 years, their work in this area has demonstrated that employee commitment to an organization can take at least three different forms (emotion-based, cost-based, and obligation-based), that each form of commitment develops in a somewhat different manner, and perhaps most importantly, that each form of commitment has quite different implications for employee behaviour, performance, and well-being. In 1997, their seminal book, *Commitment in the Workplace: Theory, Research and Application,* was selected as the Academic Book of the Year by *Choice* magazine.

In addition to their common interest and published works in organizational commitment, Drs. Meyer and Allen have separate interests and research expertise. Dr. Meyer studies work motivation, organizational justice, leadership, and organizational change. Dr. Allen investigates various psychological issues with work teams (see Chapter 10). Their collaborative and independent works have been published in leading scientific journals in the field of organizational behaviour and management.

Drs. Meyer and Allen are Fellows of the Canadian Psychological Association and the Society for Industrial and Organizational Psychology. Dr. Meyer is a former chair of Canadian Society for Industrial and Organizational Psychology and is currently editor of the OB/HRM section of the *Canadian Journal of Administrative Sciences.* Dr. Allen is a former chair of Canadian Society for Industrial/Organizational Psychology, and associate editor of the *Journal of Occupational and Organizational Psychology.*

Some of their most frequently cited works include:

"Testing the Side-bet Theory of Organizational Commitment: Some Methodological Considerations," by J.P. Meyer and N.J. Allen, N.J., published in *Journal of Applied Psychology* (1984, volume 69, pp. 372–78).

"The Measurement and Antecedents of Affective, Continuance and Normative Commitment to the Organization," by N.J. Allen and J.P. Meyer, published in *Journal of Occupational Psychology* (1990, volume 63, pp. 1–8).

"Commitment to Organizations and Occupations: Extension and Test of a 3-Component Conceptualization," by J.P. Meyer, N.J. Allen, and C.A. Smith, published in *Journal of Applied Psychology* (1993, volume 78, pp. 538–51).

"Affective, Continuance, and Normative Commitment to the Organization: An Examination of Construct Validity," by N.J. Allen and J.P. Meyer, published in *Journal of Vocational Behavior* (1996, volume 49, pp. 252–76).

Commitment in the Workplace: Theory, Research, and Application, by J.P. Meyer and N.J. Allen (Thousand Oaks, CA: Sage Publications, 1997).

WITHDRAWAL BEHAVIOUR

According to the previously mentioned study by the Conference Board of Canada, only a quarter of surveyed companies reported being confident that their current talent pool is sufficient.[45] Organizational commitment is therefore a vital concern, because the loss of even one talented employee can only worsen that situation. However, there are times when organizational commitment becomes even more critical, namely, in the face of some negative work event. To paraphrase the old saying, "When the going gets tough, the organization doesn't want you to get going." In tough times, organizations need their employees to demonstrate loyalty, not "get going" right out the door.[46] Of course, it's those same tough times that put an employee's loyalty and allegiance to the test.

Consider the following scenario: You've been working at your company for three years and served on a key product development team for the past several months. Unfortunately, the team has been struggling of late. In an effort to enhance the team's performance, the organization has added a new member to the group. This member has a solid history of product development but is, by all accounts, a horrible person with whom to work. You can easily see the employee's talent but find yourself hating every moment spent in the employee's presence. This situation is particularly distressing because the team won't finish its work for another nine months, at the earliest. What would you do in this situation?

exit A response to a negative work event by which one becomes often absent from work or voluntarily leaves the organization

3.3 What are the four primary responses to negative events at work?

Research on reactions to negative work events suggests that you might respond in one of four general ways.[47] First, you might attempt to remove yourself from the situation, either by being absent from work more frequently or by voluntarily leaving the organization. This removal is termed **exit**, defined as an active, destructive response by which an individual either ends or restricts organizational membership.[48] Second, you might attempt to change the circumstances by meeting with the new team member to attempt to work out the situation. This action is termed **voice**, defined as an active, constructive response in which individuals attempt to improve the situation.[49] Third, you might just "grin and bear it," maintaining your effort level despite your unhappiness. This response is termed **loyalty**, defined as a passive, constructive response that maintains public support for the situation while the individual privately hopes for improvement.[50] Fourth, you might just go through the motions, allowing your performance to deteriorate slowly as you mentally "check out." This reaction is termed **neglect**, defined as a passive, destructive response in which interest and effort in the job declines.[51] Sometimes neglect can be even more costly than exit because it is not as readily noticed. Employees may neglect their duties for months (or even years) before their bosses catch on to their poor behaviours. We saw a poignant example of this in the Walkerton case (Chapter 2).

voice When an employee speaks up to offer constructive suggestions for change, often in reaction to a negative work event

loyalty A passive response to a negative work event in which one publicly supports the situation but privately hopes for improvement

neglect A passive, destructive response to a negative work event in which one's interest and effort in work decline

Taken together, the exit–voice–loyalty–neglect framework captures most of the possible responses to a negative work event,[52] like the addition of a new colleague who makes work more difficult. Where does organizational commitment fit in? Organizational commitment should decrease the likelihood that an individual will respond to a negative work event with exit or neglect (the two destructive responses). At the same time, organizational commitment should increase the likelihood that the negative work event will prompt voice or loyalty (the two constructive responses). Research suggests that factors that promote affective and normative commitment indeed increase the likelihood of voice and loyalty while decreasing the likelihood of exit and neglect.[53]

3.4 What are some examples of psychological withdrawal? Of physical withdrawal? How do the different forms of withdrawal relate to each other?

It's clear from this discussion that exit and neglect represent the flipside of organizational commitment: withdrawal behaviour. How common is withdrawal behaviour within organizations? Quite common, it turns out. One study clocked employees' on-the-job behaviours over a two-year period and found that only about 51 percent of their time was actually spent working! The other 49 percent was lost to late starts, early departures, long coffee breaks, personal matters, and other forms of withdrawal.[54] As a manager, wouldn't you like to feel like there was more than a coin-flip's chance that your employees were actually working during the course of a given day?

As shown in Figure 3-4, withdrawal comes in two forms: psychological (or neglect) and physical (or exit). **Psychological withdrawal** consists of actions that provide a mental escape from the work environment.[55] When an employee is engaging in psychological withdrawal, "the lights are on, but nobody's home." Some business articles refer to psychological withdrawal as "warm-chair attrition," meaning that employees have essentially been lost even though their chairs remain occupied.[56] How big of a problem is psychological withdrawal? With roughly 40 percent of Canadian workers feeling "disengaged" from their work, it would appear that the scope of the problem is substantial.[57]

Psychological withdrawal comes in a number of shapes and sizes. The least serious is **daydreaming**, when an employee appears to be working but is actually distracted by random thoughts or concerns. **Socializing** refers to the verbal chatting about non-work topics that goes on in cubicles and offices or at the mailbox or vending machines. **Looking busy** indicates an intentional desire on the part of the employee to look like he or she is working, even when not performing work tasks.[58] Sometimes employees decide to reorganize their desks or go for a stroll around the building, even though they have nowhere to go.

psychological withdrawal Mentally escaping the work environment

daydreaming A form of psychological withdrawal in which one's work is interrupted by random thoughts or concerns

socializing A form of psychological withdrawal in which one verbally chats with co-workers about non-work topics

looking busy A form of psychological withdrawal in which one attempts to appear consumed with work when not performing actual work tasks

FIGURE 3-4 Psychological and Physical Withdrawal

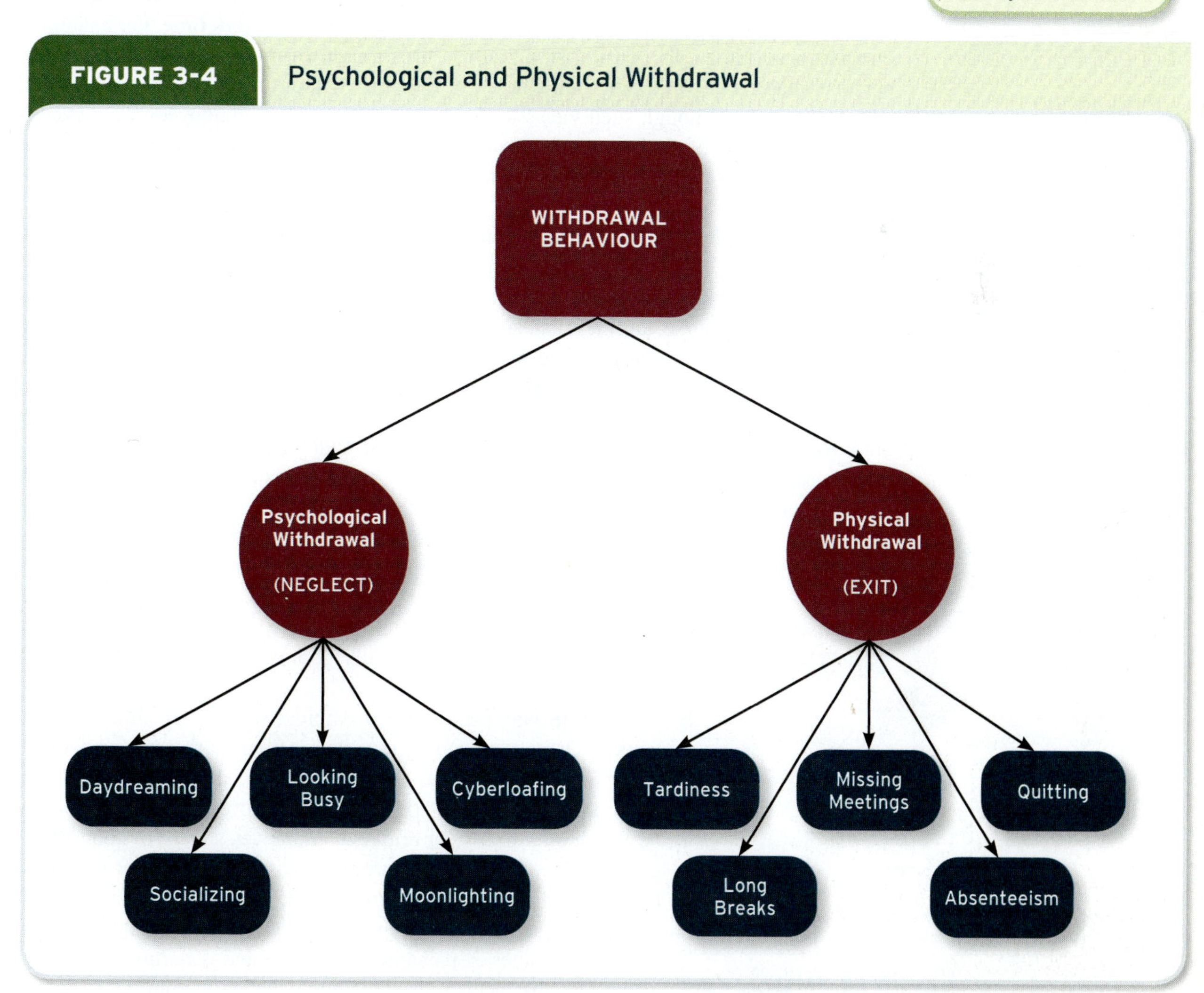

moonlighting A form of psychological withdrawal in which employees use work time and resources to do non-work-related activities

cyberloafing A form of psychological withdrawal in which employees surf the Internet, e-mail, and instant message to avoid doing work-related activities

physical withdrawal A physical escape from the work environment

tardiness A form of physical withdrawal in which employees arrive late to work or leave work early

long breaks A form of physical withdrawal in which employees take longer-than-normal lunches or breaks to spend less time at work

missing meetings A form of physical withdrawal in which employees neglect important work functions while away from the office

absenteeism A form of physical withdrawal in which employees do not show up for an entire day of work

(Those who are very good at managing impressions do such things very briskly and with a focused look on their faces!) When employees engage in **moonlighting**, they use work time and resources to complete something other than their job duties, such as assignments for another job.[59]

Perhaps the most widespread form of psychological withdrawal among white collar employees is **cyberloafing**—using Internet, e-mail, and instant messaging access for their personal enjoyment rather than work duties.[60] One recent survey of more than 3,000 employees from 750 different organizations revealed that employees spend around 40 percent of their workday responding to personal e-mails or surfing the Web.[61] Ninety-seven percent of those surveyed admitted to using the Internet primarily for personal rather than work use. To see for yourself, notice how many of your fellow students with Web-enabled laptops are responding to e-mail, instant messaging on MSN, or checking Facebook rather than taking notes during the class. You also see the same pattern of behaviour in many workplaces. Go for a stroll around the office and count how many screens you see set to Internet dating sites, the iTunes music store, personal banking sites, YouTube, travel sites, and (when the boss is clearly not watching) job hunting sites. According to some conservative estimates, workplace Internet misuse costs Canadian businesses more than $16 billion dollars in lost productivity annually.[62] Interestingly, some employees view cyberloafing as a way of "balancing the scales" when it comes to personal versus work time. For example, one participant in a cyberloafing study noted, "It is alright for me to use the Internet for personal reasons at work. After all, I do work overtime without receiving extra pay from my employer."[63] Although such views are quite reasonable, other employees view cyberloafing as a means of retaliating against negative work events. One participant in the same study noted, "My boss is not the appreciative kind; I take what I can whenever I can. Surfing the net is my way of hitting back."

Physical withdrawal consists of actions that provide a physical escape, whether short term or long term, from the work environment. Physical withdrawal also comes in a number of shapes and sizes. **Tardiness** reflects the tendency to arrive at work late (or leave work early).[64] Of course, tardiness can sometimes be unavoidable, as when employees have car trouble or must fight through bad weather, but it often represents a calculated desire to spend less time at work.[65] **Long breaks** involve longer-than-normal lunches, soda breaks, coffee breaks, and so forth that provide a physical escape from work. Ben Hamper's classic book *Rivethead: Tales of the Assembly Line*[66] is filled with examples of General Motors manufacturing employees taking excessively long breaks. For example, employees would routinely take turns covering for one another on the assembly line for half a shift so that they could spend several hours sleeping in their cars or at home, running errands, or even drinking beer at local bars. Sometimes such breaks stretch into **missing meetings**, which means employees neglect important work functions while away from the office. As a manager, you'd like to be sure that employees that leave for lunch are actually going to come back, but sometimes, that's not a safe bet!

"Hewes, it's come to my attention that you've been using our internet access to troll for babes."

Source: © The New Yorker Collection 1994 Robert Mankoff from cartoonbank.com.

Absenteeism occurs when employees miss an entire day of work.[67] Of course, people stay home from work for a variety of reasons, including illness and family emergencies. There is also a rhythm to absenteeism. For example, employees are more likely to be absent on Mondays or Fridays.[68] Moreover, streaks of good attendance create a sort of pressure to be absent, as personal responsibilities build until a day at home becomes irresistible.[69] That type of absence can sometimes be functional, because people return to work with their "batteries recharged."[70] Group and departmental norms also affect absenteeism by signalling whether an employee can get

OB FOR STUDENTS

What does withdrawal mean for you as a student? The most obvious form of withdrawal for students is missed classes—the academic version of absenteeism. Why do students choose to stay home from class on a given day? One study identified the top six reasons for missing class, ranked as follows:[71]

1. Needing to complete work for another class
2. The class is boring
3. Severe illness (e.g., flu)
4. Minor illness (e.g., cold, sore throat)
5. Tired from social activities.
6. Oversleeping

These reasons illustrate that there are a number of factors that cause people to be absent. Some are avoidable, some are unavoidable; some are related to the class, some are unrelated. Of the factors listed, the "class is boring" reason most clearly captures absenteeism as a response to a negative class-related event. Students don't like the class, so they engage in exit behaviours. There's also a rhythm and seasonality to absenteeism, as students are most likely to miss Friday classes or classes near the end of the semester (when project deadlines become most pressing).

Here's the million-dollar question for any student: Does absenteeism harm course grades? The clear answer is "yes." One study examined the correlation between class attendance and course grades across 17 different class sections and identified correlations ranging from .29 to .73.[72] Another study found that students who attend all classes average a .45 point higher GPA in the course than students who only attend half the classes.[73] This result appears even when taking into account a student's prior cumulative GPA and his or her motivation levels.

These sorts of results explain why some instructors build an attendance requirement into their classes, causing students to sign in each day to reduce absences. The benefits of this policy were tested in two sections of a psychology course.[74] One section required students to sign in to record attendance; the other section didn't. Absenteeism was one-third lower in the section that required sign-ins, and the students in that section performed significantly better on seven of the eight quizzes in the class.

The bottom line is clear for you as a student—come to class, and you'll get a better grade. Of course, showing up may be only half the battle, particularly if students are tempted to engage in neglect during lectures (e.g., reading the newspaper, surfing the Web, falling asleep). If you find yourself tempted to engage in those forms of psychological withdrawal, consider this result: Students who participate during class increase their course GPAs by an average of .23 points.[75] So there's a reason to pay attention!

away with missing a day here or there without being noticed.[76] These issues aside, a consistent pattern of absenteeism, month in and month out, is a symptom of the kind of low commitment that concerns most managers. Should absenteeism (in the form of missed classes) concern instructors as well? See our **OB for Students** feature to find out.

Finally, the most serious form of physical withdrawal is **quitting**—voluntarily leaving the organization. As with the other forms of withdrawal, employees can choose to "turn over" for a variety of reasons. The most frequent reasons include leaving for more money or a better career opportunity; dissatisfaction with supervision, working conditions, or working schedule; family factors; and health.[77] Note that many of those reasons reflect avoidable turnover, meaning that the organization could have done something to keep the

quitting A form of physical withdrawal in which employees voluntarily leave the organization employee, perhaps by offering more money, more frequent promotions, or a better work situation. Family factors and health, in contrast, usually reflect unavoidable turnover that doesn't necessarily signal a lack of commitment on the part of employees.

Regardless of their reasons, some employees choose to quit after engaging in a very thorough, careful, and reasoned analysis. Typically some sort of "shock," whether it be a critical job change or a negative work experience, jars employees enough that it triggers the thought of quitting in them.[78] Once the idea of quitting has occurred to them, employees begin searching for other places to work, compare those alternatives to their current job, and—if the comparisons seem favourable—quit.[79] This process may take days, weeks, or even months as employees grapple with the decision. In other cases, though, a shock may result in an impulsive, knee-jerk decision to quit, with little or no thought given to alternative jobs (or how those jobs compare to the current one).[80] Of course, sometimes a shock never occurs. Instead, an employee decides to quit as a result of a slow but steady decrease in happiness until a "straw breaks the camel's back" and voluntary turnover results.

Figure 3-5 shows 10 different behaviours that employees can perform to psychologically or physically escape from a negative work environment. A key question remains though: "How do all those behaviours relate to one another?" A perspective on this issue that has received the most scientific support is referred to as the progression model.[81] This model argues that the various withdrawal behaviours are connected in a progressive sequence, such that the tendency to daydream or socialize leads to the tendency to come in late or take long breaks, which leads to the tendency to be absent or quit.[82] From this perspective, knowing that an employee cyberloafs tells you that the same employee is probably going to be absent in the near future. Research has confirmed that the behaviours that are closest to each other in the sequence tend to be more highly correlated.[83] For example, quitting is more closely related to absenteeism than to tardiness, because absenteeism is right next to it in the withdrawal progression.[84] These results illustrate that withdrawal behaviours may begin with very minor actions but eventually can escalate to more serious actions that may harm the organization.

SO WHAT DOES IT MEAN TO BE A "COMMITTED" EMPLOYEE?

As shown in Figure 3-5, it means a lot of different things. It means that the employee has a strong desire to remain a member of the organization, maybe because he or she wants to stay, needs to stay, or feels he or she ought to stay. Regardless of the reasons for their attachment though, retaining employees means stopping the progression of withdrawal that begins with psychological forms and escalates to behavioural forms. Note that the negative sign (–) in Figure 3-5 illustrates that high levels of overall organizational commitment reduce the frequency of psychological and physical withdrawal. Note also that psychological withdrawal goes on to affect physical withdrawal, which represents the progressive nature of such behaviours.

As you move forward in this book, you'll notice that every chapter includes a description of how that chapter's topic relates to organizational commitment. For example, Chapter 4 on job satisfaction describes how an employee's satisfaction level influences his or her organizational commitment. You'll find that some chapter topics are more strongly correlated with affective commitment, whereas other topics correlate more strongly with continuance or normative commitment. Such differences will help you see exactly how and why a given topic, whether it be satisfaction, stress, motivation, or something else, affects organizational commitment. By the end of the book, you will have developed a good sense of the most powerful drivers of commitment.

FIGURE 3-5 What Does It Mean to Be a "Committed" Employee?

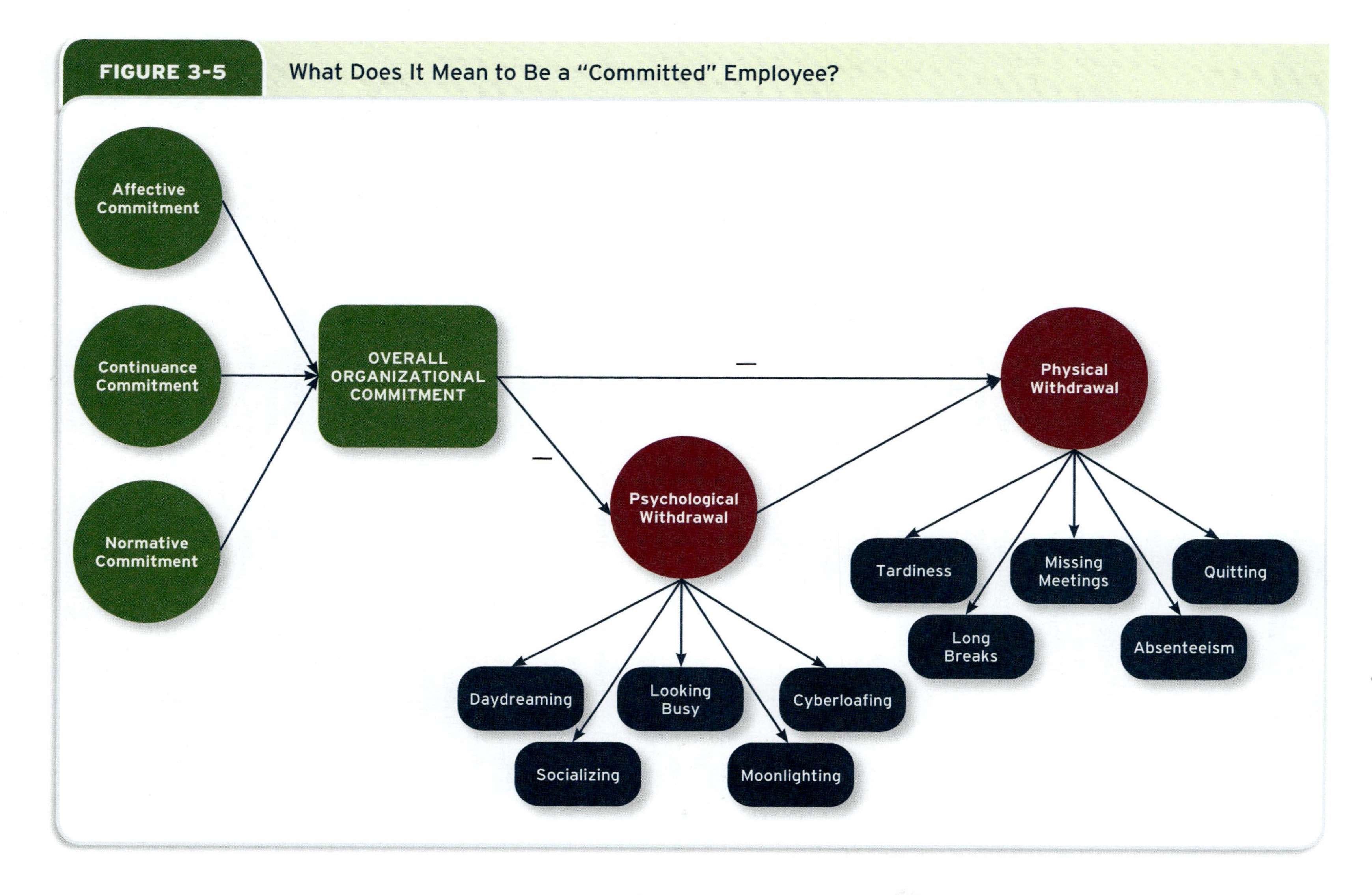

APPLICATION: COMMITMENT INITIATIVES

Now that you've gained a good understanding of organizational commitment, as well as some of the workforce trends that affect it, we close with a discussion of strategies and initiatives that can be used to maximize commitment. As the opening example of Microsoft illustrated, almost every company struggles to foster commitment at some time or another. What can they do to prevent withdrawal? From an affective commitment perspective, employer strategies could centre on increasing the bonds that link employees together. Several examples of these initiatives were presented earlier in this chapter (e.g., allowing employees time to play, social events that encourage employees to interact and develop friendships). Such opportunities promote tight bonding among employees and help to embed them within the social fabric of the organization—which may help to reduce voluntary turnover (or at least, make leaving difficult). Other commitment-enhancing initiatives centre on the nature of the work performed. Learning about ways to design the work in such a way to "engage" workers is a topic that will be covered in Chapter 4.

From a continuance commitment perspective, the priority should be to create a salary and benefits package that creates a financial need to stay. One study compared the impact of a variety of human resource management practices on voluntary turnover and found that two of the most significant predictors were average pay level and quality of the benefits package.[85] Using compensation and benefits to "lock" people into jobs, however, should be carefully considered. Although high levels of continuance commitment have been shown to lower turnover, there seems to be very little payoff in terms of job performance or citizenship behaviour.[86] One factor that goes hand in hand with salaries and benefits is advancements and promotions, because salaries cannot remain competitive if employees get stuck in neutral when climbing the career ladder.[87] Paying attention to career paths is especially important for star employees and foreign-born employees, both of whom have many options for employment elsewhere.[88]

From a normative commitment perspective, the employer can provide various training and development opportunities for employees, which means investing in them to create the sense that they owe further service to the organization. As the nature of the employee–employer relationship has changed, opportunities for development have overtaken secure employment on the list of employee priorities.[89] IBM is one company with a reputation for prioritizing development. Its "workforce management initiative" keeps a database of 33,000 resumés to develop a snapshot of employee skills. IBM uses that snapshot to plan its future training and development activities, with $400 million of the company's $750 million training budget devoted to giving employees the skills they may need in the future. If employees find developmental activities beneficial and rewarding, they may be tempted to repay those efforts with further years of service.

A final practical suggestion centres on what to do if withdrawal begins to occur. Managers are usually tempted to look the other way when employees engage in minor forms of withdrawal. After all, sometimes such behaviours simply represent a break in an otherwise busy day. However, the progression model of withdrawal shows that even minor forms of psychological withdrawal often escalate, eventually to the point of absenteeism and turnover. The implication is therefore to stop the progression in its early stages by trying to root out the source of the reduced commitment. Many of the most effective companies take great strides to investigate the causes of low commitment, whether at the psychological withdrawal stage or during exit interviews. As one senior oil executive acknowledged, the loss of a talented employee warrants the same sort of investigation as a technical malfunction that causes significant downtime on an oil rig.[90]

TAKEAWAYS

3.1 Organizational commitment is the desire on the part of an employee to remain a member of the organization. Withdrawal behaviour is a set of actions that employees perform to avoid the work situation. Commitment and withdrawal are negatively related to each other—the more committed an employee is, the less likely he or she is to engage in withdrawal.

3.2 There are three forms of organizational commitment. Affective commitment occurs when an employee *wants* to stay and is influenced by the emotional bonds between employees. Continuance commitment occurs when an employee *needs* to stay and is influenced by salary and benefits and the degree to which he or she is embedded in the community. Normative commitment occurs when an employee feels that he or she *ought* to stay and is influenced by an organization investing in its employees or engaging in charitable efforts.

3.3 Employees can respond to negative work events in four ways: exit, voice, loyalty, and neglect. Exit is a form of physical withdrawal in which the employee either ends or restricts organizational membership. Voice is an active and constructive response by which employees attempt to improve the situation. Loyalty is passive and constructive; employees remain supportive while hoping the situation improves on its own. Neglect is a form of psychological withdrawal in which interest and effort in the job decrease.

3.4 Examples of psychological withdrawal include daydreaming, socializing, looking busy, moonlighting, and cyberloafing. Examples of physical withdrawal include tardiness, long breaks, missing meetings, absenteeism, and quitting. Consistent with the progression model, withdrawal behaviours tend to start with minor psychological forms before escalating to more major physical varieties. What to do if withdrawal begins to occur? The management implication is to stop the progression in its early stages by trying to root out the source of the reduced commitment.

KEY TERMS

- absenteeism *p. 62*
- affective commitment *p. 50*
- continuance commitment *p. 51*
- cyberloafing *p. 62*
- daydreaming *p. 61*
- embeddedness *p. 56*
- erosion model *p. 55*
- exit *p. 60*
- focus of commitment *p. 52*
- long breaks *p. 62*
- looking busy *p. 61*
- loyalty *p. 60*
- missing meetings *p. 62*
- moonlighting *p. 62*
- neglect *p. 60*
- normative commitment *p. 51*
- organizational commitment *p. 49*
- physical withdrawal *p. 62*
- psychological withdrawal *p. 61*
- quitting *p. 63*
- social influence model *p. 55*
- socializing *p. 61*
- tardiness *p. 62*
- voice *p. 60*
- withdrawal behaviour *p. 50*

DISCUSSION QUESTIONS

3.1 Which form of organizational commitment (affective, continuance, or normative) do you think is most important to the majority of employees? Which do you think is most important to you?

3.2 Describe other ways that organizations can improve affective, continuance, and normative commitment, other than the strategies suggested in this chapter. How expensive are those strategies?

3.3 Consider times when you've reacted to a negative event with exit, voice, loyalty, or neglect. What was it about the situation that caused you to respond the way you did? Do you usually respond to negative events in the same way, or does your response vary across the four options?

3.4 Can organizations use a combination of monitoring and punishment procedures to reduce psychological and physical withdrawal? How might such programs work from a practical perspective? Do you think they would be effective?

3.5 Which form of organizational commitment do you feel toward the university and/ or this class?

CASE • MICROSOFT

Microsoft has one of the lowest employee turnover rates in the IT industry; however, there is room for improvement. Top talent is currently leaving Microsoft to pursue Internet start-ups or jumping ship to Google. The loss of these key employees represents a serious threat to the success of the company in the future. Recognizing this problem, Microsoft is actively identifying its top talent and developing ways to make jobs more attractive.

Employee engagement appears to be the buzz today. Studies show that employees who are engaged are more productive, profitable, and customer focused and less likely to leave the organization. According to Dr. Beverly Kaye, an expert on career issues in the workplace, what employees want is a relationship with their managers, so managers have to act more like coaches, not bosses. Some of the factors that always rank at the top with regard to what gets employees engaged and what they value in a job include career opportunities and development, great people to work with, and a great boss.

Microsoft is meeting the challenge of improving worker morale head on to retain its employees. MyMicrosoft is a program introduced by the company to provide some of the attractive amenities that other IT companies offer employees. This program will include a wide range of incentives focused on improving the working conditions and culture of the company, such as a set of lifestyle perks and a management development program. Microsoft's new program is an initial step to improve the morale of employees, but only time will tell if this program is attractive enough to retain employees.

3.1 What are the factors causing the brain drain at Microsoft? Explain.

3.2 Is Microsoft's organizational structure having an impact on its organizational commitment levels? Explain.

Sources: S. Harvey, "Getting the Stars Aligned at Microsoft," *Strategic HR Review,* March 2002; M. Goldsmith, "Engaging Employees," *BusinessWeek,* July 3, 2007; "Microsoft Struggles to Improve Worker Morale," *eweek,* June 5, 2006; M. Moeller and V. Murphy, "Outta Here at Microsoft," *BusinessWeek,* November 29, 1999; J. Persaud, "Keep the Faithful," *People Management,* June 12, 2003.

EXERCISE • REACTING TO NEGATIVE EVENTS

The purpose of this exercise is to explore how individuals react to three all-too-common scenarios that represent negative workplace events. This exercise uses groups of six participants, so your instructor will either assign you to a group of six or ask you to create your own group of six. The exercise has the following steps:

1. Individually read the following three scenarios: the annoying boss, the boring job, and pay and seniority. For each scenario, write down two specific behaviours in which you would likely engage in response to that scenario. Write down what you would actually do, as opposed to what you wish you would do. For example, you may wish that you would march into your boss's office and demand a change, but if you would actually do nothing, write down "nothing."

Annoying Boss	You've been working at your current company for about a year. Over time, your boss has become more and more annoying to you. It's not that your boss is a bad person, or even necessarily a bad boss. It's more a personality conflict—the way your boss talks, the way your boss manages every little thing, even the facial expressions your boss uses. The more time passes, the more you just can't stand to be around your boss.	Two likely behaviours:
Boring Job	You've been working at your current company for about a year. You've come to realize that your job is pretty boring. It's the first real job you've ever had, and at first it was nice to have some money and something to do every day. But the "new job" excitement has worn off, and things are actually quite monotonous. Same thing every day. It's to the point that you check your watch every hour, and Wednesdays feel like they should be Fridays.	Two likely behaviours:
Pay and Seniority	You've been working at your current company for about a year. The consensus is that you're doing a great job—you've gotten excellent performance evaluations and have emerged as a leader on many projects. As you've achieved this high status, however, you've come to feel that you are underpaid. Your company's pay procedures emphasize seniority much more than job performance. As a result, you look at other members of your project teams and see poor performers making much more than you, just because they've been with the company longer.	Two likely behaviours:

2. In groups, compare and contrast your likely responses to the three scenarios. Come to a consensus on the two most likely responses for the group as a whole. Elect one group member to write the two likely responses to each of the three scenarios on the board.
3. Class discussion (whether in groups or as a class) should centre on where the likely responses fit into the exit–voice–loyalty–neglect framework. What personal and situational factors would lead someone to one category of responses over another? Are there any responses that do not fit into the exit–voice–loyalty–neglect framework?

OB ASSESSMENTS • AFFECTIVE COMMITMENT

How emotionally attached are you to your employer? This assessment is designed to measure affective commitment—the feeling that you *want* to stay with your current organization. Think of your current job or the last job that you held (even if it was a part-time or summer job). Answer each question using the response scale provided. Then subtract your answers to the bold-faced questions from 6, with the difference being your new answers for those questions. For example, if your original answer for Question 3 was "4," your new answer is "2" (6–4). Then sum your answers for the six questions.

1 STRONGLY DISAGREE	2 DISAGREE	3 NEUTRAL	4 AGREE	5 STRONGLY AGREE

1. I would be very happy to spend the rest of my career in this organization. ______
2. I really feel as if this organization's problems are my own. ______
3. **I do not feel like "part of the family" at my organization.** ______
4. **I do not feel "emotionally attached" to this organization.** ______
5. This organization has a great deal of personal meaning for me. ______
6. **I do not feel a strong sense of belonging to my organization.** ______

SCORING

If your scores sum up to 20 or above, you feel a strong sense of affective commitment to your current or past employer, which means that you feel an emotional attachment to the company, or the people within it, that lessens the likelihood that you would leave voluntarily. If your scores sum up to less than 20, you have a weaker sense of affective commitment to your current or past employer. This result is especially likely if you responded to the questions in reference to a part-time or summer job, for which there is rarely enough time to develop a deep emotional bond.

CONNECT—Available 24/7 with instant feedback so you can study when you want, how you want, and where you want. Take advantage of the Study Plan—an innovative tool that helps students customize their own learning experience. Students can diagnose their knowledge with pre- and post-tests, identify the areas where they need help, search contents of the entire learning package for content specific to the topic they're studying, and add these resources to their study plan. Visit **www.connectob.ca** to register—take practice quizzes, run interactive scenarios, and much more. Also visit the Student Online Learning Centre for additional study tools.

Part 2 **INDIVIDUAL MECHANISMS**

CHAPTER

4 Job Satisfaction

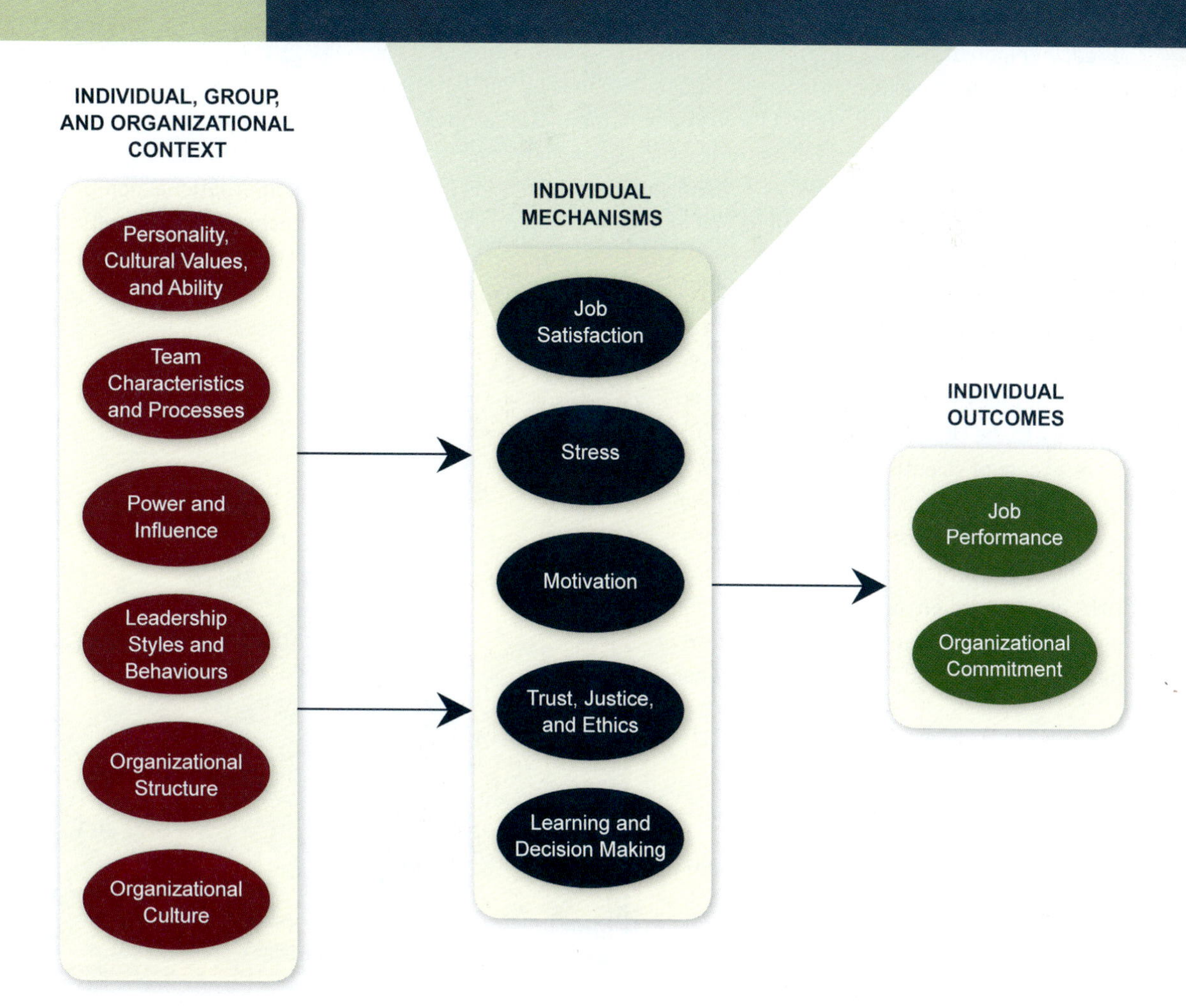

Learning Outcomes

After reading this chapter, you should be able to answer the following questions:

- 4.1 What is job satisfaction?
- 4.2 What are values, and how do they affect job satisfaction?
- 4.3 People often evaluate their job satisfaction according to specific facets. What are those facets?
- 4.4 Which job characteristics can create a sense of satisfaction with the work itself?
- 4.5 What are mood and emotions, and what specific forms do they take?
- 4.6 How does job satisfaction affect job performance and organizational commitment?

PERFORMANCE PLANTS

What if you could do something that would help prevent the suffering of millions of starving people in the third world? Imagine not having to water your front lawn or flowers, even during the hottest summer months, and still have the grass retain its fresh springlike look. What if farmers no longer had to irrigate their fields to harvest a bumper crop? Imagine if all the world's energy needs could be met from growing grass. Does all of this sound like science fiction? Well, to the 45 dedicated men and women who work at Performance Plants, solving some of the world's most challenging food-supply, energy, and environmental problems is all in a day's work!

Performance Plants Inc., founded by David Dennis in 1995, is Canada's largest agriculture biotechnology company with office and research facilities in Kingston, Ontario; Saskatoon, Saskatchewan; and Waterloo, New York.[1] Their mission is to develop science-based technologies for the purpose of enhancing the production of food, feed, and bio-fuel crops. In laymen's terms, the basic idea is to make small targeted changes to plant genetics that lead to big effects, such as dramatically increasing a plant's performance (i.e., yield) and/or increasing a plant's natural ability to withstand periods of short-term drought and extreme heat. "Performance Plants has already demonstrated in field trials the ability of its patented technologies to produce higher yields of canola—even under drought conditions," says Heather Collins, investment director with Investment Saskatchewan. "This technology is currently being tested in other crops such as corn, soybeans, rice, turf grass, and ornamental plants."[2] Recently, Performance Plants signed an agreement with the Africa Harvest Biotechnology Foundation International, an international non-profit foundation with a focus on fighting poverty, hunger, and malnutrition, to use the company's technology in a multi-year project to develop and field test drought-tolerant white maize, a staple crop in Africa. This is the first time that a Canadian company's agricultural biotech intellectual property is being transferred to Africa for non-commercial purposes.[3]

Some of the most technically demanding work is performed at the company's research facility at Innovation Place, a research park adjacent to the University of Saskatchewan.[4] Here a team of scientists perform a variety of highly specialized and interdependent activities. The role of laboratory workers is to make the targeted changes to the plant DNA and then to ensure that the resulting plant tissues can regenerate with the new genetic instructions. Walking through the

Technical specialists perform some of the more challenging work at their facility in Innovation Place, a research park adjacent to the University of Saskatchewan.

laboratory, one is reminded of the popular *CSI* television show, with characters performing DNA analyses on hair samples found at a crime scene. And just like the characters on *CSI*, it is critical for the technical experts to communicate and coordinate their activities with respect to several different projects. People not assigned to the laboratory work as greenhouse technicians in the plant nursery or outside the facility managing any number of field trials. Day-to-day supervision is shared within the team, in consultation with a respected team leader. Everyone is expected to perform a variety of different tasks in their area of expertise, which in turn, affords them an opportunity to develop and master a wide range of skills and use the "latest-and-greatest" technology and tools. Although team members perform their specialized work, frequent team meetings help everyone to see and track the fruits of their labour (e.g., finding out that three of your transgenic plants provided a yield boost in the field trial). Often faced with unique challenges, team members use their discretion to come up with innovative solutions.

Historically, turnover rate within the Saskatoon facility has been low. In the past year or two, the economy in Saskatchewan has been strengthening, which, in turn, has increased the demand for a relatively small pool of talented people. A particular concern for Performance Plants is the growing presence of several large multinational corporations (e.g., Dow AgroSciences, Bayer CropScience), and the effect of these companies on the overall satisfaction felt by members of the team. Although Performance Plants pays its employees competitive salaries for the region, the multinational corporations have a more competitive total compensation package (salary, benefits, bonus system, company vehicle, etc.). Moreover, the opportunity for promotion and career advancement in one's technical specialty tends to be higher in the larger, more complex multinational organizations. With so much excitement and worldwide demand for this crop enhancing technology, will the company be able to retain the people it needs?

JOB SATISFACTION

job satisfaction A pleasurable emotional state resulting from the appraisal of one's job or job experiences; represents how a person feels and thinks about his or her job

This chapter takes us to a new portion of our integrative model of organizational behaviour. Job satisfaction is one of several individual mechanisms that directly affect job performance and organizational commitment. To illustrate this idea with a personal example, take a moment and recall the worst job that you've held in your life, even if it was just a summer job or a short-term work assignment. What did you feel during the course of the day? How did those feelings influence the way you behaved, in terms of your time spent on task and citizenship behaviours rather than counterproductive or withdrawal behaviours? Now consider your very best job, and how that made you feel and act.

"You'll enjoy rationalizing working for this company."

Source: Reprinted with permission of Peter Vey.

Job satisfaction is defined as a pleasurable emotional state resulting from the appraisal of one's job or job experiences.[5] In other words, it represents how you *feel* about your job and what you *think* about your job.

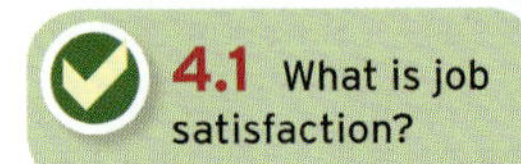

Employees with high job satisfaction experience positive feelings when they think about their duties or take part in task activities. Employees with low job satisfaction experience negative feelings when they think about their duties or take part in their task activities. Although the vast majority of Canadian workers report some degree of satisfaction with their job, only about 40 percent report being "very satisfied" and 15 percent are clearly "not satisfied."[6] Another survey of working Canadians identified corporate culture, the opportunity to use skills, the opportunity to learn, and the ability to be creative as the top drivers of job satisfaction.[7] Interestingly, financial rewards and benefits, flexible work hours, and stress were among the least cited reasons for job satisfaction.[8] Unravelling this puzzle and understanding why some employees are more satisfied than others, and what exactly drives job satisfaction levels, are issues explored in this chapter.

WHY ARE SOME EMPLOYEES MORE SATISFIED THAN OTHERS?

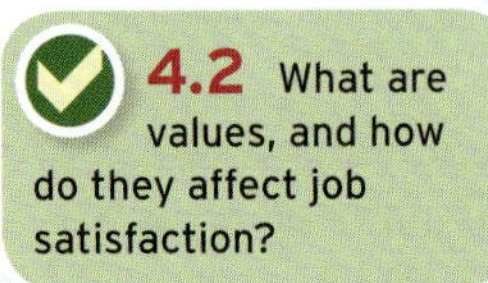

values Things that people consciously or unconsciously want to seek or attain

So what explains why some employees are more satisfied than others? At a general level, employees are satisfied when their job provides the things that they value. **Values** are those things that people consciously or subconsciously want to seek or attain.[9] Think about this question for a few moments: What do you want to attain from your job, that is, what things do you want your job to give you? A good wage? A sense of achievement? Colleagues who are fun to be around? If you had to make a list of the things you value with respect to your job, most or all of them would likely be shown in Table 4-1. This table summarizes the values assessed in the five most popular surveys of work values, broken down into more general categories.[10] Many of those values deal with the things that your work can give you, such as good pay or the chance for frequent promotions. Other values pertain to the context that surrounds your work, including whether you have a good boss or good co-workers. Still other values deal with the work itself, like whether your job tasks provide you with freedom or a sense of achievement.

Consider the list of values in Table 4-1. Which would make your top five in terms of importance right now, at this stage of your life? Maybe you have a part-time job where you value enjoyable co-workers or a comfortable work environment above everything else. Or maybe you're getting established in your career and starting a family, which makes a high salary and frequent promotions especially critical. Or perhaps you're at a point in your career that you feel a need to help others or find an outlet for your creative expression. Regardless of your top five, you can see that different people value different things and that your values may change during the course of your working life.

VALUE FULFILLMENT: VALUE-PERCEPT THEORY

value-percept theory A theory that argues that job satisfaction depends on whether the employee perceives that his or her job supplies those things that he or she values

Values play a key role in explaining job satisfaction. **Value-percept theory** argues that job satisfaction depends on whether you *perceive* that your job supplies the things that you *value*.[11] This theory can be summarized with the following equation:

$$\text{Dissatisfaction} = (V_{want} - V_{have}) \times (V_{importance})$$

In this equation, V_{want} reflects how much of a value an employee wants, V_{have} indicates how much of that value the job supplies, and $V_{importance}$ reflects how important the value is to the employee. Big differences between wants and haves create a sense of dissatisfaction, especially when the value in question is important. Note that the difference between V_{want}

TABLE 4-1 Commonly Assessed Work Values

CATEGORIES	SPECIFIC VALUES
Pay	High salary Secure salary
Promotions	Frequent promotions Promotions based on ability
Supervision	Good supervisory relations Praise for good work
Co-workers	Enjoyable co-workers Responsible co-workers
Work Itself	Utilization of ability Freedom and independence Intellectual stimulation Creative expression Sense of achievement
Altruism	Helping others Moral causes
Status	Prestige Power over others Fame
Environment	Comfort Safety

Key Question:
Which of these things are *most important* to you?

Source: Adapted from R.V. Dawis, "Vocational Interests, Values, and Preferences," in *Handbook of Industrial and Organizational Psychology*, Vol. 2, eds. M.D. Dunnette and L. M. Hough. (Palo Alto, CA: Consulting Psychologists Press, 1991), pp. 834–71.

and V_{have} gets multiplied by importance, so existing discrepancies get magnified for important values and minimized for trivial values. As an example, say that you were evaluating your pay satisfaction. You want to be earning around $70,000 a year but are currently earning $50,000 a year, so there's a $20,000 discrepancy. Does that mean you feel a great deal of pay dissatisfaction? Only if pay is one of the most important values to you from Table 4-1. If pay isn't that important, you likely don't feel much dissatisfaction.

Value-percept theory also suggests that people evaluate job satisfaction according to specific facets of the job.[12] After all, a job isn't one thing—it's a collection of tasks, relationships, and rewards.[13] The most common facets that employees consider in judging their job satisfaction appear in Figure 4-1. The figure includes the "want vs. have" calculations that drive satisfaction with pay, promotions, supervision, co-workers, and the work itself. The figure also shows how satisfaction with those five facets adds together to create "overall job satisfaction." Figure 4-1 shows that employees might be satisfied for all kinds of reasons. One person may be satisfied because she's in a high-paying job and working for a good boss. Another person may be satisfied because he has good co-workers and enjoyable work tasks. You may have noticed that a few of the values in Table 4-1, such as working for moral causes

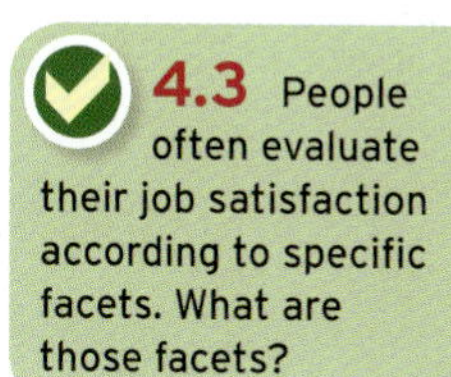

FIGURE 4-1 The Value-Percept Theory of Job Satisfaction

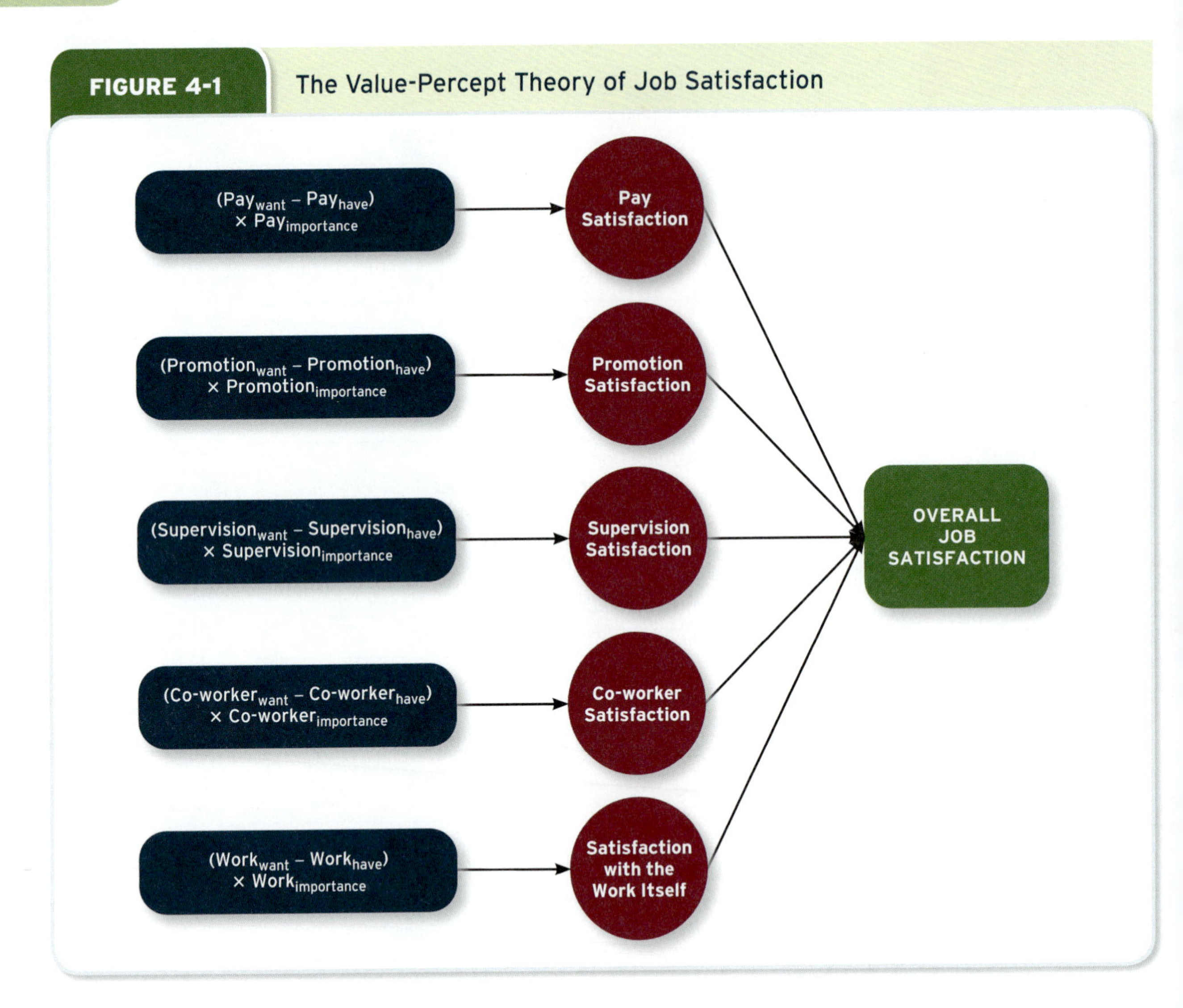

and gaining fame and prestige, are not represented in Figure 4-1. This omission is because those values are not relevant in all jobs, unlike pay, promotions, and so forth.

pay satisfaction Employees' feelings about the compensation for their jobs

The first facet in Figure 4-1, **pay satisfaction**, refers to employees' feelings about their pay, including whether it is as much as they deserve, secure, and adequate for both normal expenses and luxury items.[14] Similar to the other facets, pay satisfaction is based on a comparison of the pay that employees want and the pay they receive.[15] Although more money is almost always better, most employees base their desired pay on a careful examination of their job duties and the pay given to comparable colleagues.[16] In other words, it's not just the absolute amount of pay that matters most for satisfaction, but rather how our pay compares to others. This is exactly the issue faced by the technical staff at Performance Plants, discussed in this chapter's opening profile—knowing that they could earn more if they worked at one of the large multinational corporations in the area. It seems, however, that this isn't just a problem for Performance Plants. Pay, by a large margin, is the number one thing that working Canadians would change about their current job if they could.[17] Thus, even though we may all desire more money, it seems that we can experience satisfaction with our pay providing comparable others are "in the same boat." For more about the relationship between money and satisfaction, see our **OB Internationally** feature.

OB INTERNATIONALLY

The "money can't buy happiness" adage can be supported using national-level data. For example, survey data in the United States, Britain, and Japan show that people are no happier today than they were 50 years ago, even though average incomes have more than doubled during that span.[18] Another way of examining this issue explores the connection between national wealth and average happiness: Do wealthier nations have citizens with higher levels of satisfaction? The figure below provides a representation of the relationship between average income per citizen for a nation and the percentage of respondents who describe themselves as happy, according to population surveys.[19]

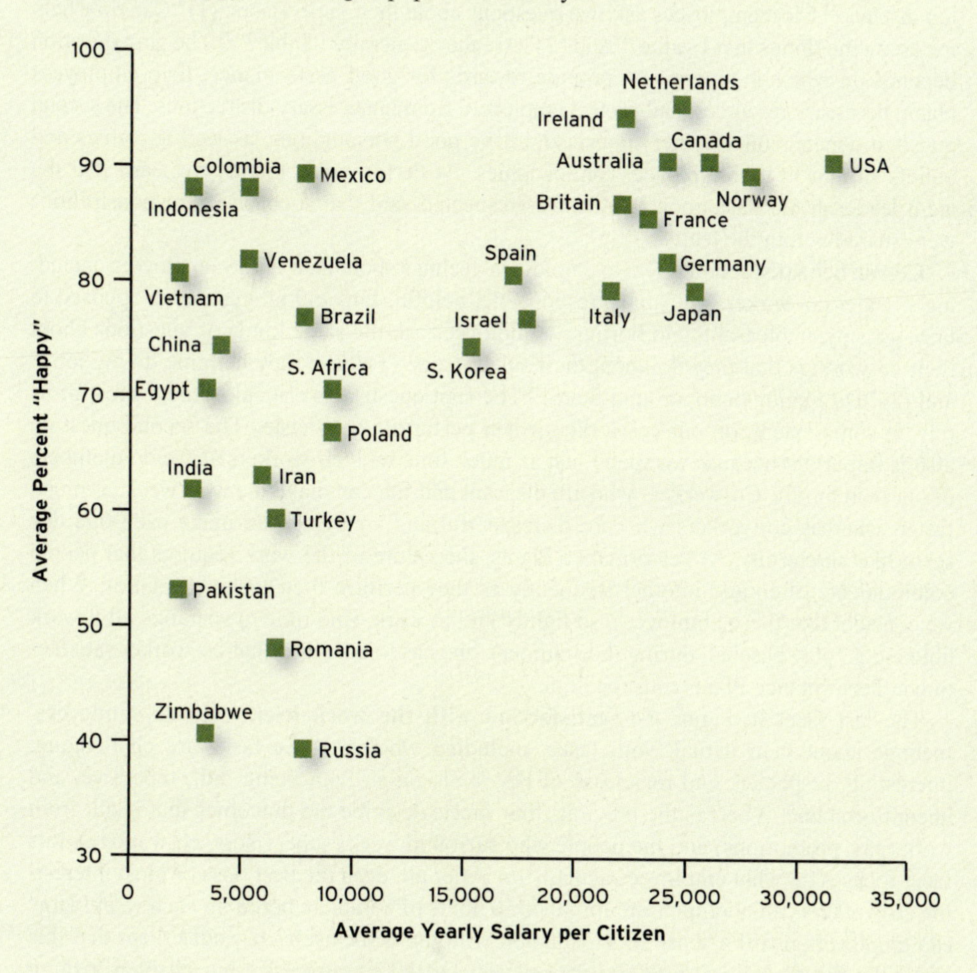

Comparing countries reveals that nations above the poverty line are indeed happier than nations below the poverty line. However, for countries with an average income of $20,000 or more, additional income is not associated with higher levels of satisfaction.[20] For example, Canada, one of the richest countries on Earth, trails nations like the Netherlands and Ireland in terms of average happiness.

promotion satisfaction Employees' feelings about how the company handles promotions

The next facet in Figure 4-1, **promotion satisfaction**, refers to employees' feelings about the company's promotion policies and their execution, including whether promotions are frequent, fair, and based on ability.[21] Unlike pay, some employees may not want frequent promotions because promotions bring more responsibility and increased work hours.[22] However, many employees value promotions because they provide opportunities for more personal growth, a better wage, and more prestige. Again, as was described in the chapter-opening profile, one of the issues facing the employees in the Saskatoon facility was the lack of promotion opportunities relative to what would be available in a larger organization.

supervision satisfaction Employees' feelings about their boss, including his or her competency, communication, and personality

Supervision satisfaction reflects employees' feelings about their boss, including whether the boss is competent, polite, and a good communicator (rather than lazy, annoying, and too distant).[23] Most employees ask two questions about their supervisors: (1) "Can they help me attain the things that I value?" and (2) "Are they generally likable?"[24] The first question depends on whether supervisors provide rewards for good performance, help employees obtain necessary resources, and protect employees from unnecessary distractions. The second question depends on whether supervisors have good personalities, as well as values and beliefs similar to the employees' philosophies. At Performance Plants, we learn that the team leader at the Saskatoon facility was respected, and that supervision responsibilities were shared within the team.

co-worker satisfaction Employees' feelings about their co-workers, including their abilities and personalities

Co-worker satisfaction refers to employees' feelings about their fellow employees, including whether co-workers are smart, responsible, helpful, fun, and interesting as opposed to lazy, gossipy, unpleasant, and boring.[25] Employees ask the same kinds of questions about their co-workers that they do about their supervisors: (1) "Can they help me do my job?" and (2) "Do I enjoy being around them?" The first question is critical because most of us rely, to some extent, on our co-workers when performing job tasks. The second question also is important because we spend just as much time with co-workers as we do members of our own family. Co-workers who are pleasant and fun can make the workweek go much faster, whereas co-workers who are disrespectful and annoying can make even one day seem like an eternity. At Performance Plants, the nature of the work requires that people communicate often and interact frequently as they perform their technical duties. When we consider that these employees, so tightly knit at work, find time to socialize after work hours (e.g., play baseball during the summer), one has to conclude that co-worker satisfaction at Performance Plants must be high.

satisfaction with the work itself Employees' feelings about their actual work tasks

The last facet in Figure 4-1, **satisfaction with the work itself**, reflects employees' feelings about their actual work tasks, including whether those tasks are challenging, interesting, respected, and make use of key skills rather than being dull, repetitive, and uncomfortable.[26] Whereas the previous four facets describe the outcomes that result from work (pay, promotions) and the people who surround work (supervisors, co-workers), this facet focuses on what employees actually *do*. After all, even the best boss or most interesting co-workers can't compensate for 40 or 50 hours of complete boredom each week! How can employers instill a sense of satisfaction with the work itself? It would seem that this particular facet of satisfaction is very relevant for the employees in our chapter-opening profile. We know, for instance, that the key drivers of job satisfaction for Canadian-based biological researchers is the flexibility in work hours and the ability to be creative.[27] We certainly see ample evidence of this at Performance Plants. The small size of the Saskatoon facility requires that the scientists and technical staff use and apply a broad range of knowledge and skills to perform work that is "cutting edge," innovative, and of great significance to others (i.e., tackling some of the environment's more complex and difficult problems).

In summary, value-percept theory suggests that employees will be satisfied when they perceive that their job offers the pay, promotions, supervision, co-workers, and work tasks that they value. Of course, this theory begs the question: Which of those ingredients is most important? In other words, which of the five facets in Figure 4-1 has the strongest influence

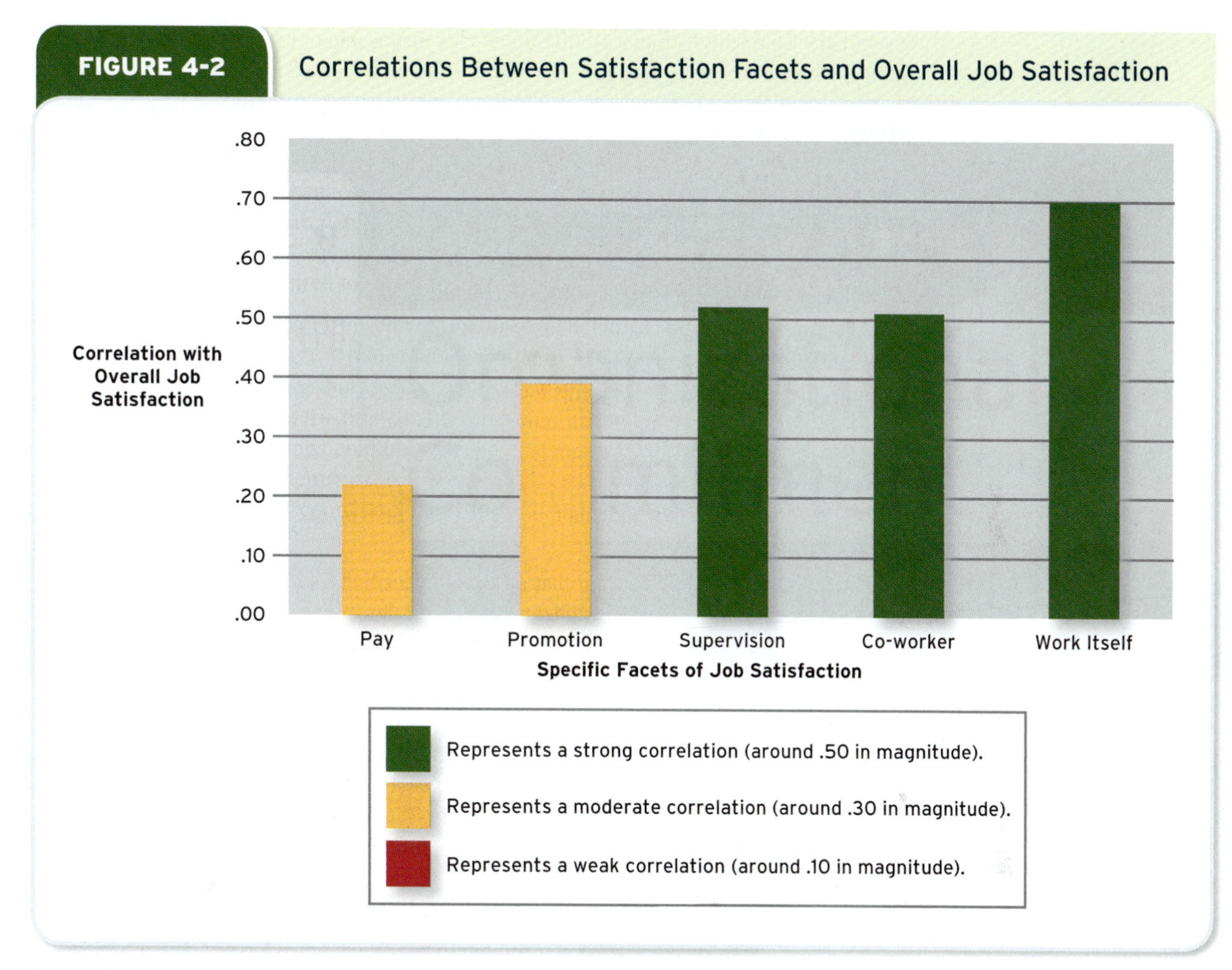

Sources: G.H. Ironson, P.C. Smith, M.T. Brannick, W.M. Gibson, and K.B. Paul, "Construction of a Job in General Scale: A Comparison of Global, Composite, and Specific Measures," *Journal of Applied Psychology* 74 (1989), pp. 193–200; S.S. Russell, C. Spitzmuller, L.F. Lin, J.M. Stanton, P.C. Smith, and G.H. Ironson, "Shorter Can Also Be Better: The Abridged Job in General Scale," *Educational and Psychological Measurement* 64 (2004), pp. 878–93.

on overall job satisfaction? Several research studies have examined these issues and come up with the results shown in Figure 4-2. The figure depicts the correlation between each of the five satisfaction facets and an overall index of job satisfaction. (Recall that correlations of .10, .30, and .50 indicate weak, moderate, and strong relationships, respectively.)

Figure 4-2 suggests that satisfaction with the work itself is the single strongest driver of overall job satisfaction.[28] Supervision and co-worker satisfaction are also strong drivers, and promotion and pay satisfaction have moderately strong effects. It would seem that a very similar pattern exists for the employees at Performance Plants. Why is satisfaction with the work itself so critical? Well, consider that a typical workweek contains around 2,400 minutes. How much of that time is spent thinking about how much money you make? 10 minutes? Maybe 20? The same is true for promotions—we may want them, but we don't necessarily spend hours a day thinking about them. We do spend a significant chunk of that time with other people though. Between lunches, meetings, hallway chats, and other conversations, we might easily spend 600 minutes a week with supervisors and co-workers. That leaves almost 1,800 minutes for just us and our work. As a result, it is difficult to be satisfied with your job if you don't like what you actually do. Of course, those of you who are full-time students might wonder what satisfaction means to you. See our **OB for Students** feature for some facets of student satisfaction.

OB FOR STUDENTS

What does satisfaction mean for you as a student? After all, pay, promotions, and supervision are less relevant for full-time students than for full-time employees. One recent study examined the facets of satisfaction for students,[29] including:

- *University satisfaction.* Do students feel good about their university choice and experience, and would they recommend their university to others?
- *Housing satisfaction.* Do students feel good about where they live and the surrounding neighbourhood?
- *Leisure satisfaction.* Do students feel good about their social life, their leisure activities, and their friendships?

The results of the study showed that all three facets had moderately strong positive correlations with an index of overall student satisfaction. So students were more satisfied when they liked the university, liked where they lived, and felt that they were having a good time. In addition, the more satisfied the students were, the better they performed in terms of their grade point average (GPA). In other words, happy students tended to be better students.

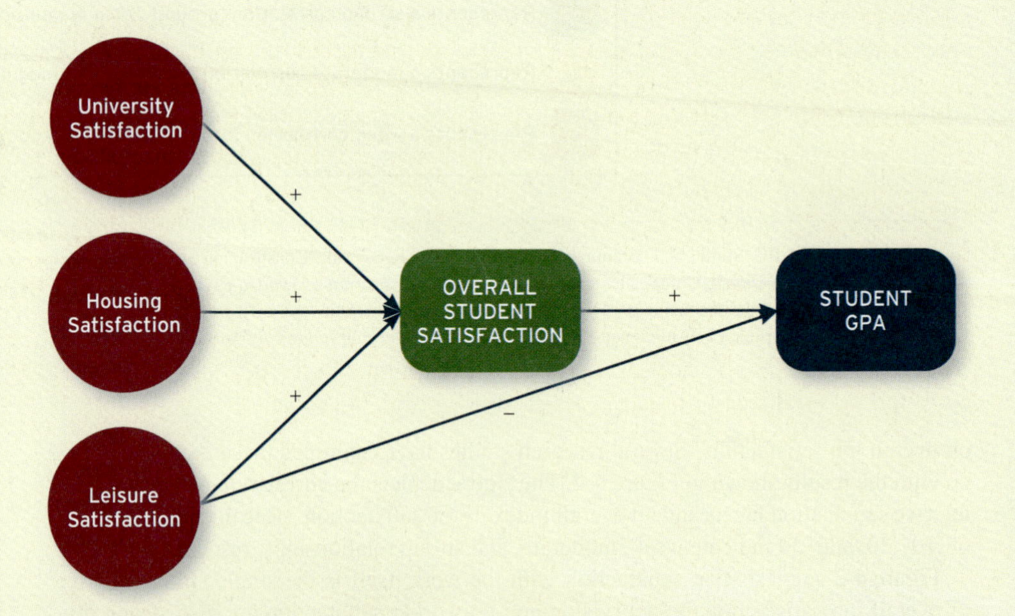

One word of caution, however. Notice the negative path from leisure satisfaction to student GPA. That path indicates that those two variables actually correlate negatively. In other words, having a lot of fun made students more satisfied, but it also made them perform less well in their classes. Moral of the story: You *can* have too much of a good thing!

SATISFACTION WITH THE WORK ITSELF: THE JOB CHARACTERISTICS MODEL

Given how important enjoyable work tasks are to overall job satisfaction, it is worth spending more time describing the kinds of tasks that most people find enjoyable. Researchers began focusing on this question in the 1950s and 1960s, partly in reaction to practices based in the "scientific management" perspective. Scientific management focuses on increasing the efficiency of job tasks by making them more simplified and specialized and using time and motion studies to plan task movements and sequences carefully.[30] The hope was that such steps would increase worker productivity and reduce the breadth of skills required to complete a job, ultimately improving organizational profitability. Instead, the simplified and routine jobs tended to lower job satisfaction while increasing absenteeism and turnover.[31] Put simply: Boring jobs may be easier, but they're not necessarily better.

So what kinds of work tasks are especially satisfying? Research suggests that three "critical psychological states" make work satisfying. The first psychological state is believing in the **meaningfulness of work**, which reflects the degree to which work tasks are viewed as something that "counts" in the employee's system of philosophies and beliefs.[32] Trivial tasks tend to be less satisfying than tasks that make employees feel like they're aiding the organization or society in some meaningful way. The second psychological state is perceiving **responsibility for outcomes**, which captures the degree to which employees feel that they are key drivers of the quality of the unit's work.[33] Sometimes employees feel like their efforts don't really matter, because work outcomes are dictated by effective procedures, efficient technologies, or more influential colleagues. Finally, the third psychological state is **knowledge of results**, which reflects the extent to which employees know how well (or how poorly) they are doing.[34] Many employees work in jobs in which they never find out about their mistakes or have notice of times when they did particularly well.

meaningfulness of work A psychological state indicating the degree to which work tasks are viewed as something that counts in the employee's system of philosophies and beliefs

responsibility for outcomes A psychological state indicating the degree to which employees feel they are key drivers of the quality of work output

knowledge of results A psychological state indicating the extent to which employees are aware of how well or how poorly they are doing

Think about times when you felt especially proud of a job well done. At that moment, you were probably experiencing all three psychological states. You were aware of the result (after all, some job had been done well). You felt you were somehow responsible for that result (otherwise, why would you feel proud?). Finally, you felt that the result of the work was somehow meaningful (otherwise, why would you have remembered it just now?). The next obvious question then becomes, "What kinds of tasks create these psychological states?" **Job characteristics theory**, which describes the central characteristics of intrinsically satisfying jobs, attempts to answer this question. As shown in Figure 4-3, job characteristics theory argues that five core job characteristics (variety, identity, significance, autonomy, and feedback, which you can remember with the acronym "VISAF") result in high levels of the three psychological states, making work tasks more satisfying.[35]

job characteristics theory A theory that argues that five core characteristics (variety, identity, significance, autonomy, and feedback) combine to result in high levels of satisfaction with the work itself

4.4 Which job characteristics can create a sense of satisfaction with the work itself?

The first core job characteristic in Figure 4-3, **variety**, is the degree to which the job requires a number of different activities that involve a number of different skills and talents.[36] When variety is high, almost every workday is different in some way, and job holders rarely feel a sense of monotony or repetition.[37] Of course, we could picture jobs that have a variety of boring tasks, such as screwing differently sized nuts onto differently coloured bolts, but such jobs do not involve a number of different skills and talents.[38] To provide some examples of low and high job variety, we offer excerpts from Studs Terkel's classic book *Working: People Talk About What They Do All Day and How They Feel About What They Do.*

variety The degree to which a job requires different activities and skills

FIGURE 4-3 Job Characteristics Theory

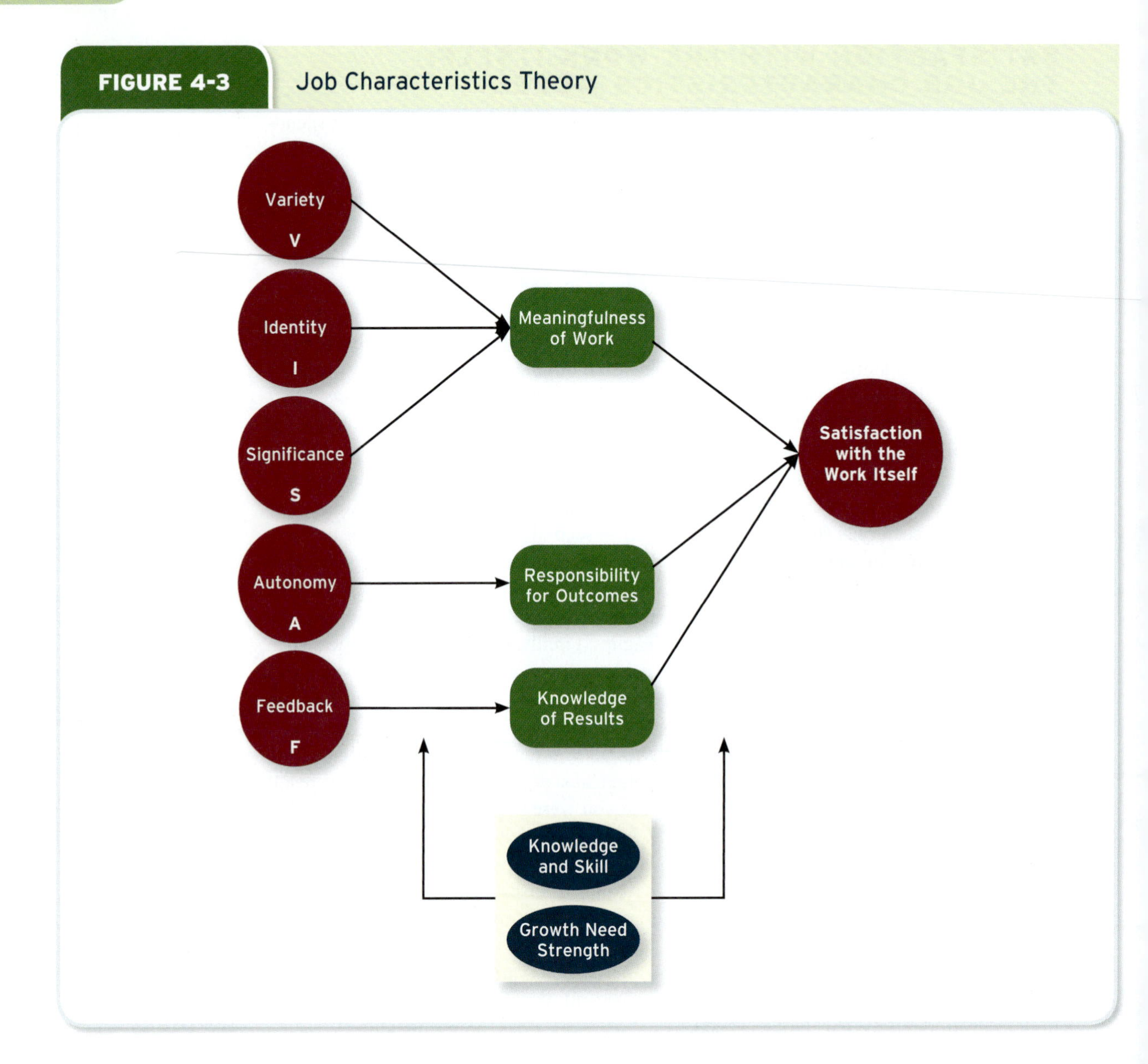

▼Low Variety: Phil Stallings, Spot-Welder

I stand in one spot, about two- or three-feet area, all night. The only time a person stops is when the line stops. We do about thirty-two jobs per car, per unit. Forty-eight units an hour, eight hours a day. Thirty-two times forty-eight times eight. Figure it out. That's how many times I push that button . . . . It don't stop. It just goes and goes and goes. I bet there's men who have lived and died out there, never seen the end of that line. And they never will—because it's endless. It's like the serpent. It's just all body, no tail. It can do things to you . . . (Laughs).[39]

▲High Variety: Eugene Russell, Piano Tuner

Every day is different. I work Saturdays and Sundays sometimes. Monday I'm tuning a piano for a record company that had to be done before nine o'clock. When I finish that, I go to another company and do at least four pianos. During that day there's a couple of harpsichords mixed in . . . . I get a big kick out of it, because there are so many facets. Other people go through a routine. At a certain time they punch a clock . . . . Then they're through with it and then their life begins. With us the piano business is an integral part of our life. I had a discussion with another tuner, who is a great guitar man. He said "Why are we tuners?" I said, "Because we want to hear good sounds."[40]

Evidence indicates that our preference for variety is hard-wired into our brains. Research in psychiatry and neuroscience shows that the brain releases a chemical called dopamine whenever a novel stimulus (a new painting, a new meal, a new work challenge) is experienced, and we tend to find this dopamine release quite pleasurable. Unfortunately, the amount of dopamine present in our brains declines over our life spans. One neuroscientist therefore suggests that the best way to protect our dopamine system is through novel, challenging experiences, writing, "The sense of satisfaction after you've successfully handled unexpected tasks or sought out unfamiliar, physically and emotionally demanding activities is your brain's signal that you're doing what nature designed you to do."[41] Something to think about next time you plan to order the same old thing at your favourite restaurant!

The second core job characteristic in Figure 4-3, **identity**, is the degree to which the job requires completing a whole, identifiable, piece of work from beginning to end with a visible outcome.[42] When a job has high identity, employees can point to something and say, "There, I did that." The transformation from inputs to finished product is very visible, and the employee feels a distinct sense of beginning and closure.[43] Think about how you feel when you work for a while on some project but don't quite get it finished—does that lack of closure bug you? If so, identity is an important concern for you. Consider these excerpts from *Working:*

identity The degree to which a job offers completion of a whole, identifiable piece of work

▼Low Identity: Mike Lefevre, Steelworker

It's not just the work. Somebody built the pyramids. Somebody's going to build something. Pyramids, Empire State Building—these things don't just happen. There's hard work behind it. I would like to see a building, say the Empire State, I would like to see on one side of it a foot-wide strip from top to bottom with the name of every bricklayer, the name of every electrician, with all the names. So when a guy walked by, he could take his son and say, "See, that's me over there on the forty-fifth floor. I put the steel beam in." Picasso can point to a painting. What can I point to? A writer can point to a book. Everybody should have something to point to.[44]

▲High Identity: Frank Decker, Interstate Truckdriver

Every load is a challenge and when you finally off-load it, you have a feeling of having completed a job—which I don't think you get in a production line. I pick up a load at the mill, going to Hotpoint in Milwaukee. I take a job and I go through all the process . . . . You feel like your day's work is well done when you're coming back. I used to have problems in the morning, a lot of heartburn, I couldn't eat. But once I off-loaded, the pressure was off. Then I could eat anything.[45]

significance The degree to which a job really matters and impacts society as a whole

Significance is the degree to which the job has a substantial impact on the lives of other people, particularly people in the world at large.[46] Virtually any job can be important if it helps put food on the table for a family, helps send kids to university, or makes employees feel like they're doing their part for the working world. That said, significance as a core job characteristic captures something beyond that—the belief that this job *really matters*. If the job was taken away, society would be the worse for it. Consider these excerpts from *Working:*

▼Low Significance: Louis Hayward, Washroom Attendant

They come in. They wash their hands after using the service—you hope. (A soft chuckle.) I go through the old brush routine, stand back, expecting a tip. A quarter is what you expect when you hand the guy a towel and a couple of licks of the broom. . . . I'm not particularly proud of what I'm doing. The shine man and I discuss it quite freely. In my own habitat I don't go around saying I'm a washroom attendant at the Palmer House. Outside of my immediate family, very few people know what I do. They do know I work at the Palmer House and let that suffice. You say Palmer House, they automatically assume you're a waiter. . . . The whole thing is obsolete. It's on its way out. This work isn't necessary in the first place. It's so superfluous. It was *never* necessary. (Laughs.)[47]

▲High Significance: Tom Patrick, Fireman

Last month there was a second alarm. I was off duty. I ran over there. I'm a bystander. I see these firemen on the roof, with the smoke pouring out around them, and the flames, and they go in . . . . You could see the pride that they were seein'. The f***** world's so f**** up, the country's f**** up. But the firemen, you actually see them produce. You see them put out a fire. You see them come out with babies in their hands. You see them give mouth-to-mouth when a guy's dying. You can't get around that s***. That's real. To me, that's what I want to be.[48]

autonomy The degree to which a job allows individual freedom and discretion regarding how the work is to be done

Autonomy is the degree to which the job provides freedom, independence, and discretion to the individual performing the work.[49] When your job provides autonomy, you view the outcomes of it as the product of your efforts rather than the result of careful instructions from your boss or a well-written manual of procedures.[50] Autonomy comes in multiple forms, including the freedom to control the timing, scheduling, and sequencing of work activities, as well as the procedures and methods used to complete work tasks.[51] To many of us, high levels of autonomy are the difference between "having a long leash" and being "micromanaged." Consider these excerpts from *Working:*

▼Low Autonomy: Beryl Simpson, Airline Reservationist

They brought in a computer called Sabre . . . . It has a memory drum and you can retrieve that information forever . . . . With Sabre being so valuable, you were allowed no more than three minutes on the telephone. You had twenty seconds, busy-out time it was called, to put the information into Sabre. Then you had to be available for another phone call. It was almost like a production line. We adjusted to the machine. The casualness, the informality that had been there previously was no longer there . . . . You took thirty minutes for lunch, not thirty-one. If you got a break, you took ten minutes, not eleven . . . . With the airline I had no free will. I was just part of that stupid computer.[52]

▲High Autonomy: Bud Freeman, Jazz Musician

I live in absolute freedom. I do what I do because I want to do it. What's wrong with making a living doing something interesting . . . ? The jazz man is expressing freedom in every note he plays. We can only please the audience doing what *we* do. We have to please ourselves first. I want to play for the rest of my life. I don't see any sense in stopping. Were I to live another thirty years—that would make me ninety-five—why not try to play? I can just hear the critics: "Did you hear that wonderful note old man Freeman played last night?" (Laughs.) As Ben Webster says, "I'm going to play this g****** saxophone until they put it on top of me."[53]

The last core job characteristic in Figure 4-3, **feedback**, is the degree to which carrying out the activities required by the job provides the worker with clear information about how well he or she is performing.[54] A critical distinction must be noted: This core characteristic reflects feedback obtained *directly from the job* as opposed to feedback from co-workers or supervisors. Most employees receive formal performance appraisals from their bosses, but that feedback occurs once or maybe twice a year. When the job provides its own feedback, that feedback can be experienced almost every day. Consider these excerpts from *Working:*

feedback In job characteristics theory, it refers to the degree to which the job itself provides information about how well the job holder is doing

Despite the need for discipline and practice, the job of a musician is one with a high degree of autonomy.

▼Low Feedback: Lilith Reynolds, Government Project Coordinator

I'm very discouraged about my job right now. . . . I'm to come up with some kind of paper on economic development. It won't be very hard because there's little that can be done. At the end of sixty days I'll present the paper. But because of the reorganization that's come up I'll probably never be asked about the paper.[55]

▲High Feedback: Dolores Dante, Waitress

When somebody says to me, "You're great, how come you're *just* a waitress?" *Just* a waitress. I'd say, "Why, don't you think you deserve to be served by me?" . . . Tips? I feel like Carmen. It's like a gypsy holding out a tambourine and they throw the coin. (Laughs.) . . . People would ask for me. . . . I would like to say to the customer, "Go to so-and-so." But you can't do that, because you feel a sense of loyalty. So you would rush, get to your customers quickly. Some don't care to drink and still they wait for you. That's a compliment.[56]

The passages in this section illustrate the potential importance of each of the five core characteristics. But how important are the core characteristics to satisfaction with the work itself? A meta-analysis of 75 different research studies showed that the five core job characteristics are moderately to strongly related to work satisfaction.[57] However, those results don't mean that *every* employee wants more variety, more autonomy, and so forth. The bottom of Figure 4-3 includes two other variables: **knowledge and skill** and **growth need strength** (which captures whether employees have strong needs for personal accomplishment or developing themselves beyond where they currently are).[58] In the jargon of theory diagrams, these variables are called "moderators." Rather than directly affecting other variables in the diagram, moderators influence the strength of the relationships between variables. If employees lack the required knowledge and skill or lack a desire for growth and development, more variety and autonomy should *not* increase their satisfaction very much.[59] However, when employees are very talented and feel a strong need for growth, the core job characteristics become even more powerful. A graphical depiction of this moderator effect appears in Figure 4-4, where you can see that the relationship between the core job characteristics and satisfaction becomes stronger when growth need strength increases.

knowledge and skill The degree to which employees have the aptitude and competence needed to succeed on their job

growth need strength The degree to which employees desire to develop themselves further

Given how critical the five core job characteristics are to job satisfaction, many organizations have employed job characteristics theory to help improve satisfaction among their employees. The first step in this process is assessing the current level of the characteristics to arrive at a "satisfaction potential score." See our **OB Assessments** feature at the end of this chapter for more about that step. The organization, together with job design consultants, then attempts to redesign aspects of the job to increase the core job characteristic levels. Often this step results in **job enrichment**, such that the duties and responsibilities associated with a job are expanded to provide more variety, identity, autonomy, and so forth. Research suggests that such enrichment efforts can indeed boost job satisfaction levels.[60] Moreover, enrichment efforts can heighten work accuracy and customer satisfaction, though training and labour costs tend to rise as a result of such changes.[61]

job enrichment When job duties and responsibilities are expanded to provide increased levels of core job characteristics

FIGURE 4-4 Growth Need Strength as a Moderator of Job Characteristic Effects

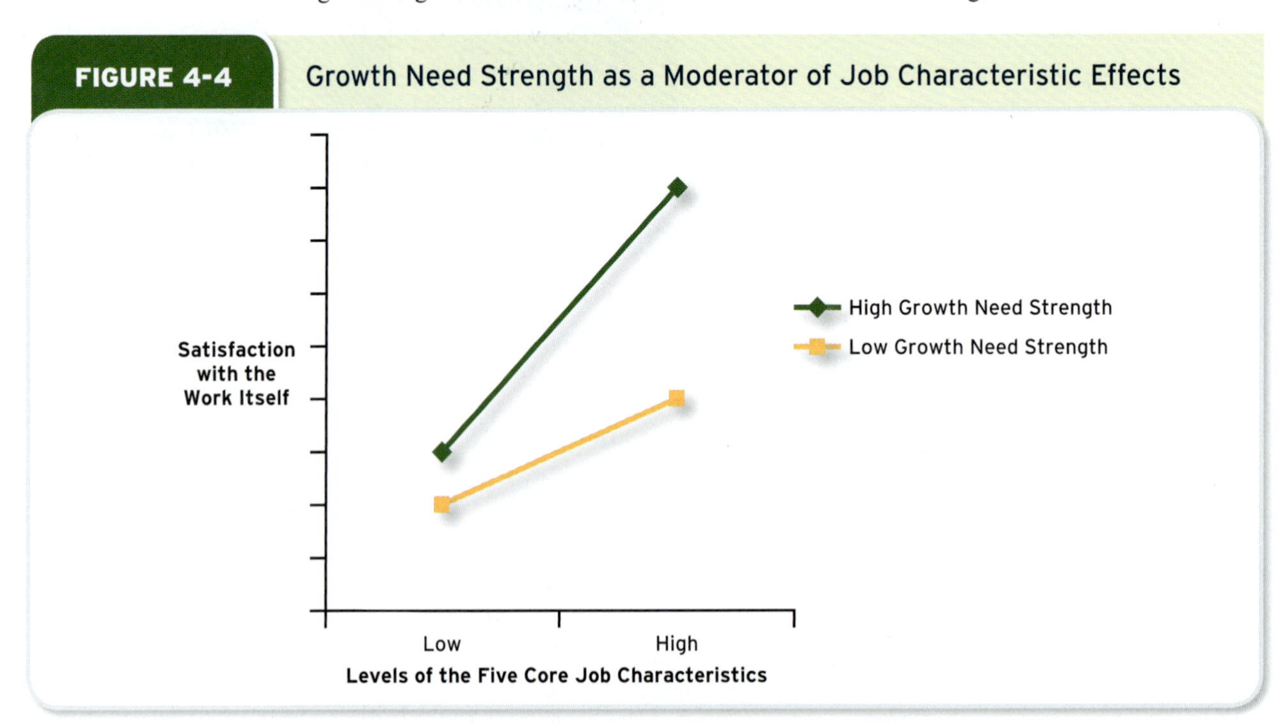

Source: Adapted from B.T. Loher, R.A. Noe, N.L. Moeller, and M.P. Fitzgerald, "A Meta-Analysis of the Relation of Job Characteristics to Job Satisfaction," *Journal of Applied Psychology* 70 (1985), pp. 280–89.

MOOD AND EMOTIONS

Let's say you're a satisfied employee, maybe because you get paid well and work for a good boss or because your work tasks provide you with variety and autonomy. Does this mean you'll definitely be satisfied at 11:00 a.m. next Tuesday? Or 2:30 p.m. the following Thursday? Obviously it doesn't. Each employee's satisfaction levels fluctuate over time, rising and falling like some sort of emotional stock market. This fluctuation might seem strange, given that people's pay, supervisors, co-workers, and work tasks don't change from one hour to the next. The key lies in remembering that job satisfaction reflects what you think and feel about your job. So part of it is rational, based on a careful appraisal of the job and the things it supplies. But another part of it is emotional, based on what you feel "in your gut" while you're at work or thinking about work. So a satisfied employee feels good about his or her job *on average,* but things happen during the course of the day to make him or her feel better at some times (and worse at others).

Figure 4-5 illustrates the satisfaction levels for one employee during the course of a workday, from around 9:00 a.m. to 5:00 p.m. You can see that this employee did a number of different things during the day, from answering e-mails to eating lunch with friends to participating in a brainstorming meeting regarding a new project. You can also see that the employee came into the day feeling relatively satisfied, though satisfaction levels had several ebbs and flows during the next eight hours. What's responsible for those ebbs and flows in satisfaction levels? Two related concepts: mood and emotions.

moods States of feeling that are mild in intensity, last for an extended period of time, and are not directed at anything

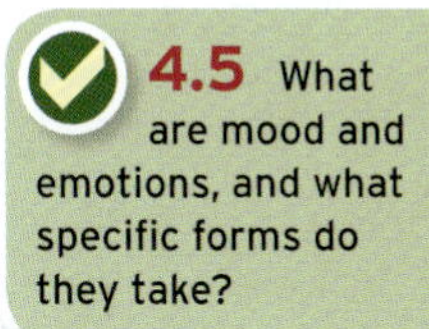

4.5 What are mood and emotions, and what specific forms do they take?

What kind of mood are you in right now? Good? Bad? Somewhere in between? Why are you in that kind of mood? Do you really even know? **Moods** are states of feeling that are often mild in intensity, last for an extended period of time, and are not explicitly directed at or caused by anything.[62] When people are in a good or bad mood, they don't always know who (or what) deserves the credit or blame; they just happen to be feeling that way for a stretch of their day. Of course, it would be oversimplifying things to call all moods either good or bad. Sometimes we're in a serene mood, and sometimes we're in an enthusiastic mood. Both are "good" but obviously feel quite different. Similarly, sometimes we're in a bored mood, and sometimes we're in a hostile mood. Both are "bad" but, again, feel quite different.

pleasantness The degree to which an employee is in a good versus bad mood

engagement How active or sluggish a mood is

It turns out that there are a number of different moods that we might experience during the workday. Figure 4-6 summarizes the different moods in which people sometimes find themselves. The figure illustrates that moods can be categorized in two ways: **pleasantness** and **engagement**. First, the horizontal axis of the figure reflects whether you feel pleasant (in a "good mood") or unpleasant (in a "bad mood").[63] The figure uses green colours to illustrate pleasant moods and red to illustrate unpleasant moods. Second, the vertical axis of the figure reflects whether you feel engaged, activated, and aroused or disengaged, deactivated, and unaroused.[64] The figure uses darker colours to convey higher levels of engagement and lighter colours to convey lower levels. Note that some moods are neither good nor bad. For example, being surprised or astonished (high engagement) and quiet or still (low engagement) are neither pleasant nor unpleasant. As a result, those latter moods are left colourless in Figure 4-6.

Figure 4-6 also illustrates that the most intense positive mood is characterized by feeling enthusiastic, excited, and elated. When employees feel this way, co-workers are likely to remark, "Wow, you're sure in a good mood!" In contrast, the most intense negative mood is characterized by feeling hostile, nervous, and annoyed. This kind of mood often triggers the question, "Wow, what's gotten you in such a bad mood?" If we return to our chart of hour-by-hour job satisfaction in Figure 4-5, what kind of mood do you think the employee was in while answering e-mails? Probably a happy, cheerful, and pleased mood. What kind of mood was the employee in during the informal meeting on the long-running project? Probably a grouchy, sad, and blue mood. Finally, what kind of mood do you think

FIGURE 4-5 Hour-by-Hour Fluctuations in Job Satisfaction during the Workday

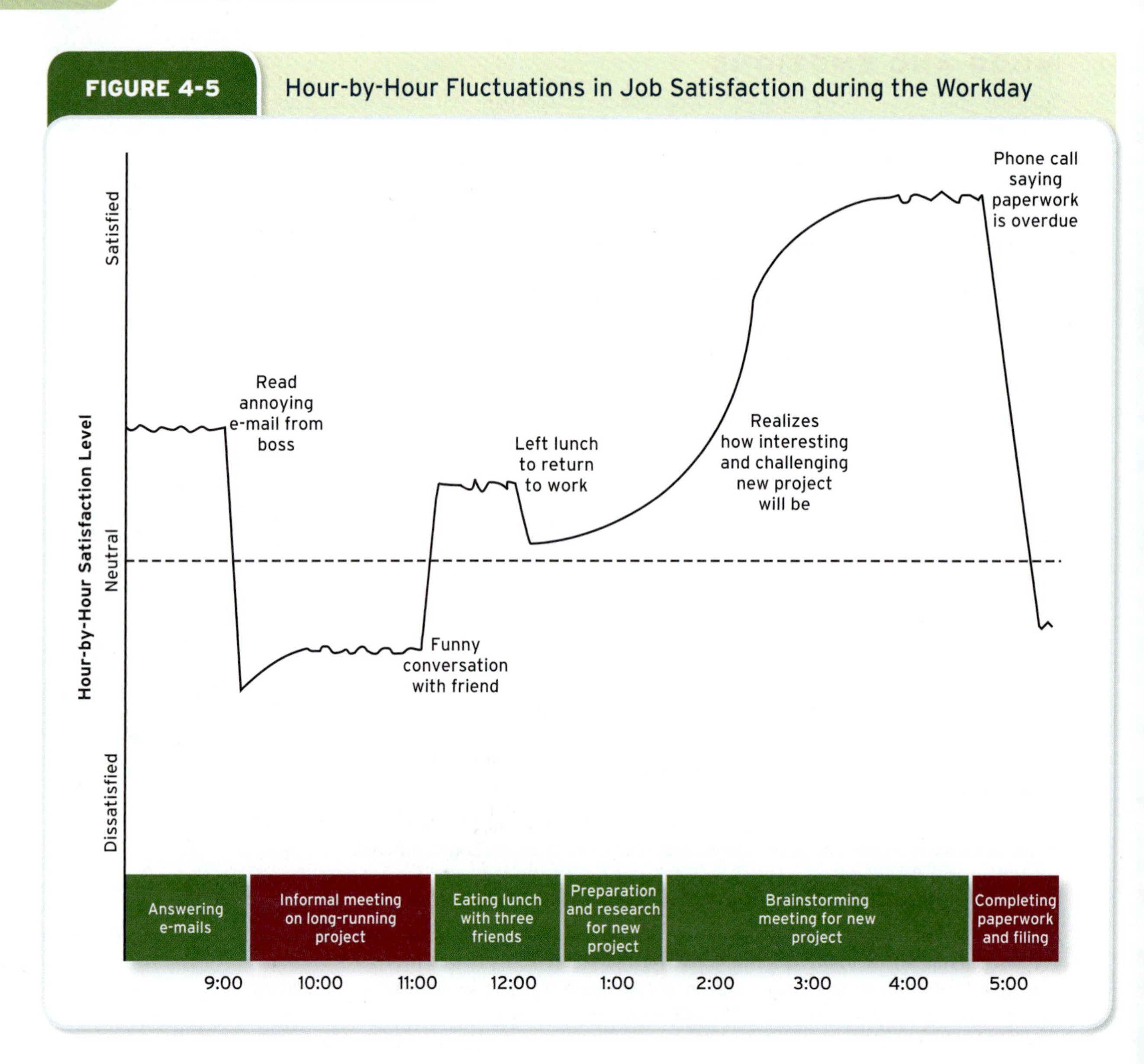

the employee was in during the brainstorming meeting for the new project? Clearly, an enthusiastic, excited, and elated mood; this employee would report especially high levels of job satisfaction at this time.

emotions Intense feelings, often lasting for a short duration, that are clearly directed at someone or some circumstance

Let's return to our chart of hour-by-hour job satisfaction in Figure 4-5. Although it's fairly easy to see the different moods that occur during the day, it also is obvious that there are events that trigger sudden changes in mood. Why does this occur? Because specific events at work cause positive and negative emotions. **Emotions** are states of feeling that are often intense, last for only a few minutes, and are clearly directed at (and caused by) someone or some circumstance. The difference between moods and emotions becomes clear in the way we describe them to others. We describe moods by saying, "I'm feeling grouchy," but we describe emotions by saying, "I'm feeling angry *at my boss*."[65] Emotions are always *about something*.

FIGURE 4-6 Different Kinds of Mood

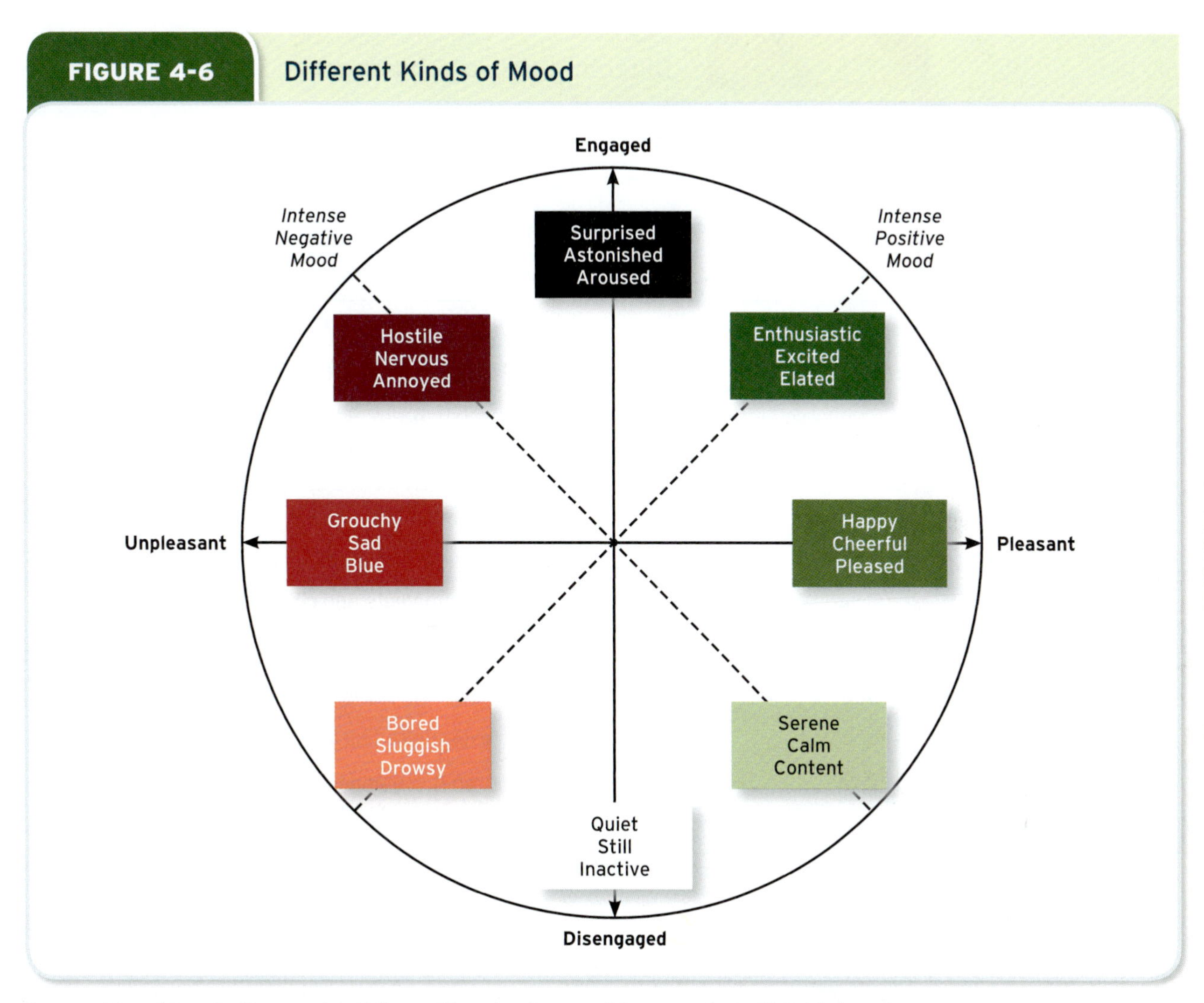

Sources: Adapted from D. Watson and A. Tellegen, "Toward a Consensual Structure of Mood," *Psychological Bulletin* 98 (1985), pp. 219–35; J.A. Russell, "A Circumplex Model of Affect," *Journal of Personality and Social Psychology* 39 (1980), pp. 1161–78; R.J. Larsen and E. Diener, "Promises and Problems with the Circumplex Model of Emotion," in *Review of Personality and Social Psychology: Emotion,* Vol. 13, ed. M.S. Clark (Newbury Park, CA: Sage, 1992), pp. 25–59.

People experience a variety of different emotions during their daily lives. Table 4-2 provides a summary of many of the most important.[66] **Positive emotions** include joy, pride, relief, hope, love, and compassion. **Negative emotions** include anger, anxiety, fear, guilt, shame, sadness, envy, and disgust. What emotion do you think the employee experienced in Figure 4-5 when reading a disrespectful e-mail from the boss? Probably anger. What emotion do you think that same employee enjoyed during a funny conversation with a friend? Possibly joy, or maybe relief that lunch had arrived and a somewhat bad day was halfway over. Leaving lunch to return to work might have triggered either anxiety (because the bad day might resume) or sadness (because the fun time with friends had ended). Luckily, the employee's sense of joy at taking on a new project that was interesting and challenging was right around the corner. The day did end on a down note, however, as the phone call signalling overdue paperwork was likely met with some mix of anger, fear, guilt, or even disgust (no one likes paperwork!).

positive emotions Employees' feelings of joy, pride, relief, hope, love and compassion

negative emotions Employees' feelings of fear, guilt, shame, sadness, envy, and disgust

TABLE 4-2 Different Kinds of Emotions

Positive Emotions	Description
Joy	A feeling of great pleasure
Pride	Enhancement of identity by taking credit for achievement
Relief	A distressing condition has changed for the better
Hope	Fearing the worst but wanting better
Love	Desiring or participating in affection
Compassion	Being moved by another's situation
Negative Emotions	
Anger	A demeaning offence against me and mine
Anxiety	Facing an uncertain or vague threat
Fear	Facing an immediate and concrete danger
Guilt	Having broken a moral code
Shame	Failing to live up to your ideal self
Sadness	Having experienced an irreversible loss
Envy	Wanting what someone else has
Disgust	Revulsion aroused by something offensive

Source: Adapted from R.S. Lazarus, *Emotion and Adaptation* (New York: Oxford University, 1991).

Of course, just because employees *feel* many of the emotions in Table 4-2 during the workday doesn't mean they're supposed to *show* those emotions. Some jobs demand that employees live up to the adage "never let 'em see you sweat." In particular, service jobs in which employees make direct contact with customers often require those employees to hide any anger, anxiety, sadness, or disgust that they may feel. Such jobs are high in what is called **emotional labour**, or the need to manage emotions to complete job duties successfully.[67] Flight attendants are trained to "put on a happy face" in front of passengers, retail salespeople are trained to suppress any annoyance with customers, and restaurant servers are trained to act like they're having fun on their job even when they're not.

emotional labour When employees manage their emotions to complete their job duties successfully

Is it a good idea to require emotional labour on the part of employees? Research on **emotional contagion** shows that one person can "catch" or "be infected by" the emotions of another person.[68] If a customer service representative is angry or sad, those negative emotions can be transferred to a customer (like a cold or disease). If that transfer occurs, it becomes less likely that customers view the experience favourably and spend more money, which potentially harms the bottom line. From this perspective, emotional labour seems like a vital part of good customer service. Unfortunately, other evidence suggests that emotional labour places great strain on employees and that their "bottled up" emotions may end up bubbling over, sometimes resulting in angry outbursts against customers or emotional exhaustion and burnout on the part of employees.[69] For more about managing emotions, see our **OB on Screen** feature.

emotional contagion The idea that emotions can be transferred from one person to another

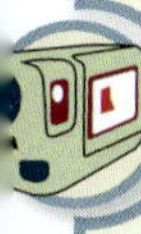

OB ON SCREEN

THE ISLAND

I wish that there was more . . . more than just waiting to go to the Island.

With those words, Lincoln Six Echo (Ewan McGregor) sums up his monotonous existence in *The Island* (Dir.: Michael Bay, DreamWorks, 2005). He gets up each morning, puts on his white jumpsuit, and goes through life within the boundaries of a sealed complex, designed to protect the survivors of "the contamination" from the pathogens that have destroyed the outside world. Life within the complex is dedicated to keeping its occupants alive and healthy over the long term, as the survivors slowly begin to repopulate the damaged planet.

Unfortunately for Lincoln, the complex seems dedicated to keeping its occupants in a relatively disengaged mood at all times: quiet, still, calm, and serene. Expressing annoyance at any little thing brings a visit from one of the security personnel. So does getting too cozy with any of the other occupants, as when Lincoln receives a "proximity warning" for touching the arm of Jordan Two Delta (Scarlett Johansson). The repeating message over the loudspeaker says it all: "Be polite, pleasant, and peaceful. A healthy person is a happy person."

Things aren't much better at Lincoln's job, where he monitors a set of thin tubes day in and day out, without even knowing where the tubes go or what's flowing through them. As he says to his friend, Jones Three Echo (Ethan Phillips), "Jones, do you ever get bored doing this . . . this boring job. . . . I mean, what are we doing here anyway?" His job is clearly low on every conceivable core job characteristic.

The only emotion that is encouraged in the complex is hope. Every day a lottery occurs in which one lucky soul wins a one-way ticket to "the island"—nature's last remaining pathogen-free zone. Each night, those who don't win the lottery are left to cling to this motto: "Your time will come." Unfortunately, things are not what they seem, and the island may not be the paradise it's made out to be. Suffice it to say that a trip to the island won't exactly result in feelings of serenity and contentment!

OB RESEARCH IN CANADA

Dr. Stéphane Côté, at the University of Toronto, is an expert on emotional intelligence and emotion regulation. Specifically, Dr. Côté's research looks at how emotional intelligence and emotion regulation impact on job stress, job performance, and leadership effectiveness. The concept of emotional intelligence refers to the ability of people to recognize and appraise emotional states in themselves and others, and to respond appropriately to these states (these ideas are developed further in Chapter 9). In addition to his work in the area of emotional intelligence, Dr. Côté's also investigates emotional contagion, a concept that was briefly reviewed in this chapter—the idea that one person can "catch" or be "infected by" the emotions of others. Selected aspects of these ideas were tested recently (see references below) where the emotional state (positive or negative mood) of a leader was found to affect the mood of group members, and the overall functioning of the team.

Presently, Dr. Côté is an associate professor of organizational behaviour and human resource management at the Joseph L. Rotman School of Management at the University of Toronto, where he teaches courses on organizational behaviour, research methods, and statistics. In 2008, Dr. Côté was a visiting scholar at the Institute for Personality and Social Research, and at the Haas School of Business, University of California, Berkeley. Dr. Stéphane Côté received his PhD and MA degrees in organizational psychology from the University of Michigan and his BSc degree in psychology from McGill University. His work has been published in leading journals in the field of organizational behaviour, such as the *Administrative Science Quarterly*, *Academy of Management Review*, *Journal of Applied Psychology*, and *Journal of Personality and Social Psychology*.

Some of Dr. Côté's recent publications include:

"Expressing Anger in Conflict: When It Helps and When It Hurts," by G.A. Van Kleef and S. Côté, published in *Journal of Applied Psychology* (2007, volume 92, pp. 1557–69).

"Emotional Intelligence, Cognitive Intelligence, and Job Performance," by S. Côté and C.T.H. Miners, published in *Administrative Science Quarterly* (2006, volumn 51, pp. 1–28).

"The Contagious Leader: Impact of the Leader's Mood on the Mood of Group Members, Group Affective Tone, and Group Processes," by T. Sy, S. Côté, and R. Saavedra, published in *Journal of Applied Psychology* (2005, volume 90, pp. 295–305).

"A Social Interaction Model of the Effects of Emotional Regulation on Work Strain," by S. Côté, published in *Academy of Management Review* (2005, volume 30, pp. 509–30).

SO WHY ARE SOME EMPLOYEES MORE SATISFIED THAN OTHERS?

As we show in Figure 4-7, answering that question requires paying attention to the more rational appraisals people make about their job and the things it supplies for them, such as pay, promotions, supervision, co-workers, and the work itself. Satisfaction with the work itself, in turn, is affected by the five core job characteristics: variety, identity, significance, autonomy, and feedback. However, answering this question also requires paying attention to daily fluctuations in how people feel, in terms of their positive and negative moods and positive and negative emotions. In this way, a generally satisfied employee may act unhappy at a given moment, just as a generally dissatisfied employee may act happy at a given moment. Understanding those sorts of fluctuations can help managers separate long-term problems (boring tasks, incompetent co-workers) from more short-lived issues (a bad meeting, an annoying interaction).

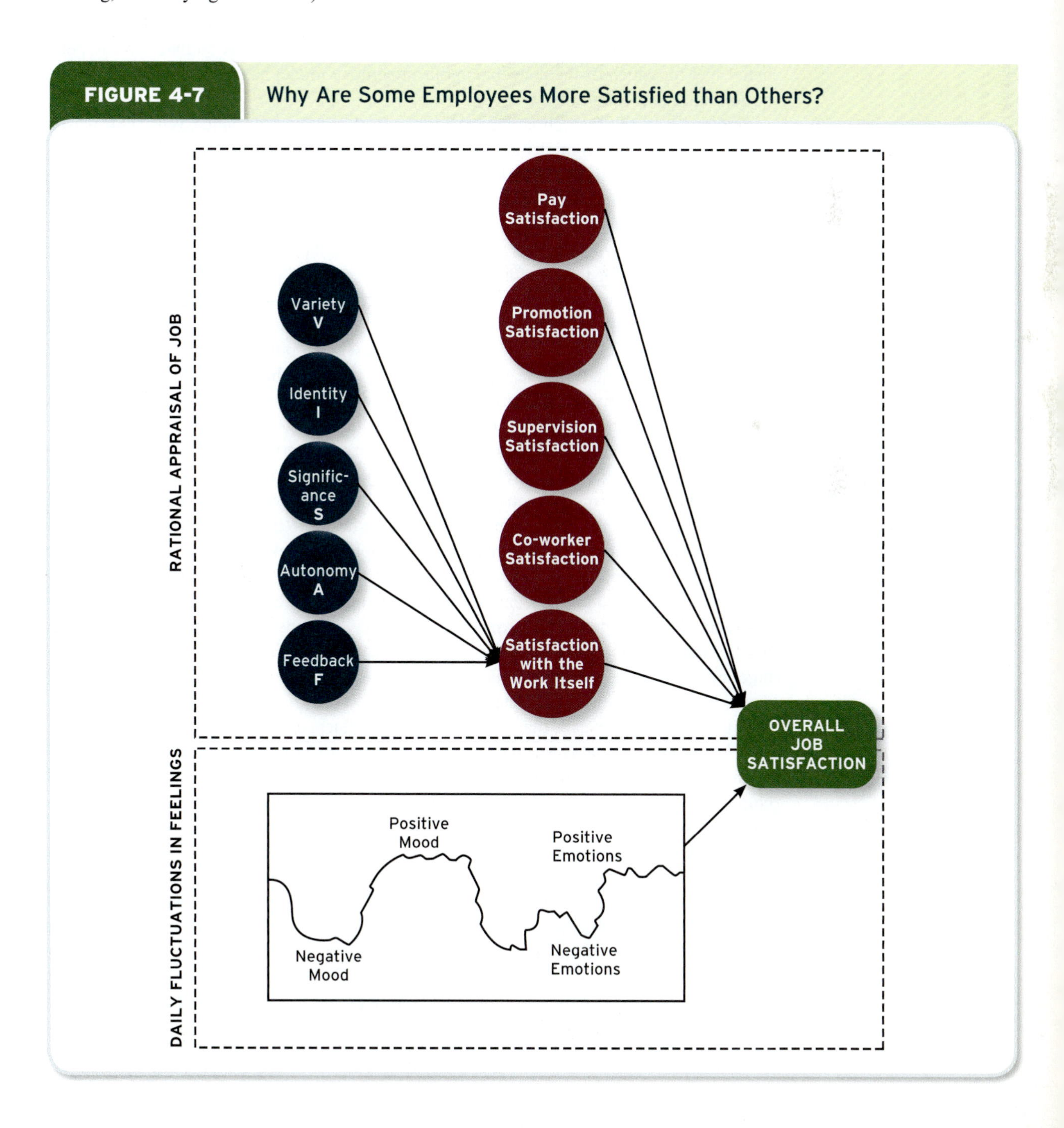

FIGURE 4-7 Why Are Some Employees More Satisfied than Others?

HOW IMPORTANT IS JOB SATISFACTION?

Several factors influence an employee's job satisfaction, from pay to co-workers to job tasks to day-to-day moods and emotions. Of course, the most obvious remaining question is, "Does job satisfaction really matter?" More precisely, does job satisfaction have a significant impact on job performance and organizational commitment—the two primary outcomes in our integrative model of OB? Figure 4-8 summarizes the research evidence linking job satisfaction to job performance and organizational commitment. This same sort of figure will appear in each of the remaining chapters of this book so that you can get a better feel for which of the concepts in our integrative model has the strongest impact on performance and commitment.

4.6 How does job satisfaction affect job performance and organizational commitment?

Figure 4-8 reveals that job satisfaction does influence job performance. Why? One reason is that job satisfaction is moderately correlated with task performance. Satisfied employees do a better job of fulfilling the duties described in their job descriptions,[70] and evidence suggests that positive feelings improve creativity, problem solving, and decision making[71] and enhance memory and recall of certain kinds of information.[72] Positive feelings also improve general activity and energy levels.[73] Apart from these sorts of findings, the benefits of job satisfaction for task performance might be explained on an hour-by-hour basis. At any given moment, employees wage a war between paying attention to a given work task and attending to "off-task" things, such as stray thoughts, distractions, interruptions, and so forth. Positive feelings when working on job tasks can pull attention away from those distractions and channel people's attention to task accomplishment.[74] When such concentration occurs, an employee is more focused on work at a given point in time. Of course, the relationship between satisfaction and task performance can work in reverse to some extent, such that people tend to enjoy jobs that they can perform more successfully.[75]

Job satisfaction also is correlated moderately with citizenship behaviour. Satisfied employees engage in more frequent "extra mile" behaviours to help their co-workers and their organization.[76] Positive feelings increase their desire to interact with others and often result in spontaneous acts of helping, because employees seek to behave in a manner that matches their current mood.[77] In addition, job satisfaction has a moderate negative correlation with counterproductive behaviour. Satisfied employees engage in fewer intentionally destructive actions that could harm their workplace.[78] Intense dissatisfaction is often the trigger that prompts an employee to "lash out" by engaging in rule breaking, theft, sabotage, or other retaliatory behaviours.[79] The more satisfied employees are, the less likely they will feel those sorts of temptations.

Figure 4-8 also reveals that job satisfaction influences organizational commitment. Why? Job satisfaction is strongly correlated with affective commitment, so satisfied employees are more likely to want to stay with the organization.[80] After all, why would employees want to leave a place where they're happy? Another reason is that job satisfaction is strongly correlated with normative commitment. Satisfied employees are more likely to feel an obligation to remain with their firm[81] and a need to "repay" the organization for whatever it is that makes them so satisfied, whether good pay, interesting job tasks, or effective supervision. However, job satisfaction is uncorrelated with continuance commitment, because satisfaction does not create a cost-based need to remain with the organization. Still, when taken together, these commitment effects become more apparent when you consider the kinds of employees who withdraw from the organization. In many cases, dissatisfied employees are those who sit daydreaming at their desks, come in late, are frequently absent, and eventually decide to quit their jobs.

FIGURE 4-8 Effects of Job Satisfaction on Performance and Commitment

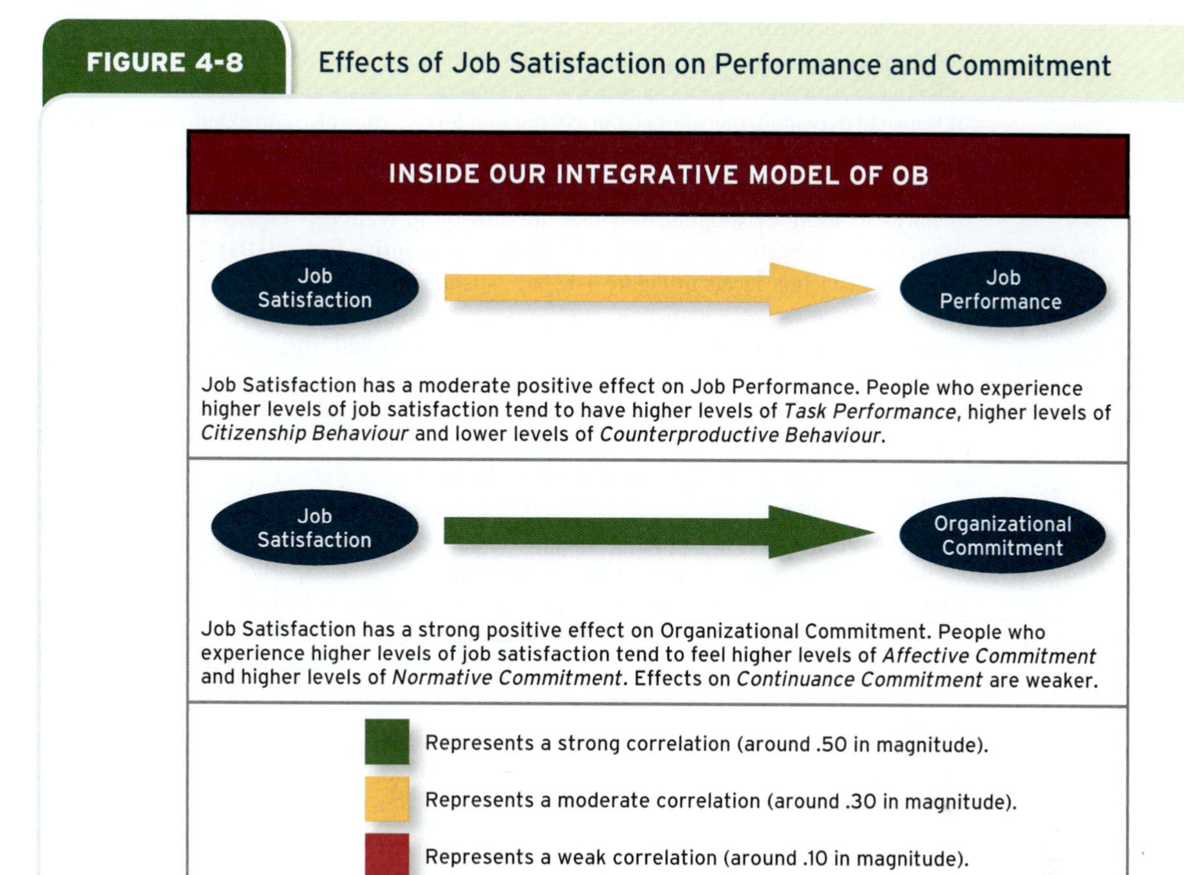

Sources: A. Cooper-Hakim and C. Viswesvaran, "The Construct of Work Commitment: Testing an Integrative Framework," *Psychological Bulletin* 131 (2005), pp. 241–59; R.S. Dalal, "A Meta-Analysis of the Relationship Between Organizational Citizenship Behaviour and Counterproductive Work Behaviour," *Journal of Applied Psychology* 90 (2005), pp. 1241–55; D.A. Harrison, D.A. Newman, and P.L. Roth, "How Important are Job Attitudes? Meta-Analytic Comparisons of Integrative Behavioural Outcomes and Time Sequences," *Academy of Management Journal* 49 (2006), pp. 305–25; T.A. Judge, C.J. Thoreson, J.E. Bono, and G.K. Patton, "The Job Satisfaction–Job Performance Relationship: A Qualitative and Quantitative Review," *Psychological Bulletin* 127 (2001), pp. 376–407; J.A. LePine, A. Erez, and D.E. Johnson, "The Nature and Dimensionality of Organizational Citizenship Behaviour: A Critical Review and Meta-Analysis," *Journal of Applied Psychology* 87 (2002), pp. 52–65; J.P. Meyer, D.J. Stanley, L. Herscovitch, and L. Topolnytsky, "Affective, Continuance, and Normative Commitment to the Organization: A Meta-Analysis of Antecedents, Correlates, and Consequences," *Journal of Vocational Behaviour* 61 (2002), pp. 20–52.

APPLICATION: TRACKING SATISFACTION

Because job satisfaction seems to be a key driver of job performance and organizational commitment, it's important for managers to understand just how satisfied their employees are. Gauging satisfaction is vital for organizations like Performance Plants, where the success of the company is directly linked to the creativity, expertise, and commitment of its employees, but it can be important in other organizations as well. Several methods assess the job satisfaction of rank-and-file employees, including focus groups, interviews, and attitude surveys. Of those three choices, attitude surveys are often the most accurate and most effective.[82] Attitude surveys can provide a "snapshot" of how satisfied the workforce is and, if repeated over time, reveal trends in satisfaction levels. They also can explore the effectiveness of major job changes by comparing attitude survey results before and after a change.

Although organizations are often tempted to design their own attitude surveys, there are benefits to using existing surveys that are already in wide use. One of the most widely administered job satisfaction surveys is the **Job Descriptive Index (JDI)**. The JDI assesses all five satisfaction facets in Figure 4-1: pay satisfaction, promotion satisfaction, supervisor satisfaction, co-worker satisfaction, and satisfaction with the work itself. The JDI also has been subjected to a great deal of research attention that, by and large, supports its accuracy.[83] Furthermore, the JDI includes a companion survey—the Job in General (JIG) scale—that assesses overall job satisfaction.[84] Excerpts from the JDI and JIG appear in Table 4-3.[85] One strength of the JDI is that the questions are written in a very simple and straightforward fashion so that they can be easily understood by most employees.

Job Descriptive Index (JDI) A facet measure of job satisfaction that assesses an individual's satisfaction with pay, promotion opportunities, supervision, co-workers, and the work itself.

The developers of the JDI offer several suggestions regarding its administration.[86] For example, they recommend surveying as much of the company as possible because any unsurveyed employees might feel that their feelings are less important. They also recommend that surveys be anonymous so that employees can be as honest as possible without worrying about being punished for any critical comments about the organization. Therefore, companies must be careful in collecting demographic information on the surveys.

TABLE 4-3 Excerpts from the Job Descriptive Index and the Job in General Scale

Think of the work you do at present. How well does each of the following words or phrases describe your work? In the blank beside each word or phrase below, write
_Y_ for "Yes" if it describes your work
_N_ for "No" if it does NOT describe it
_?_ for "?" if you cannot decide

Pay Satisfaction[a]	Co-worker Satisfaction[a]
___ Well paid	___ Stimulating
___ Bad	___ Smart
___ Barely live on income	___ Unpleasant
Promotion Satisfaction[a]	**Satisfaction with Work Itself[a]**
___ Regular promotions	___ Fascinating
___ Promotion on ability	___ Pleasant
___ Opportunities somewhat limited	___ Can see my results
Supervision Satisfaction[a]	**Overall Job Satisfaction[b]**
___ Knows job well	___ Better than most
___ Around when needed	___ Worthwhile
___ Doesn't supervise enough	___ Worse than most

[a]The Job Descriptive Index, © Bowling Green State University (1975, 1985, 1997).
[b]The Job in General Scale, © Bowling Green State University (1982, 1985).

Source: W.K. Balzer, J.A. Kihn, P.C. Smith, J.L. Irwin, P.D. Bachiochi, C. Robie, E.F. Sinar, and L.F. Parra, "Users' Manual for the Job Descriptive Index (JDI; 1997 version) and the Job in General Scales," in *Electronic Resources for the JDI and JIG,* eds. J.M. Stanton and C.D. Crossley (Bowling Green, OH: Bowling Green State University, 2000). Reprinted with permission.

Some demographic information is vital for comparing satisfaction levels across relevant groups, but too much information will make employees feel like they could be identified. Finally, the developers suggest that the survey should be administered by the firm's human resources group or an outside consulting agency. This structure will help employees feel that their anonymity is more protected.

Once JDI data have been collected, a number of interesting questions can be explored.[87] First, the data can indicate whether the organization is satisfied or dissatisfied by comparing average scores for each facet with the JDI's "neutral levels" for those facets (the "neutral levels" are available in the JDI manual). Second, it becomes possible to compare the organization's scores with national norms to provide some context for the firm's satisfaction levels. The JDI manual also provides national norms for all facets and breaks down those norms according to relevant demographic groups (e.g., managers vs. non-managers, new vs. senior employees, gender, education). Third, the JDI allows for within-organization comparisons to determine which departments have the highest satisfaction levels and which have the lowest.

The results of attitude survey efforts should then be fed back to employees so that they feel involved in the process. Of course, attitude surveys ideally should be a catalyst for some kind of improvement effort.[88] Surveys that never lead to any kind of on-the-job change eventually may be viewed as a waste of time. As a result, the organization should be prepared to react to the survey results with specific goals and action steps. For example, an organization with low pay satisfaction may react by conducting additional benchmarking to see whether compensation levels are trailing those of competitors. An organization with low promotion satisfaction might react by revising its system for assessing performance. Finally, an organization that struggles with satisfaction with the work itself could attempt to redesign key job tasks or, if that proves too costly, train supervisors in strategies for increasing the five core job characteristics on a more informal basis.

TAKEAWAYS

4.1 Job satisfaction is a pleasurable emotional state resulting from the appraisal of one's job or job experiences. It represents how you feel about your job and what you think about your job.

4.2 Values are things that people consciously or subconsciously want to seek or attain. According to value-percept theory, job satisfaction depends on whether you perceive that your job supplies those things that you value.

4.3 People often appraise their job satisfaction according to more specific facets of their job. These satisfaction facets include pay satisfaction, promotion satisfaction, supervision satisfaction, co-worker satisfaction, and satisfaction with the work itself.

4.4 Job characteristics theory suggests that five "core characteristics"—variety, identity, significance, autonomy, and feedback—combine to result in particularly high levels of satisfaction with the work itself.

4.5 Moods are states of feeling that are often mild in intensity, last for an extended period of time, and are not explicitly directed at anything. Intense positive moods include being enthusiastic, excited, and elated. Intense negative moods include being hostile, nervous, and annoyed. Emotions are states of feeling that are often intense, last only for a few minutes, and are clearly directed at someone or some circumstance.

Positive emotions include joy, pride, relief, hope, love, and compassion. Negative emotions include anger, anxiety, fear, guilt, shame, sadness, envy, and disgust.

4.6 Job satisfaction has a moderately positive relationship with job performance and a strong positive relationship with organizational commitment.

KEY TERMS

- autonomy *p. 84*
- co-worker satisfaction *p. 78*
- emotional contagion *p. 90*
- emotional labour *p. 90*
- emotions *p. 88*
- engagement *p. 87*
- feedback *p. 85*
- growth need strength *p. 86*
- identity *p. 83*
- job characteristics theory *p. 81*
- Job Descriptive Index (JDI) *p. 96*
- job enrichment *p. 86*
- job satisfaction *p. 73*
- knowledge and skill *p. 86*
- knowledge of results *p. 81*
- meaningfulness of work *p. 81*
- moods *p. 87*
- negative emotions *p. 89*
- pay satisfaction *p. 76*
- pleasantness *p. 87*
- positive emotions *p. 89*
- promotion satisfaction *p. 78*
- responsibility for outcomes *p. 81*
- satisfaction with the work itself *p. 78*
- significance *p. 84*
- supervision satisfaction *p. 78*
- value-percept theory *p. 74*
- values *p. 74*
- variety *p. 81*

DISCUSSION QUESTIONS

4.1 Which of the values in Table 4-1 on page 75 do you think are the most important to employees in general? Are there times when the values in the last three categories (altruism, status, and environment) become more important than the values in the first five categories (pay, promotions, supervision, co-workers, the work itself)?

4.2 What steps can organizations take to improve promotion satisfaction, supervision satisfaction, and co-worker satisfaction?

4.3 Consider the five core job characteristics (variety, identity, significance, autonomy, and feedback). Do you think that any one of those characteristics is more important than the other four? Is it possible to have too much of some job characteristics?

4.4 We sometimes describe colleagues or friends as "moody." What do you think it means to be "moody" from the perspective of Figure 4-6 on page 89?

4.5 Consider the list of positive and negative emotions in Table 4-2 on page 90. Which of these emotions are most frequently experienced at work? What causes them?

CASE • PERFORMANCE PLANTS

Performance Plants Inc. was founded in 1995 and is now Canada's largest agriculture biotechnology company. Working with a number of industrial partners, the company develops science-based technologies for the purpose of enhancing the production of food, feed, and bio-fuel crops. The nature of the work, and the technology used, is state of the art, with great potential to address some of the pressing problems facing the environment. With all this potential, a challenge for the company is holding on to its best and brightest. Why? People who have the talent and creativity needed to help the company realize its mission, unfortunately, are in short supply. Although Performance Plants has a core of dedicated employees across its three locations, the size of this organization pales in comparison to the big multinational corporations that can do, essentially, the same or similar work. With employees able to change jobs any time they want (i.e., suitable alternatives do exist), and, in many cases, do so without having to change their address or their morning commute, overall satisfaction and commitment play a critical role in decisions to stay or leave. At this time, satisfaction is high and turnover has been, historically, low. But it is a very fragile situation. The majority of employees who work at the Saskatoon facility are females in their early to mid-30s. There is growing pressure to satisfy their need for career advancement and development.

4.1 Put yourself in the shoes of a typical scientist at the Saskatoon facility. What might you be thinking or feeling with respect to job satisfaction, and the consequences of these thoughts and feelings. Explain.

4.2 If you did decide to move, what job satisfaction issues might you have to deal with in a larger, multinational corporation?

EXERCISE • JOB SATISFACTION ACROSS JOBS

The purpose of this exercise is to examine satisfaction with the work itself across jobs. This exercise uses groups of six participants, so your instructor will either assign you to a group of six or ask you to create your own group of six. The exercise has the following steps:

1. Use the OB Assessment below to calculate the Satisfaction Potential Score (SPS) for the following four jobs:
   a. A lobster fisherman who runs his own boat with his son
   b. A stand-up comedian
   c. A computer programmer whose assignment is to replace "98" with "1998" in thousands of lines of computer code
   d. A leader of a political party in Canada
2. Which job has the highest SPS? Which core job characteristics best explain why some jobs have high scores and other jobs have low scores? Write down the scores for the four jobs in an Excel file on the classroom computer or on the chalkboard.
3. Class discussion (whether in groups or as a class) should centre on two questions. First, is the job that scored the highest really the one that would be the most enjoyable on a day-in, day-out basis? Second, does that mean it would be the job that you would pick if you could snap your fingers and magically attain one of the jobs on the list? Why or why not? What other job satisfaction theory is relevant to this issue?

OB ASSESSMENTS • CORE JOB CHARACTERISTICS

How satisfying are your work tasks? This assessment is designed to measure the five core job characteristics derived from job characteristics theory. Think of your current job or the last job that you held (even if it was a part-time or summer job). Answer each question using the response scale provided. Then subtract your answers to the bold-faced question from 8, with the difference being your new answer for that question. For example, if your original answer for Question 2 was "5," your new answer is "3" (8 – 5). Then use the formula to compute a satisfaction potential score (SPS).

1	2	3	4	5	6	7
VERY INACCURATE	MOSTLY INACCURATE	SLIGHTLY INACCURATE	UNCERTAIN	SLIGHTLY ACCURATE	MOSTLY ACCURATE	VERY ACCURATE

V1. The job requires me to use a number of complex or high-level skills. _______

V2. The job is quite simple and repetitive. _______

I1. The job is arranged so that I can do an entire piece of work from beginning to end. _______

I2. The job provides me the chance to completely finish the pieces of work I begin. _______

S1. This job is one where a lot of other people can be affected by how well the work gets done. _______

S2. The job itself is very significant and important in the broader scheme of things. _______

A1. The job gives me a chance to use my personal initiative and judgment in carrying out the work. _______

A2. The job gives me considerable opportunity for independence and freedom in how I do the work. _______

F1. Just doing the work required by the job provides many chances for me to figure out how well I am doing. _______

F2. After I finish a job, I know whether I performed well. _______

$$SPS = \left|\frac{V1+V2+I1+I2+S1+S2}{6}\right| \times \left|\frac{A1+A2}{2}\right| \times \left|\frac{F1+F2}{2}\right|$$

$$SPS = \left|\frac{\quad}{6}\right| \times \left|\frac{\quad}{2}\right| \times \left|\frac{\quad}{2}\right|$$

$$SPS = \boxed{\quad} \times \boxed{\quad} \times \boxed{\quad} = \boxed{\quad}$$

SCORING

If your score is 150 or above, your work tasks tend to be satisfying and enjoyable. Therefore, you probably view your work as meaningful and feel that you are responsible for (and knowledgeable about) your work outcomes. If your score is less than 150, your work tasks may not be so satisfying and enjoyable. You might benefit from trying to "enrich" your job by asking your supervisor for more challenging assignments.

Sources: J.R. Hackman and G.R. Oldham, *The Job Diagnostic Survey: An Instrument for the Diagnosis of Jobs and the Evaluation of Job Redesign Projects* (New Haven, CT: Yale University, 1974); J.R. Idaszak and F. Drasgow, "A Revision of the Job Diagnostic Survey: Elimination of a Measurement Artifact," *Journal of Applied Psychology* 72 (1987), pp. 69–74.

CONNECT——Available 24/7 with instant feedback so you can study when you want, how you want, and where you want. Take advantage of the Study Plan——an innovative tool that helps students customize their own learning experience. Students can diagnose their knowledge with pre- and post-tests, identify the areas where they need help, search contents of the entire learning package for content specific to the topic they're studying, and add these resources to their study plan. Visit **www.connectob.ca** to register——take practice quizzes, run interactive scenarios, and much more. Also visit the Student Online Learning Centre for additional study tools.

www.mcgrawhill.ca/olc/colquitt

CHAPTER

5 Stress

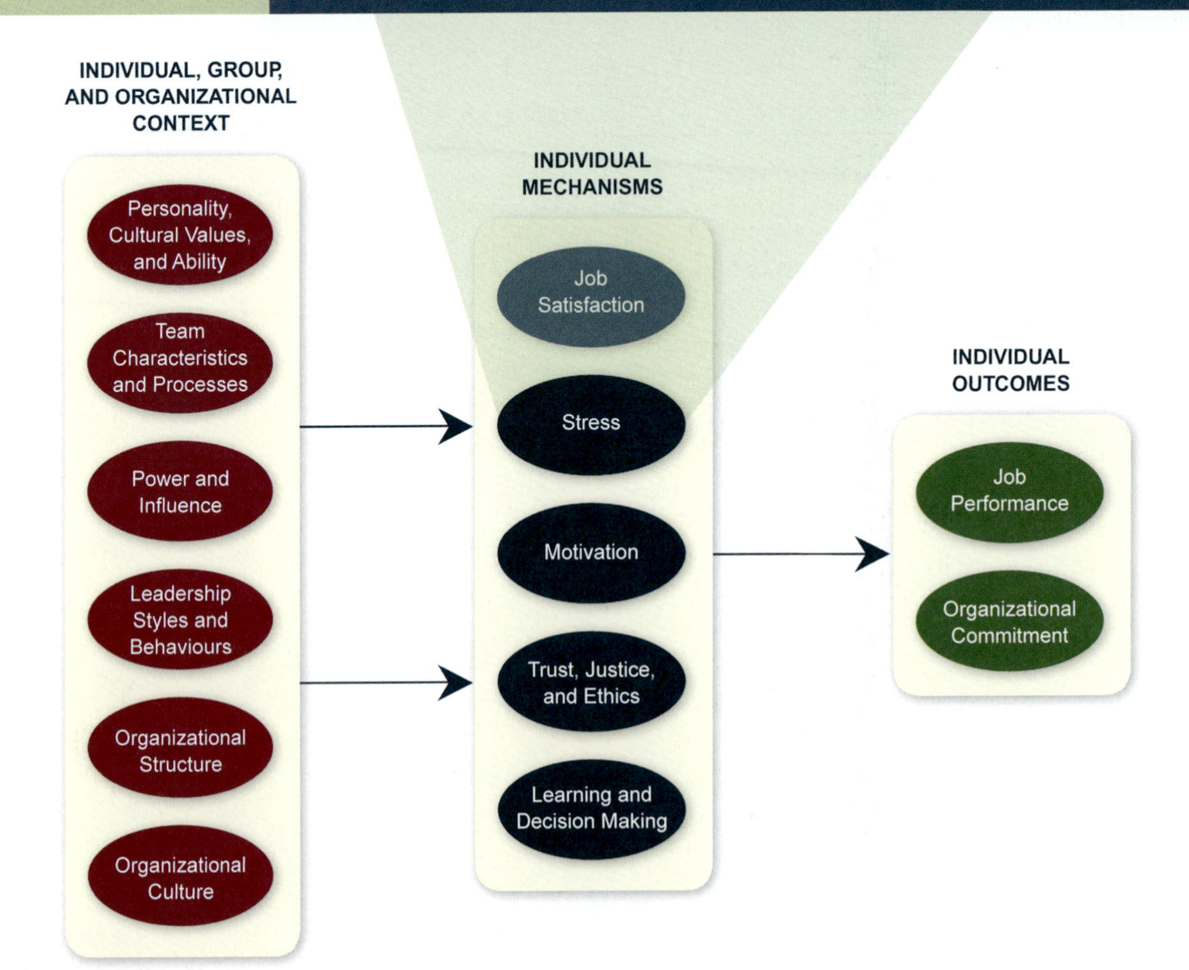

Learning Outcomes

After reading this chapter, you should be able to answer the following questions:

5.1 What is stress? What are stressors and strains? What role does appraisal play?

5.2 What are the four main types of work stressors?

5.3 How do individual employees cope with stress?

5.4 How do the Type A Behaviour Pattern and social support influence the stress process?

5.5 How does stress affect job performance and organizational commitment?

5.6 What steps can organizations take to manage employee stress?

CANADIAN IDOL

There are few experiences in this life more stressful than a job interview or audition. In fact, for many people, just the thought of being evaluated and compared to others makes us feel stressed out. Telltale signs of stress include a racing heartbeat, profuse perspiring, and feeling nauseous, which in turn, can cause us to freeze, panic, chatter aimlessly, or lose our train of thought—the very things that can undermine our chances of winning that job or opportunity. Most interviews are conducted in the privacy of a manager's office, or in front of several observers in a room. But what if that "interview" wasn't so private? What if your family and friends, and millions of strangers, could watch you perform—and then, had a say in how well you did? What if your "interview" was featured on a hit television show that was watched coast to coast?

Selection of the next *Canadian Idol* involves a very public and stressful high-stakes competition.[1] Performers sing a song of their choice, and have the opportunity to accompany themselves on guitars, pianos, and any other instrument they so choose. Auditions are open to all Canadians between the ages of 16 and 28. A four-member judging panel determines a "Top 200" from thousands of competitors who compete in regional auditions in 11 cities across Canada. This group is eventually whittled down to approximately 20 semi-finalists. Over the next three weeks, semi-finalists demonstrate their talent for a television audience, with viewers voting for their favourite candidate. Each week, candidates with the fewest votes are eliminated, leaving ten finalists at the end of the third week. The following weeks see the stakes increase dramatically as the top ten are narrowed to only two finalists, who are left to square off in the *Canadian Idol* grand finale. At stake for the winner is a guaranteed major recording contract with Sony BMG Music Canada—and instant stardom![2]

When *Canadian Idol* premiered in 2003, few would have predicted that it would become Canada's most-watched (English-language) Canadian series since the advent of electronic measurement—a record the series continues to hold. When Hamilton's Brian Melo was revealed as the 2007 *Canadian Idol* champion in the final minutes, a remarkable 2.75 million Canadians were watching.[3]

Talented performers audition in front of a large television audience to be the next *Canadian Idol.*

STRESS

Stress is an OB topic that is probably quite familiar to you. Even if you aren't planning to audition for *Canadian Idol,* consider how you feel toward the end of a semester when you have to cram for several final exams and finish a couple of term projects. At the same time, you might have also been looking for a job or planning a trip with friends or family. Although some people might be able to deal with all of these demands without becoming too frazzled, most people would say that this type of scenario causes them to feel stressed out. This stressed-out feeling might even be accompanied by headaches, stomach upsets, backaches, or sleeping difficulties. Although you might believe your stress will diminish once you graduate and settle down, high stress on the job is more prevalent than it has ever been before.[4] Statistics Canada estimates that a third of Canadian workers feel their jobs are "very stressful" or "extremely stressful."[5] Unfortunately, high stress is even more prevalent in the types of jobs that most of you are likely to have after you graduate. Table 5-1 provides a listing of where several jobs rank on the list of least to most stressful.

TABLE 5-1 Jobs Rated from Least Stressful (1) to Most Stressful (249)

LEAST STRESSFUL JOBS	STRESS LEVEL	MOST STRESSFUL JOBS	STRESS LEVEL
1. Musical instrument repairer	18.77	212. Registered nurse	62.14
2. Florist	18.80	220. Lawyer	64.33
4. Actuary	20.18	223. Newspaper reporter	65.26
6. Appliance repairer	21.12	226. Architect	66.92
8. Librarian	21.40	228. Lumberjack	67.60
10. File clerk	21.71	229. Fisherman	69.82
11. Piano tuner	22.29	230. Stockbroker	71.65
16. Vending machine repairer	23.47	233. Real estate agent	73.06
18. Barber	23.62	234. Advertising account exec	74.55
24. Mathematician	24.67	238. Public relations exec	78.52
29. Cashier	25.11	240. Air traffic controller	83.13
30. Dishwasher	25.32	241. Airline pilot	85.35
32. Pharmacist	25.87	243. Police officer	93.89
40. Biologist	26.94	244. Astronaut	99.34
44. Computer programmer	27.00	245. Surgeon	99.46
50. Astronomer	28.06	246. Taxi driver	100.49
56. Historian	28.41	248. Senior corporate exec	108.62
67. Bank teller	30.12	249. Firefighter	110.93

Source: Adapted from L. Krantz, *Jobs Rated Almanac,* 6th ed.(Fort Lee, NJ: Barricade Books, Inc., 2002)
The stress level score is calculated by summing points in 21 categories, including deadlines, competitiveness, environmental conditions, speed required, precision required, initiative required, physical demands, and hazards encountered.

Stress is defined as a psychological response to demands for which there is something at stake and coping with those demands taxes or exceeds a person's capacity or resources.[6] The particular demands that cause people to experience stress are called **stressors**. The negative consequences that occur when demands tax or exceed one's capacity or resources are called **strains**. Our definition of stress illustrates that it depends on both the nature of the demand and the person who confronts it. People differ in terms of how they evaluate stressors and the way they cope with them. As a result, they may experience different levels of stress even when confronted with the exact same situations.

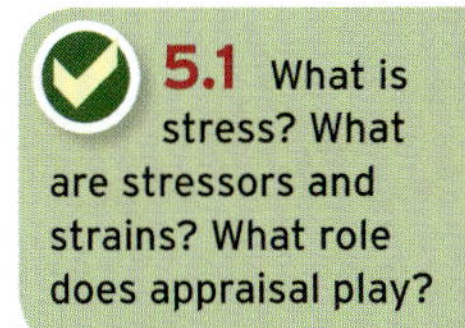

5.1 What is stress? What are stressors and strains? What role does appraisal play?

stress The psychological response to demands when there is something at stake for the individual, and where coping with these demands would tax or exceed the individual's capacity or resources

stressors Demands that cause the stress response

strains Negative consequences of the stress response

WHY ARE SOME EMPLOYEES MORE "STRESSED" THAN OTHERS?

To fully understand what it means to feel "stressed," it is necessary to describe, in more detail, how stressors are perceived and appraised. When people first encounter stressors, the process of **primary appraisal** is triggered.[7] As described in Figure 5-1, primary appraisal occurs as people evaluate the significance and the meaning of the stressors they are confronting. Here, people first consider whether a demand causes them to feel stressed, and if it does, they consider the implications of the stressor in terms of their personal goals and overall well-being.

primary appraisal Evaluation of whether a demand is stressful and, if it is, the implications of the stressor in terms of personal goals and well-being

As an example of a primary appraisal, consider the job of a cashier at a well-run convenience store. In this store, cashiers engage in routine sales transactions with customers. Customers walk in the store and select merchandise, and the cashier on duty rings up the sale and collects the money. Under normal day-to-day circumstances at this store, a well-trained cashier would not likely feel that these transactions are overly taxing or exceeding his or her capacity, so that cashier would not likely appraise these job demands as stressful. Job demands that tend not to be appraised as stressful are called **benign job demands**.

benign job demands Job demands that are not appraised as being stressful

FIGURE 5-1 Stressors and Their Appraisal

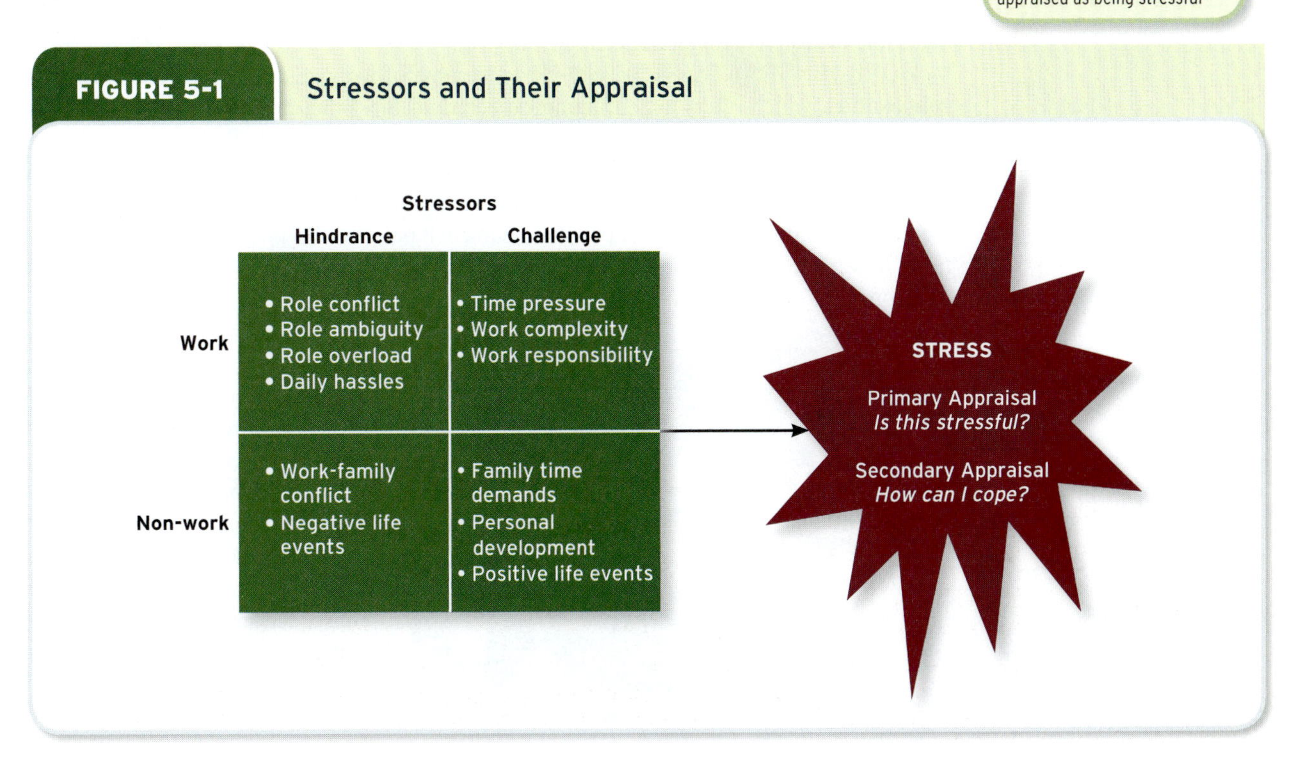

However, consider how convenience store cashiers would react in a different store in which the cash register and credit card machine break down often and without warning. The cashiers who work at this store would likely view their job as more stressful because they would have to diagnose and fix problems with equipment while dealing with customers who are growing more and more impatient. Furthermore, the cashiers in this store might appraise the stressful situation as one that unnecessarily prevents them from achieving their goal of being viewed as an effective employee in the eyes of the customers and the store manager.

Finally, consider a third convenience store in which the cashier's workload is higher due to additional responsibilities that include receiving merchandise from vendors, taking physical inventory, and training new employees. In this store, the cashiers may appraise their jobs as stressful because of the higher workload and need to balance different priorities. However, in contrast to the cashiers in the previous example, cashiers in this store might appraise these demands as providing an opportunity to learn and demonstrate the type of competence that often is rewarded with satisfying promotions and pay raises.

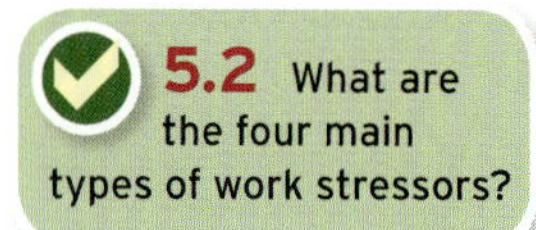

5.2 What are the four main types of work stressors?

TYPES OF STRESSORS

In the previous two examples, the cashiers were confronted with demands that a primary appraisal would label as "stressful." However, the specific demands in the two examples have an important difference. Dealing with equipment breakdowns or unhappy customers has little to no benefit to the employee in the long term. These kinds of stressors are called **hindrance stressors**—stressful demands that are perceived as hindering progress toward personal accomplishments or goal attainment.[8] Hindrance stressors tend to trigger negative emotions such as anger and anxiety. In contrast, managing additional responsibilities or higher workloads has a long-term benefit, in that it helps build the employee's skills. These kinds of stressors are called **challenge stressors**—stressful demands that are perceived as opportunities for learning, growth, and achievement. Although challenge stressors can be exhausting, they often trigger positive emotions such as pride and enthusiasm. Figure 5-1 lists a number of hindrance and challenge stressors, some of which are experienced at work and some of which are experienced outside work.[9]

hindrance stressors Stressors that tend to be appraised as thwarting progress toward growth and achievement

challenge stressors Stressors that tend to be appraised as opportunities for growth and achievement

WORK HINDRANCE STRESSORS

One type of work-related hindrance stressor is **role conflict**, which refers to conflicting expectations that other people may have of us. As an example of role conflict that occurs from incompatible demands within a single role that a person may hold, consider the job of a call centre operator. People holding these jobs are generally expected to contact as many people as possible over a given time period, which means spending as little time as possible with each person who is contacted. At the same time, however, call centre operators are also expected to be responsive to the questions and concerns raised by the people they contact. Because effectiveness in this aspect of the job may require a great deal of time, the call centre operator is put in a position in which he or she simply cannot meet both types of expectations.

role conflict When others have conflicting expectations of what an individual needs to do

Hindrance stressors like irritable customers trigger unhelpful emotions like anger and anxiety.

Role ambiguity refers to the lack of information regarding what needs to be done in a role, as well as unpredictability regarding the consequences of performance in that role.[10] Employees are sometimes asked to work on projects for which they are given very few

role ambiguity When an individual has a lack of direction and information about what needs to be done instructions or guidelines about how things are supposed to be done. In these cases, employees may not know how much money they can spend on the project, how long it's supposed to take, or what exactly the finished product is supposed to look like. Role ambiguity is often experienced among new employees who haven't been around long enough to receive instructions from supervisors or observe and model the role behaviours of more senior colleagues. Students sometimes experience role ambiguity when professors remain vague about particular course requirements or how grading is going to be performed. In such cases, the class becomes stressful because it's not quite clear what it takes to get a good grade.

Role overload occurs when the number of demanding roles a person holds is so high that the person simply cannot perform some or all of the roles very effectively. Role overload as a source of stress is becoming very prevalent for employees in many different industries. For example, the workload for executives and managers who work in investment banking, consulting, and law is so high that 80-hour workweeks are becoming the norm. Although this trend may not be surprising to some of you, people holding these jobs also indicate that they would not be able to complete most of the work that is required of them, even if they worked twice as many hours.[11] If employees actually put in enough time to meet those sorts of role demands, they might forget what life was like outside of their offices or cubicles! As our **OB Internationally** feature illustrates, there appears to be evidence that these hindrance stressors generalize across cultures.

role overload When an employee has too many demands to work effectively

OB INTERNATIONALLY

Although organizational researchers have studied job-related stress for many years, most of this work has been conducted in single countries—mainly in North America and the United Kingdom. An assumption is that work-related stressors, such as role ambiguity or role conflict, lead to feelings of stress. But is this true? Are the concepts that we have been discussing in this chapter portable to other countries and cultures? A recent study by Sharon Glazer and Terry Beehr, two respected stress researchers, was designed to address this basic question.[12] In short, the researchers wanted to know if national context matters when it comes to employees' perception of and reaction to work-related stressors.

Four countries were studied: the United States, the United Kingdom, Italy, and Hungary. Data were provided by 1,396 nurses in four hospitals in Budapest, Hungary; three hospitals each in London, England, and in northern Italy; and five hospitals in the area of Baltimore, Maryland, in the U.S. The choice to focus on health care providers, and nursing in particular, has particular relevance for Canada. Health care providers make up about 6 percent of the Canadian workforce, and nearly half (45 percent) of these workers report that most days on the job are "quite" or "extremely" stressful.[13] And of all the different professions considered to be health care providers, registered nurses have been found to be among the *most* stressed![14] Thus, it was very appropriate to focus on a profession like nursing, given the high potential for job stress.

The cross-cultural findings were quite interesting. Overall, the measures of role stressors (overload, conflict, and ambiguity) and job strain (job stress/anxiety) were in the low-to-moderate range, with nurses based in Hungary reporting the lowest scores when compared with nurses in the other three countries. Nurses based in the U.S. reported the highest level of job strain (confirming the Canadian data). Also, the patterns of correlations among the study variables were consistent across all four countries. So, do the same basic stress-related concepts exist in different countries? The answer to this question is "yes." Also, the patterns of correlations among the study variables were consistent across all four countries. So, do the same basic stress-related concepts exist in different countries? The answer to this question is "yes."[15]

daily hassles Minor day-to-day demands that interfere with work accomplishment

One final type of work-related hindrance stressor, **daily hassles**, reflects the relatively minor day-to-day demands that get in the way of accomplishing the things that we really want to accomplish. Examples of hassles include having to deal with unnecessary paperwork, office equipment malfunctions, conflict with abrasive co-workers, and useless communications. Although these examples of daily hassles may seem relatively minor, taken together, they can be extremely time consuming and stressful. Indeed, according to one survey, 40 percent of executives spend somewhere between a half day and a full day each week on communications that are not useful or necessary.[16]

time pressure The sense that the amount of time allotted to do a job is not quite enough

WORK CHALLENGE STRESSORS One type of work-related challenge stressor is **time pressure**—a strong sense that the amount of time you have to do a task is just not quite enough. Perhaps the best example of high time pressure is auditioning for *Canadian Idol.* After waiting in line for hours, along with hundreds of other *Idol* hopefuls, competitors are brought into the auditioning room in groups of five. After years of singing lessons and practice, and the chance for a major recording contract on the line, all of their hopes and dreams depend on how well each of them performs in the *next minute.*[17] Although most people appraise situations with high time pressure as rather stressful, they also tend to appraise these situations as more challenging than hindering. This is because time-pressure demands tend to be viewed as something to strive for given that success in meeting such demands can be satisfying. Even though the odds of being selected the next *Idol* are roughly 1 in 10,000 (i.e., the likelihood of being rejected is virtually 100 percent), each year people keep coming back to endure what must be a difficult, and often humiliating, process. Why? It is possible that contestants, rather than dwelling on the stressful nature of the auditioning process, see this event as a legitimate way to enter the music business that is harder and harder to penetrate.

work complexity The degree to which job requirements tax or just exceed employee capabilities

Work complexity refers to the degree to which the requirements of the work, in terms of knowledge, skills, and abilities, tax or exceed the capabilities of the person who is responsible for performing the work. As an example of work complexity, consider the nature of employee development practices that organizations use to train future executives and organizational leaders. In many cases, these practices involve giving people jobs that require skills and knowledge that the people do not yet possess. A successful marketing manager who is being groomed for an executive level position may, for example, be asked to manage a poorly performing production facility with poor labour relations in a country halfway around the world. Although these types of developmental experiences tend to be quite stressful, managers report that being stretched beyond their capacity is well worth the associated discomfort.[18]

work responsibility The number and importance of the obligations that an employee has to others

Work responsibility refers to the nature of the obligations that a person has to others. Generally speaking, the level of responsibility in a job is higher when the number, scope, and importance of the obligations in that job are higher. As an example, consider the difference in responsibility levels of a grocery store manager compared with a grocery store bagger. Although the bagger is obligated to perform an important task—efficiently placing items in bags so as not to damage the items—the store manager is obligated to ensure that the store is profitable, the customers are satisfied, and the employees are happy and safe. As with people's reactions to time pressure and work complexity, people tend to evaluate demands associated with high responsibility as both stressful and potentially positive. For an example of exceptionally high work responsibility, see our **OB on Screen** feature.

"Some of the poor wretches eventually become unable to leave the safety of their cubicles."

Source: © The New Yorker Collection 2000 Gahan Wilson from cartoonbank.com. All rights reserved.

OB ON SCREEN

PUSHING TIN

This job can be a little bit STRESS-ful!

With those words, the employees of New York's TRACON Center (Terminal Rader Approach Control) summarize what it means to be an air traffic controller in *Pushing Tin* (Dir. Mike Newell, 20th Century Fox, 1999). The TRACON employees guide 7,000 aircraft a day around the Kennedy, LaGuardia, and Newark airports, the nation's most congested airspace.

From the action depicted in the opening scenes in the movie, you should be able to appreciate that one of the most obvious stressors in the job of an air traffic controller is the high workload. Controllers sit in a darkened room trying to keep track of hundreds of blips and other pieces of information on their radar scopes, all while talking to the pilots of several aircraft. In the opening scene, for example, Nick Falzone (John Cusack) says something along the lines of, "Continental 981, 8 miles from the outer marker, turn left heading 080, maintain 2,000, until intercepting localizer, cleared ILS runway 4 right approach." Although you might be able to bark this command in less than 6 seconds, like Nick did in this scene, consider that air traffic controllers are typically responsible for directing several aircraft at the same time, each moving in different directions at speeds of up to 500 kilometres per hour.

A second key stressor for air traffic controllers is the responsibility they have for tens of thousands of lives every day. Although controller errors that result in midair collisions are extremely rare, the possibility weighs heavily on the minds of controllers, especially after they lose "the picture" (controller speak for the mental representation of an assigned airspace and all the aircraft within it) because of extreme workload, loss of concentration, or equipment malfunctions. As an example, a scene in the movie depicts the facility manager giving a tour to several elementary school children. He tells them, "Did you youngsters know that an air traffic controller is responsible for more lives in a single shift than a surgeon is in his entire life?" A young boy responds by saying, "It looks like a computer game"—to which the manager responds, "This is no game young man, I'll tell you that. If you make a mistake here, there's no reset button."

In fact, it is not unusual for air traffic controllers to experience emotional and physical strains because of the on-the-job stress they face. As one of the kids stated during the tour, "I hear that air traffic controllers have the highest rates of clinical depression, nervous breakdowns, heart attacks, and alcoholism of any profession." With statements like that, you'd probably guess that the TRACON employees view student tour groups as a hindrance stressor.

work–family conflict A form of role conflict in which the demands of a work role hinder the fulfillment of the demands in a family role (or vice versa)

negative life events Events such as a divorce or death of a family member that tend to be appraised as a hindrance

NON-WORK HINDRANCE STRESSORS Although the majority of people spend more time at the office than anywhere else,[19] there are a number of stressful demands outside of work that have implications for managing behaviour in organizations. In essence, stressors experienced outside of work may have effects that "spill over" to affect the employee at work.[20] One example of non-work hindrance stressors is **work–family conflict**, a special form of role conflict in which the demands of a work role hinder the fulfillment of the demands in a family role (or vice versa). We most often think of cases in which work demands hinder family role performance, termed "work to family conflict." For example, employees who have to deal with lots of hindrances at work may have trouble switching off the frustration after they get home, and as a consequence, they may become irritable and impatient with family and friends. However, work–family conflict can occur in the other direction as well. For example, "family to work conflict" would occur if a salesperson who is experiencing the stress of marital conflict comes to work harbouring emotional pain and negative feelings, which makes it difficult to interact with customers effectively.

Non-work hindrance stressors also come in the form of **negative life events**. Research has revealed that a number of life events are perceived as quite stressful, particularly when they result in significant changes to a person's life.[21] Table 5-2 provides a listing of some commonly experienced life events, along with a score that estimates how stressful each event is perceived to be. As the table reveals, many of the most stressful life events do not occur at work. Rather, they include family events such as the death of a spouse or close

TABLE 5-2 Stressful Life Events

LIFE EVENT	STRESS SCORE	LIFE EVENT	STRESS SCORE
Death of a spouse	100	Trouble with in-laws	29
Divorce	73	Outstanding achievement	28
Marital separation	65	Begin or end school	26
Jail term	63	Change in living conditions	25
Death of close family member	63	Trouble with boss	23
Personal illness	53	Change in work hours	20
Marriage	50	Change in residence	20
Fired at work	47	Change in schools	20
Marital reconciliation	45	Change in social activities	18
Retirement	45	Change in sleeping habits	16
Pregnancy	40	Change in family get-togethers	15
Gain of new family member	39	Change in eating habits	15
Death of close friend	37	Vacations	13
Change in occupation	36	The holiday season	12
Child leaving home	29	Minor violations of the law	11

Source: Adapted from T.H. Holmes and R.H. Rahe, "The Social Re-Adjustment Rating Scale," *Journal of Psychosomatic Research* 11 (1967), pp. 213–18.

family member, a divorce or marital separation, a jail term, or a personal illness. These events would be classified as hindrance stressors because they hinder the ability to achieve life goals and are associated with negative emotions.

NON-WORK CHALLENGE STRESSORS Of course, the non-work domain can be a source of challenge stressors as well. **Family time demands** reflect the time that a person commits to participate in an array of family activities and responsibilities. Specific examples of family time demands include time spent involved in family pursuits such as travelling, attending social events and organized activities, hosting parties, and planning and making home improvements. Examples of **personal development** activities include participation in formal education programs, music lessons, sports-related training, hobby-related self-education, participation in local government, or volunteer work. Finally, Table 5-2 includes some **positive life events** that are sources of non-work challenge stressors. For example, marriage, pregnancy, the addition of a new family member, and ending school are all stressful in their own way. However, each is associated with some positive, rather than negative, emotions.

family time demands The amount of time committed to fulfilling family responsibilities

personal development Participation in activities outside of work that foster growth and learning

positive life events Events such as marriage or the birth of a child that tend to be appraised as a challenge

HOW DO PEOPLE COPE WITH STRESSORS?

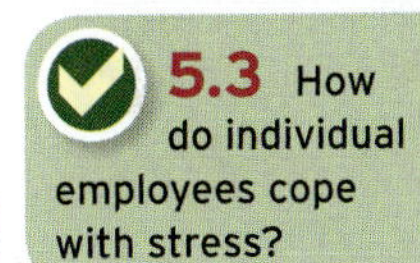

After people appraise a stressful demand, they ask themselves, "What *should* I do" and "What *can* I do" to deal with this situation? These questions, which reflect the **secondary appraisal** shown in Figure 5-1 (page 105), centre on the issue of how people cope with the various stressors that they face.[22] **Coping** refers to the behaviours and thoughts that people use to manage both the stressful demands that they face and the emotions associated with those stressful demands.[23] As Table 5-3 illustrates, coping can involve many different types of activities, and these activities can be grouped into four broad categories based on two dimensions.[24] The first dimension refers to the method of coping (behavioural versus cognitive), and the second dimension refers to the focus of coping (problem solving versus regulation of emotions).

The first part of our coping definition highlights the idea that methods of coping can be categorized on the basis of whether they involve behaviours or cognitions. **Behavioural coping** involves the set of physical activities that are used to deal with a stressful situation. In one example of behavioural coping, a person who is confronted with a lot of time pressure at work might choose to cope by working faster. In another example of behavioural coping, an employee who has several daily hassles might cope by avoiding work—coming in late, leaving early, or even staying home. As a final example of behavioural coping, employees often cope with the stress of a job by resigning and accepting a job in another organization.

secondary appraisal When people determine how to cope with the various stressors they face

coping Behaviours and thoughts used to manage stressful demands and the emotions associated with the stressful demands

behavioural coping Physical activities used to deal with a stressful situation

TABLE 5-3 Examples of Coping Strategies

	PROBLEM-FOCUSED	EMOTION-FOCUSED
Behavioural Methods	Working harder Seeking assistance Acquiring additional resources	Engaging in alternative activities Seeking support Venting anger
Cognitive Methods	Strategizing Self-motivation Changing priorities	Avoiding, distancing, and ignoring Looking for the positive in the negative Reappraising

Source: Adapted from J.C. Latack and S.J. Havlovic, "Coping with Job Stress: A Conceptual Evaluation Framework for Coping Measures," *Journal of Organizational Behaviour* 13 (1992), pp. 479–508.

cognitive coping Thoughts used to deal with a stressful situation

In contrast to behavioural coping, **cognitive coping** refers to the thoughts that are involved in trying to deal with a stressful situation. For example, the person who is confronted with an increase in time pressure might cope by thinking about different ways of accomplishing the work more efficiently. As another example of cognitive coping, the employee who is confronted with daily hassles might try to convince himself or herself that the hassles are not that bad after all.

problem-focused coping Behaviours and cognitions of an individual intended to manage the stressful situation itself

Whereas the first part of our coping definition refers to the method of coping, the second part refers to the focus of coping—that is, does the coping attempt to address the stressful demand or the emotions triggered by the demand?[25] **Problem-focused coping** refers to behaviours and cognitions intended to manage the stressful situation itself. To understand problem-focused coping, consider how some of your fellow students might cope with the time pressure associated with mid-term exams. Some people may address the time pressure by putting in more hours of studying (i.e., cramming), whereas other students may opt to keep their hours the same but work more efficiently. Although these approaches to studying differ, the focus is clearly to deal with and meet the demand rather than trying to avoid it.

emotion-focused coping Behaviours and cognitions of an individual intended to help manage emotional reactions to the stressful demands

In contrast to problem-focused coping, **emotion-focused coping** refers to the various ways in which people manage their own emotional reactions to stressful demands. The reactions to the daily hassles that we described previously illustrated two types of emotion-focused coping. For example, it is common for employees and students to use avoidance and distancing behaviours to reduce the emotional distress caused by a stressful situation. Perhaps this is why it can be so hard to start that major term paper, even though you know the deadline is approaching. Another way to reduce feelings of emotional distress is to seek an alternative activity. Have you ever felt a strong urge to clean and reorganize your room, do yardwork, or wash the dog when you should be studying for a big exam? Although people may be able to temporarily change the way they feel, by reducing the negative emotions associated with a stressful situation, the demand or problem that initially triggered the appraisal process remains.

It might be obvious to you by now that the choice of a coping strategy has important implications for how effectively people can meet or adapt to the different stressors that they face. In the work context, for example, a manager would most likely want subordinates to cope with the stress of a heavy workload by using a problem-focused strategy—working harder—rather than an emotion-focused strategy—drinking two sake bombs at lunch to create distance from the stressor. Of course, there are some situations in which emotion-focused coping may be functional for the person. As an example, consider a person who repeatedly fails to make it through the auditions for *Canadian Idol,* despite years of voice lessons and countless hours of practice. At some point, if this person did not have the capability to cope emotionally—perhaps by lowering her aspirations, or at least ignoring the judges comments—this person's self-concept could be damaged, which could translate into reduced effectiveness in other roles that she fills.

How do people choose a particular coping strategy? One factor that influences this choice is the set of beliefs that people have about how well different coping strategies can address different demands. In essence, people are likely to choose the coping strategy that they believe has the highest likelihood of meeting the demand that they face. For example, a student may come to understand that the likelihood of effectively coping with a demanding final exam is higher if she studies hard rather than trying to escape from the situation by going out until 3:00 a.m. The choice also depends on the degree to which a person believes that he or she has what it takes to execute the coping strategy

What coping strategy do you use to keep track of all your assignments, exams, and deadlines for your classes?

effectively. Returning to the previous example, if the student had already failed the first two exams in the course, despite trying hard, she may come to believe that a problem-focused coping strategy will not work. In this situation, because the student may feel helpless to address the demand directly, an emotion-focused coping strategy would be most likely.

One critical factor that determines coping strategy choice is the degree to which people believe that a particular strategy gives them some degree of control over the stressor or how they feel about it. If a person believes that a demand can be addressed with a problem-focused coping strategy, and the person also has confidence that he can use that problem-focused strategy effectively, then he will feel some control over the situation and likely use a problem-focused strategy. If a person believes that a demand cannot be addressed with a problem-focused strategy or does not believe she can effectively enact that strategy, then she likely will feel a lack of control over the situation and tend to use an emotion-focused coping strategy to decrease emotional discomfort.

So what determines how people develop a sense of control? It appears that one important factor is the nature of the stressful demand itself. In particular, people are likely to feel less control over a stressor when they appraise it as a hindrance rather than a challenge. Consider one of the life events in Table 5-2: "Trouble with boss." This event would be categorized as a hindrance stressor because it hinders goal achievement and triggers negative emotions. If you're like most people, you would want to change the behaviour of your boss so that the trouble would stop and you could go on with your work. However, it's also likely that you would feel like you have little control over this situation because bosses are in a position of power and complaining to your boss's boss might not be an option for you. The anxiety and hopelessness triggered by the situation would further erode any sense of control over the situation, likely leading to emotion-focused coping.[26]

THE EXPERIENCE OF STRAIN

Earlier in this chapter, we defined strains as the negative consequences associated with stress. How exactly does stress cause strain? Consider the case of Naomi Henderson, the CEO of RIVA, a small market-research firm in Rockville, Maryland. The job of CEO is quite demanding, and Henderson found herself working 120 hours a week to cope with the heavy workload. One night she woke up to go to the bathroom and found that she literally could not move—she was paralyzed. After being rushed to the emergency room, Henderson and her husband were told by the doctor that the diagnosis was stress. The doctor recommended rest in bed for 14 hours a day for 6 weeks.[27] Although this example may seem extreme to you, the demands of many managerial and executive level jobs are often excessive,[28] and the negative health consequences that result are fairly predictable. In fact, if you've ever been in a situation in which you've experienced heavy stress for more than a couple of days, you can probably appreciate the toll that stress can take on you. You may have noticed, for instance, that many students get sick around the middle and the end of term. Although people react to stress differently, you may have felt unusually exhausted, irritable, and achy. What might be surprising to you is that the mechanism within your body that gives you the ability to function effectively in the face of stressful demands is the same mechanism that ends up causing you these problems. So what is this mechanism?

Medical researchers who study stress have spent years examining the body's response to different sorts of stressful demands.[29] Many of these findings have been summarized in a theory called the **general adaptation syndrome (GAS)**, which is illustrated in Figure 5-2.[30] In a nutshell, GAS suggests that the body has a set of responses that allow it to adapt and function effectively in the face of stressful demands. However, when stressful demands do not ramp down or the demands occur too frequently, the body's adaptive responses become toxic. To better understand GAS, let's consider what occurs after a person is confronted with a stressful demand.

general adaptation syndrome (GAS) The process that the body uses to adapt to stressful demands so that it can continue to function effectively

OB RESEARCH IN CANADA

Dr. Julian Barling, at Queen's University, is a recognized expert in several areas of organizational behaviour, including leadership, work and family, and workplace stress and violence. His current research focuses on the nature and development of transformational leadership and unethical leadership, and how leadership can enhance an employee's psychological and physical well-being. Dr. Barling is the author of several books, including *Employment, Stress, and Family Functioning* (1990), *Changing Employment Relations: Behavioral and Social Perspectives* (with Lois Tetrick, 1995), and *Young Workers: Varieties of Experience* (with Kevin Kelloway, 1999). Dr. Barling co-edited *The Psychology of Workplace Safety* (with Michael Frone, 2003), *Handbook of Work Stress* (with Kevin Kelloway and Michael Frone, 2005), *Handbook of Workplace Violence* (with Kevin Kelloway and Joseph Hurrell, 2006), and *The SAGE Handbook of Organizational Behavior* (with Cary L. Cooper, 2008). In addition, he is the author/editor of well over 125 research articles and book chapters.

Julian Barling received his PhD in 1979 from the University of the Witwatersrand, in Johannesburg, South Africa, where he subsequently taught industrial psychology. In 1982, he joined the State University of New York at Stony Brook as a visiting professor of psychology. He joined Queen's University in 1984, initially teaching in the Department of Psychology but moving to the School of Business in 1994. From 1989 to 1991, Dr. Barling was the chairperson of the Advisory Council on Occupational Health and Safety to the Ontario Minister of Labour. In 2001, Dr. Barling received a Leaders in Business Education award from the *National Post.* In 2002, Dr. Barling was elected as a fellow of the Royal Society of Canada, and was named as one of Queen's University's Research Chairs, a position he continues to hold. In 2008, Dr. Barling was elected as a fellow of the Society of Industrial and Organizational Psychology. Presently, Dr. Julian Barling is professor of organizational behaviour and psychology in the Queen's School of Business, and associate dean with responsibility for the PhD, MSc, and research programs in the School of Business.

Some of Dr. Barling's favourite publications include:

"Predicting Workplace Aggression: Myths, Realities, and Remaining Questions," by J. Barling, K. Dupre, and E.K. Kelloway, published in *Annual Review of Psychology* (2009, volume 60, pp. 671–92).

"Transformational Leadership and Moral Reasoning, by N. Turner, J. Barling, O. Epitropaki, B. Butcher, and C. Milner, in *Journal of Applied Psychology* (2002, volume 87, pp. 304–11).

"Effects of Transformational Leadership Training on Attitudinal and Financial Outcomes: A Field Experiment," by J. Barling, E.K. Kelloway, and T. Weber, published in *Journal of Applied Psychology* (1996, volume 81, pp. 827–32).

"Member's Participation in Local Union Activities: Measurement, Prediction, Replication," by E.K. Kelloway and J. Barling, in *Journal of Applied Psychology* (1993, volume 78, pp. 262–79).

"Work Stressors and Wife Abuse," by J. Barling and A. Rosenbaum, published in *Journal of Applied Psychology* (1986, volume 71, pp. 346–48).

FIGURE 5-2 General Adaptation Syndrome

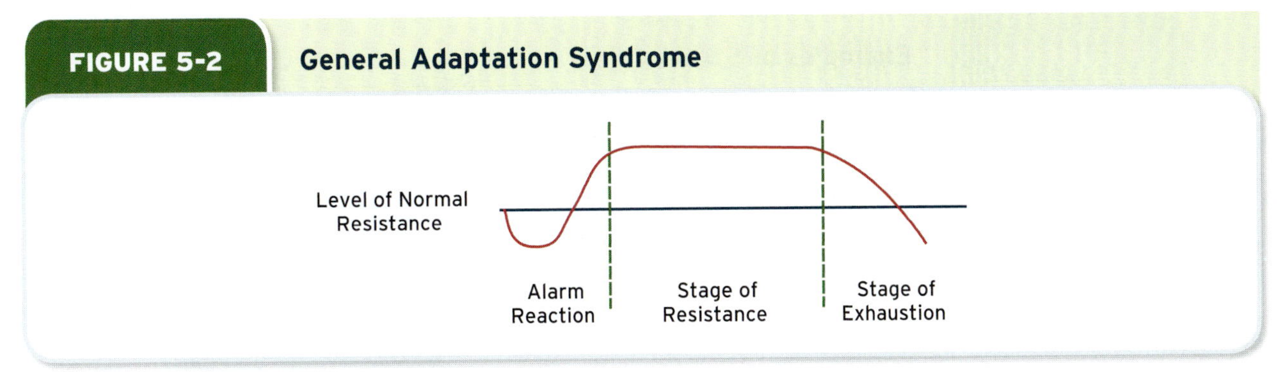

Source: Adapted from H. Seyle, *The Stress of Life*, revised ed. (New York: McGraw Hill, 1976), p. 111.

The first stage of the GAS is the alarm reaction. Upon being confronted with a stressor, there is a relatively brief period of time in which resistance to the stressor is temporarily lowered. At this point the body and mind haven't reacted yet—in essence, the stressor simply "sinks in." Immediately thereafter, the body activates several defence mechanisms to resist and counteract the stressor. At this point in the alarm reaction stage, the body (actually, the adrenal medulla and the postganglionic fibres of the sympathetic nervous system, for any future doctors in the class) begins to secrete chemical compounds (catecholamines such as adrenaline, noradrenaline, and dopamine—don't worry, these aren't in the "Key Terms" section) that circulate in the blood.[31] These chemical compounds cause increases in heart rate and blood pressure, and blood is redirected away from organs such as the spleen to the brain and skeletal muscles.

The changes that occur in the alarm stage prepare the mind and body for "fight or flight."[32] After this point, the person is in the second stage of the GAS, the stage of resistance. Here, the increased arousal of his or her mind and body caused by the secretion of chemicals helps the person respond and adapt to the demand. Unfortunately, if the chemicals in the blood remain elevated because of prolonged or repeated exposure to the stressor, the body begins to break down, and exhaustion and even death may occur. This last stage is the stage of exhaustion. Although the GAS might sound like a theory that describes reactions to extreme types of stressors—being chased through a jungle by a hungry tiger, for example—research suggests that most types of stressors evoke the same sequence of physiological events. Therefore, negative consequences to the body occur even with the more mundane stressors that most of us face in our lives. As shown in Figure 5-3, those negative consequences come in three varieties: physiological strains, psychological strains, and behavioural strains.[33]

Physiological strains that result from stressors occur in at least four systems of the human body. First, stressors can reduce the effectiveness of the body's immune system, which makes it more difficult for the body to ward off illness and infection. This probably explains why students get sick during or immediately after exam periods. Second, stressors can harm the body's cardiovascular system, cause the heart to race, increase blood pressure, and create coronary artery disease. Third, stressors can cause problems in the body's musculoskeletal system. Tension headaches, tight shoulders, and back pain have all been linked to a variety of stressors. Fourth, stressors cause gastrointestinal system problems. Symptoms of this type of strain include stomachaches, indigestion, diarrhea, and constipation.[34]

physiological strains
Reactions from stressors that harm the human body

Although you might be tempted to dismiss the importance of physiological strains because the base rate for serious illness and disease is low for people in their 20s and 30s, research shows that dismissal may be a mistake. For example, high-pressure work deadlines increase the chance of heart attack within the next 24 hours by a factor of six.[35] So, even though the likelihood of suffering a heart attack may be low for the young, who would want to increase their risk by 600 percent? Perhaps more important, the negative

FIGURE 5-3 Examples of Strain

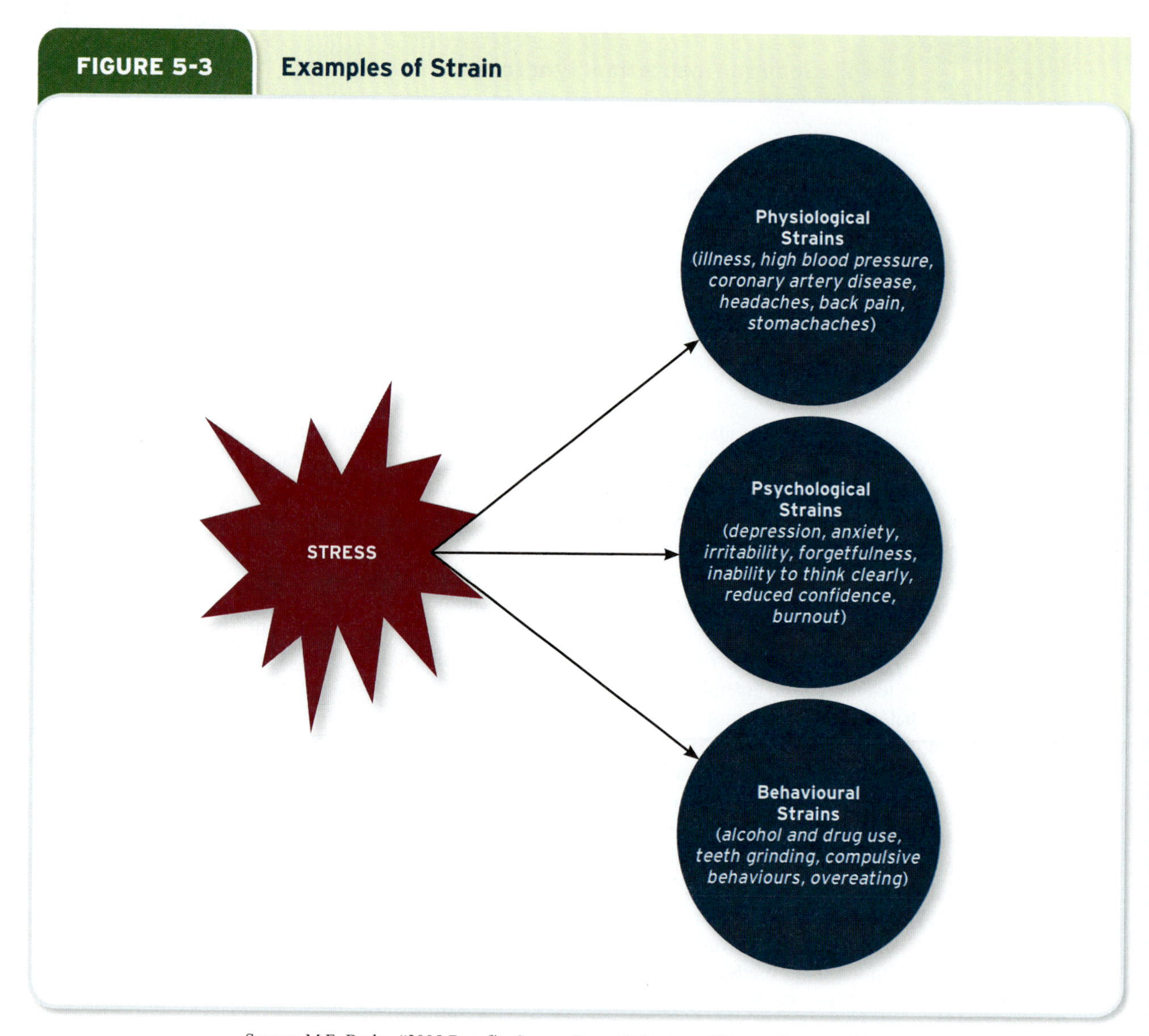

Source: M.E. Burke, "2005 Benefits Survey Report," *Society of Human Resource Management.* Reprinted with permission.

physiological effects of stress persist over time and may not become manifest until far into the future. One study showed that eye problems, allergic complaints, and chronic diseases could be attributed to stress measured eight years earlier.[36]

psychological strains Negative psychological reactions from stressors such as depression, anxiety, and anger

Psychological strains that result from stressors include depression, anxiety, anger, hostility, reduced self-confidence, irritability, inability to think clearly, forgetfulness, lack of creativity, memory loss, and (not surprising, given the rest of this list) a loss of sense of humour.[37] Although these strains are less obviously connected to GAS than the physical strains that we described in the previous paragraph, each is likely to be a symptom of **burnout**. The concept of burnout has been studied extensively by researchers, though there is not yet a complete consensus on its definition. We define it here as the emotional, mental, and physical exhaustion that results from having to cope with stressful demands on an ongoing basis.[38]

burnout The emotional, mental, and physical exhaustion from coping with stressful demands on a continuing basis

Relative to physiological and psychological strains, **behavioural strains** are the least connected to GAS. In fact, unhealthy behaviours such as grinding one's teeth at night, being overly critical and bossy, excessive smoking, compulsive gum chewing, overuse of alcohol, and compulsive eating[39] can be thought of as the behavioural symptoms of the other types of strains.

behavioural strains Patterns of negative behaviours that are associated with other strains

ACCOUNTING FOR INDIVIDUALS IN THE STRESS PROCESS

5.4 How do the Type A Behaviour Pattern and social support influence the stress process?

So far in this chapter, we've discussed how the typical or average person reacts to different sorts of stressors. Of course, people differ in terms of how they typically react to stressful demands. One way that people differ in their reaction to stress depends on whether they exhibit the **Type A Behaviour Pattern**. "Type A" people have a strong sense of time urgency and tend to be impatient, hard-driving, competitive, controlling, aggressive, and even hostile.[40] If you walk, talk, and eat at a quick pace, and if you find yourself constantly annoyed with people who do things too slowly, chances are that you're a Type A person. With that said, one way to tell for sure is to fill out the Type A questionnaire at the end of the chapter in our **OB Assessments** feature.

Type A Behaviour Pattern People who tend to experience more stressors, to appraise more demands as stressful, and to be prone to experiencing more strains

In the context of this chapter, the Type A Behaviour Pattern is important because it can influence each variable in our general model of stress. First, the Type A Behaviour Pattern may have a direct influence on the level of stressors that a person confronts. To understand why this connection might be true, consider that Type A persons tend to be hard-driving and have a strong desire to achieve. Because the behaviours that reflect these tendencies are valued by the organization, Type A individuals receive "rewards" in the form of increases in the amount and level of work required. In addition, because Type A people tend to be aggressive and competitive, they may be more prone to interpersonal conflict. We're sure that most of you would agree that conflict with peers and co-workers is an important stressor.

Second, in addition to the effect on stressors, the Type A Behaviour Pattern is important because it influences the stress process itself.[41] This effect of the Type A Behaviour Pattern is easy to understand if you consider that hard-driving competitiveness makes people hypersensitive to demands that could potentially affect their progress toward their goal attainment. In essence, Type A individuals are simply more likely to appraise demands as being stressful rather than being benign.

Third, and perhaps most important, the Type A Behaviour Pattern has been directly linked to coronary heart disease[42] and other physiological, psychological, and behavioural strains.[43] The size of the relationship between the Type A Behaviour Pattern and these strains is not so strong as to suggest that if you're a Type A person, you should immediately call 911. However, the linkage is strong enough to suggest that the risk of these problems is significantly higher for people who typically engage in Type A behaviours.

social support The help people receive from others when they are confronted with stressful demands

Another individual factor that affects the way people manage stress is the degree of **social support** that they receive. Social support refers to the help that people receive when they are confronted with stressful demands, and there are at least two major types.[44] One type of social support is called **instrumental support**, which refers to the help people receive that can be used to address the stressful demand directly. For example, if a person is overloaded with work, a co-worker could provide instrumental support by taking over some of the work or offering suggestions about how to do the work more efficiently. A second type of social support is called **emotional support**. This type of support refers to the help people receive in addressing the emotional distress that accompanies stressful demands. As an example, the supervisor of the individual who is overloaded with work might provide emotional support by showing interest in the employee's situation and appearing to be

instrumental support The help people receive from others that can be used to address a stressful demand directly

emotional support The empathy and understanding that people receive from others that can be used to alleviate emotional distress from stressful demands

Social support from friends, co-workers, and family can be a big help in managing stress, even though it usually occurs outside the stress-causing environment.

understanding and empathetic. As alluded to in these examples, social support may come from co-workers as well as from supervisors. However, social support also may be provided by family members and friends outside the context of the stressful demand.[45]

Similar to the Type A Behaviour Pattern, social support has the potential to influence the stress process in several different ways. However, most research on social support focuses on the ways that social support buffers the relationship between stressors and strains. According to this research, high levels of social support provide a person with instrumental or emotional resources that are useful for coping with the stressor, which tends to reduce the harmful consequences of the stressor to that individual. With low levels of social support, the person does not have extra coping resources available, so the stressor tends to have effects that are more harmful. In essence, this perspective casts social support as a moderator of the relationship between stressors and strains (moderators are variables that affect the strength of the relationship between two other variables). In this particular case, the relationship between stress and strain tends to be weaker at higher levels of social support and stronger at lower levels of social support. Although not every research study has found support for the buffering effect of social support,[46] the majority of research evidence has been supportive.[47]

SO WHY ARE SOME EMPLOYEES MORE "STRESSED" THAN OTHERS?

As shown in Figure 5-4, answering that question requires paying attention to the particular stressors the employee is experiencing, including hindrance and challenge stressors originating in both the work and non-work domains. However, it also depends on how those stressors are appraised and coped with, which determines whether physiological, psychological, and behavioural strains are experienced. Finally, answering the question depends on whether the employee is "Type A" or "Type B" and whether the employee has a high or low amount of social support. Understanding all of these factors can help explain why some people can shoulder stressful circumstances for weeks at a time, whereas others seem to be "at the end of their rope" when faced with even relatively minor job demands.

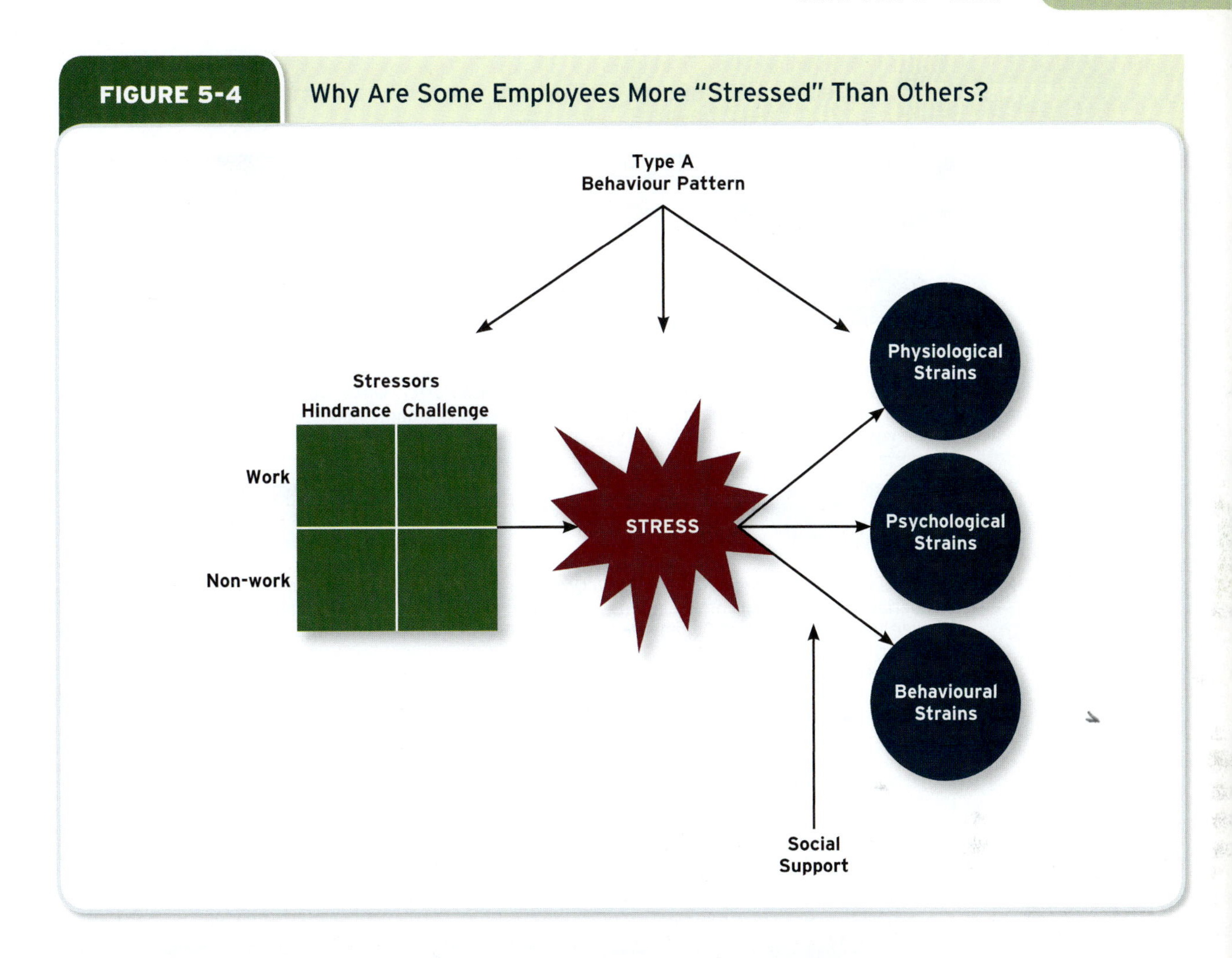

HOW IMPORTANT IS STRESS?

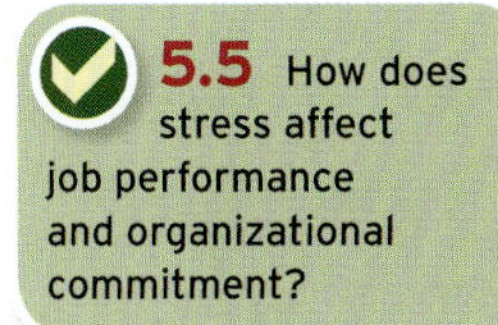

In the previous sections, we described how stressors and the stress process influence strains and, ultimately, people's health and well-being. Although these effects are important, you're probably curious about the impact that strains have on job performance and organizational commitment, the two outcomes in our integrative model of OB. Figure 5-5 summarizes the research evidence linking strains to job performance and organizational commitment.

Figure 5-5 reveals that strains have a moderately negative effect on job performance.[48] A general explanation for this negative relationship between strains and job performance is that strains reduce the overall level of energy and attention that people could otherwise bring to their job duties.[49] In fact, the reason for the negative impact of strains on performance becomes quite obvious when you consider the nature of the individual strains that we mentioned in the previous section. Certainly, you would agree that physiological, psychological, and behavioural strains in the form of illnesses, exhaustion, and drunkenness would detract from employee effectiveness in almost any job context.

Figure 5-5 also reveals that strains have a strong negative effect on organizational commitment.[50] Why might this be? Well, strains are generally dissatisfying to people, and as we discussed in the previous chapter, satisfaction has a strong impact on the degree to which people

FIGURE 5-5 Effects of Strains on Performance and Commitment

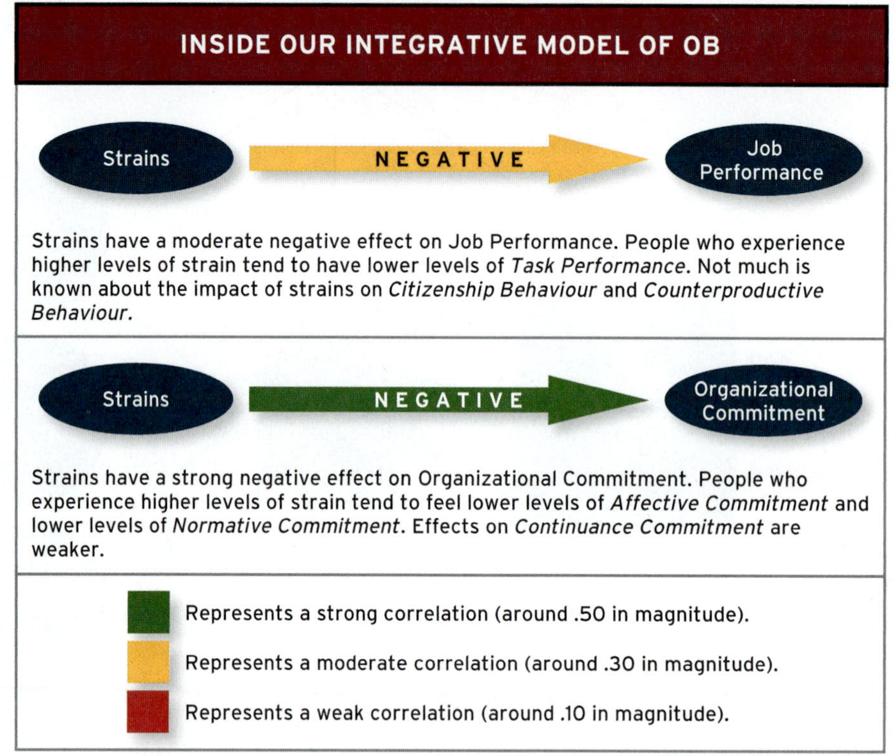

Sources: J.A. LePine, N.P. Podsakoff, and M.A. LePine, "A Meta-Analytic Test of the Challenge Stressor–Hindrance Stressor Framework: An Explanation for Inconsistent Relationships Among Stressors and Performance," *Academy of Management Journal* 48 (2005), pp. 764–75; N.P. Podsakoff, J.A. LePine, and M.A. LePine, "Differential Challenge Stressor–Hindrance Stressor Relationships with Job Attitudes, Turnover Intentions, Turnover, and Withdrawal Behavior: A Meta-Analysis," *Journal of Applied Psychology* 92 (2007). pp. 438–454.

feel committed to their organization.[51] People who work at jobs that they know are causing them to feel constantly sick and exhausted will likely be dissatisfied with their jobs and feel less desire to stay with the organization and more desire to consider alternatives.

So in this discussion and Figure 5-5, we portray stress as something that has a negative impact on both job performance and organizational commitment. But this is not quite the whole story. In fact, though all types of stressors are positively associated with strains, certain types of stressors have positive relationships with performance and commitment. But how can that be? To understand why this complexity might be true, recall from our previous discussions that challenge stressors such as time pressure and responsibility tend to evoke positive emotions and that when people are confronted with challenge stressors, they tend to deal with them using problem-focused coping strategies. The net benefits of those positive emotions and coping strategies sometimes outweigh the costs of the added strain, meaning that challenge stressors tend to have small positive relationships with performance and commitment.[52] These positive effects of challenge stressors on several important job variables have been demonstrated for executives,[53] as well as employees in lower-level jobs,[54] and as our **OB for Students** feature illustrates, the positive effect of challenge stressors applies to students as well.[55]

OB FOR STUDENTS

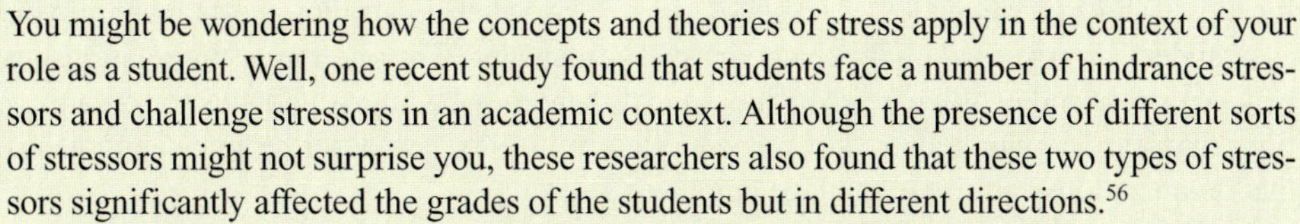

You might be wondering how the concepts and theories of stress apply in the context of your role as a student. Well, one recent study found that students face a number of hindrance stressors and challenge stressors in an academic context. Although the presence of different sorts of stressors might not surprise you, these researchers also found that these two types of stressors significantly affected the grades of the students but in different directions.[56]

Hindrance stressors included demands such as the amount of time spent on busywork for your classes, the degree to which favouritism affects final grades in your classes, and the amount of hassles you need to go through to get projects and assignments done. Challenge stressors included demands such as the difficulty of the work required in your classes, the volume of coursework that must be completed in your classes, and the time pressures experienced for completing work required in your classes. So how did these two types of stressors affect students' grades?

On the one hand, students who experienced higher levels of hindrance stressors tended to have lower grades. One reason is that coping with hindrance stressors was exhausting, and feeling this way made it more difficult to put forth the energy to study. A second reason is that hindrance stressors decreased students' motivation to learn. Students who faced a lot of hindrance stressors apparently did not believe that studying hard would result in good grades, and accordingly, they did not put forth the necessary effort.

On the other hand, students who experienced higher levels of challenge stressors tended to have higher grades. The authors' explanation for this effect was that challenge stressors motivated students to invest more effort in their learning. Although students felt that coping with challenge stressors was exhausting, the positive force of motivation was significantly more powerful. In essence, challenge stressors motivated students to work hard in spite of feeling extremely tired. So what can you do with this information?

One option might be to try and change the situation by taking action to decrease the level of hindrance stressors you experience. Although this approach might be possible with some hindrances—asking professors to provide clarifying instruction for example—the approach may be more difficult with others—such as asking the professor to reduce the amount of busywork. A second option would be to try to think of hindrances as challenges. Although it might be difficult to convince yourself that coping with hindrances such as busywork and favouritism is beneficial to your growth and learning, the research findings suggest that the effort might be worthwhile.

APPLICATION: STRESS MANAGEMENT

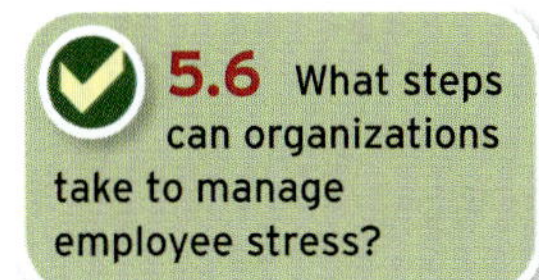

Previously, we described how employee stress results in strains that cost organizations in terms of reduced employee performance and commitment. However, there are other important costs to consider that relate to employee health. Most organizations provide some form of health care benefits for their employees. This is especially true for organizations trying to attract and retain hard-to-find skilled workers. To provide a sense of the financial cost of these benefits to employers, a national poll was conducted. When asked if they would trade their company-provided health benefits for an annual payment of $8,000, almost three-quarters of Canadians said they would keep their plan.[57] So what role does stress play in these costs?

Well, it turns out that these health-related costs are driven to a great extent by employee stress. Estimates are that between 60 percent and 90 percent of all doctor visits can be attributed to stress-related causes,[58] and the cost of providing health care to people who experience high levels of stress appears to be approximately 50 percent higher than that for those who experience lower levels of stress.[59] So what do all these costs mean to you as a student of organizational behaviour or as a manager? For one thing, the relationship between stress and health care costs means that there may be huge dividends for organizations that learn how to manage stress more effectively. Next, we describe some approaches that organizations can use to manage employee stress.

ASSESSMENT

stress audit An assessment of the sources of stress in the workplace

The first step in managing stress is to assess the level and sources of stress in the workplace. Although there are many ways to accomplish this type of evaluation, often referred to as a **stress audit**, managers can begin by asking themselves questions about the nature of the jobs in their organization to estimate whether high stress levels may be a problem.[60] The first category of questions might involve the degree to which the organization is going through change that would likely increase uncertainty among employees. As an example, a merger between two companies might increase employees' uncertainty about their job security and possible career paths. As another example, employees in an organization that has transitioned to team-based work might be concerned about how their individual performance contributions will be recognized and rewarded. A second category of questions might centre on the work itself. These questions typically focus on the level and types of stressors experienced by the employees. The third category of questions could involve the quality of relationships not only among employees but also between employees and the organization. Here, an important question to consider is whether organizational politics play a large role in administrative decisions.

REDUCING STRESSORS

job sharing When two people share the responsibilities of a single job

Once a stress audit reveals that stress may be a problem, the next step is to consider alternative courses of action. One general course of action involves managing stressors, which may be accomplished in one of two ways. First, organizations could try to eliminate or significantly reduce stressful demands. As an example of this approach, 19 percent of organizations in one recent survey used **job sharing** to reduce role overload and foster work–life balance.[61] Job sharing does not mean splitting one job into two but rather indicates that two people share the responsibilities of a single job, as if the two people were a single performing unit. The assumption underlying the practice is that "although businesses are becoming 24/7, people don't."[62]

You might be tempted to believe that job sharing would be most appropriate in lower-level jobs, where responsibilities and tasks are limited in number and relatively easy to divide. In actuality, job sharing is being used at all levels throughout the organization. Such arrangements can enable an organization to attract or retain valued employees who want more time to attend school or to care for family members. Of course, for this arrangement to work effectively it would be important that job-sharing partners be able to communicate well and coordinate their activities.[63]

PROVIDING RESOURCES

Although reducing stressors may reduce the overall level of stress that a person experiences, this approach is likely to be most beneficial when the focus of the effort is on hindrance stressors rather than challenge stressors.[64] Hindrance stressors such as role ambiguity, conflict, and politics not only cause strains but also decrease commitment and job performance. In contrast, though challenge stressors such as time pressure and responsibility cause strains, they also tend to be motivating and satisfying, and as a consequence, they generally are positively related to commitment and performance.

So as a supplement to reducing stressors, organizations can provide resources that help employees cope with stressful demands.[65] One way that organizations provide resources to employees is through **training interventions** aimed at increasing job-related competencies and skills. Employees who possess more competencies and skills can handle more demands rather than appraise the demands as overly taxing or exceeding their capacity. Training that increases employee competencies and skills is also beneficial to the extent that it promotes a sense that the demands are more controllable, and as we discussed in a previous section, a sense of control promotes problem-focused coping strategies.

training interventions Practices that increase employees' competencies and skills

A second way that organizations provide resources to employees so that they can cope more effectively is through **supportive practices** that help employees manage and balance the demands that exist in the different roles they have. Although we only have room in this chapter to describe a few of these practices, Table 5-4 lists a few examples of the steps employers can take to reduce stress and promote a healthy work–life balance.

supportive practices Ways in which organizations help employees manage and balance their demands

Organizations that use flextime give employees some degree of latitude in terms of which hours they need to be present at the workplace. Flexible working hours give employees the ability to cope with demands away from work so that they don't have to worry about these demands while they're at work. Another example is allowing workers to work at home or telecommute on a part-time basis. By providing the opportunity to work at home or some other location with computer access, employees are put in a better position to cope with demands that might be impossible to cope with otherwise (e.g., caring for a sick child or elderly parent). Making an effort to accommodate and support employees who are returning to work after a disabling injury or illness, or after a lengthy leave, not only facilitates successful reintegration but conveys a message, generally, that the organization cares about and values its members.[66] In addition to employee training mentioned earlier, managers can be trained to understand how their behaviours help or hinder their employees' efforts to cope with job stressors and balance competing work and non-work demands. For instance, to minimize role stressors (e.g., overload, ambiguity, conflict), managers can reduce the number of face-to-face meetings, clarify expectations, and allow employees more personal latitude and personal control (increased autonomy) over their day-to-day work activities.

TABLE 5-4 Examples of Supportive Practices Used by Organizations

Examples of Supportive Practices Used by Organizations
• Offer flexible hours.
• Allow workers to work from home where possible and appropriate.
• Encourage staff to stay home with sick children or elderly relatives when needed.
• Permit those returning from a leave to gradually build up to a full-time schedule.
• Train managers on how to support work-life balance.
• Eliminate unnecessary meetings.
• Communicate expectations clearly to staff.
• Allow staff to control their own priorities as much as possible.

Source: Mentally Unhealthy Workplaces Taking An Enormous Toll in Canada. Canadian Mental Health Association (May 1, 2008). http://www.cmha.ca/ ct100@mediacorp.ca

REDUCING STRAINS

relaxation techniques Calming activities to reduce stress

As an alternative to managing stressors, many organizations use practices that reduce strains.[67] One type of strain-reducing practice involves **relaxation techniques**, such as progressive muscle relaxation, meditation, and miscellaneous calming activities like taking walks, writing in a journal, and deep breathing.[68] Although these relaxation techniques differ, the basic idea is the same—they teach people how to counteract the effects of stressors by engaging in activities that slow the heart rate, breathing rate, and blood pressure.[69] As an example of a relatively simple relaxation technique, consider the recommendation of Herbert Benson, a physician and president of the Mind/Body Medical Institute in Boston. He suggests that people under stress should repeat a word, sound, prayer, phrase, or motion for 10 to 20 minutes once or twice a day and, during that time, try to completely ignore other thoughts that may come to mind.[70] As another example, recall the case of Naomi Henderson, the market research firm CEO who literally became paralyzed by all the stress in her job. Well, we're happy to say that Henderson got better, but she was able to do so only after being treated by a physician who helped her learn how to reduce her own strains by doing "mental aerobics." Those exercises involved taking breaks every hour to stretch and do deep breathing, taking short naps to replenish energy, and learning how to say no politely to unreasonable demands.[71]

cognitive-behavioural techniques Various practices that help workers cope with life's stressors in a rational manner

A second general category of strain-reducing practices involves **cognitive–behavioural techniques**. In general, these techniques attempt to help people appraise and cope with stressors in a rational manner.[72] To understand what these techniques involve, think of someone you know who not only exaggerates the level and importance of stressful demands but also predicts doom and disaster after quickly concluding that the demands simply cannot be met. If you know someone like this, you might recommend cognitive–behavioural training that involves "self-talk," a technique in which people learn to say things about stressful demands that reflect rationality and optimism. So, when confronted with a stressful demand, this person might be trained to say, "This demand isn't so tough; if I work hard I can accomplish it." In addition, cognitive–behavioural training typically involves instruction about tools that foster effective coping. So, in addition to the self-talk, the person might be trained on how to prioritize demands, manage time, communicate needs, and seek support.[73]

health and wellness programs Employee assistance programs that help workers with personal problems such as alcoholism and other addictions

A third category of strain-reducing practices involves **health and wellness programs**. Canadian organizations have begun to embrace the concept of workplace health promotion. The most recent estimate is that approximately 64 percent of employers offer their employees at least one wellness initiative.[74] Examples of workplace wellness programs that try to improve employee health and foster, in employees, a sense of well-being include smoking cessation, stress management, weight control, physical fitness, nutrition awareness, cardiovascular health/hypertension/diabetes awareness, and back care.[75]

TAKEAWAYS

5.1 Stress refers to the psychological response to demands when there is something at stake for the individual and coping with these demands would tax or exceed the individual's capacity or resources. Stressors are the demands that cause the stress response, and strains are the negative consequences of the stress response. Before stressors produce the stress response, they must first be perceived and appraised as stressful. After people appraise a stressful demand, they ask themselves, "How can I cope?"

5.2 Stressors come in two general forms: challenge stressors, which are perceived as opportunities for growth and achievement, and hindrance stressors, which are perceived as hurdles to goal achievement. These two stressors can be found in both work and non-work domains.

5.3 Coping with stress involves thoughts and behaviours that address one of two goals: addressing the stressful demand or decreasing the emotional discomfort associated with the demand.

5.4 Individual differences in the Type A Behaviour Pattern affect how people experience stress in three ways. Type A people tend to experience more stressors, to appraise more demands as stressful, and to be prone to experiencing more strains. Individual differences in social support influence the strength of the stress–strain relationship, such that more support acts as a buffer that prevents the onset of strain.

5.5 Although the body tries to adapt to different sorts of stressors, along the lines of what is described by the general adaptation syndrome (GAS), over time this adaptive response wears out the body and exhaustion and collapse may occur. The resulting strain has a moderate negative relationship with job performance and a strong negative relationship with organizational commitment.

5.6 Because of the high costs associated with employee stress, organizations assess and manage stress using a number of different practices. In general, these practices focus on reducing or eliminating stressors, providing resources that employees can use to cope with stressors, or trying to reduce the strains.

KEY TERMS

- behavioural coping *p. 111*
- behavioural strains *p. 117*
- benign job demands *p. 105*
- burnout *p. 116*
- challenge stressors *p. 106*
- cognitive coping *p. 112*
- cognitive–behavioural techniques *p. 124*
- coping *p. 111*
- daily hassles *p. 108*
- emotional support *p. 117*
- emotion-focused coping *p. 111*
- family time demands *p. 111*
- general adaptation syndrome (GAS) *p. 113*
- health and wellness programs *p. 124*
- hindrance stressors *p. 106*
- instrumental support *p. 117*
- job sharing *p. 122*
- negative life events *p. 110*
- personal development *p. 111*
- physiological strains *p. 115*
- positive life events *p. 111*
- primary appraisal *p. 105*
- problem-focused coping *p. 112*
- psychological strains *p. 116*
- relaxation techniques *p. 124*
- role ambiguity *p. 106*
- role conflict *p. 106*
- role overload *p. 107*
- secondary appraisal *p. 111*
- social support *p. 117*
- strains *p. 105*
- stress *p. 105*
- stress audit *p. 122*
- stressors *p. 105*
- supportive practices *p. 123*
- time pressure *p. 108*
- training interventions *p. 123*
- Type A Behaviour Pattern *p. 117*
- work complexity *p. 108*
- work–family conflict *p. 110*
- work responsibility *p. 108*

DISCUSSION QUESTIONS

5.1 Describe your dream job and then provide a list of the types of stressors that you would expect to be present. Is the list dominated by challenge stressors or hindrance stressors? Why do you think this is?

5.2 Think about the dream job that you described in the previous question. How much of your salary, if any at all, would you give up to eliminate the most important hindrance stressors? Why?

5.3 If you had several job offers after graduating, to what degree would the level of challenge stressors in the different jobs influence your choice of which job to take? Why?

5.4 How would you assess your ability to handle stress? Given the information provided in this chapter, what could you do to improve your effectiveness in this area?

5.5 If you managed people in an organization in which there were lots of hindrance stressors, what actions would you take to help ensure that your employees coped with the stressors using a problem-focused as opposed to an emotion-focused coping strategy?

CASE • BACKSTAGE IDOL

What really happens behind the scenes at *Canadian Idol?* According to Sheri Block, a reporter with CTV, the answer is . . . plenty! As stressful as the competition is for the thousands of *Idol* hopefuls who brave long lines and leave disappointed, can you imagine how it feels to be a backstage production assistant who helps run the city-by-city auditions?

Day one of the competition starts with a call time of 7:00 a.m. With more than 100 people already in line, Sheri and the other production assistants take their positions at the registration desk and, one by one, begin the tedious task of processing each competitor (e.g., checking that forms are completed properly, making sure that age requirements are met). After several hundred (often more) competitors are registered and assigned a number, they are organized into groups of five. Then they wait to be called.

By the time a group is called, the competitors are usually very anxious and have lots of questions, desperately looking to production assistants for advice (e.g., song selection, their outfits), reassurance, and help to remain calm—anything that might get them through to the next round. But the competition rules are very strict, and production assistants are forbidden to provide information that may give one person an advantage over another. The five competitors of each group are then escorted to the Tier 1 holding trailer where they wait, again, for their audition.

The Tier 1 audition room is small and stuffy with wood paneled walls—a far cry from a glitzy television studio. The five competitors come in and are told to stand at the back wall. They look absolutely terrified! The producer tells them to project their voice and personality. The first competitor is called and nervously comes up to sing. She darts her eyes between the producer and the production assistant, trying to read their faces as to what her fate will be. "All we can do is smile and nod in encouragement," says Sheri Block. The auditions continue like this, one by one, until the end, when the producer decides who will stay behind to sing another song. Most competitors are asked to leave, and handed over to the production assistant. Some competitors leave the room crying, while others tell us they'll just try again next year. After the group is thanked for their participation, the production assistant gets another group of five. The search for the next *Canadian Idol* continues.

5.1 Why do people allow themselves to go through a process like this, given the risks to self-esteem?

5.2 Put yourself in the shoes of a production assistant. How might you cope with the anxiety and emotional distress of the competitors?

5.3 Can you recommend some ways to reduce the level of stress experienced by competitors? Do you think your ideas would improve the selection process? Explain.

Source: Sheri Block, "Day in the Life of a Production Assistant," *Canadian Idol* website, April 28, 2008. Retrieved February 7, 2009, at www.ctv.ca/servlet/ArticleNews/story/CTVNews/20080428/CI6_ Day_in_life_PA_080428/20080918?s_name=idol2008&no_ads=.

EXERCISE • MANAGING STRESS

The purpose of this exercise is to explore ways of managing stress to reduce strain. This exercise uses groups of six participants, so your instructor will either assign you to a group of six or ask you to create your own group of six. The exercise has the following steps:

1. One method of managing stress is finding a way to reduce the hindrance stressors encountered on the job. In groups of four to six students, describe the hindrance stressors that you currently are experiencing. Each student should describe the two to three most important stressors. Other students should then offer strategies for reducing or alleviating the stressors.

HINDRANCE STRESSORS EXPERIENCED	STRATEGIES FOR MANAGING STRESSORS
Role Conflict:	
Role Ambiguity:	
Role Overload:	
Daily Hassles:	

2. Another method of managing stress is to improve work–life balance. The circle below represents how "waking hours" are divided among five types of activities: school, work, personal relaxation, time with friends, and time with family. Draw two versions of your own circle: your waking hours as they currently are, and your waking hours as you wish them to be. Other students should then offer strategies for making the necessary life changes.

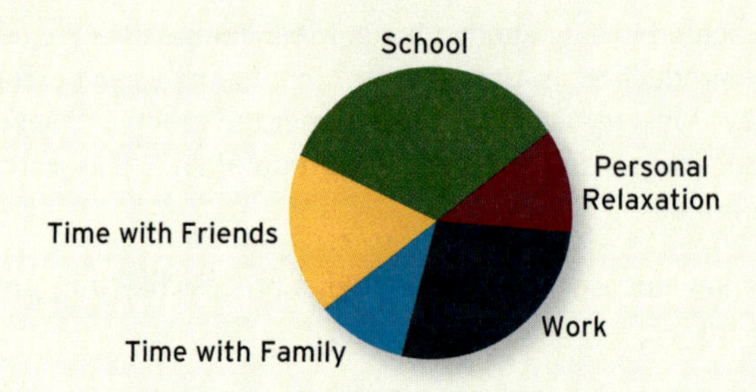

3. A third method of managing stress is improving *hardiness*—a sort of mental and physical health that can act as a buffer, preventing stress from resulting in strain. The table below lists a number of questions that can help diagnose your hardiness. Discuss your answers for each question, and then with the help of other students, brainstorm ways to increase that hardiness factor.

HARDINESS FACTOR	STRATEGIES FOR IMPROVING FACTOR
Relaxation: Do you spend enough time reading, listening to music, meditating, or pursuing your hobbies?	
Exercise: Do you spend enough time doing cardiovascular, strength, and flexibility sorts of exercises?	
Diet: Do you manage your diet adequately by eating healthily and avoiding foods high in fat?	

4. Class discussion (whether in groups or as a class) should centre on two issues. First, many of the stress-managing factors, especially in Steps 2 and 3, take up precious time. Does this make them an ineffective strategy for managing stress? Why or why not? Second, consider your Type A score in the OB Assessments below. If you are high on Type A, does that make these strategies more or less important?

OB ASSESSMENTS • TYPE A BEHAVIOUR PATTERN

Do you think that you are especially sensitive to stress? This assessment is designed to measure the extent to which you're a Type A person—someone who typically engages in hard-driving, competitive, and aggressive behaviour. Answer each question using the response scale provided. Then subtract your answers to the bold-faced questions from 8, with the difference being your new answers for those questions. For example, if your original answer for Question 3 was "2", your new answer is "6" (8 – 2). Then sum your answers for the 12 questions.

1 STRONGLY DISAGREE	2 DISAGREE	3 SLIGHTLY DISAGREE	4 NEUTRAL	5 SLIGHTLY AGREE	6 AGREE	7 STRONGLY AGREE

1. Having work to complete "stirs me into action" more than other people. ______
2. When a person is talking and takes too long to come to the point, I frequently feel like hurrying the person along. ______
3. **Nowadays, I consider myself to be relaxed and easygoing.** ______
4. Typically, I get irritated extremely easily. ______
5. My best friends would rate my general activity level as very high. ______
6. I definitely tend to do most things in a hurry. ______
7. I take my work much more seriously than most. ______
8. **I seldom get angry.** ______
9. I often set deadlines for myself work-wise. ______
10. I feel very impatient when I have to wait in line. ______
11. I put much more effort into my work than other people do. ______
12. **Compared with others, I approach life much less seriously.** ______

SCORING

If your scores sum up to 53 or above, you would be considered a Type A person, which means that you may perceive higher stress levels in your life and be more sensitive to that stress. If your scores sum up to 52 or below, you would be considered a Type B person. This means that you sense less stress in your life and are less sensitive to the stress that is experienced.

Source: C. D. Jenkins, S. J. Zyzanski, and R. H. Rosenman. "Progress Toward Validation of a Computer Scored Test for the Type A Coronary Prone Behaviour Pattern," *Psychosomatic Medicine,* 33, 193, 202 (1971). Reprinted with permission of Lippincott, Williams & Wilkins.

CONNECT——Available 24/7 with instant feedback so you can study when you want, how you want, and where you want. Take advantage of the Study Plan——an innovative tool that helps students customize their own learning experience. Students can diagnose their knowledge with pre- and post-tests, identify the areas where they need help, search contents of the entire learning package for content specific to the topic they're studying, and add these resources to their study plan. Visit **www.connectob.ca** to register——take practice quizzes, run interactive scenarios, and much more. Also visit the Student Online Learning Centre for additional study tools.

CHAPTER

6 Motivation

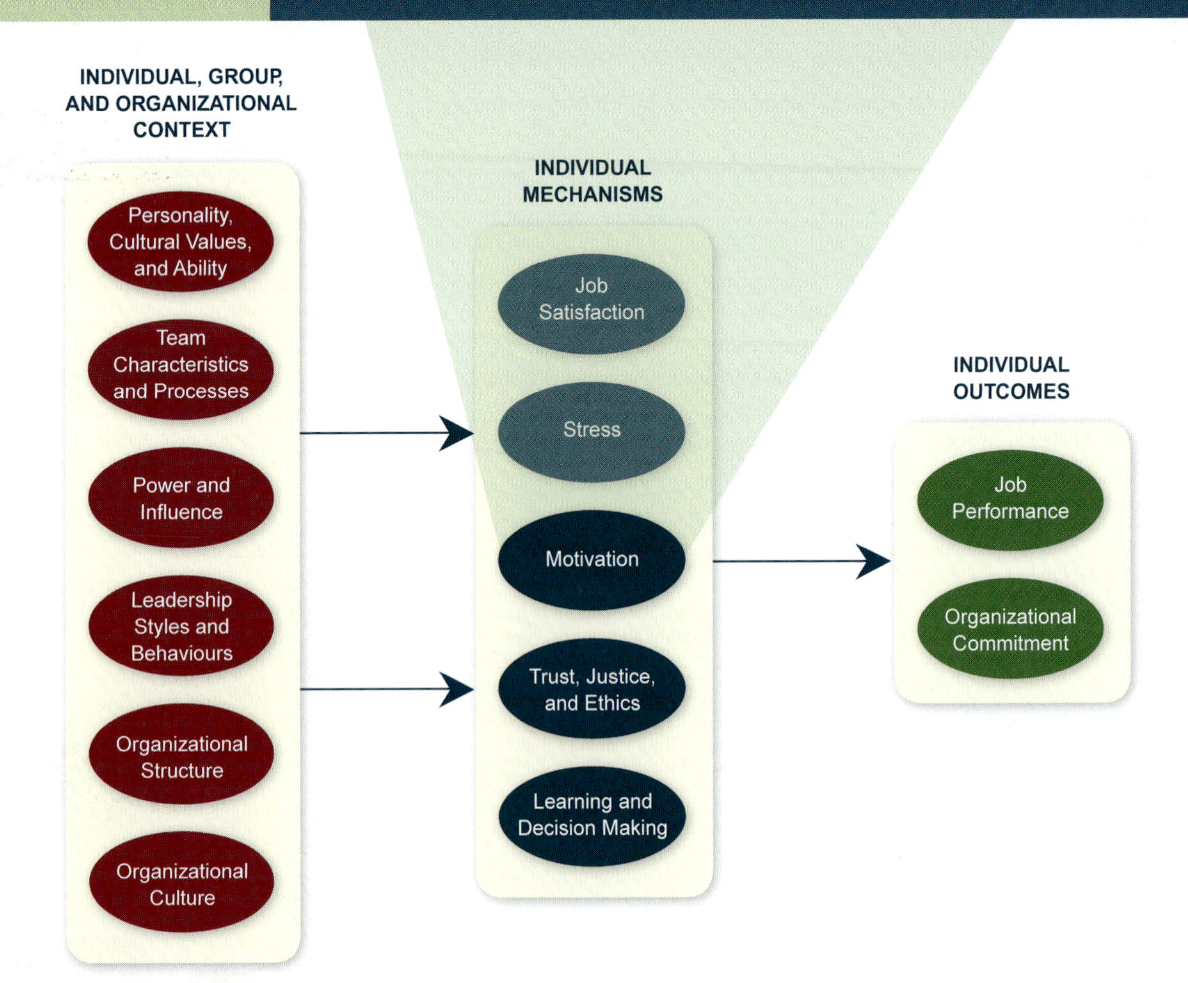

Learning Outcomes

After reading this chapter, you should be able to answer the following questions:

6.1 What is motivation?

6.2 What is expectancy theory, and what are the three beliefs that help determine how work effort is directed? What role do needs play?

6.3 What is goal setting theory? What two qualities make goals strong predictors of task performance? How and when do those effects occur?

6.4 What does it mean for rewards to be "equitable," and how are perceptions of equity determined? How do employees respond when they feel a sense of inequity?

6.5 What is psychological empowerment? What four beliefs help create a sense of empowerment among employees?

6.6 How does motivation affect job performance and organizational commitment?

6.7 What steps can organizations take to increase employee motivation?

BECAUSE OWNERS CARE

When WestJet first took to the sky 12 years ago, it was destined to play an important role in the Canadian airline industry. Founded in 1996 by a team of Calgary entrepreneurs headed by Clive Beddoe, WestJet began operations as a western Canadian regional carrier, with 200 employees and three aircraft servicing five cities.[1] Today, WestJet is Canada's leading high-value low-fare airline, offering scheduled service to 47 destinations in Canada, the United States, Mexico, and the Caribbean.[2] Discussions are currently underway with U.S.-based Southwest Airlines (an airline built on the same business model) to start a codeshare partnership that will greatly enhance each airline's capability to transport passengers anywhere in North America.[3] In 2007, the company reported revenues in excess of $2.1 billion, with net earnings coming in at a record $192.8 million.[4] In a year when many of its industry competitors faced difficulties, WestJet continued to perform well.

Since 2001, WestJet has spent over $2 billion upgrading its fleet to the more fuel-efficient Boeing next-generation 737-series aircraft. It now has 74 of these new aircraft in operation, giving WestJet one of the youngest and most fuel-efficient fleets in North America. Emissions from these aircraft are 30 percent lower on a per-person basis than the fleet of 200-series aircraft that the company replaced.[5] Other cost-saving innovations include the required navigation performance (RNP) approach technology to land aircraft. RNP utilizes global positioning system satellites to allow aircraft to fly more direct, precision approaches to airports. This in turn shortens flight time and miles flown, reducing fuel burn and emissions.[6] Why do cost savings matter so much? The answer is simple—*because owners care!* Who are these owners?

On September 26, 2005, WestJet launched the *Owners* campaign.[7] You may have heard this slogan on television: "Why do WestJetters care so much? Because we're also WestJet owners." Today, approximately 80 percent of WestJet's 6,700 employees allocate 12 percent of their base salary toward the purchase of company shares. Since the program

WestJet's "owners" program allows its employees to purchase stock and share in company profits.

began, "owners" have been rewarded with over $142 million in profit-sharing dollars. Not only has the reward system produced tangible results for employees, but it has also impacted how employees feel about their company. As one WestJetter put it, "The best sentiment we can convey to our guests is the pride we feel for our company. Our dedication is evident in the way we perform our jobs and the way we extend our renowned hospitality towards our guests."[8] WestJetters love being WestJetters, and their caring commitment to their guests and to each other has earned the company, as was featured in Chapter 1, a coveted *Most Admired Culture* award in 2005, 2006, and 2007.

MOTIVATION

6.1 What is motivation?

motivation A set of energetic forces that determine the direction, intensity, and persistence of an employee's work effort

Few OB topics matter more to employees and managers than motivation. How many times have you wondered to yourself, "Why can't I get myself going today?" Or how many times have you looked at a friend or co-worker and wondered, "Why are they working so slowly right now?" Both of these questions are asking about "motivation," which is a derivation of the Latin word for movement, *movere.*[9] Those Latin roots nicely capture the meaning of motivation, as motivated employees simply move faster and longer than unmotivated employees. More formally, **motivation** is defined as a set of energetic forces that originates both within and outside an employee, initiates work-related effort, and determines its direction, intensity, and persistence.[10] Motivation is a critical consideration because job performance is largely a function of two factors: motivation and ability (see Chapter 9 for more discussion of issues such as ability).[11]

The first part of the motivation definition illustrates that motivation is not one thing but rather a set of distinct forces. Some of those forces are internal to the employee, such as a sense of self-confidence, whereas others are external to the employee, such as the goals an employee is given. The next part of that definition illustrates that motivation determines a number of facets of an employee's work effort, as summarized in Figure 6-1, which depicts a scenario where your boss has given you an assignment to work on. Motivation determines *what* employees do at a given moment—the direction in which their effort is channelled. Every moment of the workday offers choices between task and citizenship sorts of actions or withdrawal and counterproductive sorts of actions. When it's 3:00 p.m. on a Thursday, do you keep working on the assignment your boss gave you, or do you launch Internet Explorer and start browsing for a while? Once the direction of effort has been decided, motivation goes on to determine *how hard* an employee works—the intensity of effort—and *for how long*—the persistence of effort. We all have friends or co-workers who work extremely hard for, say, 5 minutes. We also have friends or co-workers who work extremely long hours but always seem to be functioning at half-speed. Neither of those groups of people would be described as extremely motivated.

WHY ARE SOME EMPLOYEES MORE MOTIVATED THAN OTHERS?

There are a number of theories and concepts that attempt to explain why some employees are more motivated than others. The sections that follow review those theories and concepts in some detail. Most of them are relevant to each of the three motivation components described in Figure 6-1. However, some of them are uniquely suited to explaining the direction of effort, whereas others do a better job of explaining the intensity and persistence of effort.

FIGURE 6-1 Motivation and Effort

MOTIVATION DETERMINES THE . . .

DIRECTION of Effort:

What are you going to do right now?

The assignment your boss gave you yesterday?

Or are you going to send e-mails to your friends . . .

. . . or surf the Web for a while?

INTENSITY of Effort:

How hard are you going to work on it?

As hard as you can, or only at half-speed?

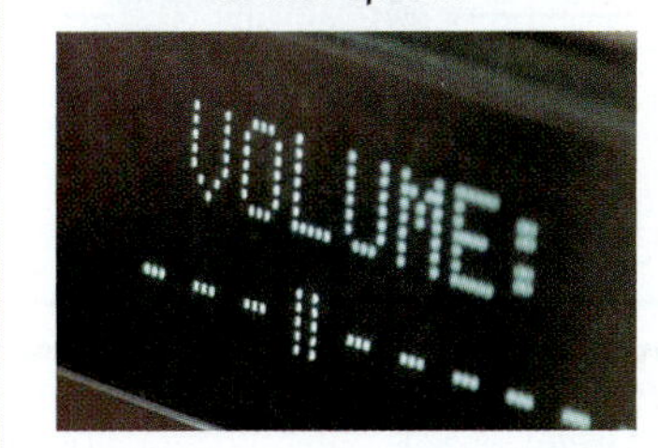

PERSISTENCE of Effort:

How long are you going to work on it?

For five hours or five minutes?

EXPECTANCY THEORY

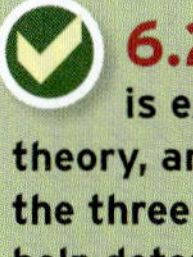

6.2 What is expectancy theory, and what are the three beliefs that help determine how work effort is directed? What role do needs play?

What makes you decide to direct your effort to work assignments rather than taking a break or wasting time? Or what makes you decide to be a "good citizen" by helping out a colleague or attending some optional company function? **Expectancy theory** describes the cognitive process that employees go through to make choices among different voluntary responses.[12] Drawing on earlier models from psychology, expectancy theory argues that employee behaviour is directed toward pleasure and away from pain or, more generally, toward certain outcomes and away from others.[13] How do employees make the choices that take them in the "right direction"? The theory suggests that our choices depend on three specific beliefs that are based in our past learning and experience: expectancy, instrumentality, and valence. These three beliefs are summarized in Figure 6-2, and we review each of them in turn.

expectancy theory A theory that describes the cognitive process employees go through to make choices among different voluntary responses

FIGURE 6-2 Expectancy Theory

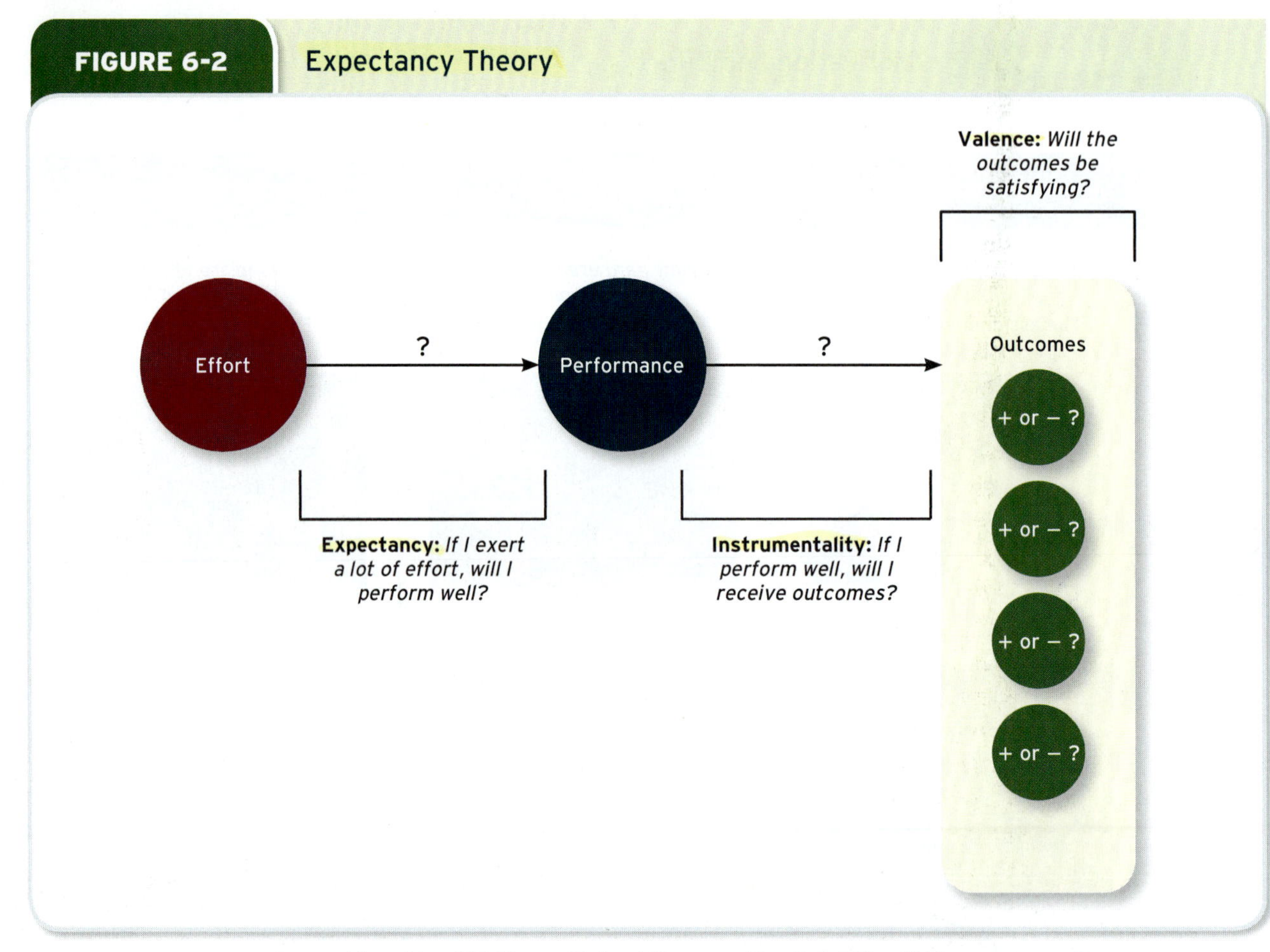

Source: Adapted from V.H. Vroom, *Work and Motivation* (New York: Wiley, 1964).

expectancy The belief that exerting a high level of effort will result in successful performance on some task

self-efficacy The belief that a person has the capabilities needed to perform the behaviours required on some task

past accomplishments The level of success or failure with similar job tasks in the past

EXPECTANCY **Expectancy** represents the belief that exerting a high level of effort will result in the successful performance of some task. More technically, expectancy is a subjective probability, ranging from 0 (no chance!) to 1 (a mortal lock!) that a specific amount of effort will result in a specific level of performance (abbreviated E → P). Think of a task at which you're not particularly good, such as writing romantic poetry. You may not be very motivated to write romantic poetry because you don't believe that your effort, no matter how hard you try, will result in a poem that "moves" your significant other. As another example, you'll be more motivated to work on the assignment described in Figure 6-1 if you're confident that trying hard will allow you to complete it successfully.

What factors shape our expectancy for a particular task? One of the most critical factors is **self-efficacy**, defined as the belief that a person has the capabilities needed to execute the behaviours required for task success.[14] Think of self-efficacy as a kind of self-confidence or a task-specific version of self-esteem.[15] Employees who feel more "efficacious" (that is, self-confident) for a particular task will tend to perceive higher levels of expectancy—and therefore be more likely to choose to exert high levels of effort. Why do some employees have higher self-efficacy for a given task than other employees? Figure 6-3 can help explain such differences.

When employees consider efficacy levels for a given task, they first consider their **past accomplishments**—the degree to which they have succeeded or failed in similar sorts of

FIGURE 6-3 Sources of Self-Efficacy

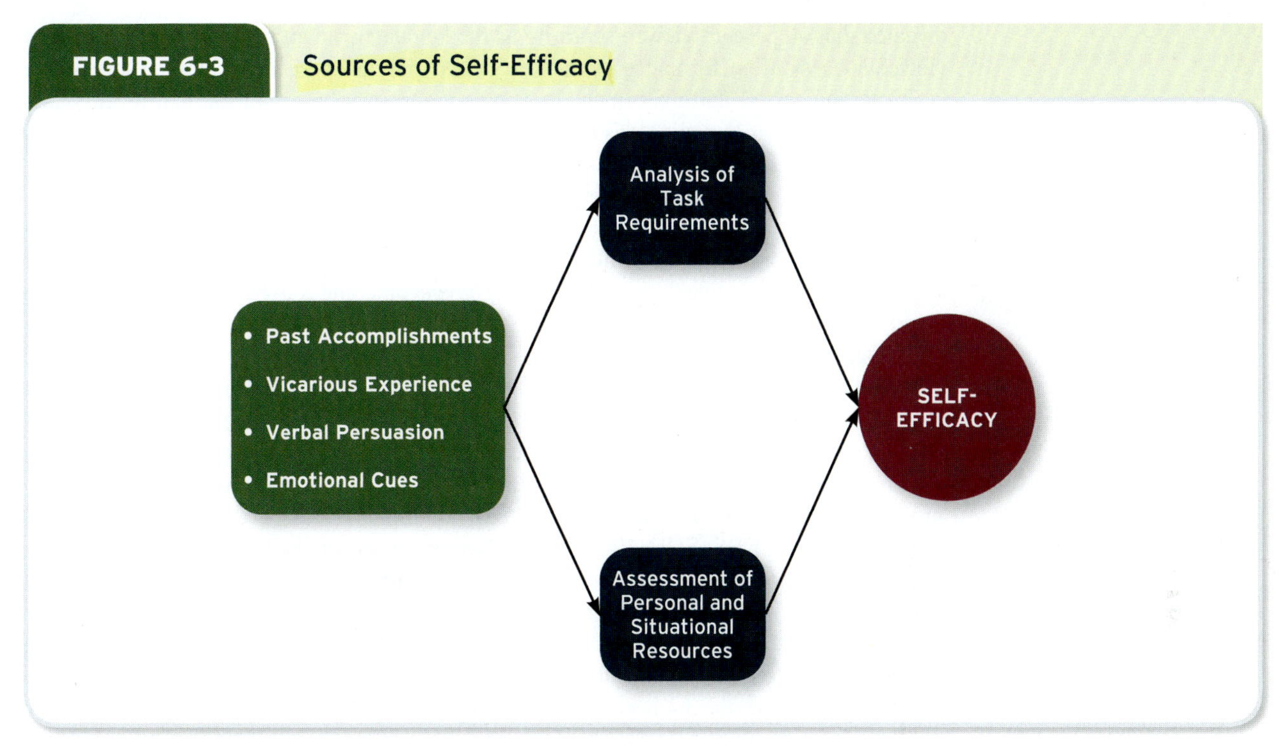

Source: Adapted from A. Bandura, "Self-Efficacy: Toward a Unifying Theory of Behavioral Change," *Psychological Review* 84 (1977), pp. 191–215; M.E. Gist and T.R. Mitchell, "Self-Efficacy: A Theoretical Analysis of its Determinants and Malleability," *Academy of Management Review* 17 (1992), pp. 183–211.

tasks in the past.[16] They also consider **vicarious experiences** by taking into account their observations and discussions with others who have performed such tasks.[17] Self-efficacy is also dictated by **verbal persuasion**, because friends, co-workers, and leaders can persuade employees that they can "get the job done." Finally, efficacy is dictated by **emotional cues**, in that feelings of fear or anxiety can create doubts about task accomplishment, whereas pride and enthusiasm can bolster confidence levels.[18] Taken together, these efficacy sources shape analyses of how difficult the task requirements are and how adequate an employee's personal and situational resources will prove to be.[19] They also explain the content of most "halftime speeches" offered by coaches during sporting events; such speeches commonly include references to past comebacks or victories (past accomplishments), pep talks about how good the team is (verbal persuasion), and cheers to rally the troops (emotional cues).

vicarious experiences Observations of and discussions with others who have performed some work task

verbal persuasion Pep talks that lead employees to believe that they can "get the job done"

emotional cues Positive or negative feelings that can help or hinder task accomplishment

INSTRUMENTALITY **Instrumentality** represents the belief that successful performance will result in some outcome(s).[20] More technically, instrumentality is a set of subjective probabilities, each ranging from 0 (no chance!) to 1 (a mortal lock!) that successful performance will bring a set of outcomes (abbreviated P → O). The term "instrumentality" makes sense when you consider the meaning of the adjective "instrumental." We say something is "instrumental" when it helps attain something else—for example, the proposed codeshare partnership with Southwest Airlines is instrumental for WestJet because it allows the company to quickly expand into the U.S. marketplace (and visa versa for Southwest Airlines into the Canadian marketplace). The "owners" program at WestJet creates a sense of instrumentality among employees, because it links the results of their efforts (e.g., providing a relaxing, enjoyable, low-cost travel experience for passengers) with a tangible outcome (profit-sharing dollars).

instrumentality The belief that successful performance will result in the attainment of some outcome(s)

Unfortunately, evidence indicates that many employees don't perceive high levels of instrumentality in their workplace. One survey of more than 10,000 employees in 2005 revealed that 60 percent viewed seniority as the key determinant of their pay.[21] Those that viewed successful performance as the key driver: only 35 percent. A similar survey one year later suggested that instrumentality perceptions vary by organizational level. When asked whether their last raise was based on their job performance, 46 percent of managers agreed, but only 29 percent of non-managers agreed.[22] Such low numbers reveal that some organizations consider factors other than performance when making pay decisions.

valence The anticipated value of the outcome(s) associated with successful performance

VALENCE **Valence** reflects the anticipated value of the outcomes associated with performance (abbreviated V).[23] Valences can be positive ("I would prefer *having* outcome X to not having it"), negative ("I would prefer *not having* outcome X to having it"), or zero ("I'm bored . . . are we still talking about outcome X?"). Salary increases, bonuses, and more informal rewards are typical examples of "positively valenced" outcomes, whereas disciplinary actions, demotions, and terminations are typical examples of "negatively valenced" outcomes.[24] In this way, employees are more motivated when successful performance helps them attain attractive outcomes, such as bonuses, while helping them avoid unattractive outcomes, such as termination. But what makes some outcomes more "positively valenced" that others? To answer this question we need to consider the role of human needs.

needs Groupings or clusters of outcomes viewed as having critical psychological or physiological consequences

ROLE OF NEEDS FOR VALENCE **Needs** can be defined as cognitive groupings or clusters of outcomes that are viewed as having critical psychological or physiological consequences.[25] In general, outcomes are deemed to be more attractive when they help to satisfy our needs. For instance, an employee with a strong growth need may find that an opportunity to take challenging training is more attractive than is an opportunity to socialize with co-workers. Note, however, that the higher positive valence associated with a "growth opportunity" outcome, in comparison to a "social opportunity" outcome, would likely be reversed if the employee's need for relatedness was stronger than her need for growth. Although scholars once suggested that certain needs are "universal" across people,[26] we now know that different people have different "need hierarchies" and that the *press* of these needs (for satisfaction) help them to evaluate potential outcomes. Table 6-1 describes many of the needs that are commonly studied in OB.[27] The terms and labels assigned to those needs often vary, so the table includes our labels as well as alternative labels that might sometimes be encountered.

Table 6-2 lists some of the most commonly considered outcomes in studies of motivation. Outcomes that are deemed particularly attractive are likely to satisfy a number of different needs. For example, praise can signal that interpersonal bonds are strong (satisfying relatedness needs) while also signalling competence (satisfying esteem needs). Note also that some of the outcomes in Table 6-2 result from other people acknowledging successful performance, whereas others are self-generated, originating in task performance itself. The former set creates **extrinsic motivation**—motivation that is controlled by some contingency that depends on task performance.[28] The latter set creates **intrinsic motivation**—motivation that is felt when task performance serves as its own reward.[29] Extrinsic and intrinsic motivation together represent an employee's "total motivation" level. For more about the distinction between intrinsic and extrinsic motivation, see our **OB on Screen** feature.

extrinsic motivation Desire to put forth work effort due to some contingency that depends on task performance

intrinsic motivation Desire to put forth work effort due to the sense that task performance serves as its own reward

You might wonder which of the outcomes in the table are most attractive to employees. That's a difficult question to answer, given that different employees emphasize different needs, but two things are clear. First, the attractiveness of outcomes varies across cultures. For example, good performance on a project in a North American company might earn a "spot award," such as an expensive watch or a trip to Las Vegas. However, a moped would likely be deemed more attractive in congested areas like India or China, and trips to alcohol- and gambling-intensive areas are taboo in parts of Asia or the Middle East.[30] Second, research suggests that employees underestimate how powerful a motivator pay is to them.[31] When employees rank the importance of outcomes like those in Table 6-2, they often put pay in fifth or sixth place. However, research studies show that financial incentives almost always have a stronger impact on motivation than other sorts of outcomes.[32]

TABLE 6-1 Commonly Studied Needs in OB

NEED LABEL	ALTERNATIVE LABELS	DESCRIPTION
Existence	Physiological, Safety	The need for the food, shelter, safety, and protection required for human existence
Relatedness	Love, Belongingness	The need to create and maintain lasting, positive, interpersonal relationships
Control	Autonomy, Responsibility	The need to be able to predict and control
Esteem	Self-regard, Growth	The need to hold a high evaluation of oneself and to feel effective and respected by others
Meaning	Self-actualization	The need to perform tasks that one cares about and that appeal to ideals and sense of purpose

Sources: Adapted from A.H. Maslow, "A Theory of Human Motivation," *Psychological Review* 50 (1943), pp. 370–96; C.P. Alderfer, "An Empirical Test of a New Theory of Human Needs," *Organizational Behavior and Human Performance* 4 (1969), pp. 142–75; E.L. Deci and R.M Ryan, "The 'What' and 'Why' of Goal Pursuits: Human Needs and the Self-Determination of Behavior," *Psychological Inquiry* 11 (2000), pp. 227–68; R. Cropanzano, Z.S. Byrne, D.R. Bobocel, and D.R. Rupp, "Moral Virtues, Fairness Heuristics, Social Entities, and Other Denizens of Organizational Justice," *Journal of Vocational Behavior* 58 (2001), pp. 164–209; K.D. Williams, "Social Ostracism," in *Aversive Interpersonal Behaviors,* ed. R.M. Kowalski (New York: Plenum Press, 1997), pp. 133–70.

Why can pay and bonuses be so motivational? One reason is that money, like many of the outcomes in Table 6-2, is relevant to multiple needs. For example, money can help satisfy existence needs by helping employees buy food, afford a house, and save for retirement. However, money also conveys a sense of esteem, as raises signal that employees are competent and well-regarded.[33] In fact, research suggests that people differ in how they view the **meaning of money**—the degree to which they view money as having symbolic, not just economic, value.[34] The symbolic value of money can be summarized in at least three dimensions: achievement (i.e., money symbolizes success), respect (i.e., money brings respect in one's community), and freedom (i.e., money provides opportunity).[35]

meaning of money The idea that money can have symbolic value (e.g., achievement, respect, freedom) in addition to economic value

Who is more likely to view money from these more symbolic perspectives? Some research suggests that men are more likely to view money as representing achievement, respect, and freedom than are women.[36] Research also suggests that employees with higher salaries are more likely to view money in achievement-related terms.[37] Younger employees are less likely to view money in a positive light, relative to older employees.[38] Differences in education do not appear to impact the meaning of money, however.[39] How do you view the meaning of money? See our **OB Assessments** feature at the end of this chapter to find out.

MOTIVATIONAL FORCE According to expectancy theory, the direction of effort is dictated by three beliefs: expectancy (E→P), instrumentality (P→O), and valence (V). More specifically, the theory suggests that the total "motivational force" to perform a given action can be described using the following formula:[40]

$$\text{Motivational Force} = \boxed{E \rightarrow P} \times \boxed{\Sigma[(P \rightarrow O) \times V]}$$

TABLE 6-2 Extrinsic and Intrinsic Outcomes

EXTRINSIC OUTCOMES	INTRINSIC OUTCOMES
Pay	Enjoyment
Bonuses	Interestingness
Promotions	Accomplishment
Benefits and perks	Knowledge gain
Spot awards	Skill development
Praise	Personal expression
Job security	(Lack of) Boredom
Support	(Lack of) Anxiety
Free time	(Lack of) Frustration
(Lack of) Disciplinary actions	
(Lack of) Demotions	
(Lack of) Terminations	

Sources: Adapted from E.E. Lawler III and J.L. Suttle, "Expectancy Theory and Job Behavior," *Organizational Behavior and Human Performance* 9 (1973), pp. 482–503; J. Galbraith and L.L. Cummings, "An Empirical Investigation of the Motivational Determinants of Task Performance: Interactive Effects Between Instrumentality–Valence and Motivation–Ability," *Organizational Behavior and Human Performance* 2 (1967), pp. 237–57; E. McAuley, S. Wraith, and T.E. Duncan, "Self-Efficacy, Perceptions of Success, and Intrinsic Motivation for Exercise," *Journal of Applied Social Psychology* 21 (1991), pp. 139–55; A.S. Waterman, S.J. Schwartz, E. Goldbacher, H. Green, C. Miller, and S. Philip, "Predicting the Subjective Experience of Intrinsic Motivation: The Roles of Self-Determination, the Balance of Challenges and Skills, and Self-Realization Values," *Personality and Social Psychology Bulletin* 29 (2003), pp. 1447–58.

The Σ symbol in the equation signifies that instrumentalities and valences are judged with various outcomes in mind, and motivation increases as successful performance is linked to more and more attractive outcomes. Note the significance of the multiplication signs in the formula: Motivational force equals zero if any one of the three beliefs is zero. In other words, it doesn't matter how confident you are if performance doesn't result in any outcomes. Similarly, it doesn't matter how well performance is evaluated and rewarded if you don't believe you can perform well.

GOAL SETTING THEORY

So, returning to the choice shown in Figure 6-1 (p. 133), let's say that you feel confident you can perform well on the assignment your boss gave you and that you also believe successful performance will bring valued outcomes. Now that you've chosen to direct your effort to that assignment, two critical questions remain: How hard will you work, and for how long? To shed some more light on these questions, you stop by your boss's office and ask her, "So, when exactly do you need this done?" After thinking about it for a while, she concludes, "Just do your best." After returning to your desk, you realize that you're still not sure how much to focus on the assignment, or how long you should work on it before turning to something else.

OB ON SCREEN

TALLADEGA NIGHTS: THE BALLAD OF RICKY BOBBY

It's because it's what you love, Ricky. It is who you were born to be. And here you sit. Thinking. Well, Ricky Bobby is not a thinker. Ricky Bobby is a driver. He is a doer, and that's what you need to do. You don't need to think . . . you need to drive. . . . When the fear rises up in your belly, you use it. And you know that fear is powerful, because it has been there for billions of years. And it is good. And you use it . . . and then you win, Ricky. You WIN! And you don't win for anybody else. You win for you. . . .

With those words, Susan (Amy Adams) tries to motivate Ricky Bobby (Will Ferrell) to return to the NASCAR circuit in *Talladega Nights* (Dir. Adam McKay, Sony Pictures, 2006). A few months earlier, no motivational speech would have been needed, as Ricky Bobby was one of the most successful drivers in all of NASCAR. At that point in his career, Ricky Bobby's motivation was based on winning and the extrinsic rewards that winning brought with it. He adopted his father's mantra: "If you ain't first, you're last!" He also opened every meal with a long list of the things he was thankful for—things that winning had brought him.

All that changed after a serious accident during a race. Ricky Bobby lost his self-efficacy in the weeks following the accident, then lost his sponsor, his house, and his wife. To add insult to injury, his dad admitted that the "If you ain't first, you're last!" philosophy had been nonsense all along. Lacking any motivation to return to NASCAR, Ricky Bobby settled for delivering pizza on a bicycle while waiting for his application to MTV's *The Real World* to be processed.

It took his former assistant, Susan, to awaken Ricky Bobby from his malaise. Her speech reminded him that he chose to become a driver in the first place for one reason and one reason only: He wanted to go fast. Driving a race car used to be intrinsically motivating for him, providing him with enjoyment and personal expression rather than the boredom that his current life possessed. Without giving away the ending, Susan's words inspired Ricky to return to NASCAR, armed with a deeper sense of intrinsic motivation for driving fast.

OB RESEARCH IN CANADA

Dr. Gary P. Latham, at the University of Toronto, is one of the world's leading experts in organizational behaviour, and probably best known for his groundbreaking work in employee motivation (goal setting theory and applications), behavioural (situational) interviewing, performance appraisal, and training. These days, Dr. Latham is actively studying ways of increasing organizational justice and organizational citizenship in the workplace. He is also working with his doctoral students on ways to help Aboriginal individuals develop career exploration, job search, and interview skills.

A native of Halifax, Dr. Latham earned a bachelor's degree at Dalhousie University and his master's and doctoral degrees, respectively, at Georgia Institute of Technology in Atlanta and the University of Akron in Ohio. He joined the University of Toronto faculty in 1990 after having served as a professor of management and organization at the University of Washington. In 1998, Dr. Latham received the Society for Industrial and Organizational Psychology's Distinguished Professional Contributions Award and in 2002 received its Distinguished Scientific Contributions Award—the only person to receive both awards. Dr. Latham is also a Fellow of the Canadian Psychological Association, the American Psychological Association, the Academy of Management, and the American Psychological Society. In 1997, he was made a Fellow of the Royal Society of Canada, and in 1999 and 2000, he was president of the Canadian Psychology Association. In 2008 and 2009, Dr. Latham served as president of the Society for Industrial and Organizational Psychology. In 2008, he received the Thomas A. Mahoney Mentoring Award from the Human Resources Division of the Academy of Management, and the Harry and Miriam Levinson Award for Exceptional Contribution to Consulting Organizational Psychology from the American Psychological Foundation.

In addition to writing 14 books/chapters, Dr. Latham has published over 120 articles in scientific journals. A sample of his most frequently cited works include:

"Goal Setting and Task Performance: 1969–1980," by E.A. Locke, L.M. Saari, K.N. Shaw, and G.P. Latham, published in *Psychological Bulletin* (1980, volume 90, pp. 125–52).

"Review of Research on Application of Goal Setting in Organizations," by G.P. Latham and G.A. Yukl, published in *Academy of Management Journal* (1975, volume 18, pp. 824–45).

"Building a Practically Useful Theory of Goal Setting and Task Motivation: A 35-Year Odyssey," by E.A. Locke and G.P. Latham, published in *American Psychologist* (2002, volume 57, pp. 705–17).

"The Situational Interview," by G.P. Latham, L.M. Saari, and E.D. Pursell, published in *Journal of Applied Psychology* (1980, volume 65, pp. 422–27).

"Training Managers to Minimize Rating Errors in Observation of Behavior," by G.P. Latham, K.N. Wexley, and E.D. Pursell, published in *Journal of Applied Psychology* (1975, volume 60, pp. 550–55).

"Keys to Motivating Tomorrow's Workforce," by G.P. Latham and C. Ernst, published in *Human Resource Management Review* (2006, volume 16, pp. 181–98).

"The Effect of Training in Verbal Self-Guidance on the Self-Efficacy and Performance of Native North Americans in the Selection Interview," by G.P. Latham and M.H. Budworth, published in *Journal of Vocational Behavior* (2006, volume 68, pp. 516–23).

Goal setting theory views goals as the primary drivers of the intensity and persistence of effort.[41] Goals are defined as the objective or aim of an action and typically refer to attaining a specific standard of proficiency, often within a specified time limit.[42] More specifically, the theory argues that assigning employees **specific and difficult goals** will result in higher levels of performance than assigning no goals, easy goals, or "do-your-best" goals.[43] Why are specific and difficult goals more effective than do-your-best ones? After all, doesn't "your best" imply the highest possible levels of effort? The reason is that few people know what their "best" is (and even fewer managers can tell whether employees are truly doing their "best"). Assigning specific and difficult goals gives people a number to shoot for—a "measuring stick" that can be used to tell them how hard they need to work and for how long. So if your boss had said, "Have the assignment on my desk by 10:30 a.m. on Tuesday, with no more than two mistakes," you would have known exactly how hard to work and for how long.

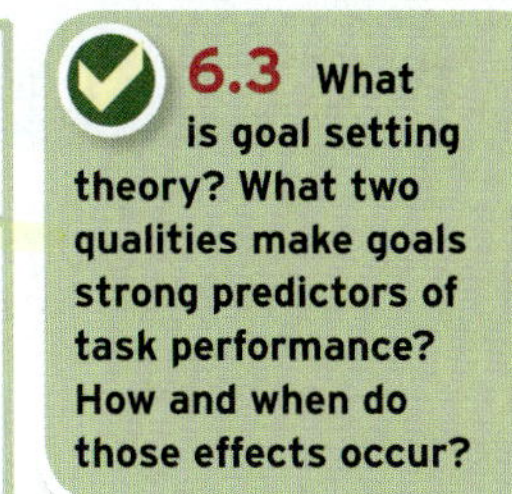

goal setting theory A theory that views goals as the primary drivers of the intensity and persistence of effort

specific and difficult goals Goals that stretch an employee to perform at his or her maximum level while still staying within the boundaries of his or her ability

Of course, a key question then becomes, "What's a difficult goal?" Figure 6-4 illustrates the predicted relationship between goal difficulty and task performance. When goals are easy, there's no reason to work your hardest or your longest, so task effort is lower. As goals move from moderate to difficult, the intensity and persistence of effort become maximized. At some point, however, the limits of a person's ability get reached, and self-efficacy begins to diminish. At that point, goals move from difficult to impossible, and employees feel somewhat helpless when attempting to achieve them. At that point, effort and performance inevitably decline. So a difficult goal is one that stretches an employee to perform at his or her maximum level while still staying within the boundaries of his or her ability.

Why exactly do specific and difficult goals have such positive effects? Figure 6-5 presents goal setting theory in more detail to understand that question better.[44] First, the assignment of a specific and difficult goal shapes people's own **self-set goals**—the internalized goals that people use to monitor their own task progress.[45] By assigning goals for employees, you

self-set goals The internalized goals that people use to monitor their own progress

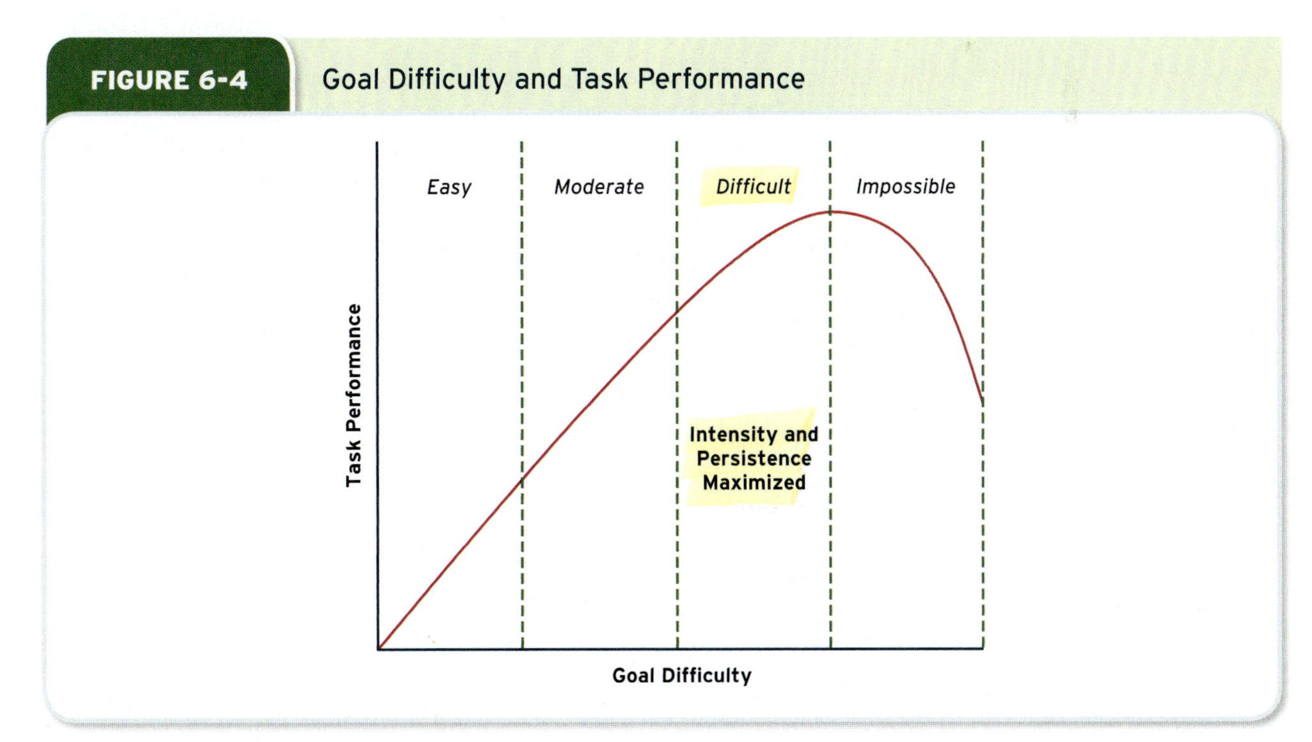

Source: Adapted from E.A. Locke and G.P. Latham, *A Theory of Goal Setting and Task Performance* (Englewood Cliffs, NJ: Prentice Hall, 1990).

FIGURE 6-5 Goal Setting Theory

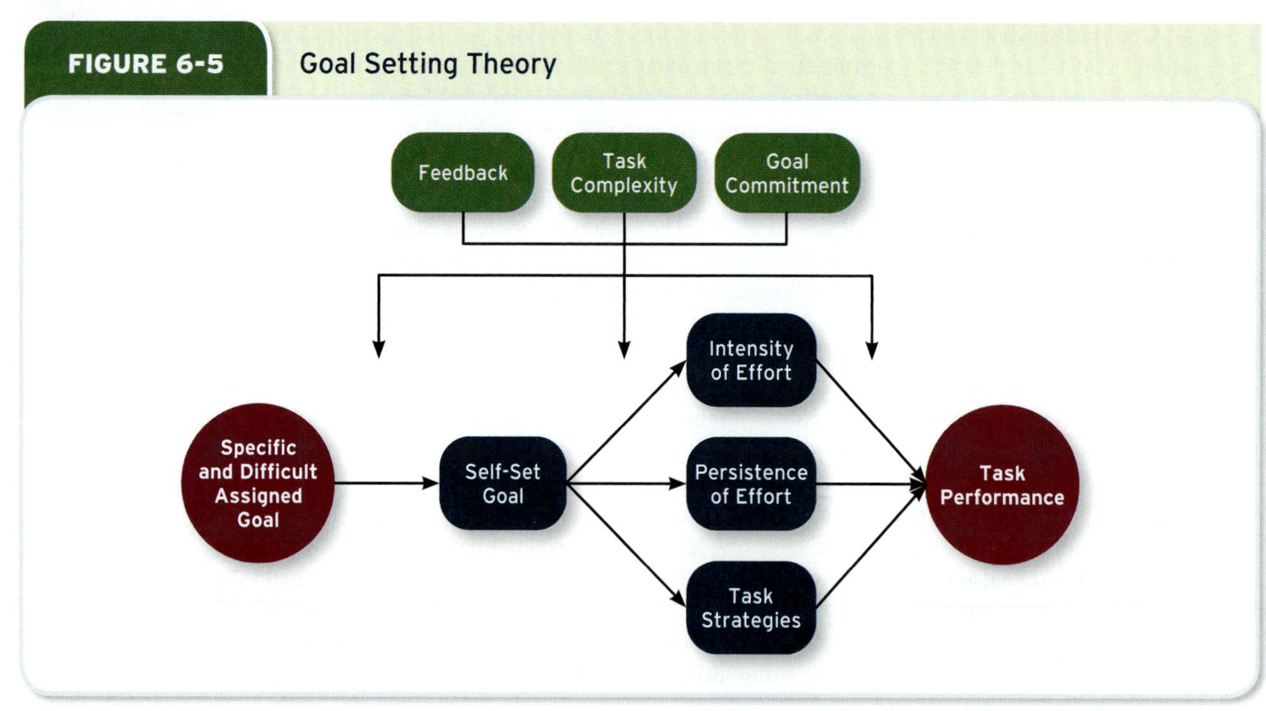

Sources: Adapted from E.A. Locke and G.P. Latham, *A Theory of Goal Setting and Task Performance* (Englewood Cliffs, NJ: Prentice Hall, 1990); E.A. Locke and G.P. Latham, "Building a Practically Useful Theory of Goal Setting and Task Motivation: A 35-Year Odyssey," *American Psychologist* 57 (2002), pp. 705–17; G.P. Latham, "Motivate Employee Performance through Goal-Setting," in *Blackwell Handbook of Principles of Organizational Behavior,* ed. E.A. Locke (Malden, MA: Blackwell, 2000), pp. 107–19.

are, in effect, shaping their personal goals or intentions (assuming that employees accept and are committed to the assigned goals). In the absence of an assigned goal, employees may not even consider what their own goals are, or they may self-set relatively easy goals that they are certain to meet. As a self-set goal becomes more difficult, the intensity of effort increases, and the persistence of effort gets extended. However, these goals have another effect; they trigger the creation of **task strategies**, defined as learning plans and problem-solving approaches used to achieve successful performance.[46] In the absence of a goal, it's easy to rely on trial-and-error to figure out how best to do a task. Under the pressure of a measuring stick, however, it becomes more effective to plan out the next move.

task strategies Learning plans and problem-solving approaches used to achieve successful performance

Figure 6-5 also includes three variables that specify when assigned goals will have stronger or weaker effects on task performance. In the jargon of theory diagrams, these variables are called "moderators." Rather than directly affecting other variables in the diagram, moderators affect the strength of the relationships between variables. One moderator is **feedback**, which consists of updates on employee progress toward goal attainment.[47] Imagine being challenged to beat a friend's score on the *Halo 3* video game but then not being told what exactly your score was as you were playing. How would you know how hard to try? Another moderator is **task complexity**, which reflects how complicated the information and actions involved in a task are, as well as how much the task changes.[48] In general, the effects of specific and difficult goals are almost twice as strong on simple tasks as on complex tasks, though the effects of goals remain beneficial even in complex cases.[49]

feedback In goal setting theory, it refers to progress updates on work goals

task complexity The degree to which the information and actions needed to complete a task are complicated

The final moderator shown in Figure 6-5 is **goal commitment**, defined as the degree to which a person accepts or internalizes an assigned goal (as a personal goal) and is determined to try to reach it.[50] When goal commitment is high, assigning specific and difficult goals to

goal commitment The degree to which a person accepts a goal and is determined to reach it

TABLE 6-3 Strategies for Fostering Goal Commitment

STRATEGY	DESCRIPTION
Rewards	Tie goal achievement to the receipt of monetary or non-monetary rewards.
Publicity	Publicize the goal to significant others and co-workers to create some social pressure to attain it.
Support	Provide supportive supervision to aid employees if they struggle to attain the goal.
Participation	Collaborate on setting the specific proficiency level and due date for a goal so that the employee feels a sense of ownership over the goal.
Resources	Provide the resources needed to attain the goal and remove any constraints that could hold back task efforts.

Sources: Adapted from J.R. Hollenbeck and H.J. Klein, "Goal Commitment and the Goal-Setting Process: Problems, Prospects, and Proposals for Future Research," *Journal of Applied Psychology* 72 (1987), pp. 212–20; H.J. Klein, M.J. Wesson, J.R. Hollenbeck, and B.J. Alge, "Goal Commitment and the Goal-Setting Process: Conceptual Clarification and Empirical Synthesis," *Journal of Applied Psychology* 84 (1999), pp. 885–96; E.A. Locke, G.P. Latham, and M. Erez, "the Determinants of Goal Commitment," *Academy of Management Review* 13 (1988), pp. 23–29; G.P. Latham, "the Motivational Benefits of Goal-Setting," *Academy of Management Executive* 18 (2004), pp. 126–29.

employees will have significant benefits for task performance. However, when goal commitment is low, those effects become much weaker.[51] The importance of goal commitment raises the question of how best to foster commitment when assigning goals to employees. Table 6-3 summarizes some of the most powerful strategies for fostering goal commitment, which range from rewards to supervisory support to employee participation.[52]

Microsoft recently revised its use of goal setting principles in an effort to boost goal commitment and task performance.[53] The company had become concerned that employees viewed their goals as objectives they *hoped* to meet rather than objectives they were *committed* to meeting. Moreover, approximately 25 percent to 40 percent of employees were working under goals that were either not specific enough or not measurable enough to offer feedback. To combat these trends, managers are now trained to identify five to seven **S.M.A.R.T. goals** for each employee (S.M.A.R.T. stands for Specific, Measurable, Achievable, Results-based, and Time-sensitive), with rewards directly linked to goal achievement. Managers and employees participate jointly in the goal setting process, and managers offer support by suggesting task strategies that employees can use to achieve the goals. In this way, managers and employees come to understand the "how" of achievement, not just the "what."[54] For insights into how goal setting operates across cultures, see our **OB Internationally** feature.

S.M.A.R.T. goals Acronym that stands for Specific, Measurable, Achievable, Results-based, Time-sensitive goals

EQUITY THEORY

6.4 What does it mean for rewards to be "equitable," and how are perceptions of equity determined? How do employees respond when they feel a sense of inequity?

Returning to our running example in Figure 6-1 (p. 133), imagine that at this point, you've decided to work on the assignment your boss gave you, and you've been told that it is due by Tuesday at 10:30 a.m. and cannot have any more than two mistakes in it. That's a specific and difficult goal, so Internet Explorer hasn't been launched in a while, and you haven't even thought about checking your e-mail. In short, you've been working very hard for a few hours, until the guy from across the hall pops his head in. You tell him what

OB INTERNATIONALLY

Research in cross-cultural OB suggests that there are some "universals" when it comes to motivation. For example, interesting work, pay, achievement, and growth are billed as motivating forces whose importance does not vary across cultures.[55] Of course, some motivation principles do vary in their effectiveness across cultures, including some of the strategies for fostering goal commitment.

Types of Goals. Should goals be given on an individual or a groupwide basis? North American employees usually prefer to be given individual goals. In contrast, employees in other countries, including China and Japan, prefer to receive team goals.[56] This difference likely reflects the stronger emphasis on collective responsibility and cooperation in those cultures.

Rewards. Rewards tend to increase goal commitment across cultures, but cultures vary in the types of rewards that they value. North American employees prefer to have rewards allocated according to merit. In contrast, employees in other countries, including China, Japan, and Sweden, prefer that rewards be allocated equally across members of the work unit.[57] Employees in India prefer a third allocation strategy—doling out rewards according to need. These cultural differences show that nations differ in how they prioritize individual achievement, collective solidarity, and the welfare of others.

Participation. National culture also affects the importance of participation in setting goals. Research suggests that employees in North America are likely to accept assigned goals because the culture emphasizes hierarchical authority. In contrast, employees in Israel, which lacks a cultural emphasis on hierarchy, do not respond as well to assigned goals.[58] Instead, employees in Israel place a premium on participation in goal setting.

Feedback. Culture also influences how individuals respond when they receive feedback regarding goal progress. As with participation, research suggests that employees in North America are more likely to accept feedback because they are comfortable with hierarchical authority relationships and have a strong desire to reduce uncertainty.[59] Other cultures, like England, place less value on reducing uncertainty, making feedback less critical to them.

you're working on, and he nods sympathetically, saying, "Yeah, the boss gave me a similar assignment that sounds just as tough. I think she realized how tough it was though, because she said I could use the company's playoff tickets if I finish it on time." Playoff tickets? Playoff tickets?? Looks like it's time to check that e-mail after all. . . .

equity theory A theory that suggests that employees create a mental ledger of the outcomes they receive for their job inputs, relative to some comparison other

Unlike the first two theories, **equity theory** acknowledges that motivation doesn't just depend on your own beliefs and circumstances but also on what happens to *other people*.[60] More specifically, equity theory suggests that employees create a "mental ledger" of the outcomes (or rewards) they get from their job duties.[61] What outcomes might be part of your mental ledger? That's completely up to you and depends on what you find valuable, though Table 6-4 provides a listing of some commonly considered outcomes. Equity theory further suggests that employees create a mental ledger of the inputs (or contributions and investments) they put into their job duties.[62] Again, the composition of your mental ledger is completely specific to you, but Table 6-4 provides a listing of some inputs that seem to matter to most employees.

TABLE 6-4 Some Outcomes and Inputs Considered by Equity Theory

OUTCOMES	INPUTS
Pay	Effort
Seniority benefits	Performance
Fringe benefits	Skills and abilities
Status symbols	Education
Satisfying supervision	Experience
Workplace perks	Training
Intrinsic rewards	Seniority

Sources: Adapted from J.S. Adams, "Inequity in Social Exchange," in *Advances in Experimental Social Psychology,* Vol. 2, ed. L. Berkowitz (New York: Academic Press, 1965), pp. 267–99.

So what exactly do you do with these mental tallies of outcomes and inputs? Equity theory argues that you compare your ratio of outcomes and inputs to the ratio of some **comparison other**—some person who seems to provide an intuitive frame of reference for judging equity.[63] There are three general possibilities that can result from this "cognitive calculus," as shown in Figure 6-6. The first possibility is that the ratio of outcomes to inputs is balanced between you and your comparison other. In this case, you feel a sense of equity, and you're likely to maintain the intensity and persistence of your effort. This situation would have occurred if you have been offered playoff tickets, just like your colleague.

comparison other Another person who provides a frame of reference for judging equity

The second possibility is that your ratio of outcomes to inputs is less than your comparison other's ratio. According to equity theory, any imbalance in ratios triggers **equity distress**—an internal tension that can only be alleviated by restoring balance to the ratios.[64] In the case of **underreward inequity** your ratio of outcomes to inputs is lower than your comparison other's ratio. Here, the equity distress likely takes the form of negative emotions such as anger or envy. One way to stop feeling those emotions is to try to restore the balance in some way; Figure 6-6 reveals two methods for doing so. You could be constructive and proactive by talking to your boss and explaining why you deserve better outcomes. Such actions would result in the growth of your outcomes, restoring balance to the ratio. Of course, anger often results in actions that are destructive rather than constructive, and research shows that feelings of underreward inequity are among the strongest predictors of counterproductive behaviours, such as employee theft (see Chapter 7 on trust, justice, and ethics for more about this issue).[65] More relevant to this chapter, another means of restoring balance is to shrink your inputs by lowering the intensity and persistence of effort. Remember, it's not the total outcomes or inputs that matter in equity theory—it's only the ratio.

equity distress An internal tension that results from being overrewarded or underrewarded relative to some comparison other

underreward inequity The ratio of outcomes to inputs is lower than some comparison other's ratio

The third possibility is **overreward inequity** where your ratio of outcomes to inputs is greater than your comparison other's ratio. Equity distress again gets experienced, and the tension likely creates negative emotions such as guilt or anxiety. Balance could be restored by shrinking your outcomes (taking less money, giving something back to the comparison other), but the theory acknowledges that such actions are unlikely in most cases.[66] Instead, the more likely solution is to increase your inputs in some way. You could increase the intensity and persistence of your task effort or decide to engage in more "extra mile" citizenship behaviours. At some point though, there may not be enough hours in the

overreward inequity The ratio of outcomes to inputs is greater than some comparison other's ratio

FIGURE 6-6 Three Possible Outcomes of Equity Theory Comparisons

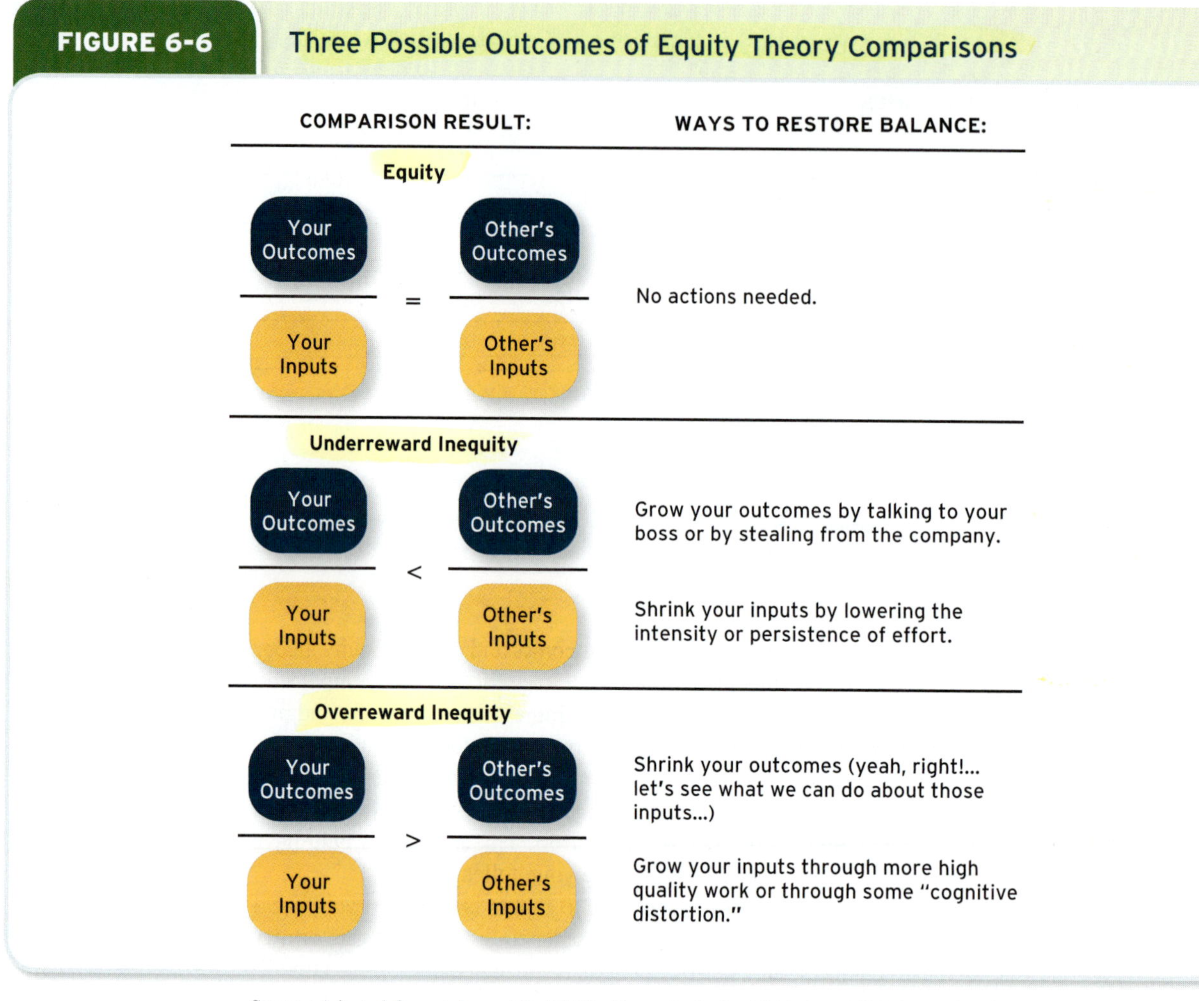

Source: Adapted from Adams, J.S. (1965). "Inequity in Social Exchange." In L. Berkowitz (Ed.), *Advances in Experimental Social Psychology* (Vol. 2, pp. 267–299). New York: Academic Press.

cognitive distortion A re-evaluation of the inputs an employee brings to a job, often occurring in response to equity distress

internal comparisons Comparing oneself to someone in your same company

external comparisons Comparing oneself to someone in a different company

day to increase your inputs any further. An alternative (and less labour-intensive) means of increasing your inputs is to simply rethink them—to re-examine your mental ledger to see if you may have "undersold" your true contributions. On second thought, maybe your education or seniority is more critical than you realized, or maybe your skills and abilities are more vital to the organization. This **cognitive distortion** allows you to restore balance mentally, without altering your behaviour in any way.

There is one other way of restoring balance, regardless of underreward or overreward circumstances, that is not depicted in Figure 6-6: Change your comparison other. After all, we compare our "lots in life" to a variety of other individuals. Table 6-5 summarizes the different kinds of comparison others that can be used.[67] Some of those comparisons are **internal comparisons**, meaning they are made using someone in the same company.[68] Others are **external comparisons**, meaning that they are made using someone in a different company. If a given comparison results in high levels of anger and envy or high levels of guilt and anxiety, the frame of reference may be shifted. In fact, research suggests that employees don't just compare themselves to one other person; instead, they make multiple comparisons to a variety of different others.[69] Although it may be possible to create a sort

TABLE 6-5 Judging Equity with Different Comparison Others

COMPARISON TYPE	DESCRIPTION AND SAMPLE SURVEY ITEM
Job Equity	Compare with others doing the same job in the same organization. Sample survey item: *Compared with others doing the same job as me in my company with similar education, seniority, and effort, I earn about:*
Company Equity	Compare with others in the same organization doing substantially different jobs. Sample survey item: *Compared with others in my company on other jobs doing work that is similar in responsibility, skill, effort, education, and working condition required, I earn about:*
Occupational Equity	Compare with others doing essentially the same job in other organizations. Sample survey item: *Compared with others doing my job in other companies in the area with similar education, seniority, and effort, I earn about:*
Educational Equity	Compare with others who have attained the same education level. Sample survey item: *Compared with people I know with similar education and responsibility as me, I earn about:*
Age Equity	Compare with others of the same age. Sample survey item: *Compared with those of my age, I earn about:*

40% less	30% less	20% less	10% less	About the same	10% more	20% more	30% more	40% more

Source: R.W. Scholl, E.A. Cooper, and J.F. McKenna, "Referent Selection in Determining Equity Perceptions: Differential Effects on Behavioral and Attitudinal Outcomes," *Personnel Psychology* 40 (1987), pp. 113–24. Reprinted with permission of Blackwell Publishing.

of "overall equity" judgment, research shows that people draw distinctions between the various equity comparisons shown in the table. For example, one study shows that job equity is the most powerful driver of citizenship behaviours, whereas occupational equity is the most powerful driver of employee withdrawal.[70]

These mechanisms make it clear that judging equity is a very subjective process. Recent data from a Salary.com report highlight that very subjectivity. A survey of 1,500 employees revealed that 65 percent of the respondents planned to look for a new job in the next three months, with 57 percent doing so because they felt underpaid. However, Salary.com estimated that only 19 percent of those workers really were underpaid, taking into account their relevant inputs and the current market conditions. In fact, it was estimated that 17 percent were actually being overpaid by their companies! On the one hand, that subjectivity is likely to be frustrating to most managers in charge of compensation. On the other hand, it is important to realize that the intensity and persistence of employees' effort is driven by their own equity perceptions, not anyone else's.

OB FOR STUDENTS

Grades are one of the primary motivators for students, as more effort is needed to earn As than Cs in most classes. Think about your own motivation levels as a student—how much of that motivation is due to trying for a higher grade?

Now here's the question we want you to consider: What would happen to your motivation to learn if your grades *became secret,* or more specifically, if your school adopted a policy that prohibited you or your university from disclosing grades to recruiters? The rationale for grade secrecy policies is twofold. First, grade secrecy is believed to reduce competitiveness between students, fostering a more cohesive atmosphere within student cohorts. Second, grade secrecy is meant to allow students to take tougher, more challenging electives without worrying about their GPA.

So what would happen to your motivation levels if grade secrecy was instituted at your school? The more salient norm of secrecy might discourage you from sharing grades with your classmates, making it more difficult to judge the equity of your grades relative to those received by other students. Grade secrecy might also reduce the valence of the grades themselves, with an A losing some of its anticipated value relative to a B or C. If those effects occurred, then motivation to learn would decline under a grade secrecy system.

Which side would you take in this debate?

Some organizations grapple with concerns about equity by emphasizing pay secrecy. One survey indicated that 36 percent of companies explicitly discourage employees from discussing pay with their colleagues, and surveys also indicate that most employees approve of pay secrecy.[71] Is pay secrecy a good idea? Although it has not been the subject of much research, there appear to be pluses and minuses associated with pay secrecy. On the plus side, such policies may reduce conflict between employees while appealing to concerns about personal privacy. On the minus side, employees may respond to a lack of accurate information by guessing at equity levels, possibly perceiving more underpayment inequity than truly exists. In addition, the insistence on secrecy might cause employees to view the company with a sense of distrust (see Chapter 7 on trust, justice, and ethics for more about this issue).[72] How might these sorts of secrecy policies affect you as a student? See our **OB for Students** feature for a discussion of grade secrecy.

PSYCHOLOGICAL EMPOWERMENT

psychological empowerment An energy rooted in the belief that tasks are contributing to some larger purpose

6.5 What is psychological empowerment? What four beliefs help create a sense of empowerment among employees?

Now we return, for one last time, to our running example in Figure 6-1 (p. 133). When last we checked in, your motivation levels had suffered because you learned your co-worker was offered the company's playoff tickets for successfully completing a similar assignment. As you browse the Web in total "time-wasting mode," you begin thinking about all the reasons you hate working on this assignment. Even aside from the issue of goals and rewards, you keep coming back to this issue: You would never have taken on this project *by choice.* More specifically, the project itself doesn't seem very meaningful, and you doubt that it will have any real impact on the functioning of the organization.

Those sentiments signal a low level of **psychological empowerment**, which reflects an energy rooted in the belief that work tasks contribute to some larger purpose.[73] Psychological empowerment represents a form of intrinsic motivation, in that merely performing the work tasks serves as its own reward and supplies many of the intrinsic outcomes shown in Table 6-2 (p. 138). The concept of psychological empowerment has much in common with our discussion of "satisfaction with the work itself" in Chapter 4 on job satisfaction. That discussion illustrated that jobs with high levels of variety, significance, and autonomy can be intrinsically satisfying.[74] Models of psychological empowerment argue that a similar set of concepts can make work tasks intrinsically motivating. Four concepts are particularly important: meaningfulness, self-determination, competence, and impact.

meaningfulness A psychological state reflecting one's feelings about work tasks, goals, and purposes, and the degree to which they contribute to society and fulfill one's ideals and passions

Meaningfulness captures the value of a work goal or purpose, relative to a person's own ideals and passions.[75] When a task is relevant to a meaningful purpose, it becomes easier to concentrate on the task and get excited about it. You might even find yourself cutting other tasks short so that you can devote more time to the meaningful one or thinking about the task outside of work hours.[76] In contrast, working on tasks that are not meaningful brings with it a sense of emptiness and detachment. As a result, you might need to mentally force yourself to keep working on the task. Managers can instill a sense of meaningfulness by articulating an exciting vision or purpose and fostering a non-cynical climate in which employees are free to express idealism and passion without criticism.[77] For their part, employees can build their own sense of meaningfulness by identifying and clarifying their own passions. What exactly makes them excited and fulfilled at work, and how can they seek out more opportunities to feel that way?

self-determination A sense of choice in the initiation and continuation of work tasks

Self-determination reflects a sense of choice in the initiation and continuation of work tasks. Employees with high levels of self-determination can choose what tasks to work on, how to structure those tasks, and how long to pursue those tasks. That sense of self-determination is a strong driver of intrinsic motivation, because it allows employees to pursue activities that they themselves find meaningful and interesting.[78] Managers can instill a sense of self-determination in their employees by delegating work tasks, rather than micromanaging them, and by trusting employees to come up with their own approach to certain tasks.[79] For their part, employees can gain more self-determination by earning the trust of their bosses and negotiating for the latitude that comes with that increased trust.

"Really, I'm fine. It was just a fleeting sense of purpose—I'm sure it will pass."

Source: © The New Yorker Collection 2000 Tom Cheney from cartoonbank.com.

Competence captures a person's belief in his or her capability to perform work tasks successfully.[80] Competence is identical to the self-efficacy concept reviewed previously in this chapter; employees with a strong sense of competence (or self-efficacy) believe they can execute the particular behaviours needed to achieve success at work. Competence brings with it a sense of pride and mastery that is itself intrinsically motivating. Managers can instill a sense of competence in their employees by providing opportunities for training and knowledge gain, expressing positive feedback, and providing challenges that are an appropriate match for employees' skill levels.[81] Employees can build their own competence by engaging in self-directed learning, seeking out feedback from their managers, and managing their own workloads.

competence The capability to perform work tasks successfully

Impact reflects the sense that a person's actions "make a difference"—that progress is being made toward fulfilling some important purpose.[82] Phrases such as "moving forward," "being on track," and "getting there" convey a sense of impact.[83] The polar opposite of impact is "learned helplessness"—the sense that it doesn't matter what a person does, nothing will make a difference. Here, phrases such as "stuck in a rut," "at a standstill," or "going nowhere" become more relevant. Managers can instill a sense of impact by celebrating milestones along the journey to task accomplishment, particularly for tasks that span a long

impact The sense that a person's actions "make a difference"—that progress is being made toward fulfilling some important purpose

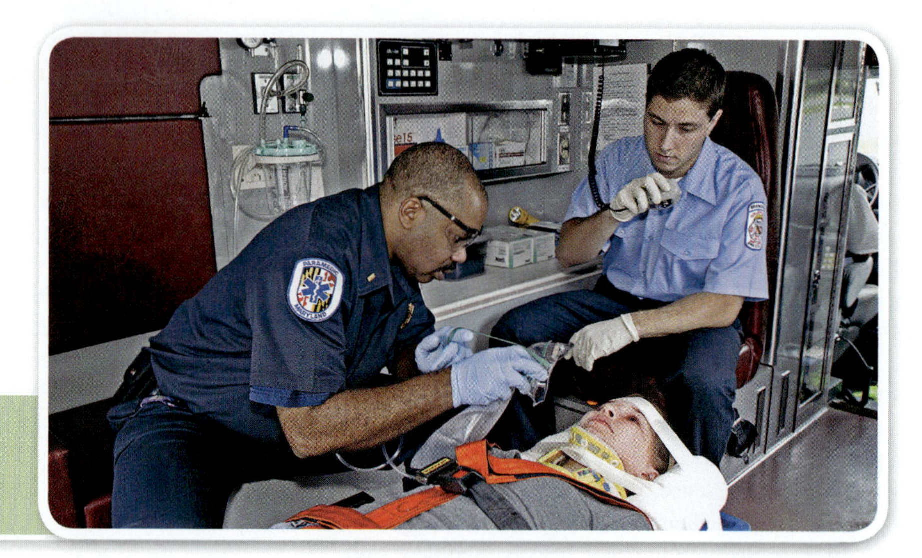

The belief that your work makes a difference, or has impact, is psychologically empowering.

time frame.[84] Employees can attain a deeper sense of impact by building the collaborative relationships needed to speed task progress and initiating their own celebrations of "small wins" along the way.

In summary, psychologically empowered employees believe their work has a meaningful purpose, that they have chosen to pursue that purpose in the way they see fit, that they are capable of succeeding in their work tasks, and that they are making progress toward achieving their work goals. Many of WestJet's initiatives could serve as a "how-to guide" for creating psychological empowerment. WestJet's supportive, close-knit culture allows employees to express their passion and ideals, and the perception of ownership and increased decision-making discretion instills a sense of self-determination and impact among all employees.

SO WHY ARE SOME EMPLOYEES MORE MOTIVATED THAN OTHERS?

As shown in Figure 6-7, answering that question requires considering all the energetic forces that initiate work-related effort, including expectancy theory concepts (expectancy, instrumentality, valence), the existence (or absence) of specific and difficult goals, perceptions of equity, and feelings of psychological empowerment. Unmotivated employees may simply lack confidence due to a lack of expectancy or competence or the assignment of an unachievable goal. Such employees may feel their performance is not properly rewarded due to a lack of instrumentality, a lack of valence, or feelings of inequity. Finally, it may be that their work simply isn't challenging or intrinsically rewarding due to the assignment of easy or abstract goals or the absence of meaningfulness, self-determination, and impact.

HOW IMPORTANT IS MOTIVATION?

Does motivation have a significant impact on the two primary outcomes in our integrative model of OB—does it correlate with job performance and organizational commitment? Answering that question is somewhat complicated, because motivation is not just one thing but rather a set of energetic forces. Figure 6-8 summarizes the research evidence linking motivation to job performance and organizational commitment. The figure expresses the likely combined impact of all those energetic forces on the two outcomes in our OB model.

FIGURE 6-7 Why Are Some Employees More Motivated Than Others?

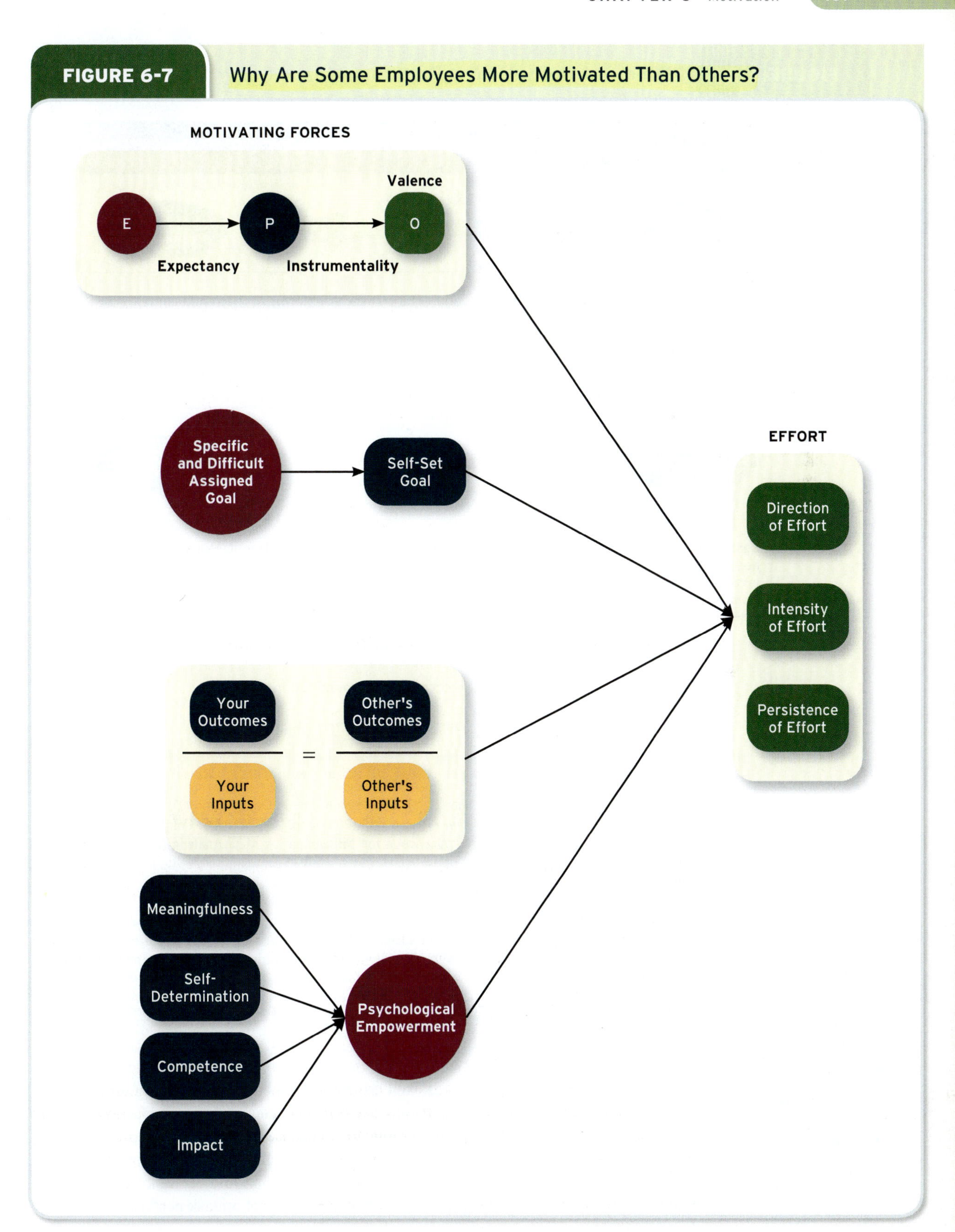

FIGURE 6-8 Effects of Motivation on Performance and Commitment

INSIDE OUR INTEGRATIVE MODEL OF OB

Motivation → Job Performance

Motivation has a strong positive effect on Job Performance. People who experience higher levels of motivation tend to have higher levels of *Task Performance*. Those effects are strongest for self-efficacy/competence and goal difficulty, followed by the valence-instrumentality-expectancy combination, and equity. Less is known about the effects of motivation on *Citizenship* and *Counterproductive Behaviour*, though equity has a moderate positive effect on the former and a moderate negative effect on the latter.

Motivation → Organizational Commitment

Less is known about the effects of Motivation on Organizational Commitment. However, equity has a moderate positive effect. People who experience higher levels of equity tend to feel higher levels of *Affective Commitment* and higher levels of *Normative Commitment*. Effects on *Continuance Commitment* are weaker.

- Represents a strong correlation (around .50 in magnitude).
- Represents a moderate correlation (around .30 in magnitude).
- Represents a weak correlation (around .10 in magnitude).

Sources: Y. Cohen-Charash and P.E. Spector, "The Role of Justice in Organizations: A Meta-Analysis," *Organizational Behavior and Human Decision Processes* 86 (2001), pp. 287–321; J.A. Colquitt, D.E. Conlon, M.J. Wesson, C.O.L.H. Porter, and K.Y. Ng, "Justice at the Millennium: A Meta-Analytic Review of 25 Years of Organizational Justice Research," *Journal of Applied Psychology* 86 (2001), pp. 425–45; E.A. Locke, and G.P. Latham. *A Theory of Goal Setting and Task Performance*. Englewood Cliffs, NJ: Prentice Hall, 1990. J.P. Meyer, D.J. Stanley, L. Herscovitch, and L. Topolnytsky, "Affective, Continuance, and Normative Commitment to the Organization: A Meta-Analysis of Antecedents, Correlates, and Consequences," *Journal of Vocational Behavior* 61 (2002), pp. 20–52; A.D. Stajkovic and F. Luthans, "Self-Efficacy and Work-Related Performance: A Meta-Analysis," Psychological Bulletin 124 (1998), pp. 240–61; W. Van Eerde and H. Thierry, "Vroom's Expectancy Models and Work-Related Criteria: A Meta-Analysis," *Journal of Applied Psychology* 81 (1996), pp. 575–86; R.E. Wood, A.J. Mento, and E.A. Locke, "Task Complexity as a Moderator of Goal Effects: A Meta-Analysis," *Journal of Applied Psychology* 72 (1987), pp. 416–25.

Turning first to job performance, literally thousands of studies support the relationships between the various motivating forces and task performance. The motivating force with the strongest performance effects are self-efficacy/competence and goals, because people who feel a sense of internal self-confidence and set higher goals outperform those who doubt their capabilities.[85] The motivational force created by high levels of valence, instrumentality, and expectancy is the next most powerful motivational variable for task performance.[86] Finally, perceptions of equity have a somewhat weaker effect on task performance.[87]

Less attention has been devoted to the linkages between motivation variables and citizenship and counterproductive behaviour. With respect to the former, employees who engage in more work-related effort would seem more likely to perform "extra-mile" sorts of actions, because those actions themselves require extra effort. The best evidence in support of that claim comes from research on equity. Specifically, employees who feel a sense of equity on the job are more likely to engage in citizenship behaviours, particularly when those behaviours aid the organization.[88] The same employees are less likely to engage in counterproductive behaviours, because such behaviours often serve as a retaliation against perceived inequities.[89]

As with citizenship behaviours, the relationship between motivation and organizational commitment seems straightforward. After all, the psychological and physical forms of withdrawal that characterize less committed employees are themselves evidence of low levels of motivation. Clearly, employees who are daydreaming, coming in late, and taking longer breaks are struggling to put forth consistently high levels of work effort. Research on equity and organizational commitment offers the clearest insights into the motivation–commitment relationship. Specifically, employees who feel a sense of equity are more emotionally attached to their firms and feel a stronger sense of obligation to remain.[90]

APPLICATION: COMPENSATION SYSTEMS

The most important area in which motivation concepts are applied in organizations is in the design of compensation systems. Table 6-6 provides an overview of many of the elements used in typical compensation systems. We use the term "element" in the table to acknowledge that most organizations use a combination of multiple approaches to compensate their employees. Two points must be noted about Table 6-6. First, the descriptions of the elements are simplistic; the reality is that each of the elements can be implemented and executed in a variety of ways.[91] Second, the elements are designed to do more than just motivate. For example, plans that put pay "at risk" rather than creating increases in base salary are geared toward control of labour costs. As another example, plans that reward unit or organizational performance are designed to reinforce collaboration, information sharing, and monitoring among employees, regardless of their impact on motivation levels.

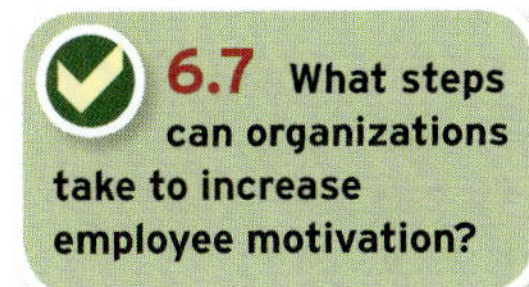

One way of judging the motivational impact of the compensation plan elements is to consider the correspondence between individual performance levels and individual monetary outcomes. After all, that correspondence influences perceptions of both instrumentality and equity. The highest instrumentality and equity levels will typically be achieved through individual-focused compensation elements. Piece-rate plans can create stronger performance–outcome contingencies but are difficult to apply outside of manufacturing, sales, and service contexts. Merit pay represents the most common element of organizational compensation plans, yet the pay increase for top performers (5.6 percent on average) is only modestly greater than the pay increase for poor performers (2.5 percent on average).[92]

A factor that hinders merit pay is the accuracy of the performance evaluations that feed into the compensation decision. Think of all the times you've been evaluated by someone else, whether in school or in the workplace. How many times have you reacted by thinking, "Where did that rating come from?" or "I think I'm being evaluated on the wrong things!" Performance evaluation experts suggest that employees should be evaluated on behaviours that are controllable by the employees (see Chapter 2 on job performance for more discussion of this issue), observable by managers, and critical to the implementation of the firm's strategy.[93] The managers who conduct evaluations also need to be trained in how to conduct them, which typically involves gaining knowledge of the relevant behaviours ahead of time and being taught to keep records of employee behaviour between evaluation sessions.[94]

TABLE 6-6 Compensation Plan Elements

ELEMENT	DESCRIPTION
Individual-Focused	
Piece-Rate	A specified rate is paid for each unit produced, each unit sold, or each service provided.
Merit Pay	An increase to base salary is made in accordance with performance evaluation ratings.
Lump-Sum Bonuses	A bonus is received for meeting individual goals but no change is made to base salary. The potential bonus represents "at risk" pay that must be re-earned each year. Base salary may be lower in cases in which potential bonuses may be large.
Recognition Awards	Tangible awards (gift cards, merchandise, trips, special events, time off, plaques) or intangible awards (praise) are given on an impromptu basis to recognize achievement.
Unit-Focused	
Gainsharing	A bonus is received for meeting unit goals (department goals, plant goals, business unit goals) for criteria controllable by employees (labour costs, use of materials, quality). No change is made to base salary. The potential bonus represents "at risk" pay that must be re-earned each year. Base salary may be lower in cases in which potential bonuses may be large.
Organization-Focused	
Profit Sharing	A bonus is received when the publicly reported earnings of a company exceed some minimum level, with the magnitude of the bonus contingent on the magnitude of the profits. No change is made to base salary. The potential bonus represents "at risk" pay that must be re-earned each year. Base salary may be lower in cases in which potential bonuses may be large.

Even if employees are evaluated on the right things by a boss who has a good handle on their performance, it's important to understand the context in which performance ratings occur. Some managers might knowingly give inaccurate evaluations due to workplace politics and a desire to not "make waves." In particular, it's tempting for managers to be very lenient in their performance evaluations so that everyone "goes home happy." Unfortunately, such practices only serve to damage instrumentality and equity because they fail to separate star employees from struggling employees. To ensure that such separation occurs, Yahoo, the California-based Internet company, has instituted a "stacked ranking" system to determine compensation, in which managers rank all the employees within their unit from top to bottom.[95] Employees at the top end of those rankings then receive higher bonuses than employees at the bottom end. Although such practices raise concerns about employee morale and excessive competitiveness, research suggests that such forced distribution systems can boost the performance of a company's workforce, especially for the first few years after their implementation.[96]

TAKEAWAYS

6.1 Motivation is defined as a set of energetic forces that originates both within and outside an employee, initiates work-related effort, and determines its direction, intensity, and persistence.

6.2 Expectancy theory describes the cognitive process that employees go through to make choices among different voluntary behaviours. Effort is directed toward behaviours when effort is believed to result in performance (expectancy), performance is believed to result in outcomes (instrumentality), and those outcomes are anticipated to be valuable (valence). Needs help us to evaluate preferences (valence) for some outcomes over others.

6.3 Goal setting theory describes the impact of assigned goals on internal goals and the intensity and persistence of effort. Goals become strong drivers of motivation and performance when they are difficult and specific. Those effects occur more frequently when employees are given feedback, tasks are not too complex, and goal commitment is high.

6.4 Rewards are equitable when a person's ratio of outcomes to inputs matches those of some relevant comparison other. A sense of inequity triggers equity distress. Underreward inequity typically results in lower levels of motivation or higher levels of counterproductive behaviour. Overreward inequity typically results in cognitive distortion, in which inputs are re-evaluated in a more positive light.

6.5 Psychological empowerment reflects an energy rooted in the belief that tasks are contributing to some larger purpose. Psychological empowerment is fostered when work goals appeal to employees' passions (meaningfulness), employees have a sense of choice regarding work tasks (self-determination), employees feel capable of performing successfully (competence), and employees feel they are making progress toward fulfilling their purpose (impact).

6.6 Motivation has a strong positive relationship with job performance and a moderate positive relationship with organizational commitment. Of all the energetic forces subsumed by motivation, self-efficacy/competence and goal difficulty have the strongest relationship with performance.

6.7 Organizations use compensation practices to increase motivation. Those practices may include individual-focused elements (piece-rate, merit pay, lump-sum bonuses, recognition awards), unit-focused elements (gainsharing), or organization-focused elements (profit sharing).

KEY TERMS

- cognitive distortion *p. 146*
- comparison other *p. 145*
- competence *p. 149*
- emotional cues *p. 135*
- equity distress *p. 145*
- equity theory *p. 144*
- expectancy *p. 134*
- expectancy theory *p. 133*
- external comparisons *p. 146*
- extrinsic motivation *p. 136*
- feedback *p. 142*
- goal commitment *p. 142*
- goal setting theory *p. 141*
- impact *p. 149*
- instrumentality *p. 135*
- internal comparisons *p. 146*
- intrinsic motivation *p. 136*
- meaningfulness *p. 149*
- meaning of money *p. 137*
- motivation *p. 132*
- needs *p. 136*
- overreward inequity *p. 145*

- past accomplishments *p. 134*
- psychological empowerment *p. 148*
- self-determination *p. 149*
- self-efficacy *p. 134*
- self-set goals *p. 141*
- S.M.A.R.T. goals *p. 143*
- specific and difficult goals *p. 141*
- task complexity *p. 142*
- task strategies *p. 142*
- underreward inequity *p. 145*
- valence *p. 136*
- verbal persuasion *p. 135*
- vicarious experiences *p. 135*

DISCUSSION QUESTIONS

6.1 Think about your needs (see Table 6-1 on page 137) and how they impact the personal choices you make, what outcomes you prefer (see Table 6-2 on page 138), and how you generally direct your attention and effort. Do you think that your needs and preferences will change as you get older?

6.2 Assume that you were working on a group project and that one of your teammates was nervous about speaking in front of the class during the presentation. Drawing on Figure 6-3 on page 135, what exactly could you do to make your classmate feel more confident?

6.3 Consider the five strategies for fostering goal commitment (rewards, publicity, support, participation, and resources). Which of those strategies do you think is most effective? Can you picture any of them having potential drawbacks?

6.4 How do you tend to respond when you experience overreward and underreward inequity? Why do you respond that way rather than with some other combination in Figure 6-6 on page 146?

6.5 Think about a job that you've held in which you felt very low levels of psychological empowerment. What could the organization have done to increase empowerment levels?

CASE • WESTJET

Since its inception, WestJet has not only challenged the conventional wisdom in the way an airline should be run but also has demonstrated an understanding that people are an important source of sustainable competitive advantage. To support a culture that motivates and empowers its members, the company has developed a compensation plan that rewards employees for their collective efforts and results. As "owners," employees seem to personally identify, and emotionally connect, with the goals and challenges faced by the organization.

The airline industry is currently going through very turbulent times. In spite of the heavy investments in a state-of-the-art fleet, the rising cost of jet fuel is a huge consideration given the recent price of crude oil on world markets. A weaker North American economy will no doubt have an effect on discretionary air travel. With the potential of lower revenues combined with higher costs, the risk for "owners" is that the company may not be as profitable as it has been in the past. To the extent this scenario is accurate, incentive systems built on profit-based payments will be adversely affected—employees and investors may not benefit from these reward systems as they have in the past. Moreover, as revenues level off or diminish there will be pressure on the organization to reduce all forms of costs (including labour), and increase its level of high-value service to attract and retain a shrinking pool of customers.

6.1 Analyze this scenario from the perspective of expectancy and equity theories. Do you think the motivation of individual employees will increase or decrease? Explain.

6.2 In the context of lower profit-sharing rewards, what would you do to keep motivation high?

EXERCISE • GEORGE LUMBER

The purpose of this exercise is to demonstrate how compensation can be used to influence motivation. This exercise uses groups of six participants, so your instructor will either assign you to a group of six or ask you to create your own group of six. George Lumber is a small, family-owned business, run by Angelo George and his father Ira. Business has been good—until last year, as seen in the chart below.

YEAR	NUMBER OF EMPLOYEES	PROFIT
2009	52	$300,000
2008	47	$700,000
2007	40	$500,000
2006	25	$300,000
2005	5	$100,000

After a careful analysis of new building starts, the cost of raw materials, taxes, and other business conditions, Angelo and Ira have come to the conclusion that the decline in profits is due to a decline in sales revenue from their weekend sales shift. The 10 weekend employees tend to be the newest salespeople hired at the company. Many of them are working part-time and either going to school during the week or holding down another job. Few of them see a position at George Lumber as a career goal, but recently, Ira has had two people from the weekend shift approach him to see if weekday work might be available. Because weekend employees are part-time, they are not generally offered benefits, though Angelo has studied the possibility. Frankly, he is not sure that these employees would even want the same benefits. How is it possible that Tina, who is 18 years of age and hoping for a career as an architect when she finishes university, might want the same things as Oscar, who is 69 years old and works to get extra money to pay for his prescription drugs every month?

Over dinner one night, Angelo and Ira brainstormed ways to motivate their employees. They came up with several ideas, including (1) giving a monthly bonus to the employee with the highest sales for that month; (2) offering a "cafeteria-style" benefits package, from which employees could select the types of benefits that would best fit their needs, up to a cost of $300 per month; (3) setting up a training program for weekend employees; (4) initiating an "on the spot" bonus of $50 for the employees who get "caught" giving superior customer service; and (5) offering to promote the employee with the highest sales at the end of the summer to a full-time position.

1. Evaluate the advantages and disadvantages of each of these motivational options from the perspective of expectancy theory, goal setting theory, and equity theory.
2. Develop a compensation plan using the elements of expectancy theory, goal setting theory, and equity theory. How would you sell your plan to Angelo and Ira?

OB ASSESSMENTS • THE MEANING OF MONEY

How do you view money—what meaning do you attach to it? This assessment will tell you where you stand on the three facets of the meaning of money—money as achievement, money as respect, and money as freedom. Answer each question using the response scale provided. Then follow the instructions below to score yourself.

1 STRONGLY DISAGREE	2 DISAGREE	3 SLIGHTLY DISAGREE	4 NEUTRAL	5 SLIGHTLY AGREE	6 AGREE	7 STRONGLY AGREE

1. Money represents one's achievement. ______
2. Money is a symbol of success. ______
3. Money is the most important goal in my life. ______
4. Money can buy everything. ______
5. Money makes people respect you in the community. ______
6. Money will help you express your competence and abilities. ______
7. Money can bring you many friends. ______
8. Money is honourable. ______
9. Money gives you autonomy and freedom. ______
10. Money can give you the opportunity to be what you want to be. ______
11. Money in the bank is a sign of security. ______
12. Money means power. ______

SCORING

Money as Achievement: Sum up items 1–4. ________

Money as Respect: Sum up items 5–8. ________

Money as Freedom: Sum up items 9–12. ________

INTERPRETATION

Money as Achievement:	High = 13 or above. Low = 12 or below.
Money as Respect:	High = 15 or above. Low = 14 or below.
Money as Freedom:	High = 20 or above. Low = 19 or below.

If you scored high on all three dimensions, then you view money as having multiple, non-economic meanings. This result means that money is likely a powerful motivator for you.

Source: Adapted from T.L. Tang, "The Meaning of Money Revisited," *Journal of Organizational Behaviour* 13 (1982), pp. 197–202.

CONNECT—Available 24/7 with instant feedback so you can study when you want, how you want, and where you want. Take advantage of the Study Plan—an innovative tool that helps students customize their own learning experience. Students can diagnose their knowledge with pre- and post-tests, identify the areas where they need help, search contents of the entire learning package for content specific to the topic they're studying, and add these resources to their study plan. Visit **www.connectob.ca** to register—take practice quizzes, run interactive scenarios, and much more. Also visit the Student Online Learning Centre for additional study tools.

www.mcgrawhill.ca/olc/colquitt

CHAPTER

7 Trust, Justice, and Ethics

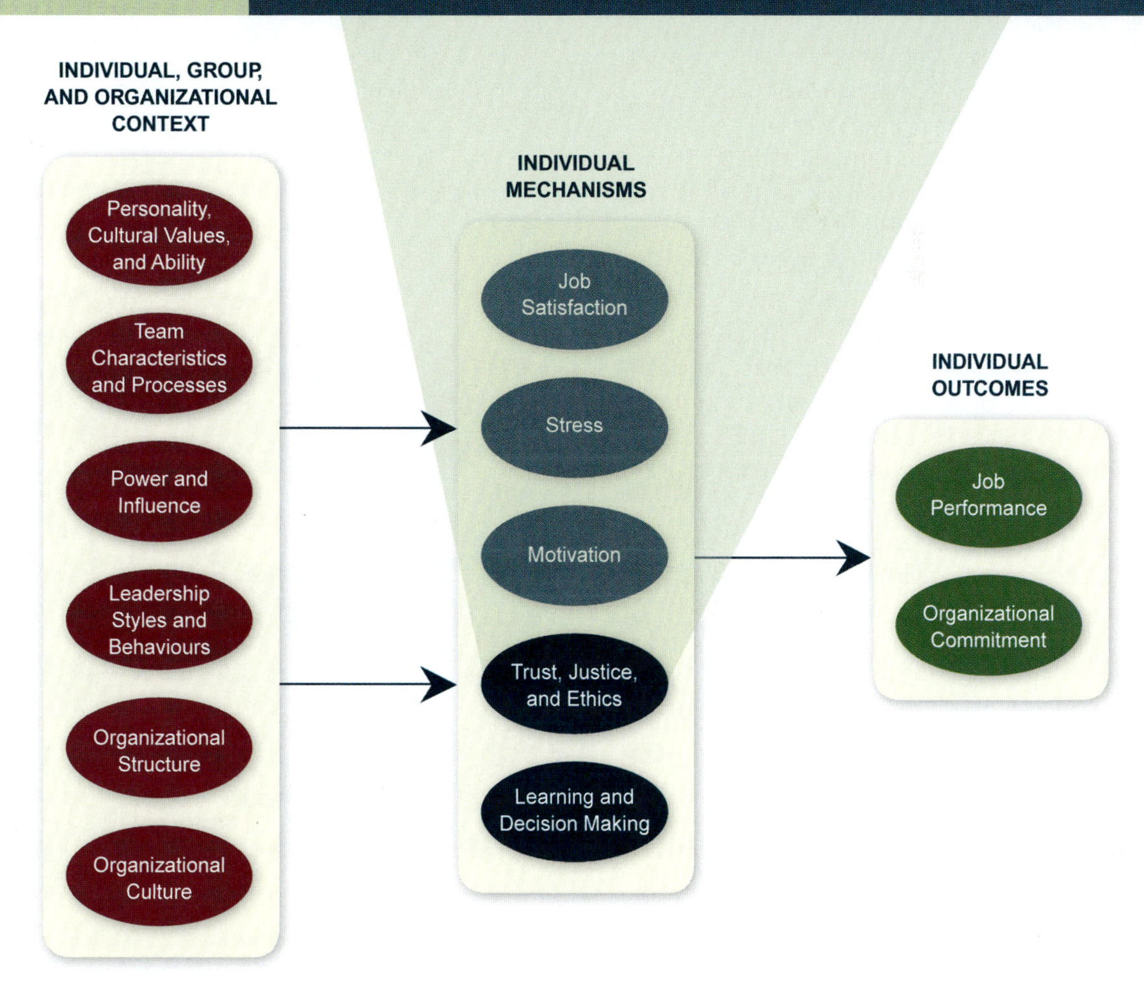

Learning Outcomes

After reading this chapter, you should be able to answer the following questions:

7.1 What is trust? What are justice and ethics?

7.2 In what three sources can trust be rooted? What dimensions can be used to describe how trustworthy an authority is?

7.3 Employees judge the fairness of an authority's decision making along four dimensions. What are those dimensions?

7.4 What is the four-component model of ethical decision making?

7.5 How does trust affect job performance and organizational commitment?

7.6 What steps can organizations take to become more trustworthy?

WAL-MART

What two words pop into your head when you hear "Wal-Mart"? For many people, "low prices" would be the answer. From this perspective, Wal-Mart is viewed as a global success story—the company founded in Bentonville, Arkansas, by a folksy entrepreneur who built a brilliant distribution system to bring products to customers at lower costs.[1] Those prices are critical to many shoppers and families, especially those who live on tight monthly budgets. As Wal-Mart describes it, the company's mission is to "lower the world's cost of living."[2] Indeed, we could argue that Wal-Mart represents the single most powerful force against inflation in the country. That low-price formula has proven so successful that Wal-Mart stands as the largest company in the history of the world,[3] with 1.8 million people on the payroll as of 2005.[4]

Wal-Mart Canada, with head offices in Mississauga, Ontario, has been a bright spot for the world's largest retailer. It has been estimated that about 80 percent to 90 percent of Canadian households shop at Wal-Mart, generating revenue of about $12 billion in 2006 (accounting for 15 percent of Wal-Mart's international sales).[5] The continued growth of Wal-Mart Canada's business is built upon a foundation that began in 1994, when Wal-Mart Canada took over operations of a struggling chain of 122 Woolco stores.[6] Today, Wal-Mart is Canada's fourth-largest employer with over 75,000 associates working in 301 stores, and is repeatedly listed among the 50 best companies to work.[7]

Other people, however, think of different words when they hear "Wal-Mart"—words like "evil empire." Those low prices often force local shops out of business.[8] Wal-Mart is also accused of forcing its suppliers to cut corners to meet its price demands, using its leverage to buy products more cheaply than its competing retailers.[9] Many of the most fervent criticisms of Wal-Mart, however, centre on how it treats its employees. Critics argue that the "always low prices" goal is built on an "always low wages" reality, with Wal-Mart offering pay and benefits that cannot be considered a living wage.[10]

Wal-Mart has long enjoyed success with its famously low prices. But the company now finds itself fighting an uphill battle to regain its reputation.

Critics note that Wal-Mart employees are paid so little that the only store they can afford to shop at is Wal-Mart![11] In 2004, the store in Jonquière, Quebec, became the only Wal-Mart store in North America to successfully unionize. Six months later, in early 2005—just prior to its first collective agreement—the Jonquière store was closed.[12] A group of laid-off workers launched an appeal, claiming that this decision was retaliation against the union. In the end the Quebec Court of Appeal ruled that the company did not transgress the province's *Labour Code*.[13] Apart from general concerns about its compensation, Wal-Mart has come under fire for illegal actions. For example, the company was recently forced to pay $78 million to 185,000 employees who claimed they were denied breaks and forced to work off the clock.[14] That $78 million pales in comparison to the class action lawsuit brought against the company by 1.5 million current and former female employees.[15] That suit, the largest of its kind in U.S. history, alleges that women get paid less than men for the same jobs and that men are promoted more frequently than women within the company. Analysts suggest that settling this discrimination case could wind up costing Wal-Mart $8 billion.[16]

One spokeswoman for the company worries that shoppers could start feeling guilty about going to Wal-Mart.[17] In response to such pressures, Wal-Mart has undertaken some important reform efforts. For example, the company hired hundreds of new human resources managers to work out in the field in an effort to improve the company's hiring and communication practices, along with employee morale and job behaviours.[18] Wal-Mart's former CEO, Lee Scott, seemed to understand the situation he's facing. At a company gathering in 2005, Scott noted, "We have to remember that any bad incident that occurs is not only a reflection on the individual who did it but on all of us here."[19] He went on to suggest that any Wal-Mart employee who does something unfair or unethical is "getting ready to take out the paint brush and put a big black mark across Wal-Mart Stores."

TRUST, JUSTICE, AND ETHICS

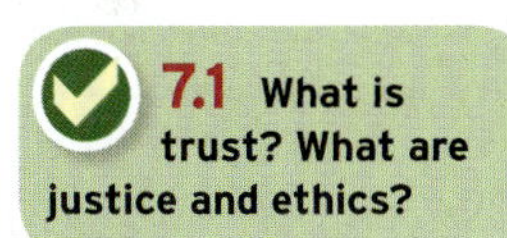
7.1 What is trust? What are justice and ethics?

When describing Wal-Mart's recent missteps, one market researcher noted, "Their reputation in the area of trust has been slipping, and trust was probably their greatest asset."[20] **Trust** is defined as the willingness to be vulnerable to an authority based on positive expectations about the authority's actions and intentions.[21] When we trust, we become willing to "put ourselves out there," even though that choice could be met with disappointment. This definition can be used to highlight the important distinction between "trust" and "risk." Actually making oneself vulnerable to an authority is a risk; trust reflects the willingness to take that risk. This definition also illustrates where trust comes from, as it is based on an assessment of how a given authority is likely to behave in a particular situation.

trust The willingness to be vulnerable to an authority based on positive expectations about the authority's actions and intentions

Who is the authority referenced in the trust definition? Sometimes that authority is person-based, as when you trust a specific Wal-Mart manager to be honest about a product's shortcomings. Sometimes that authority is organization-based, as when you trust that Wal-Mart, as a company, will treat your cousin fairly when he accepts a job. Because we don't usually have direct knowledge about the company as a whole, an organization-based version of trust depends largely on a company's reputation. It is common these days to see companies ranked in terms of their public reputations, such as "Canada's 50 Best Employers."[22] Although Wal-Mart typically makes this list, its rankings over the last few years have been slipping.[23]

Issues of trust are intertwined with two related concepts. **Justice** reflects the perceived fairness of an authority's decision making.[24] When employees perceive high levels of justice, they believe that decision outcomes are fair and that decision-making processes are designed and

justice The perceived fairness of an authority's decision making

ethics The degree to which the behaviours of an authority are in accordance with generally accepted moral norms

implemented in a fair manner. Justice concepts can be used to explain why employees judge some authorities as more trustworthy than others.[25] **Ethics** reflects the degree to which the behaviours of an authority are in accordance with generally accepted moral norms.[26] When employees perceive high levels of ethics, they believe that things are being done the way they "should be" or "ought to be" done. Ethics concepts can be used to explain why authorities decide to act in a trustworthy or untrustworthy manner.

WHY ARE SOME AUTHORITIES MORE TRUSTED THAN OTHERS?

Why are firefighters, nurses, farmers, doctors, and teachers consistently among the most trusted Canadians, whereas real estate agents, publicists, car salespeople, and politicians are among the least trusted?[27] Think about a particular boss or instructor—one with whom you've spent a significant amount of time. Do you trust that person? Would you be willing to let that person have significant influence over your professional or educational future? For example, would you be willing to let that person serve as a reference for you or write you a letter of recommendation, even though you'd have no way of monitoring what he or she said about you? When you think about the level of trust you feel for that particular authority, what exactly makes you feel that way? This question speaks to the factors that drive trust—the factors that help inspire a willingness to be vulnerable.

disposition-based trust Trust that is rooted in one's own personality, as opposed to a careful assessment of the trustee's trustworthiness

cognition-based trust Trust that is rooted in a rational assessment of the authority's trustworthiness

affect-based trust Trust that depends on feelings toward the authority that go beyond any rational assessment of trustworthiness

trust propensity A general expectation that the words, promises, and statements of individuals can be relied upon

TRUST

As shown in Figure 7-1, trust is rooted in different kinds of factors. Sometimes trust is **disposition-based**, meaning that your personality traits include a general propensity to trust others. Sometimes trust is **cognition-based**, meaning that it is rooted in a rational assessment of the authority's trustworthiness.[28] Sometimes trust is **affect-based**, meaning that it depends on feelings toward the authority that go beyond any rational assessment.[29] The sections that follow describe each of these trust forms in more detail.

DISPOSITION-BASED TRUST Disposition-based trust has less to do with the authority and more to do with the trustor. Some trustors are high in **trust propensity**—a general expectation that the words, promises, and statements of individuals and groups can be relied upon.[30] Some have argued that trust propensity represents a sort of "faith in human nature," in that trusting people view others in more favourable terms than do suspicious people.[31] The importance of trust propensity is most obvious in interactions with strangers, in which any acceptance of vulnerability would amount to "blind trust."[32] On the one hand, people who are high in trust propensity may be fooled into trusting others who are not worthy of it.[33] On the other hand, those who are low in trust propensity may be fooled by not trusting someone who is actually deserving of it. Both situations can be damaging; as one scholar noted, "We are doomed if we trust all and equally doomed if we trust none."[34] Where do you stack up on trust propensity? See our **OB Assessments** feature at the end of this chapter to find out.

Where does our trust propensity come from? As with all traits, trust propensity is a product of both nature and nurture. If our parents are dispositionally suspicious, we may either inherit that tendency genetically or model it as we watch them exhibit distrust in their day-to-day lives. Research also suggests that trust propensity is shaped by early childhood experiences.[35] In fact, trust propensity may be one of the first personality traits to develop, because infants must immediately learn to trust their parents to meet their needs. The more our needs are met as children, the more trusting we become; the more we are disappointed

FIGURE 7-1 Factors That Influence Trust Levels

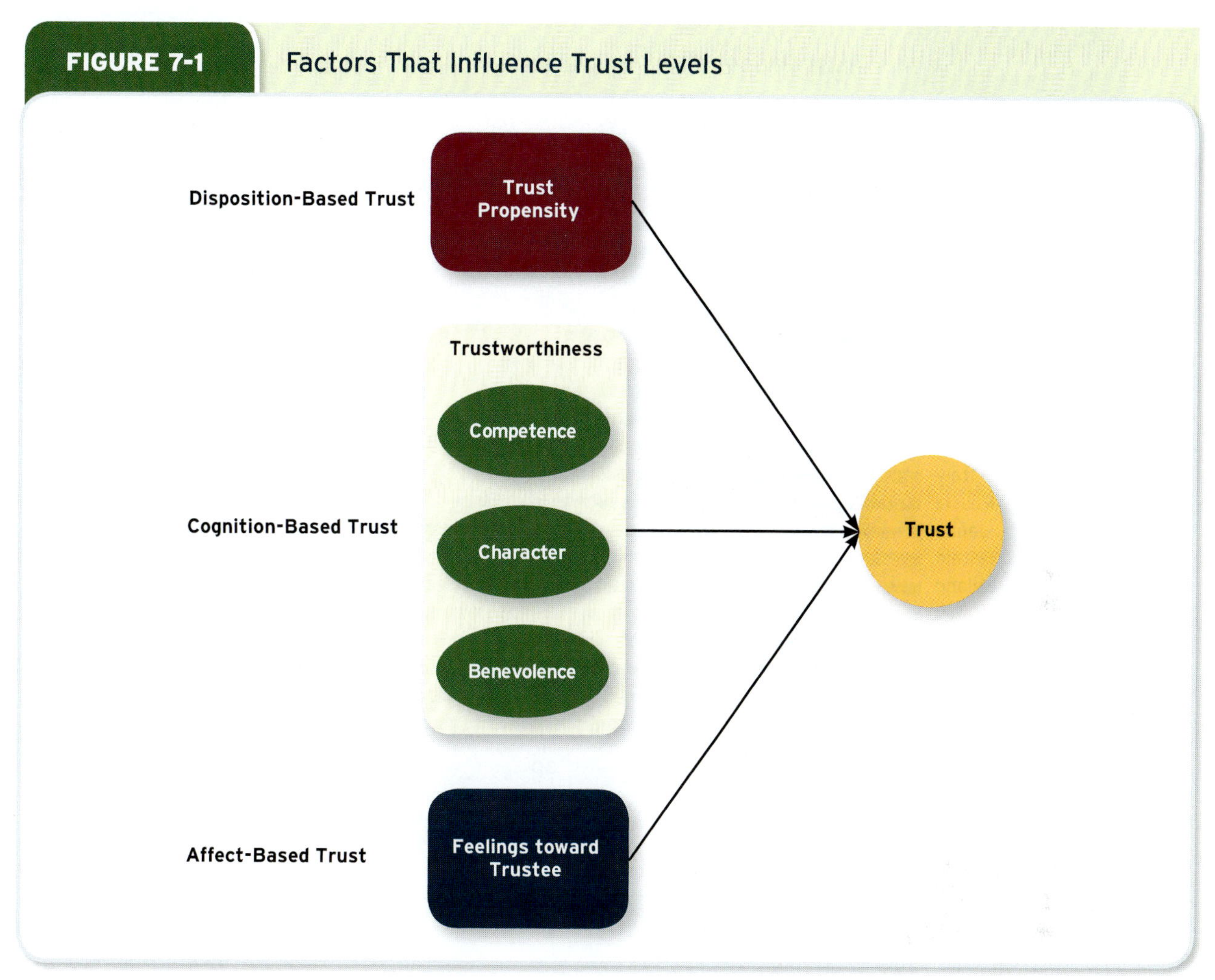

Sources: Adapted from R.C. Mayer, J.H. Davis, and F.D. Schoorman, "An Integrative Model of Organizational Trust," *Academy of Management Review* 20 (1995), pp. 709–34; D.J. McAllister, "Affect- and Cognition-Based Trust as Foundations for Interpersonal Cooperation in Organizations," *Academy of Management Journal* 38 (1995), pp. 24–59.

as children, the less trusting we become. Our propensities continue to be shaped later in life as we gain experiences with friends, schools, churches, local government authorities, and other relevant groups.[36]

The nation in which we live also affects our trust propensity. Research by the World Values Study Group examines differences between nations on various attitudes and perceptions. The study group collects interview data from 45 different societies with a total sample size of more than 90,000 participants. One of the questions asked by the study group measures trust propensity. Specifically, participants are asked, "Generally speaking, would you say that most people can be trusted or that you can't be too careful in dealing with people?" Figure 7-2 shows the percentage of participants who answered "Most people can be trusted" for this question, as opposed to "Can't be too careful," for several of the nations included in the study. The results reveal that trust propensity levels are actually relatively high in Canada, especially in relation to countries in Europe and South America.

7.2 In what three sources can trust be rooted? What dimensions can be used to describe how trust worthy an authority is?

FIGURE 7-2 Trust Propensities by Nation

Brazil
Turkey
Romania
Portugal
Chile
Argentina
France
South Africa
Mexico
South Korea
Spain
India
Italy
Russia
Japan
Britain
Ireland
United States
Canada
Netherlands
China
Sweden

0 10 20 30 40 50 60 70

Percent Agreeing "Most People Can Be Trusted"

Source: Adapted from J.J. Johnson and J.B. Cullen, "Trust in Cross-Cultural Relationships," in *Blackwell Handbook of Cross-Cultural Management,* eds. M.J. Gannon and K.L. Newman (Malden, MA: Blackwell, 2002), pp. 335–60.

COGNITION-BASED TRUST Disposition-based trust guides us in cases when we don't yet have data about a particular authority. However, eventually we gain enough knowledge to gauge the authority's **trustworthiness**, defined as the characteristics or attributes of a trustee that inspire trust.[37] At that point, our trust begins to be based on cognitions we've developed about the authority, as opposed to our own personality or disposition. In this way, cognition-based trust is driven by the authority's "track record."[38] If that track record has shown the authority to be trustworthy, then vulnerability to the authority can be accepted. If that track record is spotty however, then trust may not be warranted. Research suggests that we gauge the track record of an authority along three dimensions: competence, character, and benevolence.[39]

trustworthiness Characteristics or attributes of a person that inspire trust, including competence, character, and benevolence

Children whose needs are generally met tend to grow into trusting adults.

The first dimension of trustworthiness is **competence**, defined as the skills, abilities, and areas of expertise that enable an authority to be successful in some specific area (see Chapter 9 for more discussion of these issues).[40] Think about the decision-making process that you go through when choosing a doctor, lawyer, or mechanic.

competence The skills, abilities, and areas of expertise that enable an authority to be successful in some specific area

Clearly one of the first things you consider is competence, because you're not going to trust them if they don't know a scalpel from a retractor, a tort from a writ, or a camshaft from a crankshaft. Of course, listing a specific area is a key component of the competence definition; you wouldn't trust a mechanic to perform surgery, nor would you trust a doctor to fix your car! The competence of business authorities may be considered on a number of levels. For example, a manager may be judged according to the functional expertise of a particular industry or vocation but also according to his or her leadership skills and general business sense.[41]

The second dimension of trustworthiness is **character**, defined as the perception that the authority adheres to a set of values and principles that the trustor finds acceptable.[42] When authorities are perceived to be of sound character, it means that they have integrity—that they have honest motives and intentions. Character also conveys an alignment between words and deeds—a sense that authorities keep their promises, "walk the talk," and "do what they say they will do."[43] Unfortunately, a recent survey indicated that only around 20 percent of workers view senior managers as acting in accordance with their words.[44] The series of high-profile public scandals at companies like Enron, WorldCom, Tyco, and Hollinger International can be viewed as examples of the costs of poor character. In those cases, top management hid debt, misstated earnings, and used profits for personal gain—all of which constituted dishonest actions that went against the espoused values and principles of those companies.

character The perception that an authority adheres to a set of values and principles that the trustor finds acceptable

The third dimension of trustworthiness is **benevolence**, defined as the belief that the authority wants to do good for the trustor, apart from any selfish or profit-centred motives.[45] When authorities are perceived as benevolent, it means that they care for employees, are concerned about their well-being, and feel a sense of loyalty to them. The mentor–protegé relationship provides a good example of benevolence at work.[46] The best mentors would never do anything to hurt their protegés. They go out of their way to be helpful, even at the cost of their own personal productivity and in the absence of any financial reward. Clearly benevolence, along with competence and character, provides a set of good reasons to trust a particular authority.[47] For more about how these three trustworthiness facets can be used to gauge trust, see our **OB on Screen** feature.

benevolence The belief that an authority wants to do good for an employee, apart from any selfish or profit-centred motives

AFFECT-BASED TRUST Although competence, character, and benevolence provide three good reasons to trust an authority, the third form of trust isn't really rooted in reason at all. Affect-based trust is more emotional than rational. With affect-based trust, we trust because we have feelings for the person in question; we really like them and have a fondness for them. Those feelings are what prompt us to accept vulnerability to another person. Put simply, we trust them because we like them.

Affect-based trust acts as a supplement to the types of trust discussed previously.[48] Figure 7-3 describes how the various forms of trust can build on one another over time. In new relationships, trust depends solely on our own trust propensity. In most relationships, that propensity eventually gets supplemented by knowledge about competence, character, or benevolence, at which point cognition-based trust develops. In a select few of those relationships, an emotional bond develops, and our feelings for the trustee further increase our willingness to accept vulnerability. These relationships are characterized by a mutual investment of time and energy, a sense of deep attachment, and the realization that both parties would feel a sense of loss if the relationship were dissolved.[49]

SUMMARY Taken together, disposition-based trust, cognition-based trust, and affect-based trust provide three completely different sources of trust in a particular authority. In the case of disposition-based trust, our willingness to be vulnerable has little to do with the authority and more to do with our genes and our early life experiences. In the case of affect-based trust, our willingness to be vulnerable has little to do with a rational assessment of the authority's merits and more to do with our emotional fondness for the authority. Only in the case of cognition-based trust do we rationally evaluate the pluses and minuses of an authority, in terms of its competence, character, and benevolence. But how exactly do we gauge those trustworthiness forms? One way is to consider whether authorities adhere to rules of justice.

OB ON SCREEN

PIRATES OF THE CARIBBEAN: THE CURSE OF THE BLACK PEARL

May I ask you something? Have I ever given you reason not to trust me?

With those words, Captain Jack Sparrow (Johnny Depp) poses a difficult question in *Pirates of the Caribbean: The Curse of the Black Pearl* (Dir. Gore Verbinski, Disney, 2003). There are a whole host of reasons not to trust Jack. The most obvious comes during a sword-fight between Jack and young Will Turner (Orlando Bloom), when Jack breaks the rules of engagement by pulling his gun. "You cheated," Will pleads. "Pirate," Jack answers.

From a competence perspective, Jack actually does a lot to inspire trust. His skills at hatching a plan belie his crazy demeanour. He also happens to be a good swordsman and a remarkably good escape artist. So when Jack suggests a course of action, you're tempted to follow it. Indeed, early in the film, after Jack steals a ship from Britain's Port Royal, one of the British soldiers remarks that Jack must be the best pirate he's ever seen.

As with any pirate, however, Jack struggles with character. In addition to the afore-mentioned gun incident, Jack lies, steals, and rarely does exactly what he says he'd do. Although he appears to hold firmly to the "pirate's code," most pirates view the code more as a set of guidelines than actual rules. And that code includes such lofty sayings as, "Any-one who falls behind is left behind."

From a benevolence perspective, Jack does seem to care sincerely for Will and Eliza-beth (Keira Knightly), the British Governor's daughter for whom Will is secretly carrying a torch. In fact, Jack routinely risks his own life to save one or both of them throughout the film. But does he do so merely to further his own profit-driven motives?

Jack's nemesis, Captain Barbossa (Geoffrey Rush), sums up the uncertainty about Jack's trustworthiness, saying, "I must admit, Jack, I thought I had you figured, but it turns out you're a hard man to predict." Jack's reply: "Me? I'm dishonest, and a dishonest man you can always trust to be dishonest . . . honestly." That answer doesn't really clear things up, does it? As Elizabeth asks near the climax of the film, "Whose side is Jack on?" Will's answer: "At the moment?"

FIGURE 7-3 Types of Trust Over Time

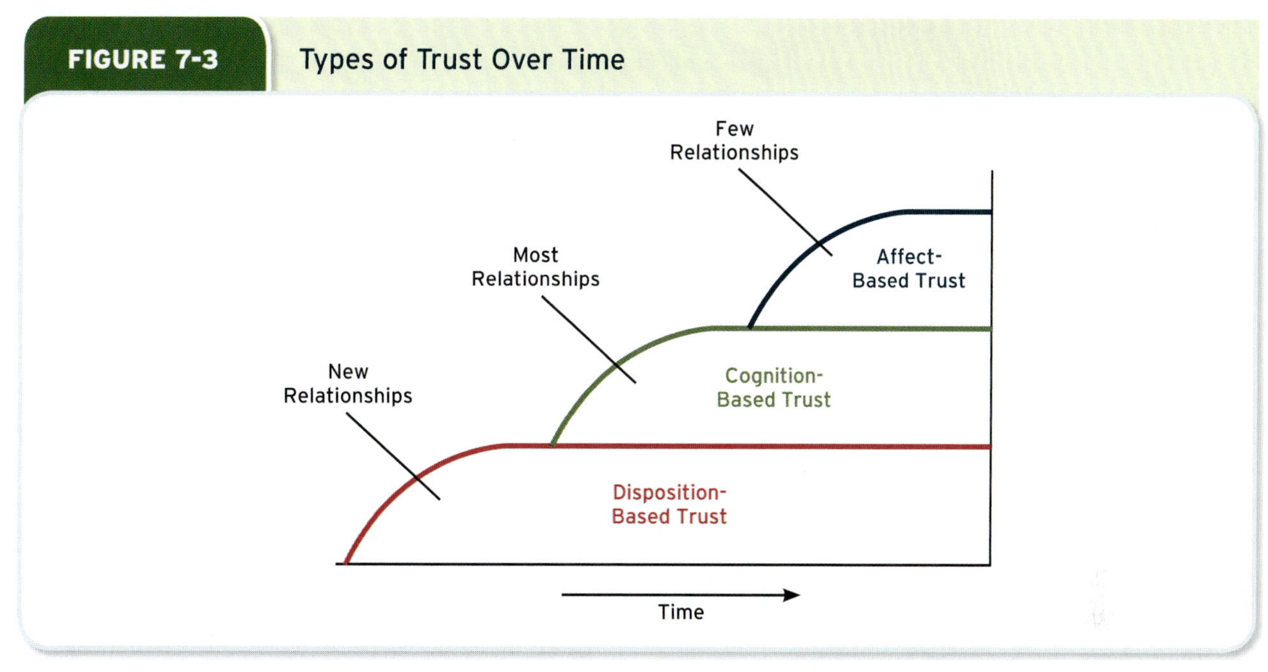

Sources: Adapted from R.J. Lewicki and B.B. Bunker, "Developing and Maintaining Trust in Work Relationships," in *Trust in Organizations: Frontiers of Theory and Research,* eds. R.M. Kramer and T.R. Tyler (Thousand Oaks, CA: Sage, 1996), pp. 114–39; R.C. Mayer, J.H. Davis, and F.D. Schoorman, "An Integrative Model of Organizational Trust," *Academy of Management Review* 20 (1995), pp. 709–34.

JUSTICE

It's often difficult to assess the competence, character, and benevolence of authorities accurately, particularly early in a working relationship. What employees need in such circumstances is some sort of observable behavioural evidence that an authority might be trustworthy. Justice provides that sort of behavioural evidence, because authorities who treat employees more fairly are usually judged to be more trustworthy.[50] As shown in Table 7-1, employees can judge the fairness of an authority's decision making along four dimensions: distributive justice, procedural justice, interpersonal justice, and informational justice.

distributive justice The perceived fairness of decision-making outcomes

DISTRIBUTIVE JUSTICE **Distributive justice** reflects the perceived fairness of decision-making outcomes.[51] Employees gauge distributive justice by asking whether decision outcomes, such as pay, rewards, evaluations, promotions, and work assignments, are allocated using proper norms. In most business situations, the proper norm is equity, with more outcomes allocated to those who contribute more inputs (see Chapter 6 on motivation for more discussion of equity). The equity norm is typically judged to be the fairest choice in situations in which the goal is to maximize the productivity of individual employees.[52]

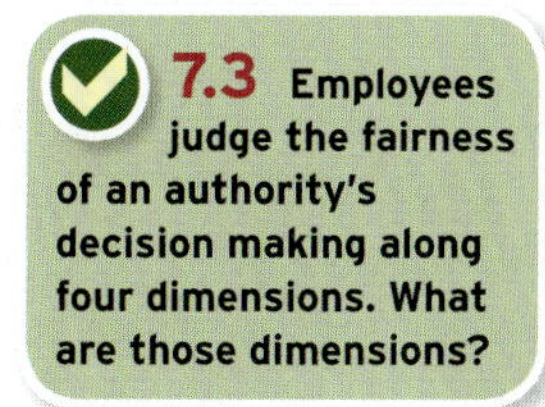

However, other allocation norms become appropriate in situations in which other goals are critical. In team-based work, building harmony and solidarity in work groups can become just as important as individual productivity. In such cases, an equality norm may be judged more fair, such that all team members receive the same amount of relevant rewards.[53] The equality norm is typically used in student project groups, in which all group members receive exactly the same grade on a project, regardless of their individual productivity levels. In cases in which the welfare of a particular employee is the critical concern, a need norm may be judged more fair. For example, PricewaterhouseCoopers, the New York–based accounting firm, wired $4,000 to 43 employees who were affected by Hurricane Katrina.[54] The company also gave those employees food, lodging, and transportation for a three-month period.

TABLE 7-1 The Four Dimensions of Justice

Distributive Justice Rules	Description
Equity vs. equality vs. need	Are rewards allocated according to the proper norm?
Procedural Justice Rules	
Voice	Do employees get to provide input into procedures?
Correctability	Do procedures build in mechanisms for appeals?
Consistency	Are procedures consistent across people and time?
Bias Suppression	Are procedures neutral and unbiased?
Representativeness	Do procedures consider the needs of all groups?
Accuracy	Are procedures based on accurate information?
Interpersonal Justice Rules	
Respect	Do authorities treat employees with sincerity?
Propriety	Do authorities refrain from improper remarks?
Informational Justice Rules	
Justification	Do authorities explain procedures thoroughly?
Truthfulness	Are those explanations honest?

Sources: J.S. Adams, "Inequity in Social Exchange," in *Advances in Experimental Social Psychology,* Vol. 2, ed. L. Berkowitz (New York: Academic Press, 1965), pp. 267–99; R.J. Bies and J.F. Moag, "Interactional Justice: Communication Criteria of Fairness," in *Research on Negotiations in Organizations,* Vol. 1, eds. R.J. Lewicki, B.H. Sheppard, and M.H. Bazerman (Greenwich, CT: JAI Press, 1986), pp. 43–55; G.S. Leventhal, "The Distribution of Rewards and Resources in Groups and Organizations," in *Advances in Experimental Social Psychology,* Vol. 9, eds. L. Berkowitz and W. Walster (New York: Academic Press, 1976), pp. 91–131; G.S. Leventhal, "What Should Be Done with Equity Theory? New Approaches to the Study of Fairness in Social Relationships," in *Social Exchange: Advances in Theory and Research,* eds. K. Gergen, M. Greenberg, and R. Willis (New York: Plenum Press, 1980), pp. 27–55; J. Thibaut and L. Walker, *Procedural Justice: A Psychological Analysis* (Hillsdale, NJ: Erlbaum, 1975).

procedural justice
The perceived fairness of decision-making processes

PROCEDURAL JUSTICE In addition to judging the fairness of a decision outcome, employees may consider the process that led to that outcome. **Procedural justice** reflects the perceived fairness of decision-making processes.[55] Procedural justice is fostered when authorities adhere to rules of fair process. One of those rules is voice, which concerns giving employees a chance to express their opinions and views during the course of decision making.[56] A related rule is correctability, which provides employees with a chance to request an appeal when a procedure seems to have worked ineffectively. Research suggests that voice improves employees reactions to decisions,[57] largely because it gives employees a sense of ownership over the decisions that occur at work. In fact, employees value voice even when it doesn't always result in the outcomes they want or when their appeals don't always reverse the decisions that were made.[58] Why? Because employees like to be heard—the expression of opinions is a valued end, in-and-of-itself, as long as employees feel those opinions were truly considered.

Aside from voice and correctability, procedural justice is fostered when authorities adhere to four rules that serve to create equal employment opportunity. The consistency, bias suppression, representativeness, and accuracy rules help ensure that procedures are neutral and objective, as opposed to biased and discriminatory. These sorts of procedural rules are relevant in many areas of working life. As one example, the rules can be used to make hiring practices more fair by ensuring that interview questions are unbiased and asked in the same manner across applications. As another example, the rules can be used to make compensation practices more fair by ensuring that accurate measures of job performance are used to provide input for merit raises.

These sorts of procedural justice rules are critical to ensure that non-relevant demographic characteristics, such as an individual's gender or ethnic or racial origin, do not bias organizational decision making. In Canada we have formal legislation that obligates federally regulated employers, as well as large private-sector contractors who provide goods and services to the federal government, to follow rules and procedures to achieve fair-treatment outcomes.[59] But even if not formally required by law to adopt an inclusive hiring strategy, many organizations have discovered that these strategies produce larger talent pools from which to select employees (i.e., with more choice, the likelihood of finding a successful match increases). Another persistent fairness issue concerns the wage gap that continues to exist between women and men who perform work of equal value.[60] Such pay differences are likely due to procedural injustice in some form, with pay-determining procedures functioning in an inconsistent, biased, and inaccurate manner across male- and female-dominated jobs. Although the wage gap has narrowed over the years, today, in Canada, full-time working women still earn an average of 72 cents for every dollar earned by full-time working men. Of course, some companies do a better job than others at achieving pay equity, promoting workplace diversity, and implementing inclusiveness decision making. Table 7-2 provides the list of employers who have been recently recognized for their exceptional fair treatment of women; members of visible minority groups; persons with disabilities; Aboriginal people; and lesbian, gay, bisexual, and transgendered peoples.[61]

You might be wondering, "Does procedural justice really matter—don't people just care about the outcomes that they receive?" To answer this question, one only has to look at the annual ranking of Canadian universities by *Maclean's* magazine. For many years, concerns have been expressed about the procedures (methodology) used to compile data and determine overall rankings—so much so that in 2006, 11 institutions decided to withdraw their participation from the process altogether. The issue for these universities was not the outcome (ranking), per se, but rather the procedures used to determine their ranks.[62] Research suggests that distributive justice and procedural justice combine to influence employee reactions, as shown in Figure 7-4.[63] It's true that when outcomes are good, people don't spend as much time worrying about how fair the process was, as illustrated by the green line in the figure, which shows that procedural justice has little impact on reactions when distributive justice is high. However, when outcomes are bad, procedural justice becomes enormously important. Research shows that negative or unexpected events trigger a thorough examination of process issues, making adherence to rules like consistency, bias suppression, and accuracy much more vital.[64]

In fact, research shows that procedural justice tends to be a stronger driver of reactions to authorities than distributive justice. For example, a meta-analysis of 183 studies showed that procedural justice was a stronger predictor of satisfaction with supervision, overall job satisfaction, and organizational commitment than distributive justice.[65] Why does the decision-making process sometimes matter more than the decision-making outcome? Likely because employees understand that outcomes come and go—some may be in your favour, while others may be a bit disappointing. Procedures, however, are more long-lasting and stay in place until the organization redesigns them or a new leader arrives to revise them.

INTERPERSONAL JUSTICE In addition to judging the fairness of decision outcomes and processes, employees might consider how authorities treat them as the procedures are implemented. **Interpersonal justice** reflects the perceived fairness of the treatment received by employees from authorities.[66] Interpersonal justice is fostered when authorities adhere to two particular rules. The respect rule pertains to whether authorities treat employees in a dignified and sincere manner, and the propriety rule reflects whether authorities refrain

interpersonal justice The perceived fairness of the interpersonal treatment received by employees from authorities

TABLE 7-2 Canada's Best Diversity Employers (listed alphabetically)

Alberta-Pacific Forest Industries Inc.	Nexen Inc.
Assiniboine Credit Union Limited	Ontario Public Service
Bell Aliant Regional Communications, LP	Pfizer Canada Inc.
Blake, Cassels & Graydon LLP	Procter & Gamble Inc.
Boeing Canada Technology Ltd., Winnipeg Division	Royal Bank of Canada
Canada Mortgage and Housing Corporation	Saskatchewan Government Insurance
Canada Post Corporation	SaskPower Corporation
Canadian Pacific Railway Ltd.	Scotiabank Group
Catholic Children's Aid Society of Toronto	Statistics Canada
Corus Entertainment Inc.	Telus Corporation
Ernst & Young LLP	Toronto Police Service
Hewlett-Packard (Canada) Co.	University Health Network
HSBC Bank Canada	University of British Columbia
Information Services Corporation of Saskatchewan	University of Toronto
Intuit Canada Limited	Vancity Group
KPMG LLP	WorkSafeBC
L'Oréal Canada Inc.	Xerox Canada Ltd.
McGill University	

Source: "Canada's Best Diversity Employers," Mediacorp Canada Inc., retrieved March 27, 2009, at www.canadastop100.com/diversity. Canada's Best Diversity Employers is a trademark of Mediacorp Canada Inc.

from making improper or offensive remarks. From this perspective, interpersonal *injustice* occurs when authorities bad-mouth employees; criticize, berate, embarrass, or humiliate them in public; or refer to them with racist or sexist labels.[67]

How common are instances of interpersonal injustice? A survey of nearly 5,000 employees found that 36 percent reported persistent hostility from authorities and co-workers, when persistent hostility was defined as experiencing one abusive act at least weekly for a period of one year.[68] How damaging are such acts? One study asked 41 employees to complete a survey on interactions with authorities and co-workers four times a day for two to three weeks using a palmtop computer.[69] Two kinds of interactions were coded—positive experiences and negative experiences—and participants also reported on their current mood (e.g., happy, pleased, sad, blue, unhappy). The results of the study showed that positive interactions were more common than negative interactions, but the effects of negative interactions on mood were five times stronger than the effects of positive interactions. Such findings suggest that violations of the respect and propriety rules loom much larger than adherence to such rules.[70] Indeed, research suggests that violations of interpersonal justice rules reduce employees' job satisfaction, life satisfaction, and organizational commitment while increasing feelings of depression, anxiety, and burnout.[71]

FIGURE 7-4 Combined Effects of Distributive and Procedural Justice

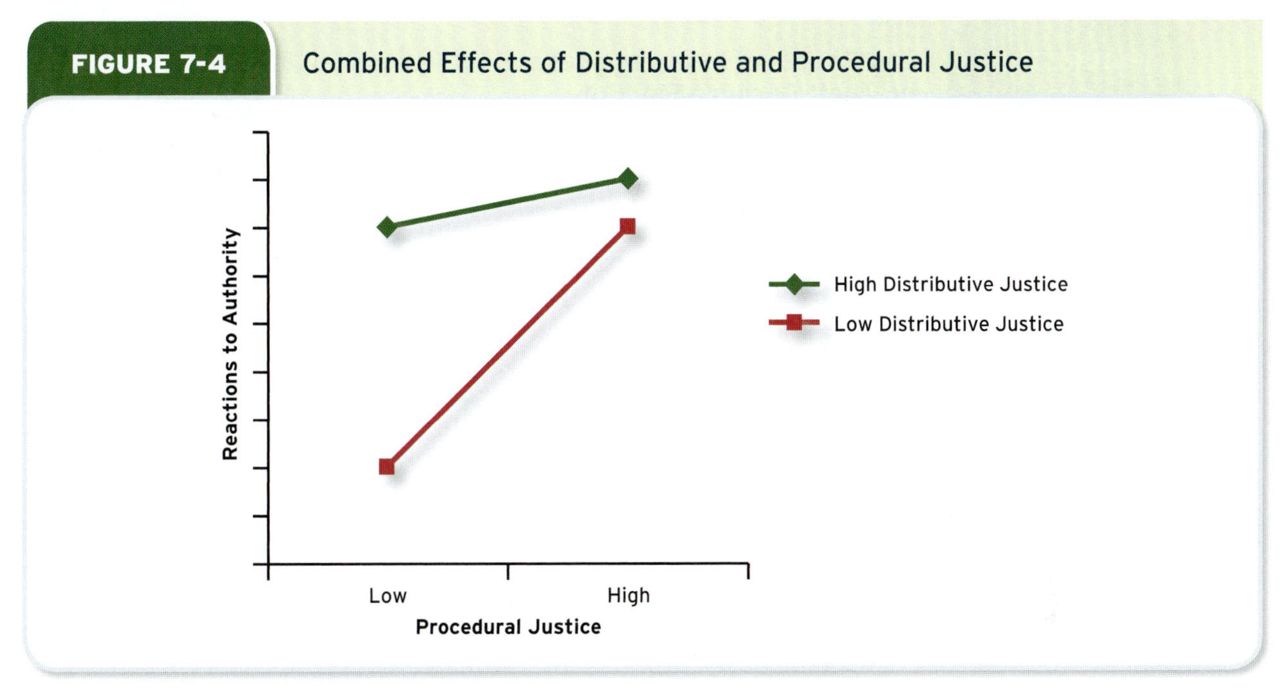

Source: Adapted from J. Brockner and B.M. Wiesenfeld, "An Integrative Framework for Explaining Reactions to Decisions: Interactive Effects of Outcomes and Procedures," *Psychological Bulletin* 120 (1996), pp. 189–208.

INFORMATIONAL JUSTICE Finally, employees may consider the kind of information that authorities provide during the course of organizational decision making. **Informational justice** reflects the perceived fairness of the communications provided to employees from authorities.[72] Informational justice is fostered when authorities adhere to two particular rules. The justification rule mandates that authorities explain decision-making procedures and outcomes in a comprehensive and reasonable manner, and the truthfulness rule requires that those communications be honest and candid. Although it seems like common sense that organizations would explain decisions in a comprehensive and adequate manner, that's often not the case. A particularly striking example of informational injustice comes from south of the border. RadioShack (operates in Canada as The Source by Circuit City) was recently criticized for firing 400 employees via e-mail.[73] Employees at the Fort Worth headquarters received messages on a Tuesday morning saying: "The work force reduction notification is currently in progress. Unfortunately your position is one that has been eliminated." After receiving the 18-word message, employees had 30 minutes to make phone calls and say goodbye to fellow employees, before packing up their belongings in boxes and plastic bags.

informational justice The perceived fairness of the communications provided to employees from authorities

These sorts of informational injustices are all too common, for a variety of reasons. One reason is that sharing bad news is the worst part of the job for most managers, leading them to distance themselves when it's time to play messenger.[74] Another reason is that managers worry about triggering a lawsuit if they comprehensively and honestly explain the real reasons for a layoff, a poor evaluation, or a missed promotion. Ironically, that defence mechanism is typically counterproductive, because research suggests that honest and adequate explanations are actually a powerful strategy for reducing retaliation responses against the organization.[75] In fact, low levels of informational justice can come back to haunt the organization if a wrongful termination claim is actually filed. How? Because the organization typically needs to provide performance evaluations for the terminated employee over the past few years, to show that the employee was fired for poor performance.[76] If managers

FIGURE 7-5 The Effects of Informational and Interpersonal Justice on Theft During a Pay Cut

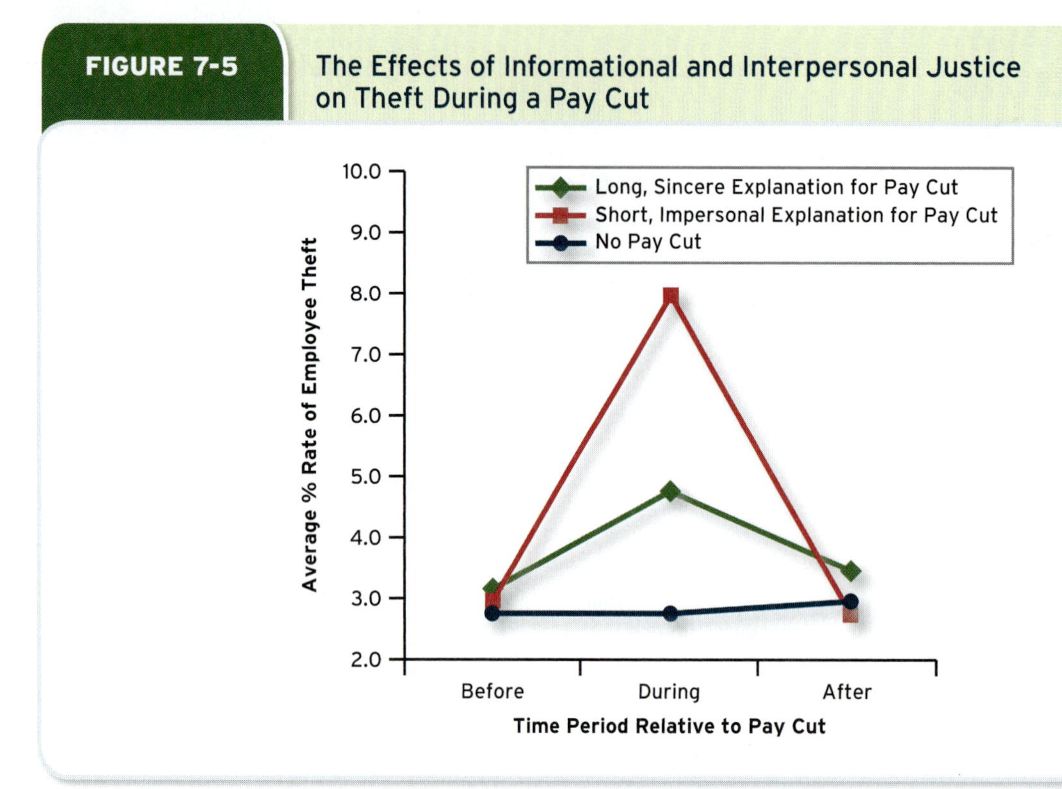

Source: Adapted from J. Greenberg, "Employee Theft as a Reaction to Underpayment Inequity: The Hidden Cost of Paycuts," *Journal of Applied Psychology* 75 (1990), pp. 561–68.

refrained from offering candid and honest explanations on those evaluations, then the organization can't offer anything to justify the termination.

One study provides a particularly effective demonstration of the power of informational justice (and interpersonal justice). The study occurred in three plants of a manufacturing company that specialized in small mechanical parts for the aerospace and automotive industries.[77] The company had recently lost two of its largest contracts and was forced to cut wages by 15 percent in two of the three plants. The company was planning to offer a short, impersonal explanation for the pay cut to both of the affected plants. However, as part of a research study, the company was convinced to offer a longer, more sincere explanation at one of the plants. Theft levels were then tracked before, during, and after the 10-week pay cut using the company's standard accounting formulas for inventory "shrinkage."

The results of the study are shown in Figure 7-5. In the plant without the pay cut, no change in theft levels occurred over the 10-week period. In the plant with the short, impersonal explanation, theft rose dramatically during the pay cut, likely as a means of retaliating for perceived inequity, before falling to previous levels once the cut had passed. Importantly, in the plant with the long, sincere explanation, the rise in theft was much less significant during the pay cut, with theft levels again falling back to normal levels once the cut had ended. Clearly, the higher levels of informational and interpersonal justice were worth it from a cost-savings perspective. The difference in theft across the two plants is remarkable, given that the long, sincere explanation was only 143 words longer than the short, impersonal explanation. What's an extra 45 seconds if it can save a few thousand dollars?

SUMMARY Taken together, distributive, procedural, interpersonal, and informational justice can be used to describe how fairly employees are treated by authorities. When an

OB RESEARCH IN CANADA

Dr. Ramona Bobocel, at the University of Waterloo, is interested in studying issues relating to justice in the workplace. According to Dr. Bobocel, there is an increasing awareness among social scientists that people's attitudes and behaviour in many domains, such as the workplace, are strongly influenced by their experience of justice or fairness. In fact, we see numerous examples of this in this chapter. Underlying Dr. Bobocel's recent research program is a continuing interest in learning how employees perceive, understand, and form judgments of fairness, with particular emphasis on (a) the effects of such judgments on attitudes (e.g., organizational commitment, leader trust), and (b) determinants of the experience of justice itself. An overarching goal is to understand the psychological mechanisms underlying fairness effects.

After receiving her PhD in 1992 from the University of Western Ontario, Dr. Bobocel joined the University of Waterloo. Presently, Dr. Bobocel is a professor in the department of psychology at the University of Waterloo. She teaches and supervises undergraduate and graduate students within the industrial and organizational psychology program at the University of Waterloo. Dr. Bobocel's research has been funded by grants from the Social Sciences and Humanities Research Council of Canada and most recently by an industry-research collaborative grant (supported by Bell Canada). She also holds the prestigious Ontario Premier's Research Excellence Award. Dr. Bobocel's research has appeared in leading academic journals, including *Journal of Applied Psychology, Journal of Personality and Social Psychology,* and *Journal of Management.* In addition to teaching and research, Dr. Bobocel is a past Chair of the Canadian Society for Industrial and Organizational Psychology (CSIOP), a division of the Canadian Psychological Association.

Some of Dr. Bobocel's favourite publications include:

"Justice Motive Theory and the Study of Justice in Work Organizations: A Conceptual Integration, by D.R. Bobocel and C.L. Hafer, published in *European Psychologist* (2007, volume 12, pp. 283–89).

"Authoritarian Dynamics and Unethical Decision Making: High SDO Leaders and High RWA Followers," by L.S. Son Hing, D.R. Bobocel, M.P. Zanna, and M.V. McBride, published in *Journal of Personality and Social Psychology* (2007, volume 1, pp. 67–81).

"How Can Explanations Be Used to Foster Organizational Justice?" by D.R. Bobocel and A. Zdaniuk, published in J. Greenberg and J. Colquitt (eds.), *The Handbook of Organizational Justice* (volume 1, pp. 469–98), Mahwah, NJ: Lawrence Erlbaum Associates, 2005.

authority adheres to the justice rules in Table 7-1, it provides behavioural data that the authority might be trustworthy. Studies show that all four justice forms have strong correlations with employee trust levels.[78] All else being equal, employees trust authorities who allocate outcomes fairly; make decisions in a consistent, unbiased, and accurate way; and communicate decision-making details in a respectful, comprehensive, and honest manner. Which authorities are most likely to adhere to these sorts of rules? Research on ethics can provide some answers.

ETHICS

Research on ethics seeks to explain why people behave in a manner consistent with generally accepted norms of morality, and why they sometimes violate those norms.[79] Some ethics studies focus on behaviours that exceed minimum standards of morality, such as charitable giving or **whistle-blowing**, which occurs when employees expose illegal actions by their employer. Other studies focus on behaviours that fall below minimum standards of morality, such as lying and cheating. Still other studies focus on behaviours that merely reach minimum standards of morality, such as obeying the law. Regardless of the particular area of focus, such research continues to be a critical area of OB because unethical acts are so common in organizations. The prevalence of unethical activities in organizational settings seems to vary across countries as is demonstrated in our **OB Internationally** feature.

whistle-blowing When employees expose illegal actions by their employer

How can we explain exactly why an authority would choose to act in an unethical manner? One set of answers can be derived from research in social psychology. As shown in Figure 7-6, the four-component model of ethical decision making argues that ethical behaviours result from a multistage sequence beginning with moral awareness, continuing on to moral judgment, and then moral intent and ethical behaviour.[80] The sections that follow review the components of this model in more detail.

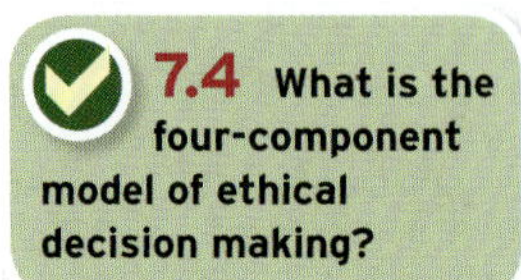

MORAL AWARENESS The first step needed to explain why an authority acts ethically is **moral awareness,** which occurs when an authority recognizes that a moral issue exists in a situation or that an ethical standard or principle is relevant to the circumstance.[81] Ethical issues rarely come equipped with "red flags" that mark them as morally sensitive—something is needed to make moral standards salient.[82] As an example, assume you worked for a videogame company whose most popular game involves assuming the role of a criminal in a big city and taking part in multiple storylines involving a variety of illegal activities, such as carjacking, bank robbery, assassination, and the killing of law enforcement personnel and innocent bystanders. A member of this game's development team has suggested embedding hidden sex scenes into the game, which is currently rated "mature" by the Entertainment Software Rating Board.

moral awareness When an authority recognizes that a moral issue exists in a situation

FIGURE 7-6 The Four-Component Model of Ethical Decision Making

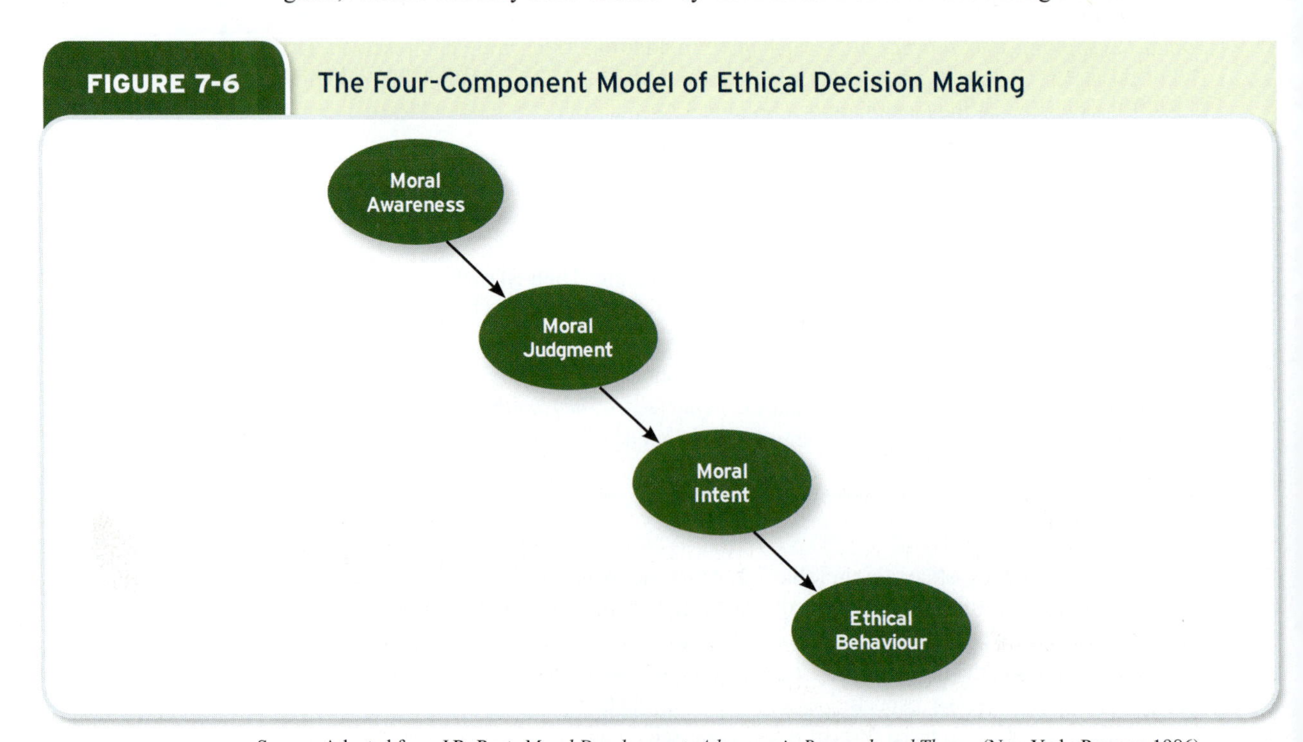

Source: Adapted from J.R. Rest, *Moral Development: Advances in Research and Theory* (New York: Praeger, 1986).

OB INTERNATIONALLY

Unethical actions can be defined as behaviours that fall below minimum standards of morality. For multinational corporations, however, the relevant question becomes "Whose standards of morality?" Research on business ethics across cultures reveals that different countries have very different baseline levels of unethical actions. Transparency International is an organization that monitors unethical practices in countries around the world. Using data from businesspeople, risk analysts, investigative journalists, country experts, and public citizens, the organization rates countries on a scale of 1 (unethical) to 10 (ethical).[83] Here are some of the scores from the 1999 version of the rankings:

SCORE	COUNTRY	SCORE	COUNTRY
10.0	Denmark	3.8	Lithuania
9.8	Finland	3.8	South Korea
9.4	Sweden	3.6	Philippines
9.2	Canada	3.6	Turkey
9.0	Netherlands	3.4	China
8.7	Australia	3.4	Mexico
8.6	Germany	3.3	Egypt
7.7	Hong Kong	3.3	Romania
7.7	Ireland	3.2	Thailand
7.5	United States	3.0	Argentina
6.8	Israel	2.9	Colombia
6.6	France	2.9	India
6.0	Japan	2.6	Ukraine
5.6	Taiwan	2.6	Venezuela
5.3	Belgium	2.6	Vietnam
5.1	Costa Rica	2.4	Russia
4.9	Greece	2.3	Kazakhstan
4.7	Italy	2.2	Pakistan
4.6	Czech Republic	2.0	Kenya
4.1	Brazil	1.6	Nigeria
3.8	Jamaica	1.5	Cameroon

These rankings reveal the challenges involved for any multinational corporation that does business in areas at the top and bottom of the rankings. Should the company have the same ethical expectations for employees in all countries, regardless of ethical norms? For now, that seems to be the most common position. For example, the Coca-Cola Company's Code of Business Conduct "applies to all the Company's business worldwide and to all Company employees."[84] The code is given to all employees along with a letter from the CEO and covers topics such as conflicts of interest, dealing with government officials, customer and supplier interactions, and political contributions. The code also describes the disciplinary actions associated with any violations of the code.

Is there an ethical issue at play here? On the one hand, you might be tempted to say that the game is already rated "mature" and that such hidden scenes are only extending the already less-than-wholesome nature of the game. Besides, "Easter eggs"—hidden objects in movies, DVDs, or computer and video games—have a long history in the entertainment industry. On the other hand, the hidden scenes constitute deception of the rating board, the customer, and potentially the customer's parents. And that deception issue stands apart from any moral issues raised by the actual content of the hidden scenes. If this story sounds familiar to you, it's because it actually happened with *Grand Theft Auto: San Andreas,* a game manufactured by a division of Take Two Interactive Software.[85] The hidden scenes, which began with the invitation, "How 'bout some coffee?" could be accessed using software available on the Internet. Take Two contends that the code for the scenes was put into early drafts of the game but was supposed to be removed before the game went to market.

ethical sensitivity The ability to recognize that a decision has ethical content

Moral awareness depends in part on the characteristics of the authority involved. An authority's **ethical sensitivity** reflects the ability to recognize that a particular decision has ethical content.[86] Ethical sensitivity can be measured by giving people a business case to read that includes a number of somewhat subtle ethical issues, along with a number of other sorts of issues (work sequencing challenges, organizing challenges, specific technical issues). Participants describe the issues that are raised in the case in an open-ended fashion, with ethical sensitivity captured by the number of ethical issues spotted within the case. In the Take Two example, it may be that the employees in charge of the *Grand Theft Auto* game weren't sensitive enough to recognize that the hidden scenes represented an ethical issue. That premise makes some sense, given that Take Two has had other ethical struggles, including having to settle charges of fraudulent accounting with the U.S. Securities and Exchange Commission.

moral intensity The degree to which an issue has ethical urgency

Moral awareness also depends on the characteristics of the issue itself. **Moral intensity** captures the degree to which the issue has ethical urgency.[87] Moral intensity is driven by six factors, summarized in Table 7-3. A particular issue is high in moral intensity if the magnitude of its consequences are high, there is strong social consensus about the act, the probability of the act occurring and having the predicted consequences is high, those consequences will occur soon, the decision makers are close to those who will be affected, and the consequences are not concentrated on a select few. In the case of the *Grand Theft Auto* hidden scenes, it may be that Take Two felt that the consequences of the act would be minor, the scenes might not be discovered, or the people who would be adversely affected are very different in a psychological sense.

moral judgment When an authority can accurately identify the "right" course of action

cognitive moral development As people age and mature, they move through several states of moral development, each more mature and sophisticated than the prior one

MORAL JUDGMENT Assuming an authority recognizes that a moral issue exists in a situation, the next step is **moral judgment**, which is when the authority accurately identifies the morally "right" course of action.[88] What factors affect moral judgment? One factor is moral development, as described by Kohlberg's theory of **cognitive moral development**.[89] This theory argues that as people age and mature, they move through several stages of moral development—each more mature and sophisticated than the prior one. These stages are shown in Figure 7-7. Research suggests that most children are at the preconventional level, so their actions are motivated by the avoidance of punishment (Stage 1) and the maintaining of "You scratch my back, I'll scratch yours" sorts of relationships

The programmers of *Grand Theft Auto* appeared to lack moral awareness when it was discovered that a hidden portion of the popular computer game, which could be easily accessed with free software, contained sex scenes.

TABLE 7-3 The Six Facets of Moral Intensity

Facet	Description
Magnitude of consequences	How much harm (or benefit) would be done to other people?
Social consensus	How much agreement is there that the proposed act would be evil (or good)?
Probability of effect	How likely is it that the act will actually occur and that the assumed consequences will match predictions?
Temporal immediacy	How much time will pass between the act and the onset of its consequences?
Proximity	How near (in a psychological or physical sense) is the authority to those who will be affected?
Concentration of effect	Will the consequences be concentrated on a limited set of people, or will they be more far-reaching?

Source: Adapted from T.M. Jones, "Ethical Decision Making by Individuals in Organizations: An Issue-Contingent Model." *Academy of Management Review* 16 (1991), pp. 366–95.

FIGURE 7-7 Stages of Cognitive Moral Development

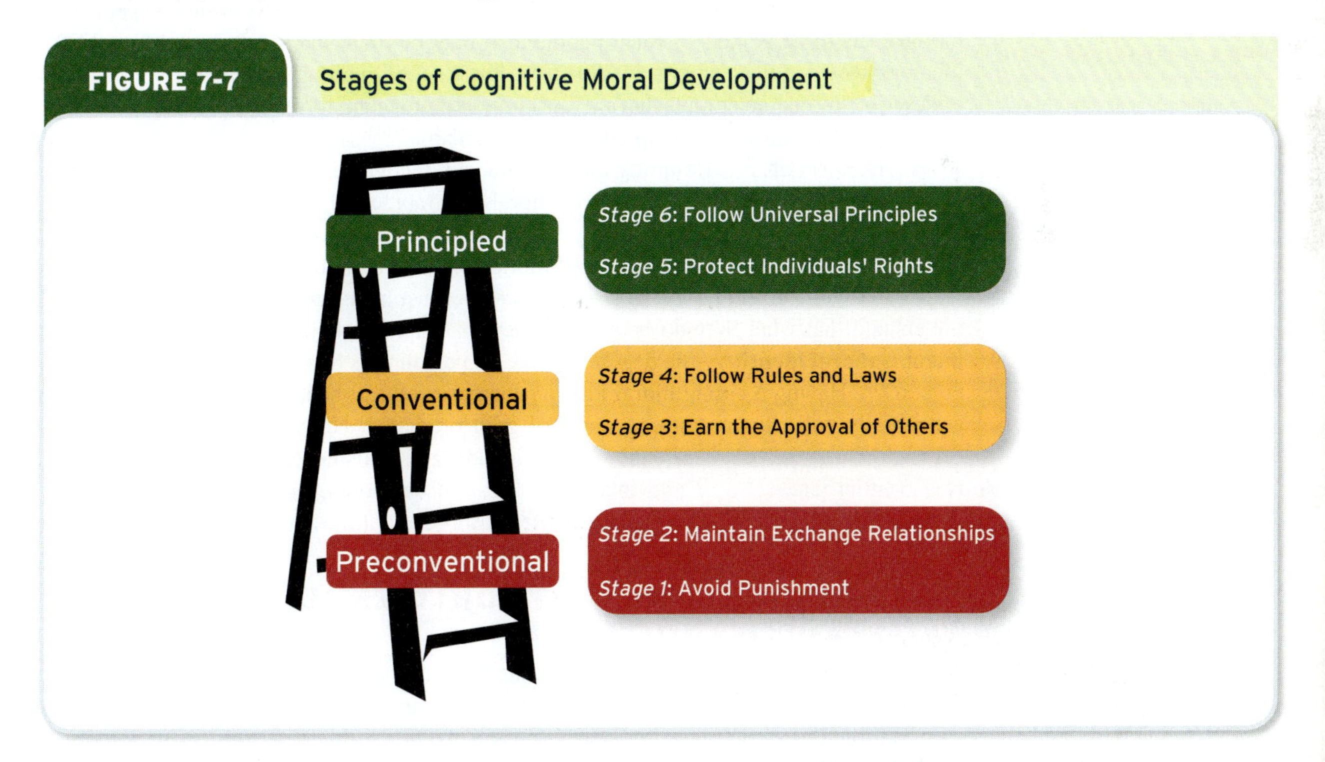

(Stage 2). Most adults, in contrast, are at the conventional level, with their ethical thinking influenced by the opinions of relevant authorities (Stage 3), along with more formal rules and standards (Stage 4).[90] That positioning is relevant for organizations because it suggests that the ethical decisions of employees can be influenced by organizational norms, practices, and reward systems.

"Miss Dugan, will you send someone in here who can distinguish right from wrong?"

Research suggests that fewer than 20 percent of North Americans reach the principled (sometimes called "postconventional") level.[91] The principles those individuals utilize during ethical decision making are called **ethical ideologies**.[92] Those in Stage 5 may be more likely to adopt a **relativism** ideology and reject the notion of universal moral rules.[93] Relativists agree with statements like, "Whether a lie is judged to be moral or immoral depends upon the circumstances surrounding the decision."[94] Such people may also be more likely to adopt a **utilitarianism** ideology where ethical actions are defined as those that achieve the most valuable ends.[95] When asked to describe the character traits that are most important to them, utilitarians prioritize traits such as "resourceful," "effective," "productive," and "winner."[96] In contrast, those in Stage 6 should be more likely to adopt an **idealism** ideology and embrace the notion of universal moral rules.[97] Idealists agree with statements like, "The existence of potential harm to others is always wrong, irrespective of the benefits to be gained."[98] Such people also may be more likely to adopt a **formalism** ideology where ethical actions are defined using a set of guiding principles.[99] When asked to describe the character traits that are most important to them, formalists prioritize traits like "trustworthy," "honest," "principled," and "dependable."[100]

ethical ideologies Principles used by individuals during ethical decision making

relativism The view that there are no universal moral rules

utilitarianism The view that ethical actions are defined as those that achieve the most valuable ends

idealism Embracing the notion of universal moral rules

formalism The view that ethical actions are defined using a set of guiding principles

moral intent An authority's degree of commitment to the moral course of action

moral identity The degree to which a person views himself or herself as a moral person

MORAL INTENT Assuming that an authority recognizes that a moral issue exists in a situation and possesses the cognitive moral development to choose the right course of action, one step remains: The authority has to *want* to act ethically. **Moral intent** reflects an authority's degree of commitment to the moral course of action.[101] The distinction between awareness, judgment, and intent is important, because many unethical people know and understand that what they do is wrong—they just don't really care. One driver of moral intent is **moral identity**—the degree to which a person sees himself or herself as a "moral person."[102] Having a strong moral identity increases ethical behaviours because failing to act morally will trigger a strong sense of guilt or shame. However, moral intent is also driven by a number of situational factors, including the existence of on-the-job pressures, role conflict, and rewards and incentives that can be more easily attained by unethical means.[103] See our **OB for Students** feature for more about these issues.

SO WHY ARE SOME AUTHORITIES MORE TRUSTED THAN OTHERS?

As shown in Figure 7-8, answering that question requires understanding the different sources in which trust can be based, including dispositions, cognitions, and affect. Disposition based trust is rooted in an individual's trust propensity, whereas affect based trust is rooted in a fondness for the authority. Cognition-based trust is driven by perceptions of trustworthiness, as employees attempt to assess the competence, character, and benevolence of authorities. Unfortunately, it is often difficult to gauge trustworthiness accurately, so employees instead look to more observable behaviours that can be used as indirect evidence of trustworthiness. Those behaviours may centre on the justice of authorities, with employees considering the

OB FOR STUDENTS

The most relevant form of unethical behaviour for students is cheating on exams and assignments. How common is cheating? One survey of almost 50,000 students at 69 schools found that 26 percent of undergraduate business majors admitted to serious cheating on exams, with 54 percent admitting to cheating on written assignments (including plagiarism or using a friend's homework).[104] Why do students cheat? One likely reason is that grade pressures reduce moral intent—even when students recognize that cheating is a moral issue and that the right decision is not to cheat, they do it anyway. Some support for this notion comes from a recent study of cheating among 5,331 students at 54 colleges and universities.[105] The students filled out anonymous surveys measuring 13 different cheating behaviours, along with four potential predictors of cheating: (1) understanding of academic integrity policies, (2) likelihood of being reported by a peer if caught cheating, (3) perceived severity of cheating penalties, and (4) how often they had observed another student cheating. Of those four potential predictors, which do you think had the strongest effect? That's right—observing another student cheating. In fact, none of the other three factors had any statistical relationship with cheating behaviours. It may be that seeing others cheat creates a sort of peer pressure to "keep up with one's classmates," particularly when classes are graded on a curve. What are some other reasons? Is it possible that students' moral judgments about the act have changed? Consider this example: Very recently, a first-year computer-science student at Ryerson University was accused of cheating after it was discovered that he helped to run a Facebook study group that was used by 146 of his fellow students.[106] The student claimed that the study group was simply a forum for other students to ask questions and help each other with their homework assignments. Do you think that this student was cheating? Do you think his behaviour or the behaviours of the other 146 students were unethical? Answers to these questions help schools gain a much deeper understanding of why students cheat if such behaviours are to be curbed.

distributive, procedural, interpersonal, and informational justice experienced at work. The ethical behaviours of authorities, which are driven by their moral awareness, their moral judgment, and their moral intent, are also relevant to trustworthiness.

HOW IMPORTANT IS TRUST?

7.5 How does trust affect job performance and organizational commitment?

Does trust have a significant impact on the two primary outcomes in our integrative model of OB? Does it correlate with job performance and organizational commitment? Figure 7-9 summarizes the research evidence linking trust to job performance and organizational commitment. The figure reveals that trust does affect job performance. Why? One reason is that trust is moderately correlated with task performance. A study of employees in eight plants of a tool manufacturing company sheds some light on why trust benefits task performance.[107] The study gave employees survey measures of their trust in two different authorities: their plant's manager and the company's top management team. Both trust measures were significant predictors of employees' **ability to focus**, which reflects the degree to which employees can devote their attention to work, as opposed to "covering their backside," "playing politics," and "keeping an eye on the boss." The ability to focus is clearly vital to task performance in many jobs, particularly when job duties become more complex.

ability to focus The degree to which employees can devote their attention to work

FIGURE 7-8 Why Are Some Authorities More Trusted Than Others?

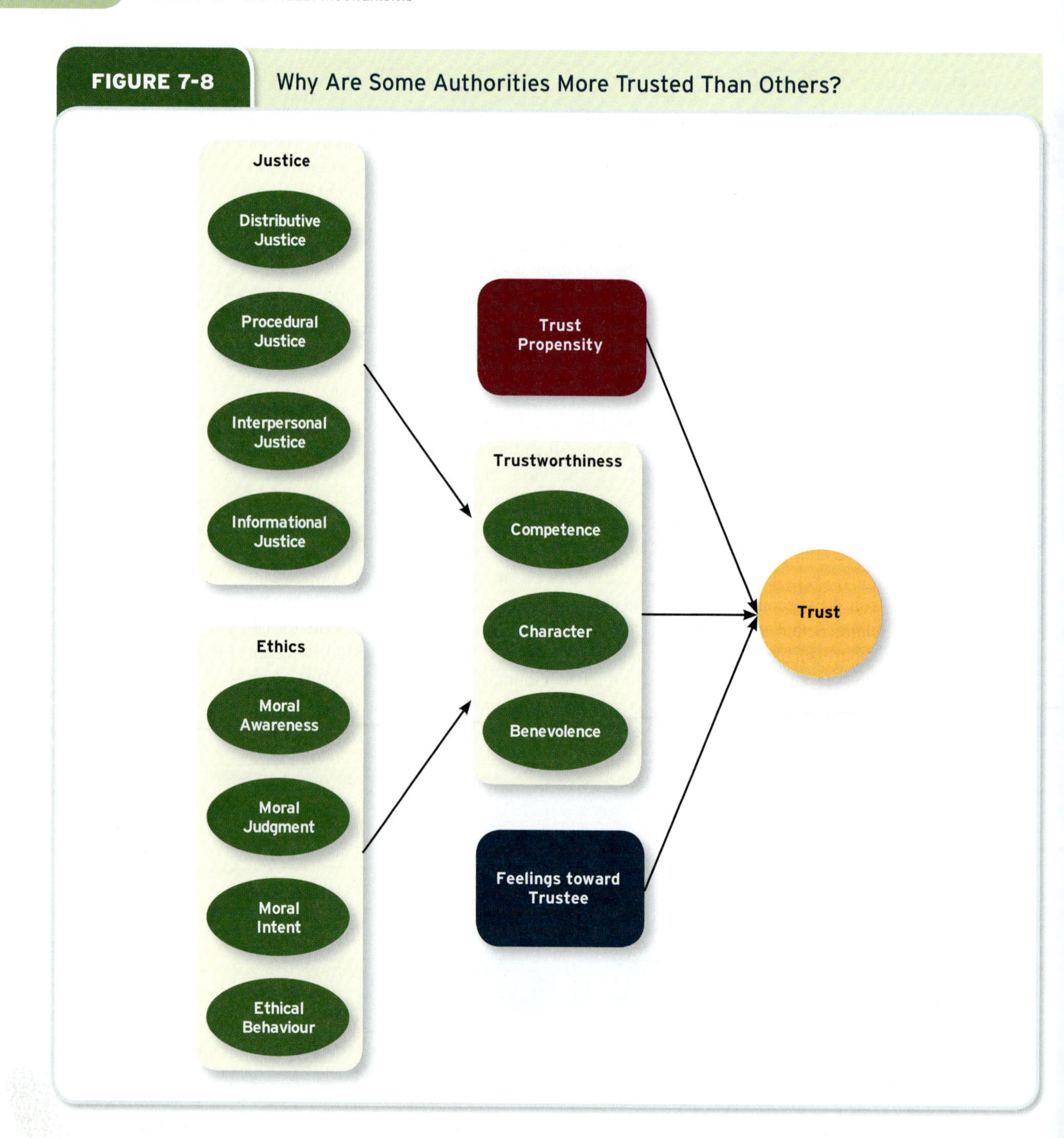

economic exchange Work relationships that resemble a contractual agreement by which employees fulfill job duties in exchange for financial compensation

Trust also influences citizenship behaviour and counterproductive behaviour. Why? One reason is that the willingness to accept vulnerability changes the nature of the employee–employer relationship. Employees who don't trust their authorities have **economic exchange** relationships that are based on narrowly defined, quid pro quo obligations that are specified in advance and have an explicit repayment schedule.[108] Economic exchanges are impersonal and resemble contractual agreements, such that employees agree to fulfill the duties in their

FIGURE 7-9 Effects of Trust on Performance and Commitment

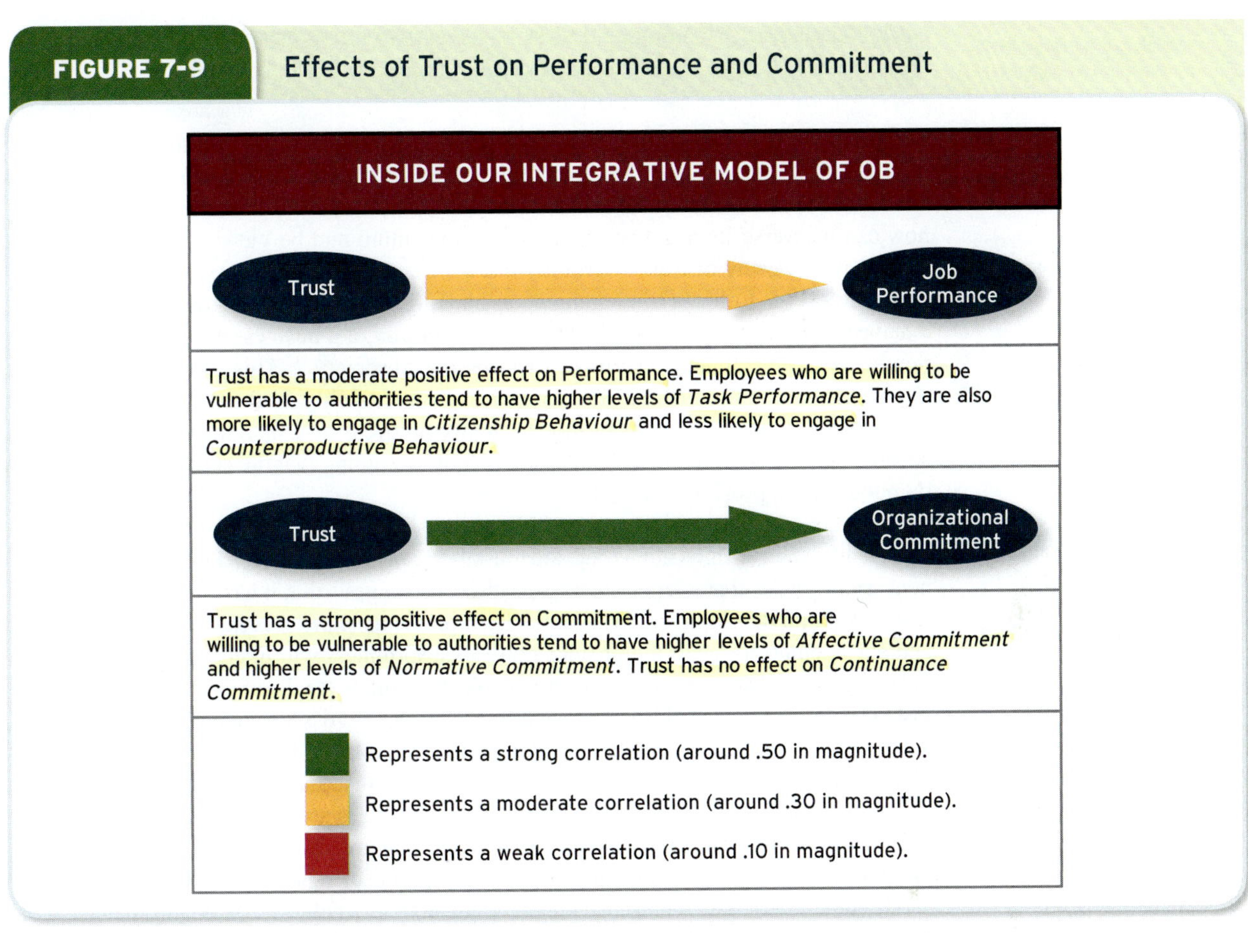

Sources: K.T. Dirks and D.L. Ferrin, "Trust in Leadership: Meta-Analytic Findings and Implications for Research and Practice," *Journal of Applied Psychology* 87 (2002), pp. 611–28; J.A. Colquitt, B.A. Scott, and J.A. LePine, "Trust, Trustworthiness, and Trust Propensity: A Meta-Analytic Test of their Unique Relationships with Risk Taking and Job Performance," *Journal of Applied Psychology* 92 (2007), pp. 909–27.

job description in exchange for financial compensation. As trust increases, **social exchange** relationships develop that are based on vaguely defined obligations that are open-ended and long term in their repayment schedule.[109] Social exchanges are characterized by mutual investment, such that employees agree to go above and beyond their duties in exchange for fair and proper treatment by authorities. In social exchange contexts, employees are willing to engage in beneficial behaviours because they trust that those efforts will eventually be rewarded.

social exchange Work relationships that are characterized by mutual investment, with employees willing to engage in "extra mile" sorts of behaviours because they trust that their efforts will eventually be rewarded

Figure 7-9 also reveals that trust affects organizational commitment. Why? One reason is that trusting an authority increases the likelihood that an emotional bond will develop,[110] particularly if that trust is rooted in positive feelings for the authority. Trusting an authority also makes it more likely that a sense of obligation will develop, because employees feel more confident that the authority deserves that obligation. When negative events occur, employees who trust the authority are willing to accept the vulnerability that comes with continued employment,[111] remaining confident in their belief that the situation will eventually improve.

APPLICATION: SOCIAL RESPONSIBILITY

Now that you understand the factors that drive trust in authorities and the importance of trust levels to performance and commitment, we turn our attention to a very practical question: "How can organizations become more trustworthy?" In the case of Wal-Mart, how can it reverse its negative reputational momentum and be viewed, once again, as an organization worthy of trust? Certainly that's a big question with no single answer. However, one start is to focus the organization's attention on **corporate social responsibility**, a perspective that acknowledges that the responsibility of a business encompasses the economic, legal, ethical, and citizenship expectations of society.[112] This perspective maintains the belief that the foundation of any business is profitability, because organizations must fulfill their economic responsibilities to their employees and shareholders. However, the social responsibility lens supplements that belief by arguing that the company's obligations do not end with profit maximization.

corporate social responsibility A perspective that acknowledges that the responsibility of a business encompasses the economic, legal, ethical, and citizenship expectations of society

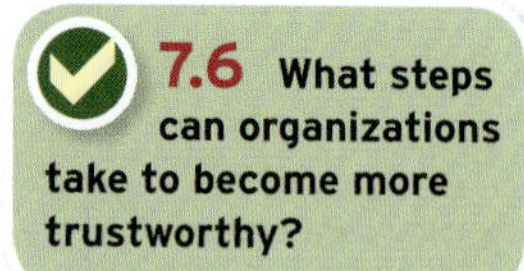

The legal component of corporate social responsibility argues that the law represents society's codification of right and wrong and must therefore be followed.[113] Fulfilling this component speaks to the character of the organization and suggests that it has reached conventional levels of moral development. Wal-Mart's legal problems signal a breach of this component, and any attempts to repair the organization's trustworthiness will likely require an end to its legal troubles. What steps can organizations take to promote legal compliance? In Canada, for instance, occupational health and safety laws are in place across the country to protect people. To raise awareness and promote healthy and safe workplaces, as well as ensure legal compliance, many organizations form internal committees made up of company and employee (or union) representatives.[114] The roles of these committees are varied, but generally include being aware of relevant safety issues and hazards, monitoring the effectiveness of on-going programs, investigating complaints, and providing annual reports for external agencies.[115] These committees often represent a tangible sign, both internally and externally, that the organization "walks the talk" with respect to caring for the well-being of its employees.

The ethical component of corporate social responsibility argues that organizations have an obligation to do what is right, just, and fair and to avoid harm.[116] Fulfilling this component is relevant to the character and benevolence of the organization and suggests that it has reached one of the principled levels of moral development. Regardless of its legal implications, the way Wal-Mart treats its employees speaks to the ethical makeup of its culture. What can organizations do to improve that culture? An example of an organization that is committed to the ethical component of corporate social responsibility is TELUS, one of the largest telecommunications companies in Canada. At TELUS, the corporate ethics policy provides guidelines for the standards of ethical conduct by all managers and employees.[117] The policy spells out, and illustrates with case examples, a set of core values that people can use to navigate day-to-day moral dilemmas.[118] In fact, to promote awareness of the corporate ethics policy all 34,000 organizational members must, each year, complete an online course as a term of employment.[119]

The citizenship component of corporate social responsibility argues that organizations should contribute resources to improve the quality of life in the communities in which they work.[120] A great example is Canadian Tire's JumpStart program, which helps kids in financial need participate in organized sport and recreation such as hockey, soccer, and swimming. Three years after its launch in 2005, JumpStart has already helped more than 100,000 kids.[121] However, the citizenship component may also involve efforts geared toward environmental sustainability. In addition to contributing to strong communities (e.g., "give where we live" program), TELUS demonstrates corporate social responsibility by reducing its carbon footprint on the environment (i.e., reducing carbon dioxide emissions).[122] Achieving these environmental goals is important for a company that operates more than 3,600 buildings and 5,400 vehicles every day.[123]

TAKEAWAYS

7.1 Trust is the willingness to be vulnerable to an authority based on positive expectations about the authority's actions and intentions. Justice reflects the perceived fairness of an authority's decision making and can be used to explain why employees judge some authorities as more trustworthy than others. Ethics reflects the degree to which the behaviours of an authority are in accordance with generally accepted moral norms and can be used to explain why authorities choose to act in a trustworthy manner.

7.2 Trust can be disposition-based, meaning that one's personality includes a general propensity to trust others. Trust can also be cognition-based, meaning that it's rooted in a rational assessment of the authority's trustworthiness. Finally, trust can be affect-based, meaning that it's rooted in feelings toward the authority that go beyond any rational assessment of trustworthiness. Trustworthiness is judged along three dimensions: competence, character, and benevolence.

7.3 The fairness of an authority's decision making can be judged along four dimensions. Distributive justice reflects the perceived fairness of decision-making outcomes. Procedural justice reflects the perceived fairness of decision-making processes. Interpersonal justice reflects the perceived fairness of the treatment received by employees from authorities. Informational justice reflects the perceived fairness of the communications provided to employees from authorities.

7.4 The four-component model of ethical decision making argues that ethical behaviour depends on three concepts. Moral awareness reflects whether an authority recognizes that a moral issue exists in a situation. Moral judgment reflects whether the authority can accurately identify the "right" course of action. Moral intent reflects an authority's degree of commitment to the moral course of action.

7.5 Trust has a moderate positive relationship with job performance and a strong positive relationship with organizational commitment.

7.6 Organizations can become more trustworthy by emphasizing corporate social responsibility, a perspective that acknowledges that the responsibility of a business encompasses the economic, legal, ethical, and citizenship expectations of society.

KEY TERMS

- ability to focus p. 179
- affect-based trust p. 162
- benevolence p. 165
- character p. 165
- cognition-based trust p. 162
- cognitive moral development p. 176
- competence p. 164
- corporate social responsibility p. 182
- disposition-based trust p. 162
- distributive justice p. 167
- economic exchange p. 180
- ethical ideologies p. 178
- ethical sensitivity p. 176
- ethics p. 162
- formalism p. 178
- idealism p. 178
- informational justice p. 171
- interpersonal justice p. 169
- justice p. 161
- moral awareness p. 174
- moral identity p. 178
- moral intensity p. 176
- moral intent p. 178
- moral judgment p. 176
- procedural justice p. 168
- relativism p. 178
- social exchange p. 181
- trust p. 161
- trust propensity p. 162
- trustworthiness p. 164
- utilitarianism p. 178
- whistle-blowing p. 174

DISCUSSION QUESTIONS

7.1 Were you aware of the ethical criticisms that Wal-Mart has received? Do those criticisms affect your likelihood of shopping there? Why or why not?

7.2 Consider the three dimensions of trustworthiness (competence, character, and benevolence). Which of those dimensions would be most important when deciding whether to trust your boss? What about when deciding whether to trust a friend? If your two answers differ, why do they?

7.3 Putting yourself in the shoes of a manager, which of the four justice dimensions (distributive, procedural, interpersonal, informational) would you find it most difficult to maximize? Which would be the easiest to maximize and why?

7.4 Which component of ethical decision making do you believe best explains student cheating: moral awareness, moral judgment, or moral intent? Why do you feel that way?

7.5 Assume you were applying for a job at a company known for its corporate social responsibility. How important would that be to you when deciding whether to apply and whether to accept a job offer?

CASE • WAL-MART

Wal-Mart has always been proud of having one of the strictest and most stringent ethics policies in the industry. Every employee in the company is encouraged to report suspicions of unethical activities. However, in recent years, Wal-Mart's business tactics have come under constant scrutiny from critics. A report by McKinsey & Co. discovered that as early as 2004, 8 percent of the company's customers had stopped shopping there due to its negative media attention. The consumer backlash against Wal-Mart's new negative image has adversely influenced the company's bottom line. Consumers have stopped shopping at Wal-Mart stores because the company is perceived as unfair to workers or bad for the economy.

Often overlooked in this debate is the good that the company has done for local communities. Wal-Mart Canada, for instance, operates one of the countries strongest community involvement programs, focused on donating and raising money and increasing awareness for Canadian charities and organizations in need. Since coming to Canada in 1994, Wal-Mart Canada and its associates have raised and donated more than $50 million to Canadian organizations through the Good Works program. Some of the programs supported include Children's Miracle Network, Breakfast Clubs of Canada, Canadian Red Cross, Juno Beach Centre, Adopt-a-School Program, Missing Children's Program in conjunction with the RCMP, and the Wal-Mart Scholarship Program.

Wal-Mart is now fighting an uphill battle to regain its reputation. Is it too late to salvage it?

7.1 How has Wal-Mart's trustworthiness been affected? Can Wal-Mart recover from so many negative events and publicity? Explain.

7.2 Poor ethics do not hinder the performance of a large corporation like Wal-Mart. Do you agree? Explain.

Sources: M. Boyle, "Wal-Mart: Desperately Seeking Ethics," *Fortune,* March 7, 2006; P. Gogoi, "Wal-Mart's Latest Ethics Controversy," *BusinessWeek,* June 13, 2007; P. Gogoi, "Wal-Mart: A Reputation Crisis," *Business Week,* October 31, 2006; P. Gogoi, "Wal-Mart's Political Payouts," *BusinessWeek,* September 29, 2006, www.businessweek.com; N. Vardi, "Would Sam Be Proud?" *Forbes,* May 3, 2007; Wal-Mart Canada website, www.walmart.ca.

EXERCISE • TRUSTWORTHINESS AND TRUST

The purpose of this exercise is to explore the factors that lead one person to trust another. This exercise uses groups of six participants, so your instructor will either assign you to a group of six or ask you to create your own group of six. The exercise has the following steps:

1. Individually, read the following paragraphs that describe three people ***who might work for you.*** For each, how comfortable would you be turning over to him or her a project that was very important to you if you could not monitor what he or she did? (1 = ***petrified;*** 10 = ***completely comfortable***).

    J.B. was promoted to his/her current position shortly before you were transferred in as head of the department. On paper, J.B. is qualified, but you have some serious doubts about his/her skills. J.B. has an MBA from a well-respected university and has been in the current position for over a year. During that time, you have found some very surprising mistakes and oversights in J.B.'s work. J.B. doesn't seem to have a grasp of how the company operates and what his/her role is supposed to be. When you have tried to explain these things, J.B. claims to understand. However, J.B.'s work doesn't seem to show it. J.B. really likes you and bends over backward to help you out whenever possible. All of J.B.'s peers seem to like him/her, and J.B. has gained a bit of a reputation among them and the customers for being very fair.

    Sandy has been with your company for a long time and has worked for you for about a year. Inasmuch as Sandy's job is fairly technical, Sandy has continued to attend seminars and read technical journals to keep up to date.

Sandy's work is always careful and complete. Sandy has on a number of occasions shown great loyalty to you, the boss. For example, just last month, Sandy blocked information from getting to your boss that would have made you look bad. On several occasions, Sandy has misled people in other departments to keep them from taking resources away from your department.

Pat recently transferred to your division from the company's East Coast division. Pat wanted to get back closer to family. Pat's former department head had tried unsuccessfully to block Pat's leaving, arguing that Pat was "just too important" to let him/her go. The quality of Pat's work appears to justify the former manager's reluctance to let Pat leave. Pat does not seem to have trouble making friends and is quite popular but has refused all of your attempts to get to know him/her. When you have gone to lunch together, Pat mostly listened to what you had to say and didn't say much. Pat often seems to have his/her guard up when talking with you. In dealings with other employees and with customers, Pat is fair and honest.

Based on your ratings, whom would you trust the most? In your groups, explain your ratings. What factors were most critical to your trust assessments?

2. Individually, read the following paragraphs that describe three people for *whom you might work*. For each, how comfortable would you be turning over to this manager control over *your destiny in the company* if you could not monitor what he or she did? (1 = petrified; 10 = completely comfortable).

   In dealing with you, Terry is a no-nonsense kind of manager. Terry has always acted on the up-and-up from everything you've seen and heard. Terry always gets things done well and is respected by all. Your attempts to go to lunch, socialize, and build a relationship have always been politely refused. Terry has a number of friends at work, but you do not seem to be one of them.

   You've worked for Taylor for several years. Taylor has always been honest with you and shown a genuine concern for others, as well as for the profitability of the business. Taylor has always been particularly good to you, and it's clear that Taylor likes and respects you. Taylor frequently has problems getting the bills paid and customers served on time and does not seem to manage the company's finances very well. Taylor does not seem to have clear objectives about what things are important for the operation of the business.

   You have always found your manager, Jesse, to have strong skills. Jesse is on the phone with another manager. You hear Jesse commit to getting a report done by Friday. Once off the phone, Jesse makes a snappy remark about hell freezing over and continues your performance review. You can recall a number of other occasions when Jesse told someone one thing and turned around and told you something entirely different. Jesse has always been nice to you and seems to like you. Jesse tells you you're meeting all your goals and should expect a promotion and pay increase within the next six months to a year.

   Based on your ratings, whom would you trust most? In your groups, explain your ratings. What factors were most critical to your trust assessments?

3. Class discussion, whether in groups or as a class, should centre on this question: What factors caused you to trust one person more than the others in the two sets of scenarios? Do the relevant factors vary when trust refers to a subordinate compared with when trust refers to a supervisor? How?

Source: Adapted from R.C. Mayer and P.M. Norman, "Exploring Attributes of Trustworthiness: A Classroom Exercise," *Journal of Management Education* 28 (2004), pp. 224–49.

OB ASSESSMENTS • TRUST PROPENSITY

Are you a trusting person or a suspicious person by nature? This assessment is designed to measure trust propensity—a dispositional willingness to trust other people. Answer each question using the response scale provided. Then subtract your answers to the bold-faced questions from 6, with the difference being your new answers for those questions. For example, if your original answer for question 4 was "4," your new answer is "2" (6–4). Then sum up your answers for the eight questions.

1 STRONGLY DISAGREE	2 DISAGREE	3 NEUTRAL	4 AGREE	5 STRONGLY AGREE

1. **One should be very cautious with strangers.** ______
2. Most experts tell the truth about the limits of their knowledge. ______
3. Most people can be counted on to do what they say they will do. ______
4. **These days, you must be alert or someone is likely to take advantage of you.** ______
5. Most salespeople are honest in describing their products. ______
6. Most repair people will not overcharge people who are ignorant of their specialty. ______
7. Most people answer public opinion polls honestly. ______
8. Most adults are competent at their jobs. ______

SCORING

If your scores sum up to 21 or above, you tend to be trusting of other people, which means you are often willing to accept some vulnerability to others under conditions of risk. If your scores sum up to 20 or below, you tend to be suspicious of other people, which means you are rarely willing to accept some vulnerability to others under conditions of risk.

Sources: R.C. Mayer and J.H. Davis, "The Effect of the Performance Appraisal System on Trust for Management: A Field Quasi-Experiment," *Journal of Applied Psychology* 84 (1999), pp. 123–36. Copyright © 1999 by the American Psychological Associated. Adapted with permission. No further reproduction or distribution is permitted without written permission from the American Psychological Association; F.D. Schoorman, R.C. Mayer, C. Roger, and J.H. Davis. "Empowerment in Veterinary Clinics: The Role of Trust in Delegation." Presented in a Symposium on Trust at the 11th Annual Conference, Society for Industrial and Organizational Psychology (SIOP), (April 1996), San Diego.

CONNECT—Available 24/7 with instant feedback so you can study when you want, how you want, and where you want. Take advantage of the Study Plan—an innovative tool that helps students customize their own learning experience. Students can diagnose their knowledge with pre- and post-tests, identify the areas where they need help, search contents of the entire learning package for content specific to the topic they're studying, and add these resources to their study plan. Visit **www.connectob.ca** to register—take practice quizzes, run interactive scenarios, and much more. Also visit the Student Online Learning Centre for additional study tools.

CHAPTER

8 Learning and Decision Making

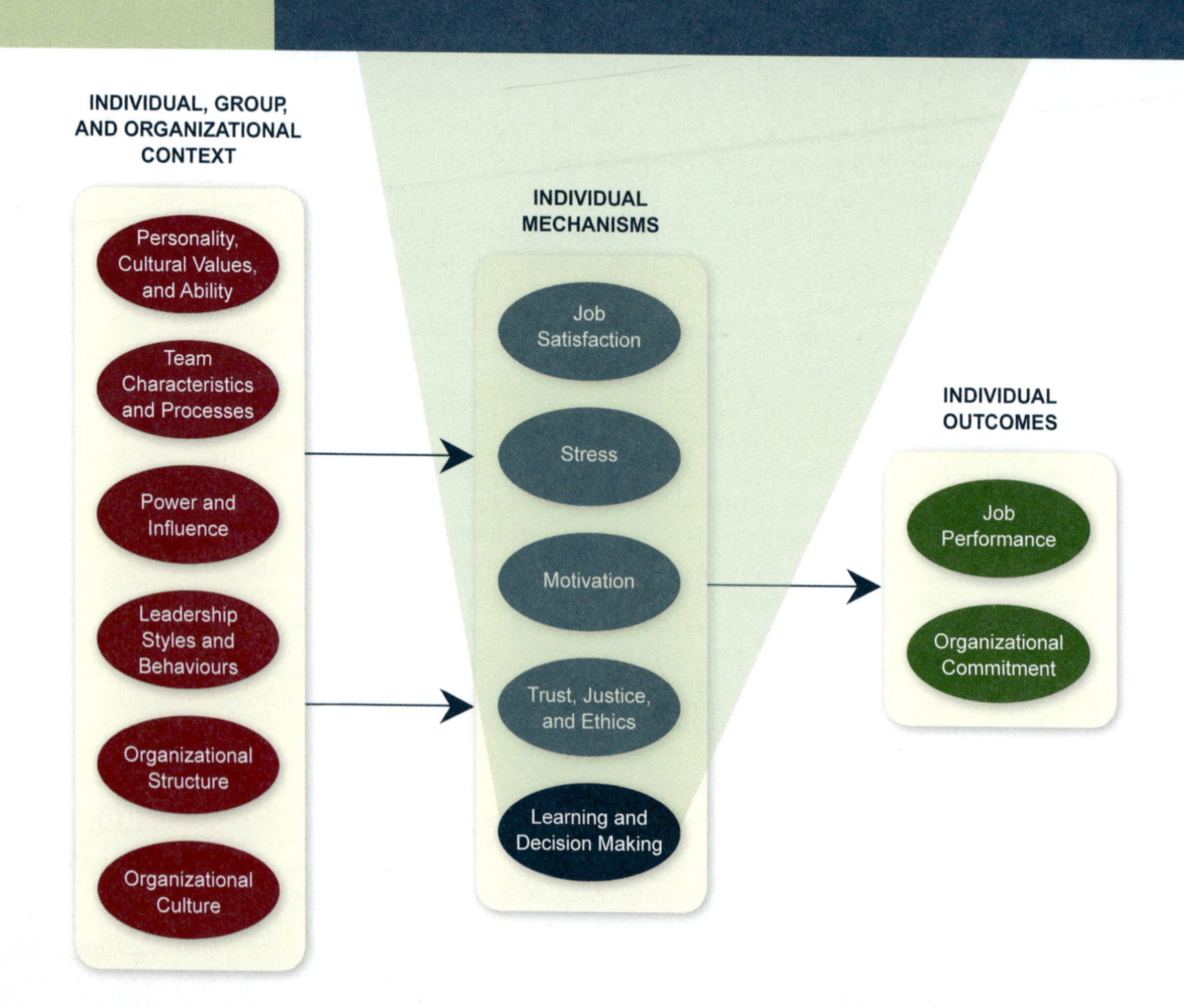

KPMG CANADA

KPMG Canada is affiliated with KPMG International, a global network of professional firms providing audit, tax, and advisory (consulting) services. The four largest accounting firms of Deloitte, KPMG International, Ernst & Young, and PricewaterhouseCoopers reported worldwide revenues of $93 billion in 2007.[1] Of this total KPMG International reported approximately 22 percent (or $20 billion).[2] KPMG Canada, with 5,000 employees in offices spread across the country, produced roughly $1 billion of revenue in 2007.[3]

One of the major challenges facing KPMG Canada is to sustain and grow a labour-intensive business at a time when many of its seasoned professional staff are approaching retirement age. An example of a large office facing this challenge is KPMG Vancouver. Each year, this office tries to hire between 40 and 60 Chartered Accountant (CA) students. Some of these CA students may have worked for the firm in co-op positions, but many come to the firm directly from university-based accounting programs. Becoming or replacing a CA is not an easy process. In addition to an appropriate university degree, CA students need several years of practical experience with a public practice accounting firm, and need to pass the Uniform Final Evaluation (UFE), which is the CA exam. Once the UFE exam is passed, employees start to be moved around to different areas of the firm, such as Canadian tax. By the employee's fifth year, the firm usually promotes the employee to manager or signals that it is time to move on to other career paths.

Lindsey Moser, 25, was one of the top accounting students in her hiring year. Growing up outside of the city, Lindsey had always wondered what it would be like to work in a downtown office. So when Lindsey was presented with an opportunity to work as a CA student at KPMG's Vancouver office, it was like a dream come true. During new-staff orientation, Lindsey quickly realized that she couldn't just rely on the

Learning Outcomes

After reading this chapter, you should be able to answer the following questions:

- 8.1 What is learning? What is decision making?
- 8.2 What types of knowledge can employees gain as they learn and build expertise?
- 8.3 What are the methods by which employees learn in organizations?
- 8.4 What two methods can employees use to make decisions?
- 8.5 What decision-making problems can prevent employees from translating their learning into accurate decisions?
- 8.6 How does learning affect job performance and organizational commitment?
- 8.7 What steps can organizations take to foster learning?

Learning how to be a professional accountant requires the mastery of many behavioural competencies that can only be acquired through on-the-job experiences.

technical competence she had mastered in her university courses. Lindsey had always impressed her professors and performed well on class assignments and exams. But this was different. Not only did KPMG expect incoming CA students to have a good working knowledge of accounting and applicable audit standards, it was also evident that new competencies would have to be acquired and mastered on-the-job. How to survive in a highly competitive and driven culture? How to work with clients (some difficult) and identify improvement opportunities for them? How to manage time and stress? How to form allies and networks to help get things done? How to portray an attitude that commands respect from people who are much more experienced? All of these questions ran through Lindsey's mind. With no classrooms, no textbooks, no lectures, and certainly no professors, how was she ever going to learn what she needed to know to be successful?

LEARNING AND DECISION MAKING

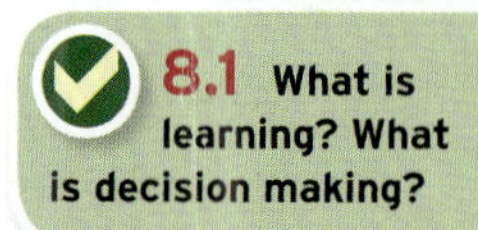
8.1 What is learning? What is decision making?

learning A relatively permanent change in an employee's knowledge or skill that results from experience

decision making The process of generating and choosing from a set of alternatives to solve a problem

Lindsey is clearly concerned about learning the ropes quickly. What Lindsey may not realize is that KPMG also shares her concern because learning and decision making are so important to the organization. **Learning** reflects relatively permanent changes in an employee's knowledge or skill that result from experience.[4] The more employees learn, the more they bring to the table when they come to work. Why is learning so important? Because it has a significant impact on **decision making**, which refers to the process of generating and choosing from a set of alternatives to solve a problem. The more knowledge and skills that employees possess, the more likely they are to make accurate and sound decisions. The risk, at KPMG and other organizations, is that less experienced employees will lack the knowledge base needed to make the right decisions when stepping into new roles.

One reason why inexperience can be so problematic is that learning is not necessarily easy. Have you ever watched "experts" perform their jobs? How is it that someone becomes an expert? How does an accountant gain the trust of her client after several brief meetings? It takes a significant amount of time to become proficient at most complex jobs. It takes most employees anywhere from three months to a year to perform at a satisfactory level.[5] To develop high levels of expertise takes significantly longer. This difficulty makes it even more important for companies to find a way to improve learning and decision making by their employees.

WHY DO SOME EMPLOYEES LEARN TO MAKE DECISIONS BETTER THAN OTHERS?

Bill Buford, a journalist interested in becoming a chef, was hired by Mario Batali's world-renowned Babbo restaurant in New York. At some point early in his tenure in the kitchen, he realized he was in over his head while he stood and watched other, more experienced cooks work at an unbelievably frantic pace. He knew right then that he had a decision to make:

> "I was at a go-forward-or-backward moment. If I went backward, I'd be saying, 'Thanks for the visit, very interesting, that's sure not me.' But how to go forward? There was no place for me. These people were at a higher level of labor. They didn't

think. Their skills were so deeply inculcated they were available to them as instincts. I didn't have skills of that kind and couldn't imagine how you'd learn them. I was aware of being poised on the verge of something: a long, arduous, confidence-bashing, profoundly humiliating experience."[6]

In this situation, Buford realized that his co-workers had more expertise than he did. **Expertise** refers to the knowledge and skills that distinguish experts from novices and less experienced people.[7] Research shows that the differences between experts and novices is almost always a function of learning as opposed to the more popular view that intelligence or other innate differences make the difference.[8] Although learning cannot be directly seen or observed, we can tell when people have learned by observing their behaviours. It is those behaviours that can be used to tell experts from novices, and it is changes in those behaviours that can be used to show that learners are gaining knowledge. Although it's sometimes easy for employees to mimic a behaviour once or twice, or get lucky with a few key decisions, true learning only occurs when changes in behaviour become relatively permanent and are repeated over time. Understanding why some employees prove better at this than others requires understanding what exactly employees learn and how they do it.

expertise The knowledge and skills that distinguish experts from novices

TYPES OF KNOWLEDGE

8.2 What types of knowledge can employees gain as they learn and build expertise?

Employees learn two basic types of knowledge, both of which have important implications for organizations. **Explicit knowledge** is the kind of information you are likely to think about when you picture someone sitting down at a desk to learn. It's information that is relatively easily communicated and a large part of what companies teach during training sessions. Think about it this way: If you can put the information or knowledge in a manual or write it down for someone else, chances are good you're talking about explicit knowledge. As you read this textbook, we're doing our best to communicate explicit knowledge to you that will be useful to you in your future job. Although such information is necessary to perform well, it winds up being a relatively minor portion of all that you need to know.

explicit knowledge Knowledge that is easily communicated and available to everyone

Tacit knowledge, in contrast, is what employees can typically learn only through experience.[9] It's not easily communicated but could very well be the most important aspect of what we learn in organizations.[10] In fact, it's been argued that up to 90 percent of the knowledge contained in organizations occurs in tacit form.[11] Did you ever get to be so good at something that you had the ability to do it but couldn't really explain it to someone else? That's a common way to explain tacit knowledge. It's been described as the "know-how," "know-what," and "know who" acquired solely through experience.[12] Others have used terms such as intuition, skills, insight, beliefs, mental models, and practical intelligence.[13] Table 8-1 lists the qualities that help explain the differences between explicit and tacit knowledge. Some would go as far as to say that explicit knowledge is what everyone can find and use, but tacit knowledge is what separates experts from common people.[14]

tacit knowledge Knowledge that employees can only learn through experience

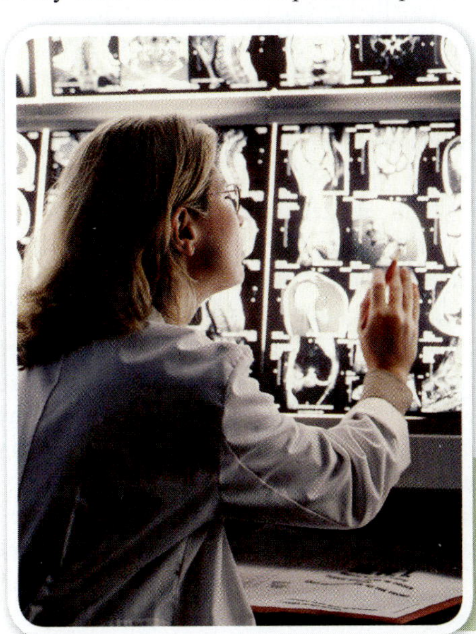

Expertise is the accumulation of superior knowledge and skills in a field that separates experts from everyone else.

TABLE 8-1 Characteristics of Explicit and Tacit Knowledge

EXPLICIT KNOWLEDGE	TACIT KNOWLEDGE
Easily transferred through written or verbal communication	Very difficult, if not impossible, to articulate to others
Readily available to most	Highly personal in nature
Can be learned through books	Based on experience
Always conscious and accessible information	Sometimes holders don't even recognize that they possess it
General information	Typically job- and/or situation-specific

Source: Adapted from R. McAdam, B. Mason, and J. McCrory, "Exploring the Dichotomies within the Tacit Knowledge Literature: Towards a Process of Tacit Knowing in Organizations," *Journal Of Knowledge Management* 11 (2007), pp. 43–59.

METHODS OF LEARNING

8.3 What are the methods by which employees learn in organizations?

Tacit and explicit knowledge are extremely important to employees and organizations. As an employee, it's hard to build a high level of tacit knowledge without some level of explicit knowledge to build off of. From an organization's perspective, the tacit knowledge that its employees accumulate may be the single most important strategic asset a company possesses.[15] The question then becomes: How do employees learn these types of knowledge? The short answer is that we learn through reinforcement (rewards and punishment), observation, and experience.

REINFORCEMENT We've known for a long time that managers use various methods of reinforcement to induce desirable or reduce undesirable behaviours by their employees. Originally known as operant conditioning, B.F. Skinner was the first to pioneer the notion that we learn by observing the link between our voluntary behaviour and the consequences that follow it. Research has continually demonstrated that people will exhibit specific behaviours if they are rewarded for doing so. Not surprisingly, we have a tendency to repeat behaviours that result in consequences that we like and to not exhibit behaviours that result in consequences we don't like. Figure 8-1 shows this operant conditioning process.

In the model shown in Figure 8-1, you notice that there are antecedents or events that precede or signal certain behaviours, which are then followed by consequences. Antecedents in organizations are typically goals, rules, instructions, or other types of information that help show employees what is expected of them. Although antecedents are useful for motivational reasons, it is primarily the consequences of actions that drive behaviour. This entire process of reinforcement is a continuous cycle, and the repetition of behaviours is strengthened to the degree that reinforcement continues to occur. There are four specific consequences typically used by organizations to modify employee behaviour, known as the **contingencies of reinforcement**.[16] Figure 8-2 summarizes these contingencies. It's important to separate these contingencies into what they are designed to do, namely, increase desired behaviours or decrease unwanted behaviours.

contingencies of reinforcement Four specific consequences used by organizations to modify employee behaviour

Two contingencies of reinforcement are used to increase desired behaviours. **Positive reinforcement** occurs when a positive outcome follows a desired behaviour. It is perhaps the most common type of reinforcement and the type we think of when an employee receives some type of "reward." Increased pay, promotions, praise from a manager or co-workers,

positive reinforcement When a positive outcome follows a desired behaviour

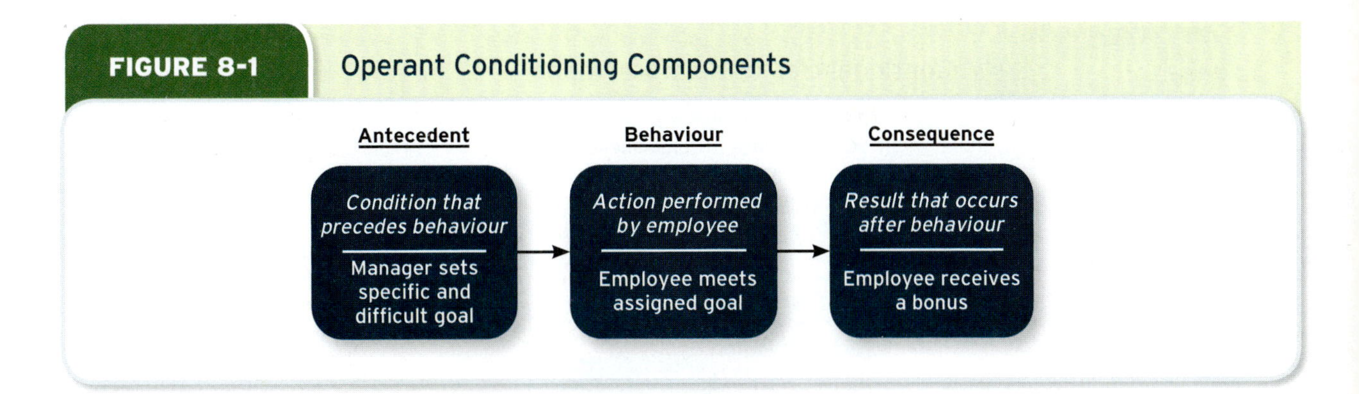

and public recognition would all be considered positive reinforcement when given as a result of an employee exhibiting wanted behaviours. For positive reinforcement to be successful, an employee needs to see a direct link between his or her behaviour and the desired outcome (see Chapter 6 on motivation for more discussion of these issues). If the consequence isn't realized until long after a specific behaviour, then the odds that the employee will link the two is minimized. **Negative reinforcement** occurs when an unwanted outcome is removed following a desired behaviour. Have you ever performed a task for the specific reason of not getting yelled at? If so, you learned to perform certain behaviours through the use of negative reinforcement. Perhaps there are some tasks your job requires that you don't enjoy. If your manager removes these responsibilities specifically because you perform well at another aspect of your job, then this could also be seen as negative reinforcement. It is important to remember that even though the word "negative" has a sour connotation to it, it is designed to *increase* desired behaviours.

negative reinforcement An unwanted outcome is removed following a desired behaviour

The next two contingencies of reinforcement are designed to decrease undesired behaviours. **Punishment** occurs when an unwanted outcome follows an unwanted behaviour. Punishment is exactly what it sounds like. In other words, the employee is given something he or she doesn't like as a result of performing a behaviour that the organization doesn't like. Suspending an employee for showing up to work late, assigning job tasks generally seen as demeaning for not following safety procedures, or even firing an employee for gross misconduct are all examples of punishment. **Extinction** occurs when there is the removal of a consequence following an unwanted behaviour. The use of extinction to reinforce behaviour can be purposeful or accidental. Perhaps an employee receives attention from co-workers when he or she acts in ways that are somewhat childish at work. Finding a way to remove the attention would be a purposeful act of extinction. Similarly though, perhaps an employee works late every now and then to finish up job tasks when work gets busy, but his or her manager stops acknowledging that hard work. Desired behaviour that is not reinforced will diminish over time. In this way, a manager who does nothing to reinforce good behaviour is actually decreasing the odds that it will be repeated!

punishment When an unwanted outcome follows an unwanted behaviour

extinction The removal of a positive outcome following an unwanted behaviour

In general, positive reinforcement and extinction should be the most common forms of reinforcement used by managers to create learning among their employees. Positive reinforcement doesn't

Positive reinforcement, such as public recognition, both encourages employees and helps to ensure that desirable behaviours will be imitated and repeated.

FIGURE 8-2 Contingencies of Reinforcement

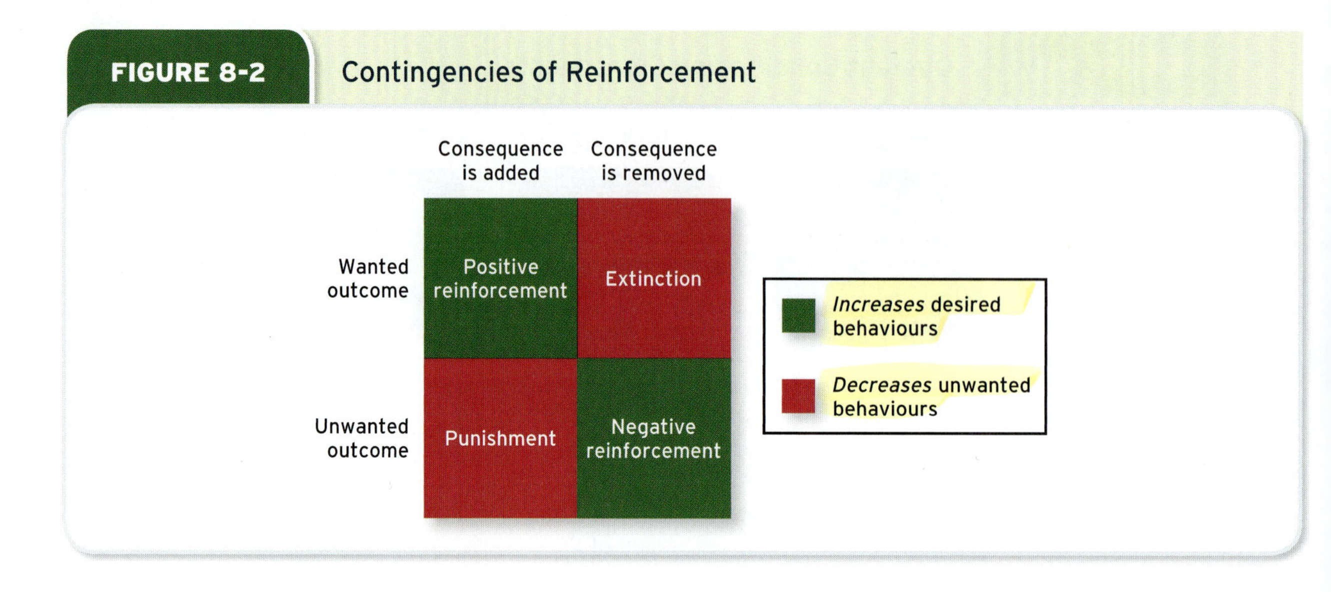

have to be in the form of material rewards to be effective. There are many ways for managers to encourage wanted behaviours. Offering praise, providing feedback, public recognition, and small celebrations are all ways to encourage employees and increase the chances they will continue to exhibit desired behaviours. At the same time, extinction is an effective way to stop unwanted behaviours. Both of these contingencies deliver their intended results, but perhaps more important, they do so without creating feelings of animosity and conflict. Although punishment and negative reinforcement will work, they tend to bring other, detrimental consequences along with them.

schedules of reinforcement The timing of when contingencies are applied or removed

Whereas the type of reinforcement used to modify behaviour is important, research also shows that the timing of reinforcement is equally important.[17] Therefore, it's important to examine the timing of when the contingencies are applied, referred to as **schedules of reinforcement**. Table 8-2 provides a summary of the five schedules of reinforcement.

continuous reinforcement A specific consequence follows each and every occurrence of a certain behaviour

Continuous reinforcement is the simplest schedule of reinforcement and happens when a specific consequence follows each and every occurrence of a desired behaviour. For most jobs, continuous reinforcement is impractical. As a manager, can you imagine providing positive reinforcement every time someone exhibits a desired behaviour? It's a good thing that research also shows that under many circumstances, continuous reinforcement might be considered the least long-lasting, because as soon as the consequence stops, the desired behaviour stops along with it.[18]

fixed interval schedule Reinforcement occurs at fixed time periods

variable interval schedule Reinforcement occurs at random periods of time

The other four schedules differ in terms of their variability and the basis of the consequences. Two schedules are interval based; that is, they distribute reinforcement based on the amount of time that passes. A **fixed interval schedule** is probably the single most common form of reinforcement schedule. With this schedule, workers are rewarded after a certain amount of time, and the length of time between reinforcement periods stays the same. Every time an employee gets a paycheque after a predetermined period of time, he or she is being reinforced on a fixed interval schedule. A **variable interval schedule** is designed to reinforce behaviour at more random points in time. A supervisor walking around at different points of time every day is a good example of a variable interval schedule. If that supervisor walked around at the same exact time every day, do you think workers would be more or less prone to exhibit good behaviours throughout the day?

fixed ratio schedule Reinforcement occurs following a fixed number of desired behaviours

The other two reinforcement schedules are based on actual behaviours. A **fixed ratio schedule** reinforces behaviours after a certain number of them have been exhibited. Some

TABLE 8-2 Schedules of Reinforcement

REINFORCEMENT SCHEDULE	REWARD GIVEN FOLLOWING	POTENTIAL LEVEL OF PERFORMANCE	EXAMPLE
Continuous	Every desired behaviour	High, but difficult to maintain	Praise
Fixed Interval	Fixed time periods	Average	Paycheque
Variable Interval	Variable time periods	Moderately high	Supervisor walk-by
Fixed Ratio	Fixed number of desired behaviours	High	Piece-rate pay
Variable Ratio	Variable number of desired behaviours	Very high	Commission pay

manufacturing plants have created piece-rate pay systems in which workers are paid according to the number of items they produce. Employees know ahead of time how many items they have to produce to be reinforced. A **variable ratio schedule** rewards people after a varying number of exhibited behaviours. Salespeople, for example, are often compensated based on commission because they receive extra pay every time they sell an item. However, a car salesman doesn't make a sale every time someone walks in the door of the dealership. Sometimes it takes exhibiting good sales behaviours to eight or nine customers to make a sale. Take a slot machine as an example. The machine doesn't reward you for every lever pull, or even for every 10 lever pulls—you never know when the next winning pull will be. Would you say that slot machines do a good job of reinforcing the behaviour that casinos would like you to have? You bet!

variable ratio schedule Behaviours are reinforced after a varying number of them have been exhibited

On the whole, research has consistently shown that variable schedules lead to higher levels of performance than fixed schedules. Think about it this way: Do you study more consistently in a class that gives pop quizzes or one that simply tests you three set times a semester? Research also shows that desired behaviours tend to disappear much more quickly when reinforcement is discontinued under fixed plans. However, variable schedules are not always appropriate for some types of reinforcement. How would you like it if your employer decided to give you your paycheques on a variable schedule? Sorry, you're not getting a paycheque this week—maybe next week! Moreover, studies suggest that continuous or fixed schedules can be better for reinforcing new behaviours or behaviours that don't occur on a frequent basis.

"Oh, not bad. The light comes on, I press the bar, they write me a check. How about you?"

Source: © The New Yorker Collection 1993 Tom Cheney from cartoonbank.com.

social learning theory Theory that argues that people in organizations learn by observing others

behavioural modelling When employees observe the actions of others, learn from what they observe, and then repeat the observed behaviour

OBSERVATION In addition to learning through reinforcement, **social learning theory** argues that people in organizations have the ability to learn through the observation of others.[19] In fact, many would argue that social learning is the primary way by which employees gain knowledge in organizations.[20] Think about where you are most likely to get your cues while working in an organization. When possible, chances are good you'll look around at other employees to figure out the appropriate behaviours on your job. Not only do employees have the ability to see the link between their own behaviours and their consequences, they can also observe the behaviours and consequences of others.[21] When employees observe the actions of others, learn from what they observe, and then repeat the observed behaviour, they are engaging in **behavioural modelling**.

For behaviour modelling to occur successfully, a number of processes have to take place. These steps are shown in Figure 8-3. First, the learner must focus attention on an appropriate model and accurately perceive the critical behaviour the model exhibits. That model might be a supervisor, a co-worker, or even a subordinate. Some organizations go out of their way to supply role models for newcomers or inexperienced workers to watch and learn from. In our opening vignette, KPMG Vancouver routinely assigned its new CA students to teams that consisted of at least one manager, and sometimes one of the firm's partners, in the hopes of capturing the tacit knowledge they had acquired. Lindsey discovered that she learned the most by simply watching her manager interact with clients—observing what he said to clients and how he responded to their questions, and what he wrote down at meetings. In fact, because tacit knowledge is so difficult to communicate, modelling might be the single best way to acquire it. For that reason, modelling is a continual process that is used at all levels of many organizations. Needless to say, choosing a good model is important, and not all models are good ones. For instance, if managers and leaders demonstrate unethical behaviours, then employees who look up to these models are likely to imitate what they see.[22]

Second, the learner actually needs to remember exactly what the model's behaviour was and how they did it. This step is easier said than done when watching experts perform their job, because so much of what they do remains unspoken and can occur at a rapid pace. Third, the learner must undertake production processes, or actually be able to reproduce what the model did. Not only must the learner have the requisite knowledge and physical skills to be able to perform the task, but also he or she must translate what he or she has

FIGURE 8-3 The Modelling Process

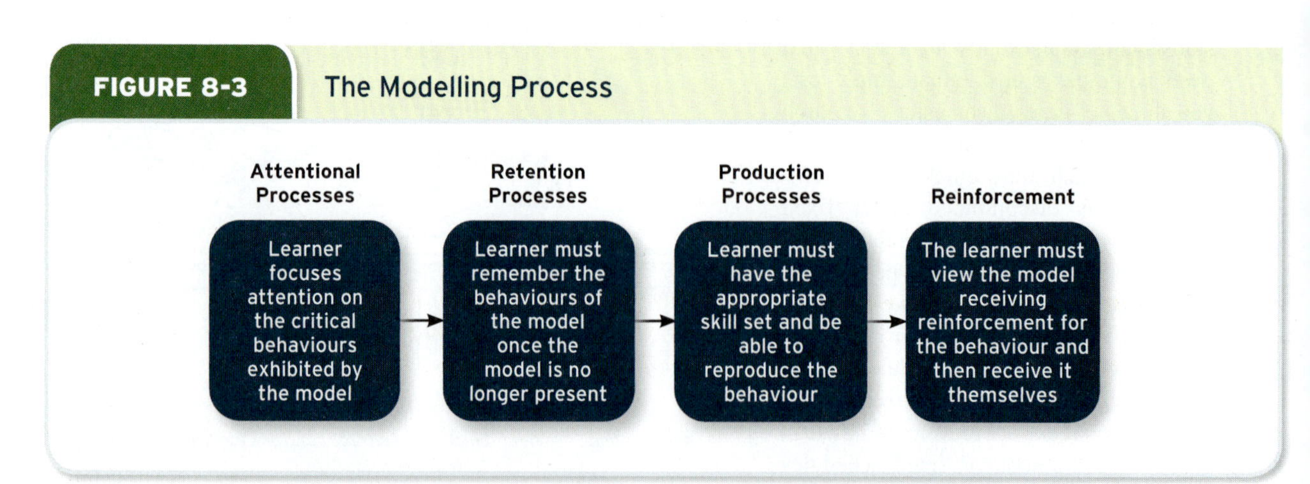

Source: Adapted from H.M. Weiss, "Learning Theory and Industrial and Organizational Psychology," in *Handbook of Industrial and Organizational Psychology*, eds. M.D. Dunnette and L.M. Hough. (Consulting Psychologists Press: Palo Alto, CA, 1990), pp. 75–169.

observed into action. Do you remember the first time you drove a car? Chances are good you'd been watching other drivers for many years, picking up bits and pieces of how to do it through observation. However, things became different when you were behind the wheel for the first time. All of a sudden, there was a lot of information to process, and years and years of observation had to be put into action.

Fourth, the last step of behavioural modelling is reinforcement. This reinforcement can come from observation, direct experience, or both. The learner can observe the consequences of the model having exhibited the behaviour (positive reinforcement or punishment), which in itself will help ingrain the desirability of performing the behaviour. In addition, it's important for the learner to receive reinforcement after replicating the behaviour. If the newly acquired behaviours are positively reinforced, the likelihood of continued behaviour increases.

GOAL ORIENTATION Before we leave this section, it's important to recognize that people learn somewhat differently according to their predispositions or attitudes toward learning and performance. These differences are reflected in different "goal orientations" that capture the kinds of activities and goals that they prioritize. Some people have what is known as a **learning orientation**, where building competence is deemed more important than demonstrating competence. "Learning-oriented" persons enjoy working on new kinds of tasks, even if they fail during their early experiences. Such people view failure in positive terms—as a means of increasing knowledge and skills in the long run.[23]

learning orientation A predisposition or attitude according to which building competence is deemed more important by an employee than demonstrating competence

For others, the demonstration of competence is deemed a more important goal than the building of competence. That demonstration of competence can be motivated by two different thought processes. Those with a **performance-prove orientation** focus on demonstrating their competence so that others think favourably of them. Those with a **performance-avoid orientation** focus on demonstrating their competence so that others will not think poorly of them. In either case, "performance-oriented" people tend to work mainly on tasks at which they're already good, preventing them from failing in front of others. Such individuals view failure in negative terms—as an indictment of their ability and competence.

performance-prove orientation A predisposition or attitude by which employees focus on demonstrating their competence so that others think favourably of them

performance-avoid orientation A predisposition or attitude by which employees focus on demonstrating their competence so that others will not think poorly of them

Research has shown that a learning goal orientation improves self-confidence, feedback-seeking behaviour, learning strategy development, and learning performance.[24] Research on the two performance orientations is more mixed. Although it would seem that focusing on performance should improve performance-based outcomes, research shows that isn't necessarily the case. On the whole, a performance-prove orientation tends to be a mixed bag, producing varying levels of performance and outcomes. What is more clear are the detrimental effects of having a performance-avoid orientation. Employees who enter learning situations with a fear of looking bad in front of others tend to learn less and have substantially higher levels of anxiety.[25] What kind of orientation do you tend to exhibit? See our **OB Assessments** feature at the end of this chapter to find out.

METHODS OF DECISION MAKING

8.4 What two methods can employees use to make decisions?

How do employees take explicit and tacit knowledge, however it's gained, and turn that knowledge into effective decision making? Sometimes that process is very straightforward. **Programmed decisions** are decisions that become somewhat automatic because a person's knowledge allows him or her to recognize and identify a situation and the course of action that needs to be taken. As shown in Figure 8-4, experts often respond to an identified problem by realizing that they've dealt with it before. That realization triggers a programmed decision that is implemented and then evaluated according to its ability to deliver the expected outcome. For experts who possess high levels of explicit and tacit knowledge, many decisions they face are of this programmed variety. That's not to say that the decisions are necessarily easy. It simply means that their experience and knowledge allows them to see the problems more easily and recognize and implement solutions more quickly.

programmed decisions Decisions that are somewhat automatic because the decision maker's knowledge allows him or her to recognize the situation and the course of action to be taken

OB RESEARCH IN CANADA

Sally Maitlis received her PhD in 1998 from the University of Sheffield, England, and is currently an associate professor at the Sauder School of Business at the University of British Columbia. One of Dr. Maitlis's areas of expertise is group and organizational decision making, with a focus on the social and emotional processes that underlie the way decisions are made. Some of the questions that Dr. Maitlis addresses in her work include: (1) How do leaders and other organizational members reach shared understandings about key decision issues? (2) Why do executives sometimes fail in their attempts to make critical strategic decisions? (3) What role does negative emotion play in organizational decision making? (4) How do the emotions expressed during team decision making affect the kinds of understandings and decisions that are reached? To study these questions, Dr. Maitlis observes and records decision processes as they unfold naturally in settings that include symphony orchestras, computer gaming companies, and not-for-profit organizations. By focusing on the social nature of decision making, and especially the role of emotions, Dr. Maitlis increases our awareness of the political and emotional aspects of organizational processes that have previously been considered quite rational.

In addition to her research activities, Dr. Maitlis teaches courses in organizational behaviour and qualitative research methods, as well as doing some executive education and coaching. She is currently associate editor for non-traditional research at the *Journal of Management Inquiry,* and sits on the editorial boards of *Academy of Management Journal, Academy of Management Review,* and *Organization Studies.* At present she is serving as international representative-at-large for the Management and Organizational Cognition division of the Academy of Management.

Some of Dr. Maitlis's favourite publications include:

"Triggers and Enablers of Sensegiving in Organizations," by S. Maitlis and T. Lawrence, published in *Academy of Management Journal* (2007, volume 50, pp. 57–84).

"The Social Processes of Organizational Sensemaking," by S. Maitlis, published in *Academy of Management Journal* (2005, volume 48, pp. 1–49).

"Toxic Decision Processes: A Study of Emotion in Organizational Decision Making," by S. Maitlis and H. Ozcelik, published in *Organization Science* (2004, volume 15, number 4, pp. 375–93).

"Taking It from the Top: How CEOs Influence and Fail to Influence Their Boards," by S. Maitlis, published in *Organization Studies* (2004, volume 25, number 8, pp. 1275–1311).

intuition An emotional judgment based on quick, unconscious, gut feelings

To experts, this kind of decision making sometimes comes across as intuition or a "gut feeling." **Intuition** can be described as emotionally charged judgments that arise through quick, unconscious, and holistic associations.[26] Because of their tacit knowledge, experts sometimes cannot put into words why they know that a problem exists, why a solution will work, or how they accomplished a task. They just "know." Of course, the difficulty arises in knowing when to trust that "gut instinct" and when not to.[27] As a general rule of thumb, you should probably ask yourself how much expertise you have in that on which you are making a judgment. In other words, don't go laying down your life savings on a spin of the roulette wheel at the casino because your intuition tells you "red"! Effective intuition results when people have a certain amount of tacit knowledge.

FIGURE 8-4 Programmed and Non-programmed Decisions

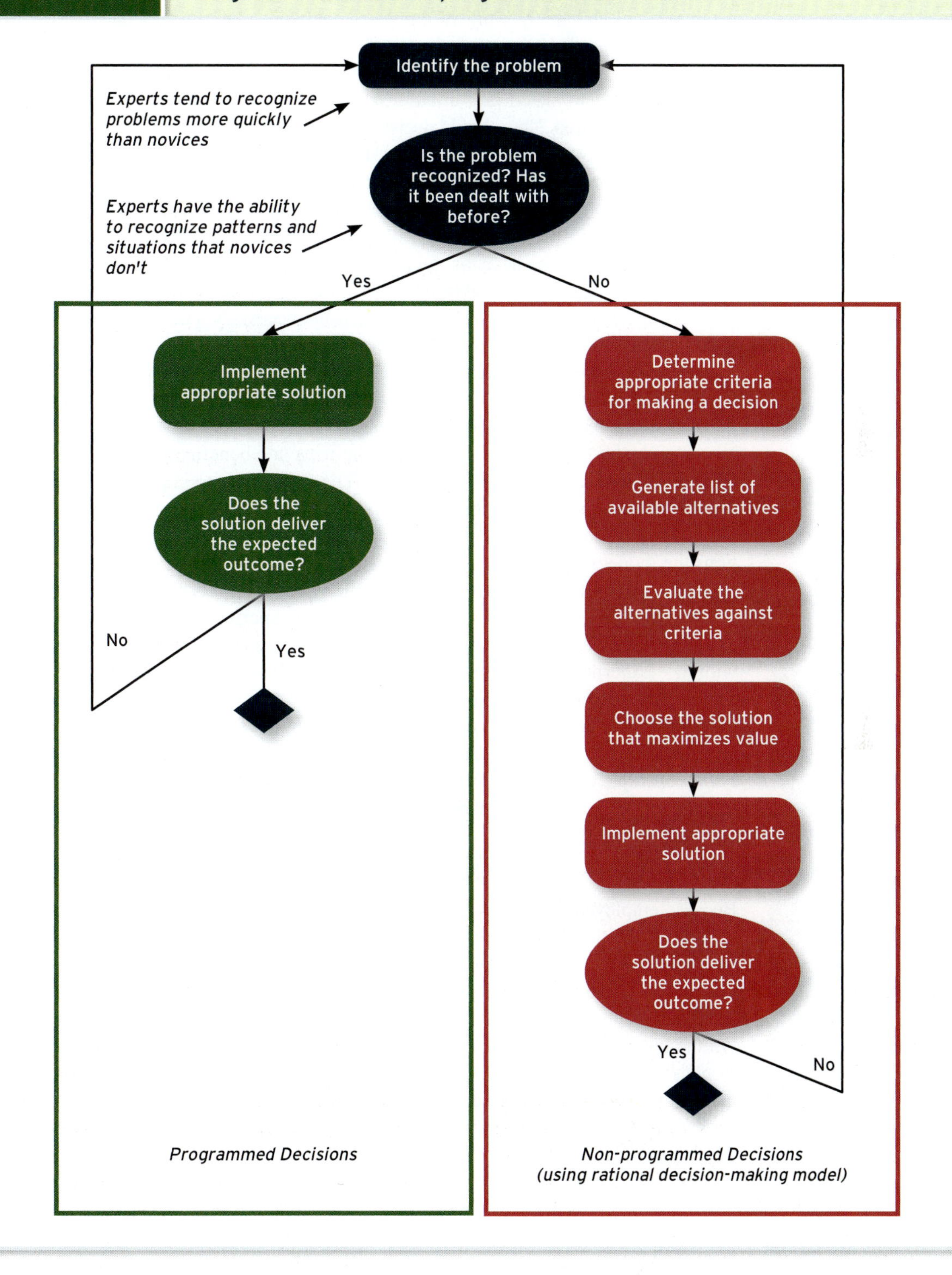

non-programmed decisions Decisions made by employees when a problem is new, complex, or not recognized

When a situation arises that is new, complex, and not recognized, it calls for a **non-programmed decision** on the part of the employee. Organizations are complex and changing environments, and many workers are faced with uncertainty on a daily basis. In these instances, employees have to make sense of their environment, understand the problems they are faced with, and come up with solutions to overcome them. As a general rule of thumb, as employees move up the corporate ladder, a larger percentage of their decisions become less and less programmed. How should decision making proceed in such contexts? The **rational decision-making model** offers a step-by-step approach to making decisions that maximize outcomes by examining all available alternatives. As shown in Figure 8-4, this model becomes relevant when people don't recognize a problem as one they have dealt with before.

rational decision-making model A step-by-step approach to making decisions that is designed to maximize outcomes by examining all available alternatives

The first step in the rational decision-making model is to identify the criteria that are important in making the decision, taking into account all involved parties. The second step is to generate a list of all available alternatives that might be potential solutions to the problem. At this point, evaluating the alternatives is not necessary. The responsibility simply lies in coming up with as many potential solutions as possible. The third step in the model is the evaluation of those alternatives against the criteria laid out in step one. Does it matter how much the alternative costs? What exactly will happen as a result of various choices? What will the side effects of the alternative be? The fourth step is to select the alternative that results in the best outcome. That is, given the costs and benefits of each alternative, which alternative provides us with the most value? The fifth step is to implement the alternative.

The rational decision-making model assumes that people are, of course, perfectly rational. However, problems immediately arise when we start to examine some of the assumptions the model makes about human decision makers. The model assumes there is a clear and definite problem to solve and that people have the ability to identify what that exact problem is. It also assumes that decision makers have perfect information—that they know and are able to identify the available alternatives and the outcomes that would be associated with those alternatives. The model further assumes that time and money are generally not issues when it comes to making a decision, that decision makers always choose the solution that maximizes value, and that they will act in the best interests of the organization. Given all these assumptions, perhaps we shouldn't label the model as "rational" after all! For an example of one decision maker who can follow the tenets of the rational decision-making model, see our **OB on Screen** feature.

DECISION-MAKING PROBLEMS

8.5 What decision-making problems can prevent employees from translating their learning into accurate decisions?

Because employees don't always make rational decisions, it's easy to second-guess decisions after the fact. Many decisions made inside organizations look good at the time and were made with perfectly good justifications to support them but turn out to have what are perceived as "bad results." The reality, however, is that it's a lot easier to question decisions in hindsight. As Warren Buffett, CEO of Berkshire Hathaway, is often quoted as saying, "In the business world, the rearview mirror is always clearer than the windshield."[28] Our responsibility here is not to rehash all the poor decisions employees and managers have made (and there are many of them!) but rather to detail some of the most common reasons for bad decision making—in other words, when are people most likely to falter in terms of the rational decision-making model and why?

bounded rationality The notion that people do not have the ability or resources to process all available information and alternatives when making a decision

LIMITED INFORMATION Although most employees perceive themselves as rational decision makers, the reality is that they are all subject to **bounded rationality**. Bounded rationality is the notion that decision makers simply do not have the ability or resources to process all available information and alternatives to make an optimal decision.[29] A comparison of bounded rationality and rational decision making is presented in Table 8-3.

OB ON SCREEN

STAR TREK: FIRST CONTACT

Data: Captain, I believe I am feeling . . . anxiety. It is an intriguing sensation. A most distracting—

Picard: (Interrupting) Data, I am sure it is a fascinating experience, but perhaps you should deactivate your emotion chip for now.

Data: Good idea sir. (click) Done.

Picard: Data, there are times when I envy you.

With these words, Captain Jean-Luc Picard (Patrick Stewart) tells Data (Brent Spiner) that he wished he had Data's ability to do what all of us would like to be able to do from time to time: make perfectly rational decisions. You see, Data is an android (a robot made to resemble a human) who serves as the chief operations officer aboard the USS Enterprise in *Star Trek: First Contact* (Dir. Jonathan Frakes, Paramount Pictures, 1996). Data, with his extremely advanced computer for a brain, is able to make close to perfect decisions by calculating probabilities with all possible available information. His brain works so quickly that a decision lasting 0.63 seconds feels "like an eternity" to him. Wouldn't we all like to have that ability?

Throughout the newer generation of *Star Trek* episodes and movies, Data exhibits an overwhelming desire to become more "human" in order to understand his shipmates. As an android with no emotions, he lacks the ability to understand why humans make the irrational mistakes they sometimes do. He doesn't comprehend humour, selfish desires, or making decisions for reasons other than achieving the optimal solution.

In a prior *Star Trek* movie, Data's creator provides him with an "emotion chip" that allows him to be distracted by the emotions and feelings that we're faced with every day. In the scene shown, Data and Captain Picard are about to enter what is an extremely dangerous, life-and-death situation. Needless to say, Captain Picard prefers that Data enter the situation with the enviable ability to turn off his emotions and make rational decisions. While Data strives to feel emotion in his quest to understand human behaviour, employees and managers often wish they had the ability to make decisions free from the distractions of emotion. However, as long as we are "human," all we can do is strive to make decisions in as rational a manner as possible.

TABLE 8-3 Rational Decision Making versus Bounded Rationality

TO BE RATIONAL DECISION MAKERS, WE *SHOULD...*	BOUNDED RATIONALITY SAYS WE *ARE LIKELY TO...*
Identify the problem by thoroughly examining the situation and considering all interested parties.	Boil the problem down to something that is easily understood.
Develop an exhaustive list of alternatives to consider as solutions.	Come up with a few solutions that tend to be straightforward, familiar, and similar to what is currently being done.
Evaluate all the alternatives simultaneously.	Evaluate each alternative as soon as we think of it.
Use accurate information to evaluate alternatives.	Use distorted and inaccurate information during the evaluation process.
Pick the alternative that maximizes value.	Pick the first acceptable alternative (satisfice).

Sources: Adapted from H.A. Simon, "Rational Decision Making in Organizations," *American Economic Review* 69 (1979), pp. 493–513; D. Kahneman, "Maps of Bounded Rationality: Psychology for Behavioural Economics," *The American Economic Review* 93 (2003), pp. 1449–75; S.W. Williams, *Making Better Business Decisions* (Thousand Oaks, CA: Sage Publications, 2002).

This limit results in two major problems for making decisions. First, people have to filter and simplify information to make sense of their complex environment and the myriad of potential choices they face.[30] This simplification leads them to miss information when perceiving problems, generating and evaluating alternatives, or judging the results. Second, because people cannot possibly consider every single alternative when making a decision, they satisfice. **Satisficing** results when decision makers select the first acceptable alternative considered.[31]

satisficing When a decision maker chooses the first acceptable alternative considered

In addition to choosing the first acceptable alternative, decision makers tend to come up with alternatives that are straightforward, familiar, and not that different from what they're already doing. When you and another person are deciding where to go out for dinner tonight, will you sit down and list every restaurant available to you within a certain radius? Of course not. You'll start listing off alternatives, generally starting with the closest and most familiar, until both parties arrive at a restaurant that is acceptable to them. Making decisions this way is no big deal when it comes to deciding where to go for dinner, because the consequences of a poor decision are minimal. However, many managers make decisions that have critical consequences for their employees and their customers. In those cases, making a decision without thoroughly looking into the alternatives becomes a problem!

FAULTY PERCEPTIONS As decision makers, employees are forced to rely on their perceptions to make decisions. Perception is the process of selecting, organizing, storing, and retrieving information about the environment. Although perceptions can be very useful, because they help us to make sense of the environment around us, they can often become distorted versions of reality. Perceptions can be dangerous in decision making, because we tend to make assumptions or evaluations on the basis of them. **Selective perception** is the tendency for people to see their environment only as it affects them and as it is consistent with their expectations. Has someone ever told you, "You only see what you want to see"? If a relative, spouse, or significant other said that to you, chances are good it probably wasn't the best experience. That person was likely upset that you did not perceive the environment (or

selective perception The tendency for people to see their environment only as it affects them and as it is consistent with their expectations what was important to them) the same way they did. Selective perception affects our ability to identify problems, generate and evaluate alternatives, and judge outcomes. In other words, we take shortcuts when we process information. In the following paragraphs, we'll discuss some of the ways in which we take perceptual shortcuts when dealing with people and situations.

One false assumption people tend to make when it comes to other people is the belief that others think, feel, and act the same way they do. This assumption is known as a **projection bias**. That is, people project their own thoughts, attitudes, and motives onto other people. "I would never do that—that's unethical" equates to "They would never do that—that's unethical." Projection bias causes problems in decision making because it limits our ability to develop appropriate criteria for a decision and evaluate decisions carefully. The bias causes people to assume that everyone's criteria will be just like theirs and that everyone will react to the decision just as they did.

projection bias The faulty perception by decision makers that others think, feel, and act the same way as they do

Another example of faulty perceptions is caused by the way we cognitively organize people into groups. **Social identity theory** holds that people identify themselves by the groups to which they belong and perceive and judge others by their group memberships.[32] There is a substantial amount of research that shows that we like to categorize people on the basis of the groups to which they belong.[33] These groups could be based on demographic information (gender, race, religion, hair colour), occupational information (scientists, engineers, accountants), workplace (Performance Plants, Microsoft, KPMG Vancouver), nationality (Canadians, Americans, Chinese), or any other subgroup that makes sense to the perceiver. You might categorize students on campus by whether they are a member of a fraternity or sorority. Those inside the Greek system categorize people by which fraternity or sorority they belong to. And people within a certain fraternity might group their own members on the basis of whom they hang out with the most. There is practically no end to the number of subgroups that people can come up with.

social identity theory A theory that people identify themselves based on the various groups to which they belong and judge others based on the groups they associate with

A **stereotype** occurs when assumptions are made about others on the basis of their membership in a social group.[34] Although not all stereotypes are bad per se, our decision-making process becomes faulty when we make inaccurate generalizations. Many companies work hard to help their employees avoid stereotyping, because doing so can lead to illegal discrimination in the workplace. Increasingly, Canadian companies, such as RBC (Chapter 1), have developed extensive diversity training programs to help their employees overcome specific cultural, racial, and gender stereotypes in the workplace.[35]

stereotype Assumptions made about others based on their social group membership

When confronted with situations of uncertainty that require a decision on our part, we often use **heuristics**—simple, efficient, rules of thumb that allow us to make decisions more easily. In general, heuristics are not bad. In fact, they lead to correct decisions more often than not.[36] However, heuristics can also bias us toward inaccurate decisions at times. Consider this example from one of the earliest studies on decision-making heuristics: "Consider the letter R. Is R more likely to appear in the first position of a word or the third position of a word?"[37] If your answer was the first position of a word, you answered incorrectly and fell victim to one of the most frequently talked about heuristics. The **availability bias** is the tendency for people to base their judgments on information that is easier to recall. It is significantly easier for almost everyone to remember words in which R is the first letter as opposed to the third. The availability bias is why more people are afraid to fly than statistics would support. Every single plane crash is plastered all over the news, making plane crashes more available in memory than successful plane landings.

heuristics Simple and efficient rules of thumb that allow one to make decisions more easily

availability bias The tendency for people to base their judgments on information that is easier to recall

Aside from the availability bias, there are many other biases that affect the way we make decisions. Table 8-4 describes 15 of the most well-researched decision-making biases. After reading all of them, you might wonder how we ever make accurate decisions at all! The answer is that we do our best to think rationally through our most important decisions prior to making them and tend to use heuristics for decisions that are less important or that need to be made more quickly. Regardless of how often we fall victim to the biases, being aware of potential decision errors can help us make them less frequently.

TABLE 8-4 Decision-Making Biases

NAME OF BIAS	DESCRIPTION
Anchoring	The tendency to rely too heavily, or "anchor," on one trait or piece of information when making decisions.
Availability bias	A biased prediction, due to the tendency to focus on the most salient and emotionally charged outcome.
Bandwagon effect	The tendency to do (or believe) things because many other people do (or believe) the same.
Choice-supportive bias	The tendency to remember one's choices as better than they actually were.
Confirmation bias	The tendency to search for or interpret information in a way that confirms one's preconceptions.
Contrast effect	The enhancement or diminishment of a weight or other measurement when compared with recently observed contrasting object.
False consensus effect	The tendency for people to overestimate the degree to which others agree with them.
Gambler's fallacy	The tendency to assume that individual random events are influenced by previous random events. For example, "I've flipped heads with this coin so many times that tails is bound to come up sooner or later."
Halo effect	The tendency for a person's positive or negative traits to "spill over" from one area of their personality to another in others' perceptions of them.
Hindsight bias	Sometimes called the "I-knew-it-all-along" effect, the inclination to see past events as being predictable.
Illusion of control	The tendency for human beings to believe they can control or at least influence outcomes that they clearly cannot.
Primacy effect	The tendency to weigh initial events more than subsequent events.
Projection bias	The tendency to unconsciously assume that others share the same or similar thoughts, beliefs, values, or positions.
Recency effect	The tendency to weigh recent events more than earlier events.
Self-fulfilling prophecy	The tendency to engage in behaviours that elicit results that will (consciously or subconsciously) confirm our beliefs.

Sources: J. Baron, *Thinking and Deciding* (3rd ed.). Cambridge, UK: Cambridge University Press, 2000; R.E. Nisbett, L. Ross, *Human Inference: Strategies and Shortcomings of Social Judgment.* Englewood Cliffs, N.J.: Prentice-Hall, 1980; D.G. Meyers, *Social Psychology.* Boston, MA: McGraw-Hill, 2005; G. Gigerenzer, P.M. Todd, ABC Research Group, *Simple Heuristics That Make Us Smart.* New York, NY, Oxford University Press, 1999; D. Kahneman, A. Tversky, & P. Slovic, *Judgment under Uncertainty: Heuristics & Biases,* Cambridge, UK: Cambridge University Press, 1982.

FAULTY ATTRIBUTIONS Another category of decision-making problems centres on how we explain the actions and events that occur around us. Research on attributions suggests that when people witness a behaviour or outcome, they make a judgment about whether it was internally or externally caused. For example, when a co-worker of yours named Joe shows up late to work and misses an important group presentation, you'll almost certainly make a judgment about why that happened. You might attribute Joe's outcome to internal factors—for example, suggesting that he is lazy or has a poor work ethic. Or you might attribute Joe's outcome to external factors—for example, suggesting that there was unusually bad traffic that day or that other factors prevented him from arriving on time.

The **fundamental attribution error** argues that people have a tendency to judge others' behaviours as due to internal factors.[38] This error suggests that you would likely judge Joe as having low motivation, poor organizational skills, or some other negative internal attribute. What if you yourself had showed up late? It turns out that we're less harsh when judging ourselves. The **self-serving bias** occurs when we attribute our own failures to external factors and our own successes to internal factors. Interestingly, evidence suggests that attributions across cultures doesn't always work the same way; see our **OB Internationally** feature for more discussion of this issue.

fundamental attribution error The tendency for people to judge others' behaviours as being due to internal factors such as ability, motivation, or attitudes

self-serving bias When one attributes one's own failures to external factors and success to internal factors

OB INTERNATIONALLY

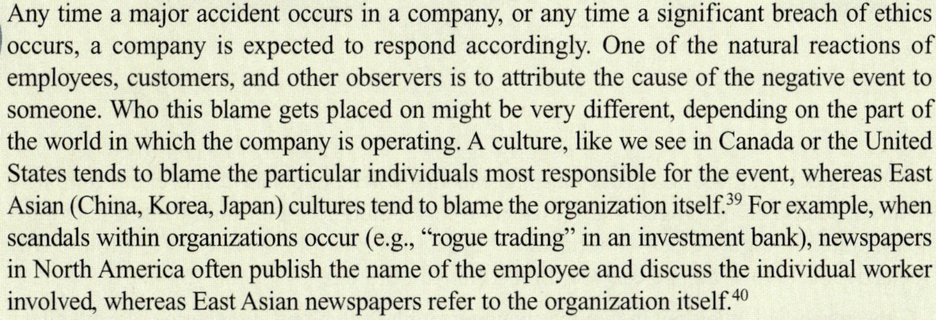

Any time a major accident occurs in a company, or any time a significant breach of ethics occurs, a company is expected to respond accordingly. One of the natural reactions of employees, customers, and other observers is to attribute the cause of the negative event to someone. Who this blame gets placed on might be very different, depending on the part of the world in which the company is operating. A culture, like we see in Canada or the United States tends to blame the particular individuals most responsible for the event, whereas East Asian (China, Korea, Japan) cultures tend to blame the organization itself.[39] For example, when scandals within organizations occur (e.g., "rogue trading" in an investment bank), newspapers in North America often publish the name of the employee and discuss the individual worker involved, whereas East Asian newspapers refer to the organization itself.[40]

Interestingly, these biases place different responsibilities on the leaders of organizations in these countries. In East Asian cultures, it's typical for the leader of an organization to take the blame for accidents, regardless of whether he or she had direct responsibility for them.[41] For example, in 2002, the director of a hospital in Tokyo was forced to resign when the cover-up of a medical accident was discovered, even though the director didn't start his job until after the cover-up took place! Similar events are common, such as the resignation of the CEO of Japan Airlines after a jet crashed, killing 500 people. In the United States, in contrast, CEOs rarely take the same level of blame. When Joseph Hazelwood crashed the Exxon Valdez into the Alaskan coastline, there were no calls for the Exxon CEO to resign. It was simply assumed by the American public that he had nothing to do with the accident.

Much of the reasoning for such differences has to do with the way the cultures view individuals and groups. East Asian cultures tend to treat groups as entities and not as individuals, whereas North American cultures tend to see individuals acting of their own accord.[42] This difference means that organizational leaders should be very cognizant of how to handle crises, depending on the country in which the negative event occurs. An apology offered by a senior leader is likely to be seen by East Asians as the company taking responsibility, whereas in Canada or the United States, it's more likely to be taken as an admission of personal guilt.[43]

FIGURE 8-5 Consensus, Distinctiveness, and Consistency

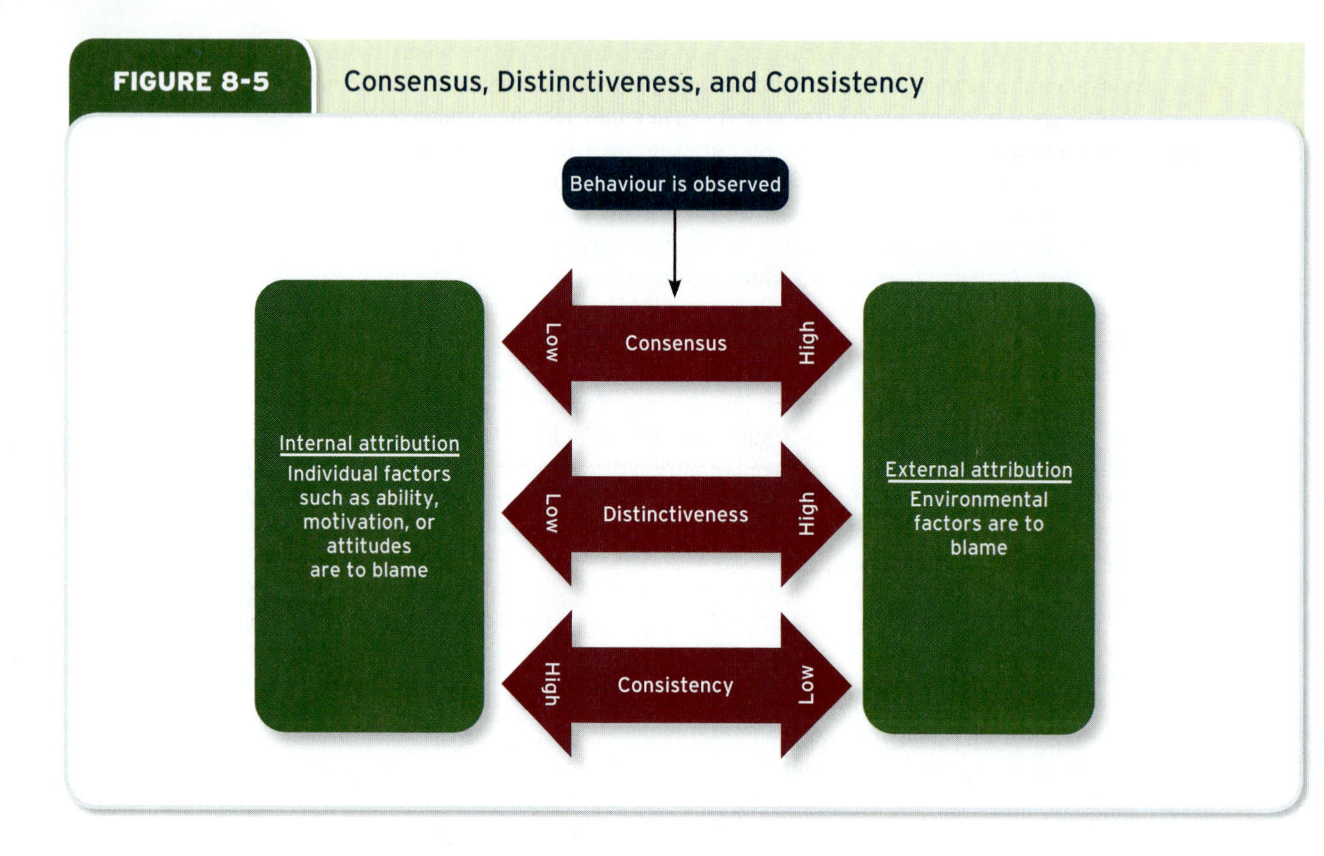

consensus Used by decision makers to attribute cause; whether other individuals behave the same way under similar circumstances

distinctiveness Used by decision makers to attribute cause; whether the person being judged acts in a similar fashion under different circumstances

consistency Used by decision makers to attribute cause; whether this individual has behaved this way before under similar circumstances

escalation of commitment A common decision-making error in which the decision maker continues to follow a failing course of action

One model of attribution processes suggests that when people have a level of familiarity with the person being judged, they'll use a more detailed decision framework. This model is illustrated in Figure 8-5.[44] To return to our previous example, if we want to explore why Joe arrived late to work, we can ask three kinds of questions:

Consensus: Did others act the same way under similar situations? In other words, did others arrive late on the same day?

Distinctiveness: Does this person tend to act differently in other circumstances? In other words, is Joe responsible when it comes to personal appointments, not just work appointments?

Consistency: Does this person always do this when performing this task? In other words, has Joe arrived late for work before?

The way in which these questions are answered will determine if an internal or external attribution is made. An internal attribution, such as laziness or low motivation for Joe, will occur if there is low consensus (others arrived on time), low distinctiveness (Joe is irresponsible with other commitments as well), and high consistency (Joe has arrived late before). An external attribution, such as bad traffic or a power outage, will occur if there is high consensus (others arrived late), high distinctiveness (Joe is responsible with other commitments), and low consistency (Joe has never come late to work before).

ESCALATION OF COMMITMENT Our last category of decision-making problems centres on what happens as a decision begins to go wrong. **Escalation of commitment** refers to the decision to continue to follow a failing course of action.[45] The expression "throwing good money after bad" captures this common decision-making error. An enormous amount of research shows that people have a tendency, when presented with a series of decisions, to escalate their commitment to previous decisions, even in the face of obvious failures.[46] Why do decision makers fall victim to this sort of error? They may feel an obligation to stick with their decision to avoid looking incompetent. They may also want to avoid admitting that they made a mistake. Those escalation tendencies become particularly strong when decision makers have invested a lot of money into the decision and when the project in question seems quite close to completion.[47]

SO WHY DO SOME EMPLOYEES LEARN TO MAKE DECISIONS BETTER THAN OTHERS?

As shown in Figure 8-6, answering that question requires understanding how employees learn, what kind of knowledge they gain, and how they use that knowledge to make decisions. Employees learn from a combination of reinforcement and observation, and that learning depends in part on whether they are learning-oriented or performance-oriented. Some of that learning results in increases in explicit knowledge, and some of that learning results in increases in tacit knowledge. Those two forms of knowledge, which combine to form an employee's expertise, are then used in decision making. If a given problem has been encountered before, decision making occurs in a more automatic, programmed fashion. If the problem is new or unfamiliar, non-programmed decision making occurs, hopefully following the rational decision-making model. Unfortunately, a number of decision-making problems can hinder the effectiveness of such decisions, including limited information, faulty perceptions, faulty attributions, and escalation of commitment.

HOW IMPORTANT IS LEARNING?

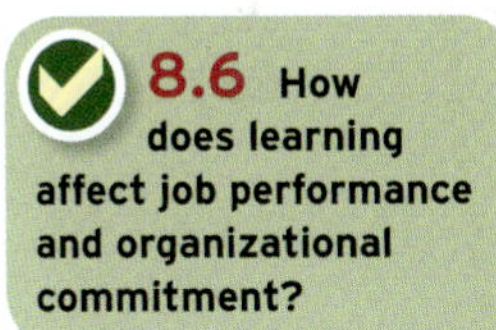

Does learning have a significant impact on the two primary outcomes in our integrative model of OB—does it correlate with job performance and organizational commitment? Figure 8-7 summarizes the research evidence linking learning to job performance and organizational commitment. The figure reveals that learning does influence job performance. Why? The primary reason is that learning is moderately correlated with task performance. It's difficult to fulfill one's job duties if the employee doesn't possess adequate levels of job knowledge. In fact, there are reasons to suggest that the moderate correlation depicted in the figure is actually an underestimate of learning's importance. That's because most of the research linking learning to task performance focuses on explicit learning, which is more practical to measure. It's difficult to measure tacit knowledge because of its unspoken nature, but clearly such knowledge is relevant to task performance. Learning seems less relevant to citizenship behaviour and counterproductive behaviour, however, given that those behaviours are often less dependent on knowledge and expertise.

Figure 8-7 also reveals that learning is only weakly related to organizational commitment.[48] In general, having higher levels of job knowledge is associated with slight increases in emotional attachment to the firm. It is true that companies that have a reputation as organizations that value learning tend to receive higher-quality applicants for jobs.[49] However, there is an important distinction between organizations that offer learning opportunities and employees who take advantage of those opportunities to actually gain knowledge. Moreover, it may be that employees with higher levels of expertise become more highly valued commodities on the job market, thereby reducing their levels of continuance commitment.

FIGURE 8-6 Why Do Some Employees Learn to Make Decisions Better Than Others?

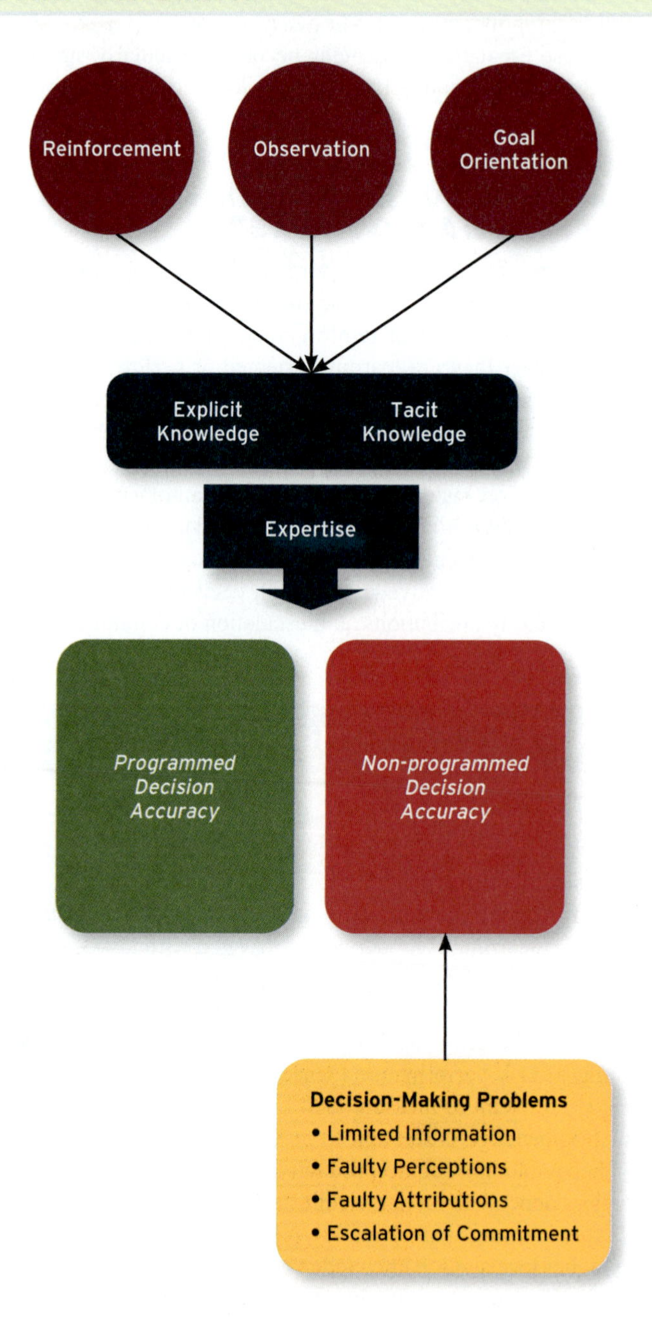

FIGURE 8-7 Effects of Learning on Performance and Commitment

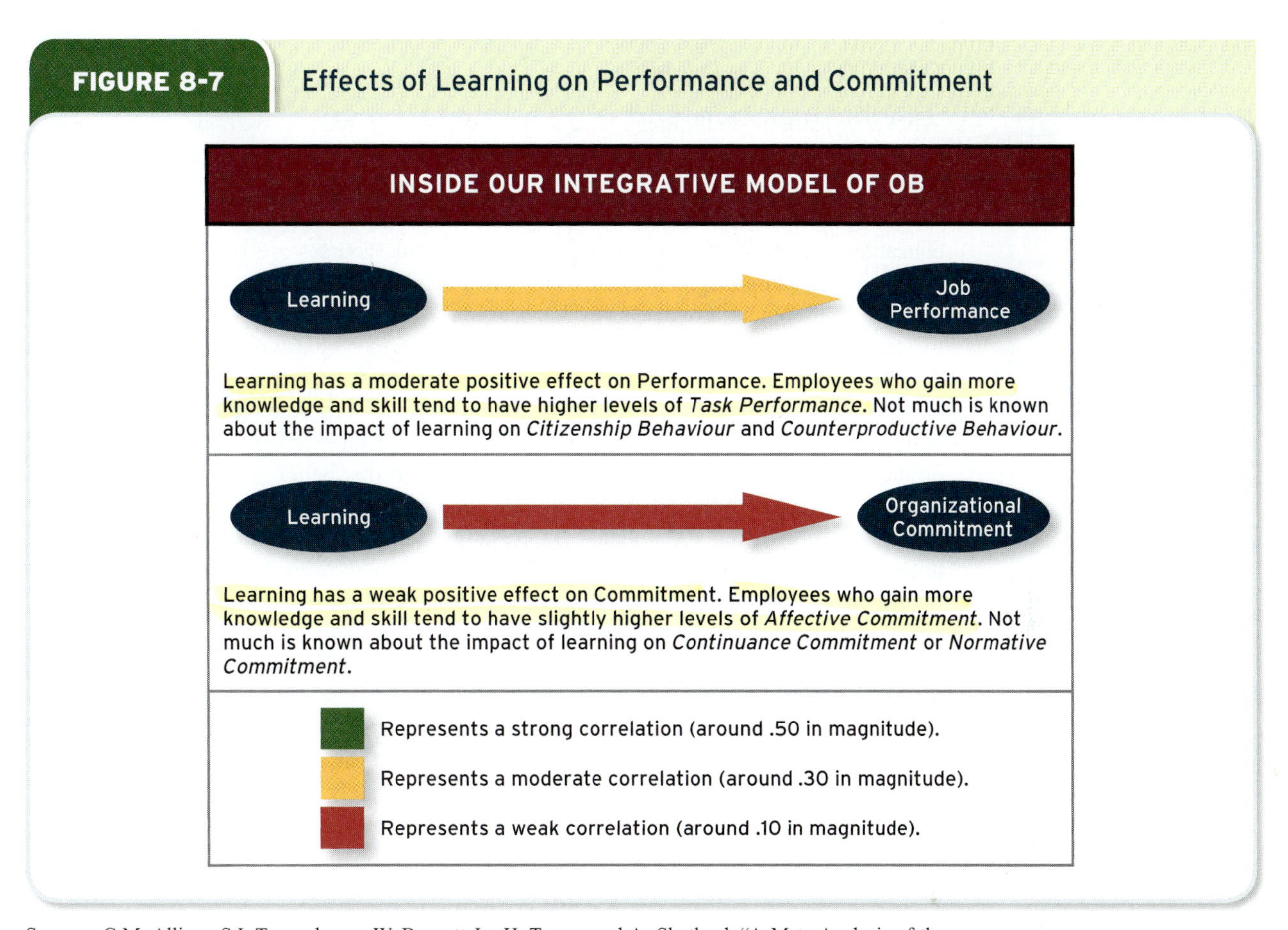

Sources: G.M. Alliger, S.I. Tannenbaum, W. Bennett Jr., H. Traver, and A. Shotland, "A Meta-Analysis of the Relations among Training Criteria," *Personnel Psychology* 50 (1997), pp. 341–58; J.A. Colquitt, J.A. Lepine, and R.A. Noe, "Toward an Integrative Theory of Training Motivation: A Meta-Analytic Path Analysis of 20 Years of Research," *Journal of Applied Psychology* 85 (2000), pp. 678–707; J.P. Meyer, D.J. Stanley, L. Herscovitch, and L. Topolnytsky, "Affective, Continuance, and Normative Commitment to the Organization: A Meta-Analysis of Antecedents, Correlates, and Consequences," *Journal of Vocational Behavior* 61 (2002), pp. 20–52.

APPLICATION: TRAINING

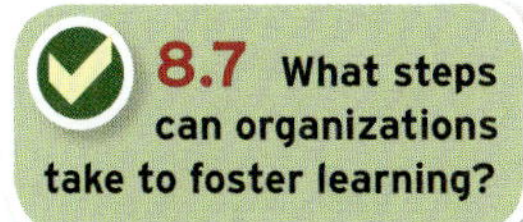

How can organizations improve learning in an effort to boost employee expertise and, ultimately, improve decision making? One approach is to rely on **training**, which represents a systematic effort by organizations to facilitate the learning of job-related knowledge and behaviour. Organizations across North America spent over $55.8 billion and approximately $1,273 per learner on formal training and development costs in 2006.[50] Estimates suggest that organizations spend three to six times that amount on informal, observational, and on-the-job training.[51] A full discussion of all the types of training companies offer is beyond the scope of this section, but suffice it to say that companies are using many different methods to help their employees acquire explicit and tacit knowledge. Technological changes are altering the way those methods are delivered, as instructor-led classroom training has declined while online self-study programs have increased.[52] As described in our **OB for Students** section, these technological changes are occurring on university campuses as well. Indeed, some of you may be working in a virtual classroom right now!

training A systematic effort by organizations to facilitate the learning of job-related knowledge and behaviour

OB FOR STUDENTS

What does learning and training have to do with you as a student? We hope this is a reasonably clear question for you already! However, there are some changes on the way in terms of how you might get taught in the future by both companies and universities. Technology and the changing marketplace (that includes you!) are forcing universities to incorporate online education as part of their ongoing strategies.[53] Online courses are growing by leaps and bounds across campuses all over the country and internationally. If you're not already experiencing virtual content in some form, chances are good many of you will have the opportunity to receive it in the not-too-distant future. Overall, higher education enrollment in North America is relatively stable, but enrollment in online courses is increasing exponentially.[54]

One of the reasons universities have been slow to incorporate online education is the belief by many faculty members that the same level of knowledge cannot be transmitted online. However, a recent meta-analysis suggests that this belief is unfounded! Research shows no difference between online and regular classroom instruction in terms of the measured learning of explicit knowledge. Interestingly enough though, the study found that the highest levels of learning occurred when the two methods were mixed (part of the class online, part in the classroom).[55] It may be that two different learning strategies are used under such scenarios, which allows different kinds of learners to take advantage of what suits them best.[56] At the moment, companies are well ahead of the curve at delivering effective online classes. Edmonton-based Intuit, the maker of personal and small business software including Quicken and TurboTax, has been using the mixed method of training for quite a while. It employs face-to-face training to establish relationships prior to moving into a virtual classroom.[57] Such corporate efforts will likely help establish a blueprint for universities to follow as they expand their online offerings.

knowledge transfer The exchange of knowledge between employees

In addition to traditional training experiences, companies are also heavily focused on **knowledge transfer** from their older, experienced workers to their younger employees. Mentoring programs, so popular today, are forms of behavioural modelling whereby employees are exposed to those in the company with significant amounts of tacit knowledge. For example, Raytheon, the Massachusetts-based defence and aerospace supplier, has created a training program called "Leave-a-Legacy" that pairs employees holding vital knowledge with high-potential subordinates. Raytheon's program is a relatively regimented program in which younger workers follow older workers around for extended periods of time, ensuring adequate opportunities for observation. Each pair of employees is also assigned a third-party coach that helps the knowledge transfer take place.[58]

communities of practice Groups of employees who learn from one another through collaboration over an extended period of time

Another form of knowledge transfer that's being used by companies more frequently is communities of practice. **Communities of practice** are groups of employees who work together and learn from one another by collaborating over an extended period of time.[59] A large number of companies are utilizing this newer form of informal social learning. John Deere, the Illinois-based manufacturer of agricultural equipment, implemented an informal training process in 2002 and now has a network of more than 300 communities dealing with issues such as mergers and acquisitions and its Deere Production System.[60] Communities of practice introduce their own unique complications, but the potential of their ability to transfer knowledge through employees is significant.[61]

transfer of training Occurs when employees retain and demonstrate the knowledge, skills, and behaviours required for their job after training ends

The success of these programs, as well as more traditional types of training, hinges on transfer of training. **Transfer of training** occurs when the knowledge, skills, and behaviours used on the job are maintained by the learner once training ends and generalized to the workplace once the learner returns to the job.[62] Transfer of training can be fostered if organizations create a **climate for transfer**—an environment that can support the use of new skills. There are a variety of factors that can help organizations foster such a climate. The degree to which the trainee's manager supports the importance of the newly acquired knowledge and skills and stresses its application to the job is perhaps the most important factor. Peer support is helpful, because having multiple trainees learning the same material reduces anxiety and allows the trainees to share concerns and work through problems. Opportunities to use the learned knowledge are also crucial, because practice and repetition are key components of learning. Because companies have a huge stake in increasing and transferring knowledge within their employee base, creating a climate for the transfer of that knowledge is imperative to the success of formal learning systems.[63]

climate for transfer An organizational environment that supports the use of new skills

TAKEAWAYS

8.1 Learning is a relatively permanent change in an employee's knowledge or skill that results from experience. Decision making refers to the process of generating and choosing from a set of alternatives to solve a problem.

8.2 Employees gain both explicit and tacit knowledge as they build expertise. Explicit knowledge is easily communicated and available to everyone. Tacit knowledge, however, is something employees can only learn through experience.

8.3 Employees learn new knowledge through reinforcement and observation of others. That learning also depends on whether the employees are learning-oriented or performance-oriented.

8.4 Programmed decisions are decisions that become somewhat automatic because a person's knowledge allows him or her to recognize and identify a situation and the course of action that needs to be taken. Many task-related decisions made by experts are programmed decisions. Non-programmed decisions are made when a problem is new, complex, or not recognized. Ideally, such decisions are made by following the steps in the rational decision-making model.

8.5 Employees are less able to translate their learning into accurate decisions when they struggle with limited information, faulty perceptions, faulty attributions, and escalation of commitment.

8.6 Learning has a moderate positive relationship with job performance and a weak positive relationship with organizational commitment.

8.7 Through various forms of training, companies can give employees more knowledge and a wider array of experiences that they can use to make decisions.

KEY TERMS

DISCUSSION QUESTIONS

8.1 In your current or past workplaces, what types of tacit knowledge did experienced workers possess? What did this knowledge allow them to do?

8.2 Companies rely on employees with substantial amounts of tacit knowledge. Why do companies struggle when these employees leave the organization unexpectedly? What can companies do to help ensure that they retain tacit knowledge?

8.3 What does the term "expert" mean to you? What exactly do experts do that novices don't?

8.4 For those of you preparing for a career, how do you expect to learn what you need to know when you start working? Do you expect the company to provide you with these opportunities, or will you have to seek them out on your own? For those of you who are currently working, what has been your experience?

8.5 Do you consider yourself a "rational" decision maker? For what types of decisions are you determined to be the most rational? What types of decisions are likely to cause you to behave irrationally?

8.6 Given your background, which of the decision-making biases listed in the chapter do you most struggle with? What could you do to overcome those biases to make more accurate decisions?

CASE • LINDSEY MOSER

Without classrooms, textbooks, lectures, or professors, how was Lindsey going to survive her challenging new job at KPMG? Well, as it turned out . . . very well! In fact, after the first year, Lindsey found herself working closely with people she liked and with high-profile clients on complex and interesting projects. It wasn't long before Lindsey was working 60 to 70 hours per week. As her reputation increased, she noticed that it was much easier to get her manager to approve training opportunities, and that key people within the firm were seeking her out. Some of her peers, however, were not as fortunate. Many were put on easy jobs that were not big money-makers or were assigned jobs that others did not want to do. This was the worst kind of punishment—to not get training opportunities or to be ignored by the "movers and shakers" within the firm! After passing the CA exam, Lindsey was quickly promoted to a management position. It would appear that her dream had, indeed, come true!

If her dream had really come true, then why did she feel so conflicted? The long working days combined with the high pressure were starting to take their toll on her happiness. Is this the life she really wanted? But after investing so many years preparing for a career in a prestigious accounting firm like KPMG, could she leave? She was aware that an alternative career in the profession would be to work as an auditor or controller in government or industry. Although the work would be more routine, potentially boring, and would require a more focused set of technical skills, it would be a lot more predictable and structured in terms of hours—she could have a life! Another thought occurred to her too. Because she had always performed so well in university, perhaps she should pursue graduate study and work toward a doctorate degree and become a professor. One of her professor's had strongly encouraged her to look at that option. Going back to school would require Lindsey leave the accounting profession altogether.

8.1 How does the organization facilitate learning of tacit knowledge?

8.2 What kind of decision is Lindsey currently faced with? What kind of information should she consider? What are the risks that may lead to a poor choice? What do you think she will do?

EXERCISE • DECISION-MAKING BIAS[1]

The purpose of this exercise is to illustrate how decision making can be influenced by decision heuristics, availability bias, and escalation of commitment. This exercise uses groups of six participants, so your instructor will either assign you to a group of six or ask you to create your own group of six. The exercise has the following steps:

1. Answer each of the problems below.
   A. A certain town is served by two hospitals. In the larger hospital, about 45 babies are born each day, and in the smaller hospital, about 15 babies are born each day. Although the overall proportion of boys is about 50 percent, the actual proportion at either hospital may be greater or less than 50 percent on any given day. At the end of a year, which hospital will have the greater number of days on which more than 60 percent of the babies born were boys?
      a. The large hospital.
      b. The small hospital.
      c. Neither; the number of days will be about the same (within 5 percent of each other).
   B. Linda is 31, single, outspoken, and very bright. She majored in philosophy in university. As a student, she was deeply concerned with discrimination and other social issues and participated in antinuclear demonstrations. Which statement is more likely:
      a. Linda is a bank teller.
      b. Linda is a bank teller and active in the feminist movement.

C. A cab was involved in a hit-and-run accident. Two cab companies serve the city: the Green, which operates 85 percent of the cabs, and the Blue, which operates the remaining 15 percent. A witness identifies the hit-and-run cab as Blue. When the court tests the reliability of the witness under circumstances similar to those on the night of the accident, he correctly identifies the colour of the cab 80 percent of the time and misidentifies it the other 20 percent. What's the probability that the cab involved in the accident was Blue, as the witness stated?

D. Imagine that you face this pair of concurrent decisions. Examine these decisions, then indicate which choices you prefer.

Decision I: Choose between:
a. A sure gain of $240, and
b. A 25 percent chance of winning $1,000 and a 75 percent chance of winning nothing.

Decision II: Choose between:
a. A sure loss of $750, and
b. A 75 percent chance of losing $1,000 and a 25 percent chance of losing nothing.

Decision III: Choose between:
a. A sure loss of $3,000, and
b. An 80 percent chance of losing $4,000 and a 20 percent chance of losing nothing.

E. a. You've decided to see a play and have bought a $40 ticket. As you enter the theatre, you realize you've lost your ticket. You can't remember the seat number, so you can't prove to the management that you bought a ticket. Would you spend $40 for a new ticket?
b. You've reserved a seat for a play, for which the ticket price is $40. As you enter the theatre to buy your ticket, you discover you've lost $40 from your pocket. Would you still buy the ticket? (Assume you have enough cash left to do so.)

F. Imagine you have operable lung cancer and must choose between two treatments: surgery and radiation. Of 100 people having surgery, 10 die during the operation, 32 (including those original 10) are dead after 1 year, and 66 are dead after 5 years. Of 100 people having radiation therapy, none dies during treatment, 23 are dead after one year, and 78 after 5 years. Which treatment would you prefer?

2. Your instructor will give you the correct answer to each problem.
3. Class discussion, whether in groups or as a class, should focus on the following questions: How accurate were the descriptions you reached? What decision-making problems were evident in the decisions you reached? Consider especially where decision heuristics, availability, and escalation of commitment may have influenced your decisions. How could you improve your decision making to make it more accurate?

[1] This exercise originally appeared in *Organizational Behavior and Management* (7th ed.) by Ivancevich, Konopaske, and Matteson (New York: McGraw-Hill, 2005); used with permission. Original exercises are based on: (1) A. Tversky and D. Kahneman, "Rational Choice and the Framing of Decisions," *Journal of Business* 59 (1986), pp. 251–78; (2) A. Tversky and D. Kahneman, "The Framing of Decisions and the Psychology of Choice," *Science* 211 (1981), pp. 453–58; (3) A. Tversky and D. Kahneman, "Extensional vs. Intuitive Reasoning: The Conjunction Fallacy in Probability Judgment," Psychological Review 90 (1983), pp. 293–315; and (4) K. McKean, "Decisions, Decisions," *Discovery Magazine*, June 1985.

OB ASSESSMENTS • GOAL ORIENTATION

What does your goal orientation look like? This assessment is designed to measure all three dimensions of goal orientation. Please write a number next to each statement that indicates the extent to which it accurately describes your attitude toward work while you are on the job. Answer each question using the response scale provided. Then sum up your answers for each of the three dimensions.

1 STRONGLY DISAGREE	2 DISAGREE	3 NEUTRAL	4 AGREE	5 STRONGLY AGREE

1. I am willing to select challenging assignments that I can learn a lot from. ______
2. I often look for opportunities to develop new skills and knowledge. ______
3. I enjoy challenging and difficult tasks where I'll learn new skills. ______
4. For me, development of my ability is important enough to take risks. ______
5. I prefer to work in situations that require a high level of ability and talent. ______
6. I like to show that I can perform better than my co-workers. ______
7. I try to figure out what it takes to prove my ability to others at work. ______
8. I enjoy it when others at work are aware of how well I am doing. ______
9. I prefer to work on projects where I can prove my ability to others. ______
10. I would avoid taking on a new task if there was a chance that I would appear incompetent to others. ______
11. Avoiding a show of low ability is more important to me than learning a new skill. ______
12. I'm concerned about taking on a task at work if my performance would reveal that I had low ability. ______
13. I prefer to avoid situations at work where I might perform poorly. ______

SCORING AND INTERPRETATION:

Learning Orientation: Sum up items 1–5.
Performance-Prove Orientation: Sum up items 6–9
Performance-Avoid Orientation: Sum up items 10–13.

For learning orientation, scores of 20 or more are above average, and scores of 19 or less are below average. For the two performance orientations, scores of 15 or more are above average, and scores of 14 or less are below average.

Source: Adapted from J.F. Brett and D. VandeWalle, "Goal Orientation and Goal Content as Predictors of Performance in a Training Program," *Journal of Applied Psychology* 84 (1999), pp. 863–7.

CONNECT——Available 24/7 with instant feedback so you can study when you want, how you want, and where you want. Take advantage of the Study Plan——an innovative tool that helps students customize their own learning experience. Students can diagnose their knowledge with pre- and post-tests, identify the areas where they need help, search contents of the entire learning package for content specific to the topic they're studying, and add these resources to their study plan. Visit **www.connectob.ca** to register——take practice quizzes, run interactive scenarios, and much more. Also visit the Student Online Learning Centre for additional study tools.

www.mcgrawhill.ca/olc/colquitt

Part 3 **INDIVIDUAL, GROUP, AND ORGANIZATIONAL CONTEXT**

CHAPTER 9

Personality, Cultural Values, and Ability

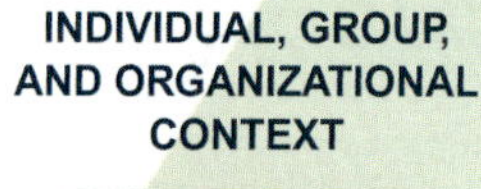

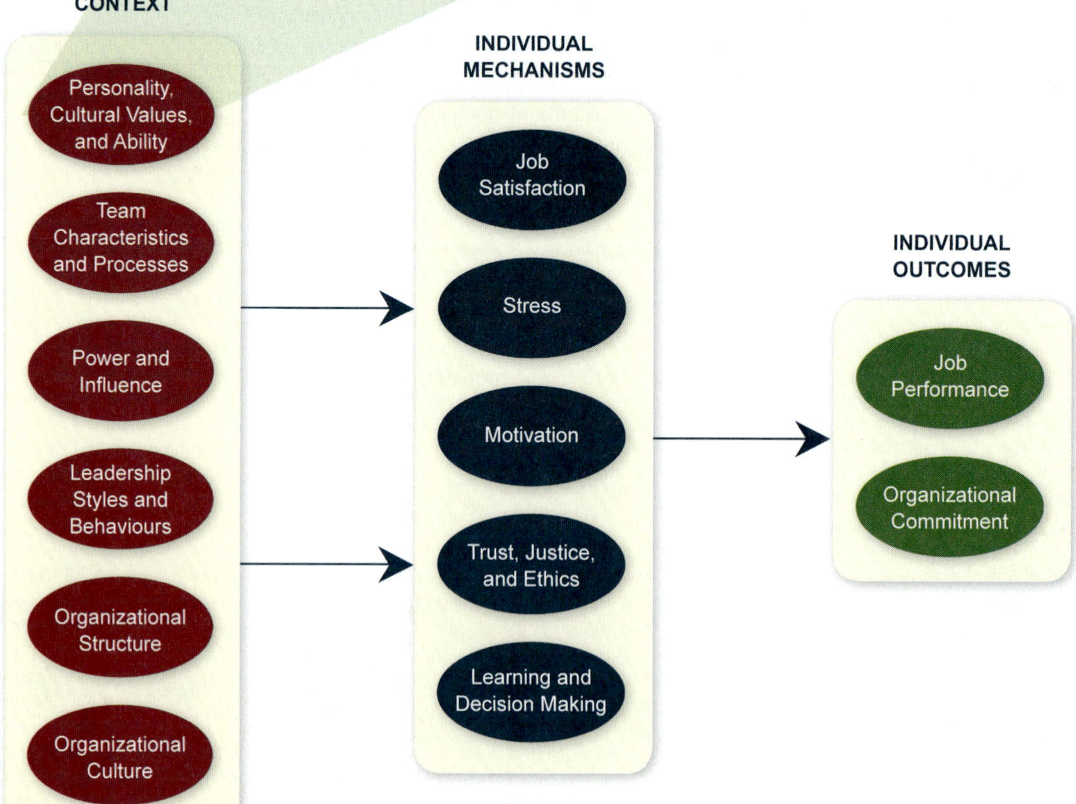

After reading this chapter, you should be able to answer the following questions:

- 9.1 What is personality, and how can it be distinguished from ability? What are cultural values?
- 9.2 What are the "Big Five?"
- 9.3 What are Hofstede's dimensions of cultural values?
- 9.4 What are the various types of cognitive ability?
- 9.5 What are the various types of emotional ability?
- 9.6 What are the various types of physical ability?
- 9.7 How do personality and ability affect job performance and organizational commitment?

GOOGLE

How long has it been since you last used Google to do a search on the Internet or navigate the Web? If you've worked on your computer today, chances are it hasn't been more than a few hours. In fact, Google has more than 300 million users across the globe[1] and is far and away the most popular Internet search engine.[2] With all this popularity has come staggering financial success. Google's revenues increased from $86.4 million in 2001 to $6.14 billion in 2006, when the company had a market value of over $115 billion. To put this in perspective, $115 billion is almost 50 percent higher than the *combined* market value of the "big three" automakers in North America.

So how did Google become so wildly successful? Well, for one thing, co-founders Larry Page and Sergey Brin developed and patented an algorithm that made Internet searches much more efficient and user friendly than what was previously available. However, another key factor that has allowed Google to achieve continued success is its strategy of hiring employees who are extremely intelligent. How does Google go about hiring the best and the brightest? The company has used a number of innovative techniques to attract and recruit a huge pool of really smart people. For example, Google placed billboards in Silicon Valley and Harvard Square with the brainteaser, "first 10-digit prime found in consecutive digits of *e*.com." People who solved the brainteaser were taken to a Web site with a more difficult brainteaser. Solving that one resulted in Google asking for the person's resume.[3]

As another example, Google developed something called the *Google Labs Aptitude Test* (GLAT for short) and published it in magazines that smart techies might read. The GLAT includes questions such as, "How many different ways can you color an icosahedron with one of three colors on each face?" and "On an infinite, two-dimensional, rectangular lattice of 1-ohm resistors, what is the resistance between two nodes that are a knight's move away?" The GLAT also includes questions for which there are no correct answers per se, but instead require originality. For example, one question asks, "Write a haiku describing methods for predicting search traffic seasonality." Another notes, "This space is intentionally left blank. Please fill it with something that improves upon emptiness."

Considered one of the best places to work, Google uses billboards like this one to catch the eye of smart and talented recruits.

Google used the GLAT as a public relations tool to attract people who are smart and who are interested in the types of problems in the test. As noted on the Official Google Blog, where the test is available, "We enjoyed writing it, and if you're our kind of uber-geek, you'll enjoy taking it, and maybe you'd enjoy life as a Googler."[4] How effective are practices like these in generating a large pool of potential Googlers? On average, Google hires about 9 people a day from the 150,000 resumes received each month—a very selective ratio.[5] The people who are brought in for an interview typically face 10-person interview panels who ask very difficult questions. For example, someone who applies for a technical job might be asked to solve math algorithms and answer technical questions about software and computer networking.[6] Clearly Google understands the need to hire smart people.[7] It also understands that if Google is not successful in beating out rivals like Yahoo and Microsoft for the best and brightest, odds are the company will go the way of AltaVista and Inktomi, two of the previous leaders in the Internet search business.

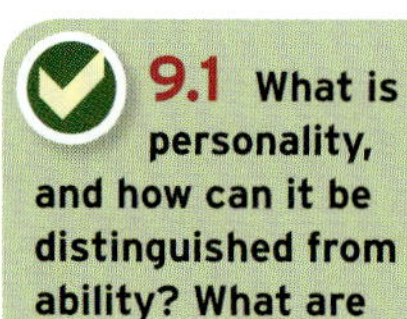
9.1 What is personality, and how can it be distinguished from ability? What are cultural values?

PERSONALITY, CULTURAL VALUES, AND ABILITY

It seems clear from the opening example that Google focuses a great deal on the personal qualities of the people it hires. **Personality** refers to the structures and propensities inside a person that explain his or her characteristic patterns of thought, emotion, and behaviour.[8] Personality creates a person's social reputation—the way he or she is perceived by friends, family, co-workers, and supervisors.[9] Even though we sometimes describe people as having "a good personality," personality is actually a collection of multiple specific traits. **Traits** are defined as recurring regularities or trends in people's responses to their environment.[10] Adjectives such as responsible, critical, organized, or achievement-oriented are all examples of traits. **Cultural values**, defined as shared beliefs about desirable end states or modes of conduct in a given culture,[11] influence the expression of a person's traits. In this way, personality and cultural values capture *what people are like*. **Ability** refers to the relatively stable capabilities people have to perform a particular range of different but related activities.[12] In contrast to skills, which can be improved over time with training and experience, ability is relatively stable. Although abilities can change slowly over time with repeated practice and repetition, the level of a given ability generally limits how much a person can improve, even with the best training in the world. In contrast to personality and values, ability captures *what people can do*. The GLAT test is an example of how Google assesses a variety of cognitive abilities deemed critical for high performance and fit with others in the company.

personality The structures and propensities inside a person that explain his or her characteristic patterns of thought, emotion, and behaviour; personality reflects what people are like and creates their social reputation

traits Recurring trends in people's responses to their environment

cultural values Shared beliefs about desirable end states or modes of conduct in a given culture that influence the expression of traits

ability Relatively stable capabilities of people for performing a particular range of related activities

HOW CAN WE DESCRIBE WHAT EMPLOYEES ARE LIKE?

We can use personality traits and cultural values to describe what employees are like. For example, how would you describe your first university roommate to one of your classmates? You'd start off using certain adjectives—maybe the roommate was funny and outgoing, or maybe polite and organized. Of course, it would take more than a few adjectives to describe your roommate fully. You could probably go on listing traits for several minutes, maybe even coming up with 100 traits or more. Although 100 traits may sound like a lot, personality researchers note that the third edition of *Webster's Unabridged Dictionary* contains 1,710 adjectives that can be used to describe someone's traits![13] Was your roommate abrasive, adulterous, agitable, alarmable, antisocial, arbitrative, arrogant, asocial, audacious, aweless, and awkward? We hope not!

THE BIG FIVE TAXONOMY

With 1,710 adjectives, you might be worrying about the length of this chapter (or the difficulty of your next exam!). Fortunately, it turns out that most adjectives are variations of five broad "factors" or "dimensions" that can be used to summarize our personalities.[14] Those five personality dimensions include **conscientiousness**, **agreeableness**, **neuroticism**, **openness to experience**, and **extraversion**. Collectively, these dimensions have been dubbed the **Big Five**.[15] Figure 9-1 lists the traits that can be found within each of the Big Five dimensions. We acknowledge that it can be hard to remember the particular labels for the Big Five dimensions, and we only wish there was some acronym that could make the process easier. Would you like to see what your Big Five profile looks like? Our **OB Assessments** feature at the end of the chapter will show you where you stand on each of the five dimensions.

conscientiousness Dimension of personality reflecting traits like being dependable, organized, reliable, ambitious, hard-working, and persevering

agreeableness Dimension of personality reflecting traits like being kind, cooperative, sympathetic, helpful, courteous, and warm

neuroticism Dimension of personality reflecting traits like being nervous, moody, emotional, insecure, jealous, and unstable

openness to experience Dimension of personality reflecting traits like being curious, imaginative, creative, complex, refined, and sophisticated

extraversion Dimension of personality reflecting traits like being talkative, sociable, passionate, assertive, bold, and dominant

Big Five The five major dimensions of personality including conscientiousness, agreeableness, neuroticism, openness to experience, and extraversion

accomplishment striving A strong desire to accomplish task-related goals as a means of expressing one's personality

CONSCIENTIOUSNESS As shown in Figure 9-1, conscientious people are dependable, organized, reliable, ambitious, hard-working, and persevering.[16] It's difficult, if not impossible, to envision a job in which those traits will not be beneficial.[17] That's not a claim we make about all of the Big Five, because some jobs require high levels of agreeableness, extraversion, or openness, while others demand low levels of those same traits. We don't want to spoil the "how important are these personal qualities?" discussion that concludes this chapter, but suffice it to say that conscientiousness has the biggest influence on job performance of any of the Big Five. Of course, the key question therefore becomes: Why is conscientiousness so valuable?

One reason can be found in the general goals that people prioritize in their working life. Conscientious employees prioritize **accomplishment striving**, which reflects a strong desire to accomplish task-related goals as a means of expressing personality.[18] People who are "accomplishment strivers" have a built-in desire to finish work tasks, channel a high proportion of their efforts toward those tasks, and work harder and longer on task assignments. As evidence of their accomplishment-striving nature, one research study showed that conscientious salespeople set higher sales goals for themselves than unconscientious salespeople and were more committed to meeting those goals.[19] Another study of salespeople showed that conscientious salespeople's organizational skills were particularly valuable during their first year of employment, and their ambitious nature became more critical as they gained tenure and experience.[20]

A third research study provides particularly compelling evidence regarding the benefits of conscientiousness.[21] The study used data from the University of California, Berkeley's Intergenerational Studies, which collected data about a set of children in the late 1920s and early 1930s. Those researchers gathered personality data using interviews and assessments of the children by trained psychologists. Follow-up studies collected data on the same sample as they reached early adulthood, middle age, and late adulthood. This last time period included assessments of career success, which included ratings of annual income and occupational prestige. The results of the study showed that childhood conscientiousness was strongly correlated with ratings of career success five decades later! In fact, those conscientiousness effects were roughly twice as strong as the effects of the other Big Five dimensions.

Such findings show that it pays to be conscientious; other research even suggests that conscientiousness is good for your health. For example, one study gathered data about the conscientiousness of 1,528 children in the early 1920s.[22] Data on health-relevant behaviours were then gathered in 1950 for 1,215 of the original participants. By 1986, 419 of the participants had died and 796 were still living. The results of the study revealed that childhood

FIGURE 9-1 Trait Adjectives Associated with the Big Five

C	A	N	O	E
Conscientiousness	Agreeableness	Neuroticism	Openness	Extraversion
• Dependable • Organized • Reliable • Ambitious • Hardworking • Persevering	• Kind • Cooperative • Sympathetic • Helpful • Courteous • Warm	• Nervous • Moody • Emotional • Insecure • Jealous • Unstable	• Curious • Imaginative • Creative • Complex • Refined • Sophisticated	• Talkative • Sociable • Passionate • Assertive • Bold • Dominant
NOT	NOT	NOT	NOT	NOT
• Careless • Sloppy • Inefficient • Negligent • Lazy • Irresponsible	• Critical • Antagonistic • Callous • Selfish • Rude • Cold	• Calm • Steady • Relaxed • At ease • Secure • Contented	• Uninquisitive • Conventional • Conforming • Simple • Unartistic • Traditional	• Quiet • Shy • Inhibited • Bashful • Reserved • Submissive

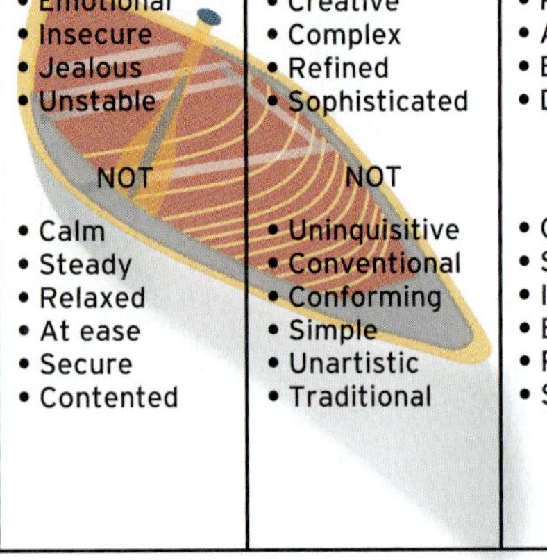

Sources: G. Saucier, "Mini-Markers: A Brief Version of Goldberg's Unipolar Big-Five Markers," *Journal of Personality Assessment* 63 (1994), pp. 506–516; L.R. Goldberg, "The Development of Markers for the Big-Five Factor Structure," *Psychological Assessment* 4 (1992), pp. 26–42; R.R. McCrae and P.T. Costa Jr., "Validation of the Five-Factor Model of Personality across Instruments and Observers," *Journal of Personality and Social Psychology* 52 (1987), pp. 81–90.

conscientiousness was negatively related to mortality, including death from injuries, death from cardiovascular disease, and death from cancer. Why did conscientious participants live longer? The study also showed that conscientiousness was negatively related to alcohol consumption and smoking during adulthood. Other research has shown that conscientious people are less likely to abuse drugs, more likely to take preventative steps to remain healthy, and less likely to perform risky behaviours as a driver or pedestrian.[23]

communion striving A strong desire to obtain acceptance in personal relationships as a means of expressing one's personality

AGREEABLENESS Agreeable people are warm, kind, cooperative, sympathetic, helpful, and courteous. Agreeable people prioritize **communion striving**, which reflects a strong desire to obtain acceptance in personal relationships as a means of expressing personality. Put differently, agreeable people focus on "getting along," not necessarily "getting ahead."[24] Unlike conscientiousness, agreeableness is not related to performance across all jobs or occupations.[25] Why not? The biggest reason is that communion striving is beneficial in some positions but detrimental in others. For example, managers often need to prioritize the effectiveness of the unit over a desire to gain acceptance. In such cases, effective job performance may demand being disagreeable in the face of unreasonable requests or demands.

Of course, there are some jobs in which agreeableness can be beneficial. The most obvious example is service jobs—jobs in which the employee has direct, face-to-face, or verbal contact with a customer. How many times have you encountered a customer service person who is cold, rude, or antagonistic? Did you tend to buy the company's product after such experiences? Research suggests that agreeable employees have stronger customer service skills.[26] One reason for their effectiveness in customer service environments is that they are reluctant to react to conflict with criticism, threats, or manipulation.[27] Instead, they tend to react to conflict by walking away, adopting a "wait-and-see" attitude, or giving in to the other person.

One study provides unique insights into the effects of agreeableness. The study used a variation of "lived day analysis," where a portion of a participant's daily routine is recorded and analyzed.[28] Ninety-six undergraduates completed assessments of the Big Five personality dimensions before being fitted with a digital recorder and an electronic microphone that could be clipped to their shirt collar. The microphone recorded 30 seconds of footage at 12-minute intervals over the course of two weekdays, with participants unable to track when footage was actually being recorded. Trained coders then rated the sounds and conversations recorded on the microphone. The results of the study revealed a number of interesting expressions of agreeableness. Agreeable participants were significantly less likely to be at home in their apartment during recordings; instead, they spent more time in public places. They were also less likely to use swear words and more likely to use words that conveyed personal rapport during conversations.

9.2 What are the "Big Five?"

EXTRAVERSION Extraverted people are talkative, sociable, passionate, assertive, bold, and dominant (in contrast to introverts, who are quiet, shy, and reserved). Of the Big Five, extraversion is the easiest to judge in **zero acquaintance situations**—situations in which two people have only just met. Consider times when you've been around a stranger in a doctor's office, in line at a grocery store, or in an airport terminal. It only takes about five minutes to figure out whether that stranger is extraverted or introverted.[29] Extraversion is also the Big Five dimension that you knew your standing on, even before taking our self-assessment. People rarely consider how open they are to new experiences or how agreeable they are, but almost everyone already self-identifies as an "extravert" or "introvert."

zero acquaintance situations Situations in which two people have just met

status striving A strong desire to obtain power and influence within a social structure as a means of expressing one's personality

positive affectivity A dispositional tendency to experience pleasant, engaging moods such as enthusiasm, excitement, and elation

Like agreeableness, extraversion is not necessarily related to performance across all jobs or occupations. However, extraverted people prioritize **status striving**, which reflects a strong desire to obtain power and influence within a social structure as a means of expressing personality.[30] Extraverts care a lot about being successful and influential and direct their work efforts toward "moving up" and developing a strong reputation. Indeed, research suggests that extraverts are more likely to emerge as leaders in social and task-related groups.[31] They also tend to be rated as more effective in a leadership role by the people who are following them.[32] One potential reason for these findings is that people tend to view extraverts, who are more energetic and outgoing, as more "leaderlike" than introverts.

In addition to being related to leadership emergence and effectiveness, research suggests that extraverts tend to be happier with their jobs. You may recall from Chapter 4 on job satisfaction that people's day-to-day moods can be categorized along two dimensions: pleasantness and engagement. As illustrated in Figure 9-2, extraverted employees tend to be high in what's called **positive affectivity**—a dispositional tendency to experience pleasant, engaging moods such as enthusiasm, excitement, and elation.[33] That tendency to experience positive moods across situations explains why extraverts tend to be more satisfied with their jobs.[34] Other research suggests that extraverts have more to be happy about than just their jobs. One study asked students to complete a "life event checklist" by indicating whether various events had happened to them in the preceding four years.[35] The results showed that extraversion was associated with more positive events, such as joining a club or athletic team, going on vacation with friends, getting a raise at work,

"I could cry when I think of the years I wasted accumulating money, only to learn that my cheerful disposition is genetic."

Source: © The New Yorker Collection 1996 J. B. Handelsman from cartoonbank.com.

OB ON SCREEN

THE BREAK-UP

Brooke: You know what Gary? I asked you to do one thing today, one very simple thing—to bring me 12 lemons—and you brought me 3.

Gary: If I knew that it was gonna be this much trouble, I would've brought home 24 lemons, even 100 lemons. You know what I wish? I wish everyone that was at that table had their own little private bag of lemons!

Brooke: It's not about the lemons. . . . I'm just saying it'd be nice if you did things that I asked. It would be even nicer if you did things without me having to ask you!

With those words, Gary (Vince Vaughn) and Brooke (Jennifer Aniston) reveal one of the biggest stumbling blocks in their relationship in *The Break-Up* (Dir.: Adam McKay, Sony Pictures, 2006). From Brooke's perspective, Gary isn't very conscientious. She put together a dinner party for their families and gave Gary one assignment: Bring home twelve lemons for a centrepiece. He brought three. After the party was over, she had one additional request—to help her do the dishes. Gary wanted to play a video game instead, noting that they could do the dishes in the morning.

Brooke isn't the only one who complains about Gary's lack of conscientiousness. Gary's brother, who co-owns their tour guide company, is constantly pleading with Gary to get his tour logs done so that he can keep the company's books straight. But Gary always has an excuse for putting off his paperwork, to the point that he's three months behind on his logs.

If Brooke and Gary decide to remain broken up, what could Brooke do to find a more conscientious boyfriend the next time around? One approach might be to turn to dating Web sites that use personality tests to assess conscientiousness. For example, eHarmony requires members to spend 45 minutes filling out a 436-question personality test that assesses 29 different personality dimensions.[36] Two of those dimensions—"industry" and "ambition"—clearly represent conscientiousness.[37] As another option, Brooke could bring a copy of this chapter's OB Assessments with her to her next social gathering. After all, it makes a great ice breaker!

FIGURE 9-2 Extraversion, Neuroticism, and Typical Moods

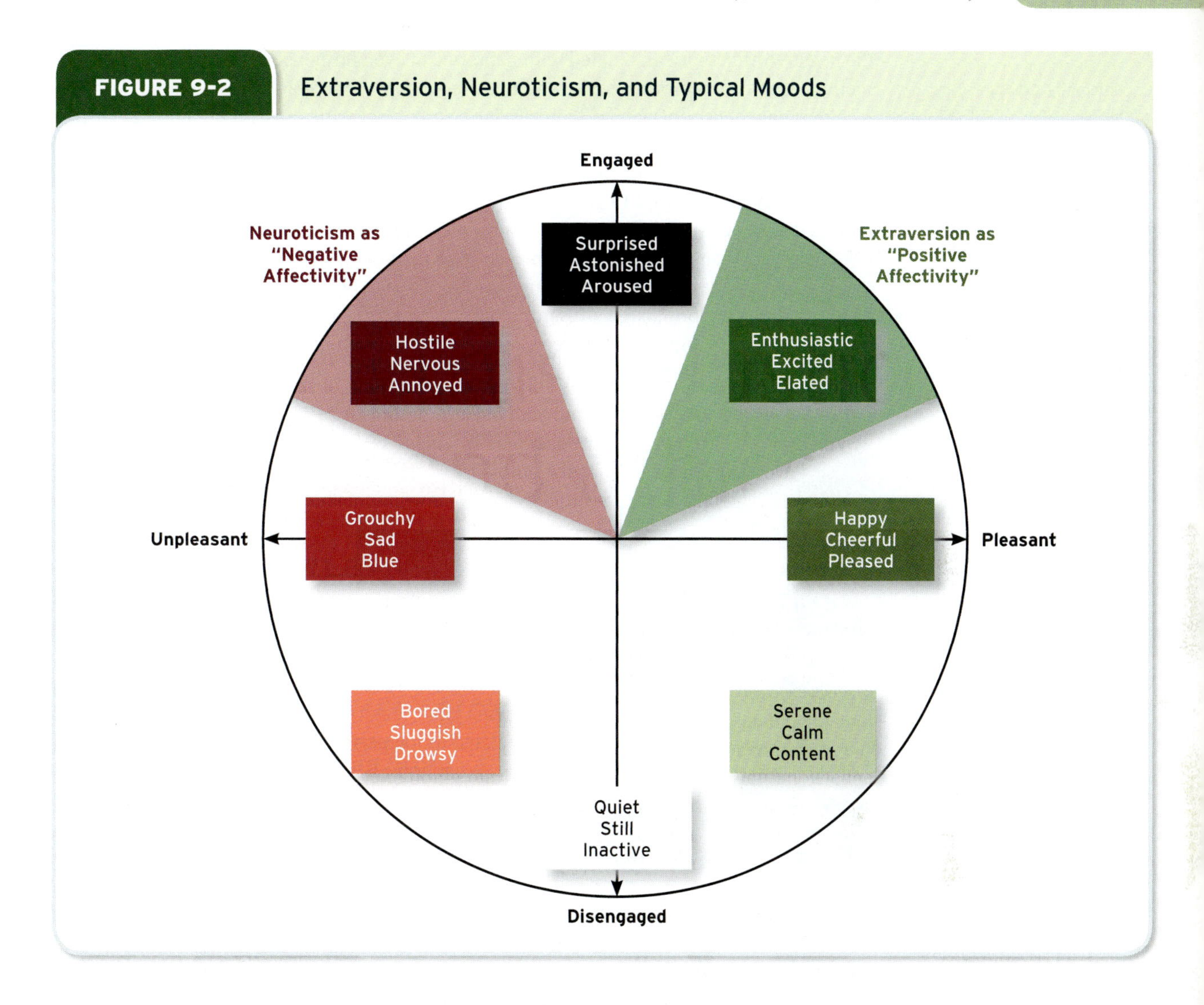

receiving an award for non-academic reasons, and getting married or engaged. Other studies have linked extraversion to the number of same-sex peers, number of dating partners, frequency of alcohol consumption, and frequency of attending parties.[38] However, extraverts spend so much time doing those things that they wind up having less frequent interactions with their family.[39]

NEUROTICISM Neurotic people are nervous, moody, emotional, insecure, and jealous. Occasionally you may see this Big Five dimension called by its flip side: "emotional stability" or "emotional adjustment." If conscientiousness is the most important of the Big Five from the perspective of job performance, neuroticism is the second-most important.[40] There are few jobs for which the traits associated with neuroticism are beneficial to on-the-job behaviours. Instead, most jobs benefit from employees who are calm, steady, and secure.

Whereas extraversion is synonymous with positive affectivity, neuroticism is synonymous with **negative affectivity**—a dispositional tendency to experience unpleasant moods such as hostility, nervousness, and annoyance (see Figure 9-2).[41] That tendency to experience negative moods explains why neurotic employees often experience lower levels of job satisfaction than their less neurotic counterparts.[42] Along with extraversion, neuroticism explains much of the impact of genetic factors on job satisfaction. Research suggests that

negative affectivity A dispositional tendency to experience unpleasant moods such as hostility, nervousness, and annoyance the negative affectivity associated with neuroticism even influences more general life satisfaction, such that neurotic people tend to be less happy with their lives in general.[43]

differential exposure Being more likely to appraise day-to-day situations as stressful, thereby feeling that stressors are encountered more frequently

differential reactivity Being less likely to believe that one can cope with the stressors experienced on a daily basis

Neuroticism also influences the way that people deal with stressful situations. Specifically, neuroticism is associated with a **differential exposure** to stressors, meaning that neurotic people are more likely to appraise day-to-day situations as stressful (and therefore feel like they are exposed to stressors more frequently).[44] Neuroticism is also associated with a **differential reactivity** to stressors, meaning that neurotic people are less likely to believe they can cope with the stressors that they experience.[45] Neuroticism is largely responsible for the Type A Behaviour Pattern that has been shown to affect employees' health and ability to manage stressful environments.[46] That is, neurotic people are much more likely to be "Type As," whereas less neurotic individuals are much more likely to be "Type Bs" (see Chapter 5 on stress for more discussion of these issues).

People who are open to new experiences tend to do well in situations that offer frequent opportunities to learn new things, such as teaching.

OPENNESS TO EXPERIENCE The final dimension of the Big Five is openness to experience. Open people are curious, imaginative, creative, complex, refined, and sophisticated. Of all the Big Five, openness to experience has the most alternative labels. Sometimes it's called "inquisitiveness" or "intellectualness" or even "culture" (not in the national culture sense—rather, in the "high culture" sense of knowing fine wine, art, and classical music). Much like agreeableness and extraversion, the traits associated with openness are beneficial in some jobs but not others. As a result, openness is not related to job performance across all occupations.

What jobs benefit from high levels of openness? Generally speaking, jobs that are very fluid and dynamic, with rapid changes in job demands. Research shows that open employees excel in learning and training environments, because their curiosity gives them a built-in desire to learn new things.[47] They also tend to be more adaptable and quick to identify when the "old way of doing things" is no longer effective, excelling at the search for a new and better approach.[48] In fact, conscientious employees are sometimes less effective than open employees in such environments, because their persevering nature sometimes prevents them from abandoning "tried-and-true" task strategies.

BMW, the German automaker, seems to understand the importance of openness to experience, along with several of the other Big Five dimensions. BMW has worked hard to create a culture of innovation in which there is never a penalty for proposing new and outlandish ways of improving its cars.[49] Those proposed improvements include a "smart card" that can be taken out of your own BMW and plugged into a rented one, passing along your music, podcast, and comfort settings to the new vehicle. Openness is needed to foster such creative thought, but agreeableness is also key to BMW's culture. Stefan Krause, BMW's chief financial officer, summarizes how to push a creative idea successfully: "You can go into fighting mode or you can ask permission and get everyone to support you. If you do it without building ties, you will be blocked."

BMW employees also draw on their conscientiousness in those critical times when a new technology is introduced or production volume is expanded. During those time periods, employees from other factories may move into temporary housing far from home to put in extra hours on another plant's line. Why are employees so devoted? For one thing, no one at BMW can remember a layoff—something that is incredibly unique in the auto industry. That's part of the reason BMW's human resources group receives more than 200,000 applications annually. Those fortunate enough to make it to the interview stage participate in elaborate, day-long drills in teams to make sure that their personalities provide a good match for the company.

The cafeteria at BMW's Leipzig facility, where the assembly line moves above to give employees a feel for the rhythm of the plant.

CULTURAL VALUES

Now that we've described a number of personality traits, we turn our attention to the cultural values that can affect the expression of those traits.[50] To some extent, cultural values provide countries with their own distinct personalities. For example, we can say that Australian people, on average, value the traits associated with extraversion more than Chinese people.[51] We can also say that Swiss people, on average, value the traits associated with openness more than Irish people. Such statements are based on research that reveals consistent between-nation differences on various personality traits. Of course, that doesn't mean that all Australian, Chinese, Swiss, and Irish citizens have exactly the same personality—merely that certain cultures tend to have higher levels of certain traits.

individualism–collectivism The degree to which a culture has a loosely knit social framework (individualism) or a tight social framework (collectivism)

power distance The degree to which a culture prefers equal power distribution (low power distance) or an unequal power distribution (high power distance)

9.3 What are Hofstede's dimensions of cultural values?

Although it's possible to describe nations on values relevant to the Big Five, as we just did, there are other values that are more commonly used to categorize nations. Many of those values are derived from a landmark study in the late 1960s and early 1970s by Geert Hofstede, who analyzed data about 88,000 IBM employees from 72 countries in 20 languages.[52] His research showed that employees working in different countries tended to prioritize different values, and those values clustered into several distinct dimensions. Those dimensions are summarized in Table 9-1 and include **individualism–collectivism**, **power distance**, **uncertainty avoidance**, **masculinity–femininity**, and **short-term vs. long-term orientation**. The table also includes cultures that tend to be high on a given dimension.

uncertainty avoidance The degree to which a culture tolerates ambiguous situations (low uncertainty avoidance) or feels threatened by them (high uncertainty avoidance)

masculinity–femininity The degree to which a culture values stereotypically male traits (masculinity) or stereotypically female traits (femininity)

short-term vs. long-term orientation The degree to which a culture stresses values that are past- and present-oriented (short-term orientation) or future-oriented (long-term orientation)

ethnocentrism One who views his or her cultural values as "right" and values of other cultures as "wrong"

The table reveals that citizens of Canada tend to be high on individualism, low on power distance, low on uncertainty avoidance, high on masculinity, and high on short-term orientation. Why is this description important to know? Because it illustrates the adjustments that Canadian employees and businesses may need to make when doing business in other cultures. Differences in cultural values can create differences in reactions to change, conflict management styles, negotiation approaches, and reward preferences.[53] Failing to understand those differences can compromise the effectiveness of multinational groups and organizations. Such problems are particularly likely if employees are high in **ethnocentrism**, defined as a propensity to view one's own cultural values as "right" and those of other cultures as "wrong."[54] For more discussion of this issue, see our **OB Internationally** feature.

Of Hofstede's five dimensions, individualism–collectivism has received the most research attention, by a wide margin.[55] Much of this research has focused on the individualism–collectivism of individual people rather than nations, sometimes referred to as "psychological individualism" or "psychological collectivism."[56] This focus on individuals rather than nations is understandable, given that some experts estimate that only 60 percent of the citizens in a collective culture actually hold collective cultural values themselves.[57] Studies of psychological collectivism have revealed that collective employees identify deeply with relevant in-groups, such as family members, close friends, or work teams. They prefer to interact with those in-groups, care for the members of those in-groups, and accept and prioritize in-group norms and goals.[58]

TABLE 9-1 Hofstede's Dimensions of Cultural Values

Individualism-Collectivism	
INDIVIDUALISM	**COLLECTIVISM**
The culture is a loosely knit social framework in which people take care of themselves and their immediate family.	The culture is a tight social framework in which people take care of the members of a broader in-group and act loyal to it.
Canada, the Netherlands, France	*Indonesia, China, West Africa*
Power Distance	
LOW	**HIGH**
The culture prefers that power be distributed uniformly where possible, in a more egalitarian fashion.	The culture accepts the fact that power is usually distributed unequally within organizations.
Canada, Germany, the Netherlands	*Russia, China, Indonesia*
Uncertainty Avoidance	
LOW	**HIGH**
The culture tolerates uncertain and ambiguous situations and values unusual ideas and behaviours.	The culture feels threatened by uncertain and ambiguous situations and relies on formal rules to create stability.
Canada, Indonesia, the Netherlands	*Japan, Russia, France*
Masculinity-Femininity	
MASCULINITY	**FEMININITY**
The culture values stereotypically male traits such as assertiveness and the acquisition of money and things.	The culture values stereotypically female traits such as caring for others and caring about quality of life.
Canada, Japan, Germany	*The Netherlands, Russia, France*
Short-Term vs. Long-Term Orientation	
SHORT TERM	**LONG TERM**
The culture stresses values that are more past- and present-oriented, such as respect for tradition and fulfilling obligations.	The culture stresses values that are more future-oriented, such as persistence, prudence, and thrift.
Canada, Russia, West Africa	*China, Japan, the Netherlands*

Sources: G. Hofstede, *Culture's Consequences: International Differences in Work Related Values* (Beverly Hills, CA: Sage, 1980); G. Hofstede, "Cultural Constraints in Management Theories," *Academy of Management Executive* 7 (1993), pp. 81–94; G. Hofstede and M.H. Bond, "The Confucius Connection: From Cultural Roots to Economic Growth," *Organizational Dynamics* 16 (1988), pp. 5–21; B.L. Kirkman, K.B. Lowe, and C.B. Gibson, "A Quarter Century of *Culture's Consequences:* A Review of Empirical Research Incorporating Hofstede's Cultural Values Framework," *Journal of International Business Studies* 37 (2006), pp. 285–320.

OB INTERNATIONALLY

Research suggests that ethnocentrism hinders the effectiveness of expatriates, who are employees working full-time in other countries. Ethnocentrism makes expatriates less likely to adjust to a new culture, less likely to fulfill the duties required of their international assignment, and more likely to withdraw from that assignment. So how can organizations identify employees with the right personalities to serve as expatriates?

One potentially useful tool is the *multicultural personality questionnaire,* which assesses five personality dimensions that can maximize the satisfaction, commitment, and performance of expatriates.[59] Those dimensions are listed below, along with some sample items for each:

Cultural empathy. A tendency to empathize with the feelings, thoughts, and behaviours of individuals with different cultural values.

- I understand other people's feelings.
- I take other people's habits into consideration.

Open-mindedness. A tendency to have an open and unprejudiced attitude toward other cultural values and norms.

- I get involved in other cultures.
- I find other religions interesting.

Emotional stability. A tendency to remain calm in the kinds of stressful situations that can be encountered in foreign environments.

- I can put setbacks in perspective.
- I take it for granted that things will turn out right.

Social initiative. A tendency to be proactive when approaching social situations, which aids in building connections.

- I easily approach other people.
- I am often the driving force behind things.

Flexibility. A tendency to regard new situations as a challenge and to adjust behaviours to meet that challenge.

- I could start a new life easily.
- I feel comfortable in different cultures.

Research has linked these five personality traits to a number of expatriate success factors. For example, individuals with a "multicultural personality" are more likely to aspire to international positions, more likely to gain international experience, more likely to adjust to new assignments, and more likely to be happy with their lives during those assignments.[60] In fact, research even suggests that expatriates who fit this profile are actually healthier, both physically and mentally.

SO HOW CAN WE DESCRIBE WHAT EMPLOYEES ARE LIKE?

As shown in Figure 9-3, many of the thousands of adjectives we use to describe people can be boiled down into the Big Five dimensions of personality. Conscientiousness reflects the reliability, perseverance, and ambition of employees. Agreeableness captures their tendency to cooperate with others in a warm and sympathetic fashion. Neuroticism reflects the tendency to experience negative moods and emotions frequently on a day-to-day basis. Individuals who are high on openness to experience are creative, imaginative, and curious. Finally, extraverts are talkative, sociable, and assertive and typically experience positive

FIGURE 9-3 How Can We Describe What Employees Are Like?

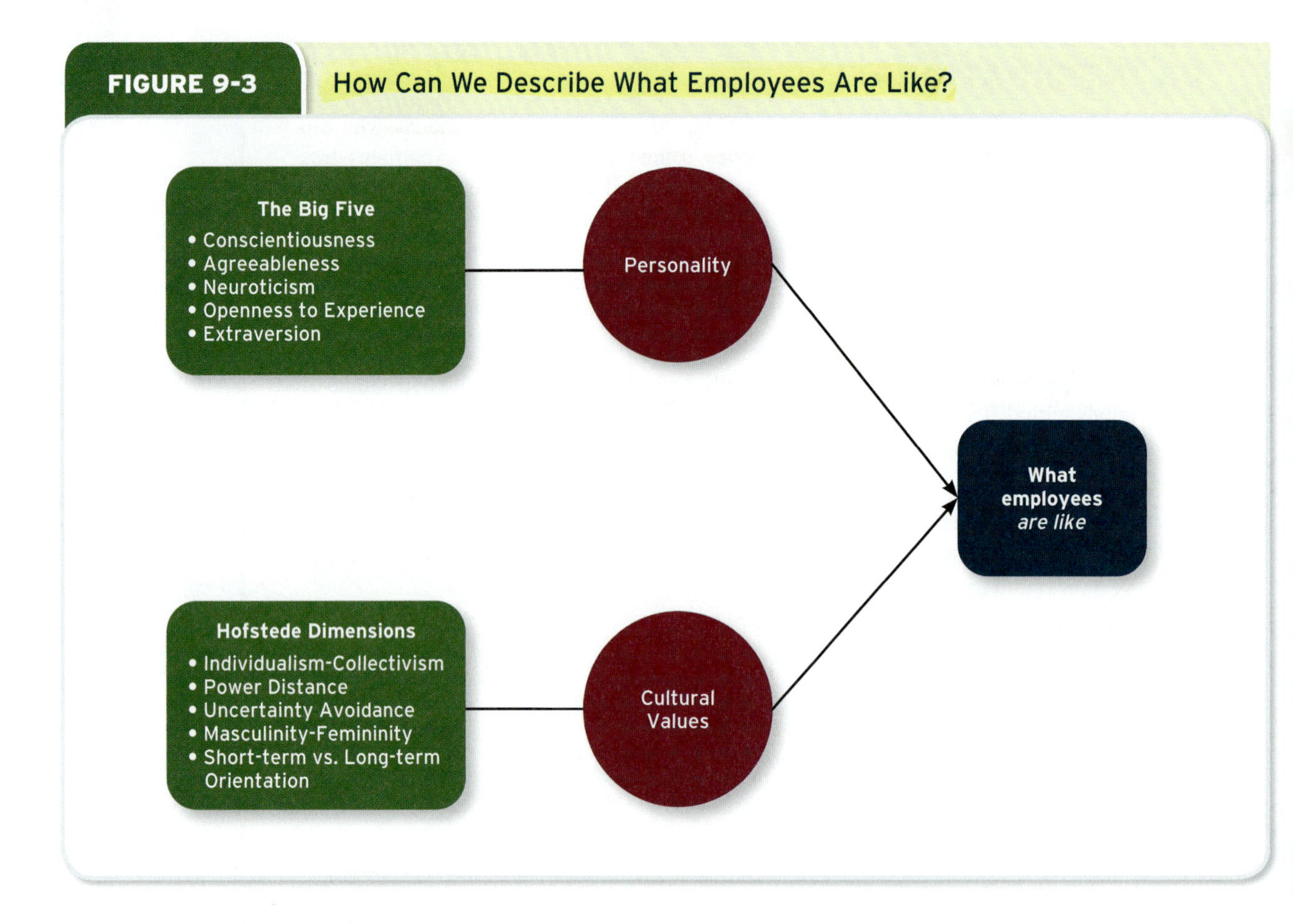

moods and emotions. Beyond personality, however, what employees are like also depends on the culture in which they were raised. Cultural values like individualism–collectivism, power distance, uncertainty avoidance, masculinity–femininity, and short-term vs. long-term orientation influence employees' thoughts, emotions, and behaviours.

WHAT DOES IT MEAN FOR AN EMPLOYEE TO BE "ABLE"?

The topic of ability is probably already familiar to you. One reason is because "ability" is an everyday word in our language, and we've all developed a pretty good understanding of our own abilities. In fact, there are many different facets of ability, and they can be grouped into subsets by considering similarities in the nature of the activities involved. As detailed in the sections to follow, abilities can be grouped into three general categories: cognitive, emotional, and physical. Taken together, these abilities capture *what people can do.* That's in contrast to personality and cultural values, which captures *what people are like.* As we saw in the opening profile, successful organizations like Google focus on findings applicants whose abilities match the requirements of a given job.

OB FOR STUDENTS

Are you psychologically collective (or are some of your fellow group members)? Past research suggests that people who hold collective values are more self-confident in group settings, are more cooperative by nature, and prefer to be evaluated and rewarded on a group-wide basis (as when student group members all receive the same grade on a class project).[61] Collective group members also perform their group duties at a higher level, engage in more citizenship behaviour, and refrain from counterproductive behaviours that could harm the group.[62] To assess your psychological collectivism, think about the work groups to which you currently belong and have belonged to in the past. The items below ask about your relationship with, and thoughts about, *those particular groups.* Respond to the following questions as honestly as possible using the response scale provided. Then sum up your scores.

1 STRONGLY DISAGREE	2 DISAGREE	3 NEUTRAL	4 AGREE	5 STRONGLY AGREE

1. I preferred to work in those groups rather than working alone. _______
2. Working in those groups was better than working alone. _______
3. I wanted to work with those groups as opposed to working alone. _______
4. I felt comfortable counting on group members to do their part. _______
5. I was not bothered by the need to rely on group members. _______
6. I felt comfortable trusting group members to handle their tasks. _______
7. The health of those groups was important to me. _______
8. I cared about the well-being of those groups. _______
9. I was concerned about the needs of those groups. _______
10. I followed the norms of those groups. _______
11. I followed the procedures used by those groups. _______
12. I accepted the rules of those groups. _______
13. I cared more about the goals of those groups than my own goals. _______
14. I emphasized the goals of those groups more than my individual goals. _______
15. Group goals were more important to me than my personal goals. _______

SCORING AND INTERPRETATION:

If you scored a 53 or above, you hold collectivistic work values, which means that you prioritize the needs and well-being of the groups to which you belong, and you adhere to the norms and goals of those groups.

Source: C.L. Jackson, J.A. Colquitt, M.J. Wesson, and C.P. Zapata-Phelan, "Psychological Collectivism: A Measurement Validation and Linkage to Group Member Performance." *Journal of Applied Psychology* 91 (2006), pp. 884–99.

COGNITIVE ABILITY

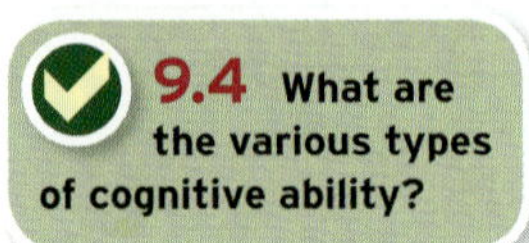
9.4 What are the various types of cognitive ability?

cognitive abilities
Capabilities related to the use of knowledge to make decisions and solve problems

Cognitive abilities are capabilities related to the acquisition and application of knowledge in problem solving.[63] Cognitive abilities are very relevant in the jobs most of you will be involved with—that is, work involving the use of information to make decisions and solve problems. Chances are good that your cognitive abilities will be tested if you apply to pursue graduate-level study, for instance, in law (LSAT; Law School Admission Test), medicine (MCAT; Medical College Admission Test), business administration (GMAT; Graduate Management Admissions Test), or the social sciences (GRE; Graduate Record Examinations). Tests like these present people with a variety of different questions; some test your ability to do math problems, whereas other questions assess your ability to complete sentences, solve logical problems, or make analogies. The different types of questions reflect that there are several specific types of cognitive ability that contribute to effectiveness on intellectual tasks. Table 9-2 lists many of these cognitive ability types, along with their specific facets and some jobs in which they are thought to be important.

TABLE 9-2 Types and Facets of Cognitive Ability

TYPE	MORE SPECIFIC FACET	JOBS WHERE RELEVANT
Verbal	***Oral*** and ***Written Comprehension:*** Understanding written and spoken words and sentences ***Oral*** and ***Written Expression:*** Communicating ideas by speaking or writing so that others can understand	Business executives; police, fire, and ambulance dispatchers; clinical psychologists
Quantitative	***Number Facility:*** Performing basic math operations quickly and correctly ***Mathematical Reasoning:*** Selecting the right method or formula to solve a problem	Treasurers; financial managers; mathematical technicians; statisticians
Reasoning	***Problem Sensitivity:*** Understanding when there is a problem or when something may go wrong ***Deductive Reasoning:*** Applying general rules to specific problems ***Inductive Reasoning:*** Combining specific information to form general conclusions ***Originality:*** Developing new ideas	Anesthesiologists; surgeons; business executives; fire inspectors; judges; police detectives; forensic scientists; cartoonists; designers
Spatial	***Spatial Orientation:*** Knowing where one is relative to objects in the environment ***Visualization:*** Imagining how something will look after it has been rearranged	Pilots; drivers; boat captains; photographers; set designers; sketch artists
Perceptual	***Speed and Flexibility of Closure:*** Making sense of information and finding patterns ***Perceptual Speed:*** Comparing information or objects with remembered information or objects	Musicians; fire fighters; police officers; pilots; mail clerks; inspectors

Source: Adapted from E.A. Fleishman, D.P. Costanza, and J. Marshall-Mies, "Abilities," in *an Occupational Information System for the 21st Century: the Development of O*Net,* eds. N.G. Peterson, M.D. Mumford, W.C. Borman, P.R. Jeanneret, and E.A. Fleishman (Washington DC: American Psychological Association, 1999), pp. 175–95.

VERBAL ABILITY Verbal ability refers to various capabilities associated with understanding and expressing oral and written communication. **Oral comprehension** is the ability to understand spoken words and sentences, and **written comprehension** is the ability to understand written words and sentences. Although these two aspects of verbal ability would seem highly related—that is, people who have high oral comprehension would tend to have high written comprehensive, and vice versa—it is not difficult to think of people who might be high on one ability but low on the other. As an example, it has been reported that as a result of his dyslexia, Tom Cruise has poor written comprehension and can only learn his lines after listening to them on tape.[64]

Because of his dyslexia, Tom Cruise struggles with written comprehension. He learns the lines for his movies by listening to them on tape.

oral comprehension The ability to understand spoken words and sentences

written comprehension The ability to understand written words and sentences

Two other verbal abilities are **oral expression**, which refers to the ability to communicate ideas by speaking, and **written expression**, which refers to the ability to communicate ideas in writing. Again, though it might seem that these abilities should be highly related, they are not necessarily. You may have taken a class with a professor who has published several well-regarded books and articles but had a very difficult time expressing concepts and theories to students effectively. Although there could be many reasons, one possible explanation is that the professor had high ability in terms of written expression but low ability in terms of oral expression.

oral expression The ability to communicate ideas by speaking

written expression The ability to communicate ideas in writing

Generally speaking, verbal abilities are most important in jobs in which effectiveness depends on understanding and communicating ideas and information to others. The effectiveness of business executives depends on their ability to consider information from reports and other executives and staff, as well as their ability to articulate a vision and strategy that promotes employee understanding. As another example, consider how important the verbal abilities of a 9-1-1 dispatcher might be if a loved one suddenly became ill and stopped breathing one evening.

QUANTITATIVE ABILITY Quantitative ability refers to two types of mathematical capabilities. The first is **number facility**, which is the capability to do simple math operations (adding, subtracting, multiplying, and dividing). The second is **mathematical reasoning**, which refers to the ability to choose and apply formulas to solve problems that involve numbers. An example of a typical problem would be as follows: "There were two trains 800 kilometres apart, and they were travelling toward each other on the same track. The first train began travelling at noon and averaged 70 kilometres per hour. The second train started off two hours later. At what speed did the second train average if the two trains smashed into each other at 10:00 p.m. of the same day"? Although number facility may be necessary to solve this problem, mathematical reasoning is crucial because the test taker needs to know which formulas to apply. Although most of us wish that problems like this would be limited to test-taking contexts (especially this particular problem), there are countless situations in which quantitative abilities are important. For example, consider the importance of quantitative ability in jobs involving statistics, accounting, and engineering. Quantitative abilities may be important in less complex, lower-level jobs as well. Have you ever been at a fast-food restaurant or convenience store when the cash register wasn't working and the clerk couldn't manage to count out change correctly or quickly? If you have, you witnessed a very good example of low quantitative ability, and perhaps some very annoyed customers.

number facility The capability to do simple math operations such as adding and subtracting

mathematical reasoning The ability to choose and apply formulas to solve problems that involve numbers

REASONING ABILITY Reasoning ability is actually a diverse set of abilities associated with sensing and solving problems using insight, rules, and logic. The first reasoning ability, **problem sensitivity**, is the ability to sense that there's a problem right now or likely

problem sensitivity The ability to sense that there is or will be a problem to be one in the near future. Anesthesiology is a great example of a job for which problem sensitivity is crucial. Before surgeries, anesthesiologists give drugs to patients so that surgical procedures can take place without the patients experiencing pain. However, during the surgery, patients can have negative reactions to the drugs that might result in the loss of life. So the ability of the anesthesiologist to sense when something is wrong even before the problem is fully apparent can be a life-or-death matter.

deductive reasoning The ability to solve problems by applying general rules

The second type of reasoning ability is called **deductive reasoning**. This ability, which refers to the use of general rules to solve problems, is important in any job in which people are presented with a set of facts that need to be applied to make effective decisions. The job of a judge requires deductive reasoning because it centres on making decisions by applying the rules of law to make verdicts. In contrast, **inductive reasoning** refers to the ability to consider several specific pieces of information and then reach a more general conclusion regarding how those pieces are related. Every episode of the television series *CSI* is filled with inductive reasoning. Crime scene investigators, like Gil Grissom, are experts at considering things like the blood splatter patterns, bruises, abrasions, DNA, fibres, and fingerprints to reach conclusions about causes of death and possible perpetrators.

inductive reasoning The ability to consider several pieces of information and then reach a more general conclusion regarding how those pieces are related

Finally, **originality** refers to the ability to develop clever and novel ways to solve problems. Larry Page and Sergey Brin, the two founders of Google, provide good examples of originality. They not only developed the search software that gave Google a competitive advantage but also created the first completely new advertising medium in nearly half a century. They also refuse to follow conventional wisdom when it comes to managerial practices and business decisions.[65] Clearly, originality is important in a wide variety of occupations, but in some jobs, originality is the most critical ability. For example, a cartoonist, designer, writer, or advertising executive without originality would find it difficult to be successful.

originality The ability to develop clever and novel ways to solve problems

SPATIAL ABILITY There are two main types of spatial abilities. The first is called **spatial orientation**, which refers to having a good understanding of where one is relative to other things in the environment. A tourist with high spatial organization would have no trouble finding her way back to her hotel on foot after a long day of sightseeing, even without a map or help from anyone on the street. The second spatial ability is called **visualization**, which is the ability to imagine how separate things will look if they were put together in a particular way. If you're good at imagining how a room would look if it were rearranged, or if your friends are impressed that you can buy things that go together well, chances are that you would score high on visualization.

spatial orientation A good understanding of where one is relative to other things in the environment

visualization The ability to imagine how separate things will look if they were put together in a particular way

PERCEPTUAL ABILITY Perceptual abilities generally refer to being able to perceive, understand, and recall patterns of information. More specifically, **speed and flexibility of closure** refers to being able to pick out a pattern of information quickly in the presence of distracting information, even without all the information present. This ability is easy to understand if you've ever seen the television show *Numb3rs*. In the show, Charlie Eppes helps the FBI solve crimes by using his genius to discover patterns in data and information. In the series premiere, for example, Charlie used the metaphor of a sprinkler to describe his unique ability, noting, "Say I couldn't see the sprinkler; from the pattern of the drops, I could calculate its precise location." Related to this ability is **perceptual speed**, which refers to being able to examine and compare numbers, letters, and objects quickly. If you can go into the produce section of a supermarket and choose the best tomatoes faster than the people around you, chances are you have high perceptual speed. Effectiveness in jobs in which people need to proofread documents, sort things, or categorize objects depends a lot on perceptual speed.

speed and flexibility of closure The ability to pick out a pattern of information quickly in the presence of distractions, even without all the information present

perceptual speed The ability to examine and compare numbers, letters, and objects quickly

GENERAL MENTAL ABILITY If you've read the preceding sections thoughtfully, you probably thought about where you stand on the different types of cognitive abilities. In doing so, you may have also reached the conclusion that you are higher on some of these abilities and lower on others. Maybe you think of yourself as being smart in verbal abilities but not as smart in quantitative abilities. In fact, most people score more similarly across

FIGURE 9-4 The "*g*-factor"

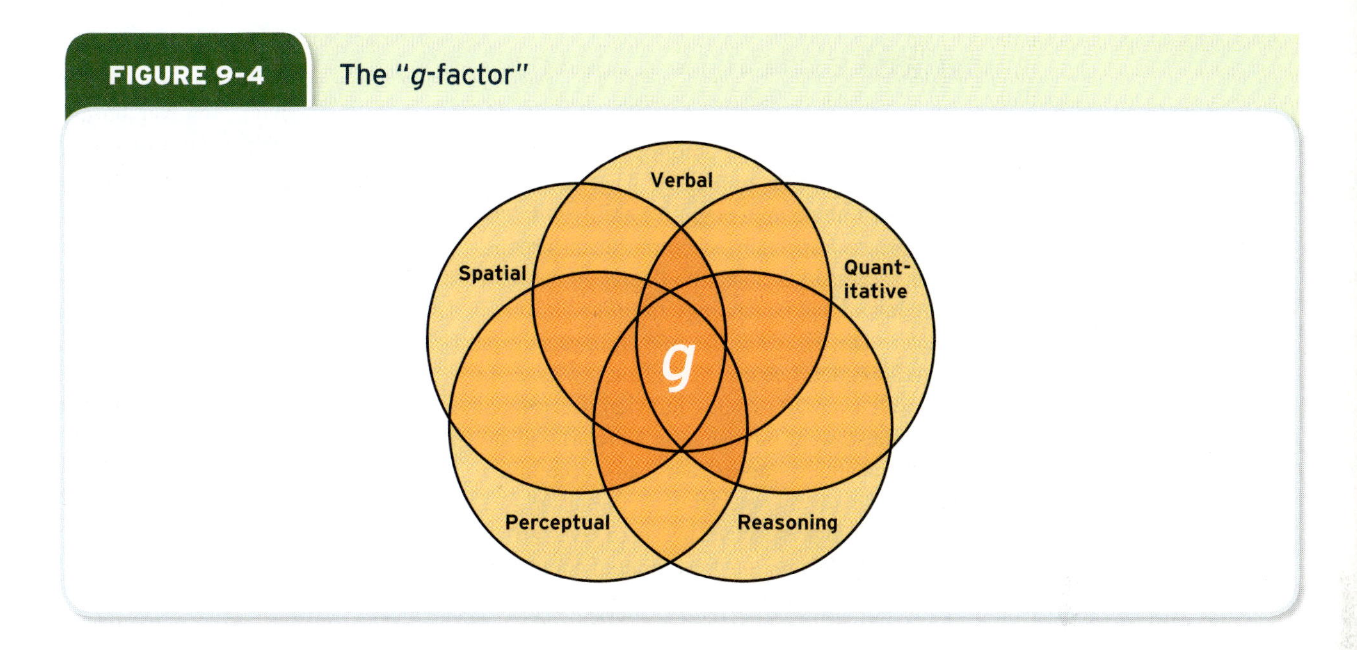

their cognitive abilities than they realize. People who are high on verbal abilities also tend to be high on reasoning, quantitative, spatial, and perceptual abilities, and people who are low on verbal abilities tend to be low on the other abilities. Although this consistency might not apply to everyone, it applies often enough that researchers have been trying to understand why this occurs for well over 100 years.[66]

The most popular explanation for the similarity in the levels of different cognitive abilities within people is that there is a **general mental ability**—sometimes called *g* or the *g factor*—that underlies or causes all of the more specific cognitive abilities we have discussed so far.[67] To understand what this ability means more clearly, consider the diagram in Figure 9-4 that depicts general mental ability as the area in common across the more specific cognitive abilities that we have discussed. This overlap exists because each of the specific abilities depends somewhat on the brain's ability to process information effectively. So, because some brains are capable of processing information more effectively than others, some people tend to score higher across the specific abilities, whereas others tend to score lower.

general mental ability The general level of cognitive ability that plays an important role in determining the more narrow cognitive abilities

"I don't have to be smart, because someday I'll just hire lots of smart people to work for me."

Source: © The New Yorker Collection 2001 David Sipress from cartoonbank.com. All rights reserved.

EMOTIONAL ABILITY

Michael Scott, who is played by Steve Carell on the television series *The Office,* believes that he's a great boss, multitalented, and super funny. He also believes that he's a people person—he thinks he really understands his employees and that his employees like and respect him. Unbeknownst to Michael, however, he comes across to all but one of his employees as insensitive and incompetent to the point of being pathetic. In this section of the chapter, we describe the concept of emotional abilities—precisely the type of ability that Michael Scott appears to lack.

OB RESEARCH IN CANADA

Dr. Kibeom Lee, at the University of Calgary, is not only an expert in human abilities and personality but also demonstrates in real life what can happen when you combine high cognitive ability with conscientiousness (especially accomplishment striving). Dr. Lee received his doctorate degree in industrial and organizational psychology from the University of Western Ontario. Over the next eight years, from 2000 to 2008, Dr. Lee and his colleagues have produced well over 50 articles in scientific journals (four of these were published in Korean) and several book chapters—an extraordinary accomplishment for a relatively new scholar! To put Dr. Lee's achievements in perspective, his six to seven articles per year is roughly *double* the output of comparable faculty at other schools. It is only fitting then that Dr. Lee studies the links between both cognitive abilities and personality traits and various criteria such as job performance.

Presently, Dr. Lee is an associate professor of psychology, and teaches courses at the undergraduate and graduate levels in personality, work attitudes, and selection and assessment. Dr. Lee is a member of the American Psychological Association, the Society for Industrial and Organizational Psychology, and the Canadian Psychological Association. The following list is a sample of Dr. Lee's published work:

"Similarity and Assumed Similarity of Personality Reports of Well-Acquainted Persons," by K. Lee, M.C. Ashton, J.A. Pozzebon, B.A. Visser, J.S. Bourdage, and B. Ogunfowora, published in *Journal of Personality and Social Psychology* (February 2009, volume 96, number 2, pp. 460–72).

"Personality Dimensions Explaining Relationships Between Integrity Tests and Counterproductive Behavior: Big Five, or One in Addition?" by B. Marcus, K. Lee, and M.C. Ashton, published in *Personnel Psychology* (2007, volume 60, pp. 1–34).

"A Meta-Analysis of the Antecedents and Consequences of Workplace Sexual Harassment," by C.R. Willness, P. Steel, and K. Lee, published in *Personnel Psychology* (2007, volume 60, pp. 127–62).

"A New Six-Dimensional Model of Personality Structure: Implications for Industrial and Organizational Psychology," by K. Lee, T–Y. Yoo, and M.C. Ashton, published in *Korean Journal of Industrial and Organizational Psychology* (2003, volume 16, pp. 89–105).

"Organizational Citizenship Behavior and Workplace Deviance: The Role of Affect and Cognitions," by K. Lee and N.J. Allen, published in *Journal of Applied Psychology* (2002, volume 87, pp. 131–42).

So how are emotional abilities different than cognitive abilities? Most of us know someone who is very smart from a "cognitive ability" or IQ standpoint, but at the same time, the person just can't manage to be effective in real-world situations that involve other people. As an example, you may have played *Trivial Pursuit* with a group of friends and found someone at the table who could not only answer the majority of the questions correctly but also managed to say odd or inappropriate things throughout the game. You may also know someone who doesn't seem very "book smart" but always seems able to get things done and says the right things at the right time. In the context of the same *Trivial Pursuit* game, such a person might have answered most of the game questions incorrectly, but sensing how uncomfortable and angry people were becoming with the annoying player, made jokes to lighten things up.

In fact, for several decades now, researchers have been investigating whether there is a type of ability that influences the degree to which people tend to be effective in social situations, regardless of their level of other cognitive abilities.[68] Although there has been some debate among these researchers,[69] many believe that there is a human ability that affects social functioning, called **emotional intelligence**.[70] Emotional intelligence is defined in terms of four different but related abilities.[71]

emotional intelligence A set of abilities related to the understanding and use of emotions that affect social functioning

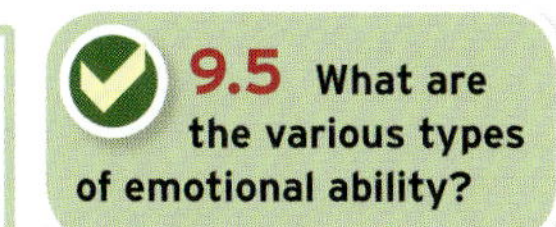

9.5 What are the various types of emotional ability?

SELF-AWARENESS The first type of emotional intelligence is **self-awareness**, or the appraisal and expression of emotions in oneself. This facet refers to the ability of an individual to understand the types of emotions he or she is experiencing, the willingness to acknowledge them, and the capability to express them naturally.[72] As an example, someone who is low in this aspect of emotional intelligence might not admit to himself or show anyone else that he is feeling somewhat anxious during the first few days of a new job. These types of emotions are perfectly natural in this job context, and ignoring them might increase the stress of the situation. Ignoring those emotions might also send the wrong signal to new colleagues, who might wonder, "Why isn't the new hire more excited about his new job?"

self-awareness The ability to recognize and understand the emotions in oneself

OTHER AWARENESS The second facet of emotional intelligence is called **other awareness**, or the appraisal and recognition of emotion in others.[73] As the name of this facet implies, it refers to a person's ability to recognize and understand the emotions that other people are feeling. People who are high in this aspect of emotional intelligence not only are sensitive to the feelings of others but also can anticipate the emotions that people will experience in different situations. In contrast, people who are low in this aspect of emotional intelligence do not effectively sense the emotions that others are experiencing, and if the emotions are negative, this inability could result in the person doing something that worsens the situation. As a specific example, have you ever had a professor who could not sense that students in class did not understand the material being presented in a lecture? When that professor continued to press on with the overheads, oblivious to the fact that the students were becoming even more confused, it was poor other awareness in action.

other awareness The ability to recognize and understand the emotions that other people are feeling

"Other awareness" is one aspect of emotional intelligence that allows us to empathize with others and understand their feelings.

EMOTION REGULATION The third facet of emotional intelligence, **emotion regulation**, refers to being able to recover quickly from emotional experiences.[74] As an example of this aspect of emotional intelligence, consider the possible responses of someone who is listening to the radio while driving to work and is cut off by an aggressive driver who, as she passes by, throws a beer can and shouts an obscenity. If this person is able to regulate his emotions effectively, he would be able to recover quickly from the initial anger and shock of the encounter. He would be able to get back to whatever he was listening to on the radio, and by the time he got to work, the incident would likely be all but forgotten. However, if this person was not able to regulate his emotions effectively, he might lose his

emotion regulation The ability to recover quickly from emotional experiences temper, tailgate the aggressive driver, and then ram into her vehicle at the next stoplight. We hope it is obvious to you that the former response is much more appropriate than the latter, which could prove quite costly to the individual. Although this example highlights the importance of regulating negative emotions, we should also point out that this aspect of emotional intelligence applies to positive emotions. Consider the response of someone who is told that she is about to receive a significant pay raise. If this person is unable to regulate her own emotions effectively, she might feel joyous and giddy the rest of the day and, as a consequence, not be able to accomplish any more work.

use of emotions The degree to which people can harness emotions and employ them to improve their chances of being successful in whatever they are seeking to do

USE OF EMOTIONS The fourth aspect of emotional intelligence is the **use of emotions**.[75] This capability reflects the degree to which people can harness emotions and employ them to improve their chances of being successful in whatever they are seeking to do. To understand this facet of emotional intelligence, consider a writer who is struggling to finish a book but is under a serious time crunch because of the contract with the publisher. If the writer was high in this aspect of emotional intelligence, she would likely psych herself up for the challenge and encourage herself to work hard through any bouts of writer's block. In contrast, if the writer is low in this aspect of emotional intelligence, she might begin to doubt her competence as a writer and think about different things she could do with her life. Because these behaviours will slow progress on the book even further, the number and intensity of self-defeating thoughts might increase, and ultimately, the writer might withdraw from the task entirely.

PHYSICAL ABILITIES

static strength The ability to lift, push, or pull very heavy objects such as boxes or heavy equipment

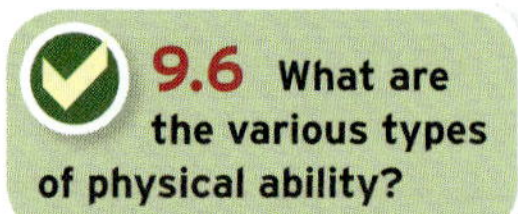
9.6 What are the various types of physical ability?

Physical abilities are likely very familiar to you because many of you took physical education classes early in your school career. Maybe you were evaluated on whether you could climb a rope to the ceiling of a gymnasium, run around a track several times, or kick a ball to a teammate who was running full stride. Or maybe you've applied for a job and had to take a test that assessed your ability to manipulate and assemble small mechanical parts. As a final example, and the one likely to be most familiar, you've probably been subjected to tests that measure the quality of your vision and hearing. Although these examples may not seem to be related, each refers to a different type of physical ability. In this section, we review a few important types of physical abilities, which are illustrated in Table 9-3.[76]

explosive strength The ability to move or move things in short bursts of energy

dynamic strength The ability to exert force for a prolonged period of time without becoming overly fatigued and giving out

STRENGTH Although strength generally refers to the degree to which the body is capable of exerting force, there are actually several different types of strength that are important, depending on the job. **Static strength** refers to the ability to lift, push, or pull very heavy objects using the hands, arms, legs, shoulder, or back. Static strength is involved in jobs in which people need to lift objects like boxes, equipment, machine parts, and heavy tools. With **explosive strength**, the person exerts short bursts of energy to move himself or an object. Employees who are required to run, jump, or throw things at work depend on their explosive strength to be effective. The final type of strength, **dynamic strength**, refers to the ability to exert force for a prolonged period of time without becoming overly fatigued and giving out. Dynamic strength is involved in jobs in which the person has to climb ropes or ladders or pull herself up onto platforms. Although jobs requiring physical strength may vary as to which category is important, there are also many jobs—such as firefighters—that require all three categories.[77]

stamina The ability to work effectively while engaging in physical activity

STAMINA **Stamina** refers to the ability of a person's lungs and circulatory system to work efficiently while he or she is engaging in prolonged physical activity. Stamina may be important in jobs that require running, swimming, and climbing. In fact, stamina is involved whenever the nature of the physical activity causes the heart rate to climb and the depth and rate of breathing to increase for prolonged periods of time.

TABLE 9-3 Physical Abilities

TYPE	MORE SPECIFIC FACET	JOBS WHERE RELEVANT
Strength	***Static:*** Lifting, pushing, pulling heavy objects ***Explosive:*** Exerting short burst of muscular force to move oneself or objects ***Dynamic:*** Exerting muscular force repeatedly or continuously	Structural iron and steel workers; tractor trailer and heavy truck drivers; farm workers; firefighters
Stamina	Exerting oneself over a period of time without circulatory system giving out	Athletes; dancers; commercial divers; firefighters
Flexibility and coordination	***Extent flexibility:*** Degree of bending, stretching, twisting of body, arms, legs ***Dynamic flexibility:*** Speed of bending, stretching, twisting of body, arms, legs ***Gross body coordination:*** Coordinating movement of body, arms, and legs in activities that involve all three together ***Gross body equilibrium:*** Ability to regain balance in contexts where balance is upset	Athletes; dancers; riggers; industrial machinery mechanics; choreographers; commercial divers; structural iron and steel workers
Psychomotor	***Fine manipulative abilities:*** Keeping hand and arm steady while grasping, manipulating, and assembling small objects ***Control movement abilities:*** Making quick, precise adjustments to a machine while operating it ***Response orientation:*** Quickly choosing among appropriate alternative movements ***Reaction time:*** Quickly responding to signals with body movements	Fabric menders; potters; timing device assemblers; jewellers; construction drillers; agricultural equipment operators; photographers; highway patrol pilots; athletes
Sensory	***Near and far vision:*** Seeing details of an object up close or at a distance ***Night vision:*** Seeing well in low light ***Visual colour discrimination:*** Detecting difference in colours and shades ***Depth perception:*** Judging relative distances ***Hearing sensitivity:*** Hearing difference in sounds that vary in terms of pitch and loudness ***Auditory attention:*** Focusing on a source of sound in the presence of other sources ***Speech recognition:*** Identifying and understanding speech of others	Electronic testers and inspectors; highway patrol pilots; tractor trailer, truck, and bus drivers; airline pilots; photographers; musicians and composers; industrial machine mechanics; speech pathologists

Source: Adapted from E.A. Fleishman, D.P. Costanza, and J. Marshall-Mies, "Abilities," in *An Occupational Information System for the 21st Century: The Development of O*NET,* eds. N.G. Peterson, M.D. Mumford, W.C. Borman, P.R. Jeanneret, and E.A. Fleishman (Washington DC: American Psychological Association, 1999), pp. 175–95.

extent flexibility The ability to execute extreme ranges of bends, twists, stretches, or reaches to complete a job

dynamic flexibility The ability to quickly and repeatedly execute bends, twists, stretches, or reaches to complete a job

gross body coordination The ability to synchronize the movements of the body, arms, and legs to do something while the whole body is in motion

gross body equilibrium The ability to maintain the balance of the body in unstable contexts or when changing directions

fine manipulative abilities The ability to keep the arms and hands steady while using the hands to do precise work

control movement abilities The ability to make precise adjustments using machinery to complete work effectively

response orientation The ability to choose the right action quickly in response to several different signals

response time The ability to respond to signalling information after it occurs

near and far vision The ability to see things up close and at a distance

night vision The ability to see things in low light

visual colour discrimination The ability to perceive colours accurately

FLEXIBILITY AND COORDINATION Generally speaking, flexibility refers to the ability to bend, stretch, twist, or reach. When a job requires extreme ranges of motion—for example, when people need to work in a cramped compartment or an awkward position—the type of flexibility involved is called **extent flexibility**. If you've ever watched a person working inside the trunk of a car installing speakers, you've seen extent flexibility. When a job requires repeated and somewhat quick bends, stretches, twists, or reaches, the type of flexibility involved is called **dynamic flexibility**. To understand what dynamic flexibility involves, picture a house painter on a ladder trying to paint some trim just within reach.

As with flexibility, there are two types of coordination that may be important in some jobs. **Gross body coordination** refers to the ability to synchronize the movements of the body, arms, and legs to do something while the whole body is in motion. In contrast, **gross body equilibrium** involves the ability to maintain the balance of the body in unstable contexts or when the person has to change directions. Jumping rope effectively requires gross body coordination; walking on a balance beam requires gross body equilibrium. Both types of coordination are important in contexts that involve quick movements. However, gross body equilibrium is more important when the work environment is artificially elevated and inherently unstable.

PSYCHOMOTOR ABILITIES There are several different examples of psychomotor abilities, which generally refer to the capacity to manipulate and control objects. **Fine manipulative abilities** refer to the ability to keep the arms and hands steady while using the hands to do precise work, generally on small or delicate objects such as arteries, nerves, gems, and watches. **Control movement abilities** are important in tasks for which people have to make different precise adjustments using machinery to complete the work effectively. Anyone who drills things for a living, whether it be wood, concrete, or teeth, needs this type of ability. The ability to choose the right action quickly in response to several different signals is called **response orientation**. It shouldn't be too difficult to imagine the importance of response orientation for an airline pilot who responds to the flashing lights, buzzers, and verbal information triggered during an in-flight emergency. The final psychomotor ability we describe is called **response time**. This ability reflects how quickly an individual responds to signalling information after it occurs. Returning to the previous example, imagine how grateful the 155 passengers and crew aboard US Airways Flight 1549 must have felt for the fast response orientation and quick response time of the pilots who were able to successful land in the Hudson River after striking a large flock of geese that took out both engines!

SENSORY ABILITIES Sensory abilities refer to capabilities associated with vision and hearing. Examples of important visual abilities include the ability to see things up close and at a distance (**near and far vision**) or in low light contexts (**night vision**), as well as the ability to perceive colours and judge relative distances between things accurately (**visual colour discrimination** and **depth perception**). There are many different jobs that emphasize only one or two of these visual abilities. For example, whereas effectiveness as a watch repairer depends on good near vision, effectiveness as an interior designer depends on visual colour discrimination. However, there are other jobs in which effectiveness might depend on almost all categories of visual abilities. A fighter pilot needs near vision to read instruments and checklists, far vision and depth perception to see enemy targets and landmarks, night vision to conduct operations in low light, and visual colour discrimination to interpret information from warning lights and computer readouts correctly.

Abilities related to hearing, also referred to as auditory abilities, include the capability to hear and discriminate sounds that vary in terms of loudness and pitch (**hearing sensitivity**), being able to focus on a single sound in the presence of many other sounds (**auditory attention**), and the ability to identify and understand the speech of another person (**speech recognition**). Perhaps the most obvious jobs for which auditory abilities would be important are musicians and composers (yes, we are going to ignore exceptions like Beethoven, who was deaf at the time he wrote his Ninth Symphony). However, with these jobs, the emphasis would likely be on hearing sensitivity and auditory attention rather than speech recognition (who listens to lyrics these days?). Another job for which auditory abilities might be crucially important is bartending, especially if the bar is crowded and noisy. In this context, a bartender needs auditory attention and speech recognition to be able to isolate and understand the words of a single patron against the backdrop of the loud chatter.

depth perception The ability to judge relative distances between things accurately

hearing sensitivity The ability to discriminate sounds that vary in terms of loudness and pitch

auditory attention The ability to focus on a single sound in the presence of many other sounds

speech recognition The ability to identify and understand the speech of another person

SO WHAT DOES IT MEAN FOR AN EMPLOYEE TO BE "ABLE"?

Thus far in the chapter, we have presented you with a fairly detailed description of the domain of human abilities, which are summarized in Figure 9-5. Although the list of abilities included in the figure may seem somewhat daunting, we hope that you can appreciate that this set of abilities describes each and every one of us. Moreover, as we have alluded to throughout the chapter, these abilities play an important role in determining how effective we can be at different tasks and jobs.

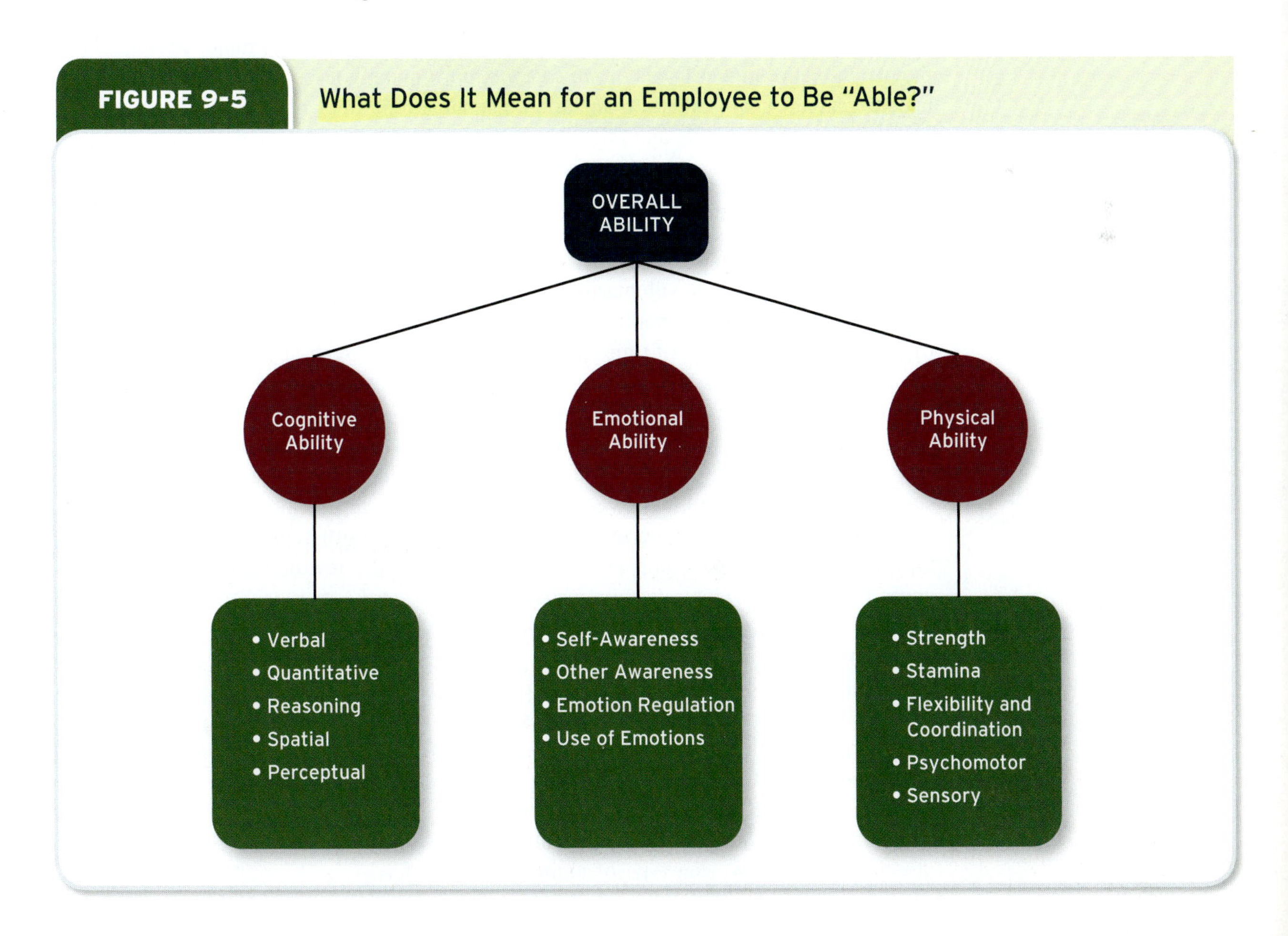

HOW IMPORTANT ARE THESE PERSONAL QUALITIES?

9.7 How do personality and ability affect job performance and organizational commitment?

typical performance Performance in the routine conditions that surround daily job tasks

maximum performance Performance in brief, special circumstances that demand a person's best effort

situational strength The degree to which situations have clear behavioural expectations, incentives, or instructions that make differences between individuals less important

trait activation The degree to which situations provide cues that trigger the expression of a given personality trait

We've already described a number of reasons why the Big Five should be important considerations, particularly in the case of conscientiousness. What if we focus specifically on the two outcomes in our integrative model of OB, performance and commitment? Figure 9-6 summarizes the research evidence linking conscientiousness to those two outcomes. The figure reveals that conscientiousness affects job performance. Of the Big Five, conscientiousness has the strongest effect on task performance,[78] partly because conscientious employees have higher levels of *motivation* than other employees.[79] They are more self-confident, perceive a clearer linkage between their effort and their performance, and are more likely to set goals and commit to them. For these reasons, conscientiousness is a key driver of what's referred to as **typical performance**, reflecting performance in the routine conditions that surround daily job tasks.[80] An employee's ability, in contrast, is a key driver of **maximum performance**, reflecting performance in brief, special circumstances that demand a person's best effort.

Conscientious employees are also more likely to engage in citizenship behaviours.[81] Why? One reason is that conscientious employees are so punctual and have such good work attendance that they are simply more available to offer "extra mile" sorts of contributions. Another reason is that they engage in so much more work-related effort that they have more energy to devote to citizenship behaviours.[82] Finally, conscientious employees are less likely to engage in counterproductive behaviours,[83] for two major reasons. First, they tend to have higher levels of *job satisfaction*,[84] making it less likely that they'll feel a need to retaliate against their organization. Second, even if they do perceive some slight or injustice, their dependable and reliable nature should prevent them from violating organizational norms by engaging in negative actions.[85]

Figure 9-6 also reveals that conscientious employees tend to be more committed to their organization.[86] They are less likely to engage in day-to-day psychological and physical withdrawal behaviours because such actions go against their work habits. They are also significantly less likely to voluntarily leave the organization.[87] Why? One reason is that the persevering nature of conscientious employees prompts them to persist in a given course of action for long periods of time. That persistence can be seen in their daily work effort, but it extends to a sense of commitment to the organization as well.[88] Another reason is that conscientious employees are better at managing *stress,* perceiving lower levels of key stressors, and being less affected by them at work.[89]

In some respects, Figure 9-6 understates the importance of conscientiousness (and personality, more generally). Why? Because personality becomes more important in some contexts than in others. The principle of **situational strength** suggests that "strong situations" have clear behavioural expectations, incentives, or instructions that make differences between individuals less important, whereas "weak situations" lack those cues.[90] Personality variables tend to be more significant drivers of behaviour in weak situations than in strong situations.[91] Similarly, the principle of **trait activation** suggests that some situations provide cues that trigger the expression of a given trait.[92] For example, a cry for help provides a cue that can trigger the expression of empathy. Personality variables tend to be more significant drivers of behaviours in situations that provide relevant cues than in situations in which those cues are lacking.

Now let's move on and consider if ability really matters? That is, does ability have a significant impact on job performance and organizational commitment? The answer to this question depends on what type of ability you are referring to—cognitive, emotional, or

FIGURE 9-6 Effects of Personality on Performance and Commitment

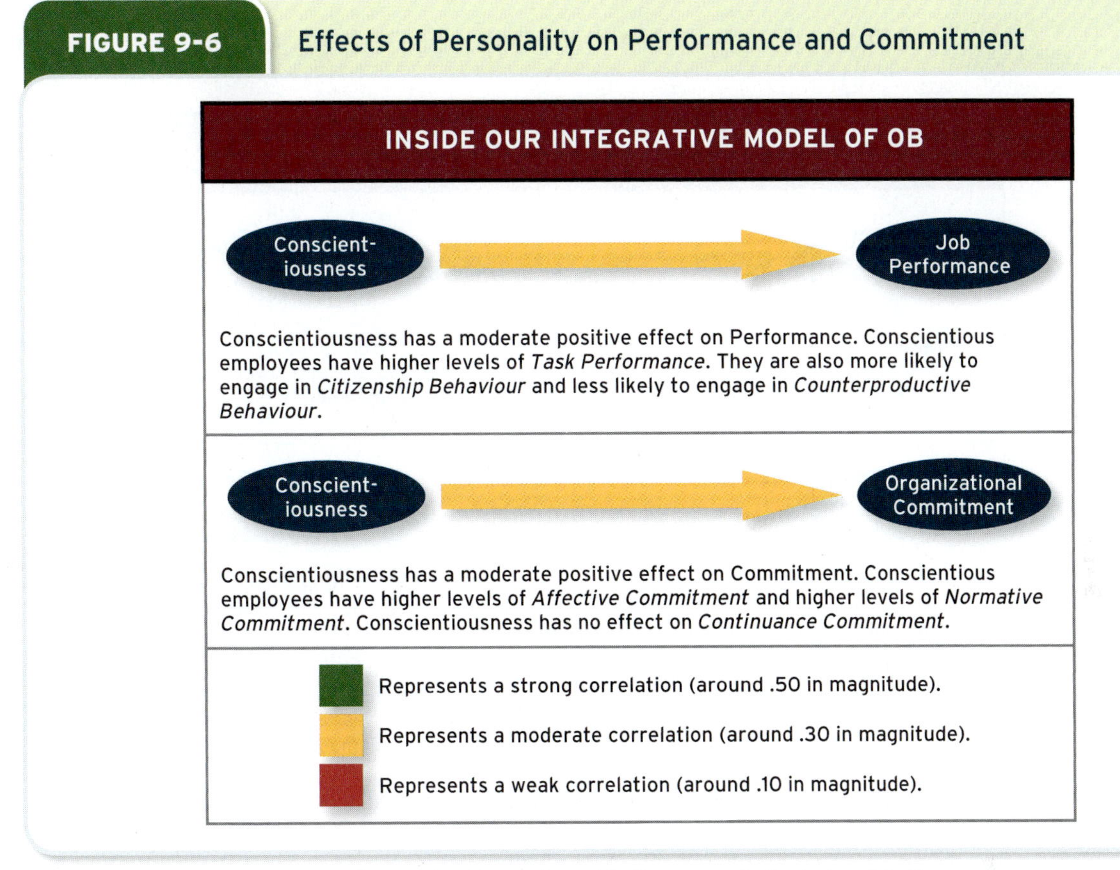

Sources: M.R. Barrick, M.K. Mount, and T.A. Judge, "Personality and Performance at the Beginning of the New Millennium: What Do We Know and Where Do We Go Next?" *International Journal of Selection and Assessment* 9 (2001), pp. 9–30; C.M. Berry, D.S. Ones, and P.R. Sackett, "Interpersonal Deviance, Organizational Deviance, and Their Common Correlates: A Review and Meta-Analysis," *Journal of Applied Psychology* 92 (2007), pp. 410–24; A. Cooper-Hakim and C. Viswesvaran, "The Construct of Work Commitment: Testing an Integrative Framework," *Psychological Bulletin* 131 (2005), pp. 241–59; L.M. Hough and A. Furnham, "Use of Personality Variables in Work Settings," in *Handbook of Psychology,* Vol. 12, eds. W.C. Borman, D.R. Ilgen, and R.J. Klimoski (Hoboken, NJ: Wiley, 2003), pp. 131–69; J.E. Mathieu and D.M. Zajac, "A Review and Meta-Analysis of the Antecedents, Correlates, and Consequences of Organizational Commitment," *Psychological Bulletin* 108 (1990), pp. 171–94; J.F. Salgado, "The Big Five Personality Dimensions and Counterproductive Behaviors," *International Journal of Selection and Assessment* 10 (2002), pp. 117–25.

physical. We focus our discussion on cognitive ability because it's the most relevant form of ability across all jobs and is likely to be important in the kinds of positions that students in an OB course will be pursuing. As it turns out, there is a huge body of research linking general cognitive ability to job performance, as summarized in Figure 9-7.[93]

The figure reveals that cognitive ability is a strong predictor of job performance—in particular, the task performance aspect. Across all jobs, smarter employees fulfill the requirements of their job descriptions more effectively than do less smart employees. In fact, of all the variables discussed in this book, none has a stronger correlation with task performance than general cognitive ability. Thousands of organizations, and many that are quite well known, assess cognitive ability in an effort to select the best candidates available for specific jobs.[94] The use of cognitive ability tests for this purpose appears to be reasonable, given that scores on such tests have a strong positive correlation with measures of performance across different types of jobs.[95]

FIGURE 9-7 Effects of General Cognitive Ability on Performance and Commitment

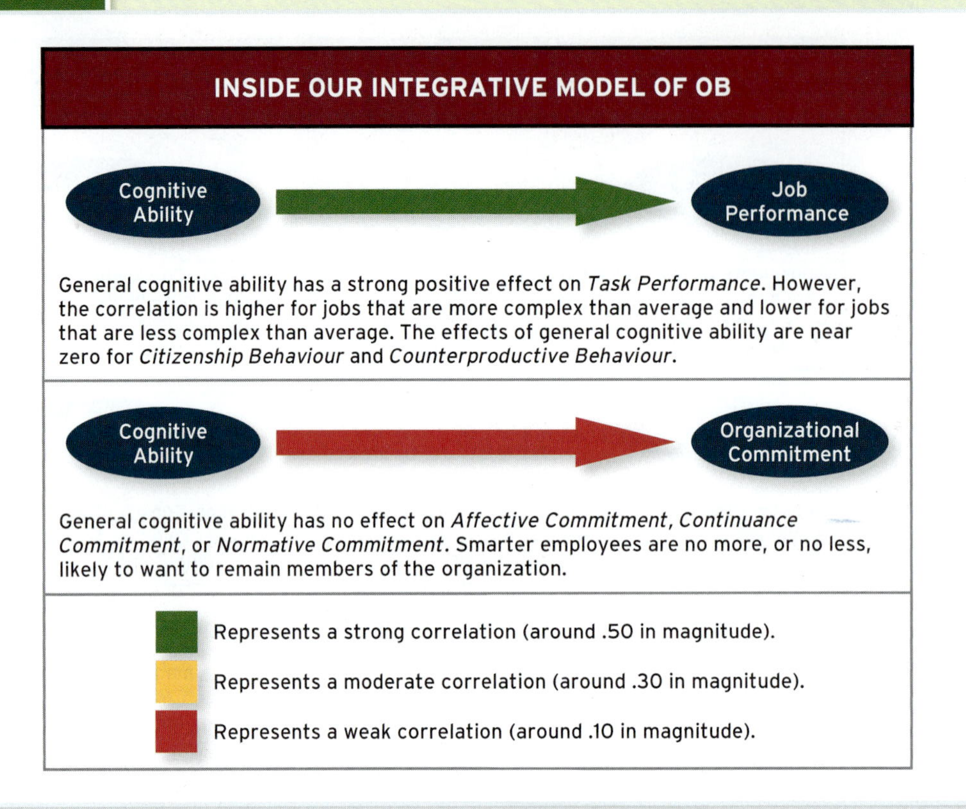

Sources: J.W. Boudreau, W.R. Boswell, T.A. Judge, and R.D Bretz, "Personality and Cognitive Ability as Predictors of Job Search Among Employed Managers," *Personnel Psychology* 54 (2001), pp. 25–50; S.M. Colarelli, R.A. Dean, and C. Konstans, "Comparative Effects of Personal and Situational Influences on Job Outcomes of New Professionals," *Journal of Applied Psychology* 72 (1987), pp. 558–66; D.N. Dickter, M. Roznowski, and D.A. Harrison, "Temporal Tempering: An Event History Analysis of the Process of Voluntary Turnover," *Journal of Applied Psychology* 81 (1996), pp. 705–16; F.L. Schmidt and J. Hunter, "General Mental Ability in the World of Work: Occupational Attainment and Job Performance," *Journal of Personality and Social Psychology* 86 (2004), pp. 162–73.

APPLICATION: PERSONALITY AND COGNITIVE ABILITY TESTS

Given how important personality and abilities can be to job performance and organizational commitment, it's not surprising that many organizations attempt to assess job applicants on these characteristics. But what's the best way to do that? Beginning with personality, it seems that many organizations try to assess an individual's traits through interviews by looking for cues that an applicant is conscientious or agreeable or has high levels of some other relevant personality dimension. Can you see a potential problem with this approach? Here's a hint: When was the last time you went into an interview and acted careless, sloppy, moody, or insecure? It's probably been a while. In fact, most interview preparation courses and books train applicants to exhibit the very personality traits that many employers are looking for!

TABLE 9-4 A Sampling of Well-Validated Measures of the Big Five

NAME OF INSTRUMENT	VENDOR	TIME REQUIRED
NEO Five-Factor Inventory (NEO-FFI)	Sigma Assessment Systems	15 minutes
Personal Characteristics Inventory (PCI)	Wonderlic	20 minutes
Personality Research Form (PRF)	Sigma Assessment Systems	45 minutes
Hogan Personality Inventory (HPI)	Hogan Assessment Systems	15 minutes
Big Five Inventory (BFI)	TestMaster	10 minutes

To examine whether interviewers can gauge the Big Five, one study asked 26 interviewers, all of whom were human resources practitioners with more than 12 years of hiring experience, to assess the personalities of undergraduate business students who were on the job market.[96] The interviewers met with an average of three students for 30 minutes and were instructed to follow the interview protocols used in their own organizations. Once the interviews had concluded, the study gathered multiple ratings of the Big Five, including ratings from the interviewer, the student, and a close friend of the student. The results of the study showed that the interviewers' ratings of extraversion, agreeableness, and openness were fairly consistent with the students' own ratings, as well as their friends' ratings. In contrast, interviewers' ratings of conscientiousness and neuroticism were only weakly related to the students' and friends' ratings. This study therefore shows that interviewers are unable to gauge the two Big Five dimensions that are most highly related to job performance.

Rather than using interviews to assess personality, more and more companies are relying on paper-and-pencil "personality tests" like the kind shown in our OB Assessments at the end of this chapter. Table 9-4 provides a list of some of the most well-validated measures of the Big Five personality dimensions. The vendors that own these measures typically offer software and services for scoring the instruments, interpreting the data against relevant population norms, and creating feedback sheets.

Given the strong relationship between general cognitive ability and job performance, it isn't surprising that many organizations apply the content of this chapter by using ability tests to hire new employees. One of the most widely used tests is the **Wonderlic Personnel Test**, a 12-minute test of general cognitive ability that consists of 50 questions. It has been in use for several decades now and given to more than 120 million people by thousands of organizations.[97] People who take the test receive one point for each correct response, and those points are summed to give a total score that can be used as a basis for selecting people for different jobs. The Wonderlic User's Manual offers recommendations for minimum passing scores for different job families, some of which are included in Table 9-5. For example, a score of 17 is the minimum suggested score for unskilled labourer, a score of 21—which is the average for high school graduates, and which corresponds to an IQ of approximately 100—is the minimum suggested score for a firefighter. A score of 28 is the minimum suggested score for upper-level managerial and executive work and is around the average for all university graduates.

Wonderlic Personnel Test A 12-minute test of general cognitive ability used to hire job applicants

TABLE 9-5 Suggested Minimum Wonderlic Scores for Various Jobs

JOB	AVERAGE SCORES
Mechanical engineer	30
Attorney	29
Executive	28
Teacher	27
Nurse	26
Office manager	25
Advertising sales	24
Manager/supervisor	23
Police officer	22
Firefighter	21
Cashier	20
Hospital orderly	19
Machine operator	18
Unskilled labourer	17
Maid-matron	16

Source: *Wonderlic Personnel Test and Scholastic Level Exam: User's Manual* (Libertyville, IL: Wonderlic Personnel Test, Inc., 1992), pp. 28–29. Reprinted with permission of Wonderlic, Inc.

TAKEAWAYS

9.1 Personality refers to the structures and propensities inside a person that explain his or her characteristic patterns of thought, emotion, and behaviour. It also refers to a person's social reputation—the way he or she is perceived by others. Cultural values are shared beliefs about desirable end states or modes of conduct in a given culture that influence the expression of traits. Ability refers to the relatively stable capabilities of people to perform a particular range of different but related activities. Personality and values capture *what people are like* (unlike ability, which reflects *what people can do*).

9.2 The "Big Five" includes conscientiousness (e.g., dependable, organized, reliable), agreeableness (e.g., warm, kind, cooperative), neuroticism (e.g., nervous, moody, emotional), openness to experience (e.g., curious, imaginative, creative), and extraversion (e.g., talkative, sociable, passionate).

9.3 Hofstede's dimensions of cultural values include individualism–collectivism, power distance, uncertainty avoidance, masculinity–femininity, and short-term vs. long-term orientation.

9.4 Cognitive abilities include verbal ability, quantitative ability, reasoning ability, spatial ability, and perceptual ability. General mental ability, or *g*, underlies all of these more specific cognitive abilities.

9.5 Emotional intelligence includes four specific kinds of emotional skills: self-awareness, other awareness, emotion regulation, and use of emotions.

9.6 Physical abilities include strength, stamina, flexibility and coordination, psychomotor abilities, and sensory abilities.

9.7 Conscientiousness has a moderate positive relationship with job performance and a moderate positive relationship with organizational commitment. It has stronger effects on these outcomes than the rest of the Big Five. General cognitive ability has a strong positive relationship with job performance, due primarily to its effects on task performance. In contrast, general cognitive ability is not related to organizational commitment.

KEY TERMS

- ability *p. 218*
- accomplishment striving *p. 219*
- agreeableness *p. 219*
- auditory attention *p. 239*
- Big Five *p. 219*
- cognitive abilities *p. 230*
- communion striving *p. 220*
- conscientiousness *p. 219*
- control movement abilities *p. 238*
- cultural values *p. 218*
- deductive reasoning *p. 232*
- depth perception *p. 239*
- differential exposure *p. 224*
- differential reactivity *p. 224*
- dynamic flexibility *p. 238*
- dynamic strength *p. 236*
- emotional intelligence *p. 235*
- emotion regulation *p. 235*
- ethnocentrism *p. 225*
- explosive strength *p. 236*
- extent flexibility *p. 238*
- extraversion *p. 219*
- fine manipulative abilities *p. 238*
- general mental ability *p. 233*
- gross body coordination *p. 238*
- gross body equilibrium *p. 238*
- hearing sensitivity *p. 239*
- individualism–collectivism *p. 225*
- inductive reasoning *p. 232*
- masculinity–femininity *p. 225*
- mathematical reasoning *p. 231*
- maximum performance *p. 240*
- near and far vision *p. 238*
- negative affectivity *p. 223*
- neuroticism *p. 219*
- night vision *p. 238*
- number facility *p. 231*
- openness to experience *p. 219*
- oral comprehension *p. 231*
- oral expression *p. 231*
- originality *p. 232*
- other awareness *p. 235*
- perceptual speed *p. 232*
- personality *p. 218*
- positive affectivity *p. 221*
- power distance *p. 225*
- problem sensitivity *p. 231*
- response orientation *p. 238*
- response time *p. 238*
- self-awareness *p. 235*
- short-term vs. long-term orientation *p. 225*
- situational strength *p. 240*
- spatial orientation *p. 232*
- speech recognition *p. 239*
- speed and flexibility of closure *p. 232*
- stamina *p. 236*
- static strength *p. 236*
- status striving *p. 221*
- trait activation *p. 240*
- traits *p. 218*
- typical performance *p. 240*
- uncertainty avoidance *p. 225*
- use of emotions *p. 236*
- visual colour discrimination *p. 238*
- visualization *p. 232*
- Wonderlic Personnel Test *p. 243*
- written comprehension *p. 231*
- written expression *p. 231*
- zero acquaintance situations *p. 221*

DISCUSSION QUESTIONS

9.1 Based on your personal observation of others, perhaps focusing on people that you have known for a few years, do you think that personality is genetically determined or developed over time through life experiences? What life experiences could make someone more conscientious? More agreeable? More neurotic? More extraverted? More open to new experiences?

9.2 Consider the profile of Canada on Hofstede's cultural values, as shown in Table 9-1 on page 226. Do you personally feel like you fit the Canadian profile, or do your values differ in some respects? If you served as an expatriate, meaning you were working in another country, which cultural value differences would be most difficult for you to deal with?

9.3 What roles do learning, education, and other experiences play in determining a person's abilities? For which type of ability—cognitive, emotional, or physical—do these factors play the largest role?

9.4 Think of experiences you've had with people who demonstrated unusually high or low levels of emotional intelligence. Then consider how you would rate them in terms of their cognitive abilities. Do you think that emotional intelligence "bleeds over" to affect people's perceptions of cognitive ability?

9.5 What combination of personality and abilities is appropriate for the job of your dreams? Do you possess those characteristics? If you fall short on any of these attributes, what could you do to improve?

CASE • GOOGLE

Google's strong magnetism has turned the technology company into the mecca for talented intellects across the world. Talented individuals from academia and respected technology companies are jumping to Google to join its unique culture and flex their intellectual power. The culture at Google encourages top talent to pursue innovative entrepreneurial projects. For example, engineers may work on their own projects for the company one day a week. For this reason, Google has attracted tech gurus such as Rob Pike, one of the creators of the Unix operating system.

In 2006, *BusinessWeek* named Google the 13th best place to launch a career. It offers many appeals for smart employees who choose to pursue a career path with the search engine behemoth. Some are attracted to the opportunity to solve enormous, unsolved technical challenges, which could benefit millions of people daily. Others are drawn to the company to get the chance to work with tech gurus who have already revolutionized the industry. Whatever the reason, Google is accumulating the most intelligent human capital in the world.

9.1 Does Google's success rely on its ability to attract and retain the most talented employees? Explain.

9.2 Which of the Big Five personality dimensions would fit best with the culture at Google? Explain

9.3 Can a company have too much intellectual human capital? Explain.

Sources: "Google Faces Brain Drain as Anniversaries Hit," April 11, 2007, www.redorbit.com/news/technology/898498/google_faces_brain_drain_as_anniversaries_hit/index.html# (June 20, 2007); K. Hafner, "New Incentive for Google Employees: Awards Worth Millions," *The New York Times,* February 1, 2005; "Revenge of the Nerds–Again," *BusinessWeek,* August 8, 2005; "The Best Places to Launch a Career," *BusinessWeek,* September 18, 2006.

EXERCISE • EMOTIONAL INTELLIGENCE

The purpose of this exercise is to help you become more aware of your emotions and the emotions of others, as well as to see how emotions can be regulated and used in your daily life. This exercise uses groups of six participants, so your instructor will either assign you to a group of six or ask you to create your own group of six. The exercise has the following steps:

1. Think about situations in which you've experienced each of the following four emotions:
   - Joy
   - Anxiety
   - Sadness
   - Indignation
2. In writing or in group discussion, answer the following questions about each situation:
   a. What, exactly, triggered your emotion in this situation?
   b. What impact did your emotions have on the outcome of the situation? Consider how your emotions affected you, others, and the general outcome of the situation. (Was it positive or negative?)
   c. What strategies did you use to deal with the emotion?
   d. What other strategies could you have used to deal with the emotion?

   For example, one student noted: "I always get anxious when I take tests. Last week, I was supposed to have a midterm in accounting, and sure enough, the upcoming test triggered my anxiety. Because I was anxious, I put off studying, and I tried to get some friends to go out to a club with me. We all had a good time that night, but the next day I got a D on my accounting test, and two of my friends failed their management midterms. I was using procrastination and avoidance as strategies for dealing with my anxiety. Another strategy I could have used was to face the anxiety head on by talking to my professor to get a better understanding of the material that was going to be on the test, or by getting a group of my friends together to form a study group for accounting."
3. Compare your responses with the responses of your fellow group members. As a group, answer the following questions:
   a. What emotional triggers do you share? In what ways are your emotional triggers different?
   b. Are there some strategies for dealing with emotions that seem especially helpful? Unhelpful?
   c. According to the stories told by the group, are there times when emotions actually help get a task done or a goal accomplished? How might you harness your emotions to help you achieve specific outcomes in the future?

Source: Adapted from material in M.A. Brackett and N.A. Katulak, "Emotional Intelligence in the Classroom: Skill-Based Training for Teachers and Students," in *Improving Emotional Intelligence: A Practitioner's Guide,* eds. J. Ciarrochi and J.D. Mayer (New York: Psychology Press/Taylor & Francis, 2006), pp. 1–27.

OB ASSESSMENTS • THE BIG FIVE

What does your personality profile look like? This assessment is designed to measure the five major dimensions of personality: conscientiousness (C), agreeableness (A), neuroticism (N), openness to experience (O), and extraversion (E). Listed below are phrases describing people's behaviours. Please write a number next to each statement that indicates the extent to which it accurately describes you. Answer each question using the response scale provided. Then subtract your answers to the boldfaced questions from 6, with the difference being your new answer for those questions. For example, if your original answer for question 6 was "2," your new answer is "4" (6 − 2).

1 VERY INACCURATE	2 MODERATELY INACCURATE	3 NEITHER INACCURATE NOR ACCURATE	4 MODERATELY ACCURATE	5 VERY ACCURATE

1. I am the life of the party. ______
2. I sympathize with others' feelings. ______
3. I get chores done right away. ______
4. I have frequent mood swings. ______
5. I have a vivid imagination. ______
6. **I don't talk a lot.** ______
7. **I am not interested in other people's problems.** ______
8. **I often forget to put things back in their proper place.** ______
9. **I am relaxed most of the time.** ______
10. **I am not interested in abstract ideas.** ______
11. I talk to a lot of different people at parties. ______
12. I feel others' emotions. ______
13. I like order. ______
14. I get upset easily. ______
15. **I have difficulty understanding abstract ideas.** ______
16. **I keep in the background.** ______
17. **I am not really interested in others.** ______
18. **I make a mess of things.** ______
19. **I seldom feel blue.** ______
20. **I do not have a good imagination.** ______

SCORING AND INTERPRETATION:

Conscientiousness: Sum up items 3, 8, 13, and 18.
Agreeableness: Sum up items 2, 7, 12, and 17.
Neuroticism: Sum up items 4, 9, 14, and 19.
Openness to Experience: Sum up items 5, 10, 15, and 20.
Extraversion: Sum up items 1, 6, 11, and 16.

Now chart your scores in the figure below to see whether you are above or below the norm for each dimension.

CONNECT—Available 24/7 with instant feedback so you can study when you want, how you want, and where you want. Take advantage of the Study Plan—an innovative tool that helps students customize their own learning experience. Students can diagnose their knowledge with pre- and post-tests, identify the areas where they need help, search contents of the entire learning package for content specific to the topic they're studying, and add these resources to their study plan. Visit **www.connectob.ca** to register—take practice quizzes, run interactive scenarios, and much more. Also visit the Student Online Learning Centre for additional study tools.

CHAPTER 10

Team Characteristics and Processes

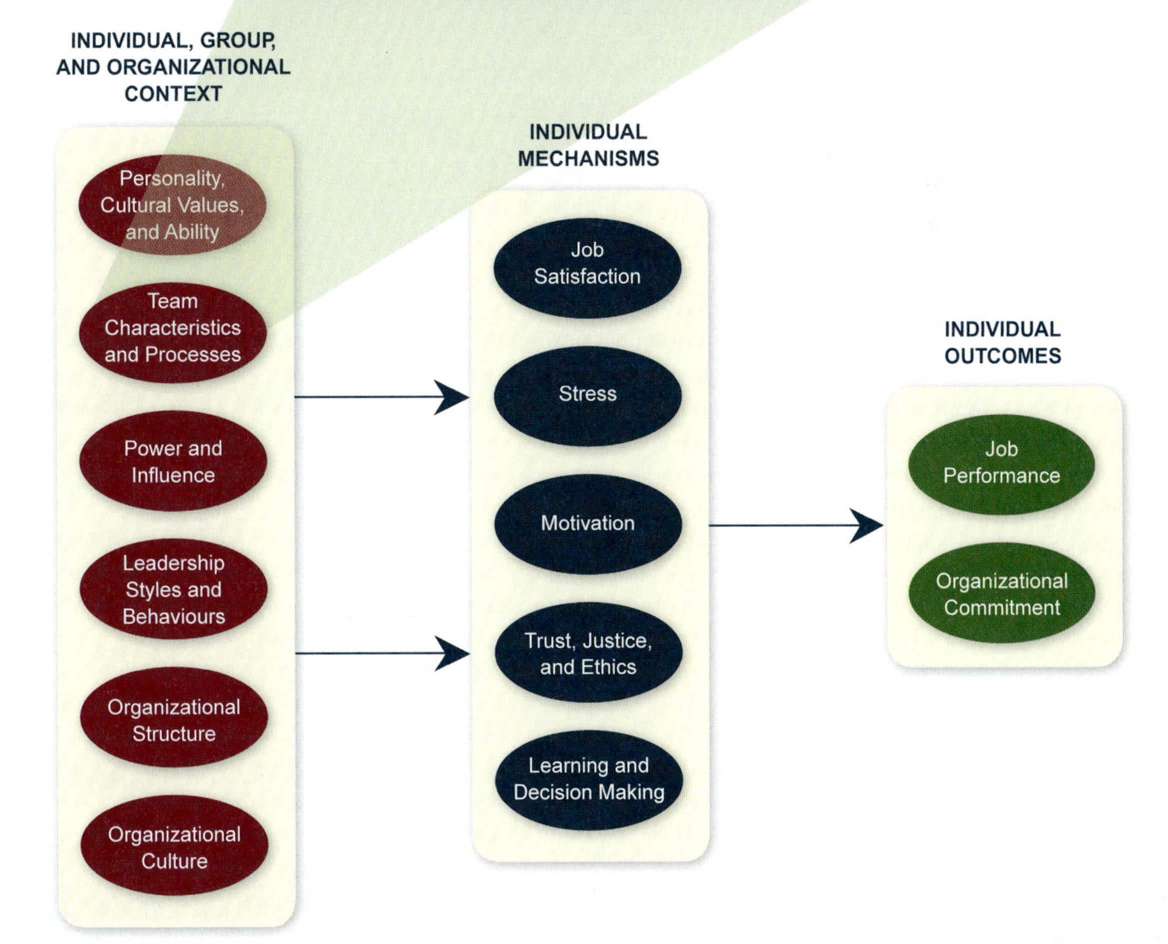

PIXAR

Chances are you've seen one of the following animated movies over the past decade or so: *Toy Story, Toy Story 2, A Bug's Life, Monster's Inc., Finding Nemo, The Incredibles, Cars, or Wall-E.* If you have, you're not alone. These critically acclaimed films, produced by Pixar, were huge hits at the box office. *Finding Nemo,* for example, had grossed over $865 million as of late 2006 and stands as one of the ten highest grossing films of all time.[1] All this success led Disney to acquire Pixar for over $7 billion—not a bad price for a 20-year-old company.[2] But how did Pixar achieve so much success in such a short period of time? The most obvious factor is that Pixar developed highly innovative computer graphics and production software for filmmaking, bringing a vibrancy and richness to its movies that had never been seen before.

A less obvious contributor to Pixar's success is that the company is built around talented people who work in highly effective teams. Perhaps the best example is the team at the top of the company: Ed Catmull, John Lasseter, and Steve Jobs.[3] Catmull dreamed up the idea of making computer-animated films and is the member most responsible for the majority of Pixar's technical achievements. Lasseter, originally a Disney animator, is the "artist" of the team. He personally directed Pixar's first three films and is the company's creative force. Finally, Steve Jobs is the CEO of Pixar and the member most responsible for the business decisions that allowed the company to grow into a multibillion dollar enterprise in less than two decades.

Even apart from its top managers, there are a number of characteristics that make the teams at Pixar effective. For example, Pixar's teams are composed of members with very different sources of expertise and knowledge, who collaborate closely with one another on most aspects of the filmmaking enterprise.[4] For example, artists directly consult with engineers to request new types of visual effects. Engineers communicate ideas for new visual effects directly to producers. This sort of direct communication between people with different functional backgrounds helps the teams cope with the sheer complexity of making animated films. It also helps Pixar's teams produce highly innovative films, which is one key to their box office success.

Learning Outcomes

After reading this chapter, you should be able to answer the following questions:

10.1 What is a team, and how are teams different than groups?

10.2 What are the three general types of team interdependence?

10.3 What factors are involved in team composition?

10.4 What is team process, and how does it relate to process gain and process loss?

10.5 What are taskwork and teamwork processes, and what are some examples of team activities that fall into these process categories?

10.6 What are team states, and what are some examples of the states that fall into this process category?

10.7 How do team characteristics and processes affect team performance and team commitment?

Teams are responsible for many elements of Pixar's success, including its production of innovative animation like the hit film *Wall-E.*

Another factor that makes Pixar's teams so effective is that the majority of the members have stayed together throughout the company's relatively brief history. This practice stands in stark contrast to the norm in the film industry of assembling a new set of actors, producers, technicians, and support personnel for each new project.[5] Why has keeping the teams together been so effective for Pixar? For one thing, it enabled team members to develop a solid understanding of how other members' knowledge and skills can help them accomplish their own tasks. Moreover, when entering new projects, team members already have a sense of everyone's strengths, weaknesses, and personality quirks. As a result, the team is more capable of avoiding the kinds of misunderstandings that can distract teams from their work.

TEAM CHARACTERISTICS AND PROCESSES

The topic of teams is likely familiar to almost anyone who might be reading this book. In fact, you've probably had first-hand experience with several different types of teams at different points in your life. As an example, most of you have played a team sport or two (yes, playing kickball in gym class counts). Most of you have also worked in student teams to complete projects or assignments for a course. Or perhaps you've worked closely with a small group of people to accomplish a task that was important to you—planning an event, raising money for a charity, or starting and running a small cash business. Finally, some of you have been members of organizational teams responsible for making a product, providing a service, or generating recommendations for solving company problems.

A **team** consists of two or more people who work interdependently over some time period to accomplish common goals related to some task-oriented purpose.[6] You can think of teams as a subset of the more general term "group," where groups are just a collection of two or more people. Teams differ from groups in two primary respects. First, the interactions within teams revolve around a deeper dependence on one another than the interactions within groups. Second, the interactions within teams occur with a specific task-related purpose in mind. Although the members of a friendship group may engage in small talk, gossip, or in-depth conversations on a frequent basis, the members of a team depend on one another for critical information, materials, and actions that are needed to accomplish their purpose. National surveys of large and small Canadian organizations have shown that almost half use some form of teamwork to accomplish work activities.[7]

team Two or more people who work interdependently over some time period to accomplish common goals related to some task-oriented purpose

Why have teams become so widespread? The most obvious reason is that the nature of the work needed to be done requires them. As work has become more complex, interaction among multiple team members has become more vital because it allows the team to pool complementary knowledge and skill. As an example, surgical teams consist of individuals who receive specialized training in the activities needed to conduct surgical procedures safely. The team consists of a surgeon who received training for the procedure in question, an anesthesiologist who received training necessary to manage patient pain, and an operating room nurse who was trained on how to provide overall care for the patient.

WHAT CHARACTERISTICS CAN BE USED TO DESCRIBE TEAMS?

In this chapter we describe team characteristics, that is, the task, unit, and member qualities that can be used to describe teams. Team characteristics provide a means of categorizing and examining teams, which is important because teams come in so many shapes and sizes. Later in the chapter we focus on processes within teams—the specific actions and behaviours that teams can engage in to achieve synergy. For now, however, we turn our attention to this question: "What characteristics can be used to describe teams?"

TYPES OF TEAMS

Let's begin by considering different types of teams and their characteristics, including the team's purpose, the length of the team's existence, and the amount of time involvement required by its individual members.

work team A relatively permanent team in which members work together to produce goods and/or provide services

WORK TEAMS **Work teams** are designed to be relatively permanent. Their purpose is to produce goods or provide services, and they generally require a full-time commitment from their members. Although all work teams have these defining characteristics, they can vary a great deal across organizations in other important ways. One way that work teams vary is in the degree to which members have autonomy in defining their roles and decision making. In traditional work teams, members have very specific sets of job duties, and their decision making is confined to the activities required by those duties. Members of self-managed work teams, in contrast, are not locked into specific jobs. Instead, they jointly decide how to organize themselves and carry out the team's work. Examples of relatively permanent work teams with decision-making discretion can be found in the MBA program at the University of Alberta. Students are typically assigned to a work team on the first day of the program and then remain with their team over a two-year period as they complete core courses together. Decisions, for instance, concerning the planning of their class assignments (e.g., scope of topics and issues covered) and the allocation of work among members (i.e., who does what) would normally be made by the team itself rather than any of the instructors who interact with the team.

management team A relatively permanent team that participates in managerial-level tasks that affect the entire organization

MANAGEMENT TEAMS **Management teams** are similar to work teams in that they are designed to be relatively permanent; however, they are also distinct in a number of important ways. Whereas work teams focus on the accomplishment of core operational-level production and service tasks, management teams participate in managerial-level tasks that affect the entire organization. Specifically, management teams are responsible for coordinating the activities of organizational subunits—typically departments or functional areas—to help the organization achieve its long-term goals.

parallel team A team composed of members from various jobs within the organization that meets to provide recommendations about important issues

PARALLEL TEAMS **Parallel teams** are composed of members from various jobs who provide recommendations to managers about important issues that run "parallel" to the organization's production process.[8] Parallel teams require only part-time commitment from members, and they can be permanent or temporary, depending on their aim. Quality circles, for example, consist of individuals who normally perform core production tasks but also meet regularly to identify production-related problems and opportunities for improvement. As an example of a more temporary parallel team, committees often form to deal with unique issues or issues that arise only periodically.

project team A team formed to take on one-time tasks, most of which tend to be complex and require input from members from different functional areas

PROJECT TEAMS **Project teams** are formed to take on "one-time" tasks that are generally complex and require a lot of input from members with different types of training and expertise.[9] Although project teams only exist as long as it takes to finish a project, some projects are quite complex and can take years to complete. Members of some project teams

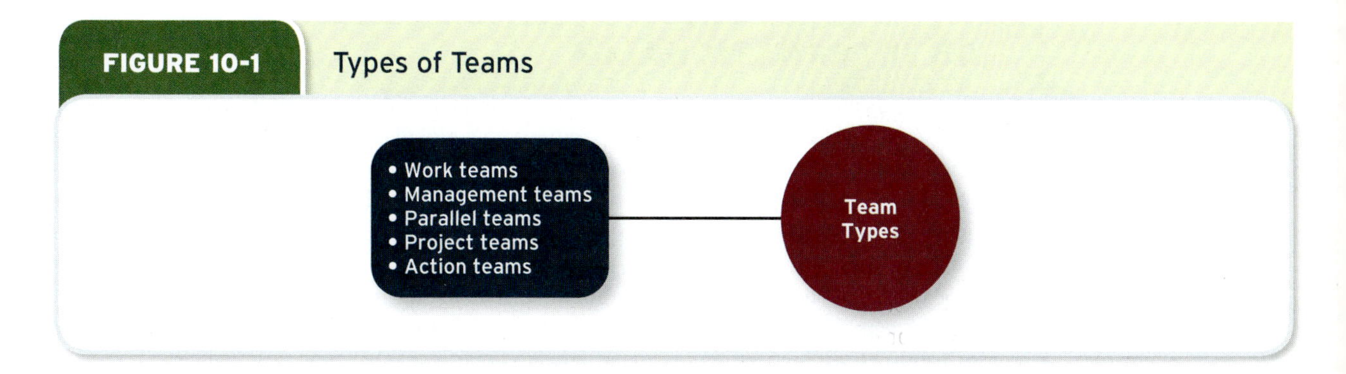

FIGURE 10-1 Types of Teams

work full-time, whereas other teams only demand a part-time commitment. A planning team comprised of engineers, architects, designers, and builders, charged with designing a suburban town centre, might work together full-time for a year or more. In contrast, the engineers and artists who constitute a design team responsible for creating an electric toothbrush might work together for a month on the project while also serving on other project teams.

action team A team of limited duration that performs complex tasks in contexts that tend to be highly visible and challenging

ACTION TEAMS **Action teams** perform tasks that are normally limited in duration. However, those tasks are quite complex and take place in contexts that are either highly visible to an audience or of a highly challenging nature.[10] Some types of action teams work together for an extended period of time. For example, sports teams remain intact for at least one season, and musical groups like the Rolling Stones may stick together for decades.

SUMMARY Figure 10-1 summarizes the five types of teams. How easy is it to classify teams into one of the types? Well, it turns out that teams often fit into more than one category. One could argue that the student teams within the MBA program at the University of Alberta have characteristics of both work teams and project teams. Another example would be the teams that produce films at Pixar. On the one hand, because the key members of Pixar's teams have stuck together for each film the company has produced, it might seem like Pixar uses work teams. On the other hand, because the creation of each film can be viewed as a project, and because members are likely involved in multiple ongoing projects, it might seem reasonable to say that Pixar uses project teams. It's probably most appropriate to say that Pixar teams have characteristics of both work teams and project teams.

VARIATIONS WITHIN TEAM TYPES

virtual team A team in which the members are geographically dispersed, and interdependent activity occurs through e-mail, Web conferencing, and instant messaging

Even knowing whether a team is a project team, an action team, or some other type of team doesn't tell you the whole story. Often there are important variations within those categories that are needed to understand a team's functioning. For example, **virtual teams** are teams in which the members are geographically dispersed, and interdependent activity occurs through electronic communications—primarily e-mail, instant messaging, and Web conferencing. In fact, recent estimates suggest that there are tens of millions of virtual teams operating today. As our **OB Internationally** feature illustrates, virtual teams are not just an efficient way to accomplish work when members are geographically separated. They may also be used to make continuous progress on work tasks without members having to work 24/7.

forming The first stage of team development, during which members try to get a feel for what is expected of them, what types of behaviours are out of bounds, and who's in charge

In addition to varying in their "virtuality," teams of any type can differ in the amount of experience they have working together. One way to understand this point is to consider what occurs in teams at different stages of their development as they progress from a newly formed to a well-established team. According to the most well-known theory of team development, teams go through a progression of four stages shown in the top panel of Figure 10-2.[11] In the first stage, called **forming**, members orient themselves by trying

OB INTERNATIONALLY

Two trends are changing the way work is accomplished in organizations today. First, businesses are increasingly conducting operations on a global basis, and as a consequence, they often employ people who live in countries around the world to perform important aspects of work. Second, communications technology has advanced to the point that it is relatively easy to communicate with groups of people located almost anywhere. Taken together, these trends have resulted in tremendous growth in the number of global virtual teams—teams of globally dispersed individuals who interact primarily through electronic communications.

Although the use of communications technology has reduced physical distance as a barrier to teamwork, differences in time zones remain a significant challenge to global virtual teams.[12] Consider the example of how Logitech developed and manufactured its flagship mouse, the Revolution. Product design and mechanical engineering took place in Ireland, electrical engineering took place in Switzerland, tooling took place in Taiwan, manufacturing took place in China, and software engineering and quality assurance took place in California.[13] Beyond obvious language issues, just imagine how difficult it must be for members of this sort of dispersed team to find convenient times to communicate with one another. If a team member in California needs to meet virtually with the team on Friday at noon (Pacific Standard Time), it would be 8:00 p.m. Friday evening in Ireland and 4:00 a.m. Friday morning in Taiwan.

Although time zone differences have been considered a hindrance to virtual teams, organizations such as IBM, Electronic Data Systems, and Logitech have begun to use them as a means of gaining a competitive advantage. In these organizations, the team's work simply *follows the sun.*[14] That is, work is accomplished continuously because members of a team who are finishing their workday in one country hand off the work to team members in another country who have just arrived at the office. Because hand-offs can occur continuously, product development and other work can be completed much more quickly.

Although "follow the sun" practices are gaining attention in many companies that operate globally, there are some issues that need to be considered.[15] As one example, language and cultural differences can create misunderstandings that prevent work from being accomplished effectively after it has been handed off. Systems that teams use to hand off work therefore need to be detailed and well understood by all team members, and members need to be willing to ask for clarification if they have questions. In addition, there are more general concerns that such "follow the sun" practices will prompt companies like IBM to ship more white-collar jobs overseas.[16]

storming The second stage of team development, during which conflict occurs due to members' ongoing commitment to ideas they bring with them to the team

norming The third stage of team development, during which members realize that they need to work together to accomplish team goals and consequently begin to cooperate

to understand the boundaries in the team. Members try to get a feel for what is expected of them, what types of behaviours are out of bounds, and who's in charge. In the next stage, called **storming**, members remain committed to ideas they bring with them to the team. This initial unwillingness to accommodate others' ideas triggers conflict that negatively affects some interpersonal relationships and harms the team's progress. During the next stage, **norming**, members realize that they need to work together to accomplish team goals, and consequently, they begin to cooperate with one another. Feelings of solidarity develop as members work toward team goals. Over time, norms and expectations develop regarding what different members are responsible for doing. In the final stage of team development, which is called **performing**, members are comfortable working within their roles, and the team makes progress toward goals.

But does this sequence of forming, storming, norming, and performing apply to the development of all types of teams? Chances are that you've had some experience with teams that would lead you to answer this question with a "no." One situation in which this developmental sequence is less applicable is when teams are formed with clear expectations regarding

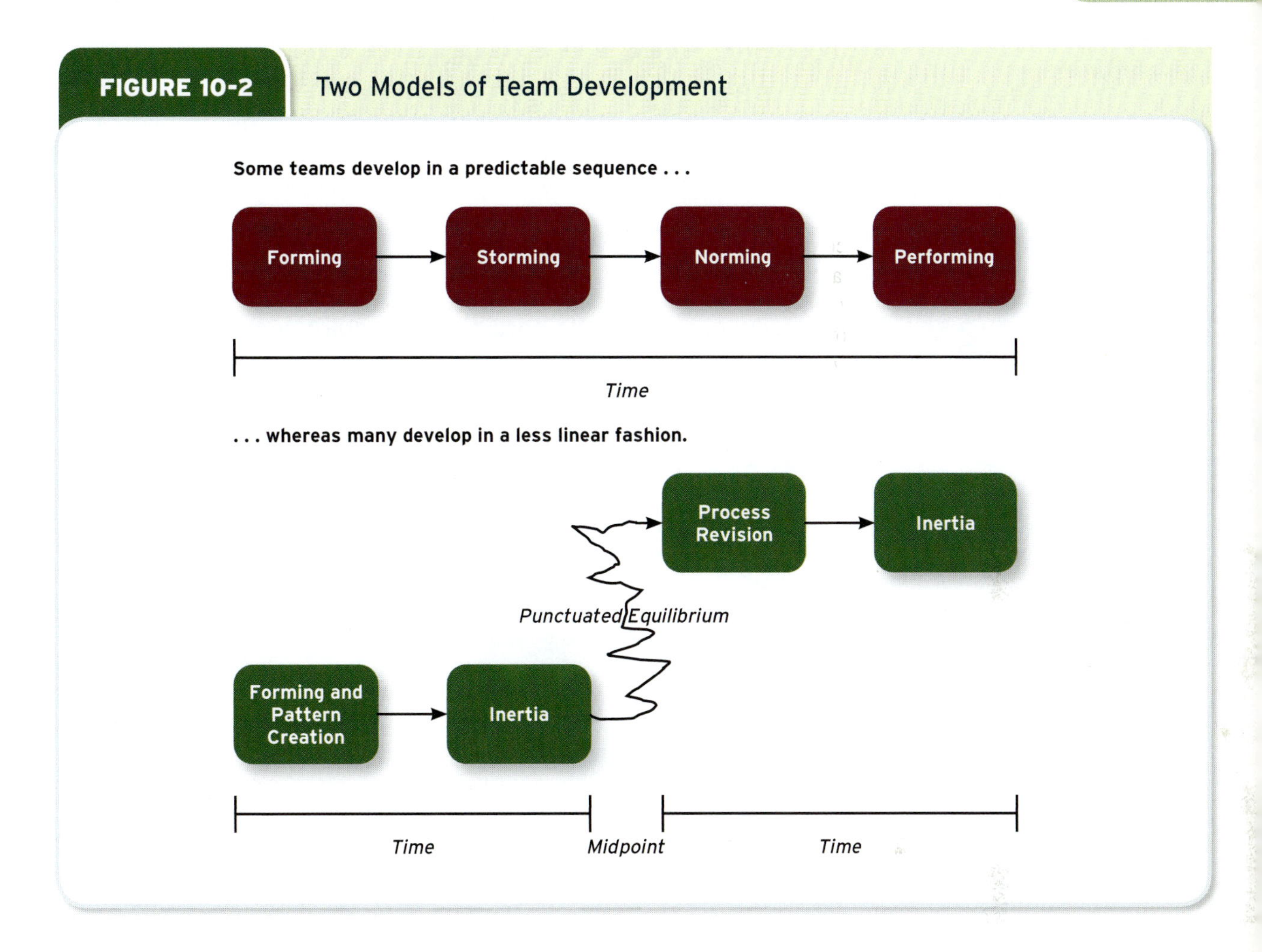

FIGURE 10-2 Two Models of Team Development

what is expected from the team and its members. As a specific example, an aircraft flight crew does not have to go through the forming, storming, norming, and performing stages to figure out that the pilot flies the plane and the flight attendant serves the beverages.

A second situation in which the development sequence is less applicable may be in certain types of project teams that follow a pattern of development called **punctuated equilibrium**.[17] This sequence appears in the bottom panel of Figure 10-2. At the initial team meeting, members make assumptions and establish a pattern of behaviour that lasts for the first half of its life. That pattern of behaviour continues to dominate the team's behaviour as it settles into a sort of inertia. At the midway point of the project—and this is true regardless of the length of the project—something remarkable happens. Members realize that they have to change their task paradigm fundamentally to complete it on time. Teams that take this opportunity to plan a new approach during this transition tend to do well, and the new framework dominates their behaviour until task completion. However, teams that do not take the opportunity to change their approach tend to persist with their original pattern and may "go down with a sinking ship."

performing The final stage of team development, during which members are comfortable working within their roles, and the team makes progress toward goals

punctuated equilibrium A sequence of team development during which not much gets done until the halfway point of a project, after which teams make necessary changes to complete the project on time

TEAM INTERDEPENDENCE

10.2 What are the three general types of team interdependence?

In addition to taxonomies of team types, we can describe teams by talking about the interdependence that governs connections among team members.

task interdependence The degree to which team members interact with and rely on other team members for information, materials, and resources needed to accomplish work for the team

TASK INTERDEPENDENCE **Task interdependence** refers to the degree to which team members interact with and rely on other team members for the information, materials, and resources needed to accomplish work for the team.[18] As Figure 10-3 illustrates, there are four primary types of task interdependence, and each requires a different degree of interaction and coordination.[19]

FIGURE 10-3 Task Interdependence and Coordination Requirements

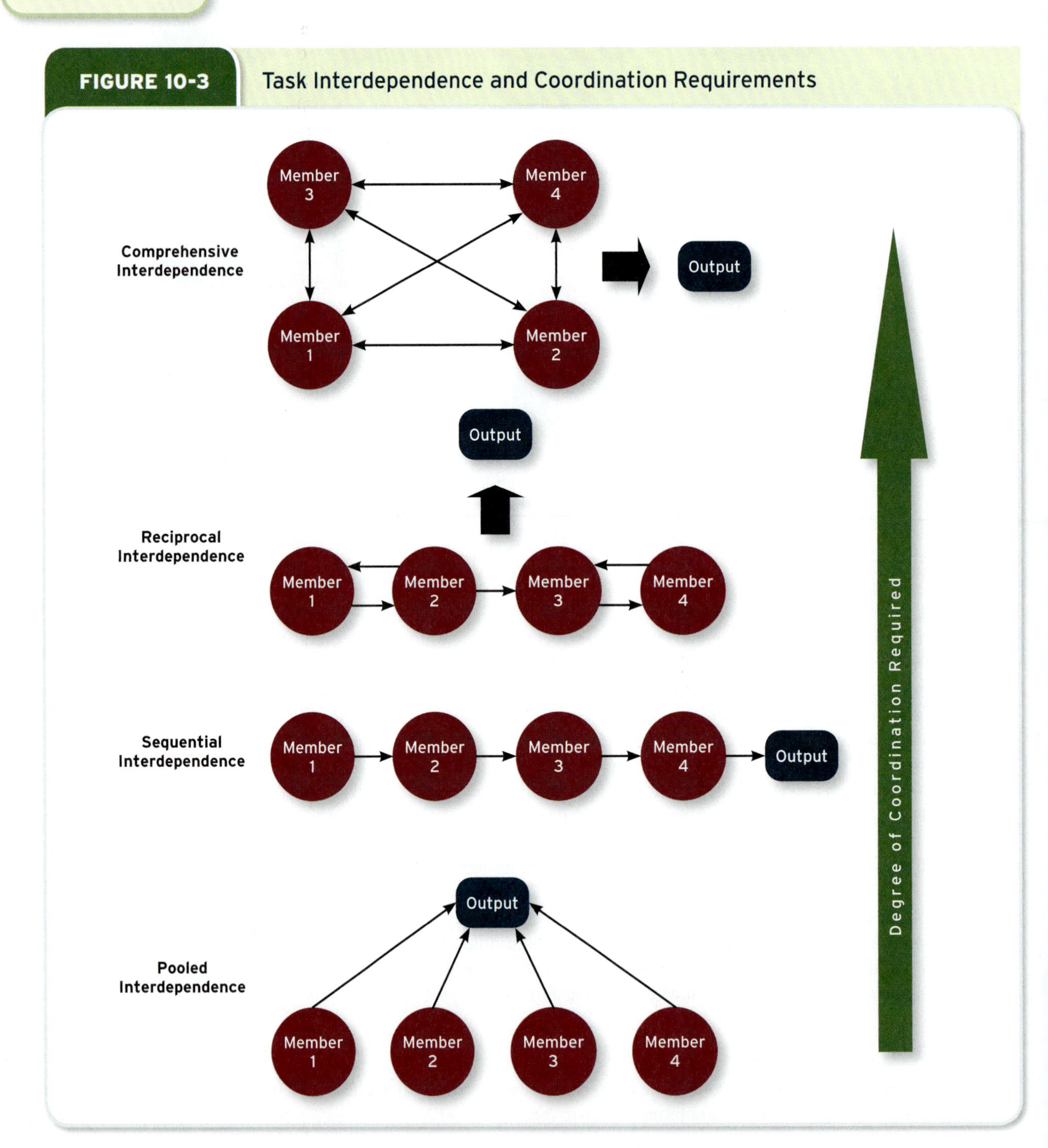

The type of task interdependence with the lowest degree of required coordination is **pooled interdependence**.[20] With this type of interdependence, group members complete their work assignments independently, and then this work is simply "piled up" to represent the group's output. A classic example of pooled interdependence would be a tug-of-war task where the total force applied to each end of the rope would be a sum of each team member's individual effort. The next type of task interdependence is called **sequential interdependence**.[21] With this type of interdependence, different tasks are done in a prescribed order, and the group is structured such that the members specialize in these tasks. Although members in groups with sequential interdependence interact to carry out their work, the interaction only occurs between members who perform tasks that are next to each other in the sequence. The classic assembly line in manufacturing contexts provides an excellent example of this type of interdependence. In this context, an employee attaches a part to the unit being built, and once this is accomplished, the unit moves on to another employee who adds another part. The process typically ends with the unit being inspected and then packaged for shipping.

pooled interdependence A form of task interdependence in which group members complete their work assignments independently, and then their work is simply added together to represent the group's output

sequential interdependence A form of task interdependence in which group members perform different tasks in a prescribed sequence, and members only depend on the member who comes before them in the sequence

Reciprocal interdependence is the next type of task interdependence.[22] Similar to sequential interdependence, members are specialized to perform specific tasks. However, instead of a strict sequence of activities, members interact with a subset of other members to complete the team's work. An example of reciprocal interdependence would be how a team of emergency room staff in a hospital work together. The nature of the patient's emergency would determine which members of the team need to coordinate and interact (e.g., having a broken leg would require a different subset of people to interact than would the delivery of a baby). Finally, **comprehensive interdependence** requires the highest level of interaction and coordination among members as they try to accomplish work.[23] In groups with comprehensive interdependence, each member has a great deal of discretion in terms of what they do and with whom they interact in the course of the collaboration involved in accomplishing the team's work. A great example of this was portrayed in the movie, *Apollo 13,* when individuals from diverse backgrounds (and orientations) came together in mission control to find solutions to novel problems (see how the carbon dioxide problem was resolved or how team members figured out how to power-up the command module for re-entry).

reciprocal interdependence A form of task interdependence in which group members interact with only a limited subset of other members to complete the team's work

comprehensive interdependence A form of task interdependence in which team members have a great deal of discretion in terms of what they do and with whom they interact in the course of the collaboration involved in accomplishing the team's work

It is important to note that there is no one right way to design teams with respect to task interdependence, and there are trade-offs associated with the different types. On the one hand, as the level of task interdependence increases, members must spend increasing amounts of time communicating and coordinating with other members to complete tasks. This type of coordination can result in decreases in productivity, which is the ratio of work completed per the amount of time worked. On the other hand, increases in task interdependence increase the ability of the team to adapt to new situations. The more members interact and communicate with other members, the more likely it is that the team will be able to devise solutions to novel problems it may face.

GOAL INTERDEPENDENCE In addition to being linked to one another by task activities, members may be linked by their goals.[24] A high degree of **goal interdependence** exists when team members have a shared vision of the team's goal and align their individual goals with that vision as a result.[25] To understand the power of goal interdependence, visualize a rowboat with several people on board, each with a paddle.[26] If each person on the boat wants to go to the exact same place on the other side of a lake, they will all row in the same direction, and the boat will arrive at the desired location. If, however, each person believes the boat should go someplace different, each person will row in a different direction, and the boat will have major problems getting anywhere.

goal interdependence The degree to which team members have a shared goal and align their individual goals with that vision

So how do you create high levels of goal interdependence? One thing to do would be to ensure that the team has a formalized mission statement that members buy in to. Mission statements can take a variety of forms, but good ones clearly describe what the team is trying to accomplish in a way that creates a sense of commitment and urgency among team members.[27] Mission statements can come directly from the organization or team leaders, but in many circumstances, it makes more sense for teams to go through the process of developing their own mission statements. This process not only helps members better understand what the team needs to do but also increases feelings of ownership toward the mission statement itself.

outcome interdependence The degree to which team members share equally in the feedback and rewards that result from the team achieving its goals

OUTCOME INTERDEPENDENCE The final type of interdependence relates to how members are linked to one another in terms of the feedback and outcomes they receive as a consequence of working in the team.[28] A high degree of **outcome interdependence** exists when team members share in the rewards that the team earns, with reward examples including pay, bonuses, formal feedback and recognition, pats on the back, extra time off, and continued team survival. Of course, because team achievement depends on the performance of each team member, high outcome interdependence also implies that team members depend on the performance of other team members for the rewards that they receive. In contrast, low outcome interdependence exists in teams in which individual members receive rewards and punishments on the basis of their own performance, without regard to the performance of the team.

team composition The mix of the various characteristics that describe the individuals who work in the team

role The behaviour a person is generally expected to display in a given context

10.3 What factors are involved in team composition?

TEAM COMPOSITION

You probably already agree that team effectiveness hinges on **team composition**—or the mix of people who make up the team. If you've been a member of a particularly effective team, you may have noticed that the team seemed to have the right mix of abilities and personalities. Team members were not only capable of performing their role responsibilities effectively, but they also cooperated and got along fairly well together. In this section, we identify the most important characteristics to consider in team composition, and we describe how these elements combine to influence team functioning and effectiveness. As shown in Figure 10-4, five aspects of team composition are crucial: roles, ability, personality, diversity, and size.

leader–staff team A type of team that consists of members who make recommendations to the leader who is ultimately responsible for team decisions

MEMBER ROLES A **role** is defined as the behaviour a person is expected to display in a given context. One obvious way to distinguish roles is to consider the role of the leader and the role of members. In **leader–staff teams**, the leader makes decisions for the team and provides direction and control over members who perform assigned tasks, so this distinction makes sense in that the responsibilities of the leader and the rest of the team are distinct.[29]

FIGURE 10-4 Five Aspects of Team Composition

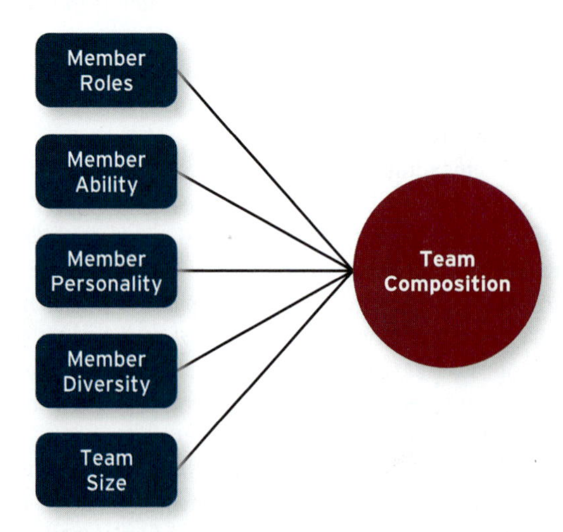

Typically, however, team members have some latitude with respect to the behaviours they exhibit. In these situations, team roles can be described in terms of the three rather broad categories: team task roles, team building roles, and individualistic roles.[30]

Team task roles refer to behaviours that directly facilitate the accomplishment of team tasks. Examples include the *orienter* who establishes the direction for the team, the *devil's advocate* who offers constructive challenges to the team's status quo, and the *energizer* who motivates team members to work harder toward team goals. In contrast to task-oriented roles, **team building roles** refer to behaviours that influence the quality of the team's social climate. Examples of team building roles include the *harmonizer* who steps in to resolve differences among teammates, the *encourager* who praises the work of teammates, and the *compromiser* who helps the team see alternative solutions that teammates can accept. Finally, **individualistic roles** reflect behaviours that benefit the individual at the expense of the team. For example, the *aggressor* "puts down" or deflates fellow teammates. The *recognition seeker* takes credit for team successes. The *dominator* manipulates teammates to acquire control and power. If you've ever had an experience in a team in which members took on individualistic roles, you probably realize just how damaging they can be. Having to deal with members who take on individualistic roles is dissatisfying and requires time and effort that would otherwise be used to accomplish productive team tasks.

team task roles Behaviours that directly facilitate the accomplishment of team tasks

team building roles Behaviours that influence the quality of the team's social climate

individualistic roles Behaviours that benefit the individual at the expense of the team

MEMBER ABILITY Team members possess a wide variety of abilities, as we have discussed in the preceding chapter. Depending on the nature of the tasks involved in the team's work, some of these may be important to consider in team design. For example, in teams involved in physical work, relevant physical abilities will be important to take into account. It is also important to take cognitive abilities into account when designing teams. General cognitive ability is important to many different types of teams. In general, smarter teams perform better because teamwork tends to be quite complex.[31] Team members not only have to be involved in several different aspects of the team's task, but they also have to learn how best to combine their individual efforts to accomplish team goals.[32]

Of course, not every member needs high levels of these physical or cognitive abilities. In fact, in tasks with an objectively verifiable best solution, the member who possesses the highest level of the ability relevant to the task will have the most influence on the effectiveness of the team. These types of tasks are called **disjunctive tasks**.[33] You may also recall situations in which it was crucial that everyone on the team possesses the relevant abilities. Consider what happens in a pit crew for a racing team: The car can't leave until all the tires are mounted, and so the length of the pit stop is determined by the physical abilities of the slowest member. Tasks like this, for which the team's performance depends on the abilities of the "weakest link," are called **conjunctive tasks**. Finally, there are **additive tasks**, for which the contributions resulting from the abilities of every member "add up" to determine team performance. For example, the amount of money raised for cancer research by volunteers going door-to-door is the is the sum of what each canvasser is able to collect on his or her own.

disjunctive tasks Tasks with an objectively verifiable best solution for which the member with the highest level of ability has the most influence on team effectiveness

conjunctive tasks Tasks for which the team's performance depends on the abilities of the team's weakest link

additive tasks Tasks for which the contributions from every member add up to determine team performance

MEMBER PERSONALITY Team members also possess a wide variety of personality traits which affect how teams function and perform as units. For example, team composition in terms of members' conscientiousness is important to teams.[34] After all, almost any team would benefit from having members who tend to be dependable and work hard to achieve team goals. What might be less obvious to you is the strong negative effect on the team of having even one member who is particularly low on conscientiousness.[35] Even if you and the other members of the team work harder to compensate for this person, it would be difficult for your team to perform as effectively as other teams in which all members are more interpersonally responsible and engaged in the team's work.

The agreeableness of team members is also an important consideration. One recent meta-analysis showed that, in team settings, the overall level of members' agreeableness may be even more important than conscientiousness.[36] Why? Because agreeable people tend to be

A task that can go only as quickly as the slowest team member, like a pit stop in a car race, is a conjunctive task.

more cooperative and trusting, tendencies that promote positive attitudes about the team and smooth interpersonal interactions. There is a caveat regarding agreeableness in teams, however. Because agreeable people tend to prefer harmony and cooperation over conflict and competition, they may be less apt to speak up and offer constructive criticisms that might help the team improve.[37] Thus, when composed of highly agreeable members, there is a chance that the team will behave in a way that enhances harmony at the expense of task accomplishment.[38]

People who are extraverted tend to perform more effectively in interpersonal contexts and are more positive and optimistic in general.[39] Therefore, it shouldn't surprise you to hear that having extraverted team members is generally beneficial to the social climate of the group, as well as to team effectiveness in the eyes of supervisors.[40] At the same time, however, research has shown that having too many members who are very high on extraversion can hurt the team. The reason for this can be attributed to extraverts' tendency to be assertive and dominant. As you would expect when there are too many members with these types of tendencies, power struggles and unproductive conflict occur with greater frequency.[41]

team diversity The degree to which team members are different from one another

MEMBER DIVERSITY Another aspect of team composition refers to the degree to which members are different from one another in terms of any attribute that might be used by someone as a basis of categorizing people. We refer to those differences as **team diversity**.[42] Trying to understand the effects of team diversity is somewhat difficult because there are so many different characteristics that may be used to categorize people. There are also several reasons diversity might influence team functioning and effectiveness, and some of these reasons seem contradictory.

value in diversity problem-solving approach A theory that supports team diversity because it provides a larger pool of knowledge and perspectives

The predominant theory that has been used to explain why diversity has positive effects is called the **value in diversity problem-solving approach**.[43] From this perspective, diversity in teams is beneficial because it provides for a larger pool of knowledge and perspectives from which a team can draw as it carries out its work. Teams that engage in work that is relatively complex and requires creativity benefit most from diversity, and research on teams that are diverse in terms of many different characteristics related to knowledge and perspectives—ethnicity, expertise, personality, attitudes—supports this idea.[44]

similarity-attraction approach A theory explaining that team diversity can be counterproductive because people tend to avoid interacting with others who are unlike them

A theory that has been used widely to explain why diversity may have detrimental effects on teams is called the **similarity-attraction approach**.[45] According to this perspective, people tend to be more attracted to others who are perceived as more similar. People also tend to avoid interacting with those who are perceived to be dissimilar to reduce the likelihood of having uncomfortable disagreements. Consistent with this perspective, research has shown

OB RESEARCH IN CANADA

Dr. Kevin Tasa received his PhD from the University of Toronto in 2002, and is currently an associate professor of organizational behaviour at the DeGroote School of Business at McMaster University. It is fitting to feature Dr. Tasa in this chapter given that his expertise is in decision making and motivational processes within team and negotiation contexts. Some of the questions that Dr. Tasa's work attempts to answer include: (1) What factors determine the level of confidence within a team? (2) Are teams more likely to interact with people or groups beyond the team's boundary when they have trust in top management? (3) What are the contextual and dispositional determinants of individual teamwork behaviour? and, (4) In negotiation situations, how do goals and self-efficacy influence a negotiator's ability to create value and avoid impasses? If you recall, some of these motivational concepts were discussed in Chapter 6. According to Dr. Tasa, these questions are important because "teams and groups are pervasive in modern organizations. By studying them, I hope to provide assistance to those who are interested in creating, supporting, and working in high functioning teams."

When Dr. Tasa is not working on his research, he teaches courses in managerial negotiations and organizational behaviour. In 2003, he was nominated for the Basu teaching award by the DeGroote MBA Association. Dr. Tasa is also an active member of the Academy of Management and the Administrative Sciences Association of Canada and is also a member of the editorial board of the *Journal of Organizational Behavior*.

Some of Dr. Tasa's favourite publications include:

"The Development of Collective Efficacy in Teams: A Multilevel and Longitudinal Perspective," by K. Tasa, S. Taggar, and G.H. Seijts, published in *Journal of Applied Psychology* (2007, volume 92, pp. 17–27).

"Collective Efficacy and Vigilant Problem Solving in Group Decision Making: A Non-linear Model," by K. Tasa, and G. Whyte, published in *Organizational Behavior and Human Decision Processes* (2005, volume 96, pp. 119–29).

"Goal Setting and Goal Orientation: An Integration of Two Different Yet Related Literatures," by G.H. Seijts, G.P. Latham, K. Tasa, and B.W. Latham, published in *Academy of Management Journal* (2004, volume 47, pp. 227–39).

that diversity on attributes such as cultural background, race, and attitudes are associated with communication problems and ultimately poor team effectiveness.[46]

So it appears that there are two different theories about diversity effects that are relevant to teams, and each has been supported in research. Which perspective is correct? As it turns out, one key to understanding the impact of team diversity requires that you consider both the general type of diversity and the length of time the team has been in existence.[47] **Surface-level diversity** refers to diversity regarding observable attributes such as race, ethnicity, sex, and age.[48] Although this type of diversity may have a negative impact on teams early in their existence because of similarity-attraction issues, those negative effects tend to disappear as members become more knowledgeable about one another. In essence, the stereotypes that members have about one another based on surface differences are replaced with knowledge regarding underlying characteristics that are more relevant to social and task interactions.[49]

surface-level diversity Diversity of observable attributes such as race, gender, ethnicity, and age

deep-level diversity Diversity of attributes that are inferred through observation or experience, such as one's values or personality

Surface-level diversity can sometimes create issues for teams as they begin their tasks, but such problems usually disappear over time.

Deep-level diversity, in contrast, refers to diversity with respect to attributes that are less easy to observe initially, but that can be inferred after more direct experience. Differences in attitudes, values, and personality are good examples of deep-level diversity.[50] In contrast to the effects of surface-level diversity, time appears to increase the negative effects of deep-level diversity on team functioning and effectiveness.[51] Over time, as team members learn about one another, differences that relate to underlying values and goals become increasingly apparent. Those differences can therefore create problems among team members that ultimately result in reduced effectiveness.

TEAM SIZE Two adages are relevant to team size: "the more the merrier" or "too many cooks spoil the pot." Which statement do you believe is true in terms of how many members to include on a team? The answer, according to the results of one recent meta-analysis, is that having a greater number of members is beneficial for management and project teams but not for teams engaged in production tasks.[52] Management and project teams engage in work that is complex and knowledge intensive, and these teams therefore benefit from the additional resources and expertise contributed by additional members.[53] In contrast, production teams tend to engage in routine tasks that are less complex. Having additional members beyond what is necessary to accomplish the work tends to result in unnecessary coordination and communication problems. Additional members may therefore be less productive because there is more socializing and they feel less accountable for team outcomes.[54]

SO WHAT CHARACTERISTICS CAN BE USED TO DESCRIBE TEAMS?

The preceding sections illustrate that there are a variety of characteristics that can be used to describe teams. As Figure 10-5 illustrates, teams can be described using taxonomies of team types. For example, teams can be described by categorizing them as a work team, a management team, a parallel team, a project team, or an action team. Teams can also be described using the nature of the team's interdependence with regards to the team's task, goals, and outcomes. Finally, teams can be described in terms of their composition.

10.4 What is team process, and how does it relate to process gain and process loss?

TEAM PROCESSES: WHY ARE SOME TEAMS MORE THAN THE SUM OF THEIR PARTS?

team process The different types of activities and interactions that occur within a team as the team works toward its goals

So far we have learned that a team consists of two or more people who work interdependently over some time period to accomplish common goals related to some task-oriented purpose.[55] **Team process** is a term that reflects the different types of activities and interactions that occur within teams that contribute to their ultimate end goals.[56] Team characteristics, like member diversity, task interdependence, team size, and so forth, affect team processes. Team processes, in turn, have a strong impact on team effectiveness. Some of the team processes we will be describing in this section are observable by the naked eye (e.g., seeing team members gathering information, building on one another's ideas, and

FIGURE 10-5 What Characteristics Can Be Used to Describe Teams?

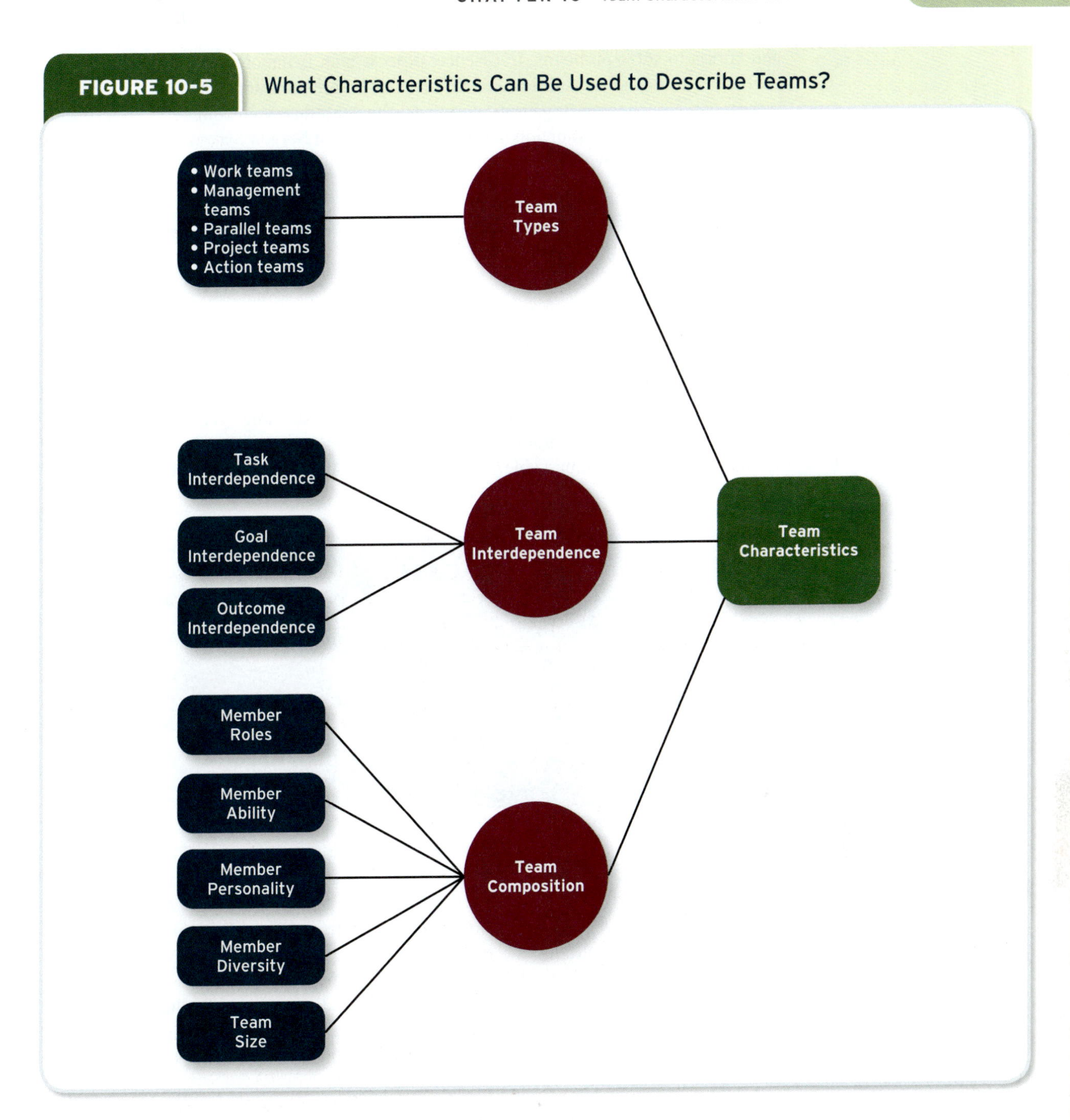

collaborating to solve some product problem), but others are invisible. For instance, an outside observer wouldn't be able to see the sense of cohesion felt by members who shared "mental models" that cause them to work together so efficiently. Thus, team processes include interactions among members that occur behaviourally, as well as the hard-to-see feelings and thoughts that coalesce as a consequence of member interactions.

Before getting started it is important to consider the concept of process gains and losses. **Process gain** is synonymous with "synergy" and is most critical in situations in which the complexity of the work is high or tasks require combinations of members' knowledge, skills,

process gain When team outcomes are greater than expected based on the capabilities of the individual members and efforts to solve problems. In essence, process gain is important because it results in useful resources and capabilities that did not exist before the team created them.[57] In other words, process gains mean getting more from the team than you would expect according to the capabilities of its individual members. Our **OB on Screen** feature illustrates vividly how a team that achieves process gain develops capabilities that help it achieve much more than what most people would rationally expect.

OB ON SCREEN

300

The world will know that free men stood against a tyrant, that few stood against many, and before this battle was over, that even a god-king can bleed.

With those words, King Leonidis (Gerard Butler) announces that his band of 300 Spartan soldiers is capable of pulling off a truly remarkable feat—standing against the Persian army led by Xerxes (Rodrigo Santoro) in *300* (Dir. Zack Snyder, Warner Brothers, 2006). Why would that feat be so remarkable? Because the Persian army includes well over 100,000 soldiers (and a few mutated elephants and rhinos).

The movie centres on the battle of Thermopylae, during which a small band of Spartans employed strategies and tactics that gave them the fighting capabilities of a much larger force. Those tactics represent process gain, because the army was able to achieve more than you'd expect if you simply added up the capabilities of the individual soldiers.

Beyond simply illustrating the concept of process gain, the movie illustrates the role that team processes play in achieving it. The clearest example occurs when the Persian Army "darkens the sky" by launching tens of thousands of arrows simultaneously. When this happens, the Spartans immediately get into a tight formation, lift their shields, and then link them together in a manner that creates a collective shield over the entire formation (think a giant turtle shell, and you get the picture).

Although the movie vividly illustrates the power of process gain, it also alludes to its fragility. For example, as long as each and every soldier executes his part of the process of creating the collective shield, the tactic is effective, and the Spartans can withstand repeated onslaughts of countless arrows. However, if just one Spartan soldier fails to raise his shield on time, it creates a breach in the formation that will only widen as the soldier is struck down (thereby exposing the soldier next to him). Thus, a single soldier's failure in the team process could lead to the destruction of the entire army. This fact was not lost on King Leonidis, who in one scene rejects a volunteer for the Spartan army because the volunteer, though a fierce fighter, could not lift his shield over his head.

Having described process gain, we now consider its polar opposite, **process loss**, that is, getting less from the team than you would expect based on the capabilities of its individual members. What factors conspire to create process loss? One factor is that in teams, members have to work to not only accomplish their own tasks but also coordinate their activities with the activities of their teammates.[58] Although this extra effort focused on integrating work is a necessary aspect of the team experience, it is called **coordination loss** because it consumes time and energy that could otherwise be devoted to task activity.[59] The second force that fosters process loss in team contexts is **motivational loss**, or the loss in team productivity that occurs when team members do not work as hard as they could.[60] Why does motivation loss occur in team contexts? One explanation is that it's often quite difficult to gauge exactly how much each team member contributes to the team. Uncertainty regarding "who contributes what" results in team members feeling less accountable for team outcomes. Those feelings of reduced accountability, in turn, cause members to exert less effort when working on team tasks than they would if they worked alone on those same tasks. This phenomenon is called **social loafing**,[61] and it can significantly hinder a team's effectiveness.[62]

process loss When team outcomes are less than expected based on the capabilities of the individual members

coordination loss Process loss due to the time and energy it takes to coordinate work activities with other team members

motivational loss Process loss due to team members' tendency to put forth less effort on team tasks than they could

social loafing A type of motivational loss resulting from members feeling less accountable for team outcomes relative to independent work that results in individually identifiable outcomes

TASKWORK PROCESSES

Having described process gains and process losses, it's time to describe the particular team processes that can help teams increase their synergy while reducing their inefficiency. One relevant category of team processes is **taskwork processes**, which are the activities of team members that relate directly to the accomplishment of team tasks. In a general sense, taskwork occurs anytime that team members interact with the tools or technologies that are used to complete their work. In this regard, taskwork is similar to the concept of task performance described in Chapter 2 on job performance. However, in the context of teams, especially those that engage in knowledge work, three types of taskwork processes are crucially important: creative behaviour, decision making, and boundary spanning. These three taskwork processes are shown in Figure 10-6.

taskwork processes The activities of team members that relate directly to the accomplishment of team tasks

CREATIVE BEHAVIOUR

When teams engage in creative behaviour, their activities are focused on generating novel and useful ideas and solutions.[63] The team environment is also uniquely suited to fostering creative behaviour. As a consequence, organizations like Pixar rely on teams to come together and combine their members' unique sets of knowledge and skill in a manner that results in novel and useful ideas. However, achieving such outcomes depends on much more than just putting a diverse mix of people together and letting them go at it. In fact, as we noted in the opening vignette, creative behaviour in teams can be fostered when members participate in a specific set of activities.

FIGURE 10-6 Taskwork Processes

Creative Behaviour
Decision Making
Boundary Spanning
Taskwork Processes

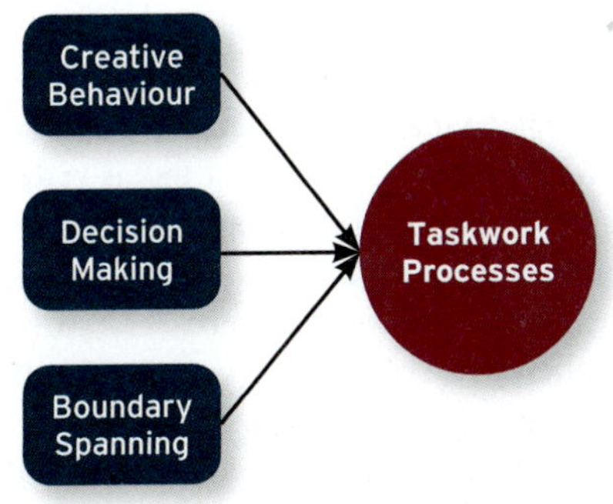

brainstorming A team process used to generate creative ideas

Perhaps the best known activity that teams use to foster creative behaviour is **brainstorming**. Generally speaking, brainstorming involves a face-to-face meeting of team members in which each offers as many ideas as possible about some focal problem or issue.[64] Most brainstorming sessions centre around the following rules:

1. Express all ideas that come to mind (no matter how strange).
2. Go for quantity of ideas rather than quality.
3. Don't criticize or evaluate the ideas of others.
4. Build on the ideas of others.

The theory is that if a team follows these rules, it will develop a large pool of ideas that it can use to address the issue at hand.[65] It may surprise you to learn then that such brainstorming sessions rarely work as well as intended. In fact, research suggests that team members would be better off coming up with ideas on their own, as individuals, before pooling those ideas and evaluating them to arrive at a solution.[66]

Why doesn't brainstorming work as well as individual idea generation? There appear to be at least three reasons.[67] First, there may be a tendency for people to social loaf in group brainstorming contexts. That is, members may not work as hard thinking up ideas as they would if they had to turn in an individually generated list with their name on it. Second, though the brainstorming rules explicitly forbid criticizing others' ideas, members may be hesitant to express ideas that seem silly or not well-thought-out. Third, brainstorming typically requires that members wait their turn to express their ideas. This waiting around consumes time that could otherwise be used by individuals to generate new ideas. Given the problems associated with brainstorming, why do organizations continue to use it? One reason is that the general idea of brainstorming is well-known, and common sense leads people to believe that it works as advertised. Another reason is that there are benefits of brainstorming beyond just generating ideas. For example, brainstorming builds morale and results in the sharing of knowledge that might otherwise be locked inside the minds of the individual team members.[68] Although this knowledge may not be useful for the particular problem that's being debated, it might be useful for issues that arise in the future.

DECISION MAKING In Chapter 8 on learning and decision making, we described how people use information and intuition to make specific decisions. In team contexts, however, decision making involves multiple members gathering and considering information that is relevant to their area of specialization, and then making recommendations to a team leader who is ultimately responsible for the final decision.[69] If you have ever watched the TV show *The Apprentice*, you should be able to understand this process quite clearly. The show typically begins with Donald Trump assigning two teams a fairly complex task. A member from each team then volunteers to be project leader, and this person assigns roles like marketing, logistics, and sales to the other team members. Throughout the project, members make suggestions and recommendations to the leader, who ultimately is responsible for making the decisions that determine the success of the project. Of course, project success is important because someone from the losing team—most often the project leader—gets to hear Trump say those famous words: "You're fired."

decision informity The degree to which team members possess adequate information about their own task responsibilities

staff validity The degree to which team members make good recommendations to the team leader

hierarchical sensitivity The degree to which the team leader effectively weighs the recommendations of the members

What factors account for a team's ability to make effective decisions? At least three factors appear to be involved.[70] The first factor is **decision informity**, which reflects whether members possess adequate information about their own task responsibilities. Project teams on *The Apprentice* often fail, for example, because the team member in charge of marketing does not gather information necessary to help the team understand the desires and needs of the client. The second factor is **staff validity**, which refers to the degree to which members make good recommendations to the leader. Team members can possess all the information needed to make a good recommendation but then fail to do so because of a lack of ability, insight, or good judgment. The third factor is **hierarchical sensitivity**,

Like many teams in the real world, the teams on the popular television show *The Apprentice* often struggle to make good decisions.

which reflects the degree to which the leader effectively weighs the recommendations of the members. Whom does the leader listen to, and whom does the leader ignore? Teams that make good decisions tend to have leaders that do a good job giving recommendations the weight they deserve.

The decision informity, staff validity, and hierarchical sensitivity concepts can be used to make specific recommendations for improving team decision making. For example, research shows that more experienced teams tend to make better decisions because they develop an understanding of the information that's needed and how to use it, and leaders develop an understanding of which members provide the best recommendations.[71] As another example, team decision making may be improved by giving members feedback about the three variables involved in the decision-making process.[72] For example, a team can improve its decision making if the members are told that they have to share and consider additional pieces of information before making recommendations to the leader. Although this recommendation may seem obvious, all too often teams only receive feedback about their final decision. In addition, there may be a benefit to separating the process of sharing information from the process of making recommendations and final decisions, at least in terms of how information is communicated among members.[73] Whereas teams tend to share more information when they meet face to face, leaders do a better job considering recommendations and making final decisions when they're away from the members. Once they're separated, they don't have to deal with pressure from members who may be more assertive or better at articulating and defending their positions.

BOUNDARY SPANNING The third type of taskwork process is **boundary spanning**, which involves activities with individuals and groups other than those who are considered part of the team. **Ambassador activities** refer to communications that are intended to protect the team, persuade others to support the team, or obtain important resources for the team. As you might have guessed from this description, members who engage in ambassador activities typically communicate with people who are higher up in the organization. For example, a member of a marketing team might meet with senior management to request an increase in the budget for an expanded television ad campaign. **Task coordinator activities** involve communications that are intended to coordinate task-related issues with people or groups in other functional areas. Continuing with the marketing team example,

boundary spanning Interactions among team members and individuals and groups who are not part of the team

ambassador activities Boundary-spanning activities that are intended to protect the team, persuade others to support the team, or obtain important resources for the team

task coordinator activities Boundary-spanning activities that are intended to coordinate task-related issues with people or groups in other functional areas

scout activities Boundary-spanning activities that are intended to obtain information about technology, competitors, or the broader marketplace

a member of the team might meet with someone from manufacturing to work out how a coupon might be integrated into the product packaging materials. Finally, **scout activities** refer to things team members do to obtain information about technology, competitors, or the broader marketplace. The marketing team member who meets with an engineer to seek information about new materials is engaging in scout activities. Taken together, research suggests that these boundary-spanning activities may be as important to determining team success as the processes that occur entirely within the team.[74]

10.5 What are taskwork and teamwork processes, and what are some examples of team activities that fall into these process categories?

TEAMWORK PROCESSES

Another category of team processes that helps teams increase their process gain while minimizing their process loss is teamwork processes. **Teamwork processes** refer to the interpersonal activities that facilitate the accomplishment of the team's work but do not directly involve task accomplishment itself.[75] You can think of teamwork processes as the behaviours that create the setting or context in which taskwork can be carried out. So what types of behaviours do teamwork processes involve? Figure 10-7 summarizes the set of teamwork processes discussed in this chapter.[76]

teamwork processes The interpersonal activities that promote the accomplishment of team tasks but do not involve task accomplishment itself

transition processes Teamwork processes, such as mission analysis and planning, that focus on preparation for future work in the team

action processes Teamwork processes, such as helping and coordination, that aid in the accomplishment of teamwork as the work is actually taking place

TRANSITION PROCESSES

Teamwork processes become important right when teams first begin their work. **Transition processes** are teamwork activities that focus on preparation for future work. For example, mission analysis involves an analysis of the team's task, the challenges that face the team, and the resources available for completing the team's work. Strategy formulation refers to the development of courses of action and contingency plans, and then adapting those plans in light of changes that occur in the team's environment. Finally, goal specification involves the development and prioritization of goals related to the team's mission and strategy. Each of these transition processes is relevant before the team actually begins to conduct the core aspects of its work. However, these transition processes also may be important between periods of work activity. For example, think about the adjustments made by a hockey team that is losing after the first period of play. The team could consider the strengths of its opponent and develop a new strategy intended to neutralize them. In this way, teams may switch from transition processes to taskwork, and then back to transition processes.

ACTION PROCESSES

Whereas transition processes are important before and between periods of taskwork, **action processes** are important as the taskwork is being accomplished. One type of action process involves monitoring progress toward goals. Teams that pay attention to goal-related information—perhaps by charting the team's performance relative to team goals—are typically in a good position to realize when they are "off-track" and need to make changes. Systems monitoring involves keeping track of things that the team needs to accomplish its work. A team that does not engage in systems monitoring may fail because it runs out of inventory, time, or other necessary resources. Helping behaviour involves members

FIGURE 10-7 Teamwork Processes

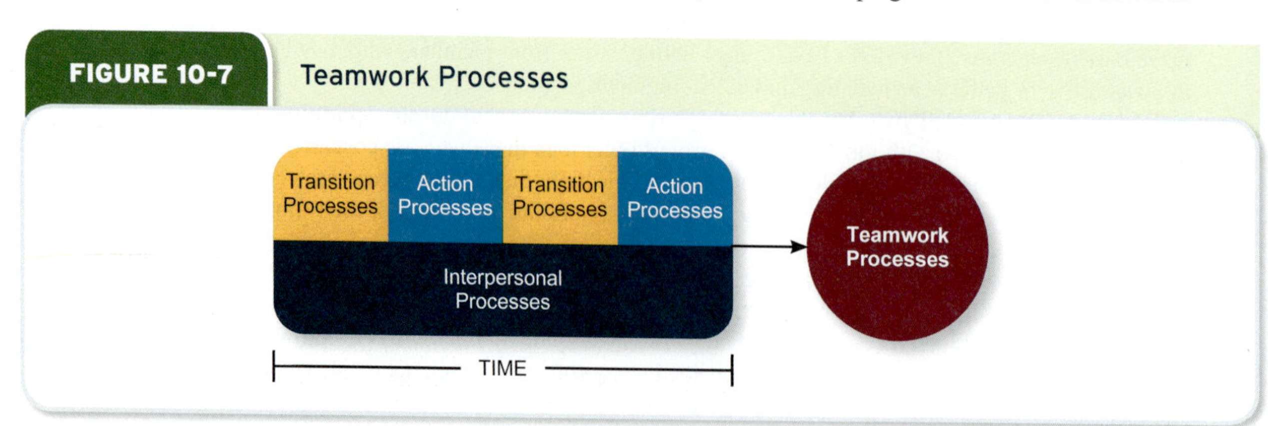

going out of their way to help or back up other team members. Team members can provide indirect help to their teammates in the form of feedback or coaching, as well as direct help in the form of assistance with members' tasks and responsibilities. Coordination refers to synchronizing team members' activities in a way that makes them mesh effectively and seamlessly. Poor coordination results in team members constantly having to wait on others for information or other resources necessary to do their part of the team's work.[77]

INTERPERSONAL PROCESSES The third category of teamwork processes is called **interpersonal processes**. The processes in this category are important before, during, or in between periods of taskwork, and each relates to the manner in which team members manage their relationships. The first type of interpersonal process is motivating and confidence building, which refers to things team members do or say that affect the degree to which members are motivated to work hard on the team's task. Expressions that create a sense of urgency and optimism are examples of communications that would fit in this category. Similarly, affect management involves activities that foster a sense of emotional balance and unity. If you've ever worked in a team in which members got short-tempered when facing pressure or blamed one another when there were problems, you have firsthand experience with poor affect management.

interpersonal processes Teamwork processes, such as motivating and confidence building, that focus on the management of relationships among team members

Another important interpersonal process is conflict management, which involves the activities that the team uses to manage conflicts that arise in the course of its work. Conflict tends to have a negative impact on a team, but the nature of this effect depends on the focus of the conflict as well as the manner in which the conflict is managed.[78] **Relationship conflict** refers to disagreements among team members in terms of interpersonal relationships or incompatibilities with respect to personal values or preferences. This type of conflict centres on issues that are not directly connected to the team's task. Relationship conflict is not only dissatisfying to most people, but it also tends to result in reduced team performance. **Task conflict**, in contrast, refers to disagreements among members about the team's task. In the abstract, this type of conflict can be beneficial to teams if it stimulates conversations that result in the development and expression of new ideas.[79] Research findings, however, indicate that task conflict tends to result in reduced team effectiveness unless two conditions are present.[80] First, members need to trust one another and be confident that they can express their opinions openly without fear of reprisals. Second, team members need to engage in effective conflict management processes.

relationship conflict Disagreements among team members with regard to interpersonal relationships or incompatibilities in personal values or preferences

task conflict Disagreements among members about the team's task

What does effective conflict management involve? First, when trying to manage conflict, it's important for members to stay focused on the team's mission. If members do this, they can rationally evaluate the relative merits of each position.[81] Second, any benefits of task conflict disappear if the level of the conflict gets too heated, if parties appear to be acting in self-interest rather than in the best interest of the team, or if there is high relationship conflict.[82] Third, to effectively manage task conflict, members need to discuss their positions openly and be willing to exchange information in a way that fosters collaborative problem solving.[83] If you've ever had an experience in an ongoing relationship in which you tried to avoid uncomfortable conflict by ignoring it, you probably already understand that this strategy only tends to make things worse in the end. Our **OB for Students** feature provides an example of how conflict management can have a significant impact on the effectiveness of student teams.

For task conflict to be productive, team members must feel free to express their opinions and know how to manage conflict effectively.

OB FOR STUDENTS

Conflict among team members about the team's task can result in improved team performance, for several reasons. Primarily, task conflict can foster the sharing of information that results in superior solutions to the problems that arise in the team's work. However, if you have experience working in student teams in your courses, you know that this type of conflict can have some really negative consequences—not the least of which is the discomfort it provokes and the huge waste of time that can ensue. To avoid this dissatisfying experience, many students try to avoid conflict in their team. One strategy that may be familiar to you involves splitting up parts of the assignment, performing the work independently, and finally slapping the parts together to produce the team outcome. Although a team might be able to complete assignments using this strategy, the end product tends not to be as good as it could be.

Might there be a better way for student teams to manage task conflict? One study of teams of undergraduate business students investigated the role that task conflict had on two important team outcomes—the grade on a semester-long team project and members' satisfaction with the team experience.[84] The results of the study indicated that the effects of task conflict on these two outcomes depended a lot on the way the team managed its conflict.

First, higher levels of task conflict tended to result in higher scores on team projects, but only for teams that approached the conflict proactively. Members of these teams openly discussed points of disagreement and tried to resolve their disagreements collaboratively. In contrast, teams tended to perform less well on team projects when the members managed high levels of task conflict in a more passive way. These teams tended to avoid openly expressing disagreements or ended potential disagreement prematurely by being overly accommodating of other members' positions.

Second, higher levels of task conflict resulted in higher levels of satisfaction with the team experience, but only for teams that managed conflict in an agreeable manner. Individuals in these teams expressed opposing positions in a relaxed and non-confrontational way. When members expressed their positions harshly or in a more emotional way, higher levels of task conflict tended to reduce member satisfaction.

TEAM STATES

team states Specific types of feelings and thoughts that coalesce in the minds of team members as a consequence of their experience working together

A third category of team processes that helps teams increase their process gain while minimizing their process loss is less visible to the naked eye. **Team states** refer to specific types of feelings and thoughts that coalesce in the minds of team members as a consequence of their experience working together. Although there are many types of team states that we could review in this chapter, Figure 10-8 summarizes the set of team states we discuss.

cohesion A team state that occurs when members of the team develop strong emotional bonds to other members of the team and to the team itself

groupthink Behaviours that support conformity and team harmony at the expense of other team priorities

COHESION For a number of different reasons, members of teams can develop strong emotional bonds to other members of their team and to the team itself. This emotional attachment, which is called **cohesion**,[85] tends to foster high levels of motivation and commitment to the team, and as a consequence, cohesiveness tends to promote higher levels of team performance.[86] But is a cohesive team necessarily a good team? According to researchers, the answer to this question is no. In highly cohesive teams, members may try to maintain harmony by striving toward consensus on issues without ever offering, seeking, or seriously considering alternative viewpoints and perspectives. This drive toward conformity at the expense of other team priorities is called **groupthink** and is thought to be associated with feelings of overconfidence about the team's capabilities.[87] In the end, groupthink has been blamed for decision-making fiascos. Famous examples include NASA's disastrous decision

FIGURE 10-8 Team States

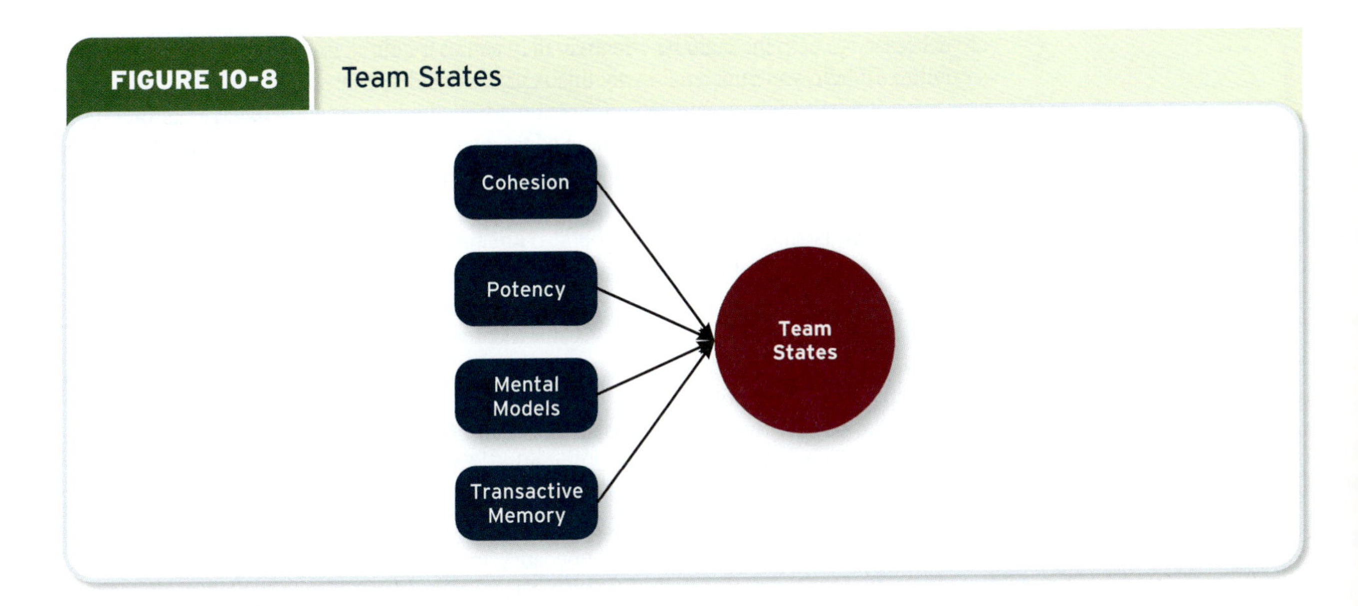

to launch the space shuttle *Challenger* in unusually cold weather,[88] and Enron's board of directors' decisions to ignore illegal accounting practices.[89]

So how do you leverage the benefits of cohesion without taking on the potential costs? One way is to acknowledge that cohesion can potentially have detrimental consequences. A good first step in this regard would be to assess the team's cohesion using a scale such as the one in our **OB Assessments** feature at the end of this chapter. A high score on this sort of assessment indicates the team may be vulnerable to groupthink. A second step in preventing problems associated with cohesion would be to formally institute the role of devil's advocate. The person filling this role would be responsible for evaluating and challenging prevailing points of view in a constructive manner and also bringing in fresh perspectives and ideas to the team. Although the devil's advocate role could be filled by an existing team member, it's also possible that the team could bring in an outsider to fill that role.

10.6 What are team states, and what are some examples of the states that fall into this process category?

POTENCY The second team state, **potency**, refers to the degree to which members believe that the team can be effective across a variety of situations and tasks.[90] When a team has high potency, members are confident that their team can perform well, and as a consequence, they focus more of their energy on achieving team goals. When a team has low potency, members are not as confident about their team, and so they begin to question the team's goals and one another. Ultimately, this reaction can result in members focusing their energies on activities that don't benefit the team. As a result, research studies have shown that potency has a strong positive impact on team performance.[91] So how does high potency develop in teams? Team members' confidence in their own capabilities, their trust in other members' capabilities, and feedback about past performance are all likely to play a role. Specifically, team potency is promoted in teams in which members are confident in themselves and their teammates and when the team has found success in the past.

potency A team state reflecting the degree of confidence among team members that the team can be effective across situations and tasks

MENTAL MODELS **Mental models** refer to the level of common understanding among team members with regard to important aspects of the team and its task.[92] A team may have shared mental models with respect to the capabilities that members bring to the team as well as the processes the team needs to use to be effective.[93] How can these two types of mental models foster team effectiveness? When team members share in their understanding of one another's capabilities, they're more likely to know where to go for the help they might need to complete their work. In addition, they should be able to anticipate when another member needs help to do his or her work. When members have a shared understanding of which processes

mental models The degree to which team members have a shared understanding of important aspects of the team and its task are necessary to help the team be effective, they can carry out these processes efficiently and smoothly. To help you understand why this is true, consider what would happen in a team of students who had different understandings about how the team should manage conflict. Few disagreements would get resolved if some of the members believed that direct confrontation was best, whereas others believed that avoidance was best.

transactive memory The degree to which team members' specialized knowledge is integrated into an effective system of memory for the team

TRANSACTIVE MEMORY Whereas mental models refer to the degree to which the knowledge is shared among members, **transactive memory** refers to how specialized knowledge is distributed among members in a manner that results in an effective system of memory for the team.[94] This concept takes into account the idea that not everyone on a team has to possess the same knowledge. Instead, team effectiveness requires that members understand when their own specialized knowledge is relevant to the team and how their knowledge should be combined with the knowledge of other members to accomplish team goals. If you've ever worked on a team that had effective transactive memory, you may have noticed that work got done very efficiently.[95] Everyone focused on his or her specialty and what he or she did best, members knew exactly where to go to get information when there were gaps in their knowledge, and the team produced synergistic results. Of course, transactive memory can also be fragile because the memory system depends on each and every member.[96] If someone is slow to respond to another member's request for information or forgets something important, the team's system of memory fails. Alternatively, if a member of the team leaves, you lose an important node in the memory system.

SO WHY ARE SOME TEAMS MORE THAN THE SUM OF THEIR PARTS?

As shown in Figure 10-9, teams become more than the sum of their parts if their team process achieves process gain rather than process loss. Teams can accomplish that goal by engaging in activities that are involved in taskwork processes, teamwork processes, and team states. Important taskwork processes include creative behaviour, decision making, and boundary spanning. Important teamwork processes include transition processes, action processes, and interpersonal processes. Finally, team states refer to variables such as cohesion, potency, mental models, and transactive memory. In contrast to the taskwork and teamwork processes, team states offer less visible and observable reasons why some teams possess an effective synergy whereas others seem quite inefficient.

HOW IMPORTANT ARE TEAM CHARACTERISTICS AND PROCESSES?

Having described team characteristics and processes, our questions now concern how each of these influence team performance and commitment (which is sometimes called team viability).

team viability Team commitment; the likelihood a team can work together effectively into the future

Team viability refers to the likelihood that the team can work together effectively into the future.[97] If the team experience is not satisfying, members may become disillusioned and focus their energy on activities away from the team. Although a team with low viability might be able to work together on short-term projects, over the long run, a team such as this is bound to have significant problems.[98] We first turn our attention to team characteristics.

Of course, it's difficult to summarize the relationship between team characteristics and team performance and commitment when there are so many characteristics that can be used to describe teams. Here we focus our discussion on the impact of task interdependence, because high task interdependence is one of the things that distinguishes true teams from mere groups of individuals. As Figure 10-10 shows, it turns out that the relationship

FIGURE 10-9 Why Are Some Teams More Than the Sum of Their Parts?

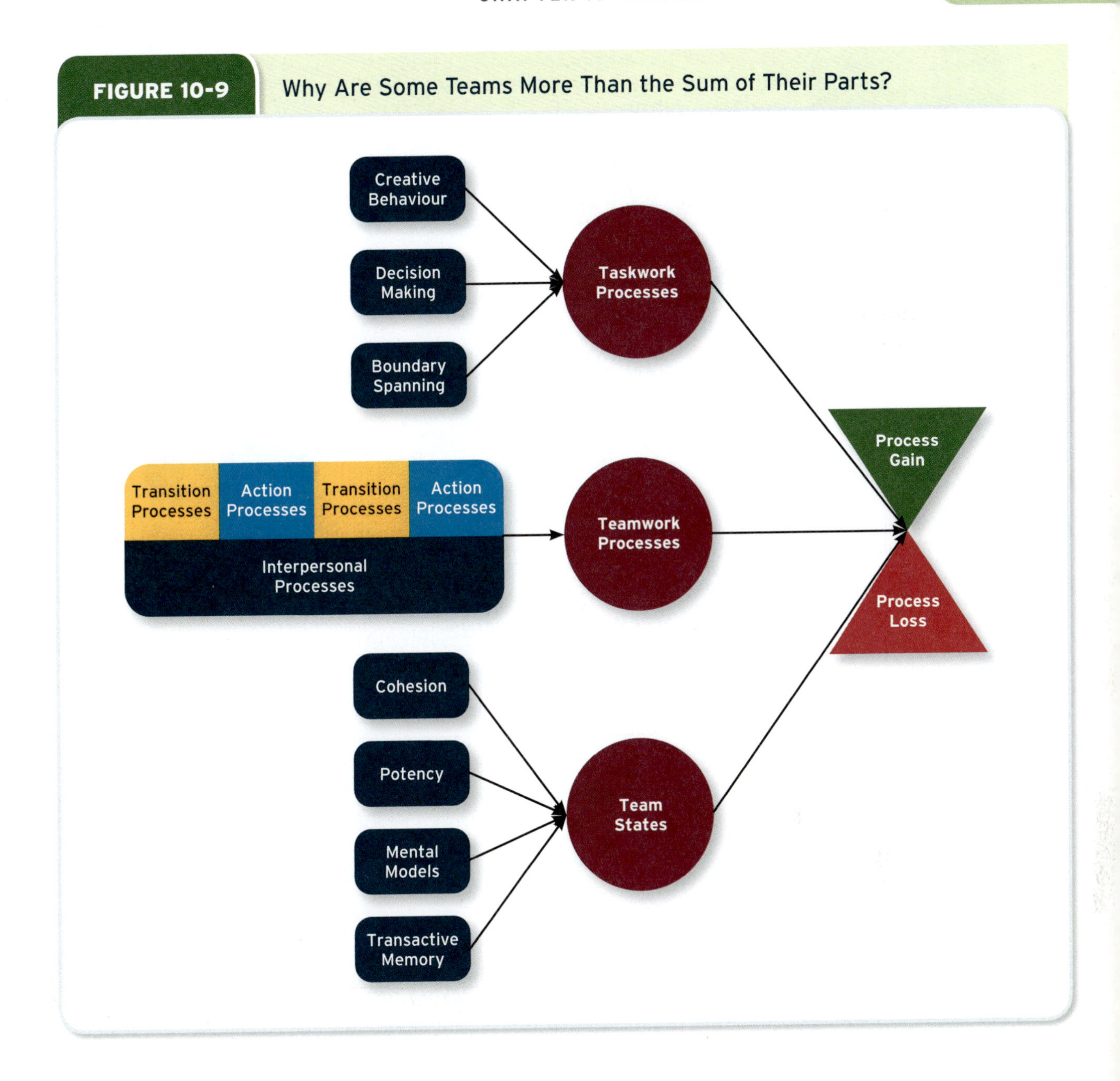

between task interdependence and team performance is moderately positive.[99] That is, task performance tends to be higher in teams in which members depend on one another and have to coordinate their activities rather than when members work more or less independently. It's important to mention that the relationship between task interdependence and team performance is significantly stronger in teams that are responsible for completing complex knowledge work rather than simple tasks. When work is more complex, interdependence is necessary because there is a need for members to interact and share resources and information. When work is simple, sharing information and resources is less necessary because members can do the work by themselves.

In the lower portion of Figure 10-10, you can see that the relationship between task interdependence and team commitment is weaker.[100] Teams with higher task interdependence

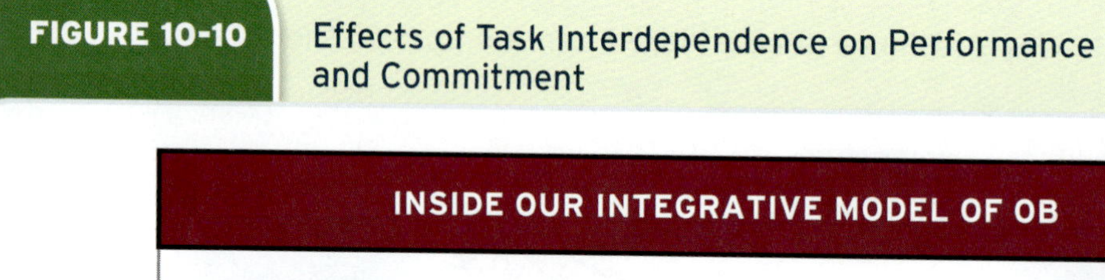

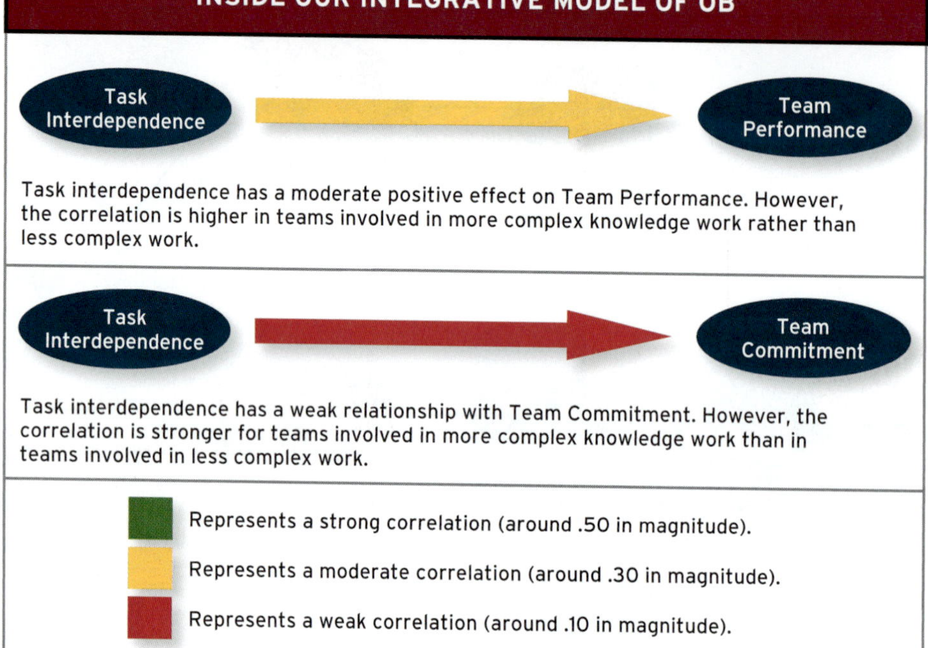

Sources: M.A. Campion, G.J. Medsker, and A.C. Higgs, "Relations Between Work Group Characteristics and Effectiveness: Implications for Designing Effective Work Groups," *Personnel Psychology* 46 (1993), pp. 823–49; M.A. Campion, E.M. Papper, and G.J. Medsker, "Relations Between Work Team Characteristics and Effectiveness: A Replication and Extension," *Personnel Psychology* 49 (1996), pp. 429–52; G.L. Stewart, "A Meta-Analytic Review of Relationships Between Team Design Features and Team Performance," *Journal of Management* 32 (2006), pp. 29–54.

10.7 How do team characteristics and processes influence team effectiveness?

have only a slightly higher probability of including members who are committed to their team's continued existence. As with the relationship with team performance, task interdependence has a stronger effect on viability for teams doing complex knowledge work. Apparently, sharing resources and information in a context in which it is unnecessary is dissatisfying to members and results in a team with reduced prospects of continued existence.

Do team processes affect performance and commitment? In Figure 10-11, we characterize the relationship between team processes and performance and commitment by focusing specifically on research involving teamwork processes. The figure therefore represents a summary of existing research on transition processes, action processes, and interpersonal processes.

Research conducted in a wide variety of team settings has shown that teamwork processes have a moderate positive relationship with team performance.[101] This same moderate positive relationship appears to hold true, regardless of whether the research examines transition processes, action processes, or interpersonal processes. Why might the relationships between these different types of processes and team performance be so similarly positive? Apparently, effectiveness with respect to a wide variety of interactions is needed to help teams achieve process gain and, in turn, perform effectively. The interpersonal activities

FIGURE 10-11 Effects of Teamwork Process on Performance and Commitment

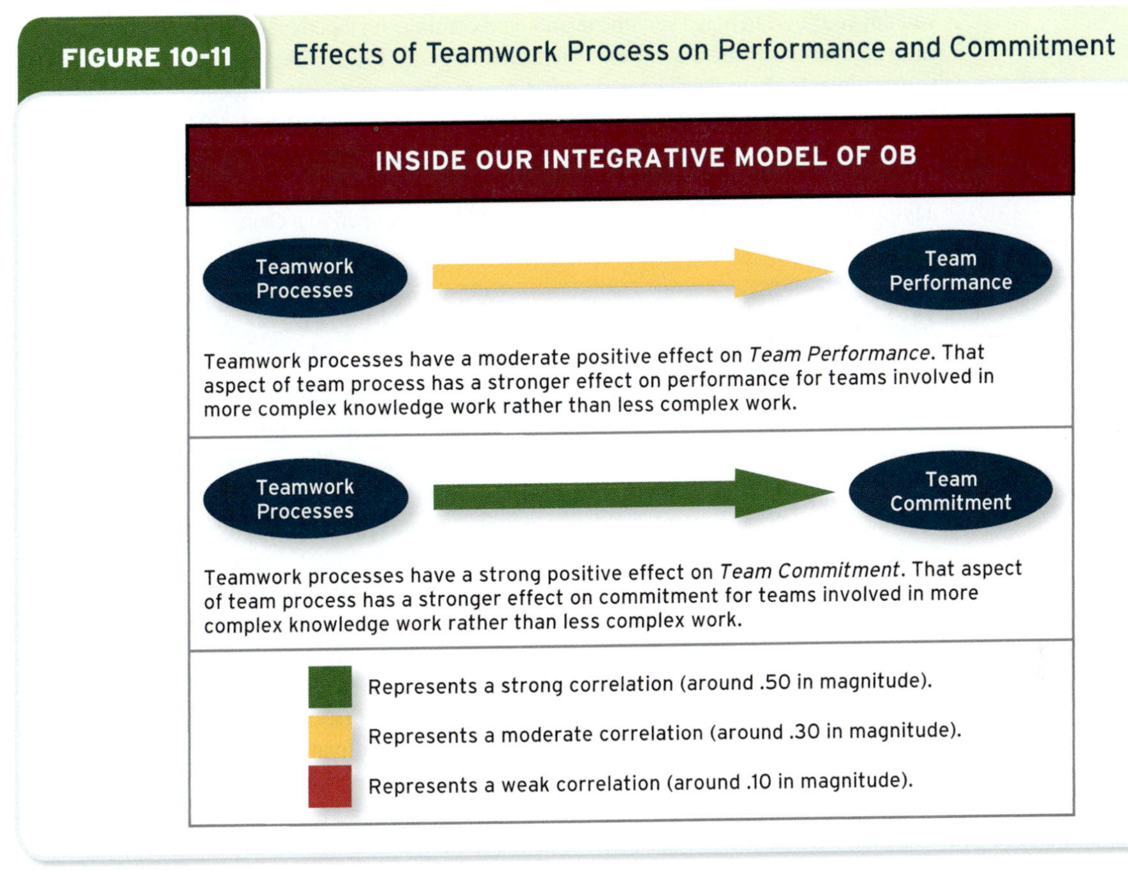

Source: J.A. LePine, R.F. Piccolo, C.L. Jackson, J.E. Mathieu, and J.R. Saul, "A Meta-Analysis of Team Process: Towards a Better Understanding of the Dimensional Structure and Relationships with Team Effectiveness Criteria," *Personnel Psychology* 61 (2008), pp. 273–307.

that prepare teams for future work appear to be just as important as those that help members integrate their taskwork and those that build team confidence and a positive team climate.

Research also indicates that teamwork processes have a strong positive relationship with team commitment.[102] In other words, teams that engage in effective teamwork processes tend to continue to exist together into the future. Why should teamwork and team commitment be so strongly related? One reason is that people tend to be satisfied in teams in which there are effective interpersonal interactions, and as a consequence, they go out of their way to do things that they believe will help the team stick together. Think about a team situation that you've been in when everyone shared the same goals for the team, work was coordinated smoothly, and everyone was positive, pleasant to be around, and willing to do their fair share of the work. If you've ever actually been in a situation like this—and we hope that you have—chances are that

A rare orchestra that performs without a conductor, the Orpheus Chamber Orchestra exhibits such teamwork and commitment that it has had a successful history of over 35 years of performance. While all members of the orchestra help refine the interpretation and execution of each work in its repertoire, they also select a concertmaster and principal players to lead each piece.

you did your best to make sure the team could continue on together. It's likely that you worked extra hard to make sure that the team achieved its goals. It's also likely that you expressed positive sentiments about the team and your desire for the team to remain together. Of course, just the opposite would be true in a team context in which members had different goals for the team, coordination was difficult and filled with emotional conflict, and everyone was pessimistic and disagreeable. Members of a team like this would not only find the situation dissatisfying but, also make it known that they would be very open to a change of scenery.

APPLICATION: TEAM COMPENSATION

Although all team characteristics have implications for managerial practices, outcome interdependence is particularly relevant for two reasons. First, outcome interdependence has obvious connections to compensation practices in organizations,[103] and most of us are interested in factors that determine how we get paid. If you work for an organization with compensation that has high outcome interdependence, a higher percentage of your pay will depend on how well your team does. If you work for an organization with compensation that has low outcome interdependence, a lower percentage of your pay will depend on how well your team does.

A second reason outcome interdependence is important to consider is that it presents managers with a tough dilemma. High outcome interdependence promotes higher levels of cooperation because members understand that they share the same fate—if the team wins, everyone wins, and if the team fails, everyone fails.[104] However at the same time, high outcome interdependence may result in reduced motivation, especially among higher performing members. The reason is that high performers may perceive that they are not paid in proportion to what they contributed to the team and that their teammates are taking advantage of this inequity for their own benefit.[105]

hybrid outcome interdependence When team members receive rewards based on both their individual performance and that of the team to which they belong

One solution to this dilemma has been to design team reward structures with **hybrid outcome interdependence**, which means that members receive rewards that are dependent on both their team's performance and how well they perform as individuals.[106] The majority of organizations that use teams use some sort of hybrid outcome interdependence, and the portion of pay based on team performance is probably lower than you would think. For example, the size of team-based pay in the goods and service sectors is around 10 percent to 12 percent of an employee's base pay.[107] It may also surprise you to learn that hybrid outcome interdependence, in and of itself, may not always be that effective. Research conducted at Xerox, for example, showed that service teams with hybrid outcome interdependence were less effective than service teams with very high or very low levels of outcome interdependence.[108]

An alternative approach to solving the dilemma of outcome interdependence has been to implement a level that matches the level of task interdependence. Members tend to be more productive in high task interdependence situations when there is also high outcome interdependence. Similarly, members prefer low task interdependent situations when there is low outcome interdependence.[109] To understand the power of aligning task and outcome interdependence, consider scenarios in which there is not a good match. For example, how would you react to a situation if you worked very closely with your teammates on a team project in one of your classes, and though your professor said the team's project was outstanding, she awarded an A to one of your team members, a B to another, and a C to you? Similarly, consider how you would react to a situation if you scored enough points for an A on your final exam, but your professor averaged everyone's grades together and gave all students a C. Chances are you wouldn't be happy with either scenario.

TAKEAWAYS

10.1 Teams are comprised of two or more people who work interdependently over some time period to accomplish common goals related to some task-oriented purpose. Teams are more interdependent and task focused than groups.

10.2 Teams can be interdependent in terms of the team task, goals, and outcomes. Each type of interdependence has important implications for team functioning and effectiveness.

10.3 Team composition refers to the characteristics of the members who work in the team. These characteristics include roles, ability, personality, and member diversity, as well as the number of team members. Depending on the team's task, it may be important to consider the average ability of the members, the ability of the most able, or the ability of the least able. The effect of diversity on the team depends on time and whether the diversity is surface-level or deep-level. The effects of surface-level diversity tend to diminish with time, whereas the effects of deep-level diversity tend to increase over time.

10.4 Team process reflects the different types of activities and interactions that occur within teams that contribute to their ultimate end goals. When teams have process gain, they become more than the sum of their parts through interactions that create synergy among members. When teams have process loss, they become less than the sum of their parts through interactions that create inefficiencies between members.

10.5 Taskwork processes are the activities of team members that relate directly to the accomplishment of team tasks. Taskwork processes include creative behaviour, decision making, and boundary spanning. Teamwork processes refer to the interpersonal activities that facilitate the accomplishment of the team's work but do not directly involve task accomplishment itself. Teamwork processes include transition processes, action processes, and interpersonal processes.

10.6 Team states refer to specific types of feelings and thoughts that coalesce in the minds of team members as a consequence of their experience working together. Team states include cohesion, potency, mental models, and transactive memory.

10.7 Task interdependence has a moderate positive relationship with team performance and a weak relationship with team commitment. Teamwork processes have a moderate positive relationship with team performance and a strong positive relationship with team commitment. Outcome interdependence has important effects on teams, which can be managed with compensation practices that take team performance into account.

KEY TERMS

- action processes *p. 268*
- action team *p. 253*
- additive tasks *p. 259*
- ambassador activities *p. 267*
- boundary spanning *p. 267*
- brainstorming *p. 266*
- cohesion *p. 270*
- comprehensive interdependence *p. 257*
- conjunctive tasks *p. 259*
- coordination loss *p. 265*
- decision informity *p. 266*
- deep-level diversity *p. 262*

- disjunctive tasks *p. 259*
- forming *p. 253*
- goal interdependence *p. 257*
- groupthink *p. 270*
- hierarchical sensitivity *p. 266*
- hybrid outcome interdependence *p. 276*
- individualistic roles *p. 259*
- interpersonal processes *p. 269*
- leader–staff team *p. 258*
- management team *p. 252*
- mental models *p. 271*
- motivational loss *p. 265*
- norming *p. 254*
- outcome interdependence *p. 258*
- parallel team *p. 252*
- performing *p. 255*
- pooled interdependence *p. 257*
- potency *p. 271*
- process gain *p. 263*
- process loss *p. 265*
- project team *p. 252*
- punctuated equilibrium *p. 255*
- reciprocal interdependence *p. 257*
- relationship conflict *p. 269*
- role *p. 258*
- scout activities *p. 268*
- sequential interdependence *p. 257*
- similarity-attraction approach *p. 260*
- social loafing *p. 265*
- staff validity *p. 266*
- storming *p. 254*
- surface-level diversity *p. 261*
- task conflict *p. 269*
- task coordinator activities *p. 267*
- task interdependence *p. 256*
- taskwork processes *p. 265*
- team *p. 251*
- team building roles *p. 259*
- team composition *p. 258*
- team diversity *p. 260*
- team process *p. 262*
- team states *p. 270*
- team task roles *p. 259*
- team viability *p. 272*
- teamwork processes *p. 268*
- transactive memory *p. 272*
- transition processes *p. 268*
- value in diversity problem-solving approach *p. 260*
- virtual team *p. 253*
- work team *p. 252*

DISCUSSION QUESTIONS

10.1 In which types of teams have you worked? Were these teams consistent with the team types discussed in this chapter, or were they a combination of types?

10.2 Think about your student teams. Which aspects of both models of team development apply the most and least to teams in this context?

10.3 How does diversity relate to the two types of effectiveness in your student teams?

10.4 Think of a team you worked in that performed poorly. Were any of the causes of the poor performance related to the forces that tend to create process loss? If so, which force was most particularly problematic? What steps, if any, did your team take to deal with the problem?

10.5 Think of a team you worked in that performed exceptionally well. What type of taskwork process did the team engage in? Which teamwork processes did the team seem to depend on most to produce the exceptional results?

10.6 Think about the team states described in this chapter. If you joined a new team, how long do you think it would take you to get a feel for those team states? Which states would you be able to gauge first? Which would take longer?

10.7 Describe boundary-spanning activities in the context of a student team. Have student teams you worked in done any of these effectively? Are there boundary-spanning activities that you could engage in that would promote your learning, grades, or overall satisfaction?

10.8 Which types of teamwork training would your student team benefit most from? What exactly would this training cover? What specific benefits would you expect? What would prevent a team from training itself on this material?

CASE • PIXAR

In a little over a decade, Pixar has managed to produce eight blockbuster hits. Its leadership in producing animated motion pictures results from an amalgamation of contributing factors, including the three individuals who lead this innovative organization. Ed Catmull, John Lasseter, and Steve Jobs represent the driving forces behind one of the most cohesive teams in the industry. Pixar consists of three departments: animators, the story department, and the art department. Cross-functional teams comprise members of each of these departments who are integrated together to facilitate communication and thus produce groundbreaking movies.

Companies rise and fall quickly within the moviemaking industry, yet Pixar has managed to pull all of its resources together to create something magical each and every time it produces a movie. How is this success achieved? Pixar has retained the majority of the employees who started with the company at its initiation, which has been a huge advantage. Employees within each team know the strengths and weaknesses of every other team member and therefore can collaborate effectively. Pixar also has established Pixar University to train new employees, which enables them to have an immediate impact after they complete their three-month training program. The success of Pixar thus is rooted in the team atmosphere created by the organization.

10.1 Are cross-functional teams a necessity for the continued success of Pixar? Explain.

10.2 What makes teams at Pixar different from other teams? Explain.

Sources: C. Conley, "Innovation All the Time," *BusinessWeek Online,* September 19, 2006; "Corporate Overview," www.pixar.com/companyinfo/about_us/overview.htm (June 26, 2007); S. Dowling, "How Pixar Changed Animation–for Good," October 10, 2003, http://newsvote.bbc.co.uk (June 26, 2007); E. Millard, "What Makes Pixar Run?" May 2004, www.technewsworld.com/story/34107.html (June 26, 2007).

EXERCISE • PAPER PLANE CORPORATION

The purpose of this exercise is to analyze the advantages and disadvantages of sequential versus pooled interdependence on a team production project. This exercise uses groups of six participants, so your instructor will either assign you to a group of six or ask you to create your own group of six. The exercise has the following steps.

1. Your professor will supply you with the materials you need to create your final product (as many paper airplanes as you can fold to quality standards in three five-minute rounds). Instructions for folding the paper airplanes and judging their quality are provided below. Before you start work on your airplanes, do the following:

a. As a group, select a team manager (who will supervise operations and get additional resources as needed) and a team inspector (who will judge the quality of the work on airplanes).

b. Familiarize yourself with how to make a paper airplane by folding one according to the instructions shown on the next page.

c. Be sure you are in a space where all of the team members can work comfortably.

d. To the extent possible, move away from other groups.

e. Familiarize yourself with the information about the Paper Plane Corporation.

2. Your group is the complete workforce for the Paper Plane Corporation. Established in 1943, Paper Plane has led the market in paper plane production. Presently under new management, the company is contracting to make aircraft for the Canadian Forces. You must determine the most efficient method for producing these aircraft. You must make your contract with the Air Force under the following conditions:
   a. The Canadian Forces will pay $200,000 per airplane.
   b. The aircraft must pass a strict inspection by a quality control manager.
   c. A penalty of $250,000 per airplane will be subtracted for failure to meet the production requirements.
   d. Labour and other overhead will be computed at $3,000,000.
   e. Cost of materials will be $30,000 per bid plane. If you bid for 10 but only make 8, you must pay the cost of materials for those you failed to make or those that did not pass inspection.

Plane Folding Instructions

3. In the first round of airplane manufacturing process, you have been asked to focus on individuality. Each Paper Plane worker should manufacture his or her own planes from start to finish. When each plane is finished, it should be put in a central location for quality inspection. When time is called, you will record your team profit on the Summary Sheet.
4. In the second round of manufacturing, you have been asked to give each worker a specific job. In other words, the manufacturing process will take place in an assembly-line fashion. When planes come off the assembly line, they will be given directly to the quality control manager for inspection. When time is called, you will record your team profit on the Summary Sheet.
5. In the final round of manufacturing, your team has been asked to devise a manufacturing process that will maximize both efficiency and effectiveness. You may do whatever you like in terms of creating paper airplanes. You will have the same amount of time that you did in the two previous rounds. When time is called, you will record your team profit on the Summary Sheet.
6. Class discussion (whether in groups or as a class) should centre on the following questions:
   a. Did pooled interdependence (Round 1) or sequential interdependence (Round 2) work better for your group in terms of the number of planes made correctly? Why do you think you got the result you did?
   b. How did you change your work structure in Round 3? Did the changes you implemented help you achieve better productivity? Why or why not?
   c. From your perspective, what are the advantages and disadvantages of pooled and/or sequential interdependence?

Sources: Adapted from J.M. Ivancevich, R. Konopaske, and M. Matteson, *Organizational Behavior and Management,* 7th ed. (Chicago: McGraw-Hill/Irwin, 2005). Original exercise by Louis Potheni in F. Luthans, *Organizational Behavior* (New York: McGraw-Hill, 1985), p. 555.

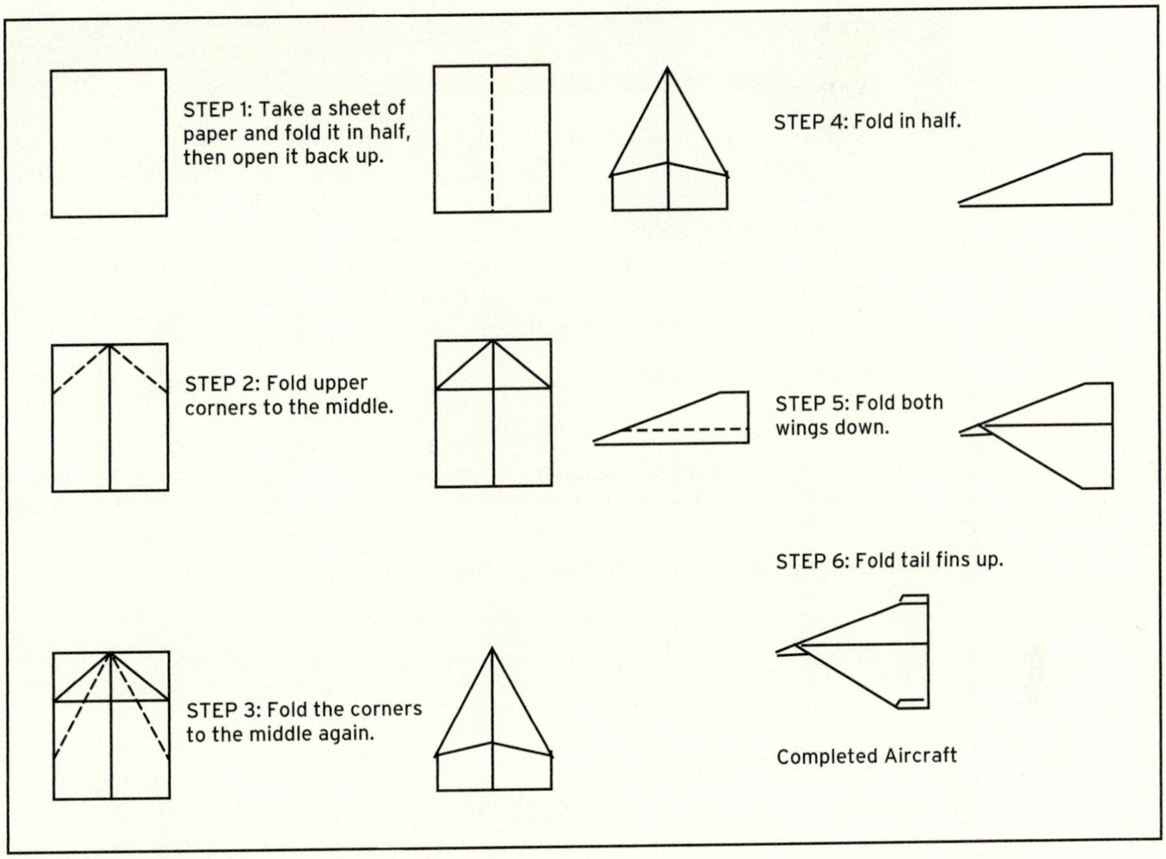

STEP 1: Take a sheet of paper and fold it in half, then open it back up.

STEP 2: Fold upper corners to the middle.

STEP 3: Fold the corners to the middle again.

STEP 4: Fold in half.

STEP 5: Fold both wings down.

STEP 6: Fold tail fins up.

Completed Aircraft

Summary Sheet

Round 1

Bid: ______ Aircraft @ $200,000 per aircraft = ____________________

Results: ______ Aircraft @ $200,000 per aircraft = ____________________

Subtract: $3,000,000 overhead + ______ × $30,000 cost of raw materials +
______ × $250,000 penalty for not completing a bid plane = ____________________

Profit: ____________________

Round 2

Bid: ______ Aircraft @ $200,000 per aircraft = ____________________

Results: ______ Aircraft @ $200,000 per aircraft = ____________________

Subtract: $3,000,000 overhead + ______ × $30,000 cost of raw materials +
______ × $250,000 penalty for not completing a bid plane = ____________________

Profit: ____________________

Round 3

Bid: ______ Aircraft @ $200,000 per aircraft = ____________________

Results: ______ Aircraft @ $200,000 per aircraft = ____________________

Subtract: $3,000,000 overhead + ______ × $30,000 cost of raw materials +
______ × $250,000 penalty for not completing a bid plane = ____________________

Profit: ____________________

OB ASSESSMENTS • COHESION

How cohesive is your team? This assessment is designed to measure cohesion—the strength of the emotional bonds that develop among members of a team. Think of your current student project team or an important team that you belong to in your job. Answer each question using the response scale provided. Then subtract your answers to the bold-faced questions from 8, with the difference being your new answers for those questions. For example, if your original answer for question 6 was "5", your new answer is "3" (8 − 5). Then sum up your answers for the eight questions.

1 STRONGLY DISAGREE	2 DISAGREE	3 SLIGHTLY DISAGREE	4 NEUTRAL	5 SLIGHTLY AGREE	6 AGREE	7 STRONGLY AGREE

1. **If given a chance, I would choose to leave my team to join another.** _______
2. The members of my team get along well together. _______
3. The members of my team will readily defend each other from criticism. _______
4. I feel that I am really a part of my team. _______
5. I look forward to being with the members of my team every day. _______
6. **I find that I generally do not get along with other members of my team.** _______
7. I enjoy belonging to this team because I am friends with many members. _______
8. The team to which I belong is a close one. _______

SCORING

If your scores sum up to 48 or above, you feel a strong bond to your team, suggesting that your team is cohesive. If your scores sum up to less than 48, you feel a weaker bond to your team, suggesting that your team is not as cohesive.

Source: G.H. Dobbins and S.J. Zacarro, "The Effects of Group Cohesion and Leader Behavior on Subordinate Satisfaction," *Group and Organization Management* 11 (1986), pp. 203–19. Copyright © 1986 Sage Publications Inc. Reproduced via permission from Copyright Clearance Center.

CONNECT—Available 24/7 with instant feedback so you can study when you want, how you want, and where you want. Take advantage of the Study Plan—an innovative tool that helps students customize their own learning experience. Students can diagnose their knowledge with pre- and post-tests, identify the areas where they need help, search contents of the entire learning package for content specific to the topic they're studying, and add these resources to their study plan. Visit **www.connectob.ca** to register—take practice quizzes, run interactive scenarios, and much more. Also visit the Student Online Learning Centre for additional study tools.

CHAPTER

11 Power and Influence

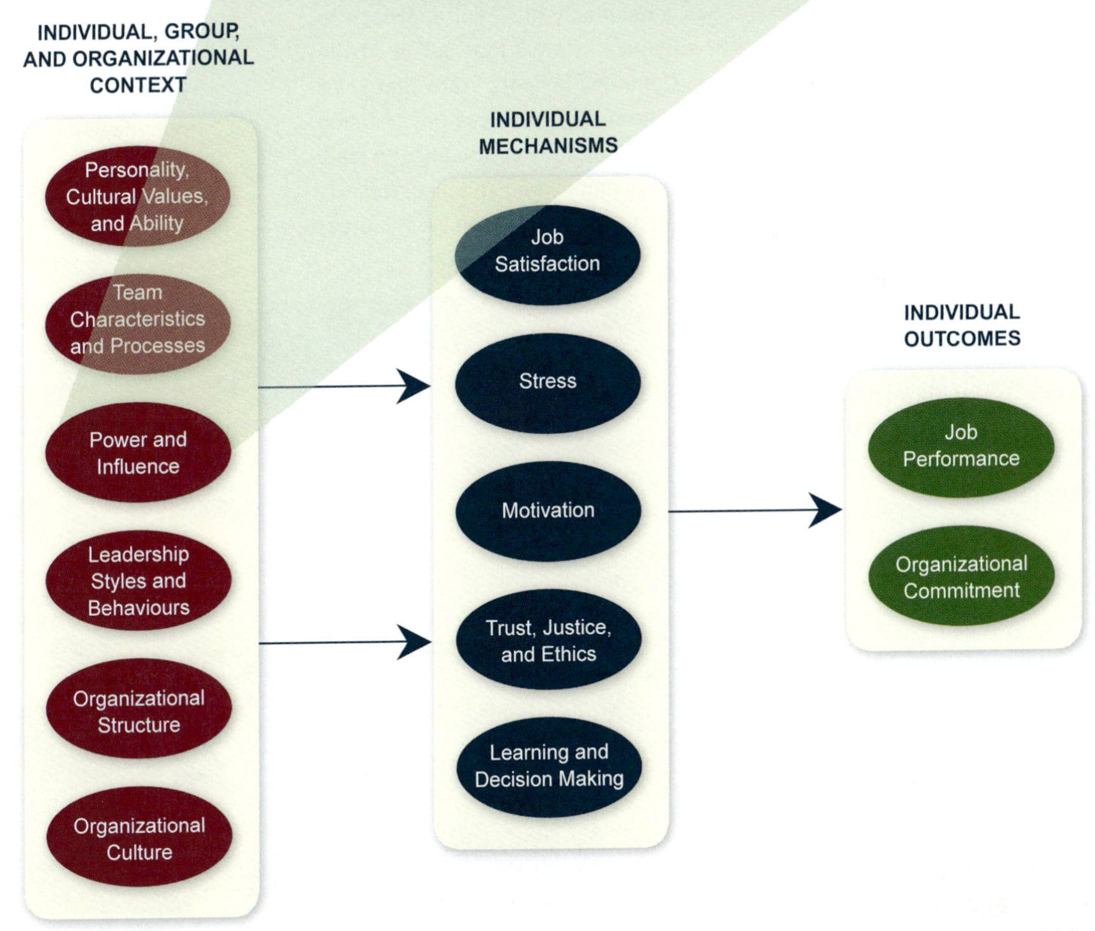

Learning Outcomes

After reading this chapter, you should be able to answer the following questions:

11.1 What is power?

11.2 What are the different types of power that people possess, and when can they use those types most effectively?

11.3 What behaviours do people exhibit when trying to influence others? Which of these behaviours is most effective?

11.4 What is organizational politics? When is political behaviour most likely to occur?

11.5 How do individuals use their power and influence to resolve conflicts in the workplace?

11.6 How do power and influence affect job performance and organizational commitment?

11.7 What are the ways in which individuals negotiate in the workplace?

HEWLETT-PACKARD

In 2005, when Mark Hurd took over the responsibilities as CEO of Hewlett-Packard (HP), the California-based maker of printers and computers, the company was in the midst of the largest crisis in its history. HP was faced with seemingly insurmountable financial and strategic obstacles, employed a completely demoralized workforce, and was saddled with a board of directors rife with political battles (the result of which was a highly publicized corporate spying scandal in 2006).[1] Doesn't that sound like a job everyone would want? Fortunately for HP, Mark Hurd was just the kind of leader it needed at the time. In the span of two years, Hurd, through the smart use of power and influence, turned HP around to take its place as the largest technology company in the world with $92 billion in sales.

Part of Hurd's mystique as a leader is that he is the complete opposite of the CEO who preceded him: Carleton ("Carly") Fiorina. Dismissed three months prior to Hurd's arrival by the board of directors, Fiorina was known as a very smooth, polished, out-in-front CEO who enjoyed the limelight. However, she was also more of a top-down, power-conscious leader who attempted to change a deeply instilled culture within HP by setting a vision that employees came to resent and resist.[2] In fact, Hurd became known as the "Un-Carly," as he took on the role of coach in opposition to Fiorina's quarterbacking.[3] He took a decidedly different approach to leadership and used his power and influence in ways that better fit the culture of the company he took over. Company insiders state that Hurd is "low-key, self-effacing, and a bread-and-butter business guy."[4] Using more personal forms of power and "softer" methods of influence to lead, Hurd was able to build commitment among employees and investors. He didn't walk in the door with set ideas and a grandiose vision for the organization. In fact, Hurd changed nothing when he first arrived—the CEO's office remained exactly the way it was when Fiorina left. Moreover, to this day, Hurd refuses to pose for pictures that will place him on the cover of magazines by himself.[5]

Mark Hurd, CEO of Hewlett-Packard, uses power very differently from his predecessor, Carly Fiorina. Hurd's low-key approach to leadership and his interpersonal strategies for building commitment among employees demonstrate just one way in which managers can lead. Fiorina's more assertive style was another; both have their advantages.

Hurd came to HP from NCR, the California-based manufacturer of retail and financial technology, a position that afforded him "outsider" status at HP. Hurd therefore made it a point to consult with his employees to formulate a plan for HP's future. He encouraged employees to contact him directly with ideas, receiving over 5,000 e-mails. Using his own areas of expertise and supplying rational arguments to help drive decisions, he generated a level of commitment among his workforce that hadn't been seen in years.[6] Hurd also made a point of visiting and collecting information from all areas of the company while maintaining an open mind. Explained Hurd, "I never like people to think I'm interviewing them. I either want to bring them towards the view I've formed, or better, yet, have them argue me down."[7]

Hurd also did his best to tear down some of the uncertainty that had created a highly charged political atmosphere within HP. He brought in outsiders to play key roles in the company, simplified reward systems, and refused to use outside consultants in an effort to minimize the coalitions that had formed within the organization.[8] He also refused to be unduly influenced by political behaviours, noting, "When someone gets a job, it better be clear what they did to get it. If the organization thinks it's because they gave good PowerPoint presentations or because they were nice to Hurd when he showed up, you've got a problem. But if it's because she built a strong team and delivered strong operating results, the next person may think, 'Well, that's what I ought to do.'"[9] Part of his ability to influence as a leader is the creation of common goals, as Hurd explained: "In the end, we've got to do what's best for the company, not what's best for its CEO or the management, or what's best for any single one person."[10]

POWER AND INFLUENCE

11.1 What is power?

power The ability to influence the behaviour of others and resist unwanted influence in return

As evidenced by the turnaround at Hewlett-Packard, knowing how to use power skillfully can make a huge difference. **Power** can be defined as the ability to influence the behaviour of others and resist unwanted influence in return.[11] Note that this definition gives us a couple of key points to think about. First, just because a person has the ability to influence others does not mean he or she will actually choose to do so. In fact, many times in organizations, the most powerful employees don't even realize how influential they could be! Second, in addition to influencing others, power can be seen as the ability to resist the influence attempts of others.[12] This resistance could come in the form of the simple voicing of a dissenting opinion, the refusal to perform a specific behaviour, or the organization of an opposing group of co-workers.[13] Sometimes leaders need to resist the influence of other leaders or higher-ups to do what's best for their own unit. Other times leaders need to resist the influence of their own employees to avoid being a "pushover" when employees try to go their own way. In this chapter we focus on how people acquire power and how power can be used to influence the actions of others.

WHY ARE SOME PEOPLE MORE POWERFUL THAN OTHERS?

What exactly comes to mind when you think of the term "power"? Does it raise a positive or negative image for you? Certainly it's easy to think of people who have used power for what we would consider good purposes, but it's just as easy to think of those who have used power for unethical or immoral purposes. For now, try not to focus on how people use power but instead on how they acquire that power.

ACQUIRING POWER

11.2 What are the different types of power that people possess, and when can they use those types most effectively?

Think about the people you currently work with or have worked with in the past, or think of students who are involved in many of the same activities you are. Do any of those people seem to have especially high levels of power, meaning that they have the ability to influence your behaviour? What is it that gives them that power? In some cases, their power may come from some formal position (e.g., supervisor, team leader, teaching assistant, resident advisor). However, sometimes the most powerful people we know lack any sort of formal authority. It turns out that power in organizations can come from a number of different sources. Specifically, there are five major types of power that can be grouped along two dimensions: organizational power and personal power.[14] These types of power are illustrated in Figure 11-1.

legitimate power A form of organizational power based on authority or position

ORGANIZATIONAL POWER The three types of organizational power derive primarily from a person's position within the organization. These types of power are considered to be more formal in nature.[15] **Legitimate power** is derived from a position of authority inside the organization and is sometimes referred to as "formal authority." People with legitimate power have some title—some term on an organizational chart or on their door that says, "Look, I'm supposed to have influence over you." Those with legitimate power have the understood right to ask others to do things that are considered within the scope of their authority. When a manager asks an employee to stay late to work on a project, work on one task instead of another, or work faster, they are exercising legitimate power. The higher up in an organization a person is, the more legitimate power he or she generally possesses. Since 1997, the Women's Executive Network (WXN), a Toronto-based networking and advocacy group, has identified the most powerful women in Canada. As shown in Table 11-1, all of these women possess legitimate power, in that the position they hold affords them the ability to influence others.[16]

FIGURE 11-1 Types of Power

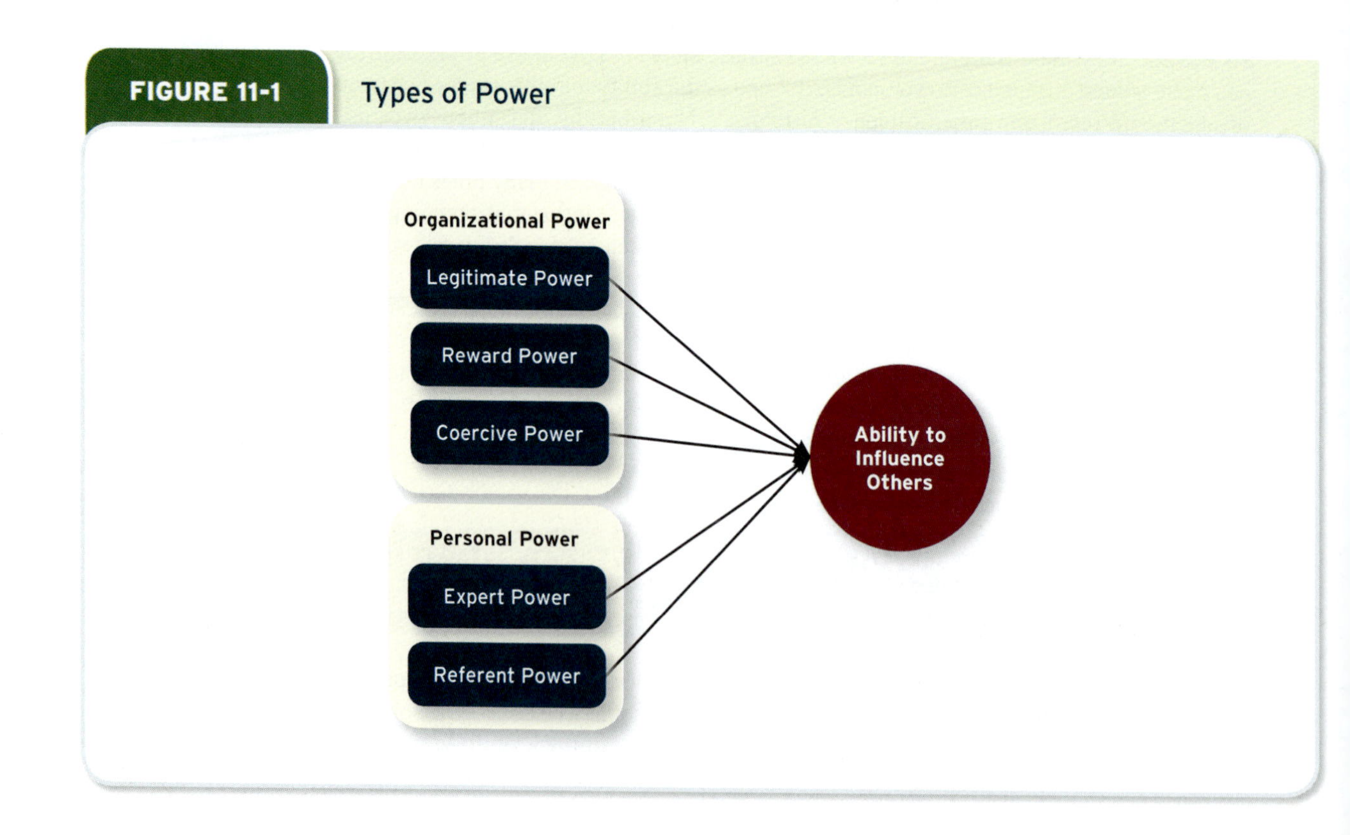

TABLE 11-1 Powerful Women in Canadian Business

NAME (ALPHABETICAL)	COMPANY	POSITION
Stacey Allerton Firth	Ford Motor Company of Canada	Vice President, Human Resources
Sonia Baxendale	Canadian Imperial Bank of Commerce	Senior Executive Vice President, CIBC Retail Markets & Wealth Management
Francine Blackburn	Royal Bank of Canada	Executive Vice President and Chief Internal Auditor
Sherri Brillon	EnCana	Executive Vice President, Strategic Planning & Portfolio Management
Shauneen Bruder	Royal Bank of Canada	Executive Vice President, Business & Commercial Banking
Teri Currie	Toronto Dominion Bank Financial Group	Executive Vice President, Human Resources
Heather Gavin	OPSEU Pension Trust	Chief Administration Officer and Plan Manager
Greta R. Cusworth	Sun Life Financial	Senior Vice President, International Initiatives
Laura Dottori-Attanasio	National Bank of Canada	Senior Vice President, Risk Management
Lauren Flaherty	Nortel Networks	Chief Marketing Officer
Françoise Guénette	ING Canada	Senior Vice President, Corporate and Legal Services, and Secretary
Sandra Hanington	Bank of Montreal	Executive Vice President, Customer Strategies & Marketing, Personal and Commercial
Wendy Hannam	Bank of Nova Scotia	Executive Vice President, Domestic Personal Banking & Distribution
Zabeen Hirji	Royal Bank of Canada	Executive Vice President & Chief Human Resources Officer
Victoria Hubbell	Hospitals of Ontario Pension Plan	Senior Vice President , Strategy and Stakeholder Relations
Stephani Kingsmill	Manulife Financial	Senior Vice President & GM, Real Estate
Christina Kramer	Canadian Imperial Bank of Commerce	Executive Vice President, Retail Markets
Louise Le Brun	Fédération des caisses Desjardins du Québec	Senior Vice President, Operations and Administration
Barbara Mason	Bank of Nova Scotia	Executive Vice President, Wealth Management

(continued on next page)

TABLE 11-1 Powerful Women in Canadian Business (continued)

NAME (ALPHABETICAL)	COMPANY	POSITION
Kim McKenzie	Bank of Nova Scotia	Executive Vice President, Information Technology & Solutions
Rosemarie McClean	Ontario Teachers' Pension Plan	Senior Vice President, Member Services
Karen Metrakos	Bank of Montreal	Executive Vice President, Operations
Wendy Millar	Bank of Montreal	Executive Vice President and Senior Risk Officer, Personal & Commercial/Private Client Group
Jacqueline Moss	Canadian Imperial Bank of Commerce	Executive Vice President, Human Resources
Patricia Nesbitt	Great-West Life Assurance Co.	Senior Vice President, Canadian Equities, GWL Investment Management Ltd.
Monica Norminton	Alberta Pensions Administration Corporation	Chief Executive Officer/President
Maarika Paul	Bell Canada	Senior Vice President Real Estate Development & Corporate Responsibility
Tracy Redies	HSBC Bank Canada	Executive Vice President, Personal Financial Services and Wealth Management
Carol Ring	Rogers Communications	President of Cable, Greater Toronto Area
Belinda Stronach	Magna International	Executive Vice Chairman
Tamara Vrooman	Vancity Credit Union	Chief Executive Officer

Source: "WXN 2008 Canada's Most Powerful Women: Top 100 Winners." Women's Executive Network. Retrieved April 16, 2009, at www.wxnetwork.com/files/WXN-2008_Top100Winners.pdf.

Legitimate power does have its limits, however. It doesn't generally give a person the right to ask employees to do something outside the scope of their jobs or roles within the organization. For example, if a manager asked an employee to wash her car or mow his lawn, it would likely be seen as an inappropriate request. As we'll see later in this chapter, there is a big difference between having legitimate power and using it effectively. When used ineffectively, legitimate power can be a very weak form of power. In our opening example, Mark Hurd and Carly Fiorina each had the same level of legitimate power inside Hewlett-Packard, but the ways in which they used that power were quite different. As a result, the perceptions of them as leaders and the reactions they received were also quite different.

reward power A form of organizational power based on the control of resources or benefits

The next two forms of organizational power are somewhat intertwined with legitimate power. **Reward power** exists when someone has control over the resources or rewards another person wants. For example, managers generally have control over raises, performance evaluations, awards, more desirable job assignments, and the resources an employee might require to perform a job effectively. Those with reward power have the ability to influence others if those being influenced believe they will get the rewards by behaving in a certain way. **Coercive power** exists when a person has control over punishments in an organization. Coercive power operates primarily on the principle of fear. It exists when one person believes that another has the ability to punish him or her and is willing to use that power. For example, a manager might have the right to fire, demote, suspend, or lower the pay of an employee. Sometimes the limitations of a manager to impose punishments are formally spelled out in an organization. However, in many instances, managers have a considerable amount of leeway in this regard. Coercive power is generally regarded as a poor form of power to use regularly, because it tends to result in negative feelings toward those that wield it.

"Hank, when you're finished firing this gentleman I have some rather unfortunate news for you as well."

Source:

coercive power A form of organizational power based on the ability to hand out punishment

PERSONAL POWER Of course, the women in Table 11-1 do not appear on that list just because they have some formal title that affords them the ability to reward and punish others. There's something else about them as people that provides them additional capabilities to influence others. Personal forms of power capture that "something else." **Expert power** is derived from a person's expertise, skill, or knowledge on which others depend. When people have a track record of high performance, the ability to solve problems, or specific knowledge that is necessary to accomplish tasks, they are more likely to be able to influence other people who need that expertise. Consider a lone programmer who knows how to operate a piece of antiquated software, a machinist who was recently trained to operate a new piece of equipment, or the only engineer who has experience working on a specific type of project. All these individuals will have a degree of expert power because of what they individually bring to the organization. **Referent power** exists when others have a desire to identify and be associated with a person. This desire is generally derived from an affection, admiration, or loyalty toward a specific individual.[17] Although our focus is on individuals within organizations, there are many examples of Canadians who seem to possess high levels of referent power. General Rick Hillier, Avril Lavigne, and Sidney Crosby all possess referent power to some degree because others want to emulate them. For more discussion of referent power (and legitimate power), see our **OB on Screen** feature.

expert power A form of organizational power based on expertise or knowledge

referent power A form of organizational power based on the attractiveness and charisma of the leader

Of course, it's possible for a person to possess all of the forms of power at the same time. In fact, the most powerful people—like those in Table 11-1—have bases of power that include all five dimensions. From an employee's perspective, it's sometimes difficult to gauge what form of power is most important. Why exactly do you do what your boss asks you to do? Is it because the boss has the formal right to provide direction, because the boss controls your evaluations, or because you admire and like the boss? Many times, we don't know exactly what type of power a person has until they attempt to use it. Generally speaking, the personal forms of power are more strongly related to organizational commitment and job performance than are the organizational forms. If you think about the authorities for whom you worked the hardest, they probably possessed some form of expertise and charisma, rather than just an ability to reward and punish. Some useful guidelines for wielding each of the forms of power can be found in Table 11-2.

OB ON SCREEN

THE QUEEN

Queen Elizabeth: *I rather envy you being able to vote. Not the actual ticking of the box, although, I suppose, it would be nice to experience that ONCE. But the sheer joy of being partial.*

Artist: Yes. One forgets that as Sovereign, you are not entitled to vote.

Queen Elizabeth: *No.*

Artist: Still, you won't catch me feeling sorry for you. You might not be allowed to vote, Ma'am. But it IS your Government.

Queen Elizabeth: *Yes . . . I suppose that is some consolation.*

These words at the very beginning of the movie help explicate the seemingly contradictory and confusing forms of power that permeate *The Queen* (Dir. Stephen Frears, Miramax Films, 2006). The movie itself is primarily a story about the week during which Diana, Princess of Wales, was killed in a Paris car crash. Queen Elizabeth II (Helen Mirren) is initially adamant that the princess's funeral will be a private affair and not a public one. What the Queen incorrectly estimates is the affection the public had toward Diana and the outpouring of public support she would receive.

The movie is a stark portrayal of the reactions some people have toward various forms of power. The Queen clearly perceives herself as having a great deal of legitimate power due to her royal position. However, in a real sense, her duties and responsibilities are largely ceremonial, as she has no real formal authority to do anything. What she slowly must come to grips with is that people's responses to legitimate power aren't quite the same as those to more personal forms of power.

Tony Blair (Michael Sheen) correctly estimates that the public has much larger affections toward Diana than the Queen perceives and attempts to counsel her to that effect. He goes so far as to dub Diana the "people's princess." The Queen is baffled throughout the movie at the outpouring of support for the princess, because she never realized the extreme level of referent power that Diana possessed. Diana's entry into the royal family through marriage, her high-profile support of charitable causes, and her charisma caused the larger public to identify with and develop an emotional attachment to her to a degree they never could with the Queen.

TABLE 11-2 Guidelines for Using Power

TYPE OF POWER	GUIDELINES FOR USE
Legitimate	Make polite, clear requests. Explain the reason for the request. Don't exceed your scope or authority. Follow up to verify compliance. Insist on compliance if appropriate.
Reward	Offer the types of rewards people desire. Offer rewards that are fair and ethical. Don't promise more than you can deliver. Explain the criteria for giving rewards and keep it simple. Provide rewards as promised if requirements are met. Don't use rewards in a manipulative fashion.
Coercive	Explain rules and requirements and ensure people understand the serious consequences of violations. Respond to infractions promptly and without favouritism. Investigate to get facts before following through. Provide ample warnings. Use punishments that are legitimate, fair, and commensurate with the seriousness of non-compliance.
Expert	Explain the reasons for a request and why it's important. Provide evidence that a proposal will be successful. Don't make rash, careless, or inconsistent statements. Don't exaggerate or misrepresent the facts. Listen seriously to the person's concerns and suggestions. Act confidently and decisively in a crisis.
Referent	Show acceptance and positive regard. Act supportive and helpful. Use sincere forms of ingratiation. Defend and back up people when appropriate. Do unsolicited favours. Make self-sacrifices to show concern. Keep promises.

Source: Adapted and partially reprinted G. Yukl, *Leadership in Organization,* 5th ed. (Upper Saddle River, NJ: Prentice Hall, 2002).

CONTINGENCY FACTORS There are certain situations in organizations that are likely to increase or decrease the degree to which people can use their power to influence others. Most of these situations revolve around the idea that the more dependent an individual or group is on you, the more influential you become to them. A person can have high levels of expert and referent power, but if he or she works alone and performs tasks that nobody sees, the ability to influence others is greatly reduced. That being said, there are four factors that have an effect on the strength of a person's ability to use power to influence others.[18] These factors are summarized in Table 11-3. **Substitutability** is the degree to which people have alternatives in accessing resources. Individuals that are able to control resources to which no one else has access can use their power to gain greater influence. **Discretion** is the degree to which individuals have the right to make decisions on their own.

substitutability The degree to which people have alternatives in accessing the resources that a leader controls

discretion The degree to which managers have the right to make decisions on their own

TABLE 11-3 The Contingencies of Power

CONTINGENCY	AN INDIVIDUAL'S ABILITY TO INFLUENCE OTHERS INCREASES WHEN . . .
Substitutability	There are no substitutes for the rewards or resources the individual controls.
Centrality	The individual's role is important and interdependent with others in the organization.
Discretion	The individual has the freedom to make his or her own decisions without being restrained by organizational rules.
Visibility	Others know about this individual and the resources he or she can provide.

centrality How important a person's job is and how many people depend on that person to accomplish their tasks

visibility How aware others are of a leader and the resources that leader can provide

For example, if your boss is forced to follow organizational policies and rules, her ability to influence your actions is reduced. **Centrality** represents how important a person's job is and how many people depend on that person to accomplish their tasks. An individual who performs critical tasks and interacts with others regularly has a greater ability to use his or her power to influence others. **Visibility** is how aware others are of an individual's power and position. For instance, if everyone knows that an individual has a certain level of power, the ability to use that power to influence others is likely to be high.

Ken Loughridge, an information technology manager working for MWH Global—an environmental and engineering consulting firm based in England—took these ideas to heart when he changed jobs within the organization. He used a survey the company had done to map out the "social network" within his organization. He used that network map to tell where his employees went for information, who possessed certain types of expertise, and who offered the most help to his employees. He then went to each of the most well-connected individuals so that he could meet them face-to-face. In a sense, he was seeking out and networking with the individuals in his organization that were likely to have the most power.[19] Companies are increasingly using such networking maps to understand the power structures in their organizations.

11.3 What behaviours do people exhibit when trying to influence others? Which of these behaviours is most effective?

USING INFLUENCE

Up until now, we have discussed the types of power that people possess and when their opportunities to use that power will grow or diminish. Now we turn to the specific strategies that people use to translate their power into actual influence.

influence The use of behaviours to cause behavioural or attitudinal changes in others

Recall that having power increases our *ability* to influence behaviour. It does not mean that we will use or exert that power. **Influence** is the use of an actual behaviour that causes behavioural or attitudinal changes in others.[20] There are two important aspects of influence to keep in mind. First, influence can be seen as directional. It most frequently occurs downward (managers influencing employees) but can also be lateral (peers influencing peers) or upward (employees influencing managers). Second, influence is all relative. The absolute power of the "influencer" and "influencee" isn't as important as the disparity between them.[21]

rational persuasion The use of logical arguments and hard facts to show someone that a request is worthwhile

INFLUENCE TACTICS Individuals depend on a number of tactics to cause behavioural or attitudinal changes in others. In fact, there are 10 types of influence tactics that are commonly used.[22] These tactics and their general levels of effectiveness are illustrated in Figure 11-2. The four most effective tactics have been shown to be rational persuasion, inspirational appeals, consultation, and collaboration. **Rational persuasion** is the use of logical arguments and hard facts to show the target that the request is a worthwhile one. Research shows that rational persuasion is most effective when it helps show that the proposal is important and feasible.[23] Rational persuasion is particularly important because it's the only tactic that is consistently successful in the case of upward influence.[24] Returning to our Hewlett-Packard example, Mark Hurd suggests that he uses this tactic most often to influence others and that it is the tactic that most often influences him when used by employees.[25] An **inspirational appeal** is a tactic designed to appeal to the target's values and ideals, thereby creating an emotional or attitudinal reaction. To use this tactic effectively, it is important to have insight into what kinds of things are important to the target. **Consultation** occurs when the target is allowed to participate in deciding how to carry out or implement a request. This tactic increases commitment from the target, who now has a stake in seeing that his or her opinions were right. A leader may use **collaboration** by attempting to make it easier for the target to complete the request. Collaboration could involve the leader helping complete the task, providing required resources, or removing obstacles that make task completion difficult.[26]

Four other influence tactics are sometimes effective and sometimes not. **Ingratiation** is the use of favours, compliments, or friendly behaviour to make the target feel better about the influencer. You might more commonly hear this referred to as "sucking up," especially when used in an upward influence sense. Ingratiation has been shown to be more effective when used as a long-term strategy and not nearly as effective when used immediately prior to making an influence attempt.[27] **Personal appeals** are when the requestor asks for something based on personal friendship or loyalty. The stronger the friendship, the more successful the attempt is likely to be. As described in our **OB Internationally** feature, there are cultural differences when it comes to this kind of an appeal, as there are with other influence attempts. An **exchange tactic** is used when the requestor offers a reward or resource to the target in return for performing a request. This type of request requires that the requestor have something of value to offer.[28] Finally, **apprising** occurs when the requestor clearly explains why performing the request will benefit the target personally. It differs from rational persuasion in that it focuses solely on the benefit to the target as opposed to simple logic or benefits to the group or organization. It differs from exchange in that the benefit is not necessarily something that the requestor gives to the target but rather something that results from the action.[29]

inspirational appeal An influence tactic designed to appeal to one's values and ideals, thereby creating an emotional or attitudinal reaction

consultation An influence tactic whereby the target is allowed to participate in deciding how to carry out or implement a request

collaboration An influence tactic whereby the leader makes it easier for the target to complete a request by offering to work with and help the target

ingratiation The use of favours, compliments, or friendly behaviour to make the target feel better about the influencer

personal appeals An influence tactic in which the requestor asks for something based on personal friendship or loyalty

exchange tactic An influence tactic in which the requestor offers a reward in return for performing a request

apprising An influence tactic in which the requestor clearly explains why performing the request will benefit the target personally

FIGURE 11-2 Influence Tactics and Their Effectiveness

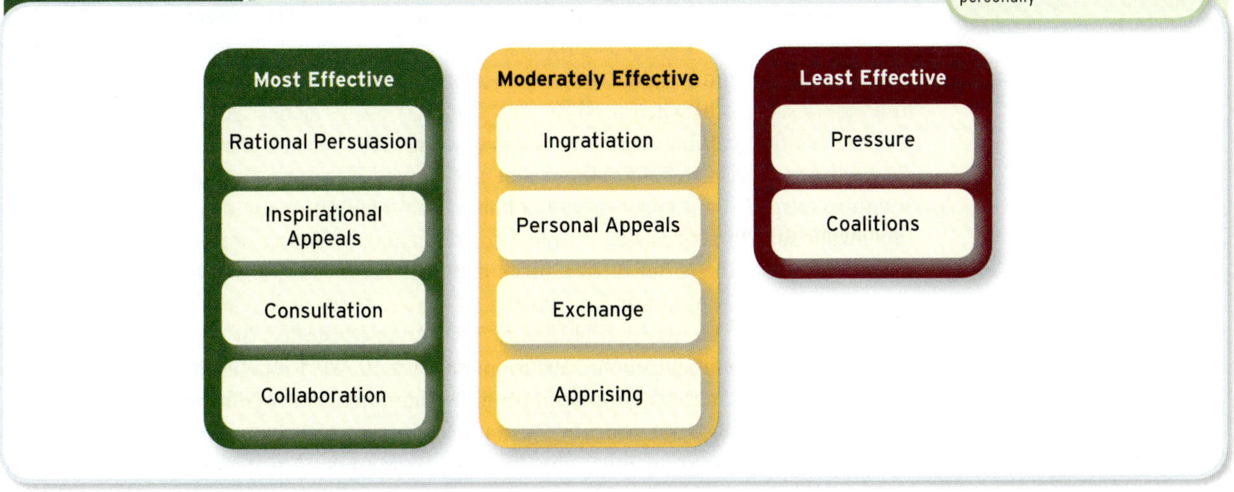

Most Effective	Moderately Effective	Least Effective
Rational Persuasion	Ingratiation	Pressure
Inspirational Appeals	Personal Appeals	Coalitions
Consultation	Exchange	
Collaboration	Apprising	

OB INTERNATIONALLY

When Google hired Kai-Fu Lee to be vice president of engineering and president of Google Greater China, with a compensation package worth more than $10 million, the company was counting on his continued ability to use the same skills that allowed him to be a huge success at Microsoft. What was it that Lee possessed that made him so worthwhile? Lee argues that it was his understanding of *guanxi* (pronounced gwan-she).[30] In the Chinese culture, guanxi (literally translated "relationships") is the ability to influence decisions by creating obligations between parties based on personal relationships.

Guanxi represents a relationship between two people that involves both sentiment and obligation.[31] Individuals with high levels of guanxi tend to be tied together on the basis of shared institutions, such as kinship, places of birth, schools attended, and past working relationships.[32] Although such shared institutions might "get someone in the door" in the United States, in China, they become a higher form of obligation. Influence through guanxi just happens—it's an unspoken obligation that must be followed through on.[33] It is, in a sense, a blending of both formal and personal relationships that exists at a different level than in the United States. There is no such thing as a "business-only" relationship, and the expectation is simply that if you take, you must also give back.[34]

American managers who go to work overseas must be conscious of these different but influential relationships. In addition to understanding the power of guanxi, evidence suggests that Chinese managers from different areas of the country (e.g., Hong Kong, Taiwan, mainland China) have different beliefs when it comes to which influence tactics are the most effective.[35] If anything, it goes to show that managers need to be acutely aware of both general and more specific cultural differences when trying to influence others in China.

pressure An influence tactic in which the requestor attempts to use coercive power through threats and demands

coalition An influence tactic in which the influencer enlists other people to help influence the target

The two tactics that have been shown to be least effective and could result in resistance from the target are pressure and coalitions. Of course this does not mean that they aren't used or can't be effective at times. **Pressure** is the use of coercive power through threats and demands. As we have discussed previously, coercion is a poor way to influence others and may only bring benefits over the short term. The last tactic is the formation of coalitions. **Coalitions** occur when the influencer enlists other people to help influence the target. These people could be peers, subordinates, or one of the target's superiors. Coalitions are generally used in combination with one of the other tactics. For instance, if rational persuasion is not strong enough, the influencer might bring in another person to show that that person agrees with the logic of the argument.

Two points should be noted about the use of influence tactics. First, influence tactics tend to be most successful when used in combination.[36] Many tactics have some limitations or weaknesses that can be overcome using other tactics. Second, the influence tactics that tend to be most successful are those that are "softer" in nature. Rational persuasion, consultation, inspirational appeals, and collaboration take advantage of personal rather than organizational forms of power. People who are the most effective at influencing others will generally rely on the softer tactics, make appropriate requests, and ensure the tactics they use match the types of power they have.

engagement In the context of influence tactics, occurs when one agrees and becomes committed to an influencer's request

compliance When targets of influence are willing to do what the leader asks but do it with a degree of ambivalence

RESPONSES TO INFLUENCE TACTICS As illustrated in Figure 11-3, there are three possible responses people have to influence tactics.[37] **Engagement** occurs when the target of influence agrees with and becomes committed to the influence request.[38] For a leader, this is the best outcome, because it results in employees putting forth the greatest level of effort in accomplishing what they are asked to do. Engagement reflects a shift in both the behaviours and the attitudes of employees. **Compliance** occurs when targets of

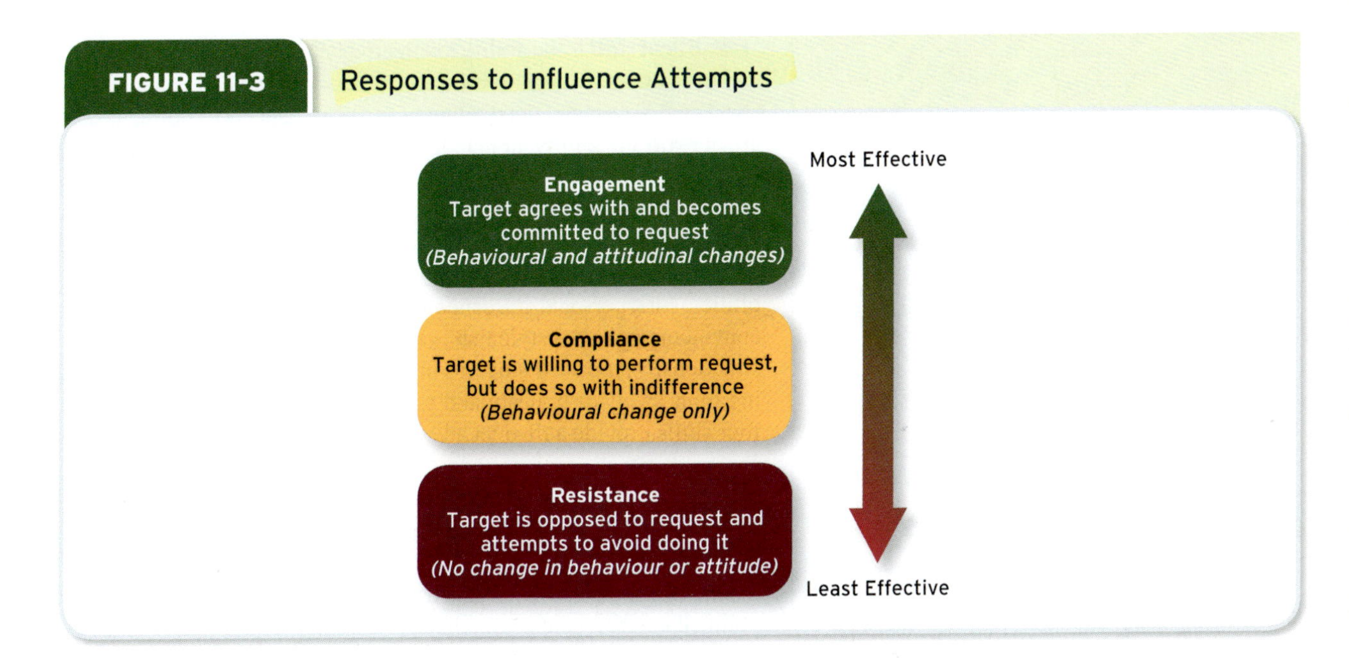

influence are willing to do what the leader asks, but they do it with a degree of ambivalence. Compliance reflects a shift in the behaviours of employees but not their attitudes. This behaviour is the most common response to influence attempts in organizations, because anyone with some degree of power who makes a reasonable request is likely to achieve compliance. That response allows leaders to accomplish their purpose but it doesn't bring about the highest levels of employee effort and dedication. Still, it's clearly preferable to **resistance**, which occurs when the target refuses to perform the influence request and puts forth an effort to avoid having to do it. Employee resistance could come in the form of making excuses, trying to influence the requestor in return, or simply refusing to carry out the request. Resistance is most likely when the influencer's power is low relative to the target or when the request itself is inappropriate or unreasonable.[39]

resistance When a target refuses to perform a request and puts forth an effort to avoid having to do it

POWER AND INFLUENCE IN ACTION

In this section, we look at two major areas in which people have the ability to use power to influence others. The first is through navigating the environment of organizational politics within the organization. The second is through using power and influence to help solve conflicts within the organization. As it turns out, it's easy for these two areas to coincide with each other.

ORGANIZATIONAL POLITICS If there was perhaps one term that had a more negative connotation than power, it might be politics. You've probably had people give you career advice such as, "Stay away from office politics" or "Avoid being seen as political." The truth is that you cannot escape it; politics are a fact of life in organizations![40] **Organizational politics** can be seen as actions by individuals that are directed toward the goal of furthering their own self-interests.[41] Although there's generally a negative perception of politics, it's important to note that this definition doesn't imply that furthering one's self-interests is necessarily in opposition to the company's interests. A leader needs to be able to push his or her own ideas and influence others through the use of organizational politics. Research has recently supported the notion that, to be effective, leaders must have a certain degree of political skill.[42] In fact, universities and some organizations such as Becton, Dickinson, and Company—a leading global medical technology company—are training their future leaders to be attuned to their political environment and develop their political skill.[43]

organizational politics Individual actions directed toward the goal of furthering a person's own self-interests

"You have no idea how political this place is."

Source: © The New Yorker Collection 2001 Alex Gregory from cartoonbank.com. All rights reserved.

Political skill is the ability to effectively understand others at work and use that knowledge to influence others in ways that enhance personal and/or organizational objectives.[44] Two aspects of political skill are networking ability, or an adeptness at identifying and developing diverse contacts, and social astuteness, or the tendency to observe others and accurately interpret their behaviour.[45] To see where you stand on these two dimensions, see our **OB Assessments** feature at the end of the chapter. Political skill also involves two other capabilities. Interpersonal influence involves having an unassuming and convincing personal style that is flexible enough to adapt to different situations.[46] Apparent sincerity involves appearing to others as having high levels of honesty and genuineness.[47] Taken together, these four skills provide a distinct advantage when navigating the political environments in organizations.

Although organizational politics can lead to positive outcomes, people's perceptions of politics are generally negative. This perception is certainly understandable, as anytime someone acts in a self-serving manner, it is potentially to the detriment of others.[48] In a highly charged political environment in which people are trying to capture resources and influence one another toward potentially opposing goals, it's only natural that some employees will feel stress about the uncertainty they face at work. Environments that are perceived as extremely political have been shown to cause lower job satisfaction, increased strain, lower job performance, and lower organizational commitment among employees.[49] In fact, high levels of organizational politics have even been shown to be detrimental to company performance as a whole.[50]

political skill The ability to understand others and the use of that knowledge to influence them to further personal or organizational objectives

As a result, organizations (and their members) do their best to minimize the perceptions of self-serving behaviours that are associated with organizational politics. This goal requires identifying the particular organizational circumstances that cause politics to thrive. As illustrated in Figure 11-4, organizational politics are driven by both personal characteristics and organizational characteristics. Some employees have a strong need for power that provides them with an incentive to engage in political behaviours. Others are high in self-monitoring, meaning that they have a tendency to be closely guarded in their actions and behaviours.[51] Still others have "Machiavellian" tendencies, meaning that they are willing to manipulate and deceive others to acquire power.[52]

Organizational factors that are the most likely to increase politics are those that raise the level of uncertainty in the environment. When people are uncertain about an outcome or event, they will generally act in ways that help reduce that uncertainty. A number of events can trigger uncertainty, including limited or changing resources, ambiguity in role requirements, high performance pressures, or unclear performance evaluation measures.[53] These sorts of organizational factors generally have a much stronger effect on political behaviour than do personal factors. That's actually a good thing for organizations, because it may be easier to clarify performance measures and roles than it is to change the personal characteristics of a workforce.

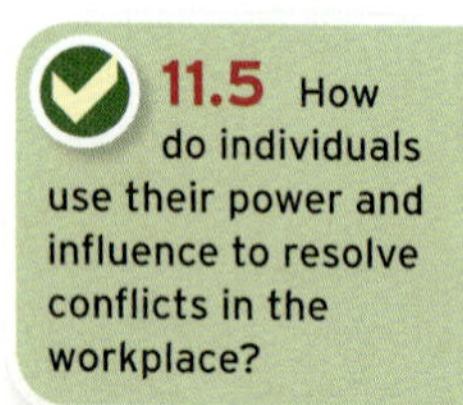
11.5 How do individuals use their power and influence to resolve conflicts in the workplace?

CONFLICT RESOLUTION In addition to using their power to shape office politics, individuals can use their influence in the context of conflict resolution. Conflict arises when two or more individuals perceive that their goals are in opposition (see Chapter 10 for more discussion of such issues). Conflict and politics are clearly intertwined, because the pursuit of one's own self-interests often breeds conflict in others. As illustrated in Figure 11-5, there are five different approaches to handling conflict, each of which is appropriate in different circumstances.[54] The five styles can be viewed as combinations of two separate factors: how *assertive* individuals want to be in pursuing their own goals and how *cooperative* they are with regard to the concerns of others.

FIGURE 11-4 The Organizational Politics Process

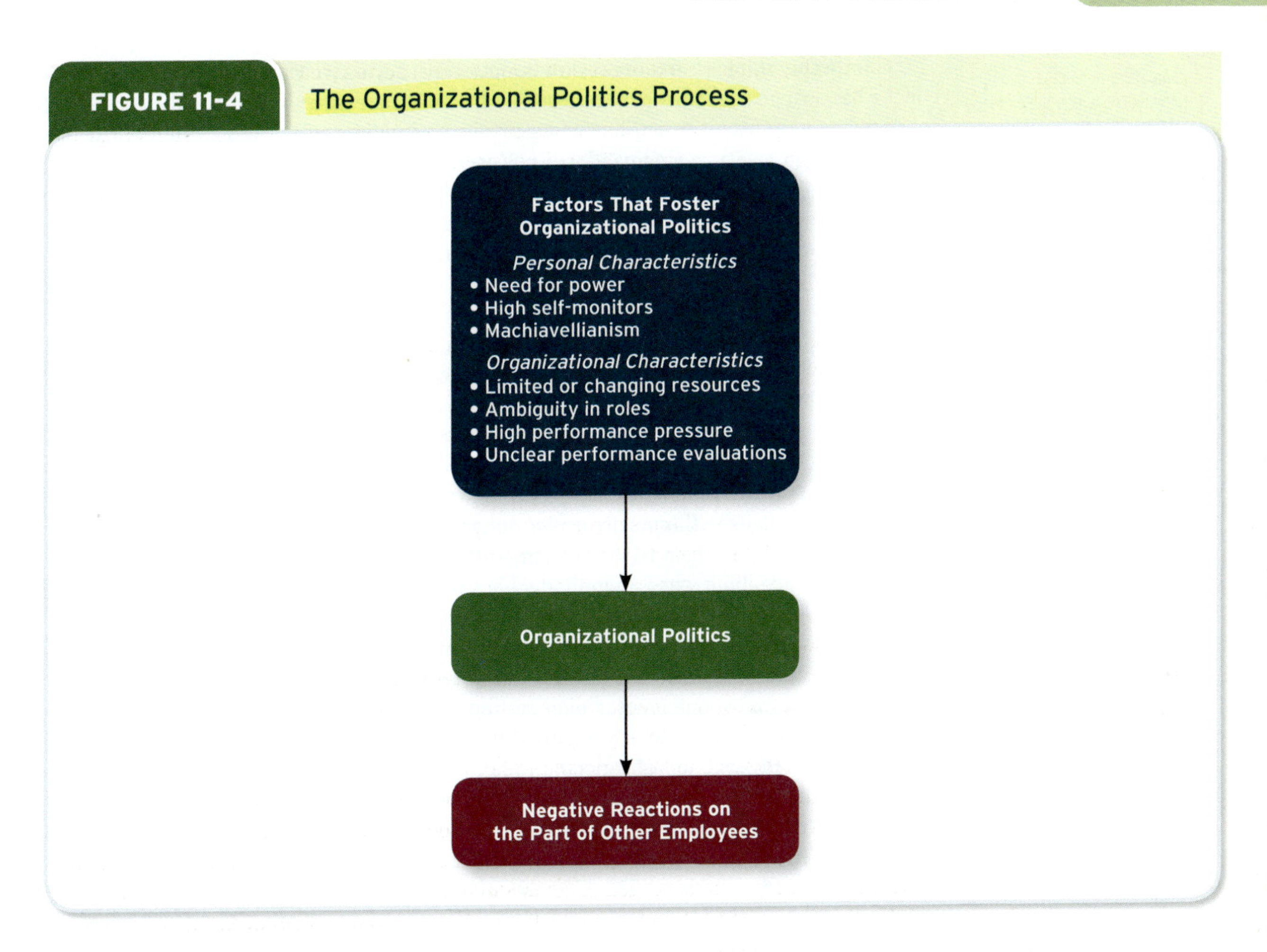

FIGURE 11-5 Styles of Conflict Resolution

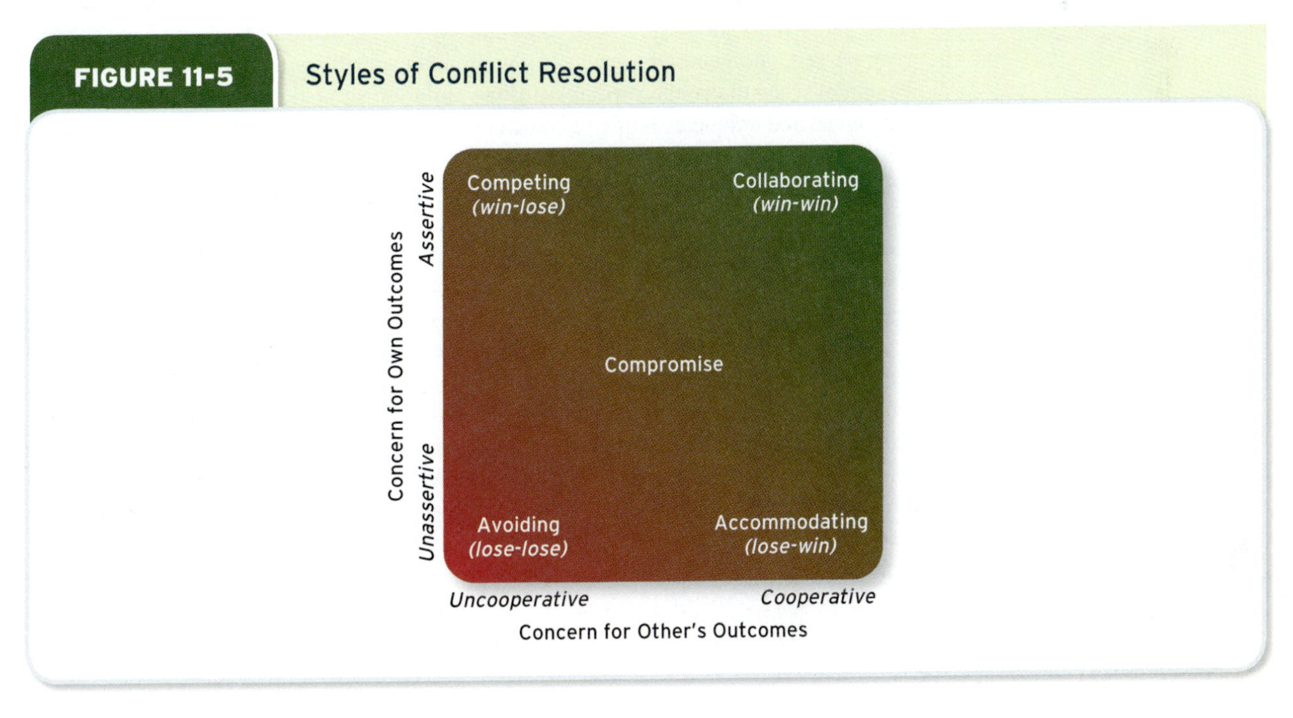

competing A conflict resolution style by which one party attempts to get his or her own goals met without concern for the other party's results

Competing (high assertiveness, low cooperation) occurs when one party attempts to get his or her own goals met without concern for the other party's results. It could be considered a win–lose approach to conflict management. Competing occurs most often when one party has high levels of organizational power and can use legitimate or coercive power to settle the conflict. It also generally involves the hard forms of influence, such as pressure or coalitions. Although this strategy for resolving conflict might get the result initially, it won't win an individual many friends, given the negative reactions that tend to accompany such tactics. It's best used in situations in which a leader knows he or she is right and a quick decision needs to be made.

avoiding A conflict resolution style by which one party wants to remain neutral, stay away from conflict, or postpone the conflict to gather information or let things cool down

accommodating A conflict resolution style by which one party gives in to the other and acts in a completely unselfish way

Avoiding (low assertiveness, low cooperation) occurs when one party wants to remain neutral, stay away from conflict, or postpone the conflict to gather information or let things cool down. Avoiding usually results in an unfavourable outcome for everyone, including the organization, and may result in negative feelings toward the leader. Most important, avoiding never really resolves the conflict. **Accommodating** (low assertiveness, high cooperation) occurs when one party gives in to the other and acts in a completely unselfish way. Individuals will typically use an accommodating strategy when the issue is really not that important to them but is very important to the other party. It's also an important strategy to think about when an individual has less power than the other party. If individuals know they are going to lose the conflict due to their lack of power anyway, it might be a better long-term strategy to give in to the demands from the other party.

collaboration A conflict resolution style whereby both parties work together to maximize outcomes

compromise A conflict resolution style by which conflict is resolved through give-and-take concessions

Collaboration (high assertiveness, high cooperation) occurs when both parties work together to maximize outcomes. Collaboration is seen as a win–win form of conflict resolution. Collaboration is generally regarded as the most effective form of conflict resolution, especially in reference to task-oriented rather than personal conflicts.[55] However, it's also the most difficult to come by because it requires full sharing of information by both parties, a full discussion of concerns, relatively equal power between parties, and a lot of time investment to arrive at a resolution. However, this style also results in the best outcomes and reactions from both parties. **Compromise** (moderate assertiveness, moderate cooperation) occurs when conflict is resolved through give-and-take concessions. Compromise is perhaps the most common form of conflict resolution whereby each party's losses are offset by gains and vice versa. It is seen as an easy form of resolution, maintains relations between parties, and generally results in favourable evaluations for the leader.[56] For more discussion of when to use the various conflict resolution strategies, see Table 11-4.

One recent and unique example of conflict resolution is occurring through the One Laptop Per Child project. Nicolas Negroponte is the founder and chairperson of this non-profit organization whose mission is to make millions of $100 laptops for undereducated children in the world's poorest nations. Needless to say, manufacturing a $100 laptop (named the XO) is no small feat. Negroponte is leading a network of vastly different individuals, all working on their own time or on loan from other organizations, through a painstaking collaborative process of design and manufacturing. The process hasn't always been easy. There have been times when Negroponte has had to adopt a competing style of conflict resolution to make a custom wireless system for the laptop function. This competitive response upset a faction of volunteers who subsequently quit the project. However, other times Negroponte has facilitated collaboration among very disparate groups. As a leader with varying degrees of power, Negroponte constantly has to balance the needs of the project with the needs of individuals and attempt to resolve conflict effectively.[57]

TABLE 11-4 When to Use Conflict Resolution Styles

RESOLUTION STYLE	USE DURING THE FOLLOWING SITUATIONS:
Competing	• When quick decisive action is vital (i.e. emergencies). • On important issues for which unpopular actions need implementation. • On issues vital to company welfare when you know you're right. • Against people who take advantage of non-competitive people.
Avoiding	• When an issue is trivial or more important issues are pressing. • When you perceive no chance of satisfying your concerns. • When potential disruption outweighs the benefits of resolution. • To let people cool down and regain perspective. • When gathering information supersedes an immediate decision. • When others can resolve the conflict more effectively. • When issues seem tangential or symptomatic of other issues.
Collaborating	• To find an integrative solution when both sets of concerns are too important to be compromised. • When your objective is to learn. • To merge insights from people with different perspectives. • To gain commitment by incorporating concerns into a consensus. • To work through feelings that have interfered with a relationship.
Accommodating	• When you find you are wrong, to allow a better position to be heard, to learn, and to show your reasonableness. • When issues are more important to others than yourself, to satisfy others and maintain cooperation. • To build social credits for later issues. • To minimize loss when you are outmatched and losing. • When harmony and stability are especially important. • To allow subordinates to develop by learning from mistakes.
Compromising	• When goals are important but not worth the effort of potential disruption of more assertive modes. • When opponents with equal power are committed to mutually exclusive goals. • To achieve temporary settlements to complex issues. • To arrive at expedient solutions under time pressure. • As a backup when collaboration or competition is unsuccessful.

Source: Reprinted from K.W. Thomas, "Toward Multi-Dimensional Values in Teaching: The Example of Conflict Behaviors," *Academy of Management Review* 2 (1977), pp. 484–90.

The One Laptop Per Child project intends to provide millions of $100 laptops for the world's poorest children. Founder and director Nicholas Negroponte has put together a large team of volunteers and "borrowed" workers from many different organizations and has worked to establish an effective collaboration among them by adopting a wide variety of conflict-resolution strategies, even the competing style.

SO WHY ARE SOME PEOPLE MORE POWERFUL THAN OTHERS?

As shown in Figure 11-6, answering that question requires an understanding of the types of power that people acquire, what kinds of influence tactics they have available to them, and how they can use that influence to alter the attitudes and behaviours of others. People acquire both organizational (legitimate, reward, coercive) and personal (expert, referent) forms of power, which gives them the ability to influence others. They can then use that power to influence others through influence tactics. Those tactics can help achieve organizational goals or may be applied more specifically to dealing with organizational politics or conflict resolution situations. In the end, there are three possible responses to influence attempts: engagement, compliance, and resistance. The effectiveness of those attempts will depend on an individual's skill at performing them and how well they match the forms of power they have with the appropriate types of influence.

HOW IMPORTANT ARE POWER AND INFLUENCE?

11.6 How do power and influence affect job performance and organizational commitment?

How important is an individual's ability to use power and influence? Does a leader's power and influence correlate with the job performance and organizational commitment of her employees? Figure 11-7 summarizes the research evidence linking power and influence to job performance and organizational commitment. The figure reveals that power and influence are moderately correlated with job performance. When used correctly and focused on task-related outcomes, power and influence can create engagement in workers such that they are both behaviourally and attitudinally focused on high levels of task performance. That engagement also helps increase citizenship behaviour, whereas the compliance associated

FIGURE 11-6 Why Are Some People More Powerful Than Others?

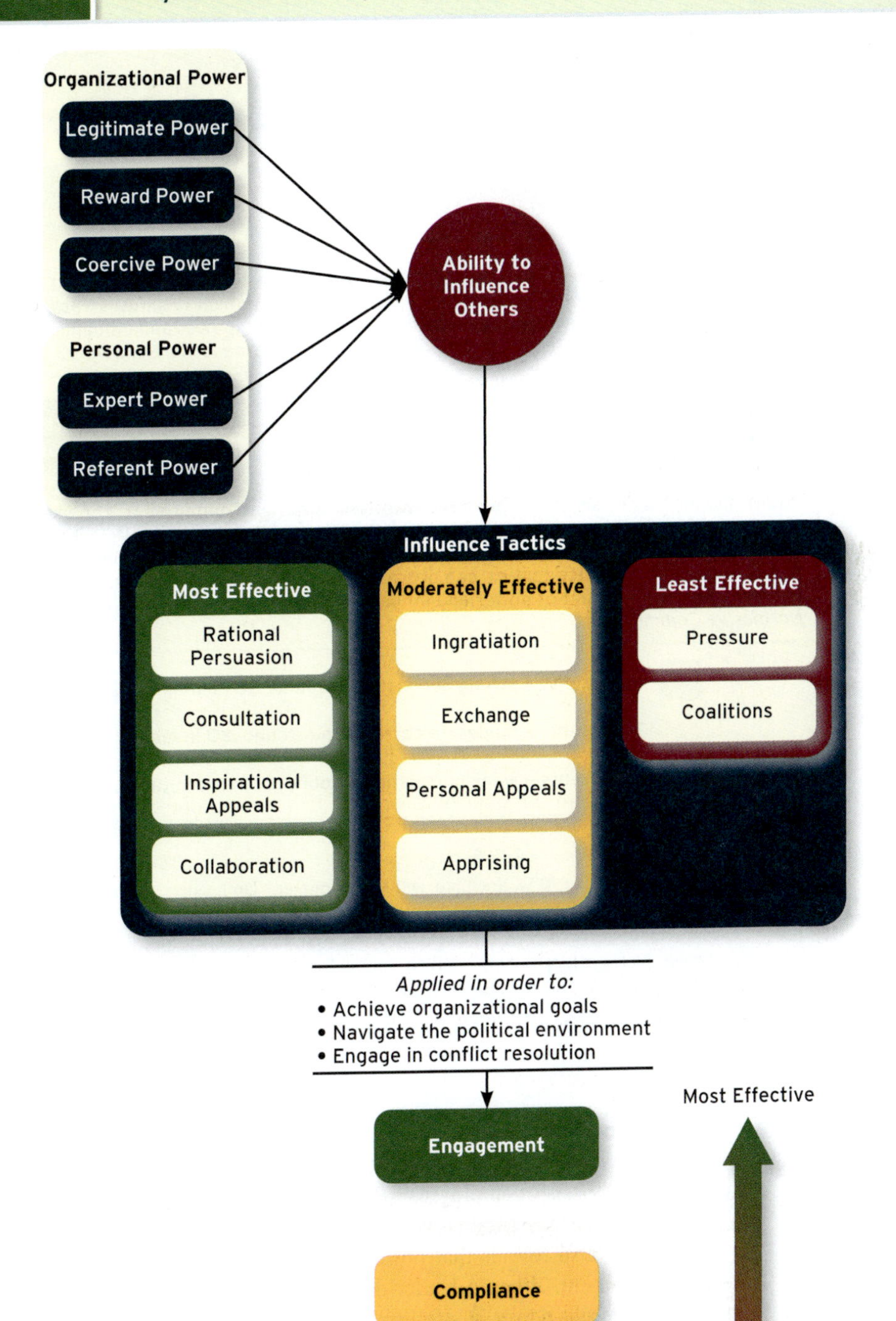

FIGURE 11-7 Effects of Power and Influence on Performance and Commitment

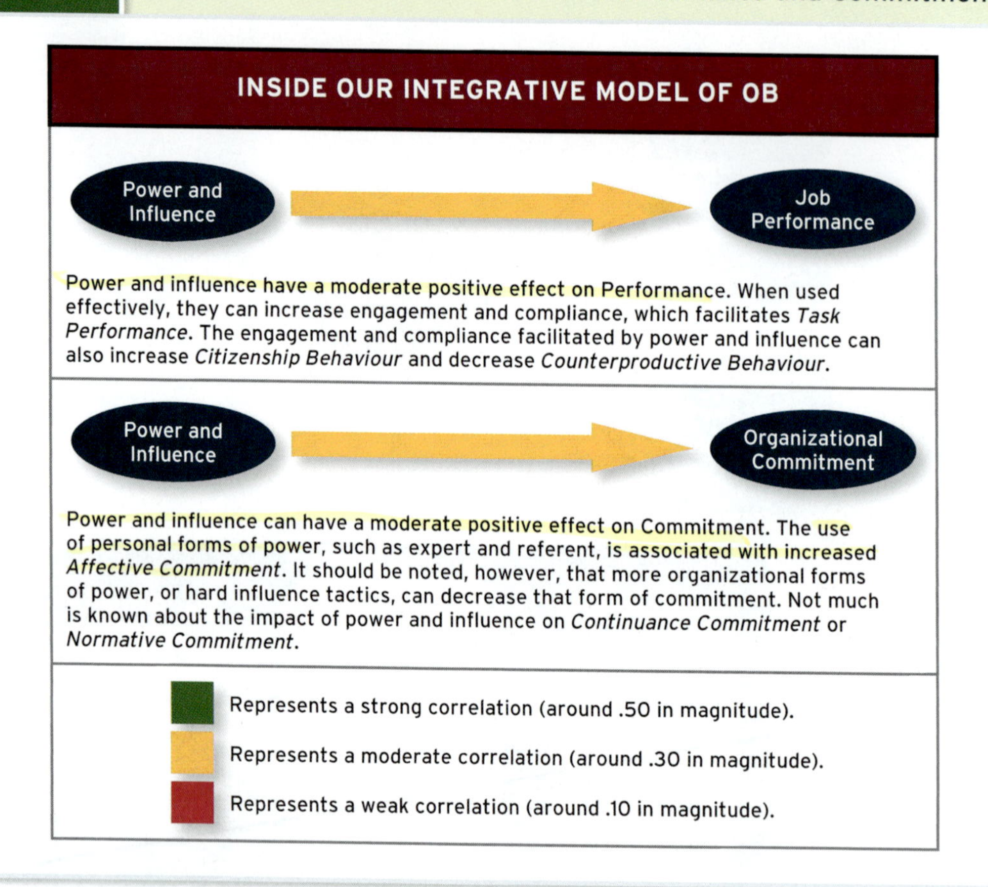

Sources: R.T. Sparrowe, B.W. Soetjipto, and M.L. Kraimer, "Do Leaders' Influence Tactics Relate to Members' Helping Behavior? It Depends on the Quality of the Relationship," *Academy of Management Journal* 49 (2006), pp. 1194–1208; G. Yukl, H. Kim, and C.M. Falbe, "Antecedents of Influence Outcomes," *Journal of Applied Psychology* 81 (1996), pp. 309–17; P.P. Carson, K.D. Carson, and C.W. Rowe, "Social Power Bases: A Meta-Analytic Examination of Interrelationships and Outcomes," *Journal of Applied Social Psychology* 23 (1993), pp. 1150–69.

with power and influence can decrease counterproductive behaviour. These job performance benefits make sense given that the effective use of power and influence can increase the *motivation* levels of employees, whereas the ineffective use of power and influence can increase *stress* levels of employees.

Figure 11-7 also reveals that power and influence are moderately related to organizational commitment. When a leader draws on personal sources of power, such as expert power and referent power, a stronger emotional bond can be created with the employee, boosting affective commitment. The effective use of such power should increase *job satisfaction* and a sense of *trust* in the leader, all of which are associated with increased commitment levels. As with job performance, however, it is important to note that an ineffective use of power can also decrease commitment levels. In particular, repeated uses of coercive power or repeated reliance on hard influence tactics such as pressure or coalitions could actually decrease organizational commitment levels.

OB RESEARCH IN CANADA

Dr. Marylène Gagné is an associate professor of organizational behaviour in the John Molson School of Business at Concordia University in Montreal. Before moving to Concordia University, Dr. Gagné earned her PhD at the University of Rochester. Dr. Gagné's research looks at how organizations, through their structures, cultures, rewards, tasks, and managerial/leadership styles, affect people's attitudes, motivational orientation, and behaviours. When asked why she is drawn to the study of organizational behaviour, Dr. Gagné replied, "I like to know what energizes people, and how this affects their passion for work and life. For me, studying how managers and leaders use their power and influence is one way to understand employees' experiences." Reference to some of Dr. Gagné's work was made in Chapter 6 on motivation (see intrinsic and extrinsic motivation). Dr. Gagné has been the recipient many research awards, such as the John Molson School of Business Junior Researcher Award and the Canadian Psychological Association's New Researcher Award, and her published work can be found in many organizational behaviour and psychology journals.

Some of Dr. Gagné's favourite publications include:

"The Study of Compensation Systems Through the Lens of Self-Determination Theory: Reconciling 35 Years of Debate," by M. Gagné and J. Forest, published in *Canadian Psychology* (2008, volume 49, pp. 225–32).

"Self-Determination Theory as a New Framework for Understanding Organizational Behavior," by M. Gagné and E.L. Deci, published in *Journal of Organizational Behavior* (2005, volume 26, pp. 331–62).

"Facilitating Acceptance of Organizational Change: The Importance of Self-Determination," by M. Gagné, R. Koestner, and M. Zuckerman, published in *Journal of Applied Social Psychology* (2000, volume 30, pp. 1843–52).

APPLICATION: NEGOTIATIONS

11.7 What are the ways in which individuals negotiate in the workplace?

There is perhaps no better place for individuals to use their power, influence, political, and conflict resolution skills than when conducting negotiations. **Negotiation** is a process in which two or more interdependent individuals discuss and attempt to come to an agreement about their different preferences.[58] Negotiations can take place inside the organization or when dealing with organizational outsiders. Negotiations can involve settling a contract dispute between labour and management, determining a purchasing price for products, haggling over a performance review rating, or determining the starting salary for a new employee. Clearly, negotiations are a critical part of organizational life, for both leaders and employees.

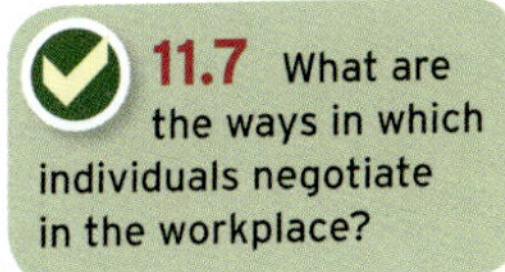

negotiation A process in which two or more interdependent individuals discuss and attempt to reach agreement about their differences

distributive bargaining
A negotiation strategy in which one person gains and the other person loses

There are two general strategies individuals must choose between when it comes to negotiations: distributive bargaining and integrative bargaining.[59] **Distributive bargaining** involves win–lose negotiating over a "fixed-pie" of resources.[60] That is, when one person gains, the other person loses (also known as a "zero-sum" condition). The classic example of a negotiation in which distributive bargaining is used is the purchasing of a car. When you walk into a car dealership, there's a stated price on the side of the car that's known to be negotiable. In these circumstances though, every dollar you save is a dollar the dealership loses. Similarly, every dollar the salesperson negotiates for, you lose. Distributive bargaining is similar in nature to a competing approach to conflict resolution. Some of the most visible negotiations that have traditionally been approached with a distributive bargaining tactic are union–management labour negotiations. Whether it be automobile manufacturers, airlines, or nurses at hospitals, the negotiations for these sessions are typically viewed through a win–lose lens. For an example of a negotiation that might interest you, see this chapter's **OB for Students** feature.

integrative bargaining
A negotiation strategy that achieves an outcome that is satisfying for both parties

Many negotiations within organizations, including labour–management sessions, are beginning to occur with a more integrative bargaining strategy. **Integrative bargaining** is aimed at accomplishing a win–win scenario.[61] It involves the use of problem solving and mutual respect to achieve an outcome that is satisfying for both parties. Individuals who thoroughly understand the conflict resolution style of collaboration are likely to thrive in these types of negotiations. In general, integrative bargaining is a preferable strategy whenever

OB FOR STUDENTS

Nine out of ten recruiters say that their initial compensation offer to a job candidate is lower than they are prepared to pay.[62] Many of you are in the midst of or starting to consider a job search as you graduate. Research has plenty to say about your ability to negotiate and secure an acceptable salary. One major issue is that the majority of us never attempt to negotiate the offered salary.[63] A second major issue is that those who do negotiate do a pretty poor job of it. Although the conventional wisdom that men negotiate more often than women is false, a study of MBA students showed that men do perhaps negotiate more effectively than their female counterparts and that these differences could account for a lot of money over time.[64] Regardless, here are some suggestions for negotiating your salary:[65]

1. Know your worth going in. You should know the approximate salaries for others within your major or functional area. You can ask your career centre for this information in many cases.
2. You need to know your "BATNA," or your best alternative to a negotiated agreement. What is the lowest possible offer that you would be willing to accept? At what point would you be willing to walk away? Negotiators with a clear BATNA generally walk away with higher results.
3. What is your goal for a salary? Do not be afraid to put this number on the table. Avoid vague responses such as, "I want more money," which does nothing to help further the negotiation process.
4. You need to be prepared to sell yourself. What value do you bring to the table that they might not know about? If you want to convince the company that raising your offer is a win–win result, you need to be able to convince the company that your value is more significant than it thought it was.
5. Last but not least: Don't threaten to leave the table unless you really are prepared to do it. Do you indeed have a worthwhile backup plan?

possible, because it allows a long-term relationship to form between the parties (because neither side feels like the loser). In addition, integrative bargaining has a tendency to produce a higher level of outcome favourability when both parties' views are considered than distributive bargaining.[66] However, not all situations are appropriate for integrative bargaining. Integrative bargaining is most appropriate in situations in which multiple outcomes are possible, there is an adequate level of trust, and parties are willing to be flexible.[67] Please don't approach your next used car purchase with an integrative bargaining strategy!

TAKEAWAYS

11.1 Power is the ability to influence the behaviour of others and resist unwanted influence in return. Power is necessary, in that it gives individuals the ability to influence others.

11.2 There are potentially five types of power available to individuals within organizations. There are three organizational forms of power: Legitimate power is based on authority or position; reward power is based on the distribution of resources or benefits; and coercive power is based on the handing out of punishments. There are two personal forms of power: Expert power is derived from expertise and knowledge, whereas referent power is based on the attractiveness and charisma of the individual. These types of power can be used most effectively when the individuals are central to the work process, highly visible, have discretion, and are the sole controllers of resources and information.

11.3 Ten different influence tactics are commonly used in organizational settings. The most effective are rational persuasion, inspirational appeals, consultation, and collaboration. The least effective are pressure and the forming of coalitions. Tactics with moderate levels of effectiveness are ingratiation, personal appeals, exchange, and apprising.

11.4 Organizational politics are individual actions that are directed toward the goal of furthering a person's own self-interests. Political behaviour is most likely to occur in organizational situations in which individual outcomes are uncertain.

11.5 Power and influence can be used to resolve conflicts in five distinct ways: avoidance, competing, accommodating, collaborating, and compromising. The most effective and also most difficult tactic is collaboration.

11.6 Power and influence have moderate positive relationships with job performance and organizational commitment. However, for these beneficial effects to be realized, individuals must wield their power effectively and rely on effective influence tactics.

11.7 People use both distributive and integrative bargaining to negotiate outcomes.

KEY TERMS

- accommodating *p. 298*
- apprising *p. 293*
- avoiding *p. 298*
- centrality *p. 292*
- coalition *p. 294*
- coercive power *p. 289*
- collaboration *pp. 293, 298*
- competing *p. 298*

- compliance *p. 294*
- compromise *p. 298*
- consultation *p. 293*
- discretion *p. 291*
- distributive bargaining *p. 304*
- engagement *p. 294*
- exchange tactic *p. 293*
- expert power *p. 289*
- influence *p. 292*
- ingratiation *p. 293*
- inspirational appeal *p. 293*
- integrative bargaining *p. 304*
- legitimate power *p. 286*
- negotiation *p. 303*
- organizational politics *p. 295*
- personal appeals *p. 293*
- political skill *p. 296*
- power *p. 285*
- pressure *p. 294*
- rational persuasion *p. 292*
- referent power *p. 289*
- resistance *p. 295*
- reward power *p. 288*
- substitutability *p. 291*
- visibility *p. 292*

DISCUSSION QUESTIONS

11.1 Can a leader influence others without power? How exactly would that influence take place?

11.2 Which forms of power do you consider to be the strongest? Which types of power do you currently have? How could you go about obtaining higher levels of the forms that you're lacking?

11.3 Who is the most influential person you have come in contact with personally? What forms of power did he or she have and which types of influence did he or she use to accomplish objectives?

11.4 Think of a time when you resisted an influence attempt at work. What made you resist? Could the person attempting to influence you have done anything differently to get you to behave the way he or she wanted?

11.5 What would it take to have a "politically free" environment? Is that possible?

11.6 Think about the last serious conflict you had with a co-worker or group member. How was that conflict resolved? Which approach did you take to resolve it?

11.7 Think of a situation in which you negotiated an agreement. Which approach did you take? Was it the appropriate one? How might have the negotiation process gone more smoothly?

CASE • HEWLETT-PACKARD

Hewlett-Packard had to make a tough decision to replace Carly Fiorina to guide the company out of a crisis. The board appointed Mark Hurd, a low-profile CEO with a proven record of success. Hurd's personality was the complete opposite of Fiorina's and exactly what the company needed. Fiorina was a celebrity CEO with a flare for marketing, whereas Hurd is a straight-edged CEO who frequently seeks the inputs of his employees from every level of the organization. Hurd's leadership style has been embraced by his internal and external constituencies.

Only several months into his tenure, Hurd has made several significant moves that have positively affected the company. First, Hurd is changing the culture that focused on innovating the next big thing every day. Instead, he is attempting to re-create HP's culture to focus on execution and accountability and thus rebuild the company's reputation as a consistent performer. Second, he has simplified the bonus system to reflect the performance of employees' business units and the overall company. Third, Hurd made a strategic decision to undergo a restructuring process that would cut HP's costs and make the company leaner. Therefore, HP decided to lay off 14,500 employees from its 150,000-employee workforce. This cost-cutting decision will allow the company to be more competitive in the long term. It seems evident so far that Hurd's personality and business sense will lead HP back to its once prestigious stature.

11.1 Describe the sources of power that are available to Hurd. How does this compare with the previous CEO?

11.2 Consider the various influence tactics used by Hurd. Why was his approach so effective?

Sources: P. Burrow, "HP Says Goodbye to Drama," *BusinessWeek,* 2005, www.businessweek.com; P. Burrows and B. Elgin, "HP's New Low-Profile Boss," *BusinessWeek,* 2005, www.businessweek.com; A. Hesseldahl, "The Cuts Aren't Over at HP," *BusinessWeek,* 2006, www.businessweek.com; P. Thibodeau, "Dunn Out at HP; Hurd Put on Hot Seat," *Computerworld* 40 (2006), pp. 1–14.

EXERCISE • LOBBYING FOR INFLUENCE

The purpose of this exercise is to give you experience in using influence tactics to modify the behaviour of others. This exercise uses groups of six participants, so your instructor will either assign you to a group of six or ask you to create your own group of six. The exercise has the following steps:

1. During this exercise, your objective is to get other people in the class to give you their points. If you get more than 50 percent of the total number of points distributed to the whole class, you will win. Each person in the class has a different number of points, as shown in the class list. You can keep or give away your points in whatever manner you choose, as long as you follow the rules for each round of the process. There are five rounds, described next.

   Round 1. In this round, you will write memos to your classmates. You can say whatever you want in your memos, and write them to whomever you choose, but for the 10-minute writing period, there will be no talking, only writing. You will deliver all your messages at one time, at the end of the 10-minute writing period.

   Round 2. In this round, you will respond in writing to the messages you received in the first round. You can also write new memos as you see fit. Again, there is to be no talking! At the end of 15 minutes, you can distribute your memos.

   Round 3. In Round 3, you can talk as much as you like. You will have 15 minutes to talk with anyone about anything.

   Round 4. In this round, you will create ballots to distribute your points any way you see fit. To distribute your points, put a person's name on an index card, along with the number of points you want that person to have. If you choose to keep any of your points, put your own name on the card, along with the number of points you want to keep. Do not hand in your cards until asked to do so by the professor.

Round 5. If there is no clear winner, Round 5 will be used to repeat steps 3 and 4.

2. Either individually or in your groups, answer the following discussion questions:
   - What kinds of social influence attempts did you make during this exercise?
   - How successful were you at influencing others to go along with you?
   - What kinds of influence did others use on you?
   - What was the most successful way you saw someone else use influence during the memo-writing and discussion sections?
   - What other factors determined how you voted?

Source: Adapted from "Voting for Dollars," in the Instructor's Manual for D.A. Whetten and K.S. Cameron, *Developing Management Skills,* 7th ed. (Englewood Cliffs, NJ: Prentice Hall, 2007).

OB ASSESSMENTS • POLITICAL SKILL

How much political skill do you have? This assessment is designed to measure two dimensions of political skill. Please write a number next to each statement that indicates the extent to which it accurately describes your attitude toward work while you were on the job. Alternatively, consider the statements in reference to school rather than work. Answer each question using the response scale provided. Then sum up your answers for each of the dimensions.

1 STRONGLY DISAGREE	2 DISAGREE	3 NEUTRAL	4 AGREE	5 STRONGLY AGREE

1. I spend a lot of time and effort networking with others. ______
2. I know a lot of important people and am well connected. ______
3. I am good at using my connections and networks to make things happen. ______
4. I have developed a large network of colleagues and associates whom I can call on for support when I really need to get things done. ______
5. I spend a lot of time making connections. ______
6. I always seem to instinctively know the right thing to say or do to influence others. ______
7. I have a good intuition or savvy about how to present myself to others. ______
8. I am particularly good at sensing the motivations and hidden agendas of others. ______
9. I pay close attention to people's facial expressions. ______
10. I understand people very well. ______

SCORING AND INTERPRETATION

Networking Ability: Sum up items 1–5. ________

Social Astuteness: Sum up items 6–10. ________

For networking ability, scores of 18 or more are above average and scores of 17 or less are below average. For social astuteness, scores of 19 or more are above average and scores of 18 or less are below average.

Source: Adapted from G.R. Ferris, D.C. Treadway, R.W. Kolodinsky, W.A. Hochwarter, C.J. Kacmar, C. Douglas, and D.D. Frink, "Development and Validation of the Political Skill Inventory," *Journal of Management* 31 (2005), pp. 126–52.

CONNECT—Available 24/7 with instant feedback so you can study when you want, how you want, and where you want. Take advantage of the Study Plan—an innovative tool that helps students customize their own learning experience. Students can diagnose their knowledge with pre- and post-tests, identify the areas where they need help, search contents of the entire learning package for content specific to the topic they're studying, and add these resources to their study plan. Visit **www.connectob.ca** to register—take practice quizzes, run interactive scenarios, and much more. Also visit the Student Online Learning Centre for additional study tools.

www.mcgrawhill.ca/olc/colquitt

CHAPTER

12 Leadership Styles and Behaviours

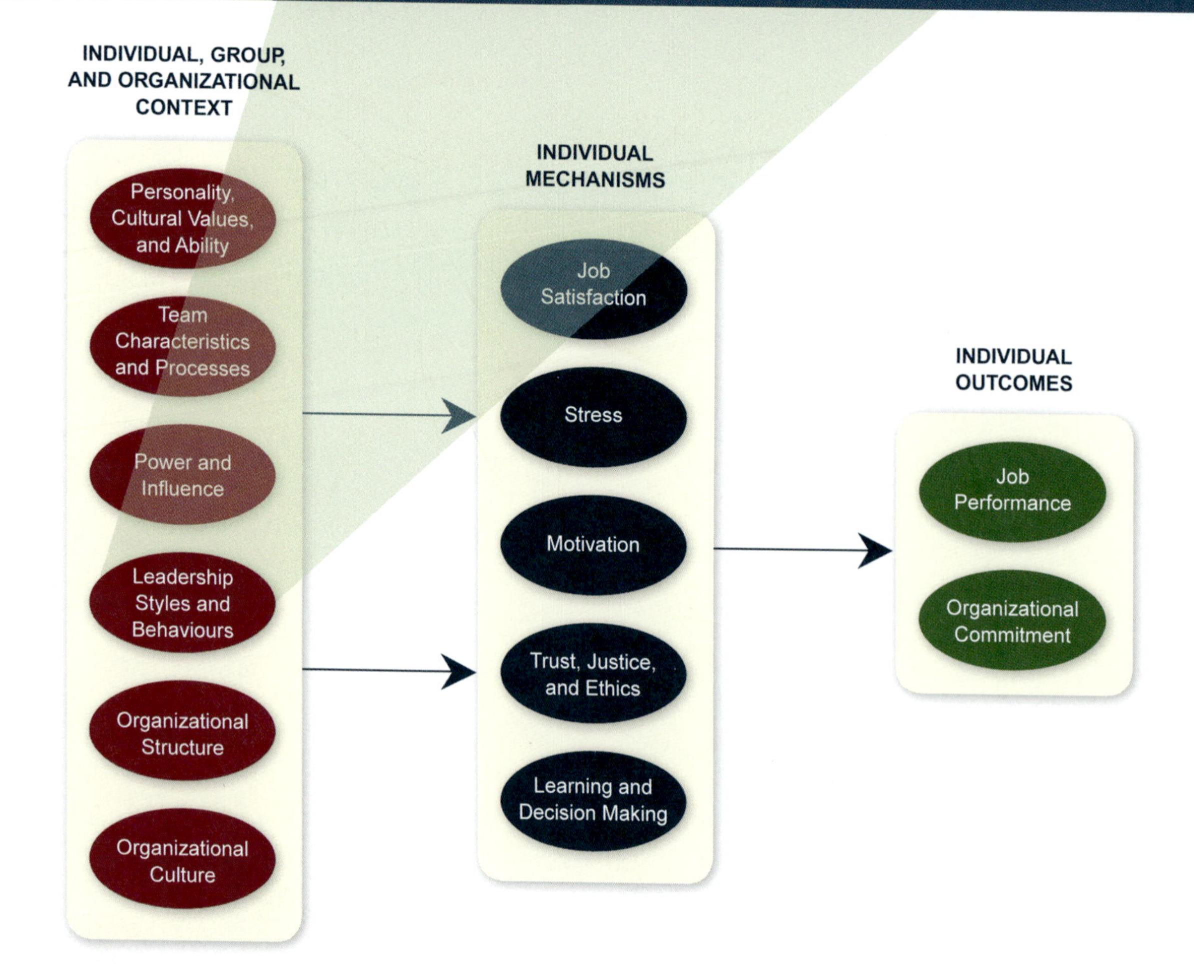

APPLE

On January 24, 1984, Apple Computer introduced the Macintosh to the world.[1] The Macintosh represented the marriage of two different visions.[2] The first vision belonged to Steve Jobs, who co-founded Apple with Steve Wozniak and who wanted to introduce the graphical user interface and mouse, developed at Xerox's Palo Alto Research Center, to mainstream computing. The second vision belonged to Jef Raskin, the computer scientist who chose the Macintosh name and wanted to create an "all-in-one" computer that customers could just plug in to get started. The Macintosh began as a fringe product for Apple, which was still focused on updating the Apple II—the computer that had essentially started the personal computer industry in 1977 and remained the market leader before being eclipsed by the IBM PC. To stave off IBM's threat, Jobs knew that Apple needed a product that would be "so important that it will make a dent in the universe."[3]

The development of the Macintosh was dominated by Jobs's leadership, for better and for worse.[4] Two phrases captured the spirit he created within the Macintosh team. "Let's Be Pirates" reflected the renegade nature of the group as it fought against the rest of the industry and even Apple's existing products. "Working 90 Hours a Week and Loving It!" reflected the impossible odds the team faced in bringing the Macintosh to market in only two years. One team member described Jobs's leadership style as "hands-on management," saying that Jobs "would march right into your cubicle, invade your space, sit right down, and start playing with whatever you were working on." Jobs's impatience and legendary temper were balanced only by his considerable charisma. As one Apple employee noted, "He doesn't know that anything is impossible because, well, he's always been able to do anything he wanted. So even as he's being a jerk, he's got this incredibly seductive aura around him that keeps you bound to him, keeps you near his flame, keeps you on the team."

After reading this chapter, you should be able to answer the following questions:

12.1 What is leadership? What does it mean for a leader to be "effective"?

12.2 What traits and characteristics are related to leader emergence? What traits and characteristics are related to leader effectiveness?

12.3 What four styles can leaders use to make decisions? According to the time-driven model of leadership, what factors combine to make some styles more effective in a given situation?

12.4 What two dimensions capture most of the day-to-day leadership behaviours that leaders engage in?

12.5 How does transformational leadership differ from transactional leadership?

12.6 How does leadership affect job performance and organizational commitment?

12.7 Can leaders be trained to be more effective?

Apple's Steve Jobs, then and now—on the left with the original Macintosh, on the right with the iPod.

The introduction of the Macintosh should have been a crowning achievement for Jobs. Apple sold 70,000 units in the 100 days following the product announcement, meeting even the most optimistic expectations.[5] However, sales declined sharply over the summer as customers realized that the Macintosh didn't have enough memory, wasn't expandable, and didn't have enough software, particularly for business customers. Market research could have warned of such problems, but Jobs chose not to do any research because of his ambitious timetable and his own belief that he knew what consumers wanted. As Jobs explained, "Did Alexander Graham Bell do any market research when he invented the telephone? Of course not." Such sentiments were reinforced by Apple's marketing director who noted, "Steve did his market research by looking into the mirror every morning." Added to those missteps was the fateful decision to ask Microsoft, the company founded by Bill Gates and Paul Allen, to develop a word processing program for the Macintosh. Although Microsoft delivered the program on time, its experience with the Macintosh enabled it eventually to incorporate the graphical user interface into its Windows operating system, seriously damaging the Macintosh's market niche. Less than two years later, Jobs lost an internal power struggle and left the company he co-founded.

Of course, that's not the end of the story. Fast-forward a decade later and Apple found itself in dire straits—a company with a meagre 2 percent market share in computers,[6] no new products,[7] and a CEO in Gil Amelio who didn't fit the company's culture.[8] Desperate for a new operating system to satisfy Apple's customers and certain that his in-house talent couldn't provide it, Amelio began looking outside the company for help. Enter Steve Jobs. During the preceding decade, Jobs had founded NeXT, a computer company that had initially specialized in upscale hardware for educational environments but was now more notable for its NeXTSTEP software. Jobs also bought a computer graphics company from George Lucas, the creator of the *Star Wars* franchise. Although Jobs was initially attracted to the company's hardware and software, it was Pixar's animation division that wound up making Jobs's investment so profitable. Fresh off Pixar's debut of *Toy Story*, Apple acquired NeXT, and Steve Jobs was back where he belonged, eventually assuming the role of Apple's CEO in 1997. Jobs quickly fast-tracked some innovative new hardware offerings, including the iMac, which returned to the all-in-one roots of the original Macintosh while also demonstrating a new appreciation for software with the development of programs like iPhoto, iMovie, and iTunes.[9] Of course, the masterstroke of Jobs's second go-around was the realization that online music would be the "next big thing" and that existing music players were about as user friendly as the IBM PC had once been. Demonstrating a new willingness to go outside Apple for designs, Jobs hired a company called PortalPlayer to develop a revolutionary product that would complement iTunes—a product that eventually became the iPod. As the iPod set the stage for the iPhone, the return of Steve Jobs set Apple up as a significant player in three different industries.

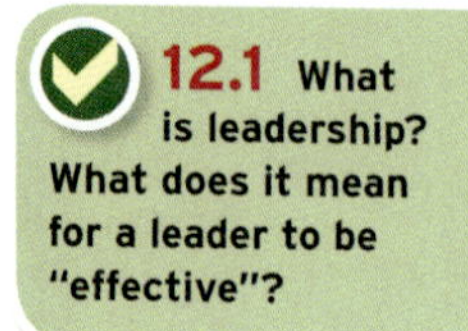

LEADERSHIP STYLES AND BEHAVIOURS

leadership The use of power and influence to direct the activities of followers toward goal achievement

There is perhaps no subject that's written about more in business circles than the topic of leadership. A quick search on Amazon.com of the topic "leadership" will generate a list of more than 200,000 books! That number doesn't even count the myriad of videos, podcasts, CDs, and other items, all designed to help people become better leaders. Given all the interest in this topic, a natural question becomes, "What exactly is a leader?" We define **leadership** as the use of power and influence to direct the activities of followers toward goal achievement.[10] That direction can affect followers' interpretation of events, the organization of their work activities, their commitment to key goals, their relationships with other followers, and their access to cooperation and support from other work units.[11] In this chapter we will discover that there are many different types of leaders, many of whom can excel given the right circumstances. In the case of Steve Jobs at Apple, his power is derived from his former role as Apple's CEO; his expertise in hardware, software, and the user experience; and his remarkable charisma. Since his return, Jobs has clearly used his power and influence effectively, as Apple's stock price has climbed 1,025 percent since the launch of the iPod, reaching a total market value of $72 billion as of 2007.[12]

Of course, most leaders can't judge their performance by pointing to changes in stock price. In fact, it turns out that leader effectiveness can be gauged in a number of ways. Leaders can be judged by objective evaluations of unit performance, such as profit margins, market share, sales, returns on investment, productivity, quality, costs in relation to budgeted expenditures, and so forth.[13] If those sorts of indices are unavailable, the leader's superiors may judge the performance of the unit on a more subjective basis. Other approaches to judging leader effectiveness centre more around followers, including indices such as absenteeism, retention of talented employees, grievances filed, requests for transfer, and so forth.[14] Those sorts of indices can be complemented by employee surveys that assess the perceived performance of the leader, the perceived respect and legitimacy of the leader, and employee commitment, satisfaction, and psychological well-being. The top panel of Table 12-1 provides one example of these sorts of measures.

One source of complexity when judging leader effectiveness, particularly with more subjective employee-centred approaches, is "Whom do you ask?" The members of a given unit often disagree about how effective their leader is. **Leader–member exchange theory**, which describes how leader–member relationships develop over time on a dyadic basis, can explain why those differences exist.[15] The theory argues that new leader–member relationships are typically marked by a phase called **role taking**, during which a manager describes role expectations to an employee and the employee attempts to fulfill those expectations with his or her job behaviours.[16] In this period of sampling and experimentation, the leader tries to get a feel for the talent and motivation levels of the employee. For some employees, that initial role taking phase may eventually be supplemented by **role making**, during which the employee's own expectations for the dyad get mixed in with those of the leader.[17] The role-making process is marked by a free-flowing exchange in which the leader offers more opportunities and resources and the employee contributes more activities and effort.

leader-member exchange theory A theory describing how leader-member relationships develop over time on a dyadic basis

role taking The phase in a leader-follower relationship when a leader provides an employee with job expectations and the follower tries to meet those expectations

role making The phase in a leader-follower relationship when a follower voices his or her own expectations for the relationship, resulting in a free-flowing exchange of opportunities and resources for activities and effort

Over time, the role-taking and role-making processes result in two general types of leader–member dyads, as shown in Figure 12-1. One type is the "high-quality exchange" dyad, marked by the frequent exchange of information, influence, latitude, support, and attention. Those dyads form the leader's "in-group" and are characterized by higher levels of mutual trust, respect, and obligation.[18] The other type is the "low-quality exchange" dyad, marked by a more limited exchange of information, influence, latitude, support, and attention. Those dyads form the leader's "out-group" and are characterized by lower levels of trust, respect, and obligation.[19] Tests of the theory suggest that employees who are competent, likable, and similar to the leader in personality will be more likely to end up in the leader's in-group, with those factors proving more impactful than age, gender, or racial similarity.[20] Leader–member exchange theory would suggest that leader effectiveness should be judged by gauging how effective the most critical leader–member dyads appear to be. The bottom panel of Table 12-1 provides one example of this sort of measure, with more agreement indicating a higher-quality exchange relationship and thus, higher levels of leader effectiveness on a dyadic basis.[21]

TABLE 12-1 Employee-Centred Measures of Leader Effectiveness

Unit-Focused Approach
Ask all members of the unit to fill out the following survey items, and then average the responses across the group to get a measure of leader effectiveness.
1. My supervisor is effective in meeting our job-related needs.
2. My supervisor uses methods of leadership that are satisfying.
3. My supervisor gets us to do more than we expected to do.
4. My supervisor is effective in representing us to higher authority.
5. My supervisor works with us in a satisfactory way.
6. My supervisor heightens our desire to succeed.
7. My supervisor is effective in meeting organizational requirements.
8. My supervisor increases our willingness to try harder.
9. My supervisor leads a group that is effective.
Dyad-Focused Approach
Ask members of the unit to fill out the following survey items in reference to their particular relationship with the leader. The responses are not averaged across the group; rather, differences across people indicate differentiation into "in-groups" and "out-groups" within the unit.
1. I always know how satisfied my supervisor is with what I do.
2. My supervisor understands my problems and needs well enough.
3. My supervisor recognizes my potential.
4. My supervisor would use his/her power to help me solve work problems.
5. I can count on my supervisor to "bail me out" at his/her expense if I need it.
6. My working relationship with my supervisor is extremely effective.
7. I have enough confidence in my supervisor to defend and justify his/her decisions when he/she is not present to do so.

Sources: Adapted from B. Bass and B. Avolio, *MLQ Manual* (Menlo Park, CA: Mind Garden, Inc., 2004); G.B. Graen and M. Uhl-Bien, "Relationship-Based Approach to Leadership: Development of Leader–Member Exchange (LMX) Theory of Leadership over 25 Years: Applying a Multi-Level Multi-Domain Perspective," *Leadership Quarterly* 6 (1995), pp. 219–47.

FIGURE 12-1 Leader-Member Exchange Theory

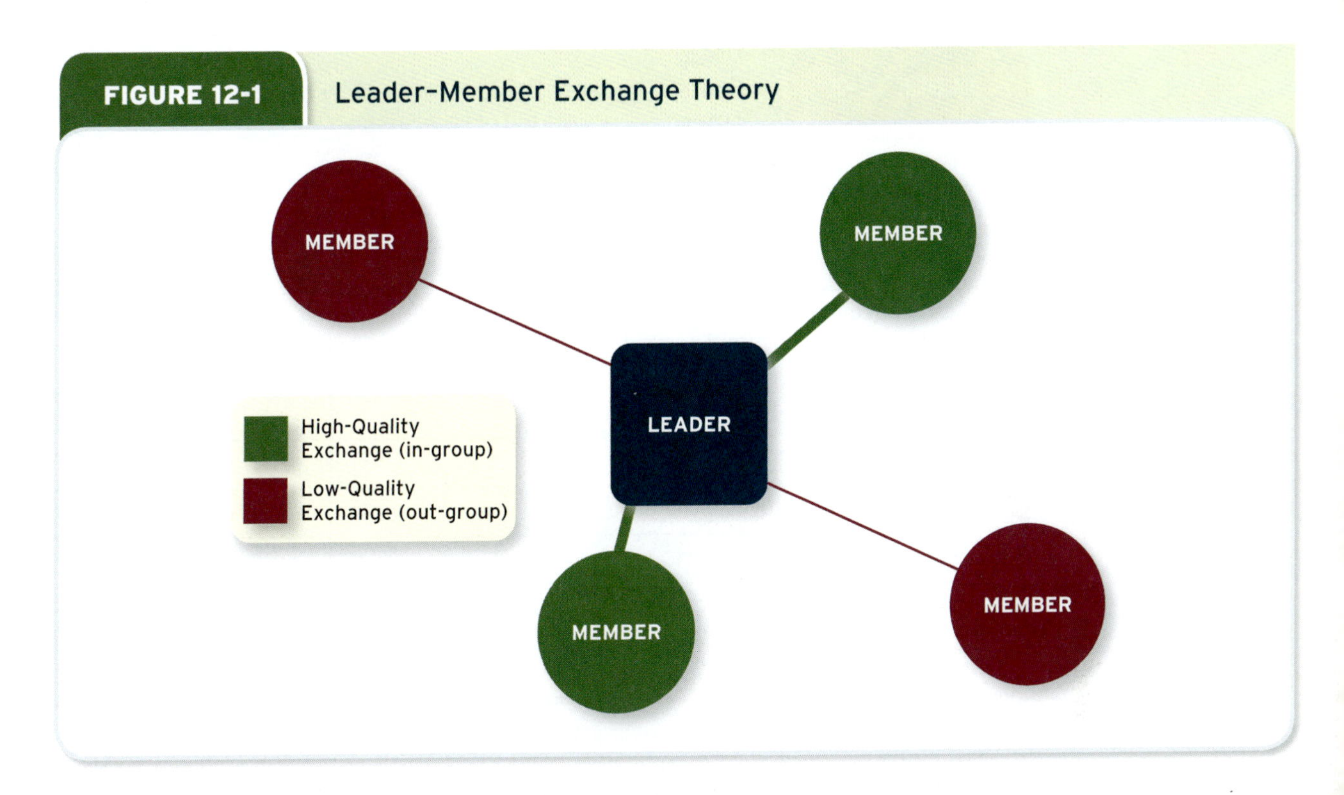

WHY ARE SOME LEADERS MORE EFFECTIVE THAN OTHERS?

12.2 What traits and characteristics are related to leader emergence? What traits and characteristics are related to leader effectiveness?

For our purposes, **leader effectiveness** will be defined as the degree to which the leader's actions result in the achievement of the unit's goals, the continued commitment of the unit's employees, and the development of mutual trust, respect, and obligation in leader–member dyads. Now that we've described what it means for a leader to be effective, we turn to the critical question in this chapter: "Why are some leaders more effective than others?" That is, why exactly are some leaders viewed as more effective on a unitwide basis, and why exactly are some leaders better at fostering high-quality exchange relationships? Beginning as far back as 1904, research on leadership has attempted to answer such questions by looking for particular traits or characteristics of effective leaders.[22] The search for traits and characteristics is consistent with "great person" theories of leadership that suggest that "leaders are born, not made."[23] Early research in this area frequently focused on physical features (e.g., gender, height, physical attractiveness, energy level), whereas subsequent research focused more squarely on personality and ability (see Chapter 9 on personality, cultural values, and ability for more discussion of those topics).

leader effectiveness The degree to which the leader's actions result in the achievement of the unit's goals, the continued commitment of the unit's employees, and the development of mutual trust, respect, and obligation in leader-member dyads

After a century of research, leadership scholars now acknowledge that there is no generalizable profile of effective leaders from a trait perspective.[24] In fact, most studies have concluded that traits are more predictive of **leader emergence** (i.e., who becomes a leader in the first place) than they are of leader effectiveness (i.e., how well people actually do in a leadership role). Table 12-2 reviews some of the traits and characteristics frequently examined in organizational behaviour research in general and leadership research in particular.

leader emergence The process of becoming a leader in the first place

TABLE 12-2 Traits/Characteristics Related to Leader Emergence and Effectiveness

DESCRIPTION OF TRAIT/ CHARACTERISTIC	LINKED TO EMERGENCE?	LINKED TO EFFECTIVENESS?
High conscientiousness	√	
Low agreeableness	√	
Low neuroticism		
High openness to experience	√	√
High extraversion	√	√
High general cognitive ability	√	√
High energy level	√	√
High stress tolerance	√	√
High self-confidence	√	√

Sources: Adapted from T.A. Judge, J.E. Bono, R. Ilies, and M.W. Gerhardt, "Personality and Leadership: A Qualitative and Quantitative Review," *Journal of Applied Psychology* 87 (2002), pp. 765–80; T.A. Judge, A.E. Colbert, and R. Ilies, "Intelligence and Leadership: A Quantitative Review and Test of Theoretical Propositions," *Journal of Applied Psychology* 89 (2004), pp. 542–52; G. Yukl, *Leadership in Organizations,* 4th ed. (Englewood Cliffs, NJ: Prentice-Hall, 1998).

The table draws a distinction between traits and characteristics that predict leader emergence and those that predict leader effectiveness. Although a number of traits and characteristics are relevant to leadership, two limitations of this work have caused leadership research to move in a different direction. First, many of the trait–leadership correlations are weak in magnitude, particularly when leader effectiveness serves as the outcome. Second, the focus on leader traits holds less practical relevance than a focus on leader actions. What exactly can leaders *do* that can make them more effective? This chapter will review three types of leader actions: decision-making styles, day-to-day behaviours, and behaviours that fall outside of a leader's typical duties.

LEADER DECISION-MAKING STYLES

12.3 What four styles can leaders use to make decisions? According to the time-driven model of leadership, what factors combine to make some styles more effective in a given situation?

Of course, one of the most important things leaders do is make decisions. Think about the job you currently hold or the last job you had. Now picture your boss. How many decisions did he or she have to make in a given week? How did he or she go about making those decisions? A leader's decision-making style reflects the process the leader uses to generate and choose from a set of alternatives to solve a problem (see Chapter 8 on learning and decision making for more about such issues). Decision-making styles capture *how* a leader decides as opposed to *what* a leader decides.

The most important element of a leader's decision-making style is this: Does the leader decide most things for him- or herself, or does the leader involve others in the process? We've probably all had bosses (or professors, or even parents) who made virtually all decisions by themselves, stopping by to announce what had happened once the call had been made. We've

FIGURE 12-2 Leader Decision-Making Styles

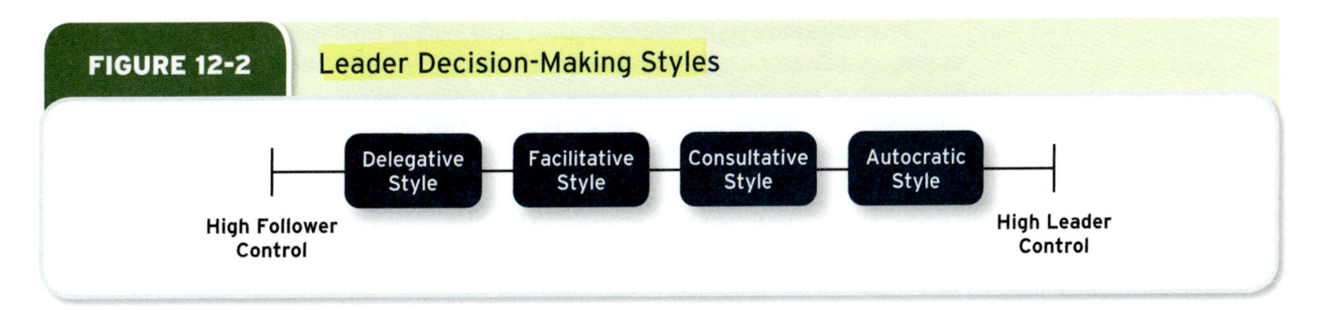

probably also had other bosses (or professors, or parents) who tended to do the opposite—involving us, asking our opinions, or seeking our vote even when we didn't even care about what was being discussed. It turns out that this issue of leader versus follower control can be used to define some specific decision-making styles. Figure 12-2 shows those styles, arranged on a continuum from high follower control to high leader control.

autocratic style A leadership style where the leader makes the decision alone without asking for opinions or suggestions of the employees in the work unit

consultative style A leadership style where the leader presents the problem to employees asking for their opinions and suggestions before ultimately making the decision him- or herself

facilitative style A leadership style where the leader presents the problem to a group of employees and seeks consensus on a solution, making sure that his or her own opinion receives no more weight than anyone else's

DEFINING THE STYLES With an **autocratic style**, the leader makes the decision alone without asking for the opinions or suggestions of the employees in the work unit.[25] The employees may provide information that the leader needs but are not asked to generate or evaluate potential solutions. In fact, they may not even be told about the decision that needs to be made, knowing only that the leader wants information for some reason. An example of this is the autocratic manner in which professors often have to approach course-related decisions. It is common for professors to select the topics covered and the background readings, as well as to determine the nature and weighting of assignments and exams, without consulting with the students who will be taking the course.

The next two styles in Figure 12-2 (moving from right to left on the continuum) offer more employee involvement. With a **consultative style**, the leader presents the problem to individual employees or a group of employees, asking for their opinions and suggestions before ultimately making the decision him- or herself.[26] With this style, employees do "have a say" in the process, but the ultimate authority still rests with the leader. An example of a consultative style would be a professor who asks students to share their opinions and preferences before assigning an in-class or take-home final exam. Ultimate decision-making authority changes with a **facilitative style**, in which the leader presents the problem to a group of employees and seeks consensus on a solution, making sure that his or her own opinion receives no more weight than anyone else's.[27] With this style, the leader is more facilitator than decision maker. An example of a facilitative style would be a professor who carefully describes the virtues and pitfalls of randomly assigned versus self-selected project teams, but then allows individual students in the class to form their own groups or opt for random assignment.

"I'd like your honest, unbiased and possibly career-ending opinion on something."

Source: © The New Yorker Collection 2003 Alex Gregory from cartoonbank.com.

delegative style A leadership style where the leader gives the employee the responsibility for making decisions within some set of specified boundary conditions

With a **delegative style**, the leader gives an individual employee or a group of employees the responsibility for making the decision within some set of specified boundary conditions.[28] The leader plays no role in the deliberations unless asked, though he or she may offer encouragement and provide necessary resources behind the scenes. An example of a delegative style would be when the professor describes her expectations with respect to a final product, but allows the project teams to decide how best to achieve this outcome.

WHEN ARE THE STYLES MOST EFFECTIVE? Which decision-making style is best? As you may have guessed, there is no one decision-making style that's effective across all situations, and all styles have their pluses and minuses. There are many factors to consider when leaders choose a decision-making style.[29] The most obvious consideration is the quality of the resulting decision, because making the correct decision is the ultimate means of judging the leader. However, leaders also have to consider whether employees will accept and commit to their decision. Research studies have repeatedly shown that allowing employees to participate in decision making increases their job satisfaction.[30] Such participation also helps develop employees' own decision-making skills.[31]

Of course, such participation has a downside for employees because it takes up time. Many employees view meetings as an interruption of their work. One recent study found that employees spend, on average, six hours a week in scheduled meetings, and that time spent in meetings was negatively related to job satisfaction when employees didn't depend on others in their jobs, were focused on their own task accomplishment, and felt that meetings were run ineffectively.[32] Consider the case of Paul Pressler, whose five-year term as CEO of Gap Inc. ended in 2007.[33] Pressler had been hired from Disney to use his expertise to bring discipline to the struggling company. His tenure was criticized for its increase in meetings, with employees asked to explain incredibly specific details to Gap Inc.'s new chief financial officer. One former employee describes the demands as "the antithesis of being creative and nimble. It was talking about the work vs. doing the work." Criticisms about decision-making style were also levelled at Cynthia Harriss, whom Pressler had hired to lead the Gap brand. "She made no decisions," says one employee. "She defaulted to Paul, who made no decisions."

time-driven model of leadership A model that suggests that seven factors, including the importance of the decision, the expertise of the leader, and the competence of the followers, combine to make some decision-making styles more effective than others in a given situation

How can leaders effectively manage their choice of decision-making styles? The **time-driven model of leadership** offers one potential guide.[34] The model suggests that the focus should shift away from autocratic, consultative, facilitative, and delegative *leaders* to autocratic, consultative, facilitative, and delegative *situations*. More specifically, the model suggests that seven factors combine to make some decision-making styles more effective in a given situation and other styles less effective. Those seven factors include:

- *Decision significance:* Is the decision significant to the success of the project or the organization?
- *Importance of commitment:* Is it important that employees "buy in" to the decision?
- *Leader expertise:* Does the leader have significant knowledge or expertise regarding the problem?
- *Likelihood of commitment:* How likely is it that employees will trust the leader's decision and commit to it?
- *Shared objectives:* Do employees share and support the same objectives, or do they have an agenda of their own?
- *Employee expertise:* Do the employees have significant knowledge or expertise regarding the problem?
- *Teamwork skills:* Do the employees have the ability to work together to solve the problem, or will they struggle with conflicts or inefficiencies?

Figure 12-3 illustrates how these seven factors can be used to illustrate the most effective decision-making style in a given situation. The figure asks whether levels of each of the seven factors are "high" (H) or "low" (L). The figure functions like a funnel moving from

FIGURE 12-3 The Time-Driven Model of Leadership

START HERE → END HERE

Decision Significance	Importance of Commitment	Leader Expertise	Likelihood of Commitment	Shared Objectives	Employee Expertise	Teamwork Skills	Style
H	H	H	H	-	-	-	Autocratic
H	H	H	L	H	H	H	Delegative
H	H	H	L	H	H	L	Consultative
H	H	H	L	H	L	-	Consultative
H	H	H	L	L	-	-	Consultative
H	H	L	H	H	H	H	Facilitative
H	H	L	H	H	H	L	Consultative
H	H	L	H	H	L	-	Consultative
H	H	L	H	L	-	-	Consultative
H	H	L	L	H	H	H	Facilitative
H	H	L	L	H	H	L	Consultative
H	H	L	L	H	L	-	Consultative
H	H	L	L	L	-	-	Consultative
H	L	H	-	-	-	-	Autocratic
H	L	L	-	H	H	H	Facilitative
H	L	L	-	H	H	L	Consultative
H	L	L	-	H	L	-	Consultative
H	L	L	-	L	-	-	Consultative
L	H	-	H	-	-	-	Autocratic
L	H	-	L	-	-	H	Delegative
L	H	-	L	-	-	L	Facilitative
L	L	-	-	-	-	-	Autocratic

Source: Adapted from V.H. Vroom, "Leadership and the Decision-Making Process," *Organizational Dynamics* 28 (2000), pp. 82–94.

left to right, with each answer bringing you closer to the eventual recommended style (dashes mean that a given factor can be skipped with that combination). Although the model seems complex on first look, the principles within it are straightforward. Autocratic styles are reserved for decisions that are insignificant or decisions for which employee commitment is unimportant. The only exception is when the leader's expertise is high and the leader is trusted. Going with the autocratic style in these situations should result in an accurate decision that makes the most efficient use of employees' time. Delegative styles are reserved for circumstances in which employees have strong teamwork skills and aren't likely to just commit to whatever decision the leader provides. Deciding between the remaining two styles—consultative and facilitative—is more nuanced and requires a more complete consideration of all seven factors.

Research has tended to support many of the time-driven model's propositions, particularly when the research uses practicing managers as participants.[35] For example, one study asked managers to recall past decisions, the context surrounding those decisions, and the eventual successes (or failures) of their decisions.[36] When managers used the decision-making styles recommended by the model, those decisions were rated as successful 68 percent of the time. When managers went against the model's prescriptions, their decisions were only rated as successful 22 percent of the time. It's also interesting to note that studies suggest that managers tend to choose the style recommended by the model only around 40 percent of the time and exhibit less variation in styles than the model suggests they should.[37] In particular, managers seem to overuse the consultative style and underutilize autocratic and facilitative styles. For a more informal test (and "test drive") of the model, see our **OB on Screen** feature.

OB ON SCREEN

THIRTEEN DAYS

There's something immoral about abandoning your own judgment.

With those words, President John F. Kennedy (Bruce Greenwood) foreshadows the decision-making style he's going to use during the Cuban missile crisis, as depicted in *Thirteen Days* (Dir. Roger Donaldson, New Line, 2001). During a conversation with his brother, Robert Kennedy (Steven Culp), and his chief-of-staff, Kenny O'Donnell (Kevin Costner), Kennedy voices regret over his past decision to support the Bay of Pigs invasion, when U.S.-backed Cuban refugees attempted to overthrow the government of Fidel Castro. He doesn't want to repeat the same mistakes when dealing with a new crisis: the installation of Soviet missiles in Cuba. Kennedy assembles the best team of advisors he can to deal with the crisis, but the question remains: What decision-making style should he use?

If we work our way through Figure 12-3, it seems clear that the decision is significant (the missiles can reach every major city in the United States, except for Seattle). O'Donnell himself notes how important it is for U.S. generals to commit to the decision, and it's clear that Kennedy doesn't have the expertise needed to drive the discussions.

Unfortunately for Kennedy, the movie's depiction of the events shows that his generals don't trust him (they view him as an "appeaser," like his father was), resulting in a low likelihood of commitment. To make matters worse, the generals appear to have their own objectives, seeming to want to use the missile crisis as an excuse to invade Cuba and take out Castro once and for all. If you're scoring at home, our journey through Figure 12-3 results in H-H-L-L-L, suggesting that the most effective decision-making style for Kennedy is consultative.

Did Kennedy use that style? In the end, Kennedy's advisors present him with two feasible options. One is an invasion of Cuba to take out the missiles, and the other is a blockade, an action that prevents additional missiles from being delivered while giving the Russians a chance to pull back from the brink of war. Once those options are delivered, Kennedy doesn't call for a show of hands and makes no attempt to bring the room to consensus. He asks his speechwriters to get time on the network news the next day and write up speeches for invasion and for blockade. Then he tells the room he'll give them *his decision* in the morning. Thus, Kennedy did exactly what the time-driven model of leadership suggests he should have done: Gather the opinions and suggestions of others but maintain the ultimate authority for himself.

DAY-TO-DAY LEADERSHIP BEHAVIOURS

Leaving aside how they go about making decisions, what do leaders *do* on a day-to-day basis? When you think about bosses that you've had, what behaviours do they tend to perform as part of their daily leadership responsibilities? A series of studies at Ohio State University in the 1950s attempted to answer that question. The studies began by generating a list of all the behaviours leaders engage in—around 1,800 in all.[38] Those behaviours were trimmed down to 150 specific examples, then grouped into several categories, as shown in Table 12-3.[39] The table reveals that many leaders spend their time engaging in a mix of initiating, organizing, producing, socializing, integrating, communicating, recognizing, and representing behaviours. Although eight categories are easier to remember than 1,800 behaviours, further analyses suggested that the categories in Table 12-3 really boil down to just two dimensions: initiating structure and consideration.[40]

Initiating structure reflects the extent to which the leader defines and structures the roles of employees in pursuit of goal attainment.[41] Leaders who score high on initiating structure play a more active role in directing group activities and prioritize planning, scheduling, and trying out new ideas. They might emphasize the importance of meeting deadlines, describe explicit standards of performance, ask employees to follow formalized procedures, and criticize poor work when necessary.[42] **Consideration** reflects the extent to which

12.4 What two dimensions capture most of the day-to-day leadership behaviours that leaders engage in?

initiating structure A pattern of behaviour where the leader defines and structures the roles of employees in pursuit of goal attainment

consideration A pattern of behaviour where the leader creates job relationships characterized by mutual trust, respect for employee ideas, and consideration of employee feelings

TABLE 12-3 Day-to-Day Behaviours Performed by Leaders

BEHAVIOUR	DESCRIPTION
Initiating Structure	
Initiation	Originating, facilitating, and sometimes resisting new ideas and practices
Organization	Defining and structuring work, clarifying leader versus member roles, coordinating employee tasks
Production	Setting goals and providing incentives for the effort and productivity of employees
Consideration	
Membership	Mixing with employees, stressing informal interactions, and exchanging personal services
Integration	Encouraging a pleasant atmosphere, reducing conflict, promoting individual adjustment to the group
Communication	Providing information to employees, seeking information from them, showing an awareness of matters that affect them
Recognition	Expressing approval or disapproval of the behaviours of employees
Representation	Acting on behalf of the group, defending the group, and advancing the interests of the group

Source: J.K. Hemphill and A.E. Coons, "Development of the Leader Behaviour Description Questionnaire," in *Leader Behaviour: Its Description and Measurement,* eds. R.M. Stogdill and A.E. Coons. (Columbus, OH: Bureau of Business Research, Ohio State University, 1957), pp. 6–38.

leaders create job relationships characterized by mutual trust, respect for employee ideas, and consideration of employee feelings.[43] Leaders who score high on consideration create a climate of good rapport and strong, two-way communication and exhibit a deep concern for the welfare of employees. They might do personal favours for employees, take time to listen to their problems, "go to bat" for them when needed, and treat them as equals.[44]

The Ohio State studies argued that initiating structure and consideration were (more or less) independent concepts, meaning that leaders could be high on both, low on both, or high on one and low on the other. That view differed from a series of studies conducted at the University of Michigan during the same time period. Those studies identified concepts similar to initiating structure and consideration, calling them production-centred (or task-oriented) and employee-centred (or relations-oriented) behaviours.[45] However, the Michigan studies framed their task-oriented and relations-oriented concepts as two ends of one continuum, implying that leaders couldn't be high on both dimensions.[46] In fact, a recent meta-analysis of 78 studies showed that initiating structure and consideration are only weakly related—knowing whether a leader engages in one brand of behaviour says little about whether he or she engages in the other brand.[47] To see how much initiating structure and consideration you engage in during leadership roles, see our **OB Assessments** feature at the end of the chapter.

After an initial wave of research on initiating structure and consideration, leadership experts began to doubt the usefulness of the two dimensions for predicting leadership effectiveness.[48] More recent research has painted a more encouraging picture, however. A meta-analysis of 103 studies showed that initiating structure and consideration both had beneficial relationships with a number of outcomes.[49] For example, consideration had a strong positive relationship with perceived leader effectiveness, employee motivation, and employee job satisfaction. It also had a moderate positive relationship with overall unit performance. For its part, initiating structure had a strong positive relationship with employee motivation and moderate positive relationships with perceived leader effectiveness, employee job satisfaction, and overall unit performance.

life cycle theory of leadership A theory stating that the optimal combination of initiating structure and consideration depends on the readiness of the employees in the work unit

Although initiating structure and consideration tend to be beneficial across situations, there may be circumstances in which they become more or less important. The **life cycle theory of leadership** (sometimes also called the situational model of leadership) argues that the optimal combination of initiating structure and consideration depends on the readiness of the employees in the work unit.[50] **Readiness** is broadly defined as the degree to which employees have the ability and the willingness to accomplish their specific tasks.[51] As shown in Figure 12-4, the theory suggests that readiness varies from R1 (unable and unwilling) to R2 (unable but willing) to R3 (able but unwilling) to R4 (able and willing). It is important to note that employees may be unwilling to perform their tasks because they lack commitment or motivation or merely because they are insecure due to a lack of experience.[52]

readiness The degree to which employees have the ability and the willingness to accomplish their specific tasks

To find the optimal behavioural combination for those levels of readiness, put your finger on the relevant R level then move it straight down to the recommended combination. For example, the optimal combination for the R1 readiness level is **telling**—high initiating structure and low consideration—in which case the leader provides specific instructions and closely supervises performance.[53] Here the leader tells employees what to do, where to do it, and how to do it, because such guidance and direction is needed in the absence of employee ability, motivation, or confidence. The optimal combination for the R2 readiness level is **selling**—high initiating structure and high consideration—so the leader explains key issues and provides opportunities for clarification.[54] Some guidance and direction is still needed due to a lack of employee ability, but the increased explanation and persuasion can help foster the emerging motivation and confidence.

telling When the leader provides specific instructions and closely supervises performance

selling When the leader explains key issues and provides opportunities for clarification

As employees gain more ability, the nature of their job becomes more complex, potentially renewing concerns about their confidence. The optimal combination for the R3 readiness level is **participating**—low initiating structure and high consideration—as the leader shares

participating When the leader shares ideas and tries to help the group conduct its affairs

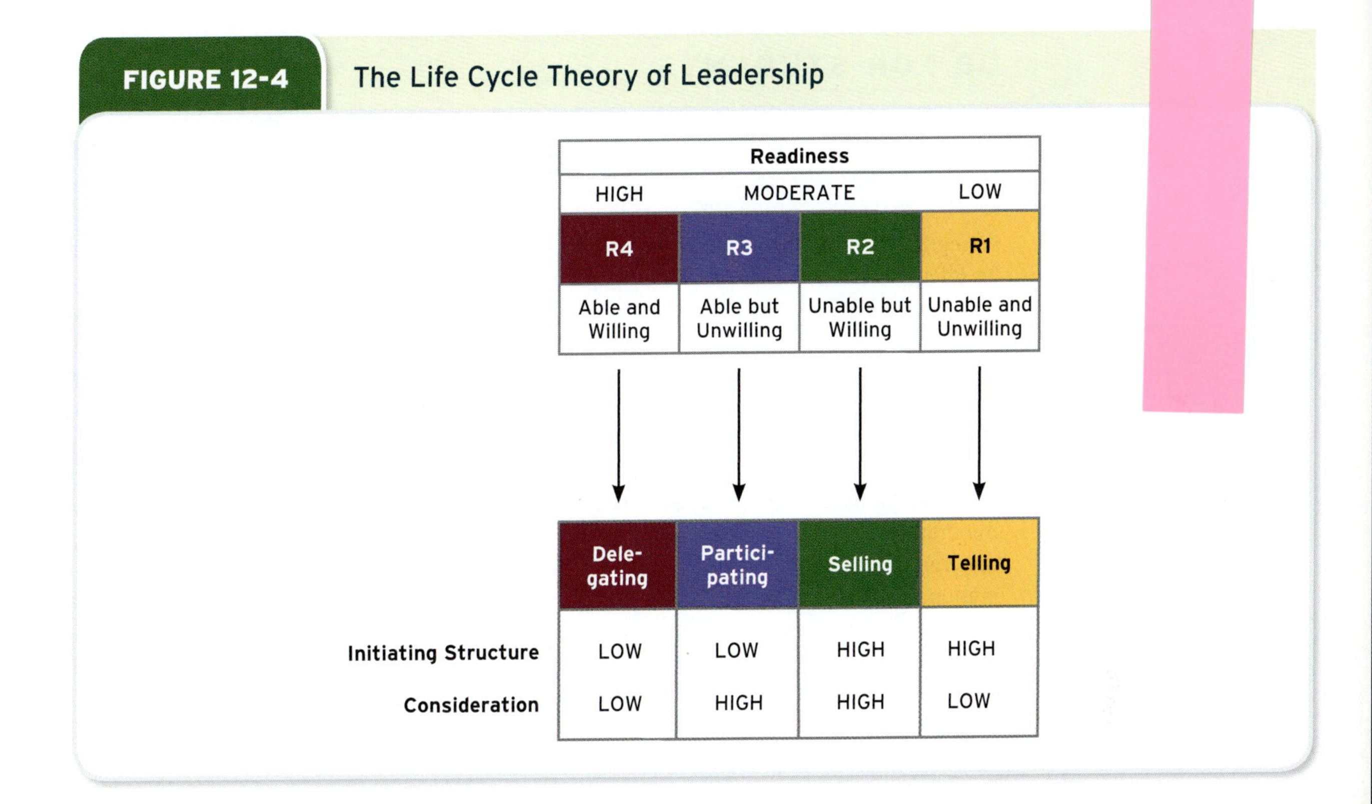

ideas and tries to help the group conduct its affairs.[55] Here guidance is no longer needed because employee ability is high. What is needed is some combination of collaborating and facilitating to support employees during this shift in their role requirements. Finally, the optimal combination for the R4 readiness level is **delegating**—low initiating structure and low consideration—such that the leader turns responsibility for key behaviours over to the employees.[56] Here the leader "gives them the ball and lets them run with it." All that is needed from the leader is some degree of observation and monitoring to make sure that the group's efforts stay on track.

delegating When the leader turns responsibility for key behaviours over to employees

Estimates suggest that the life cycle theory has been incorporated into leadership training programs, with more than one million managers exposed to it annually.[57] Unfortunately, the application of the theory has outpaced scientific testing of its propositions. The research that has been conducted supports the theory's predictions only for low readiness situations, suggesting that telling and selling sorts of behaviours may be more effective when ability, motivation, or confidence are lacking.[58] When readiness is higher, these tests suggest that leader behaviours simply matter less, regardless of their particular combinations. Tests also suggest that leaders only use the recommended combinations of behaviours between 14 and 37 percent of the time,[59] likely because many leaders adhere to the same leadership philosophy regardless of the situation. It should also be noted that tests of the theory have been somewhat more supportive when conducted on an across-job, rather than within-job, basis. For example, research suggests that the performance of lower-ranking university employees (e.g., maintenance workers, custodians, landscapers) depends more on initiating structure and less on consideration than the performance of higher-ranking university employees (e.g., professors, instructors).[60] To see the potential relevance of the life cycle theory for students, see our **OB for Students** feature.

Although the scientific validity of the life cycle theory remains in question, its predictions often seem to play out in professional sports. General managers often hire coaches with

OB FOR STUDENTS

Even if you aren't currently working and haven't worked in the past, the life cycle theory of leadership has some relevance to you. After all, you've experienced at least two kinds of leaders already: parents and teachers.

The originators of the life cycle theory suggest that it offers predictions for how parenting behaviours should vary over the course of a child's time at home.[61] Telling should be effective early in life, because initiating structure is needed as children learn to navigate their daily lives. As the child enters school and begins to demonstrate his or her own responsibility and work ethic, telling should give way to selling to build trust and mutual respect. As the child moves into high school and college or university, the responsibility for key decisions becomes his or her own, with the parent offering mostly support in accordance with a participating style. Finally, as the now young adult makes his or her own living and starts a family, a delegating style seems most appropriate.

Although those predictions have never been formally tested, research has supported the importance of parenting behaviours to academic success in university. One study of 236 undergraduates asked the students to rate their parents on three types of behaviours: consideration, demandingness (one aspect of initiating structure), and autonomy granting (reflecting the use of a more participating and delegating style).[62] The students were asked to rate those behaviours in reference to two time periods: now and during their childhood (around 8 years old). As would be expected based on the life cycle theory, current levels of autonomy granting were significantly related to student GPA, but childhood levels were not. However, autonomy granting at both time periods was related to students' confidence, persistence, involvement, and rapport with instructors. Its importance did not vary, as would be expected by the theory. Similarly, the study showed that consideration was related to students' confidence and persistence in the classroom and their rapport with their instructors, again regardless of whether the behaviours occurred currently or in childhood. For its part, demandingness had little impact on student outcomes, regardless of the relevant time period.

a "hands-on" directive philosophy for youthful teams with several rookies or new starters. Over time, those teams mature and become more experienced, at which point the coach's style begins to wear on the veterans. The general managers then bring in coaches with a more "hands-off" style (often referred to as a "player's coach"). This same dynamic recently played out at Home Depot. Controversial CEO Bob Nardelli agreed to resign in early 2007 after a six-year tenure, with one observer noting, "The fact is that this retail organization never really embraced his leadership style."[63] Nardelli has been described as a detail-obsessed manager devoted to building a disciplined corps predisposed to following orders.[64] He believes in a command-and-control sort of environment and is fond of saying, "Facts are friendly."[65] You can probably already guess the adjectives associated with Nardelli's replacement. The co-founder of Home Depot describes new CEO Frank Blake as more "people oriented," lacking Nardelli's sharp edges while playing the role of consensus builder.[66]

TRANSFORMATIONAL LEADERSHIP BEHAVIOURS

By describing decision-making styles and day-to-day leader behaviours, we've covered a broad spectrum of what it is that leaders do. Still, something is missing. Take a small piece of scrap paper and jot down five people who are famous for their effective leadership. They can come from inside or outside the business world and can be either living people or historical figures. All that's important is that their name be practically synonymous with

OB RESEARCH IN CANADA

Dr. Rick D. Hackett, at the DeGroote School of Business, McMaster University, has published widely on leadership and its influence on employee attitudes, performance, and organizational citizenship behaviours. Following a two-year visiting appointment at the Hong Kong University of Science and Technology, his more recent research explores whether leadership styles effective in North America and Western European countries are also effective in China, a society known for its high collectivism and power distance values. His interest in leadership was piqued by his observations over the years on just how much influence leaders can have on the morale and productivity of the workplace.

Dr. Hackett's publications have appeared in several journals, such as the *Academy of Management Journal*, *Journal of Applied Psychology,* and *Organizational Behaviour and Human Decision Processes.* Moreover, much of his research has received coverage in the media, including the *Wall Street Journal,* the *Globe and Mail, Report on Business* magazine, CTV NewsNet, and the *Toronto Star.* His studies have received "Best Paper" honours at the Academy of Management Conference and the Administrative Sciences Association of Canada. Dr. Hackett is also past president of the Canadian Society for Industrial and Organizational Psychology, is a fellow of the Canadian Psychological Association, and is listed in *Who's Who in Canada.*

Dr. Hackett's favourite publications include:

"Individual-Level Cultural Values as Moderators of the Perceived Support-Employee Outcomes Relationship in China: Comparing the Effects of Power Distance and Traditionality," by J.L. Farh, R.D. Hackett, and J. Liang, published in *Academy of Management Journal* (2007, volume 50, pp. 715–29).

"Leader-Member Exchange as a Mediator of the Relationship Between Transformational Leadership and Followers' Performance and Organizational Citizenship Behavior," by H. Wang, K.S. Law, R.D. Hackett, D. Wang, and Z. Chen, published in *Academy of Management Journal* (2005, volume 48, pp. 420–32).

"Further Assessments of Bass's (1985) Conceptualization of Transactional and Transformational Leadership," by P. Bycio, R.D. Hackett, and J.S. Allen, published in *Journal of Applied Psychology* (1995, volume 80, pp. 468–78).

"Absenteeism Among Hospital Nurses: An Idiographic-Longitudinal Analysis," by R.D. Hackett, P. Bycio, and R.M. Guion, published in *Academy of Management Journal* (1989, volume 32, pp. 424–53).

great leadership. Once you've compiled your list, take a look at the names. Do they appear on your list because they tend to use the right decision-making styles in the right situations and engage in effective levels of consideration and initiating structure? What about the case of Steve Jobs? Do decision-making styles and day-to-day leadership behaviours explain his importance to Apple? What about U.S. President Barack Obama? What was it about his election campaign in 2008 that engaged and inspired so many young people across the

Mother Teresa's inspiring humanitarian work with India's sick and poor, and her founding of the influential Missionaries of Charity, became known around the world and suggest that she was a transformational leader. She was awarded the Nobel Peace Prize in 1979.

transformational leadership A pattern of behaviour where the leader inspires followers to commit to a shared vision that provides meaning to their work while also serving as a role model who helps followers develop their own potential and view problems from new perspectives

laissez-faire leadership When the leader avoids leadership duties altogether

transactional leadership A pattern of behaviour where the leader rewards or disciplines the follower based on performance

passive management-by-exception When the leader waits around for mistakes and errors, then takes corrective action as necessary

active management-by-exception When the leader arranges to monitor mistakes and errors actively and takes corrective action when required

United States and around the world? What about the many prominent Canadians who, over the years, have demonstrated great leadership, such as Terry Fox or David Suzuki? What is it about these leaders that attract others to their causes—be it finding a cure for cancer or saving the environment?

The missing piece of this leadership puzzle is what leaders do to motivate their employees to perform beyond expectations. **Transformational leadership** involves inspiring followers to commit to a shared vision that provides meaning to their work while also serving as a role model who helps followers develop their own potential and view problems from new perspectives.[67] Transformational leaders heighten followers' awareness of the importance of certain outcomes while increasing their confidence that those outcomes can be achieved.[68] What gets "transformed" is the way followers view their work, causing them to focus on the collective good more than just their own short-term self-interests and to perform beyond expectations as a result.[69]

Transformational leadership is viewed as a more motivational approach to leadership than other managerial approaches. Figure 12-5 contrasts various approaches to leadership according to how active or passive they are and, ultimately, how effective they prove to be. The coloured cubes in the figure represent five distinct approaches to motivating employees, and the depth of the cubes represent how much a leader prioritizes each of the approaches. The figure therefore represents an optimal leadership approach that prioritizes more effective and more active behaviours. That optimal approach includes low levels of **laissez-faire** (i.e., hands-off) leadership, represented by the red cube, which is the avoidance of leadership altogether.[70] Important actions are delayed, responsibility is ignored, and power and influence go unutilized. One common measure of leadership reflects laissez-faire styles with this statement: "The leader avoids getting involved when important issues arise."[71]

The three yellow cubes represent **transactional leadership**, which occurs when the leader rewards or disciplines the follower depending on the adequacy of the follower's performance.[72] With **passive management-by-exception**, the leader waits around for mistakes and errors, then takes corrective action as necessary.[73] After all, "if it ain't broke, don't fix it!"[74] This approach is represented by statements like: "The leader takes no action until complaints are received."[75] With **active management-by-exception**, the leader arranges

FIGURE 12-5 Laissez-Faire, Transactional, and Transformational Leadership

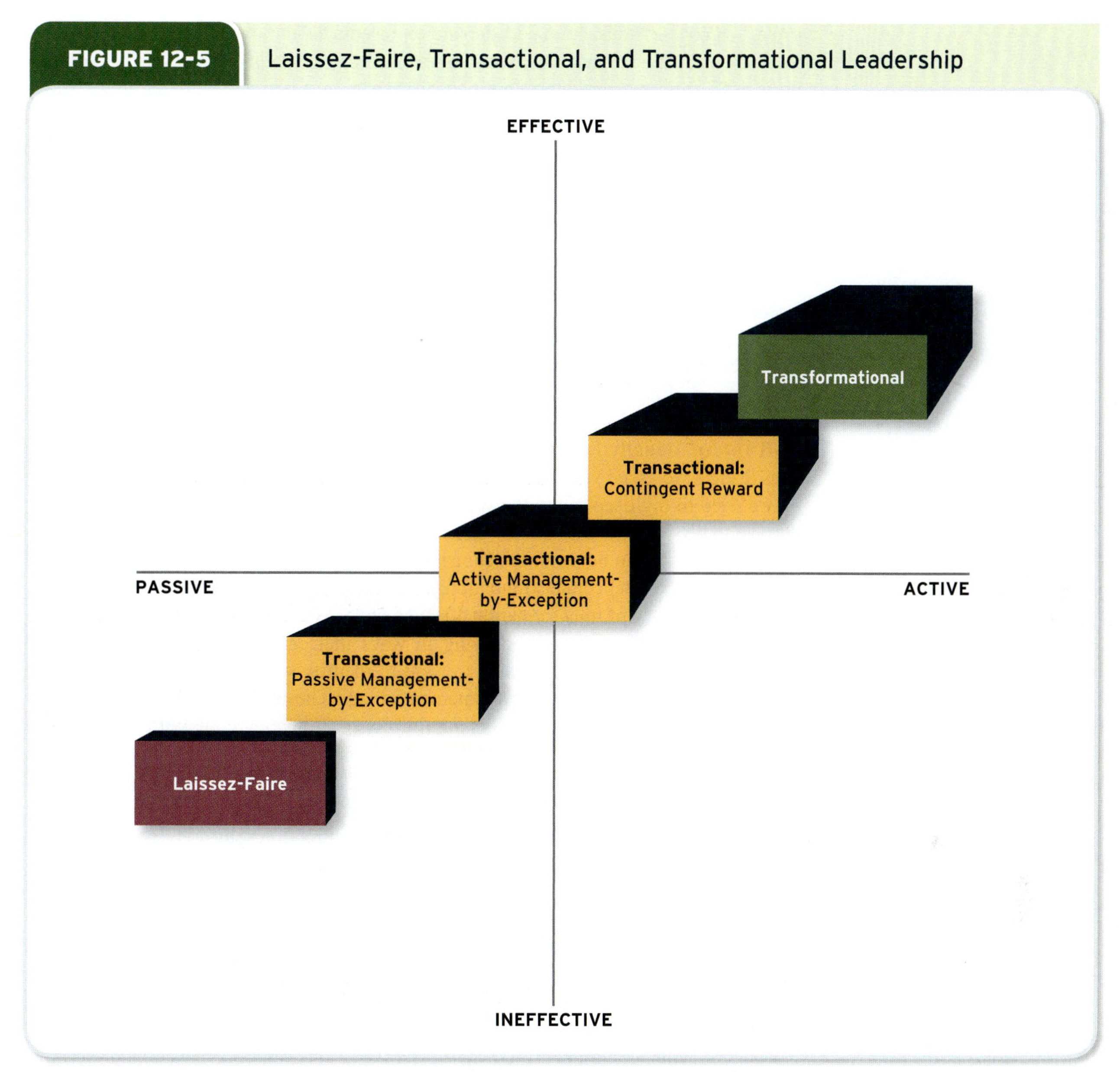

Source: Adapted from B.M. Bass and R.E. Riggio, *Transformational Leadership,* 2nd ed. (Mahwah, NJ: Lawrence Erlbaum Associates, 2006).

to monitor mistakes and errors actively and again takes corrective action when required.[76] This approach is represented by statements like: "The leader directs attention toward failures to meet standards."[77] **Contingent reward** represents a more active and effective brand of transactional leadership, in which the leader attains follower agreement on what needs to be done using promised or actual rewards in exchange for adequate performance.[78] Statements like "The leader makes clear what one can expect to receive when performance goals are achieved" exemplify contingent reward leadership.[79]

contingent reward When the leader attains follower agreement on what needs to be done using rewards in exchange for adequate performance

Transactional leadership represents the "carrot-and-stick" approach to leadership, with management-by-exception providing the "sticks" and contingent reward supplying the "carrots." Of course, transactional leadership represents the dominant approach to motivating employees in most organizations, and research suggests that it can be effective. A meta-analysis of 87 studies showed that contingent reward was strongly related to follower motivation and perceived leader effectiveness[80] (see Chapter 6 on motivation for more discussion of contingent reward issues). Active management-by-exception was only weakly related to follower motivation and perceived leader effectiveness, however, and passive management-by-exception seems to actually harm those outcomes.[81] Such results support the progression shown in Figure 12-5, with contingent reward standing as the most effective approach under the transactional leadership umbrella.

12.5 How does transformational leadership differ from transactional leadership?

Finally, the green cube represents transformational leadership—the most active and effective approach in Figure 12-5. How effective is transformational leadership? Well, we'll save that discussion for the "How Important Is Leadership" section that concludes this chapter, but suffice it to say that transformational leadership has the strongest and most beneficial effects of any of the leadership variables described in this chapter. It's also the leadership approach that is most universally endorsed across cultures, as described in our **OB Internationally** feature. In addition, it probably captures the key qualities of the famous leaders we asked you to list a few paragraphs back. To understand why it's so powerful, we need to dig deeper into the specific kinds of actions and behaviours that leaders can utilize to become more transformational. It turns out that the full spectrum of transformational leadership can be summarized using four dimensions: idealized influence, inspirational motivation, intellectual stimulation, and individualized consideration. Collectively, these four dimensions of transformational leadership are often called "the Four I's."[82]

idealized influence When the leader behaves in ways that earn the admiration, trust, and respect of followers, causing followers to want to identify with and emulate the leader

Idealized influence involves behaving in ways that earn the admiration, trust, and respect of followers, causing followers to want to identify with and emulate the leader.[83] Idealized influence is represented by statements like: "The leader instills pride in me for being associated with him/her."[84] Idealized influence is synonymous with *charisma*—a Greek word that means "divinely inspired gift"—which reflects a sense among followers that the leader possesses extraordinary qualities.[85] Charisma is a word often associated with Steve Jobs. One observer noted that, even though Jobs could be very difficult to work with, his remarkable charisma created a mysterious attraction that drew people to him, keeping them loyal to his collective sense of mission.[86]

To some extent, discussions of charisma serve as echoes of the "great person" view of leadership that spawned the trait research described in Table 12-2 (page 316). In fact, research suggests that there is a genetic component to charisma specifically and to transformational leadership more broadly. Studies on identical twins reared apart show that such twins have very similar charismatic profiles, despite their differing environments.[87] Indeed, such research suggests that almost 60 percent of the variation in charismatic behaviour can be explained by genes. One explanation for such findings is that genes influence the personality traits that give rise to charisma. For example, research suggests that extraversion, openness to experience, and agreeableness have significant effects on perceptions of leader charisma,[88] and all three of those personality dimensions have a significant genetic component (see Chapter 9 on personality, cultural values, and ability for more discussion of such issues).

inspirational motivation When the leader behaves in ways that foster an enthusiasm for and commitment to a shared vision of the future

Inspirational motivation involves behaving in ways that foster an enthusiasm for and commitment to a shared vision of the future.[89] That vision is transmitted through a sort of "meaning-making" process in which the negative features of the status quo are emphasized while highlighting the positive features of the potential future.[90] Inspirational motivation is represented by statements like: "The leader articulates a compelling vision of the future."[91] At Apple, Steve Jobs is renowned for spinning a "reality distortion field" that reshapes employees' views of the current work environment.[92] One Apple employee explained, "Steve has this power of vision that is almost frightening. When Steve believes in something, the power of that vision can literally sweep aside any objections, problems, or whatever. They just cease to exist."[93]

OB INTERNATIONALLY

Does the effectiveness of leader styles and behaviours vary across cultures? Answering that question is one of the objectives of *Project GLOBE* (Global Leadership and Organizational Behaviour Effectiveness), a collection of 170 researchers from 62 cultures who have studied leadership with 17,300 managers in 951 organizations since 1991.[94] In part, Project GLOBE represents a test of *culturally endorsed implicit leadership theory,* which argues that effective leadership is "in the eye of the beholder" and that cultural variables can alter how people define such leadership.[95] To test that theory, the GLOBE researchers asked participants to rate a number of leader styles and behaviours using a 1–7 scale, where 1 represents the perception that the style or behaviour inhibits a person from being an outstanding leader and 7 represents the perception that the style or behaviour contributes greatly to a person being an outstanding leader. The figure below shows how three of the styles and behaviours described in this chapter were rated across 10 different regions (note that the term "Anglo" represents people of English ethnicity, including the United States, Canada, and Australia).

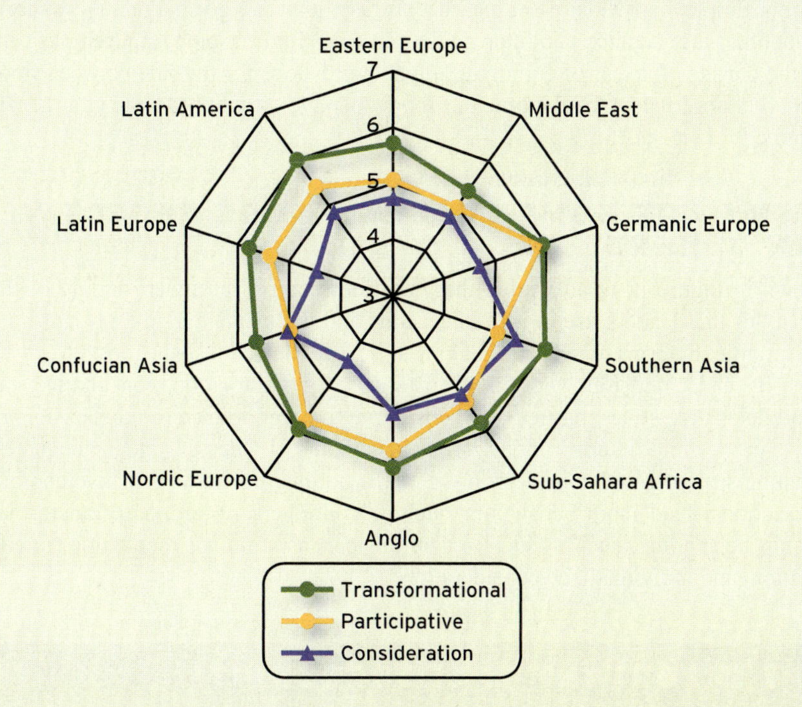

It turns out that transformational leadership is the most universally accepted approach to leadership of any of the concepts studied by Project GLOBE,[96] receiving an average rating near 6 among the citizens of every region except the Middle East. That universal appeal is likely explained by the fact that transformational leaders appeal to values like idealism and virtue that are accepted and endorsed in almost all countries.[97] The figure also shows that participative decision-making styles are favourably viewed in most countries, though more variation is evident, with the Middle East and Asia endorsing that style less than European and Anglo regions. Even more variation is seen with consideration behaviours, which are endorsed a bit less across the board but especially in Europe. These results suggest that participative styles and consideration behaviours appeal to cultural values that differ across regions. Understanding these kinds of results can help organizations select, counsel, and train managers who will better fit the profile of an effective leader in a given region.

intellectual stimulation When the leader behaves in ways that challenge followers to be innovative and creative by questioning assumptions and reframing old situations in new ways

Intellectual stimulation involves behaving in ways that challenge followers to be innovative and creative by questioning assumptions and reframing old situations in new ways.[98] Intellectual stimulation is represented by statements like: "The leader gets others to look at problems from many different angles."[99] Intellectual stimulation has been a staple of Jobs's tenure at Apple. He pushed for a different power supply on the Apple II so that the fan could be removed, preventing it from humming and churning like other computers of the time. Years later, he insisted on removing the floppy drive from the iMac because it seemed silly to transfer data one megabyte at a time, a decision that drew merciless criticism when the iMac debuted.

individualized consideration When the leader behaves in ways that help followers achieve their potential through coaching, development, and mentoring

Individualized consideration involves behaving in ways that help followers achieve their potential through coaching, development, and mentoring.[100] Not to be confused with the consideration behaviour derived from the Ohio State studies, individualized consideration represents treating employees as unique individuals with specific needs, abilities, and aspirations that need to be tied into the unit's mission. Individualized consideration is represented by statements like: "The leader spends time teaching and coaching."[101] Of the four facets of transformational leadership, Steve Jobs seems lowest on individualized consideration. Employees who are not regarded as his equals are given a relatively short leash and sometimes face an uncertain future in the company. In fact, some Apple employees resist riding the elevator for fear of ending up trapped with Jobs for the ride between floors. As one observer describes it, by the time the doors open, you might have had your confidence undermined for weeks.[102]

SO WHY ARE SOME LEADERS MORE EFFECTIVE THAN OTHERS?

As shown in Figure 12-6, answering that question requires an understanding of the particular styles that leaders use to make decisions and the behaviours they perform in their leadership role. In terms of decision-making styles, do they choose the most effective combination of leader and follower control in terms of the autocratic, consultative, facilitative, and delegative styles, particularly considering the importance of the decision and the expertise in the unit? In terms of day-to-day behaviours, do they engage in adequate levels of initiating structure and consideration? Finally, do they utilize an effective combination of transactional leadership behaviours, such as contingent reward, and transformational leadership behaviours, such as idealized influence, inspirational motivation, intellectual stimulation, and individualized consideration?

HOW IMPORTANT IS LEADERSHIP?

12.6 How does leadership affect job performance and organizational commitment?

How important is leadership? As with some other topics in organizational behaviour, that's a complicated question because "leadership" isn't just one thing. Instead, all of the styles and behaviours summarized in Figure 12-6 have their own unique importance. However, transformational leadership stands apart from the rest to some extent, with particularly strong effects in organizations. For example, transformational leadership is more strongly related to unit-focused measures of leadership effectiveness, like the kind shown in the top panel of Table 12-1 (page 314).[103] Units led by a transformational leader tend to be more financially successful and bring higher-quality products and services to market at a faster rate.[104] Transformational leadership is also more strongly related to dyad-focused measures of leader effectiveness, like the kind shown in the bottom panel of Table 12-1. Transformational leaders tend to foster leader–member exchange relationships that are of higher quality, marked by especially strong levels of mutual respect and obligation.[105]

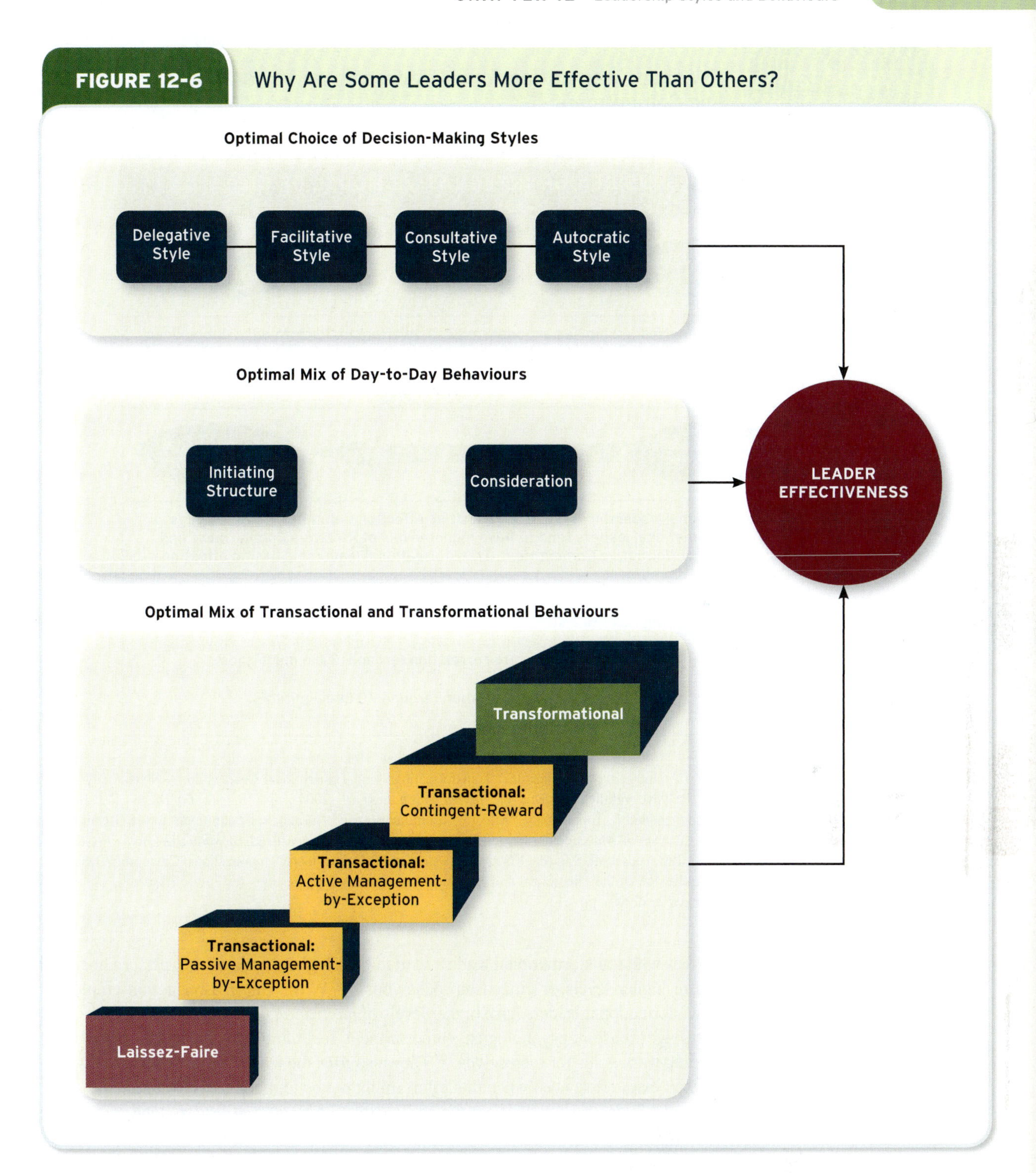

What if we focus specifically on the two outcomes in our integrative model of OB: performance and commitment? Figure 12-7 summarizes the research evidence linking transformational leadership to those two outcomes. The figure reveals that transformational leadership indeed affects the job performance of the employees who report to the leader.

FIGURE 12-7 Effects of Transformational Leadership on Performance and Commitment

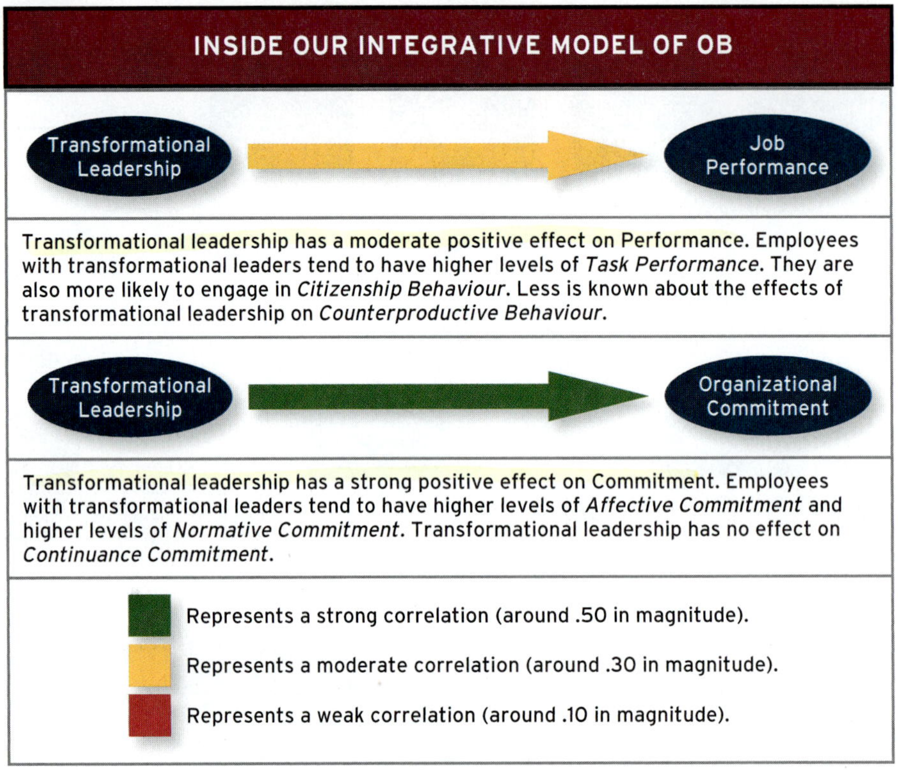

INSIDE OUR INTEGRATIVE MODEL OF OB

Transformational Leadership → Job Performance

Transformational leadership has a moderate positive effect on Performance. Employees with transformational leaders tend to have higher levels of *Task Performance*. They are also more likely to engage in *Citizenship Behaviour*. Less is known about the effects of transformational leadership on *Counterproductive Behaviour*.

Transformational Leadership → Organizational Commitment

Transformational leadership has a strong positive effect on Commitment. Employees with transformational leaders tend to have higher levels of *Affective Commitment* and higher levels of *Normative Commitment*. Transformational leadership has no effect on *Continuance Commitment*.

Represents a strong correlation (around .50 in magnitude).

Represents a moderate correlation (around .30 in magnitude).

Represents a weak correlation (around .10 in magnitude).

Sources: T.A. Judge and R.F. Piccolo, "Transformational and Transactional Leadership: A Meta-Analytic Test of Their Relative Validity," *Journal of Applied Psychology* 89 (2004), pp. 755–68; J.P. Meyer, D.J. Stanley, L. Herscovitch, and L. Topolnytsky, "Affective, Continuance, and Normative Commitment to the Organization: A Meta-Analysis of Antecedents, Correlates, and Consequences," *Journal of Vocational Behavior* 61 (2002), pp. 20–52; P.M. Podsakoff, S.B. MacKenzie, J.B. Paine, and D.G. Bachrach, "Organizational Citizenship Behaviors: A Critical Review of the Theoretical and Empirical Literature and Suggestions for Future Research," *Journal of Management* 26 (2000), pp. 513–63.

Employees with transformational leaders tend to have higher levels of task performance and engage in higher levels of citizenship behaviours.[106] Why? One reason is that employees with transformational leaders have higher levels of *motivation* than other employees.[107] They feel a stronger sense of psychological empowerment, feel more self-confident, and set more demanding work goals for themselves.[108] They also *trust* the leader more, making them willing to exert extra effort even when that effort might not be immediately rewarded.[109]

Figure 12-7 also reveals that employees with transformational leaders tend to be more committed to their organization.[110] They feel a stronger emotional bond with their organization and a stronger sense of obligation to remain present and engaged in their work. Why? One reason is that employees with transformational leaders have higher levels of *job satisfaction* than other employees.[111] One study showed that transformational leaders can make employees feel that their jobs have more variety and significance, enhancing intrinsic satisfaction with the work itself.[112] Other studies have shown that charismatic leaders express positive emotions more frequently and that those emotions are "caught" by employees through a sort of "emotional contagion" process.[113] For example, followers of transformational leaders tend to feel more optimism and less frustration during their workday, which makes it a bit easier to stay committed to work.

Although leadership is very important to unit effectiveness and the performance and commitment of employees, there are contexts in which the importance of the leader can be reduced. The **substitutes for leadership model** suggests that certain characteristics of the situation can constrain the influence of the leader, making it more difficult for the leader to influence employee performance.[114] Those situational characteristics come in two varieties, as shown in Table 12-4. **Substitutes** reduce the importance of the leader while simultaneously providing a direct benefit to employee performance. For example, a cohesive work group can provide its own sort of governing behaviours, making the leader less relevant, while providing its own source of motivation and job satisfaction. **Neutralizers**, in contrast, only reduce the importance of the leader—they themselves have no beneficial impact on performance.[115] For example, spatial distance lessens the impact of a leader's behaviours and styles, but distance itself has no direct benefit for employee job performance.

substitutes for leadership model A model that suggests that characteristics of the situations can constrain the influence of the leader, which makes it more difficult for the leader to influence employee performance

substitutes Situational characteristics that reduce the importance of the leader while simultaneously providing a direct benefit to employee performance

neutralizers Situational characteristics that reduce the importance of the leader and do not improve employee performance in any way

The substitutes for leadership model offers a number of prescriptions for a better understanding of leadership in organizations. First, it can be used to explain why a leader who seemingly "does the right things" doesn't seem to be making any difference.[116] It may be that the leader's work context possesses high levels of neutralizers and substitutes. Second, it can be used to explain what to do if an ineffective person is in a leadership role with no immediate replacement waiting in the wings.[117] If the leader can't be removed, perhaps the organization can do things to make that leader more irrelevant. Studies on the substitutes for leadership model have been inconsistent in showing that substitutes and neutralizers actually make leaders less influential in the predicted manner.[118] What is more clear is that the substitutes in Table 12-4 have beneficial effects on the job performance and organizational commitment of employees. In fact, the beneficial effects of the substitutes are sometimes even greater

TABLE 12-4 Leader Substitutes and Neutralizers

SUBSTITUTES	DESCRIPTION
• Task feedback	Receiving feedback on performance from the task itself
• Training and experience	Gaining the knowledge to act independently of the leader
• Professionalism	Having a professional specialty that offers guidance
• Staff support	Receiving information and assistance from outside staff
• Group cohesion	Working in a close-knit and interdependent work group
• Intrinsic satisfaction	Deriving personal satisfaction from one's work
NEUTRALIZERS	
• Task stability	Having tasks with a clear, unchanging sequence of steps
• Formalization	Having written policies and procedures that govern one's job
• Inflexibility	Working in an organization that prioritizes rule adherence
• Spatial distance	Being separated from one's leader by physical space

Source: Adapted from S. Kerr and J.M. Jermier, "Substitutes for Leadership: Their Meaning and Measurement," *Organizational Behaviour and Human Performance* 22 (1978), pp. 375–403.

than the beneficial effects of the leader's own behaviours and styles. Some leadership experts even recommend that leaders set out to create high levels of the substitutes in their work units wherever possible, even if the units might ultimately wind up "running themselves."[119]

APPLICATION: LEADERSHIP TRAINING

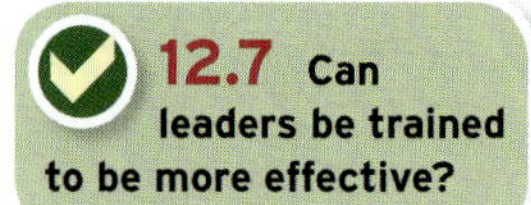

Given the importance of leadership, what can organizations do to maximize the effectiveness of their leaders? One method is to spend more time training them. Leadership training programs often focus on very specific issues, like conducting more accurate performance evaluations, being a more effective mentor, structuring creative problem solving, or gaining more cultural awareness and sensitivity.[120] However, training programs can also focus on much of the content covered in this chapter. For example, content could focus on contextual considerations that alter the effectiveness of decision-making styles or particular leader behaviours, such as initiating structure and consideration. What about transformational leadership? Given how dependent charisma is on personality and genetic factors, is it possible that transformational leaders can only be born, not made?

It turns out that many training programs focus on transformational leadership content, and research suggests that those programs can be effective.[121] One study of transformational leadership training occurred in one of the largest bank chains in Canada.[122] Managers at all of the branches in one region were randomly assigned to either a transformational training group or a control group. The managers in the training group took part in a one-day training session that began by asking the managers to describe the best and worst leaders they had ever encountered. Where applicable, the behaviours mentioned as belonging to the best leaders were framed around transformational leadership. The transformational dimensions were then described in a lecture-style format. Participants set goals for how they could behave more transformationally and engaged in role-playing exercises to practise those behaviours. The managers then created specific action plans, with progress on those plans monitored during four "booster sessions" over the next month. The results of the study showed that managers who participated in the training were rated as more transformational afterward. More important, their employees reported higher levels of organizational commitment, and their branches enjoyed better performance in terms of personal loan sales and credit card sales.

TAKEAWAYS

12.1 Leadership is defined as the use of power and influence to direct the activities of followers toward goal achievement. An "effective leader" improves the performance and well-being of his or her overall unit, as judged by profit margins, productivity, costs, absenteeism, retention, employee surveys, and so forth. An "effective leader" also cultivates high-quality leader–member exchange relationships on a dyadic basis through role-taking and role-making processes.

12.2 Leader emergence has been linked to a number of traits, including conscientiousness, disagreeableness, openness, extraversion, general cognitive ability, energy level, stress tolerance, and self-confidence. Of that set, the last six traits also predict leader effectiveness.

12.3 Leaders can use a number of styles to make decisions. Beginning with high leader control and moving to high follower control, they include autocratic, consultative, facilitative, and delegative styles. According to the time-driven model of leadership, the appropriateness of these styles depends on decision significance, the importance of commitment, leader expertise, the likelihood of commitment, shared objectives, employee expertise, and teamwork skills.

12.4 Most of the day-to-day leadership behaviours that leaders engage in are examples of either initiating structure or consideration. Initiating structure behaviours include initiation, organization, and production sorts of duties. Consideration behaviours include membership, integration, communication, recognition, and representation sorts of duties.

12.5 Transactional leadership emphasizes "carrot-and-stick" approaches to motivating employees, whereas transformational leadership fundamentally changes the way employees view their work. More specifically, transformational leadership inspires them to commit to a shared vision or goal that provides meaning and challenge to their work. The specific behaviours that underlie transformational leadership include the "Four I's": idealized influence, inspirational motivation, intellectual stimulation, and individualized consideration.

12.6 Transformational leadership has a moderate positive relationship with job performance and a strong positive relationship with organizational commitment. It has stronger effects on these outcomes than other leadership behaviours.

12.7 Leaders can be trained to be effective. In fact, such training can be used to increase transformational leadership behaviours, despite the fact that charisma is somewhat dependent on personality and genetic factors.

KEY TERMS

- active management-by-exception p. 326
- autocratic style p. 317
- consideration p. 321
- consultative style p. 317
- contingent reward p. 327
- delegating p. 323
- delegative style p. 318
- facilitative style p. 317
- idealized influence p. 328
- individualized consideration p. 330
- initiating structure p. 321
- inspirational motivation p. 328
- intellectual stimulation p. 330
- laissez-faire leadership p. 326
- leader effectiveness p. 315
- leader emergence p. 315
- leader–member exchange theory p. 313
- leadership p. 312
- life cycle theory of leadership p. 322
- neutralizers p. 333
- participating p. 322
- passive management-by-exception p. 326
- readiness p. 322
- role making p. 313
- role taking p. 313
- selling p. 322
- substitutes p. 333
- substitutes for leadership model p. 333
- telling p. 322
- time-driven model of leadership p. 318
- transactional leadership p. 326
- transformational leadership p. 326

DISCUSSION QUESTIONS

12.1 Before reading this chapter, which statement did you feel was more accurate: "Leaders are born" or "Leaders are made"? How do you feel now, and why do you feel that way?

12.2 The time-sensitive model of leadership argues that leaders aren't just concerned about the accuracy of their decisions when deciding among autocratic, consultative, facilitative, and delegative styles; they're also concerned about the efficient use of time. What other considerations could influence a leader's use of the four decision-making styles?

12.3 The time-sensitive and life cycle models of leadership both potentially suggest that leaders should use different styles and behaviours for different followers. Can you think of any negative consequences of that advice? How could those negative consequences be managed?

12.4 Consider the four dimensions of transformational leadership: idealized influence, inspirational motivation, intellectual stimulation, and individualized consideration. Which of those dimensions would you respond to most favourably? Why?

12.5 Can you think of any potential downsides to transformational leadership? What would they be?

CASE • APPLE

Steve Jobs has managed single-handedly to change the entire world with his innovative products. His vision to place digital media in the hands of the common public became a reality in the past decade while he served as CEO of Apple. Lee Clow, chairman of TBWA/Chiat/Day, stated that "From the time he was a kid, Steve thought his products could change the world." The leadership persona of Steve Jobs is well-known throughout the company, as well as to the public. Jobs is a perfectionist who likes to have a hand in every major project, from start to finish. The influence exerted by Jobs has turned Apple into the most innovative company in the world for the past three years.

Obviously Steve Jobs has the desire to innovate great products to revolutionize the world. But what separates him from everyone else? He has an uncanny ability to execute his strategies. This ability appears to be becoming a lost art in the world of business. Jobs also has the focus to take an idea and transform it into a product. This focus is what drives his employees to achieve high standards. A recent poll by *BusinessWeek* revealed that fans of Apple believe Steve Jobs is the "king." Nearly 90 percent of respondents consider him either very good or excellent. Apple has a bright future ahead of it in the hands of a man who has made a career out of innovation and success.

12.1 How effective is Steve Jobs as the leader of Apple? Explain.

12.2 Would you consider Steve Jobs to be a transformational leader? Explain.

Sources: "Grading Steve Jobs," *BusinessWeek,* April 24, 2002, www.businessweek.com; "Steve Jobs' Magic Kingdom," *BusinessWeek,* February 6, 2006, www.businessweek.com; "Steve Jobs: He Thinks Different," *BusinessWeek,* November 1, 2004, www.businessweek.com; "The World's 25 Most Innovative Companies," *BusinessWeek,* May 14, 2007.

EXERCISE • EMPLOYEE INVOLVEMENT

The purpose of this exercise is to use the time-driven model of leadership (shown in Figure 12-3 on page 319) to determine whether to involve employees in various decisions. This exercise uses groups of six participants, so your instructor will either assign you to a group of six or ask you to create your own group of six. The exercise has the following steps:

1. Review the case below, and then answer on your own the discussion questions that appear in Step 2.

Case: Canadian Coast Guard

You are the captain of a 60-metre Canadian Coast Guard cutter, with a crew of 16, including officers. Your mission is general search and rescue at sea. At 2:00 this morning, while en route to your home port after a routine 28-day patrol, you received word from the nearest Coast Guard station that a small plane had crashed 100 kilometres offshore. You obtained all the available information about the location of the crash, informed your crew of the mission, and set a new course for the scene at maximum speed to commence a search for survivors and wreckage.

You have now been searching for 20 hours. Your search operation has been increasingly impaired by rough seas, and there is evidence of a severe storm building. The atmospherics associated with the deteriorating weather have made communications with the Coast Guard station impossible. A decision must be made shortly about whether to abandon the search and place your vessel on a course that would ride out the storm (thereby protecting the vessel and your crew but relegating any possible survivors to almost certain death from exposure) or continue a potentially futile search and the risks it would entail.

Before losing communications, you received an updated weather advisory about the severity and duration of the storm. Although your crew members are extremely conscientious about their responsibilities, you believe they would be divided on the decision of leaving or staying.

2. Come to a group consensus on the following questions:
   a. To what extent should your subordinates be involved in making this decision? Select one of the following levels of involvement:
      - *No involvement:* You make the decision alone without any participation from subordinates.
      - *Low involvement:* You ask one or more subordinates for information relating to the problem, but you don't ask for their recommendations and might not mention the problem to them.
      - *Medium involvement:* You describe the problem to one or more subordinates (alone or in a meeting) and ask for any relevant information as well as their recommendations on the issue. However, you make the final decision, which might or might not reflect their advice.
      - *High involvement:* You describe the problem to subordinates. They discuss the matter, identify a solution without your involvement (unless they invite your ideas), and implement that solution. You have agreed to support their decision.

   b. What factors led you to choose this level of employee involvement rather than the others?

3. Class discussion (whether in groups or as a class) should focus on this question: What problems might occur if less or more involvement was granted in these cases?

Source: Case adapted from *The New Leadership: Managing Participation in Organizations*, by V.H. Vroom and A.G. Jago (Englewood Cliffs, NJ: Prentice Hall, 1988).

OB ASSESSMENTS • INITIATING STRUCTURE AND CONSIDERATION

How do you act when you're in a leadership role? This assessment is designed to measure the two dimensions of leaders' day-to-day behaviours: initiating structure and consideration. Please write a number next to each statement that reflects how frequently you engage in the behaviour described. Answer each question using the response scale provided. Then subtract your answers to the bold-faced questions from 6, with the difference being your new answer for that question. For example, if your original answer for question 16 was "4," your new answer is "2" (6 – 4). Then sum up your answers for each of the dimensions.

1 NEVER	2 SELDOM	3 OCCASIONALLY	4 OFTEN	5 ALWAYS

1. I let group members know what is expected of them. ______
2. I encourage the use of uniform procedures. ______
3. I try out my ideas in the group. ______
4. I make my attitudes clear to the group. ______
5. I decide what shall be done and how it shall be done. ______
6. I assign group members to particular tasks. ______
7. I make sure that my part in the group is understood by the group members. ______
8. I schedule the work to be done. ______
9. I maintain definite standards of performance. ______
10. I ask group members to follow standard rules and regulations. ______
11. I am friendly and approachable. ______
12. I do little things to make it pleasant to be a member of the group. ______
13. I put suggestions made by the group into operation. ______
14. I treat all group members as equals. ______
15. I give advance notice of changes. ______
16. **I keep to myself.** ______
17. I look out for the personal welfare of group members. ______
18. I am willing to make changes. ______
19. **I refuse to explain my actions.** ______
20. **I act without consulting the group.** ______

SCORING AND INTERPRETATION:

Initiating Structure: Sum up items 1–10.

Consideration: Sum up items 11–20.

For initiating structure, scores of 38 or more are above average, and scores of 37 or less are below average. For consideration, scores of 40 or more are above average, and scores of 39 or less are below average.

Source: R.M. Stogdill, *Manual for the Leader Behaviour Description Questionnaire–Form XII* (Columbus, OH: Bureau of Business Research, The Ohio State University, 1963).

CONNECT——Available 24/7 with instant feedback so you can study when you want, how you want, and where you want. Take advantage of the Study Plan——an innovative tool that helps students customize their own learning experience. Students can diagnose their knowledge with pre- and post-tests, identify the areas where they need help, search contents of the entire learning package for content specific to the topic they're studying, and add these resources to their study plan. Visit **www.connectob.ca** to register——take practice quizzes, run interactive scenarios, and much more. Also visit the Student Online Learning Centre for additional study tools.

www.mcgrawhill.ca/olc/colquitt

CHAPTER

13 Organizational Structure

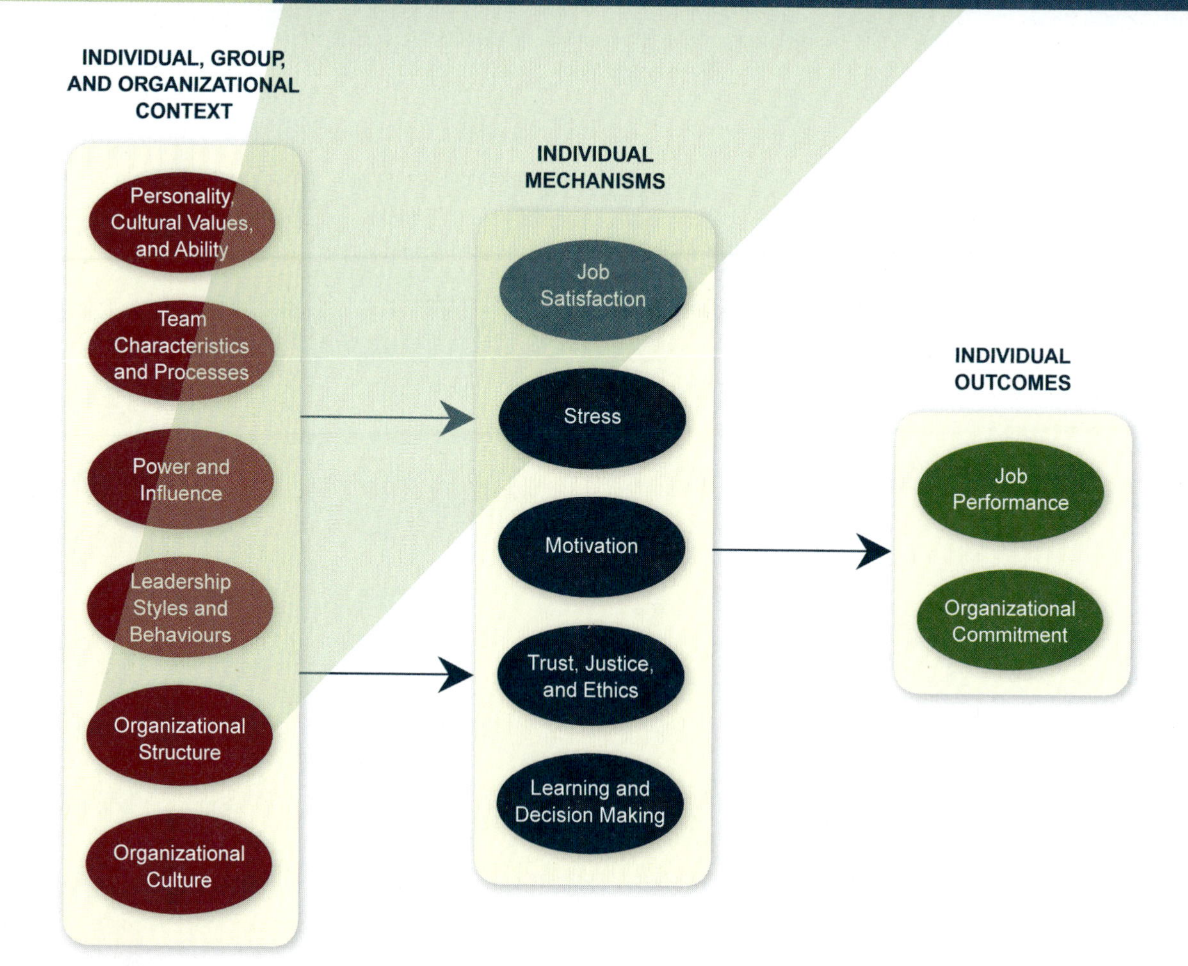

Learning Outcomes

After reading this chapter, you should be able to answer the following questions:

13.1 What is an organization's structure, and what does it consist of?

13.2 What are the major elements of an organizational structure?

13.3 What is organizational design? What factors does the organizational design process depend on?

13.4 What are some of the more common organizational forms that an organization might adopt for its structure?

13.5 When an organization makes changes to its structure, how does that restructuring affect job performance and organizational commitment?

SONY CORPORATION

Sony is one of the most recognized brand names in the world for audio and video equipment, televisions, information and communications equipment, semiconductors, and a variety of electronic components. In Canada, Sony employs approximately 1,100 people and is divided into two major sales and marketing groups: wholesale sales and retail sales.[1] The wholesale group is responsible for marketing and sales of Sony products to consumers through a dealer network, and to professionals through multiple direct sales channels. The retail group operates approximately 80 Sony Style retail locations across the country. Few people may realize that behind the scenes, supporting the sales and marketing activities of Sony Canada Ltd., is one of the most bureaucratic organizations in the world—Sony Corporation of Japan.

Sir Howard Stringer. Perhaps not the name you would expect for the CEO of Sony Corporation. Stringer is now the first non-Japanese head of Sony. When Stringer took over as CEO, the corporation consisted of multiple, diverse business units that, for the most part, operated independently and without regard for one another. As a result, Sony's performance had slipped dramatically in both profits and market share. Indeed, the once proud and respected technology giant was now considered a laggard, and its 160,000-employee workforce lacked the ability to work together toward common goals.[2]

One of the major reasons for Sony's problems was the development of "silos" or "fiefdoms" that divided up the company's business. Many of these silos were created by separating workers according to the type of work that they performed. In Sony's case, one of the biggest problems originated from separating hardware engineers from software developers. Sony grouped its hardware engineers together to encourage them to be creative and focus on major technological advances. This strategy worked very well for a long time as Sony developed hardware, like the Sony Walkman, that was smaller and lighter than that offered by its competitors.[3]

Howard Stringer, Sony's CEO, faces the challenge of helping the company recover its leadership position while addressing organizational structure problems that have hurt it in the past. Sony has 160,000 employees in its various departments.

However, significant environmental changes required better integration between the hardware engineers and software developers. Specifically, consumers began to want their various electronic devices to "talk to one another" and be easier to use than ever before. Both of those new demands required hardware engineers and software developers to collaborate—something that Sony had inadvertently discouraged.

One of the greatest capitalizers on this networking trend was Apple: Its iPod became the epitome of everything people wanted in a portable, personal music player. Much of this appeal emerged because the iPod's software allowed even the most computer illiterate user to download and network digital music. Apple had beaten Sony at its own game. One of the biggest disappointments for Sony was its development of the digital-based "Network Walkman"—two years prior to the creation of the iPod! However, because Sony's engineers and software developers didn't communicate or work together, the Network Walkman was unbelievably complicated to use. The way Sony organized its workers—its organizational structure—had essentially kept the company from taking advantage of the biggest shift in music media in the past 20 years.

Even today, Sony has an incredibly complex organizational structure. Entertainment units are split by geographic regions and operate completely independently of one another. Consumer electronics divisions each have their own marketing departments that often compete for the same customer![4] However, using the same structure that cost it in its competition with Apple also allowed Sony to finish producing the most advanced gaming system in the world: the PlayStation 3. Howard Stringer's challenge is to find a way to organize Sony to take advantage of what many believe is the greatest accumulation of assets in the entertainment industry. He has to find a way to structure the organization so that it builds synergy between the company's movie, games, music, and consumer electronics divisions—all while preparing Sony to react to the "next big change" in entertainment.

ORGANIZATIONAL STRUCTURE

13.1 What is an organization's structure, and what does it consist of?

As the preceding example illustrates, an organization's structure can have a significant impact on its financial performance and ability to manage its employees. The decisions that Howard Stringer makes regarding Sony's organizational structure will have an impact on how employees communicate and cooperate with one another, how power is distributed, and how individuals view their work environment. In fact, an organization's structure dictates more than you might think. We've spent a great deal of time in this book talking about how employee attitudes and behaviours are shaped by individual characteristics, such as personality and ability, and group mechanisms, such as teams and leaders. In this and the following chapter, we discuss how the organization as a whole affects employee attitudes and behaviour.

Think about some of the jobs you've held in the past (or perhaps the job you hope to have after graduation). What types of employees did you interact with on a daily basis? Were they employees who performed the same tasks that you performed? Or maybe they didn't do exactly what you did, but did they serve the same customer? How many employees did your manager supervise? Was every decision you made scrutinized by your supervisor, or were you given a "long leash"? The answers to all of these questions are influenced by organizational structure. An **organizational structure** formally dictates how jobs and tasks are divided and coordinated between individuals and groups within the company. Organizational structures can be relatively simple when a company only has five to twenty employees but grow incredibly complex in the case of Sony's 160,000 employees who produce thousands of different kinds of products.

organizational structure Formally dictates how jobs and tasks are divided and coordinated between individuals and groups within the company

"No, now all of our pillaging is done electronically from a centralized office."

Source: © The New Yorker Collection 2003 Christopher Weyant from cartoonbank.com. All rights reserved.

WHY DO SOME ORGANIZATIONS HAVE DIFFERENT STRUCTURES THAN OTHERS?

One way of getting a feel for an organization's structure is by looking at an organizational chart. An **organizational chart** is a drawing that represents every job in the organization and the formal reporting relationships between those jobs. It helps organizational members and outsiders understand and comprehend how work is structured within the company. Figure 13-1 illustrates two sample organizational charts. In a real chart, the boxes would generally be filled with actual names and job titles. As you can imagine, as companies grow larger, their organizational charts get more complex. Can you imagine drawing an organizational chart that included every one of Sony's 160,000 employees? Not only would that require a lot of boxes and a lot of paper, it would probably take a couple of years to put together. (Plus, as soon as someone left the organization, it would be time to update the chart!)

organizational chart A drawing that represents every job in the organization and the formal reporting relationships between those jobs

ELEMENTS OF ORGANIZATIONAL STRUCTURE

The organizational charts described in this chapter are relatively simple and designed to illustrate specific points; if you want to see how complex some of these charts can get, do a search on the Internet for "organizational chart," and you'll begin to see how varied organizations can be in the way they design their company. Specifically, charts like those in Figure 13-1 can illustrate the five key elements of an organization's structure. Those five key elements, summarized in Table 13-1, describe how work tasks, authority relationships, and decision-making responsibilities are organized within the company. These elements will be discussed in the next several sections.

FIGURE 13-1 Two Sample Organizational Structures

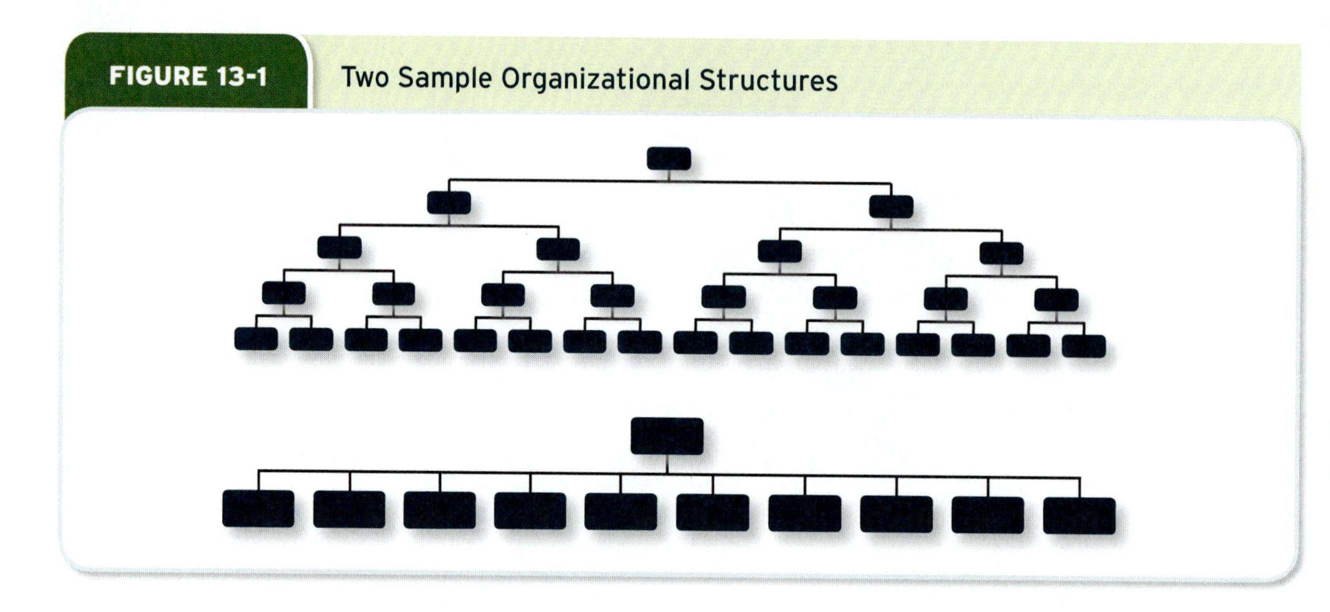

TABLE 13-1 Elements of Organizational Structure

ORGANIZATIONAL STRUCTURE DIMENSION	DEFINITION
Work specialization	The degree to which tasks in an organization are divided into separate jobs.
Chain of command	Answers the question of "who reports to whom?" and signifies formal authority relationships.
Span of control	Represents how many employees each manager in the organization has responsibility for.
Centralization	Refers to where decisions are formally made in organizations.
Formalization	The degree to which rules and procedures are used to standardize behaviours and decisions in an organization.

13.2 What are the major elements of an organizational structure?

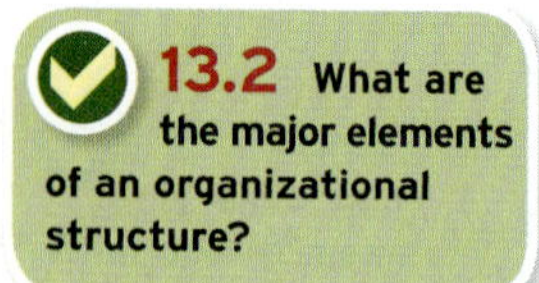

work specialization The degree to which tasks in an organization are divided into separate jobs

WORK SPECIALIZATION **Work specialization** is the way in which tasks in an organization are divided into separate jobs. In some organizations, this categorization is referred to as a company's division of labour. How many tasks does any one employee perform? To some degree, work specialization is a never-ending trade-off among productivity, flexibility, and worker motivation. Take an assembly line worker at Ford as an example. Henry Ford was perhaps the earliest (and clearly most well-known) believer in high degrees of work specialization. He divided tasks among his manufacturing employees to such a degree that each employee might only perform one single task, over and over again, all day long. Having only one task to perform allowed those employees to be extremely productive at doing that one thing. It also meant that training new workers was much easier when replacements were needed.

However, there are trade-offs when organizations make jobs highly specialized. Highly specialized jobs can cause organizations to lose the ability for their employees to be flexible in what they do. By spending all their time performing specialized tasks well, employees fail to update or practise other skills. Accounting majors, for example, might specialize in taxes or auditing. Some larger companies might hire these graduates for their ability to do either auditing or tax—but not both. Other companies might be looking for an accountant who can perform either aspect well, depending on how they divide up accounting duties within their organization. Still other companies might want to hire "general managers" who understand accounting, finance, management, marketing, and operations as a part of their job. Thus, high levels of specialization may be acceptable in larger firms with more employees but can be problematic in smaller firms in which employees must be more flexible in their job duties.

Organizations may also struggle with employee job satisfaction when they make jobs highly specialized. If you recall Chapter 4 on job satisfaction, we discussed five core characteristics of jobs that significantly affect satisfaction. One of those characteristics was variety, or the degree to which the job requires a number of different activities involving a number of different skills and talents.[5] Employees tend to be more satisfied with jobs that require them to perform a number of different kinds of activities. Even though you might be very efficient and productive performing a job with only one task, how happy would you be to perform that job on a daily basis? One of the most famous films in early motion picture history was *Modern Times,* a film in which Charlie Chaplin was relegated to performing the same task over and over, very quickly. The movie ridiculed work specialization and the trend of treating employees as machines.

Charlie Chaplin in *Modern Times* (1932) has a job with an extremely high degree of work specialization.

CHAIN OF COMMAND The **chain of command** within an organization essentially answers the question "Who reports to whom?" Every employee in a traditional organizational structure has one person to whom they report. That person then reports to someone else, and on and on, until the buck stops with the CEO (though in a public company, even the CEO is responsible to the board of directors). The chain of command can be seen as the specific flow of authority down through the levels of an organization's structure. Organizations depend on this flow of authority to attain order, control, and predictable performance.[6] Some newer organizational structures make this chain of command a bit more complex. It has become common to have positions that report to two or more different managers. For example, Intel recently placed two people apiece in charge of the two largest divisions of their organization. Questions have arisen as to how their duties will be split up and whether employees will know who it is to whom they should report.[7]

chain of command Answer to the question of "who reports to whom?" and signifies formal authority relationships

SPAN OF CONTROL A manager's **span of control** represents how many employees he or she is responsible for in the organization. The organizational charts in Figure 13-1 provide an illustration of the differences in span of control. In the top chart, each manager is responsible for leading two subordinates. In most instances, this level would be considered a narrow span of control. In the bottom chart, the manager is responsible for 10 employees. Typically, this number would be considered a wide span of control. Of course, the key question in many organizations is how many employees one manager can supervise effectively. Answering that question requires a better understanding of the benefits of narrow and wide spans of control.

span of control Represents how many employees each manager in the organization has responsibility for

Narrow spans of control allow managers to be much more hands-on with employees, giving them the opportunity to use directive leadership styles while developing close mentoring relationships with employees. A narrow span of control is especially important if the manager has substantially more skill or expertise than the subordinates. Early writings on management assumed that the narrower the span of control, the more productive employees would become.[8] However, a narrow span of control requires organizations to hire many managers, which can significantly increase labour costs. Moreover, if the span of control becomes too narrow, employees can become resentful of their close supervision and long for more latitude in their day-to-day decision making. In fact, current research suggests that a moderate span of control is best for an organization's productivity.[9] This relationship is illustrated in Figure 13-2. Note that organizational performance increases as span of control increases, but only up to the point that managers no longer have the ability to coordinate and supervise the large numbers of employees underneath them. Most organizations work hard to try to find the right balance, and this balance differs for every organization, depending on its unique circumstances. However, there is no question that spans of control in organizations have increased significantly in recent years.[10] Organizations such as Coca-Cola have vice presidents with up to 90 employees reporting to them![11]

An organization's span of control affects how "tall" or "flat" its organizational chart becomes. For example, the top panel of Figure 13-1 depicts a tall structure with many hierarchical levels and a narrow span of control, whereas the bottom panel depicts a flat organization with few levels and a wide span of control. Think about what happens when an organization becomes "taller." First, more layers of management means having to pay more management salaries. Second, communication in the organization becomes more complex as each new layer becomes one more point through which information must pass when travel-

FIGURE 13-2 The Relationship between Span of Control and Organizational Performance

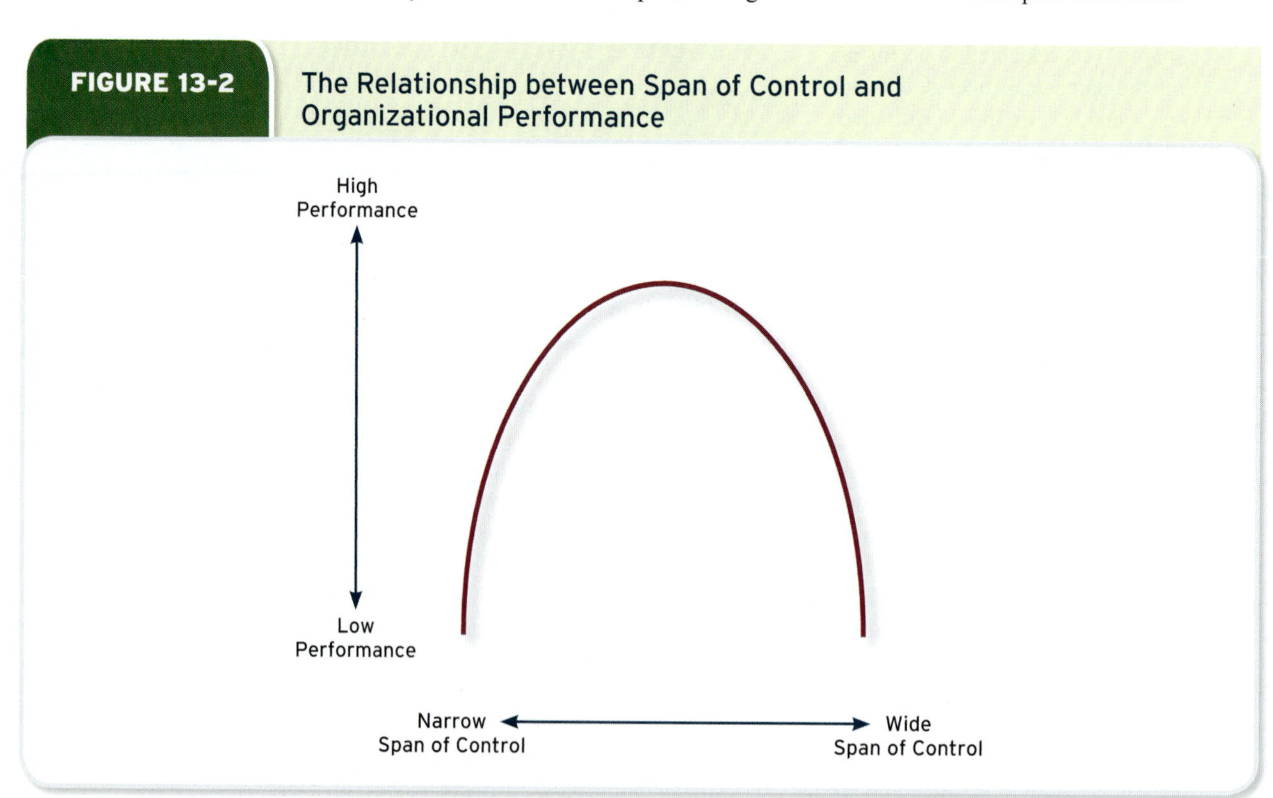

Source: Adapted from N.A. Theobald and S. Nicholson-Crotty, "The Many Faces of Span of Control: Organizational Structure Across Multiple Goals," *Administration and Society* 36 (2005), pp. 648–60.

ling upward or downward. Third, the ability for an organization to make decisions becomes slower because approval for decisions has to be authorized at every step of the hierarchy.

Throughout the 1990s and into the current millennium, organizations have worked to become flatter to reduce the costs associated with multiple layers of management and increase their ability to adapt to their environment. Intel, for example, recently announced a reduction in its managerial ranks of 1,000 positions (or 1 percent of its 100,000 employees). A spokesperson from Intel announced that "This [layoff] is designed to improve costs and improve decision making and communications across the company."[12] Later in the chapter we describe how the administration of health care delivery in Alberta has moved from a governance structure of 193 separate boards prior to 1994 to one super board today.

CENTRALIZATION **Centralization** reflects where decisions are formally made in organizations. If only the top managers within a company have the authority to make final decisions, we would say that the organization has a highly "centralized" structure. In contrast, if decision-making authority is pushed down to lower-level employees and these employees feel empowered to make decisions on their own, an organization has a "decentralized" structure. Decentralization becomes necessary as a company grows larger. Sooner or later, the top management of an organization cannot make every single decision within the organization. Centralized organizational structures tend to concentrate power and authority within a relatively tight group of individuals in the firm, because they are the ones who have formal authority over important decisions. This point is illustrated at a cosmic level in our **OB on Screen** feature.

centralization Refers to where decisions are formally made in organizations

Many organizations are moving toward a more decentralized structure. A manager can't have 20 employees reporting to him or her if those employees aren't allowed to make some decisions on their own. However, it's also important to realize that some organizations might choose to centralize a few functions while leaving other decisions in the hands of lower-level managers. Aon Insurance is a perfect example of this approach. Through a series of mergers and acquisitions over the past 20 years, Aon had grown to a size of 47,000 employees in 500 locations around the world. Each of those offices had the authority to make its own decisions regarding human resource practices, such as who to hire and how to pay people. This decentralization led to employees being treated differently depending on the location where they worked, creating feelings of animosity and unfairness. These inconsistent decisions could have been made more efficiently by the organization as a whole.[13] Have the organizations where you have worked been largely centralized or decentralized? See our **OB Assessments** feature at the end of this chapter to find out.

FORMALIZATION A company is high in **formalization** when there are many specific rules and procedures used to standardize behaviours and decisions. Although not something you can necessarily see on an organizational chart, the impact of formalization is felt throughout the organization. Rules and procedures are a necessary mechanism for control in every organization. Although the word "formalization" has a somewhat negative connotation, think about your reaction if every McDonald's made its french fries in different ways at each location. Or think about this: Would it bother you if the quality of health care you receive depended on where you live in the province? Formalization is a necessary coordination mechanism that organizations rely on to get a standardized product or to deliver a standardized service.

formalization The degree to which rules and procedures are used to standardize behaviours and decisions in an organization

ELEMENTS IN COMBINATION You might have noticed that some elements of an organization's structure seem to go hand-in-hand with other elements. For example, wide spans of control tend to be associated with decentralization in decision making. A high level of work specialization tends to bring about a high level of formalization. Moreover, if you take a closer look at the elements, you might notice that many of the elements capture the struggle between efficiency and flexibility. **Mechanistic organizations** are efficient, rigid, predictable, and standardized organizations that thrive in stable environments. Mechanistic organizations are typified by a structure that relies on high levels of formalization, a rigid

mechanistic organizations Efficient, rigid, predictable, and standardized organizations that thrive in stable environments

OB ON SCREEN

STAR WARS II: ATTACK OF THE CLONES

"It is with great reluctance that I have agreed to this calling. I love democracy . . . . I love the Republic. But I am mild by nature, and I do not desire to see the destruction of democracy. The power you give me I will lay down when this crisis has abated, I promise you. And as my first act with this new authority, I will create a grand army of the Republic to counter the increasing threats of the separatists."

With those words, Supreme Chancellor Palpatine (Ian McDiarmid) takes control of the Republic in *Star Wars II: Attack of the Clones* (Dir. George Lucas, 20th Century Fox, 2002). Even in distant worlds, organizations are a way of life. Although the six Star Wars movies during the past 30 years have included a lot of space battles, they have also witnessed the formation, transformation, and ruling of a galaxy through the use of organizational structure.

One of the main plot lines in Episodes I through III of the Star Wars saga revolves around Chancellor Palpatine. He is the elected leader of the Galactic Senate, which serves as the governing body for the Galactic Republic (a group of hundreds of planets whose members agreed to form an organization for mutual protection and economic alliance). The Jedi Order is a group of mystical warriors that exist to protect the Republic. Unfortunately for Palpatine, his powers as Chancellor are extremely limited because all his decisions require a vote from all participating senators. Moreover, the Jedi are loyal to the Senate, not to him.

Unbeknownst to those around him, Chancellor Palpatine is really a Sith Lord named Darth Sidious. The Sith are an evil group of Jedi who use their mystical powers—known as "The Force"—for evil purposes. Palpatine secretly controls a group known as the Trade Federation, which he uses to attack and threaten members of the Republic. Episodes II and III of the Star Wars saga show Palpatine using this threat to have the Republic grant him centralized decision-making authority. That centralized authority gives him the power and authority needed to create a grand Army of the Republic. Once that army is created, they get transformed into Storm Troopers who help him change the Republic into his own personal Empire. That centralized authority (together with his ability to shoot "force lightning"), helps Palpatine rule the galaxy—until one Luke Skywalker comes along . . . .

organic organizations
Flexible, adaptive, outward-focused organizations that thrive in dynamic environments

and hierarchical chain of command, high degrees of work specialization, centralization of decision making, and narrow spans of control. In contrast, **organic organizations** are flexible, adaptive, outward-focused organizations that thrive in dynamic environments. Organic organizations are typified by a structure that relies on low levels of formalization, weak or multiple chains of command, low levels of work specialization, and wide spans of control. Table 13-2 sums up the differences between the two types of organizations.

If you think about the differences between the two types, it probably wouldn't be too difficult to come up with a few companies that fall more toward one end of the continuum or

OB RESEARCH IN CANADA

Dr. Michael Withey is a professor of organizational behaviour in the Faculty of Business Administration at Memorial University of Newfoundland. He received his PhD from Queen's University in 1986. A topic that has long fascinated Dr. Withey is the principle of situational strength (see Chapter 9): Why do employee characteristics, like attitudes or personality, have a much more pronounced effect on work behaviours in weak rather than strong situations? What makes a situation strong or weak? Well, one consideration would be the structural characteristics of the organization where the work is done. A recent study by Dr. Withey and his colleagues has extended some of the ideas presented in this chapter by examining how bureaucratic organizational structures, characterized as having high work specialization, centralization, and formalization, affect the motivation, attitudes, and perceptions of its members. The question he is trying to answer is whether these organizational designs enable or disable employees—if you think about it, arguments can be made either way. Another of Dr. Withey's research interests is employee responses to dissatisfaction—recall the exit–voice–loyalty–neglect (EVLN) framework mentioned in Chapter 3? According to Dr. Withey, "The EVLN framework is interesting because it considers a range of employee responses at the same time. There is a lot of research on each of the responses separately, but the study of them together and the ability to consider trade-offs and sequences of responses opens a whole other realm."

Some of Dr. Withey's favourite publications include:

"The Strong Situation Hypothesis," by W.H. Cooper and M.J. Withey, published in *Personality and Social Psychology Review* (2009, volume 13, pp. 62–72).

"The Moderating Effect of Situational Strength on the Relationship Between Personality and Effort Expenditure," by M.J. Withey, I.R. Gellatly, and M. Annett, published in *Journal of Applied Social Psychology* (2005, volume 35, pp. 1587–1608).

"Predicting Exit, Voice, Loyalty and Neglect," by M.J. Withey, and W.H. Cooper, published in *Administrative Science Quarterly* (1989, volume 34, pp. 521–39).

"Measures of Perrow's Work Unit Technology: An Empirical Assessment and a New Scale," by M.J. Withey, R.L. Daft, and W.H. Cooper, published in *Academy of Management Journal* (1983, volume 26, pp. 45–63).

the other. However, it is important to remember that few organizations are perfect examples of either of these extremes. Most fall somewhere near the middle, with certain areas within the organization having mechanistic qualities and others being more organic in nature. Although it is tempting to label mechanistic as "bad" and organic as "good," this perception is not necessarily true. Being mechanistic is the only way for many organizations to survive, and it can be a highly appropriate and fruitful way to structure work functions. To find out why that's the case, we need to explore why organizations develop the kinds of structures they do.

TABLE 13-2 Characteristics of Mechanistic vs. Organic Structures

MECHANISTIC ORGANIZATIONS	ORGANIC ORGANIZATIONS
High degree of work specialization; employees are given a very narrow view of the tasks they are to perform.	Low degree of work specialization; employees are encouraged to take a broad view of the tasks they are to perform.
Very clear lines of authority; employees know exactly whom they report to.	Although there might be a specified chain of command, employees think more broadly in terms of where their responsibilities lie.
High levels of hierarchical control; employees are not encouraged to make decisions without their manager's consent.	Knowledge and expertise are decentralized; employees are encouraged to make their own decisions when appropriate.
Information is passed through vertical communication between an employee and his or her supervisor.	Lateral communication is encouraged, focusing on information and advice as opposed to orders.
Employees are encouraged to develop firm-specific knowledge and expertise within their area of specialization.	Employees are encouraged to develop knowledge and expertise outside of their specialization.

Source: Adapted from T. Burns and G.M. Stalker, *The Management of Innovation* (London: Tavistock, 1961).

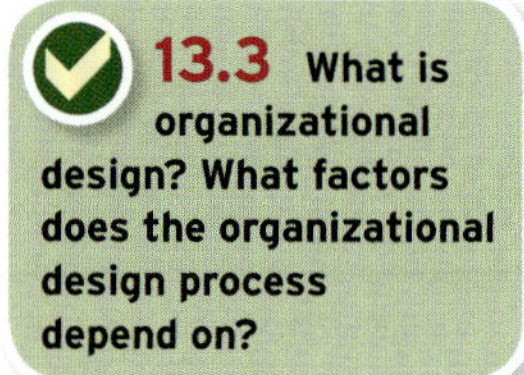

ORGANIZATIONAL DESIGN

organizational design The process of creating, selecting, or changing the structure of an organization

business environment The outside environment, including customers, competitors, suppliers, and distributors, which all have an impact on organizational design

company strategy An organization's objectives and goals and how it tries to capitalize on its assets to make money

Organizational design is the process of creating, selecting, or changing the structure of an organization. Ideally, organizations don't just "let" a structure develop on its own; they proactively design it to match their specific circumstances and needs. However, some organizations aren't that proactive and find themselves with a structure that has unintentionally developed on its own, without any careful planning. Those organizations may then be forced to change their structure to become more effective. A number of factors influence the process of organizational design. Those factors include the environment in which the organization does business, its strategy and technology, and the size of the firm.

BUSINESS ENVIRONMENT An organization's **business environment** consists of its customers, competitors, suppliers, distributors, and other factors external to the firm, all of which have an impact on organizational design. One of the biggest factors in an environment's effect on structure is whether the outside environment is stable or dynamic. Stable environments do not change frequently, and any changes that do occur happen very slowly. Stable environments allow organizations to focus on efficiency and require little change over time. In contrast, dynamic environments change on a frequent basis and require organizations to have structures that are more adaptive.[14] In the opening example for this chapter, Sony failed to meet the needs of its changing business environment to match Apple's iPod. Because it took it so long to recognize and adapt to that environmental shift, Sony has struggled to be profitable. Some would argue that the world is changing so fast that the majority of companies can no longer keep up.

COMPANY STRATEGY A **company strategy** describes an organization's objectives and goals and how it tries to capitalize on its assets to make money. Although the myriad of organizational strategies is too cumbersome to discuss here, two common strategies revolve around being either a low-cost producer or a differentiator.[15] Companies that focus on a low-cost producer strategy rely on selling products at the lowest possible cost. To do this well, they have to focus on being as efficient as they can be. Such companies are more likely to take a mechanistic approach to organizational design. Other companies might follow a differentiation strategy. Rather than focusing on supplying a product or service at the lowest cost, these companies believe that people will pay more for a product that is unique in some way. It could be that their product has a higher level of quality or offers features that a low-cost product doesn't. A differentiation strategy often hinges on adjusting to changing environments quickly, which often makes an organic structure more appropriate.

TECHNOLOGY An organization's **technology** is the method by which it transforms inputs into outputs. Very early on in the study of organizations, it was assumed that technology was the major determinant of an organization's structure.[16] Since then, the picture has become less clear regarding the appropriate relationship between technology and structure.[17] Although not completely conclusive, research suggests that the more routine a technology is, the more mechanistic a structure should be. In many ways, this suggestion makes perfect sense: If a company makes the exact same thing over and over, it should focus on creating that one thing as efficiently as possible by having high levels of specialization, formalization, and centralization. However, if technologies need to be changed or altered to suit the needs of various consumers, it follows that decisions would be more decentralized and the rules and procedures the organization relies on would need to be more flexible.

technology The method by which an organization transforms inputs to outputs

COMPANY SIZE There is no question that there is a significant relationship between **company size,** or total number of employees, and structure.[18] As organizations become larger, they need to rely on some combination of specialization, formalization, and centralization to control their activities and thus become more mechanistic in nature. When it comes to organizational performance, however, there is no definite answer as to when an organization's structure should be revised, or "how big is too big."[19] As many organizations get bigger, they attempt to create smaller units within the firm to create a "feeling of smallness."

company size The number of employees in a company

COMMON ORGANIZATIONAL FORMS

Our discussion of organizational design describes how an organization's business environment, strategy, technology, and size conspire to make some organizational structures more effective than others. Now we turn our attention to a logical next question: What structures do most organizations utilize? The sections that follow describe some of the most common organizational forms. As you read their descriptions, think about whether these forms would fall on the mechanistic or organic side of the structure continuum. You might also consider what kinds of design factors would lead an organization to choose that particular form.

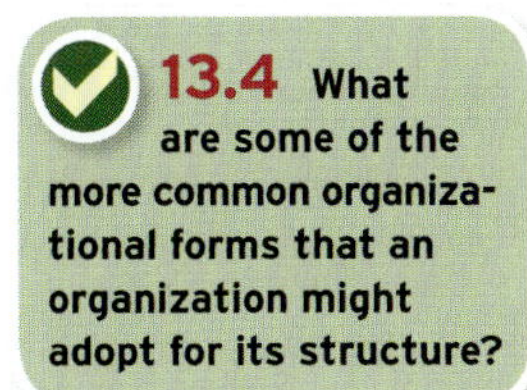

SIMPLE STRUCTURES **Simple structures** are perhaps the most common form of organizational design, primarily because there are more small organizations than large ones. In fact, more than 80 percent of employing organizations have fewer than 19 employees.[20] Small accounting and law firms, family-owned grocery stores, individual-owned retail outlets, independent churches, and landscaping services are all organizations that are likely to use a simple structure. Figure 13-3 shows a simple structure for a manager-owned restaurant. The figure reveals that simple structures are just that: simple. Simple structures are generally used by extremely small organizations in which the manager, president, and owner are all the same person. A simple structure is a flat organization with one person as the central decision-making figure; it is not large enough to have a high degree of formalization and will only have very basic differences in work specialization.

simple structure An organizational form that features one person as the central decision-making figure

A simple structure makes perfect sense for a small organization, because employees can come and go with no major ripple effects on the organization. However, as the business grows, the coordinating efforts on the part of the owner/manager become increasingly more complex. In the case of our restaurant, let's assume that the growth of the restaurant requires

FIGURE 13-3 An Organizational Structure for a Small Restaurant

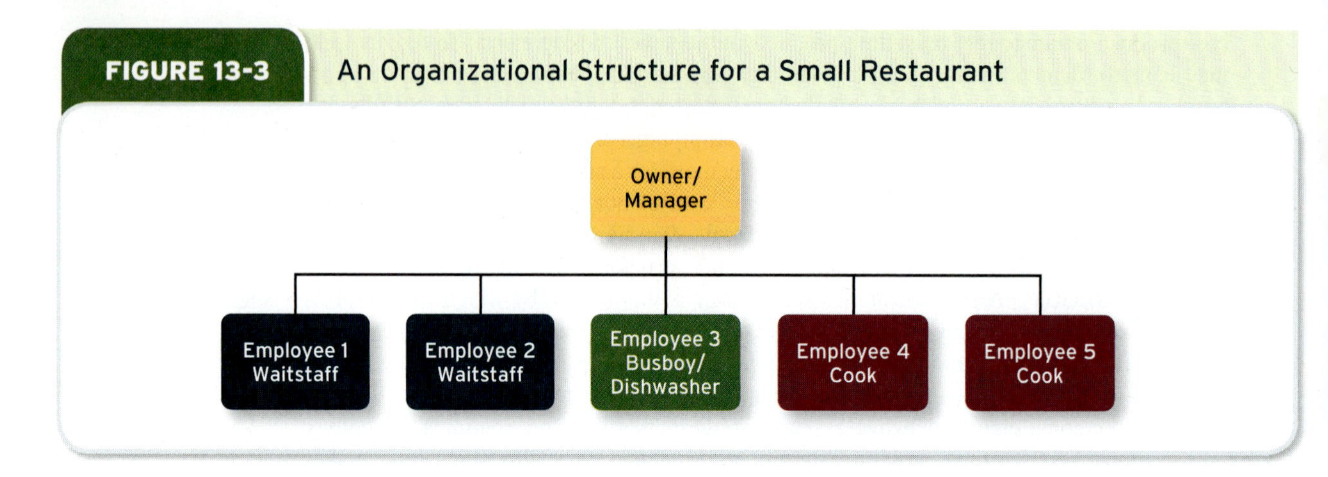

the owner to spend time doing lots of little things to manage the employees. Now the manager has lost the ability to spend time focusing on the actual business at hand. The manager then decides to add a supervisor to handle all of the day-to-day organizing of the restaurant. This arrangement works well until the owner decides to open a second restaurant that needs to have its own supervisor. Now let's assume that this second restaurant is much larger, leading the owner to decide to have separate supervisors directly in charge of the servers and the kitchen. All of the sudden, our little restaurant has three layers of management!

BUREAUCRATIC STRUCTURES When you think of the word "bureaucracy," what thoughts come to mind? Stuffy, boring, restrictive, formal, hard to change, and needlessly complex are some of the terms that have a tendency to be associated with bureaucracies. Those unflattering adjectives aside, chances are very good that you either currently work in a bureaucracy or will after you graduate. A **bureaucratic structure** is an organizational form that exhibits many of the facets of the mechanistic organization. Bureaucracies are designed for efficiency and rely on high levels of work specialization, formalization, centralization of authority, rigid and well-defined chains of command, and relatively narrow spans of control. Are you attracted to these structures? How do think it would feel to work in a bureaucratic organization? For more insights see our **OB for Students** feature below and our **OB Research in Canada** box on page 349.

bureaucratic structure An organizational form that exhibits many of the facets of a mechanistic organization

There are numerous types of bureaucratic structures on which we might focus. The most basic of these is the **functional structure**. As shown in Figure 13-4, a functional structure groups employees by the functions they perform for the organization. For example, employees with marketing expertise are grouped together, those with finance duties are grouped together, and so on. The success of the functional structure is based on the efficiency advantages that come with having a high degree of work specialization that is centrally coordinated.[21] Managers have expertise in an area and interact with others with the same type of expertise to create the most efficient solutions for the company. As illustrated in our previous example of the fast-growing restaurant, many small companies naturally evolve into functionally based structures as they grow larger.

functional structure An organizational form in which employees are grouped by the functions they perform for the organization

However, small companies experiencing rapid growth are not the only organizations to benefit from a functional structure. Smurfit-Stone Container Corporation, a leading paper and packaging manufacturer with 25,000 employees at 140 locations, is moving toward a more traditional functional structure. Smurfit-Stone was organized like other companies in the paper industry, with a structure relying on a large number of plants operating under different general managers. CEO Patrick Moore made the decision to move toward a more functional structure, noting that the move "allows us to drive a standardization of operating practices within the organization, which is critical. In addition, it allows us to drive scale

OB FOR STUDENTS

Whether it's obvious to you or not, structure has a significant effect on you as a student. What organizations are you a part of? Fraternities, sororities, professional associations, student government, and other campus organizations all have structures that influence how decisions are made, where the power lies, and how involved members are in the day-to-day goings on. Indeed, even your university as a whole affects you by the way it is structured.

As you begin to search for jobs, there is some evidence that you will be attracted to certain organizations on the basis of their organizational structure. On the whole, university-level job seekers tend to find centralization in organizations an unattractive company characteristic. It's not hard to picture why. Most job seekers like the idea of being able to work in an organization in which they will be able to make decisions on their own without someone else's approval.

Does anyone find centralization attractive? Not usually, but there is evidence that some job seekers are less affected by centralization than others. For example, research has shown that job seekers with high self-esteem are less bothered by centralization.[22] That is, the negative effect of centralization on organizational attractiveness is weaker for them. Perhaps they feel confident that they can "fight the bureaucracy" if they need to!

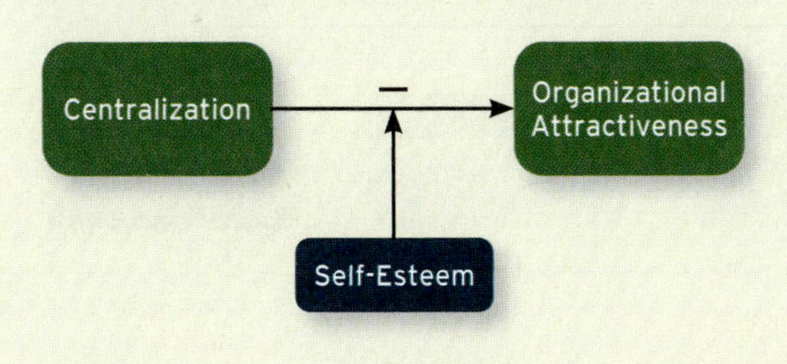

Regardless, when you begin your search for a job, some good questions to ask in an interview might revolve around the organizational structure of the company. How many people will be working for your immediate supervisor? How does the group you are looking to work for fit in with the rest of the organization? Will you be working for one direct supervisor or have reporting responsibilities to a number of managers? You are likely to find that questions like these will impress your interviewer. Understanding these aspects of organizational structure might also help you make a decision between multiple job offers.

and efficiency, which has suffered with the series of acquisitions that provided too many smaller, inefficient plants."[23] Smurfit-Stone hopes that the efficiencies generated by the change in structure will afford it enough cost savings to get a jump on its competitors.

Functional structures are extremely efficient when the organization as a whole has a relatively narrow focus, fewer product lines or services, and a stable environment. The biggest weaknesses of a functional structure tend to revolve around the fact that individuals within each function get so wrapped up in their own goals and viewpoints that they lose sight of the bigger organizational picture. In other words, employees don't communicate as well across functions as they do within functions. The Sony example in this chapter's opening vignette describes this danger, as the hardware engineers failed to communicate with the software developers. That lack of communication prevented the hardware and software people from seeing all the pieces of the puzzle.

In contrast to functional structures, **multi-divisional structures** are bureaucratic organizational forms in which employees are grouped into divisions around products, geographic regions, or clients (see Figure 13-4). Each of these divisions operates relatively autonomously from the others and has its own functional groups. Multi-divisional structures

multi-divisional structure An organizational form in which employees are grouped by product, geography, or client

FIGURE 13-4 Functional and Multi-Divisional Structures

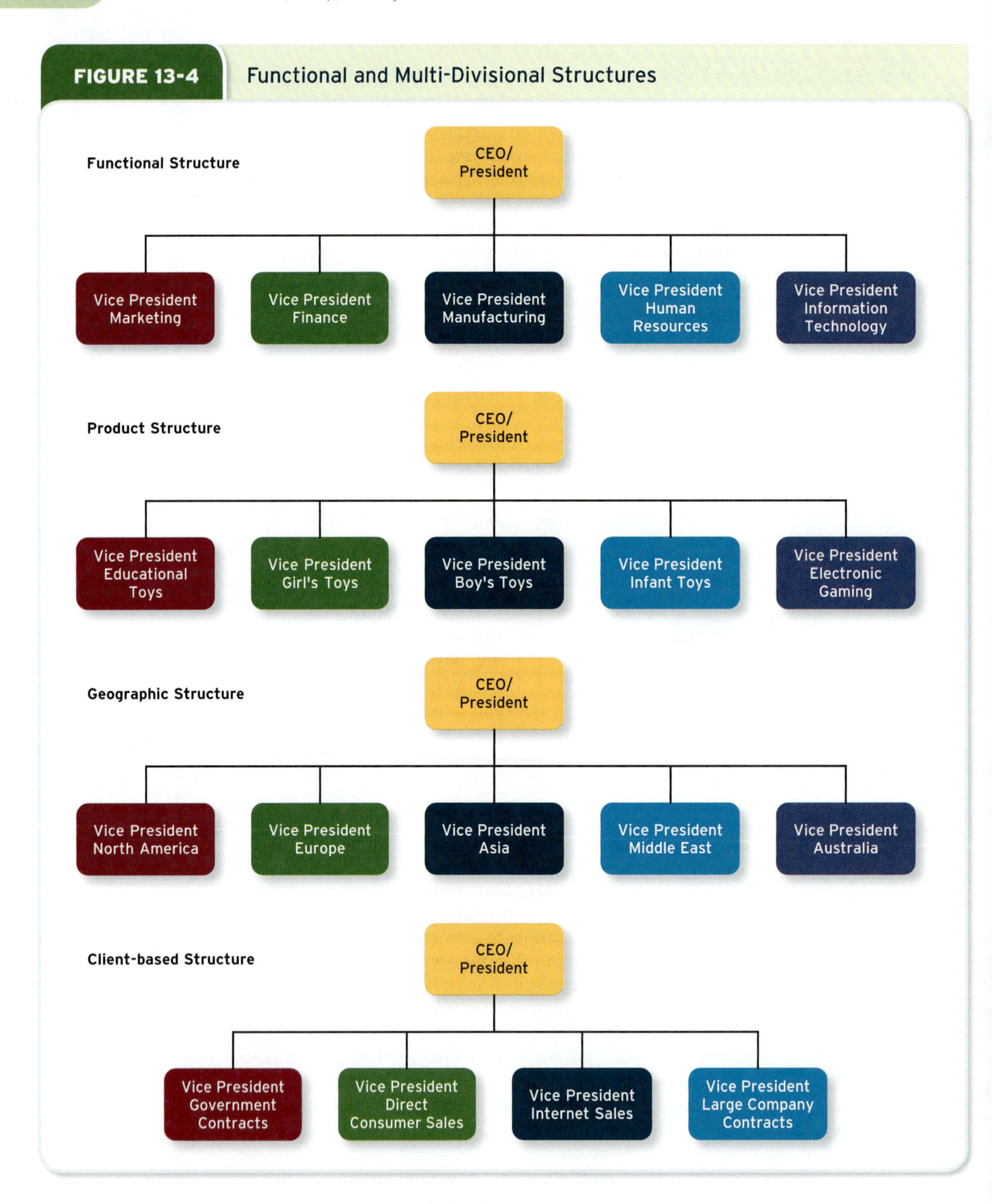

generally develop from companies with functional structures whose interests and goals become too diverse for that structure to handle. For example, if a company with a functional structure begins to add customers that require localized versions of its product, the company might adopt a geographic structure to handle the product variations. Which form a company chooses will likely depend on where the diversity in its business lies.

Product structures group business units around different products that the company produces. Each of those divisions becomes responsible for manufacturing, marketing, and doing research and development for the products in its own division. Boeing, Hewlett-Packard, and Sony are companies that have developed product structures. Product structures make sense when firms diversify to the point that the products they sell are so different that managing them becomes overwhelming. CEO Mark Hurd changed Hewlett-Packard's organizational structure to become more product-based. He was inspired to do so because his sales force (in a centralized functional structure) simply had way too many products to sell (from the largest servers to the smallest printers). Shifting the sales force into three different product-based divisions allowed the salespeople to concentrate on a core set of products, reinvigorating the Hewlett-Packard sales force.[24]

product structure An organizational form in which employees are grouped around different products that the company produces

Geographic structures are generally based around the different locations where the company does business. The functions required to serve a business are placed under a manager who is in charge of a specific location. Reasons for developing a geographic structure revolve around the different tastes of customers in different regions, the size of the locations that need to be covered by different salespeople, or the fact that the manufacturing and distribution of a product are better served by a geographic breakdown. When the Regus Group (a U.K.-based company) and HQ Global Workplaces (a U.S.-based company) merged, they came together to form the world's largest supplier of meeting spaces and office suites. The new Regus group now has 750 office-suite facilities in 350 cities in 60 countries. When they merged, HQ and Regus had different structures. Given its necessarily geographic-based type of business (i.e., the distances between facilities and the range of their customers), the new Regus group is structured by geographic region.[25] Many global companies are also organized by geographic location. IBM was one of the first, but that might be changing, as described in our **OB Internationally** feature.

geographic structure An organizational form in which employees are grouped around the different locations where the company does business

One last form of multi-divisional structure is the **client-based structure**. When organizations have a number of very large customers or groups of customers that all act in a similar way, they might organize their businesses around serving those customers. For example, small banks traditionally organize themselves into divisions such as personal banking, small business banking, personal lending, and commercial lending. Similarly, consulting firms often organize themselves into divisions that are responsible for small business clients, large business clients, and federal clients.

client-based structure An organizational form in which employees are organized around serving customers

Matrix structures are more complex forms of organizational design that try to take advantage of two types of structures at the same time. Companies such as Xerox, General Electric, and Dow Corning were among the first to adopt this type of structure.[26] Figure 13-5 provides an example of a matrix structure. In this example, employees are distributed into teams or projects within the organization on the basis of both their functional expertise and the product that they happen to be working on. Thus, the matrix represents a combination of a functional structure and a product structure. There are two important points to understand about the matrix structures. First, the matrix allows an organization to put together very flexible teams based on the experiences and skills of their employees.[27] This flexibility enables the organization to adjust much more quickly to the environment than a traditional bureaucratic structure would.

matrix structure A complex form of organizational structure that combines a functional and multi-divisional grouping

Second, the matrix gives each employee two chains of command, two groups with which to interact, and two sources of information to consider. This doubling of traditional structural elements can create high stress levels for employees if the demands of their functional

OB INTERNATIONALLY

Traditionally, IBM has structured its 200,000-employee organization along geographic lines. In fact, some might argue that IBM was the company that pioneered the first multinational geographic structure by setting up mini-IBMs in countries around the globe. Each country in which IBM operated had its own workforce and management team that reacted to the clients for whom it provided services in each country. It was a structure that made perfect sense in a world where consultants needed to be on location with their clients when those customers were having software or computer issues. However, IBM's environmental factors are changing rapidly. Competitors, such as those out of India, are providing many of the same services for significantly less money.

To change with its competitors, IBM is reorganizing its workforce by creating and utilizing what it calls competency centres. These centres will group employees from around the world on the basis of the specific skill sets that they have to offer clients. Some workers will be grouped into one location that can service clients all over the world through the use of technology. In Boulder, Colorado, IBM employs 6,200 professionals as part of a "call centre" that monitors clients' computing functions worldwide. If something goes wrong in one of IBM's 426 data centres, employees in Boulder will more than likely be the ones to handle it or send it to someone who can. Other IBM workers will be grouped by broader geographic locations so that they can still be in relatively close proximity to their customers. When these employees are needed by a client, IBM has a computer database that allows it to put together teams of highly specialized consultants by examining the skill sets listed on 70,000 IBM resumés.

Does this change in structure sound familiar to you? It should: Though IBM is maintaining some of it geographical structure, its organizational structure is becoming more functional. As the world becomes flatter through technology, clients expect the best talent from around the world, not just the best talent that happens to be sitting in their city. These structural changes will allow IBM to give clients just that. For IBM, these are the necessary changes that come with being a global company. It's not just about structure though, according to IBM Senior Vice President Robert W. Moffat Jr.: "Globalization is more than that. Our customers need us to put the right skills in the right place at the right time."[28]

grouping are at odds with the demands of their product- or client-based grouping.[29] The situation can become particularly stressful if one of the two groupings has more power than the other. For example, it may be that the functional manager assigns employees to teams, conducts performance evaluations, and decides raises—making that manager more powerful than the product- or client-based manager.[30] Although matrix structures have been around for an extremely long time, the number of organizations using them is growing as teams become a more common form of organizing work. They have also become more common in global companies, with the functional grouping balanced by a geographic grouping. For example, Areva NP, a French company that designs and builds nuclear power plants, has a matrix structure based on products (plants, fuel, services, and equipment) and geographical locations (France, Germany, and North America).[31]

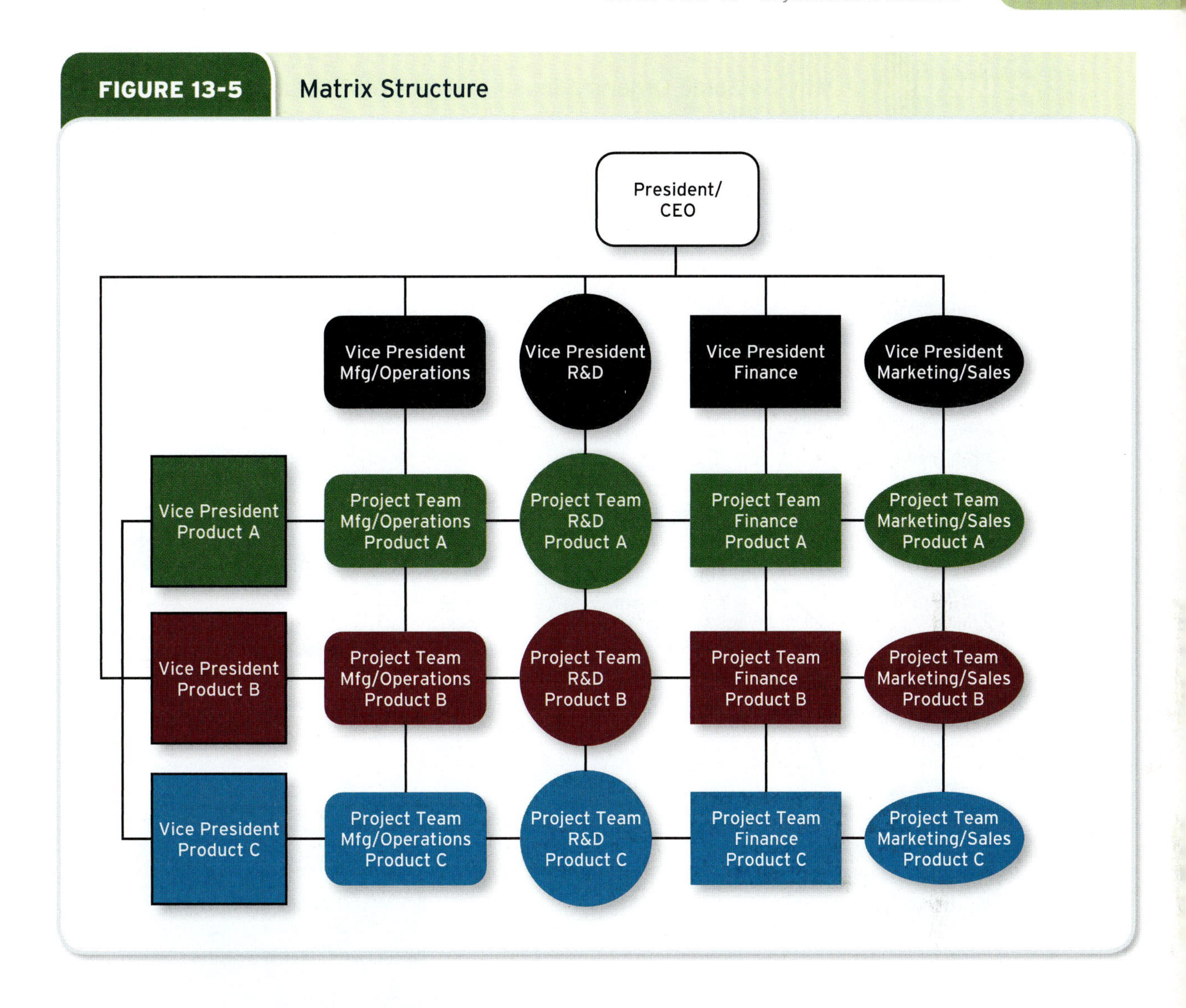

SO WHY DO SOME ORGANIZATIONS HAVE DIFFERENT STRUCTURES THAN OTHERS?

As shown in Figure 13-6, differences in the business environment, company strategy, technology, and firm size cause some organizations to be designed differently than others. These differences create variations in the five elements of organizational structure: work specialization, chain of command, span of control, centralization, and formalization. These elements then combine to form one of a number of common organizational forms, including: (1) a simple structure; (2) a bureaucratic structure, which may come in functional, product, geographic, or client-based forms; or (3) a matrix structure. Some of these forms are more mechanistic, whereas others are more organic. Taken together, these structures explain how work is organized within a given company.

FIGURE 13-6 Why Do Some Organizations Have Different Structures Than Others?

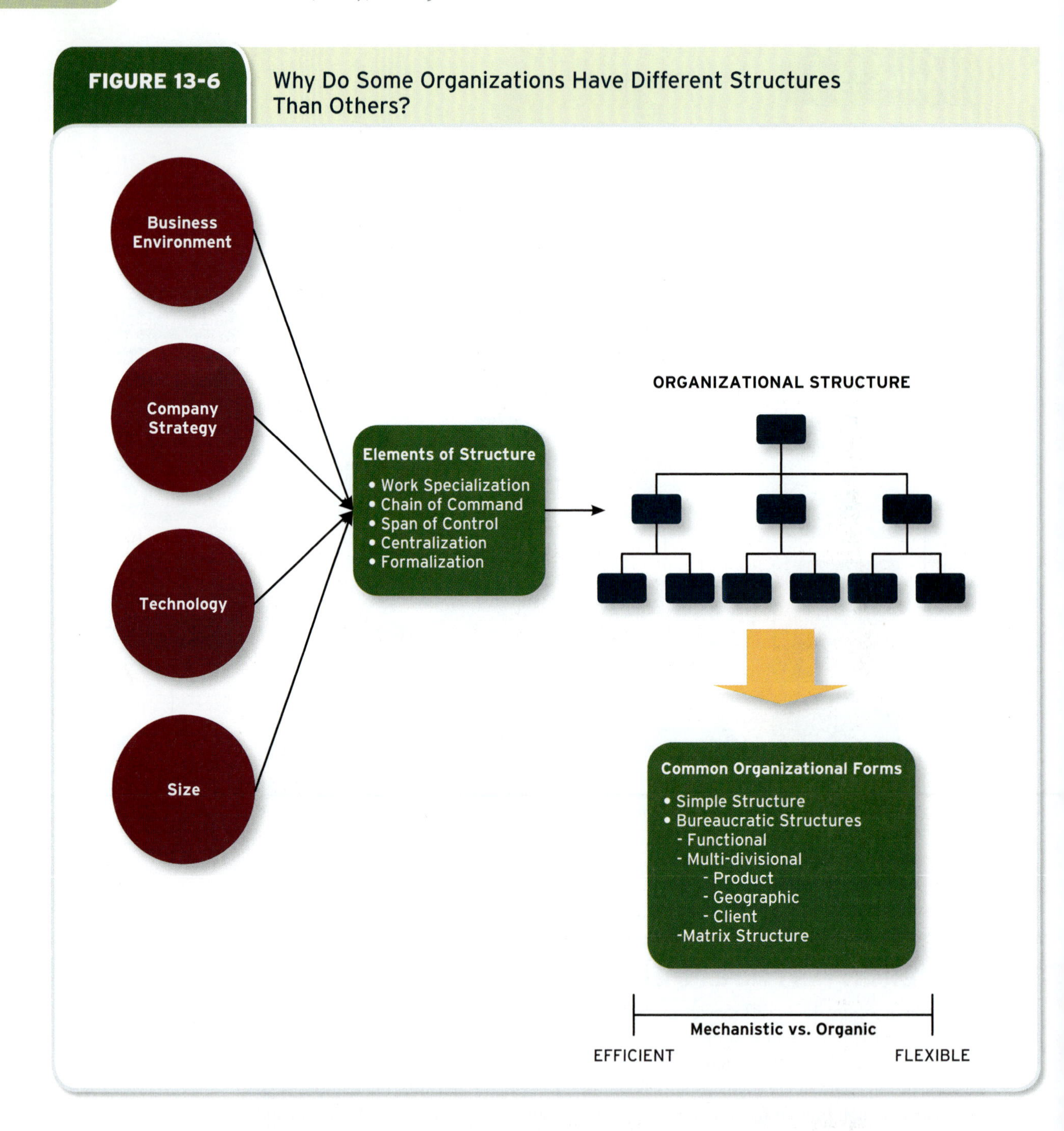

HOW IMPORTANT IS STRUCTURE?

To some degree, an organization's structure provides the foundation for almost everything in organizational behaviour. Think about some of the things that organizational structure affects: communication patterns between employees, the tasks an employee performs, the types of groups an organization uses, the freedom employees have to innovate and try new things, how power and influence are divided up in the company . . . we could go on and on. Picture the walls of a house. The occupants within those walls can decorate or personalize the structure as best they can. They can make it more attractive according to their individual preferences by adding and taking away furniture, but at the end of the day, they are still stuck with that structure. They have to work within the confines that the builder envisioned (unless they are willing to tear down walls or build new ones at considerable time, effort, and expense!). Organizational structures operate in much the same way for employees and their managers. A given manager can do many things to try to motivate, inspire, and set up an effective work environment so that employees have high levels of performance and commitment. At the end of the day, however, that manager must work within the structure created by the organization.

Given how many organizational forms there are, it is almost impossible to give an accurate representation of the impact of organizational structure on job performance. In fact, we might even say that an organization's structure determines what job performance is supposed to look like! In addition, the elements of structure are not necessarily good or bad for performance. For example, a narrow span of control is not necessarily better than a broad one; rather, the organization must find the optimal "middle ground." One thing we can say, as illustrated in Figure 13-7, is that changes to an organization's structure can have negative effects on the employees who work for the company, at least in the short term. The process of changing an organization's structure is called **restructuring**. Research suggests that restructuring has a small negative effect on task performance, likely because changes in specialization, centralization, or formalization may lead to confusion about how exactly employees are supposed to do their jobs, which hinders *learning* and *decision making*. Restructuring has a more significant negative effect on organizational commitment, however. Restructuring efforts can increase *stress* and jeopardize employees' *trust* in the organization. There is some evidence that the end result is a lower level of affective commitment on the part of employees, because they feel less emotionally attached to the firm.

restructuring The process of changing an organization's structure

APPLICATION: RESTRUCTURING

As you have read through our discussion of organizational structure, you may have noticed how important it is for organizations to adapt to their environment. The first step in adapting is recognizing the need to change. The second (and sometimes much more problematic) step is actually doing it by restructuring. Restructuring efforts come in a variety of shapes and sizes. Organizations may change from a product-based structure to a functional structure, from a functional structure to a geographic-based structure, and on and on. However, the most common kind of restructuring in recent years has been a "flattening" of the organization. Why do so many organizations do this? Think back to our discussion of tall and flat organizational hierarchies, in which we noted that taller organizations have more layers of management. Many restructuring efforts are designed to remove one or more of those layers to increase efficiency.

Restructuring, as an adaptive response to changing environments, can be a slow, ongoing process. Consider how the Alberta government has changed the way health care services are delivered to its residents. Since the early 1990s, this province has experienced a dramatic increase in population. The problem facing the government was how to provide consistent, standardized, cost-effective, and equitable access to health services—regardless of whether you lived in an urban centre like Calgary or Edmonton, or in one of the smaller towns or villages. Prior to 1994, 128 acute care hospital boards, 25 public health boards, and 40 long-term-care boards reported to Alberta Health and Wellness. Each of these 193

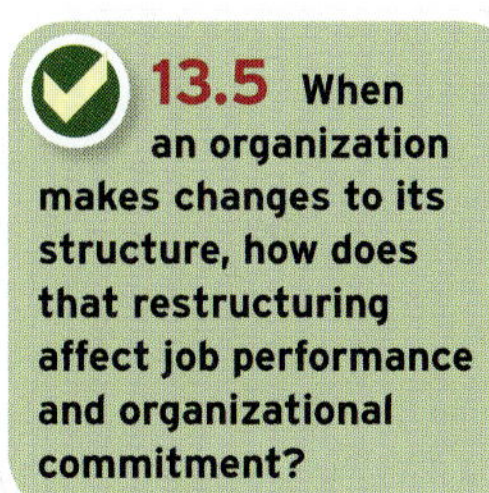

FIGURE 13-7 Effects of Organizational Structure on Performance and Commitment

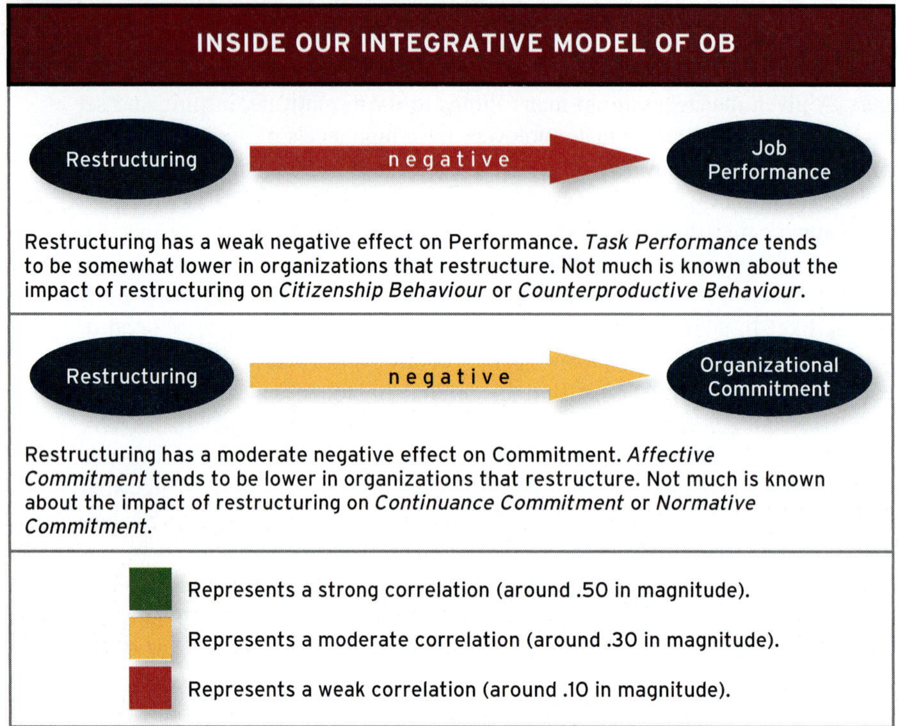

Sources: C. Gopinath and T.E. Becker, "Communication, Procedural Justice, and Employee Attitudes: Relationships under Conditions of Divestiture," *Journal of Management* 26 (2000), pp. 63–83; J. Brockner, G. Spreitzer, A. Mishra, W. Hockwarter, L. Pepper, and J. Weinberg, "Perceived Control as an Antidote to the Negative Effects of Layoffs on Survivors' Organizational Commitment and Job Performance," *Administrative Science Quarterly* 49 (2004), pp. 76–100.

boards, in effect, managed its own operational decision making. Although responsive to local needs, with so many boards it was becoming harder and harder for the province to manage the challenges of escalating health care costs, standardization, and equal access. Thus, a different administrative structure was needed, one that stressed increased centralization of decision making and formalization. Seventeen health regions were established in 1994 to oversee operational decision making across the province. The 17 health regions were reduced to 9 regions in 2003 (Chinook, Capital Health, Calgary Health, David Thompson, East Central, Aspen, Peace Country, Northern Lights, and Palliser), plus the Alberta Mental Health Board, the Alberta Cancer Board, and the Alberta Alcohol and Drug Abuse Commission. In early 2008, these 12 entities were replaced by one super board that is responsible for all health services delivery in Alberta. "Moving to one provincial governance board will ensure a more streamlined system for patients and health professionals across the province," said provincial Minister of Health and Wellness Ron Liepert.[32]

One of the ways in which managers can do their best to help a restructuring succeed is to help manage layoff survivors (employees that remain with the company following a layoff). Many layoff survivors are known to experience a great deal of guilt and remorse following an organization's decision to remove some employees from the company.[33] Researchers and practitioners recently have been trying to understand layoff survivors better, as well as how to help them adjust more quickly. One of the major problems for layoff survivors is the increased job demands placed on them. After all, that co-worker or boss the employee had was doing *something*. Layoff survivors are generally burdened with having to pick up the leftover tasks that used to be done by somebody else.[34] This burden creates a sense of uncertainty and stress. Recent research suggests that one of the best ways to help layoff survivors adjust is to do things that give them a stronger sense of control.[35] Allowing survivors to have a voice in how to move forward or help set the plans about how to accomplish future goals are two ways managers can help employees feel more in control. In addition, honest and frequent communication with layoff survivors greatly helps reduce their feelings of uncertainty and stress.[36]

TAKEAWAYS

13.1 An organization's structure formally dictates how jobs and tasks are divided and coordinated between individuals and groups within the organization. This structure, partially illustrated through the use of organizational charts, provides the foundation for organizing jobs, controlling employee behaviour, shaping communication channels, and providing a lens through which employees view their work environment.

13.2 There are five major elements to an organization's structure: work specialization, chain of command, span of control, centralization of decision making, and formalization. These elements can be organized in such a way as to make an organization more mechanistic in nature, which allows it to be highly efficient in stable environments, or more organic in nature, which allows it to be flexible and adaptive in changing environments.

13.3 Organizational design is the process of creating, selecting, or changing the structure of an organization. Factors to be considered in organizational design include a company's business environment, its strategy, its technology, and its size.

13.4 There are literally thousands of organizational forms. The most common is the simple structure, which is used by most small companies. Larger companies adopt a more bureaucratic structure. This structure may be functional in nature, such that employees are grouped by job tasks, or multi-divisional, such that employees are grouped by product, geography, or client. Organizations may also adopt a matrix structure that combines functional and multi-divisional grouping.

13.5 Organizational restructuring efforts have a weak negative effect on job performance. They have a more significant negative effect on organizational commitment, because employees tend to feel less emotional attachment to organizations that are restructuring.

KEY TERMS

- bureaucratic structure *p. 352*
- business environment *p. 350*
- centralization *p. 347*
- chain of command *p. 345*
- client-based structure *p. 355*
- company size *p. 351*
- company strategy *p. 350*
- formalization *p. 347*
- functional structure *p. 352*
- geographic structure *p. 355*
- matrix structure *p. 355*
- mechanistic organizations *p. 347*
- multi-divisional structure *p. 353*
- organic organizations *p. 348*
- organizational chart *p. 343*
- organizational design *p. 350*
- organizational structure *p. 342*
- product structure *p. 355*
- restructuring *p. 359*
- simple structure *p. 351*
- span of control *p. 345*
- technology *p. 351*
- work specialization *p. 344*

DISCUSSION QUESTIONS

13.1 Is it possible to be a great leader of employees in a highly mechanistic organization? What special talents or abilities might be required?

13.2 Why do the elements of structure, such as work specialization, formalization, span of control, chain of command, and centralization, have a tendency to change together? Which of the five do you feel is the most important?

13.3 Which is more important for an organization: the ability to be efficient or the ability to adapt to its environment? What does this say about how an organization's structure should be set up?

13.4 Which of the organizational forms described in this chapter do you think leads to the highest levels of motivation among workers? Why?

13.5 If you worked in a matrix organization, what would be some of the career development challenges that you might face? Does the idea of working in a matrix structure appeal to you? Why or why not?

13.6 Should an organization consult with rank-and-file employees before it restructures? Should it be open about its intentions to restructure or more secretive about key details? Why?

CASE • SONY CORPORATION

In his role as CEO, Sir Howard Stringer could not have arrived at a more critical time for the company. Sony's organizational structure has become bloated with multiple "silos" that divide the company into seemingly separate entities. The different silos are not committed to a common Sony vision, which has caused the organization to fail to capitalize on market shifts. Sony also includes a number of non-core businesses that have taken capital away from key areas that historically were successful. Thus, Sony's organizational structure is not integrated with its organizational strategy.

Currently, Sony is attempting to create a leaner company to combat the competitive problems facing its core businesses. The television division represents a significant portion of its revenue and is in need of restructuring. Stringer will attempt to revitalize this division by focusing plant production on HDTV products rather than cathode ray tube TV products. Sony also will begin integrating the various divisions of the company to create, build, and market HDTV products. Another division within Sony needing restructuring is the computer entertainment arm. Sony's PlayStation3 is struggling to break even in fiscal 2007, largely due to the lack of communication among various departments of the company. Because the various divisions of Sony are separate, the company cannot effectively compete with its competitors. Stringer will have an uphill battle to restructure Sony to integrate the various divisions of the company to regain its stature in the industry.

13.1 Evaluate Sony's organizational structure in terms of its inability to compete effectively with its competitors.

13.2 Why has Sony been missing the mark with its recent product releases?

Sources: B. Bremner, "Is a Slimmer Sony Coming?" *BusinessWeek,* September 16, 2005; E. Rusli, "Game Over for Father of PlayStation," *Forbes,* April 27, 2007, www.forbes.com (June 26, 2007); "Time for Sony to Call the TV Repairman," *BusinessWeek,* August 15, 2005; J. Yang, "What Should Sony Spin Off?" *BusinessWeek,* April 13, 2005.

EXERCISE • CREATIVE CARDS, INC.

The purpose of this exercise is to demonstrate the effects of structure on organizational efficiency. Creative Cards, Inc., is a small but growing company, started 10 years ago by Angela Naom, a graphic designer. The company has added many employees over the years but without a master plan. Now Angela wants to reorganize the company. The current structure of Creative Cards, Inc. looks like this:

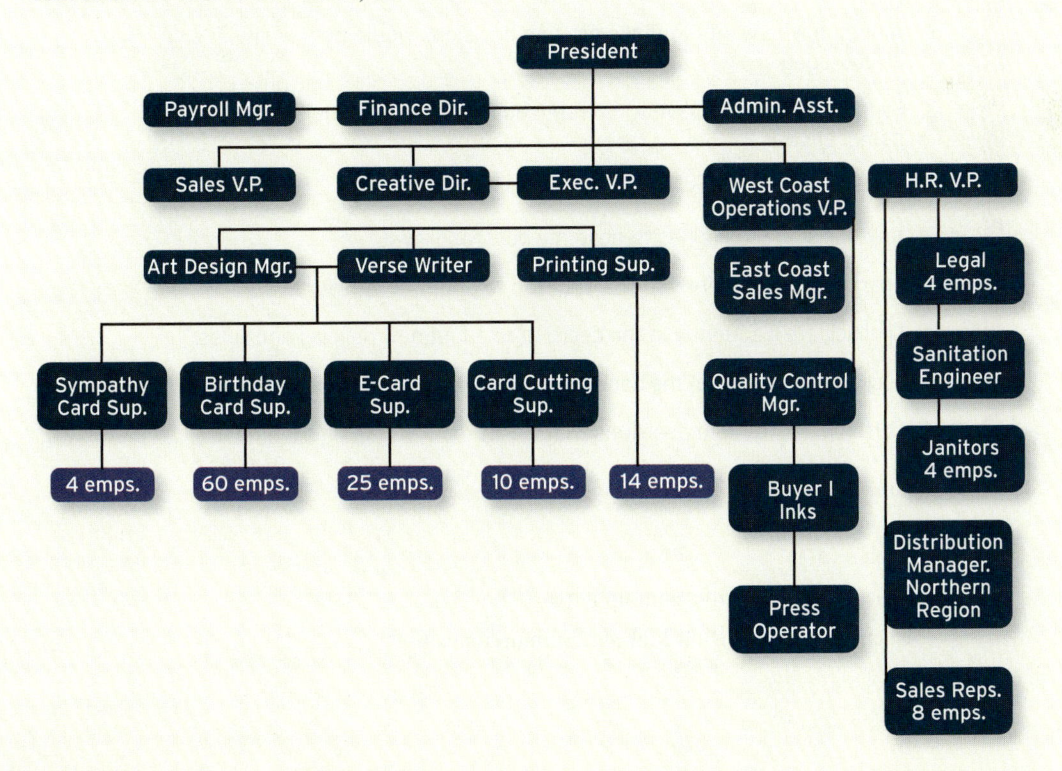

This exercise uses groups of six participants, so your instructor will either assign you to a group of six or ask you to create your own group of six. The exercise has the following steps:

1. Review the organizational chart and identify at least 10 problems with the design of Creative Cards, Inc. Be sure to consider work specialization, chain of command, span of control, centralization, and formalization in developing your answer.
2. Create a new organizational design that you think would help the company operate more efficiently and effectively.

OB ASSESSMENTS • CENTRALIZATION

Have you experienced life inside an organization with a highly centralized structure? This assessment is designed to measure two facets of what would be considered a centralized organizational structure. Those two facets are hierarchy of authority, which reflects the degree to which managers are needed to approve decisions, and participation in decision making, which reflects how involved rank-and-file employees are in day-to-day deliberations. Think about the last job you held (even if it was a part-time or summer job). Alternatively, think about a student group of yours that seems to have a definite "leader." Then answer each question using the response scale provided.

1 STRONGLY DISAGREE	2 DISAGREE	3 NEUTRAL	4 AGREE	5 STRONGLY AGREE

1. There can be little action here until a supervisor approves a decision. ________
2. A person who wants to make his own decisions would be quickly discouraged. ________
3. Even small matters have to be referred to someone higher up for a final answer. ________
4. I have to ask my boss before I do almost anything. ________
5. Any decision I make has to have my boss' approval. ________
6. I participate frequently in the decision to adopt new programs. ________
7. I participate frequently in the decision to adopt new policies and rules. ________
8. I usually participate in the decision to hire or adopt new group members. ________
9. I often participate in decisions that affect my working environment. ________

SCORING

Hierarchy of Authority: Sum up items 1–5. ________

Participation in Decision Making: Sum up items 6–9. ________

INTERPRETATION

A centralized structure would be one in which Hierarchy of Authority is high and Participation in Decision Making is low. If your score is above 20 for Hierarchy of Authority and below 8 for Participation in Decision Making, your organization (or student group) has a highly centralized structure. Think about the implications that this structure has on your view toward work and your interactions with your co-workers or boss.

Source: Adapted from M. Schminke, R. Cropanzano, and D.E. Rupp, "Organization Structure and Fairness Perceptions: The Moderating Effects of Organizational Level," *Organizational Behavior and Human Decision Processes* 89 (2002), pp. 881–905.

CONNECT—Available 24/7 with instant feedback so you can study when you want, how you want, and where you want. Take advantage of the Study Plan—an innovative tool that helps students customize their own learning experience. Students can diagnose their knowledge with pre- and post-tests, identify the areas where they need help, search contents of the entire learning package for content specific to the topic they're studying, and add these resources to their study plan. Visit **www.connectob.ca** to register—take practice quizzes, run interactive scenarios, and much more. Also visit the Student Online Learning Centre for additional study tools.

www.mcgrawhill.ca/olc/colquitt

CHAPTER

14 Organizational Culture

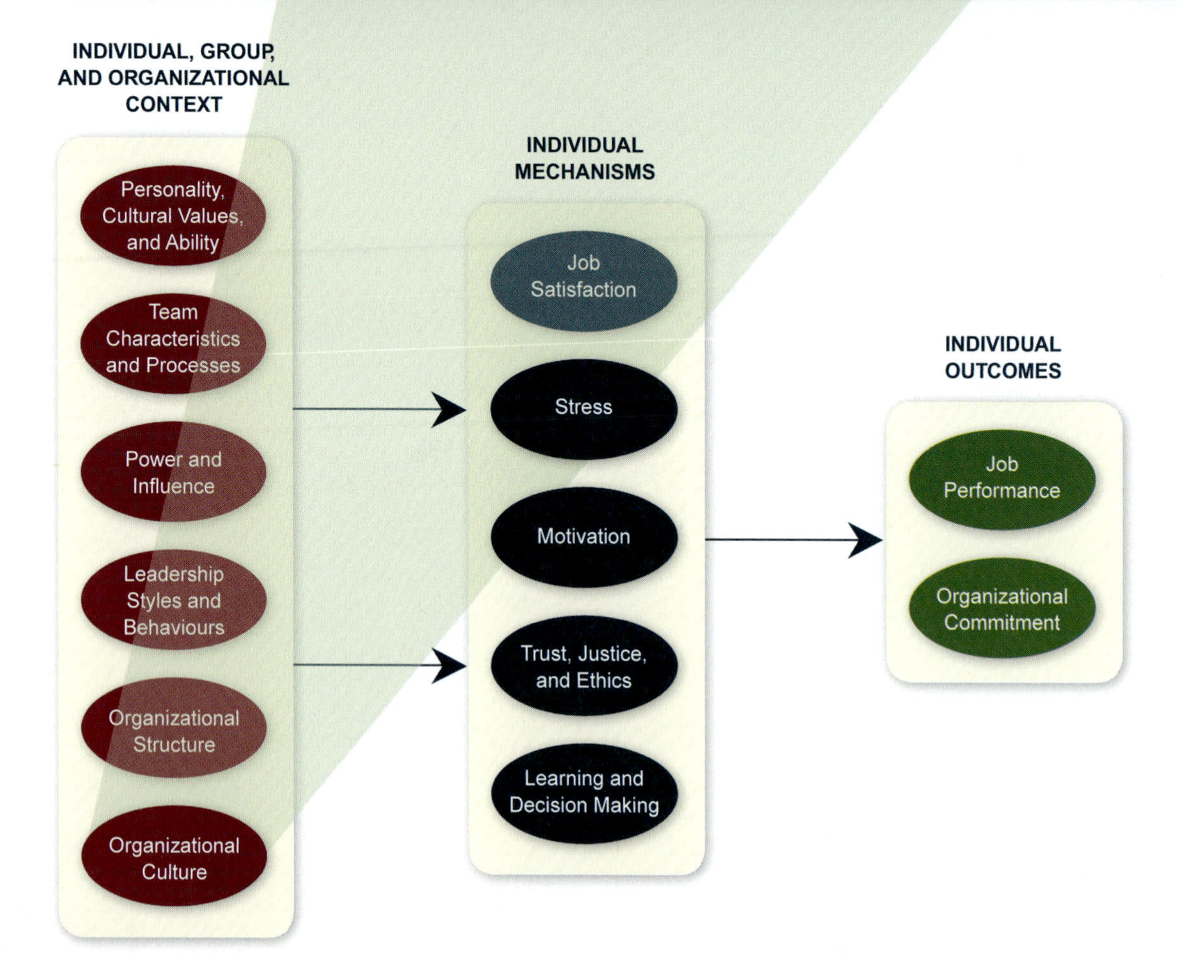

Learning Outcomes

After reading this chapter, you should be able to answer the following questions:

14.1 What is organizational culture, and what are its components?

14.2 What general and specific types can be used to describe an organization's culture?

14.3 What is a strong culture, and what makes a culture strong? Is a strong culture necessarily good?

14.4 How do organizations maintain their culture? How do they change it?

14.5 What is person-organization fit? How does fitting with an organization's culture affect job performance and organizational commitment?

14.6 What steps can organizations take to make sure that newcomers will fit with their culture?

GENERAL ELECTRIC AND ENRON

General Electric. Enron. Not two companies that you would expect to be mentioned in the same breath at the beginning of a textbook chapter. After all, General Electric was recently named the World's Most Admired Company by *Fortune* magazine,[1] and Enron will go down in history as one of the greatest organizational failures and financial scandals ever.[2] So why would we mention both of these firms together? Because the fact is that throughout the 1990s and into the early 2000s, these companies actually approached their businesses and treated their employees in very similar ways. Both were extremely successful enterprises whose stock performance rewarded investors handsomely and caused them to be recognized as companies of excellence by numerous publications of all types.[3] On the surface, both companies used terms like "creativity," "competitiveness," "people," "integrity," and "excellence" to describe their core values. On an annual basis, GE and Enron both fired managers who were at the bottom of their performance scales, with Enron removing the bottom 20 percent of performers and GE removing the bottom 10 percent. Employees were paid well above average market levels, and managers received large bonuses that were tied directly to performance goals. Both had strong-minded and well-respected leaders—GE was led by Jack Welch, who has been described as a legend, a hero, and the world's greatest business leader,[4] and Enron was led by Jeff Skilling, known as a brilliant visionary and perhaps one of the smartest CEOs on the planet.[5]

Underneath the surface though, these two organizations could not have been more different. What was it that made these two companies move in such opposite directions? One potential answer lies with organizational culture. Whereas GE's culture led to continued success, high levels of employee commitment and performance, low employee turnover, and generally a perception as one of the top companies in world, Enron's culture failed miserably over the long term on almost every level.

The company practices of General Electric (led by Jack Welch) and of Enron (led by Jeff Skilling) had many similarities, despite the dramatically different fates of the two firms.

Many blame Enron's failure on a culture of greed that favoured maximizing real or perceived profits to boost stock prices.[6] In the late 1990s, an Enron taskforce put together to help communicate Enron's "Visions and Values" considered replacing words such as "integrity," "excellence," "trust," and "respect" with words like "smart," "bold," and "aggressive."[7] The changes were never made, but the fact that they were considered says quite a bit about the underlying culture within Enron. There was also no doubt that the culture at Enron had a powerful effect on employees. Jeff Skilling told others, "People didn't just go to work for Enron; it became a part of your life, just as important as your family. *More* important than your family."[8]

ORGANIZATIONAL CULTURE

In almost every chapter up to this point, we have simply given you definitions of important topics. However, in this case, it is important for you to understand that there are just about as many definitions of organizational culture as there are people who study it. In fact, research on organizational culture has produced well over 50 different definitions![9] It seems that the term "culture" means a great many things to a great many people. Definitions of culture have ranged from as broad as, "The way we do things around here"[10] to as specific as . . . well, let's just suffice it to say that they can get complicated. Not surprisingly, the various definitions of organizational culture stem from how people have studied it. Sociologists study culture using a broad lens and anthropological research methods, like those applied to study tribes and civilizations. Psychologists tend to study culture and its effects on people using survey methods. In fact, many psychologists actually prefer the term "climate," but for our purposes, we'll use the two terms interchangeably. In this chapter, we define **organizational culture** as the shared social knowledge within an organization regarding the rules, norms, and values that shape the attitudes and behaviours of its employees.[11]

organizational culture The shared social knowledge within an organization regarding the rules, norms, and values that shape the attitudes and behaviours of its employees

"I don't know how it started, either. All I know is that it's part of our corporate culture."

Source:

This definition helps highlight a number of facets of organizational culture. First, culture is social knowledge among members of the organization. Employees learn about most important aspects of culture through other employees. This transfer of knowledge might be through explicit communication, simple observation, or other, less obvious methods. In addition, culture is shared knowledge, which means that members of the organization understand and have a degree of consensus regarding what the culture is. Second, culture tells employees what the rules, norms, and values are within the organization. What are the most important work outcomes to focus on? What behaviours are appropriate or inappropriate at work? How should a person act or dress while at work? Indeed, some cultures even go so far as to say how employees should act when they aren't at work. Third, organizational culture shapes and reinforces certain employee attitudes and behaviours by creating a system of control over employees.[12] There is evidence that your individual goals and values will grow over time to match those of the organization for which you work.[13] This development really isn't that hard to imagine, given how much time employees spend working inside an organization.

14.1 What is organizational culture, and what are its components?

WHY DO SOME ORGANIZATIONS HAVE DIFFERENT CULTURES THAN OTHERS?

One of the most common questions people ask when you tell them where you are employed is, "So, tell me . . . what's it like there?" The description you use in your response is likely to have a lot to do with what the organization's culture is all about. In calculating your response to the question, you might consider describing the kinds of people who work at your company. More than likely, you will do your best to describe the work atmosphere on a regular day. Perhaps you will painstakingly describe the facilities you work in or how you feel the employees are treated. You might even go as far as to describe what it is that defines "success" at your company. All of those answers give clues that help organizational outsiders understand what a company is actually like. To give you a feel for the full range of potential answers to the "what's it like there?" question, it's necessary to review the facets of culture in more detail.

CULTURE COMPONENTS

There are three major components to any organization's culture: observable artifacts, espoused values, and basic underlying assumptions. You can understand the differences among these three components if you view culture like an onion, as in Figure 14-1. Some components of an organization's culture are readily apparent and observable, like the skin of an onion. However, other components are less observable to organizational outsiders or newcomers. Such outsiders can observe, interpret, and make conclusions based on what they see on the surface, but the inside remains a mystery until they can peel back the outside layers to gauge the values and assumptions that lie beneath. The sections that follow review the culture components in more detail.

OBSERVABLE ARTIFACTS **Observable artifacts** are the manifestations of an organization's culture that employees can easily see or talk about. They supply the signals that employees interpret to gauge how they should act during the workday. Artifacts supply the primary means of transmitting an organization's culture to its workforce. It is difficult to overestimate the importance of artifacts, because they help show not only current employees but also potential employees, customers, shareholders, and investors what the organization is all about. There are six major types of artifacts: symbols, physical structures, language, stories, rituals, and ceremonies.[14]

observable artifacts Aspects of an organization's culture that employees and outsiders can easily see or talk about

FIGURE 14-1 The Three Components of Organizational Culture

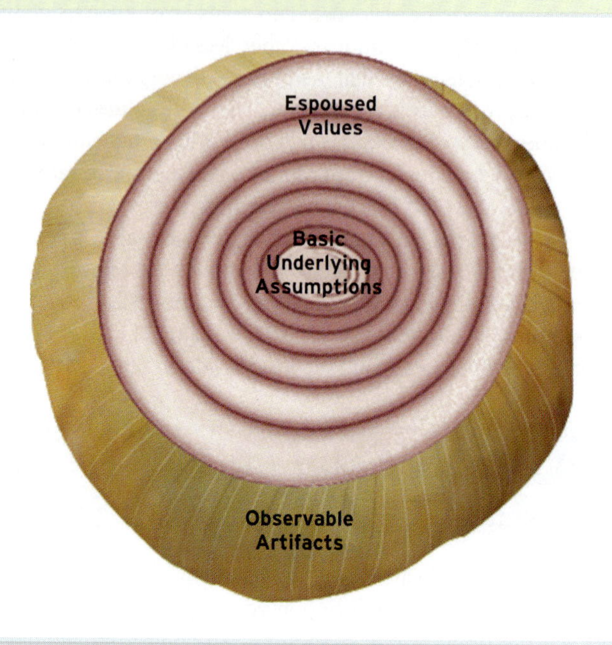

symbols The images an organization uses, which generally convey messages

Symbols can be found throughout an organization, from its corporate logo to the images it places on its Web site to the uniforms its employees wear. Think about what Nike's "swoosh" represents: speed, movement, velocity. What might that symbol convey about Nike's culture? Or consider Apple's "apple" logo. That symbol brings to mind Newton's discovery of gravity under the apple tree, conveying the importance of innovation within Apple's culture. When you think of the words "dark suit, white shirt, tie," what company do you think of? For many, the symbol represents IBM because that represents the company's long-standing dress code. Even though that dress code hasn't been in place at IBM for 10 years, it still symbolizes a formal, bureaucratic, and professional culture.

physical structures The organization's buildings and internal office designs

Physical structures also say a lot about a culture. Is the workplace open? Does top management work in a separate section of the building? Is the setting devoid of anything unique, or can employees express their personalities? Have you noticed that the physical layout of an office, in particular the positioning of the desk and chairs in the room, conveys information about culture? What message is conveyed when a large desk divides the office so that you have sit across from your professor when you meet? Compare that assessment to when the desk is positioned against a side wall so that you have to sit beside your professor? Which of these two desk configurations conveys a collaborative, informal orientation toward students? What would it say about the culture of an organization if employees were allowed to have beach-themed office furniture?

language The jargon, slang, and slogans used within an organization

Language reflects the jargon, slang, and slogans used within the walls of an organization. Do you know what a CTR, CPC, or Crawler is? Chances are you don't. If you worked for Yahoo, however, those terms would be second nature to you. CTR stands for click-through rate, CPC stands for cost-per-click, and a Crawler is a computer program that gathers information from other Web sites. Home Depot maintains a "stack it high and watch it fly" slogan, which reflects its approach to sales. Yum Brands Inc., which owns Pizza Hut, Taco Bell, KFC, and other fast-food restaurants, expects employees to be "customer maniacs"[15]—language that conveys its culture for customer interaction.

Stories consist of anecdotes, accounts, legends, and myths that are passed down from cohort to cohort within an organization. When the global conglomerate Unilever purchased Ben & Jerry's Homemade Inc. in 2001, the Unilever chairman first walked into the Vermont-based company to a sight he didn't often see: All the employees were wearing togas![16] This story captures the cultural differences between Unilever and Ben & Jerry's and serves to illustrate the unique identity shared by the ice cream company's employees.

stories Anecdotes, accounts, legends, and myths passed down from cohort to cohort within an organization

Rituals are the daily or weekly planned routines that occur in an organization. A popular ritual that many white-collar organizations have adopted is called "casual Fridays." One day a week, employees are permitted to leave the suit at home and come to work dressed in their jeans or other casual attire. This weekly dress ritual reinforces the idea that work can be relaxed and fun. Another variation on this theme would be to permit employees to bring their pets to work on a designated day each month. An annual ritual for Telus Corporation is that every employee must take and pass a course on ethics.[17] Now consider some of the rituals that you or your family regularly perform—what messages to these rituals convey about what is valued?

rituals The daily or weekly planned routines that occur in an organization

Ceremonies are formal events, generally performed in front of an audience of organizational members. Graduates and their families experience a public celebration of hard work, achievement, and accomplishment during their convocation ceremony. Organizations frequently use public reward ceremonies to recognize individuals and teams who best exemplify what the culture values (e.g., safety; high performance; cost-saving suggestions). Ceremonies can also be used to convey important cultural changes. For example, in the process of turning around the company, Continental Airlines held a ceremony to burn an 800-page policy manual that was despised by employees. This manual was later replaced by a new 80-page manual.[18]

ceremonies Formal events, generally performed in front of an audience of organizational members

ESPOUSED VALUES **Espoused values** are the beliefs, philosophies, and norms that a company explicitly states. Espoused values can range from published documents, such as a company's vision or mission statement, to verbal statements made to employees by executives and managers. A great example of espoused values is found in the corporate constitution of Calgary-based EnCana Corporation. Explicit statements in this formal document spell out to both managers and employees what is valued within their high-performance culture. The constitution explicitly states that *EnCanans* value accountability, imagination, adaptability, leadership, and urgency, and that these values need to be demonstrated daily. Also explicit in this document are statements about what is not valued—*EnCanans* do not tolerate knowledge without action, action without knowledge, avoiding accountability, wasting time and resources, uncaring efforts, and failure without learning.[19]

espoused values The beliefs, philosophies, and norms that a company explicitly states

It is certainly important to draw a distinction between espoused values and enacted values. It is one thing for a company to outwardly say something is important; it is another thing for employees to consistently act in ways that support those espoused values. When a company holds to its espoused values over time and regardless of the situations it operates in, the values become more believable both to employees and outsiders. However, in times of economic downturns, staying true to espoused values is not always easy. Our opening example of Enron helps to illustrate the differences between espoused and enacted values.

BASIC UNDERLYING ASSUMPTIONS **Basic underlying assumptions** are taken-for-granted beliefs and philosophies that are so ingrained that employees simply act on them rather than questioning the validity of their behaviour in a given situation.[20] These assumptions represent the deepest and least observable part of a culture and may not be consciously apparent, even to organizational veterans. Edgar Schein, one of the pre-eminent scholars on the topic of organizational culture, uses the example of safety in an engineering firm. He states, "In an occupation such as engineering, it would be inconceivable to deliberately design something that is unsafe; it is a taken-for-granted assumption that things should be safe."[21] Whatever a company's underlying assumptions are, its hidden beliefs are those that are the most likely to dictate employee behaviour and affect employee attitudes. They are also the aspects of an organizational culture that are the most long-lasting and difficult to change.[22]

basic underlying assumptions The ingrained beliefs and philosophies of employees

14.2 What general and specific types can be used to describe an organization's culture?

fragmented culture An organizational culture type in which employees are distant and disconnected from one another

mercenary culture An organizational culture type in which employees think alike but are not friendly to one another

networked culture An organizational culture type in which employees are friendly to one another, but everyone thinks differently and does his or her own thing

communal culture An organizational culture type in which employees are friendly to one another and all think alike

GENERAL CULTURE TYPES

If we can consider the combination of an organization's observable artifacts, espoused values, and basic underlying assumptions, we can begin to classify its culture along various dimensions. Of course, there are many different types of organizational cultures, just like there are many different types of personalities. Many researchers have tried to create general typologies that can be used to describe the culture of any organization. For instance, one popular general typology divides organizational culture along two dimensions: solidarity and sociability. Solidarity is the degree to which group members think and act alike, and sociability represents how friendly employees are to one another.[23] Figure 14-2 shows how we might describe organizations that are either high or low on these dimensions. Organizations that are low on both dimensions have a **fragmented culture** in which employees are distant and disconnected from one another. Organizations that have cultures in which employees think alike but aren't friendly to one another can be considered **mercenary cultures**. These types of organizations are likely to be very political, "what's in it for me" environments. Cultures in which all employees are friendly to one another, but everyone thinks differently and does his or her own thing, are **networked cultures**. Many highly creative organizations have a networked culture. Organizations with friendly employees who all think alike are **communal cultures**.

SPECIFIC CULTURE TYPES

The typology shown in Figure 14-2 is general enough to be applied to almost any organization. However, there are obviously other ways to classify an organization's culture. In fact, many organizations attempt to manipulate observable artifacts and espoused values to create specific cultures that help them achieve their organizational goals. Some of these specific cultures are more relevant in some industries than in others. Although the number of specific cultures that an organization might strive for are virtually endless, we focus on four examples: customer service cultures, safety cultures, diversity cultures, and creativity cultures.

FIGURE 14-2 A Typology of Organizational Culture

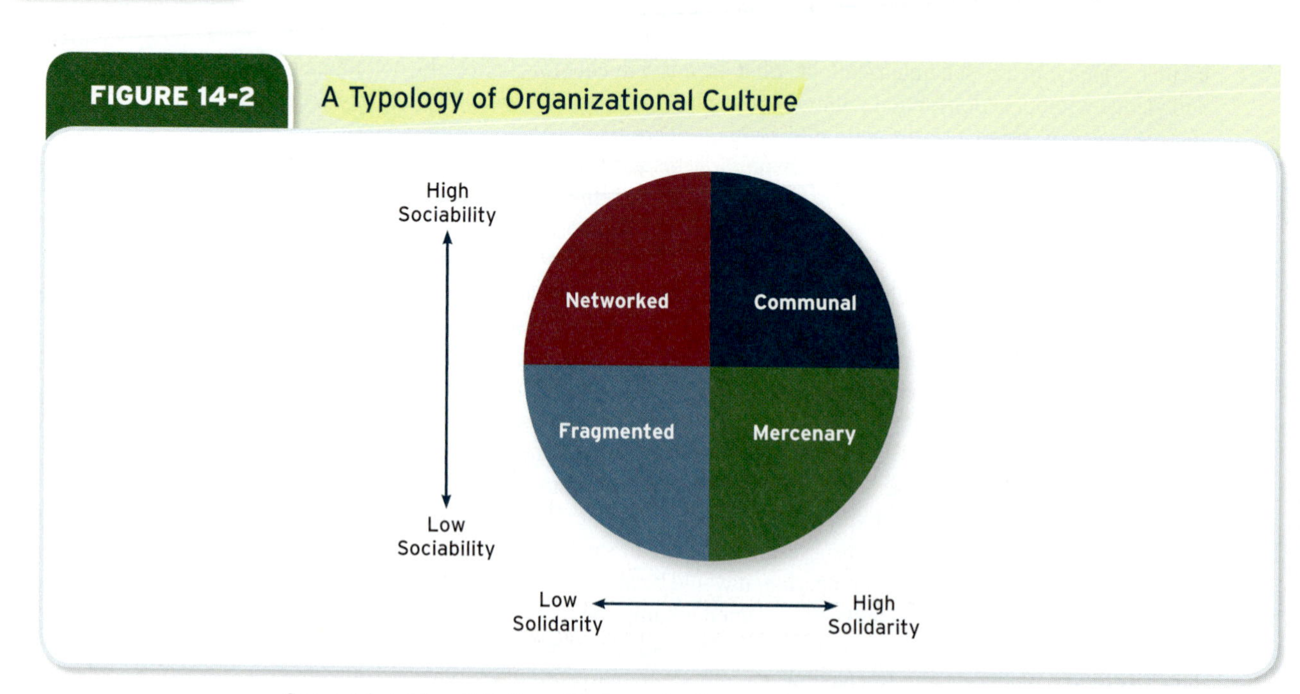

Source: Adapted from R. Goffee and G. Jones, *The Character of a Corporation* (New York: Harper Business, 1998).

FIGURE 14-3 The Service Culture Process

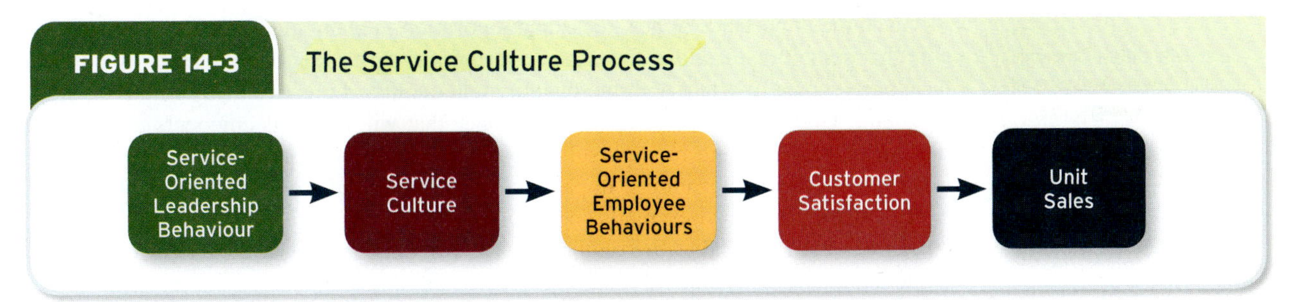

Source: Adapted from B. Schneider, M.G. Ehrhart, D.M. Mayer, J.L. Saltz, and K. Niles-Jolly, "Understanding Organization–Customer Links in Service Settings," *Academy of Management Journal* 48 (2005), pp. 1017–32.

Many organizations try to create a **customer service culture** focused on service quality. Organizations that have successfully created a service culture have been shown to change employee attitudes and behaviours toward customers.[24] These changes in attitudes and behaviours then manifest themselves in higher levels of customer satisfaction and sales.[25] Figure 14-3 illustrates the process of creating a service culture and the effects it has on company results. If you may recall from the opening profile in Chapter 1, we introduced WestJet as an organization that is widely recognized for having a strong customer service culture—a culture that fosters a common set of values among its members, such as being friendly, passionate, and showing appreciation for their "guests."[26]

customer service culture A specific culture type focused on service quality

Some companies require that their employees work in environments where the risk of accidents or injuries is very high. For these organizations, creating a **safety culture** is of paramount importance.[27] The payoff for these organizations is often an increased level of safety-related awareness and behaviours, and lower accidents.[28] Syncrude Canada Ltd. is one of several major organizations that process the vast oil sands deposit in northeastern Alberta. For this company, safety is critical given that each stage of the processing (i.e., mining, extraction, and upgrading/refining) is so dangerous—as one engineer put it, "We can launch things here." The question is how you instill core safety values in well over 4,500 employees, who are performing hundreds of different technical jobs. For Syncrude, the answer includes strong management commitment to protecting and promoting safety, careful selection and training of its new employees, extensive and mandatory safety rules and procedures, required safety-knowledge training and testing, and opportunities for members to participate in world-class emergency response teams. How has its safety culture affected the company? Well, Syncrude consistently reports among the lowest time-lost records in the industry![29] As with many changes, it is very important that what management says about safety is also how it acts. One study found that employees were highly cynical of a safety program when they perceived a mismatch between espoused and enacted safety values by management.[30]

safety culture A specific culture type focused on the safety of employees

There are a number of reasons why an organization might want to foster a **diversity culture**. For Royal Bank of Canada (RBC), having a culture that values diversity has helped the bank to fully leverage the talents of women, aging baby boomers, Aboriginals, visible minorities, and newcomers to the country. According to Zabeen Hirji, executive vice president and chief human resources officer at RBC, striving to foster an inclusive work environment that brings out the best in everyone contributes to the creation of innovative solutions for clients and communities—in short, "Differences in people are seen as valuable and potential assets."[31] Examples of activities that RBC uses to implement its diversity strategy include hiring people who have the technical, behavioural, and diversity requirements for the position being filled, investing heavily in training throughout the company, and by promoting internal mentoring relationships.[32]

diversity culture A specific culture type focused on fostering or taking advantage of a diverse group of employees

creativity culture A specific culture type focused on fostering a creative atmosphere

Given the importance of new ideas and innovation in many industries, it is understandable that some organizations focus on fostering a **creativity culture**. Creativity cultures have been shown to affect both the quantity and quality of creative ideas within an organization.[33] Google recently put policies in place that will allow its engineers to spend 20 percent of their working time pursuing projects that they feel passionate about to foster innovation at the organization.[34] In part to foster a culture of creativity, Pfizer Canada has banned all e-mails and voice mails on weekends and after 6 p.m. on weekdays to keep their employees fresh while they are on the job. The company feels that this 12-hour break has led to a higher-quality flow of ideas and provided a morale boost to go along with it.[35] To see whether you've spent time working in a creativity culture, see our **OB Assessments** feature at the end of the chapter.

CULTURE STRENGTH

culture strength The degree to which employees agree about how things should happen within the organization and behave accordingly

Although most organizations seem to strive for one, not all companies have a culture that creates a sense of definite norms and appropriate behaviours for their employees. If you've worked for a company and can't identify whether it has a strong culture, it probably doesn't. A high level of **culture strength** exists when employees definitively agree about the way things are supposed to happen within the organization (high consensus) and when their subsequent behaviours are consistent with those expectations (high intensity).[36] As shown in Figure 14-4, a strong culture serves to unite and direct employees. Weak cultures exist when employees disagree about the way things are supposed to be or what is expected of them, meaning that there is nothing to unite or direct their attitudes and actions.

FIGURE 14-4 Culture Strength and Subcultures

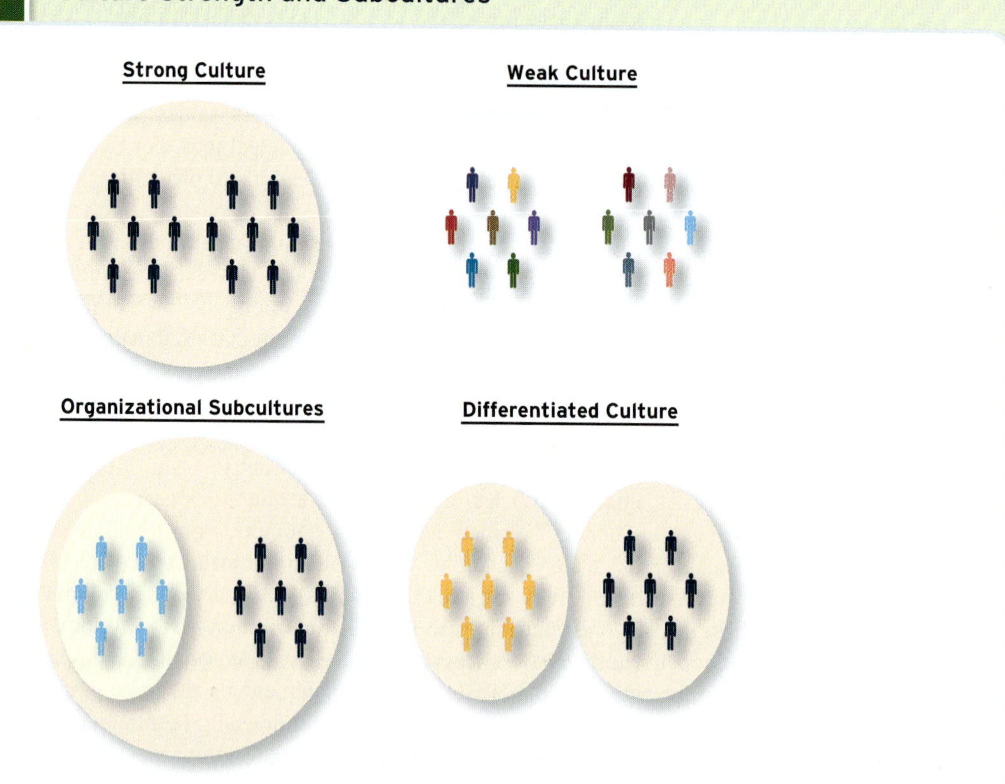

TABLE 14-1 Pros and Cons of a Strong Culture

ADVANTAGES OF A STRONG CULTURE	DISADVANTAGES OF A STRONG CULTURE
Differentiates the organization from others	Makes merging with another organization more difficult
Allows employees to identify themselves with the organization	Attracts and retains similar kinds of employees, thereby limiting diversity of thought
Facilitates desired behaviours among employees	Can be "too much of a good thing" if it creates extreme behaviours among employees
Creates stability within the organization	Makes adapting to the environment more difficult

Strong cultures take a long time to develop and are very difficult to change. Individuals working within strong cultures are typically very aware of it. However, this discussion brings us to an important point: "Strong" cultures are not always "good" cultures. Strong cultures guide employee attitudes and behaviours, but that doesn't always mean that they guide them toward the most successful organizational outcomes. As such, it is useful to recognize some of the positive and negative aspects of having a strong organizational culture. Table 14-1 lists some of the advantages and disadvantages.[37] You might have noticed that all of the advantages in the left-hand column of Table 14-1 allow the organization to become more efficient at whatever aspect of culture is strong within the organization. The right-hand column's disadvantages all lead toward an organization's inability to adapt.

14.3 What is a strong culture, and what makes a culture strong? Is a strong culture necessarily good?

In some cases, the culture of an organization is not really strong or weak. Instead, there might be **subcultures** that unite a smaller subset of the organization's employees. These subgroups may be created because there is a strong leader in one area of the company who engenders different norms and values or because different divisions in a company act independently and create their own cultures. As shown in Figure 14-4, subcultures exist when the overall organizational culture is supplemented by another culture governing a more specific set of employees. Subcultures are more likely to exist in large organizations than they are in small companies.[38] Most organizations don't mind having subcultures, to the degree that they do not interfere with the values of the overall culture. In fact, subcultures can be very useful for organizations if there are certain areas of the organization that have different demands and needs for their employees.[39] However, when their values don't match those of the larger organization, we call subcultures **countercultures.** Countercultures can sometimes serve a useful purpose by challenging the values of the overall organization or signifying the need for change.[40] In extreme cases, however, countercultures can split the organization's culture right down the middle, resulting in the differentiated culture in Figure 14-4.

subculture A culture created within a small subset of the organization's employees

counterculture When a subculture's values do not match those of the organization

MAINTAINING AN ORGANIZATIONAL CULTURE

Clearly an organization's culture can be described in many ways, from espoused values and basic underlying assumptions, to general dimensions such as solidarity or sociability, to more specific types such as service cultures or safety cultures. No matter how we describe an organization's culture, however, that culture will be put to the test when an organization's founders and original employees begin to recruit and hire new members. If those new

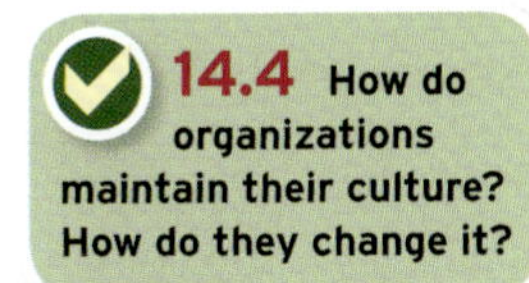

members do not fit the culture, then the culture may become weakened or differentiated. However, two processes can conspire to help keep cultures strong: attraction–selection–attrition and socialization.

ASA framework A theory (Attraction-Selection-Attrition) that states that employees will be drawn to organizations with cultures that match their personality, organizations will select employees that match, and employees will leave or be forced out when they are not a good fit

ATTRACTION-SELECTION-ATTRITION (ASA) The **ASA framework** holds that potential employees will be attracted to organizations whose cultures match their own personality, meaning that some potential job applicants won't apply due to a perceived lack of fit.[41] In addition, organizations will select candidates based on whether their personalities fit the culture, further weeding out potential "misfits." Finally, those people who still don't fit will either be unhappy or ineffective when working in the organization, which leads to attrition (i.e., voluntary or involuntary turnover).

Several companies can provide an example of ASA in action. FedEx has worked hard to create a culture of ethics. The executives at FedEx believe that a strong ethical culture will attract ethical employees who will strengthen moral behaviour at FedEx.[42] The Cheesecake Factory, a U.S.-based restaurant chain, believes that selection is where maintaining a culture begins. Management suggests that its heavily service-oriented culture calls for certain types of employees. They believe that teaching people how to perform regular restaurant duties is possible, but teaching people to have the right personality and attitudes is not. As a company, it consistently tries to identify the traits that allow employees to thrive in a Cheesecake Factory environment.[43] Of course, attraction and selection processes do not always align employees' personalities with organizational culture—one reason voluntary and involuntary turnover occurs in every organization.

SOCIALIZATION In addition to taking advantage of attraction–selection–attrition, organizations also maintain an organizational culture by shaping and moulding new employees. Starting a new job with a company is a stressful, complex, and challenging undertaking for both employees and organizations.[44] In reality, no outsider can fully grasp or understand the culture of an organization simply by looking at artifacts visible from outside the company. A complete understanding of organizational culture is a process that happens over time.

socialization The primary process by which employees learn the social knowledge that enables them to understand and adapt to the organization's culture

Socialization is the primary process by which employees learn the social knowledge that enables them to understand and adapt to the organization's culture. It is a process that begins before an employee starts work and doesn't end until an employee leaves the organization.[45] What is it that an employee needs to learn and adapt to in order to be socialized into his or her new role within an organization? Most of the important information can be grouped into six dimensions, highlighted in Figure 14-5.[46] Research shows that each of these six dimensions is an important area in the process of socialization. Each has unique contributions to job performance, organizational commitment, and person–organization fit.[47]

anticipatory stage A stage of socialization that begins as soon as a potential employee develops an image of what it would be like to work for a company

Socialization happens in three relatively distinct stages. The **anticipatory stage** happens prior to an employee spending even one second on the job. It starts the moment a potential employee hears the name of the organization. When you see the company name "Microsoft," what does it make you think about? What are the images that come to your mind? Anticipatory socialization begins as soon as a potential employee develops an image of what it must be like to work for a given company. The bulk of the information acquired during this stage occurs during the recruitment and selection processes that employees go through prior to joining an organization. Relevant information includes the way employees are treated during the recruitment process, the things that organizational insiders tell them about the organization, and any other information that employees acquire about what the organization is like and what working there entails.

encounter stage A stage of socialization beginning the day an employee starts work, during which the employee compares the information as an outsider to the information learned as an insider

The **encounter stage** begins the day an employee starts work. There are some things about an organization and its culture that can only be learned once a person becomes an organizational insider. During this stage, new employees compare the information they acquired as outsiders during the anticipatory stage with what the organization is really like now that they are insiders. To the degree that the information in the two stages is similar, employees

FIGURE 14-5 Dimensions Addressed in Most Socialization Efforts

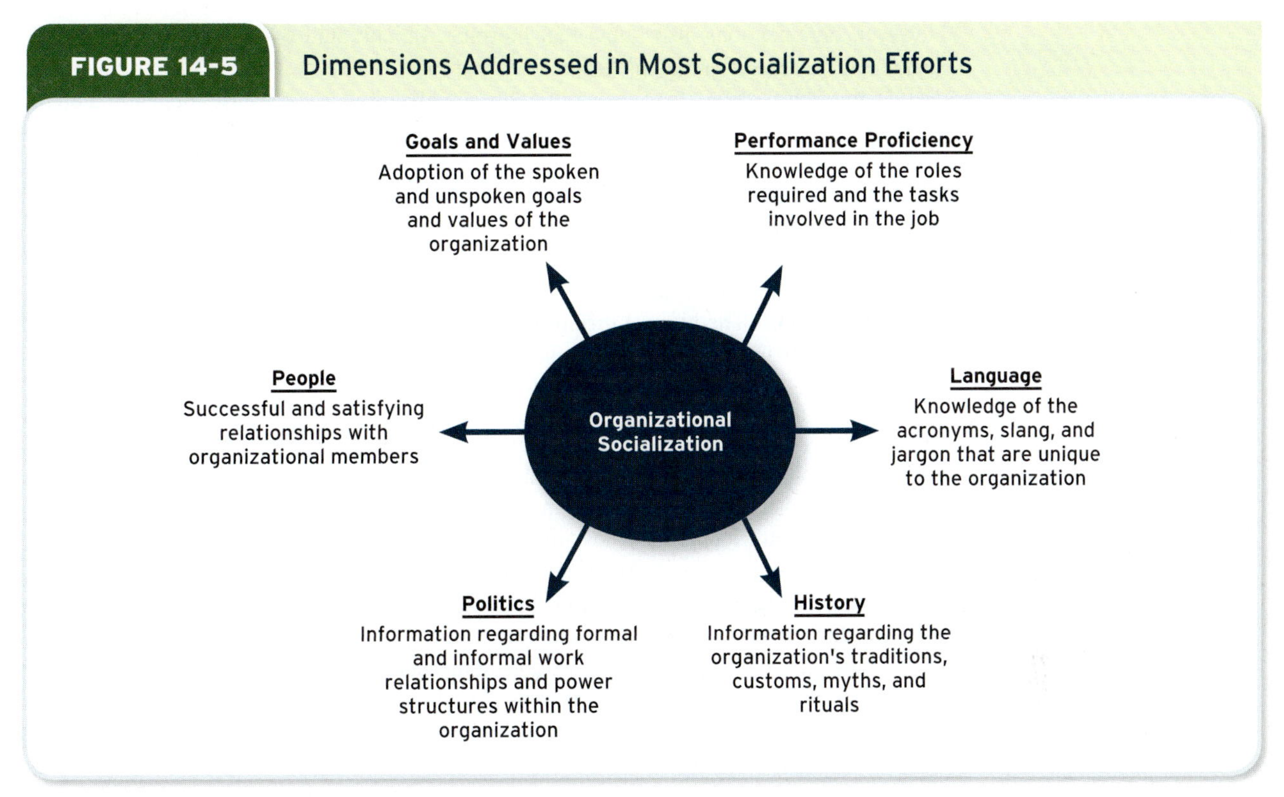

Source: G.T. Chao, A.M. O'Leary-Kelly, S. Wolf, H.J. Klein, and P.D. Gardner, "Organizational Socialization: Its Content and Consequences," *Journal of Applied Psychology* 79 (1994), pp. 730–43. Copyright © 1994 by the American Psychological Association. Adapted with permission. No further reproduction or distribution is permitted without written permission from the American Psychological Association.

will have a smoother time adjusting to the organization. Problems occur when the two sets of information don't quite match. This mismatch of information is called **reality shock**. Reality shock is best exemplified by hearing an employee say something to the effect of, "Working at this company is not nearly what I expected it to be." Surveys suggest that as many as one-third of new employees leave an organization within the first 90 days as a result of unmet expectations.[48] The goal of the organization's socialization efforts should be to minimize reality shock as much as possible. We'll describe some ways that organizations can do this effectively in our Application section near the end of this chapter.

reality shock A mismatch of information that occurs when an employee finds that aspects of working at a company are not what the employee expected it to be

The final stage of socialization is one of **understanding and adaptation**. During this stage, newcomers come to learn the content areas of socialization and internalize the norms and expected behaviours of the organization. The important part of this stage is change on the part of the employee. By looking back at the content areas of socialization in Figure 14-5, you can begin to picture what a perfectly socialized employee looks like. The employee has adopted the goals and values of the organization, understands what the organization has been through, and can converse with others in the organization using technical language and specific terms that only insiders would understand. In addition, the employee enjoys and gets along with other employees in the organization, knows who to go to in order to make things happen, and understands and can perform the key functions of his or her job. Talk about the perfect employee! Needless to say, that is quite a bit of information to gain—it is not a process that happens overnight. Some would say that this last stage of socialization never truly ends, as an organization's culture continues to change and evolve over time.[49]

understanding and adaptation The final stage of socialization, during which newcomers come to learn the content areas of socialization and internalize the norms and expected behaviours of the organization

However, organizations also know that the more quickly and effectively an employee is socialized, the sooner that employee becomes a productive worker within the organization.

It is important to note that the length of the socialization process varies depending on the characteristics of the employee, not just the company. For example, some employees might progress more rapidly through the stages because of the knowledge they possess, their ability to recognize cultural cues, or their adaptability to their environment. In fact, there is growing evidence that proactivity on the part of employee being socialized has a significant effect on socialization outcomes.[50] Some organizations might help their employees socialize more quickly because they have stronger cultures or cultures that are more easily understandable. The biggest difference though is that some organizations simply work harder at socializing their employees than others.

CHANGING AN ORGANIZATIONAL CULTURE

Given all the effort it takes to create and maintain a culture, changing a culture once one has been established is perhaps even more difficult. In fact, estimates put the rate of successful major culture change at less than 20 percent.[51] Mark Fields, head of Ford Motor Company's North and South American auto operations, knows how difficult it can be to change the culture at an organization. Prior CEOs at Ford have tried, unsuccessfully, to change a culture that current employees call "toxic," "cautious," "hierarchical," and "cliquish." To instigate a change, Fields took drastic measures, including purposefully creating a sense of stress and crisis among employees. Ford is calling its new attempt at major culture change the "Way Forward." In the "Way Forward" war room (where Fields and colleagues map out the drastic changes the company needs to make), big sheets of white paper hang on the wall reading, "Culture eats strategy for breakfast," and "Culture is unspoken, but powerful. It develops over time—difficult to change." Fields has gone to many extremes to create a climate for change among those responsible for helping him with the plans to overhaul Ford's culture. He has banned PowerPoint presentations, uses phrases such as "change or die" in meetings, and makes employees wear blue wristbands with "Red, White and Bold" inscribed on them, signifying a new Ford.[52] In practice, there are two primary ways to change a culture: changes in leadership and mergers or acquisitions.

CHANGES IN LEADERSHIP There is perhaps no bigger driver of culture than the leaders and top executives of organizations. Just as the founders and originators of organizations set the tone and develop the culture of a new company, subsequent CEOs and presidents leave their mark on the culture. Many times, leaders are expected simply to sustain the culture that has already been created.[53] At other times, leaders have to be the driving force for change as the environment around the organization shifts. This expectation is one of the biggest reasons that organizations change their top leadership. For example, Nortel Networks recently hired two former Cisco executives into the roles of chief operating officer and chief technology officer. It was Nortel's hope that these executives would help bring some of Cisco's culture of aggressiveness to Nortel and thus allow it to compete more effectively in the high-technology industry environment.[54]

MERGERS AND ACQUISITIONS Merging two companies with two distinct cultures is a surefire way to change the culture in an organization. The problem is that there is just no way to know what the culture will look like after the merger takes place. What the new culture will resemble is a function of both the strength of the two cultures involved in the merger and how similar they are to each other.[55] Ideally, a new culture would be created out of a compromise in which the best of both companies is represented by the new culture. Mergers rarely result in the strong culture that managers hope will appear when they make the decision to merge. In fact, most merged companies operate under a differentiated culture for an extended period of time. Some of them never really adopt a new identity, and when they do,

OB INTERNATIONALLY

As mentioned in the chapter, there is perhaps no more perilous journey for a company to take than merging with or acquiring another large firm. These problems are exacerbated when the two companies are from different countries. As few as 30 percent of international mergers and acquisitions create shareholder value.[56] Nevertheless, 2006 set a record pace for global mergers and acquisitions.[57] Why is this the case? Hopefully, we've illustrated the inherent difficulties of simply trying to merge two different cultures when the organizations are in the same country. These cultural differences can be magnified when international culture plays a role as well. Chances are good that your experiences in university have shown you that different countries have different cultures, just like organizations. People that come from different countries tend to view the world differently and have different sets of values as well. For instance, DaimlerChrysler bought a controlling stake in Mitsubishi Motors, thinking that a strong alliance between the two would result in high levels of value for both companies. Unfortunately, this merger broke up for reasons that have been attributed to international culture differences between the two firms (Japan vs. U.S. and Germany).[58] Japanese managers had a tendency to avoid "unpleasant truths" and stay away from major change efforts—a tendency that DaimlerChrysler never confronted.

There are many stories of failed international mergers, and one of the greatest reasons for them is that corporations do not recognize the impact that national culture differences (in addition to organizational culture differences) have on their ability to be successful. One such merger that doesn't intend to fall victim to this issue is the creation of a joint venture between telecommunication giants Nokia (Finland) and Siemens (Germany). This merger between two very different firms is projected to earn annual sales of $20 billion. The CEOs of the two companies (Siemens's Klaus Kleinfeld and Nokia's Olli-Pekka Kallasvuo) are determined not to let differences in national or organizational cultures cause the merger fatal problems. Toward this end, cultural integration has been in the forefront of their minds. Although much of the main business will be located in Germany, headquarters for the new company will be in Helsinki. Both CEOs are determined for each company to learn from the other.[59]

many of them are seen as failures by the outside world. This perception is especially true in global mergers, in which each of the companies not only has a different organizational culture but is from a different country as well. See our **OB Internationally** box for more details.

Merging two different cultures has major effects on the attitudes and behaviours of organizational employees. Companies merge for many different strategic reasons, and though many managers and executives may realize its importance, whether the cultures will match is rarely the deciding criterion.[60] Slightly less troublesome but still a major hurdle to overcome are acquisitions. In most instances, the company doing the acquiring has a dominant culture to which the other is expected to adapt. A recent example is the acquisition of Mail Boxes Etc. by UPS. Strategically, the acquisition had many advantages and was supposed to allow UPS to compete better with FedEx. However, the culture clash between the efficiency and rigidness of UPS and the entrepreneurial spirit of Mail Boxes Etc. franchisees has caused UPS some major headaches.[61] We've noted how difficult it is just to get one person to adapt to an established culture through the socialization process. Can you imagine how difficult it is to change an entire organization at the same time? See our **OB on Screen** feature for one potential answer.

OB ON SCREEN

IN GOOD COMPANY

I'm not sure I understand what you are talking about. . . . What I mean is, what do computers have to do with sports? Are you literally saying that there should be a section in the magazine about computers? Who's going to want to read that?

By interjecting those words, Dan Forman (Dennis Quaid) interrupts Globecom CEO Teddy K (Malcolm McDowell) in the middle of a division-wide speech during *In Good Company* (Dir. Paul Wietz, Universal, 2005). Globecom purchased *Sports America* magazine in a hostile takeover, hoping that the company would be a cash cow. However, problems arise when the two cultures of the companies don't mesh. Dan's words at the meeting speak volumes about what each *Sports America* employee is thinking but doesn't say out of fear for their jobs: "We simply don't fit the Globecom culture!"

Teddy K's Globecom is a no-holds-barred, dog-eat-dog, profit-means-everything type of firm whose employees use language like "synergy" to describe what leads to success. In fact, it very much resembles a mercenary culture. One telling example of the culture emerges when Globecom appoints an inexperienced, 26-year-old Carter Duryea (Topher Grace) to take 51-year-old Dan Forman's place because the CEO remembered that Carter had done "something with cellphones." Carter soon finds that *Sports America* is a more traditional, family-oriented company that values employees and relationships with customers. His fast-talking, smooth-moving ways don't exactly go over well with his new subordinates. And it really doesn't help when he starts dating Dan's daughter (Scarlett Johansson).

The lack of fit between Globecom and *Sports America* isn't unlike many acquisitions that take place in corporate America. Two very different cultures that value different things are thrown together for the sake of "potential." Carter is essentially expected to change the *Sports America* culture to fit with Globecom. However, he actually finds that he likes the *Sports America* culture much better, as it seems to have a better "fit" with his own personality. In the end, the culture clash between the two firms is too much, and Globecom sells *Sports America.* You'll have to rent the movie to find out what happens to Dan and Carter.

SO WHY DO SOME ORGANIZATIONS HAVE DIFFERENT CULTURES THAN OTHERS?

As shown in Figure 14-6, attraction–selection–attrition (ASA) processes, socialization, changes in leadership, and mergers and acquisitions shape the three components of organizational culture: basic underlying assumptions, espoused values, and observable artifacts. Specific combinations of those culture components then give rise to both general and specific culture types. For example, cultures can be categorized on the basis of solidarity and sociability into fragmented, mercenary, networked, and communal types. Cultures can also be categorized into more specific types such as customer service, safety, diversity, and creativity. Finally, those general and specific types can be further classified according to the strength of the culture. Taken together, these processes explain "what it's like" within the hallways of a given organization.

HOW IMPORTANT IS ORGANIZATIONAL CULTURE?

Normally, this section is where we summarize the importance of organizational culture by describing how it affects job performance and organizational commitment—the two outcomes in our integrative model of OB. However (similar to organizational structure in Chapter 13), it's difficult to summarize the importance of culture in this way because there are so many different types and dimensions of the concept. High solidarity cultures, high sociability cultures, diversity cultures, creativity cultures, and so forth all have different effects on performance and commitment—effects that likely vary across different types of organizations and industries.

14.5 What is person-organization fit? How does fitting with an organization's culture affect job performance and organizational commitment?

Regardless of the type of culture we're talking about, however, one concept remains important for any employee in any business: fit. Think for a moment about working for an organization whose culture doesn't match your own values. Maybe you work for an organization that produces a product that you don't believe in or that might be harmful to others, such as Rothmans, Benson and Hedges, or Labatt Breweries of Canada. Maybe your employer is an organization that expects you to perform questionable behaviours from an ethical standpoint or produces a product that is of poor quality. **Person–organization fit** is the degree to which a person's personality and values match the culture of an organization. Employees judge fit by thinking about the values they prioritize the most, and then judging whether the organization shares those values. Table 14-2 provides a set of values that many people have used to judge fit. Which of these values would you say are the most important to you?

person-organization fit The degree to which a person's values and personality match the culture of the organization

A recent meta-analysis illustrated the importance of person–organization fit to employees.[62] When employees feel that their values and personality match those of the organization, they experience higher levels of *job satisfaction* and feel less *stress* about their day-to-day tasks. They also feel higher levels of *trust* toward their managers. Taken together, those results illustrate why person–organization fit is so highly correlated with organizational commitment, one of the two outcomes in our integrative model of OB (see Figure 14-7). When employees feel they fit with their organization's culture, they are much more likely to develop an emotional attachment to the company. The effects of fit on job performance are weaker, however. In general, person–organization fit is more related to citizenship behaviours than task performance. Employees who sense a good fit are therefore more likely to help their colleagues and "go the extra mile" to benefit the company.

FIGURE 14-6 Why Do Some Organizations Have Different Cultures Than Others?

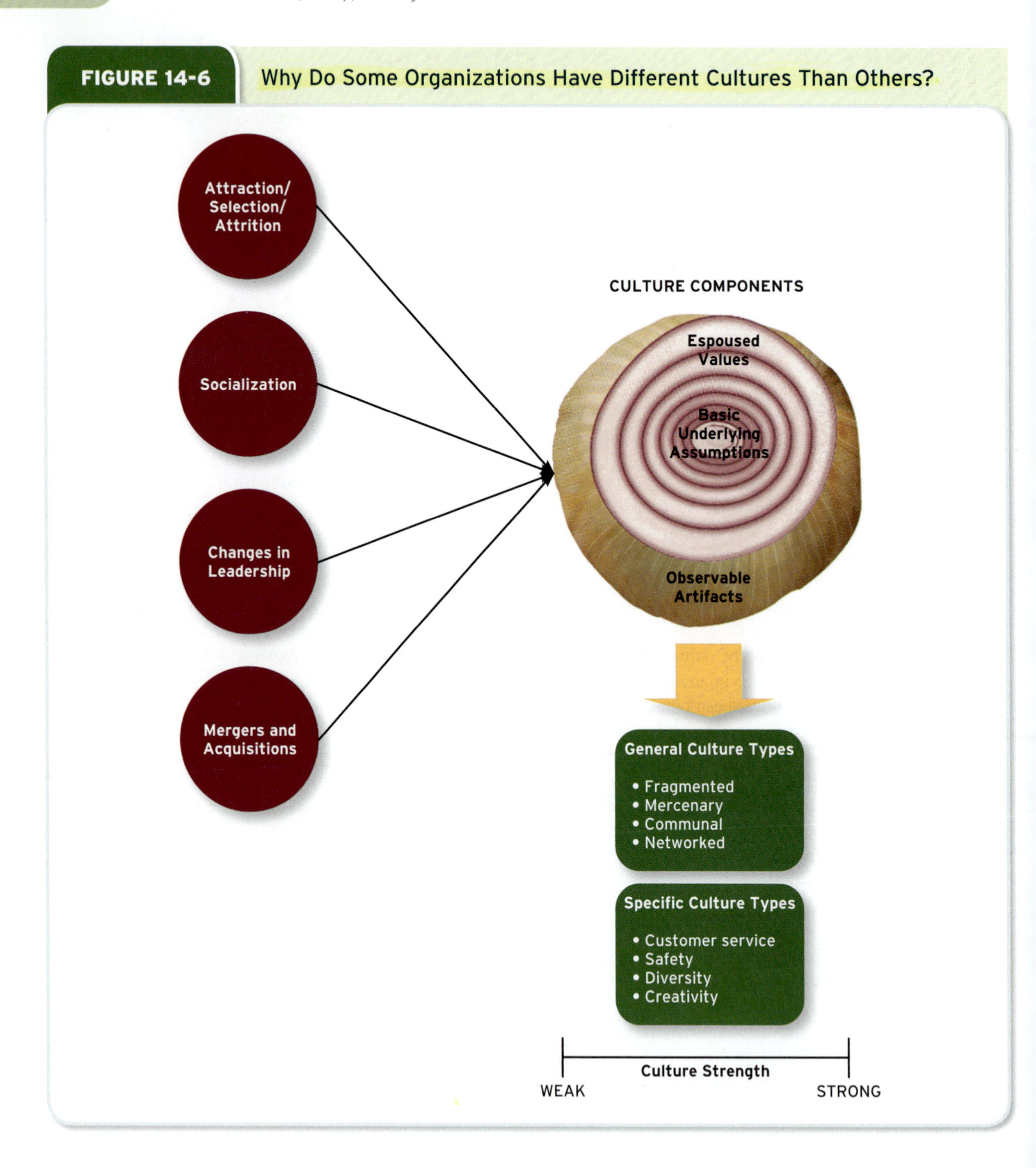

TABLE 14-2 Values Used to Judge Fit with an Organizational Culture

PERSONAL AND CULTURAL VALUES	
Flexibility	Adaptability
Stability	Predictability
Being innovative	Take advantage of opportunities
A willingness to experiment	Risk taking
Being careful	Autonomy
Being rule oriented	Being analytical
Paying attention to detail	Being precise
Being team oriented	Sharing information freely
Emphasizing a single culture	Being people oriented
Fairness	Respect for the individual's rights
Tolerance	Informality
Being easygoing	Being calm
Being supportive	Being aggressive
Decisiveness	Action orientation
Taking initiative	Being reflective
Achievement orientation	Being demanding
Taking individual responsibility	High expectations for performance
Opportunities for growth	High pay for good performance
Security of employment	Offers praise for good performance
Low level of conflict	Confronting conflict directly
Developing friends at work	Fitting in
Working in collaboration with others	Enthusiasm for the job
Working long hours	Not being constrained by rules
Having an emphasis on quality	Being distinctive from others
Having a good reputation	Being socially responsible
Being results oriented	Having a clear guiding philosophy
Being competitive	Being highly organized

Source: C.A. O'Reilly, J.A. Chatman, and D.F. Caldwell, "People and Organizational Culture: A Profile Comparison Approach to Assessing Person–Organization Fit," *Academy of Management Journal* 34 (1991), pp. 487–516.

FIGURE 14-7 Effects of Person-Organization Fit on Performance and Commitment

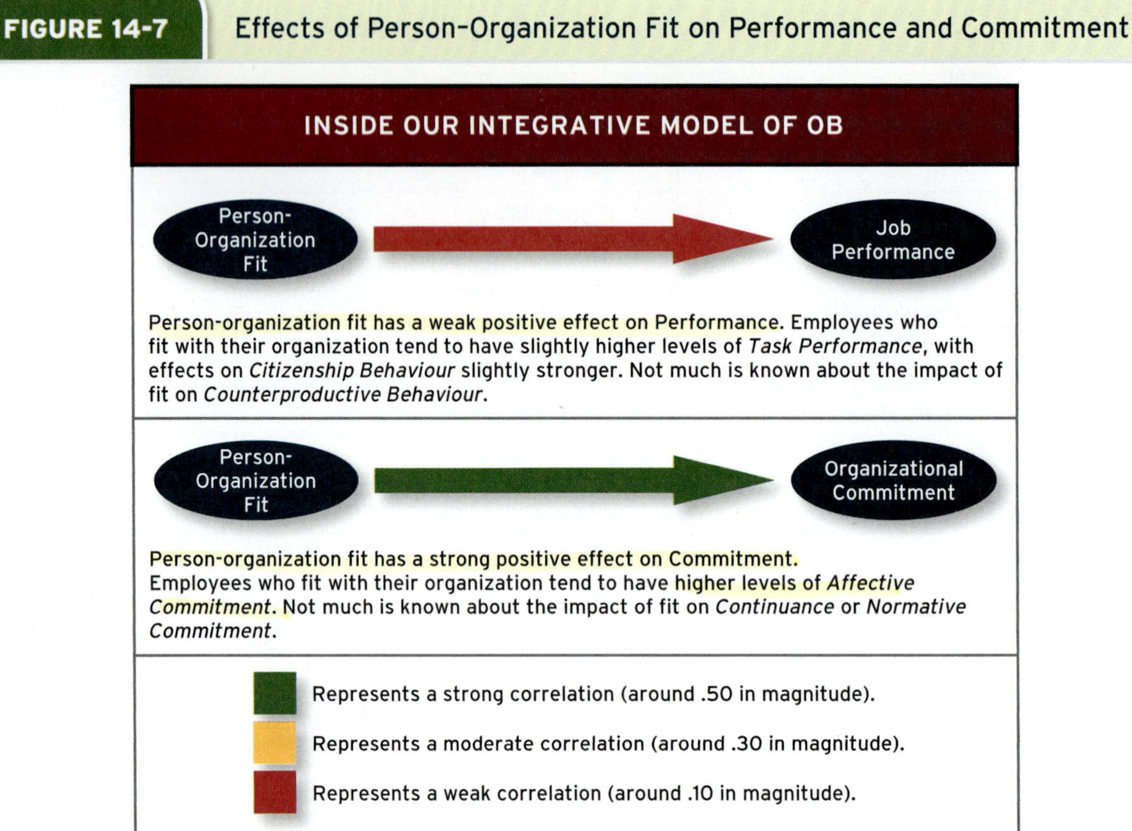

Sources: A.L. Kristof-Brown, R.D. Zimmerman, and E.C. Johnson, "Consequences of Individuals' Fit at Work: A Meta-Analysis of Person–Job, Person–Organization, Person–Group, and Person–Supervisor Fit," *Personnel Psychology* 58 (2005), pp. 281–342. Reprinted with permission of Blackwell Publishing.

APPLICATION: MANAGING SOCIALIZATION

Most organizations recognize the importance of having employees adapt to the culture of their organization quickly. Luckily, there are a number of actions that organizations can take to help their employees adapt from the first day they walk in the door. Table 14-3 on page 386 highlights some of the different tactics that organizations can use when socializing their employees. Note that companies can take two very different approaches to the socialization process. The left-hand column represents a view of socialization in which the goal of the process is to have newcomers adapt to the organization's culture. This view assumes that the organization has a strong culture and definite norms and values that it wants employees to adopt, which is not always the case. Some organizations don't have a strong culture that they want employees to adapt to, or they might be trying to change their culture and want new employees to come in and "shake things up." The socialization tactics listed in the right-hand column of Table 14-3 might be more appropriate in such circumstances. In addition to the socialization tactics listed in the table, there are three other major ways in which organizations routinely and effectively help speed up the socialization process of newcomers: realistic job previews, orientation programs, and mentoring.

OB RESEARCH IN CANADA

Jia Lin Xie received her PhD in 1992 from Concordia University and is currently a professor in the Rotman School of Management at the University of Toronto. Dr. Xie's expertise within the field of organizational behaviour includes job design, job stress, cross-cultural organizational behaviour, and knowledge management. Her cross-cultural research focuses on the comparisons between Chinese and North Americans on job-related attitudes and behaviour. A recent paper (see below) illustrates some of this work. It is common to view the Chinese as holding collective and interdependent cultural values (Chapter 9). By tracking a group of 486 Chinese employees, Dr. Xie found evidence of variation in these traditional values, and that these variations were linked to stress coping and health. In other work, she was able to show how perceptions of organizational culture influence individual behaviours, such as absenteeism. It seems that employees in both China and Canada base their decisions to attend or be absent from work, in part, on what they believe to be a legitimate and acceptable (expected) level of absence within the group.

Jia Lin Xie has held a faculty position at University of Toronto since 1992, and has been invited to give lectures at various executive programs in China, Hong Kong, and Europe. In addition to her research and teaching, Dr. Xie has devoted much of her time and effort promoting an internationalization of management knowledge. Currently she is serving as senior vice president for the International Association for Chinese Management Research, an Academy of Management–affiliated academic association with over 4,600 members from more than 25 countries and regions.

Some of Dr. Xie's favourite publications include:

"Theories of Job Stress and the Role of Traditional Values: A Longitudinal Study in China," by J.L. Xie, J. Schaubroeck, and S. Lam, published in *Journal of Applied Psychology* (2008, volume 93, pp. 831–48).

"Collective Efficacy Versus Self-Efficacy in Coping Responses to Stressors and Control: A Cross-Cultural Study," by J. Schaubroeck, S. Lam, and J.L. Xie, published in *Journal of Applied Psychology* (2000, volume 85, pp. 512–25).

"Interactive Effects of Absence Culture Salience and Group Cohesiveness: A Multi-level and Cross-level Analysis of Work Absenteeism in the Chinese Context," by J.L. Xie and G. Johns, published in *Journal of Occupational and Organizational Psychology* (2000, volume 73, pp. 31–52).

"Perception of Absence from Work: People's Republic of China Versus Canada," by G. Johns and J.L. Xie, published in *Journal of Applied Psychology* (1998, volume 83, pp. 515–30).

"Karasek's Model in the People's Republic of China: Effects of Job Demands, Control, and Individual Differences," by J.L. Xie, published in *Academy of Management Journal* (1996, volume 39, pp. 1594–1618).

TABLE 14-3 Tactics Organizations Use to Socialize New Employees

TACTICS DESIGNED TO ENCOURAGE ADAPTATION TO THE ORGANIZATION'S CULTURE	TACTICS DESIGNED TO DISCOURAGE ADAPTATION TO THE ORGANIZATION'S CULTURE
Orient new employees along with a group of other new employees.	Orient new employees by themselves.
Put newcomers through orientation apart from current organizational members.	Allow newcomers to interact with current employees while they are being oriented.
Provide hurdles that are required to be met prior to organizational membership.	Allow organizational membership regardless of whether any specific requirements have been met.
Provide role models for newcomers.	Use no examples of what an employee is supposed to be like.
Constantly remind newcomers that they are now part of a group and that this new group helps define who they are.	Constantly affirm to newcomers that they are to be themselves and that they were chosen for the organization based on who they are.

Source: Adapted from G.R. Jones, "Socialization Tactics, Self-Efficacy, and Newcomers' Adjustments to Organizations," *Academy of Management Journal* 29 (1986), pp. 262–79; J. Van Maanen and E.H. Schein, "Toward a Theory of Organizational Socialization," *Research in Organizational Behavior* 1 (1979), pp. 209–64.

realistic job previews
The process of ensuring that a potential employee understands both the positive and negative aspects of the potential job

REALISTIC JOB PREVIEWS One of the most inexpensive and effective ways of reducing early turnover among new employees is the use of **realistic job previews**.[63] Realistic job previews (RJPs) occur during the anticipatory stage of socialization during the recruitment process. These RJPs involve making sure a potential employee has an accurate picture of what working for an organization is going to be like by providing both the positive *and* the negative aspects of the job.[64] Kal Tire, a leading Canadian automotive retail outlet, allows job candidates to spend an entire day inside the company becoming familiar with the organization and the job they are applying for. By allowing applicants to see what the organization's idea of customer service is and the job demands of road tire repairs, Kal Tire is effectively reducing the likelihood of significant reality shock and shortening the encounter stage that generally accompanies initial employment.[65]

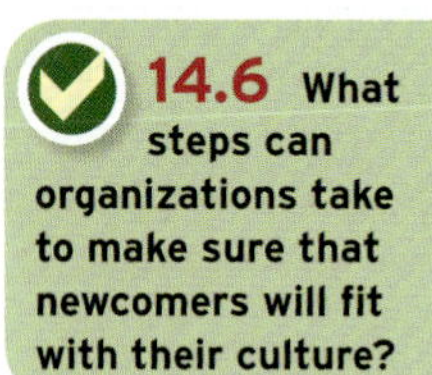
14.6 What steps can organizations take to make sure that newcomers will fit with their culture?

ORIENTATION PROGRAMS One effective way to start the socialization process is by having new employees attend some form of **newcomer orientation** session. Apparently most organizations agree, given that 64 percent to 93 percent of all organizations use some form of orientation training process.[66] Not all orientation programs are alike however, and different types of orientation training can be more effective than others.[67] Orientation programs have been shown to be effective transmitters of socialization content, such that those employees who complete orientation have higher levels of satisfaction, commitment, and performance than those who don't.[68] General Motors has a unique orientation program set up for its new hires, called JumpStart. The program is designed to indoctrinate new employees into the GM culture, which GM believes will allow these employees to become productive much more quickly. Each new employee is able to join up to five different committees that represent a different aspect of GM's culture, in which they learn about key values, network with employees from different areas of the country, and interact with business leaders.[69]

newcomer orientation
The process of ensuring that a potential employee understands both the positive and negative aspects of the potential job

MENTORING One of the most popular pieces of advice given to university students as they begin their careers is that they need to find a mentor or coach within their organization.[70]

Mentoring is a process by which a junior-level employee (protegé) develops a deep and long-lasting relationship with a more senior-level employee (mentor) within the organization. The mentor can provide social knowledge, resources, and psychological support to the protegé both at the beginning of employment and as the protegé continues his or her career with the company. Mentoring has always existed in companies on an informal basis. However, as organizations continue to learn about the strong benefits of these relationships, they are more frequently instituting mentoring programs that formally match newcomers with mentors.[71] Formal programs allow the company to provide consistent information, train mentors, and ensure that all newcomers have the opportunity to develop one of these fruitful relationships. If you may recall from our discussion in Chapter 1, one of the ways that RBC promotes its diversity culture is through a formal mentoring program that pairs protegés with seasoned mentors. Mentoring does not just occur in business organizations, however. See our **OB for Students** feature for a discussion of mentoring for university students.

mentoring The process by which a junior-level employee develops a deep and long-lasting relationship with a more senior-level employee within the organization

OB FOR STUDENTS

What does culture mean for you as a student? Think back on all the things you had to learn and all the ambiguity you faced during your first semester in university. Just as organizational newcomers experience reality shock when they enter an organization, so do first-year students when they initially enter the university culture. Just as organizations have a culture that affects employees, universities have a culture that affects students. One recent study at a university investigated whether it was worthwhile to help socialize students in much the same way that organizations socialize new employees. The university set up a mentoring program to help facilitate the transition toward being a successful student.

As shown in the diagram below, whether a first-year student was provided a mentor and the quality of the relationship he or she had with that mentor positively affected both satisfaction with and commitment to the university. In turn, levels of satisfaction with and commitment to the university had positive effects on the student's intention to graduate.

Of course, many of you are now wondering why your university didn't do this for you! Many of you probably had some type of informal mentor to rely on to some degree. Some of you, however, might have lacked such a resource. That disadvantage explains why formal mentoring programs can be important: Formal programs help ensure equal access for everyone. If your university doesn't have a formal mentoring program or orientation session, you might consider being an informal mentor to an incoming first-year student.

Source: Adapted from R.J. Sanchez, T.N. Bauer, and M.E. Paronto, "Peer-Mentoring Freshmen: Implications for Satisfaction, Commitment, and Retention to Graduation," *Academy of Management Learning and Education* 5 (2006), pp. 25–37.

TAKEAWAYS

14.1 Organizational culture is the shared social knowledge within an organization regarding the rules, norms, and values that shape the attitudes and behaviours of its employees. There are three components of organizational culture: observable artifacts, espoused values, and basic underlying assumptions. Observable artifacts include symbols, physical structures, language, stories, rituals, and ceremonies.

14.2 An organization's culture can be described on dimensions such as solidarity and sociability to create four general culture types: networked, communal, fragmented, and mercenary. Organizations often strive to create a more specific cultural emphasis, as in customer service cultures, safety cultures, diversity cultures, and creativity cultures.

14.3 Strong cultures have the ability to influence employee behaviours and attitudes. Strong cultures exist when employees agree on the way things are supposed to happen and their behaviours are consistent with those expectations. Strong cultures are not necessarily good or bad. Generally, a culture's effectiveness depends on how well it matches the company's outside environment. To this degree, adaptive cultures can be very useful.

14.4 Organizations maintain their cultures through attraction–selection–attrition (ASA) processes and socialization practices. Organizations change their cultures by changing their leadership or through mergers and acquisitions.

14.5 Person–organization fit is the degree to which a person's values and personality match the culture of the organization. Person–organization fit has a weak positive effect on job performance and a strong positive effect on organizational commitment.

14.6 There are a number of practices organizations can utilize to improve the socialization of new employees, including realistic job previews, orientation programs, and mentoring.

KEY TERMS

- anticipatory stage *p. 376*
- ASA framework *p. 376*
- basic underlying assumptions *p. 371*
- ceremonies *p. 371*
- communal culture *p. 372*
- counterculture *p. 375*
- creativity culture *p. 374*
- culture strength *p. 374*
- customer service culture *p. 373*
- diversity culture *p. 373*
- encounter stage *p. 376*
- espoused values *p. 371*
- fragmented culture *p. 372*
- language *p. 370*
- mentoring *p. 387*
- mercenary culture *p. 372*
- networked culture *p. 372*
- newcomer orientation *p. 386*
- observable artifacts *p. 369*
- organizational culture *p. 368*
- person–organization fit *p. 381*
- physical structures *p. 370*
- realistic job previews *p. 386*
- reality shock *p. 377*
- rituals *p. 371*
- safety culture *p. 373*
- socialization *p. 376*
- stories *p. 371*
- subculture *p. 375*
- symbols *p. 370*
- understanding and adaptation *p. 377*

DISCUSSION QUESTIONS

14.1 Have you or a family member worked for an organization that you would consider to have a strong culture? If so, what made the culture strong? Did you or they enjoy working there? What do you think led to that conclusion?

14.2 Is it possible for an employee to have personal values that are inconsistent with the values of the organization? If so, how is this inconsistency likely to affect the employee's behaviour and attitudes while at work?

14.3 If you had to describe the culture of your university, what would it be like? What observable artifacts are present to be perceived by students? Are there any underlying assumptions that guide your behaviour at your university?

14.4 How can two companies with very different cultures that operate in the same industry both be successful? Shouldn't one company's culture automatically be a better fit for the environment?

14.5 If an organization wanted to foster a diversity culture, what steps might management take to ensure that employees will support the new culture? What observable artifacts might a company change to instill this culture?

14.6 When you think of the registrar's office at your school, what kinds of words come to mind? Where do these impressions come from? Do you think your impressions are accurate? What has the potential to make them inaccurate?

14.7 Think about the last job you started. What are some unique things that companies might do to reduce the amount of reality shock that new employees encounter? Are these methods likely to be expensive?

CASE • GENERAL ELECTRIC AND ENRON

General Electric and Enron can be compared on the basis of their seemingly similar company practices throughout the 1990s and into the early 2000s. From the outside looking in, both companies attracted the best and the brightest by offering premium wages and other financial bonuses. Each company had a similar policy to retain only their best performing employees; Enron annually retained its top 80 percent of employees, whereas General Electric retained its top 90 percent. Both companies also developed cultures driven by success. But Enron's culture actually caused its downward spiral that led to its ultimate demise.

Was it Enron's accounting practices, initiated at the top of the company, that caused its organizational failure? Although accounting was a major piece of the equation, another factor really enabled one of the largest financial scandals in history. The so-called "entrepreneurial culture" emphasized the importance of financial performance and aggressive employee initiatives. The ends justified the means at Enron, which may explain why a distinct lack of controls monitored the performance of employees.

General Electric's fixation on bottom-line performance and risk taking is complemented by its core values, which include a high sense of ethical behaviour. The culture that Jack Welch helped establish at GE remains relatively the same, even since the new

CEO, Jeffrey R. Immelt, took control of the company. Immelt has realized that GE's culture, focused on teamwork, innovation, ethics, and financial performance, is a culture that can continue to give the company a competitive advantage in the future.

14.1 Is corporate culture the underlying cause of corporate scandals? Explain.

14.2 Is General Electric's absolute employee evaluation process (firing the bottom 10 percent) a good strategic decision? Explain.

Sources: "At Enron, 'the Environment Was Ripe for Abuse,'" *BusinessWeek,* February 25, 2002; "The Immelt Revolution," *BusinessWeek,* March 28, 2005; "What Really Went Wrong with Enron? A Culture of Evil?" 2002, www.scu.edu/ethics/publications/ethicalperspectives/enronpanel.html (June 26, 2007).

EXERCISE • UNIVERSITY CULTURE

The purpose of this exercise is to explore how organizational culture is transmitted through observable artifacts. This exercise uses groups of six participants, so your instructor will either assign you to a group of six or ask you to create your own group of six. The exercise has the following steps:

1. Consider the observable artifacts that transmit the organizational culture of your university.

Symbols	Think about the logo and images associated with your university. What message do they convey about the university's culture?
Physical structures	Think about the most visible physical structures on campus. What do those structures say about your university's culture?
Language	Think about the jargon, slang, slogans, and sayings associated with your university. What insights do they offer into the university's culture?
Stories	What anecdotes, accounts, legends, and myths are associated with your university? What messages do they convey about your university's culture?
Rituals	What are the daily or weekly routines that occur at your university, and what do they say about the culture?
Ceremonies	What are the formal events and celebrations that occur at your university, and what cultural signals do they convey?

2. Consider the sorts of values listed in Table 14-2 on page 383. If you consider the symbols, physical structures, language, stories, rituals, and ceremonies identified in Step 1, what core values seem to summarize your university's culture? Using a transparency, laptop, or chalkboard, list the one value that seems to be most central to your university's culture. Then list the three cultural artifacts that are most responsible for transmitting that core value. Present your results to the class.
3. Discuss (in groups or as a class) two main questions. First, do you like how your university's culture is viewed, as represented in the group presentations? Why or why not? Second, if you wanted to change the university's culture to represent other sorts of values, what process would you use to change the culture?

OB ASSESSMENTS • CREATIVITY CULTURE

Have you experienced a creativity culture? This assessment is designed to measure two facets of that type of culture. Think of your current job, or the last job that you held (even if it was a part-time or summer job). If you haven't worked, think of a current or former student group that developed strong norms for how tasks should be done. Answer each question using the response scale provided. Then subtract your answers to the bold-faced questions from 6, with the difference being your new answer for that question. For example, if your original answer for question 7 was "4," your new answer is "2" (6 – 4). Then sum up for your scores for the two facets.

1 STRONGLY DISAGREE	2 DISAGREE	3 UNCERTAIN	4 AGREE	5 STRONGLY AGREE

1. New ideas are readily accepted here. ________
2. This company is quick to respond when changes need to be made. ________
3. Management here is quick to spot the need to do things differently. ________
4. This organization is very flexible; it can quickly change procedures to meet new conditions and solve problems as they arise. ________
5. People in this organization are always searching for new ways of looking at problems. ________
6. It is considered extremely important here to follow the rules. ________
7. **People can ignore formal procedures and rules if it helps to get the job done.** ________
8. Everything has to be done by the book. ________
9. **It is not necessary to follow procedures to the letter around here.** ________
10. **Nobody gets too upset if people break the rules around here.** ________

SCORING

Innovation: Sum up items 1–5. ________

Formalization: Sum up items 6–10. ________

INTERPRETATION

If your score is 22 or above for either facet, your organization or workgroup is high on that particular dimension. Creative cultures tend to be high on innovation and low on formalization. So if your score was 22 or above for innovation and 21 or below for formalization, then chances are you've experienced a strong creativity culture.

Source: M.G. Patterson, M.A. West, V.J. Shackleton, J.F. Dawson, R. Lawthom, S. Maitlis, D.L. Robinson, and A.M. Wallace, "Validating the Organizational Climate Measure: Links to Managerial Practices, Productivity and Innovation," *Journal of Organizational Behavior* 26 (2005), pp. 379–408. Copyright © 2005 John Wiley & Sons Limited. Reproduced with permission.

Glossary

A

ability Relatively stable capabilities of people for performing a particular range of related activities. (218)

ability to focus The degree to which employees can devote their attention to work. (179)

absenteeism A form of physical withdrawal in which employees do not show up for an entire day of work. (62)

abuse Employee assault or endangerment from which physical and psychological injuries may occur. (38)

accommodating A conflict resolution style by which one party gives in to the other and acts in a completely unselfish way. (298)

accomplishment striving A strong desire to accomplish task-related goals as a means of expressing one's personality. (219)

action processes Teamwork processes, such as helping and coordination, that aid in the accomplishment of teamwork as the work is actually taking place. (268)

action team A team of limited duration that performs complex tasks in contexts that tend to be highly visible and challenging. (253)

active management-by-exception When the leader arranges to monitor mistakes and errors actively and takes corrective action when required. (326)

adaptive task performance Thoughtful responses by an employee to unique or unusual task demands. (29)

additive tasks Tasks for which the contributions from every member add up to determine team performance. (259)

affect-based trust Trust that depends on feelings toward the authority that go beyond any rational assessment of trustworthiness. (162)

affective commitment An employee's desire to remain a member of an organization due to a feeling of emotional attachment. (50)

agreeableness One of the Big Five dimensions of personality reflecting traits like being kind, cooperative, sympathetic, helpful, courteous, and warm. (219)

ambassador activities Boundary-spanning activities that are intended to protect the team, persuade others to support the team, or obtain important resources for the team. (267)

anticipatory stage A stage of socialization that begins as soon as a potential employee develops an image of what it would be like to work for a company. (376)

apprising An influence tactic in which the requestor clearly explains why performing the request will benefit the target personally. (293)

ASA framework A theory (Attraction-Selection-Attrition) that states that employees will be drawn to organizations with cultures that match their personality, organizations will select employees that match, and employees will leave or be forced out when they are not a good fit. (376)

auditory attention The ability to focus on a single sound in the presence of many other sounds. (239)

autocratic style A leadership style where the leader makes the decision alone without asking for opinions or suggestions of the employees in the work unit. (317)

autonomy The degree to which a job allows individual freedom and discretion regarding how the work is to be done. (84)

availability bias The tendency for people to base their judgments on information that is easier to recall. (203)

avoiding A conflict resolution style by which one party wants to remain neutral, stay away from conflict, or postpone the conflict to gather information or let things cool down. (298)

B

basic underlying assumptions The ingrained beliefs and philosophies of employees. (371)

behavioural coping Physical activities used to deal with a stressful situation. (111)

behaviourally anchored rating scales (BARS) Use of examples of critical incidents to evaluate an employee's job performance behaviours directly. (42)

behavioural modelling When employees observe the actions of others, learn from what they observe, and then repeat the observed behaviour. (196)

behavioural strains Patterns of negative behaviours that are associated with other strains. (117)

benevolence The belief that an authority wants to do good for an employee, apart from any selfish or profit-centred motives. (165)

benign job demands Job demands that are not appraised as being stressful. (105)

Big Five The five major dimensions of personality including conscientiousness, agreeableness, neuroticism, openness to experience, and extraversion. (219)

boosterism Positively representing the organization when in public. (35)

boundary spanning Interactions among team members and individuals and groups who are not part of the team. (267)

bounded rationality The notion that people do not have the ability or resources to process all available information and alternatives when making a decision. (200)

brainstorming A team process used to generate creative ideas. (266)

bureaucracy An organizational form that emphasizes the control and coordination of its members through a strict chain of command, formal rules and procedures, high specialization, and centralized decision making. (4)

bureaucratic structure An organizational form that exhibits many of the facets of a mechanistic organization. (352)

burnout The emotional, mental, and physical exhaustion from coping with stressful demands on a continuing basis. (116)

business environment The outside environment, including customers, competitors, suppliers, and distributors, which all have an impact on organizational design. (350)

C

centrality How important a person's job is and how many people depend on that person to accomplish their tasks. (292)

centralization Refers to where decisions are formally made in organizations. (347)

ceremonies Formal events, generally performed in front of an audience of organizational members. (371)

chain of command Answer to the question of "who reports to whom?" and signifies formal authority relationships. (345)

challenge stressors Stressors that tend to be appraised as opportunities for growth and achievement. (106)

character The perception that an authority adheres to a set of values and principles that the trustor finds acceptable. (165)

citizenship behaviour Voluntary employee behaviours that contribute to organizational goals by improving the context in which work takes place. (33)

civic virtue Participation in company operations at a deeper-than-normal level through voluntary meetings, readings, and keeping up with news that affects the company. (35)

client-based structure An organizational form in which employees are organized around serving customers. (355)

climate for transfer An organizational environment that supports the use of new skills. (211)

coalition An influence tactic in which the influencer enlists other people to help influence the target. (294)

coercive power A form of organizational power based on the ability to hand out punishment. (289)

cognition-based trust Trust that is rooted in a rational assessment of the authority's trustworthiness. (162)

cognitive abilities Capabilities related to the use of knowledge to make decisions and solve problems. (230)

cognitive-behavioural techniques Various practices that help workers cope with life's stressors in a rational manner. (124)

cognitive coping Thoughts used to deal with a stressful situation. (112)

cognitive distortion A re-evaluation of the inputs an employee brings to a job, often occurring in response to equity distress. (146)

cognitive moral development As people age and mature, they move through several states of moral development, each more mature and sophisticated than the prior one. (176)

cohesion A team state that occurs when members of the team develop strong emotional bonds to other members of the team and to the team itself. (270)

collaboration An influence tactic whereby the leader makes it easier for the target to complete a request by offering to work with and help the target; a conflict resolution style whereby both parties work together to maximize outcomes. (293, 298)

communal culture An organizational culture type in which employees are friendly to one another and all think alike. (372)

communion striving A strong desire to obtain acceptance in personal relationships as a means of expressing one's personality. (220)

communities of practice Groups of employees who learn from one another through collaboration over an extended period of time. (210)

company size The number of employees in a company. (351)

company strategy An organization's objectives and goals and how it tries to capitalize on its assets to make money. (350)

comparison other Another person who provides a frame of reference for judging equity. (145)

competence The capability to perform work tasks successfully; the skills, abilities, and areas of expertise that enable an authority to be successful in some specific area. (149, 164)

competing A conflict resolution style by which one party attempts to get his or her own goals met without concern for the other party's results. (298)

compliance When targets of influence are willing to do what the leader asks but do it with a degree of ambivalence. (294)

comprehensive interdependence A form of task interdependence in which team members have a great deal of discretion in terms of what they do and with whom they interact in the course of the collaboration involved in accomplishing the team's work. (257)

compromise A conflict resolution style by which conflict is resolved through give-and-take concessions. (298)

conjunctive tasks Tasks for which the team's performance depends on the abilities of the team's weakest link. (259)

conscientiousness One of the Big Five dimensions of personality reflecting traits like being dependable, organized, reliable, ambitious, hard-working, and persevering. (219)

consensus Used by decision makers to attribute cause; whether other individuals behave the same way under similar circumstances. (206)

consideration A pattern of behaviour where the leader creates job relationships characterized by mutual trust, respect for employee ideas, and consideration of employee feelings. (321)

consistency Used by decision makers to attribute cause; whether this individual has behaved this way before under similar circumstances. (206)

consultation An influence tactic whereby the target is allowed to participate in deciding how to carry out or implement a request. (293)

consultative style A leadership style where the leader presents the problem to employees asking for their opinions and suggestions before ultimately making the decision him- or herself. (317)

contingencies of reinforcement Four specific consequences used by organizations to modify employee behaviour. (192)

contingent reward When the leader attains follower agreement on what needs to be done using rewards in exchange for adequate performance. (327)

continuance commitment An employee's desire to remain a member of an organization due to an awareness of the costs of leaving. (51)

continuous reinforcement A specific consequence follows each and every occurrence of a certain behaviour. (194)

control movement abilities The ability to make precise adjustments using machinery to complete work effectively. (238)

coordination loss Process loss due to the time and energy it takes to coordinate work activities with other team members. (265)

coping Behaviours and thoughts used to manage stressful demands and the emotions associated with the stressful demands. (111)

corporate social responsibility A perspective that acknowledges that the responsibility of a business encompasses the economic, legal, ethical, and citizenship expectations of society. (182)

correlation The statistical relationship between two variables; abbreviated r, it can be positive or negative and range from 0 (no statistical relationship) to ±1 (a perfect statistical relationship). (18)

counterculture When a subculture's values do not match those of the organization. (375)

counterproductive behaviour Employee behaviours that intentionally hinder organizational goal accomplishment. (35)

courtesy Sharing important information with co-workers. (34)

co-worker satisfaction Employees' feelings about their co-workers, including their abilities and personalities. (78)

creativity culture A specific culture type focused on fostering a creative atmosphere. (374)

cultural values Shared beliefs about desirable end states or modes of conduct in a given culture that influence the expression of traits. (218)

culture strength The degree to which employees agree about how things should happen within the organization and behave accordingly. (374)

customer service culture A specific culture type focused on service quality. (373)

cyberloafing A form of psychological withdrawal in which employees surf the Internet, e-mail, and instant message to avoid doing work-related activities. (62)

D

daily hassles Minor day-to-day demands that interfere with work accomplishment. (108)

daydreaming A form of psychological withdrawal in which one's work is interrupted by random thoughts or concerns. (61)

decision informity The degree to which team members possess adequate information about their own task responsibilities. (266)

decision making The process of generating and choosing from a set of alternatives to solve a problem. (190)

deductive reasoning The ability to solve problems by applying general rules. (232)

deep-level diversity Diversity of attributes that are inferred through observation or experience, such as one's values or personality. (262)

delegating When the leader turns responsibility for key behaviours over to employees. (323)

delegative style A leadership style where the leader gives the employee the responsibility for making decisions within some set of specified boundary conditions. (318)

depth perception The ability to judge relative distances between things accurately. (239)

differential exposure Being more likely to appraise day-to-day situations as stressful, thereby feeling that stressors are encountered more frequently. (224)

differential reactivity Being less likely to believe that one can cope with the stressors experienced on a daily basis. (224)

discretion The degree to which managers have the right to make decisions on their own. (291)

disjunctive tasks Tasks with an objectively verifiable best solution for which the member with the highest level of ability has the most influence on team effectiveness. (259)

disposition-based trust Trust that is rooted in one's own personality, as opposed to a careful assessment of the trustee's trustworthiness. (162)

distinctiveness Used by decision makers to attribute cause; whether the person being judged acts in a similar fashion under different circumstances. (206)

distributive bargaining A negotiation strategy in which one person gains and the other person loses. (304)

distributive justice The perceived fairness of decision-making outcomes. (167)

diversity culture A specific culture type focused on fostering or taking advantage of a diverse group of employees. (373)

dynamic flexibility The ability to quickly and repeatedly execute bends, twists, stretches, or reaches to complete a job. (238)

dynamic strength The ability to exert force for a prolonged period of time without becoming overly fatigued and giving out. (236)

E

economic exchange Work relationships that resemble a contractual agreement by which employees fulfill job duties in exchange for financial compensation. (180)

embeddedness An employee's connection to and sense of fit in the organization and community. (56)

emotional contagion The idea that emotions can be transferred from one person to another. (90)

emotional cues Positive or negative feelings that can help or hinder task accomplishment. (135)

emotional intelligence A set of abilities related to the understanding and use of emotions that affect social functioning. (235)

emotional labour When employees manage their emotions to complete their job duties successfully. (90)

emotional support The empathy and understanding that people receive from others that can be used to alleviate emotional distress from stressful demands. (117)

emotion-focused coping Behaviours and cognitions of an individual intended to help manage emotional reactions to the stressful demands. (112)

emotion regulation The ability to recover quickly from emotional experiences. (235)

emotions Intense feelings, often lasting for a short duration, that are clearly directed at someone or some circumstance. (88)

encounter stage A stage of socialization beginning the day an employee starts work, during which the employee compares the information as an outsider to the information learned as an insider. (376)

engagement In the context of mood, it represents how active or sluggish a mood is. In the context of influence tactics, it occurs when one agrees and becomes committed to an influencer's request. (87, 294)

equity distress An internal tension that results from being over-rewarded or underrewarded relative to some comparison other. (145)

equity theory A theory that suggests that employees create a mental ledger of the outcomes they receive for their job inputs, relative to some comparison other. (144)

erosion model A model that suggests that employees with fewer bonds with co-workers are more likely to quit the organization. (55)

escalation of commitment A common decision-making error in which the decision maker continues to follow a failing course of action. (206)

espoused values The beliefs, philosophies, and norms that a company explicitly states. (371)

ethical ideologies Principles used by individuals during ethical decision making. (178)

ethical sensitivity The ability to recognize that a decision has ethical content. (176)

ethics The degree to which the behaviours of an authority are in accordance with generally accepted moral norms. (162)

ethnocentrism One who views his or her cultural values as "right" and values of other cultures as "wrong." (225)

exchange tactic An influence tactic in which the requestor offers a reward in return for performing a request. (293)

exit A response to a negative work event by which one becomes often absent from work or voluntarily leaves the organization. (60)

expectancy The belief that exerting a high level of effort will result in successful performance on some task. (134)

expectancy theory A theory that describes the cognitive process employees go through to make choices among different voluntary responses. (133)

expertise The knowledge and skills that distinguish experts from novices. (191)

expert power A form of organizational power based on expertise or knowledge. (289)

explicit knowledge Knowledge that is easily communicated and available to everyone. (191)

explosive strength The ability to move or move things in short bursts of energy. (236)

extent flexibility The ability to execute extreme ranges of bends, twists, stretches, or reaches to complete a job. (238)

external comparisons Comparing oneself to someone in a different company. (146)

extinction The removal of a positive outcome following an unwanted behaviour. (193)

extraversion One of the Big Five dimensions of personality reflecting traits like being talkative, sociable, passionate, assertive, bold, and dominant. (219)

extrinsic motivation Desire to put forth work effort due to some contingency that depends on task performance. (136)

F

facilitative style A leadership style where the leader presents the problem to a group of employees and seeks consensus on a solution, making sure that his or her own opinion receives no more weight than anyone else's. (317)

family time demands The amount of time committed to fulfilling family responsibilities. (111)

feedback In job characteristics theory, it refers to the degree to which the job itself provides information about how well the job holder is doing. In goal setting theory, it refers to progress updates on work goals. (85, 142)

fine manipulative abilities The ability to keep the arms and hands steady while using the hands to do precise work. (238)

fixed interval schedule Reinforcement occurs at fixed time periods. (194)

fixed ratio schedule Reinforcement occurs following a fixed number of desired behaviours. (194)

focus of commitment The people, places, and things that inspire a desire to remain a member of an organization. (52)

formalism The view that ethical actions are defined using a set of guiding principles. (178)

formalization The degree to which rules and procedures are used to standardize behaviours and decisions in an organization. (347)

forming The first stage of team development, during which members try to get a feel for what is expected of them, what types of behaviours are out of bounds, and who's in charge. (253)

fragmented culture An organizational culture type in which employees are distant and disconnected from one another. (372)

functional structure An organizational form in which employees are grouped by the functions they perform for the organization. (352)

fundamental attribution error The tendency for people to judge others' behaviours as being due to internal factors such as ability, motivation, or attitudes. (205)

G

general adaptation syndrome (GAS) The process that the body uses to adapt to stressful demands so that it can continue to function effectively. (113)

general mental ability The general level of cognitive ability that plays an important role in determining the more narrow cognitive abilities. (233)

geographic structure An organizational form in which employees are grouped around the different locations where the company does business. (355)

goal commitment The degree to which a person accepts a goal and is determined to reach it. (142)

goal interdependence The degree to which team members have a shared goal and align their individual goals with that vision. (257)

goal setting theory A theory that views goals as the primary drivers of the intensity and persistence of effort. (141)

gossiping Casual conversations about other people in which the facts are not confirmed as true. (38)

gross body coordination The ability to synchronize the movements of the body, arms, and legs to do something while the whole body is in motion. (238)

gross body equilibrium The ability to maintain the balance of the body in unstable contexts or when changing directions. (238)

groupthink Behaviours that support conformity and team harmony at the expense of other team priorities. (270)

growth need strength The degree to which employees desire to develop themselves further. (86)

H

harassment Unwanted physical contact or verbal remarks from a colleague. (38)

health and wellness programs Employee assistance programs that help workers with personal problems such as alcoholism and other addictions. (124)

hearing sensitivity The ability to discriminate sounds that vary in terms of loudness and pitch. (239)

helping Assisting co-workers who have heavy workloads, aiding them with personal matters, and showing new employees the ropes when they are first on the job. (34)

heuristics Simple and efficient rules of thumb that allow one to make decisions more easily. (203)

hierarchical sensitivity The degree to which the team leader effectively weighs the recommendations of the members. (266)

hindrance stressors Stressors that tend to be appraised as thwarting progress toward growth and achievement. (106)

history A collective pool of experience, wisdom, and knowledge created by people that benefits the organization. (10)

human relations movement Field of study that recognizes that the psychological attributes of individual workers and the social forces within workgroups have important effects on work behaviours. (5)

human resource management Field of study that focuses on the applications of OB theories and principles in organizations. (4)

hybrid outcome interdependence When team members receive rewards based on both their individual performance and that of the team to which they belong. (276)

hypotheses Written predictions that specify relationships between variables. (17)

I

idealism Embracing the notion of universal moral rules. (178)

idealized influence When the leader behaves in ways that earn the admiration, trust, and respect of followers, causing followers to want to identify with and emulate the leader. (328)

identity The degree to which a job offers completion of a whole, identifiable piece of work. (83)

impact The sense that a person's actions "make a difference"—that progress is being made toward fulfilling some important purpose. (149)

incivility Communication that is rude, impolite, discourteous, and lacking in good manners. (38)

individualism-collectivism The degree to which a culture has a loosely knit social framework (individualism) or a tight social framework (collectivism). (225)

individualistic roles Behaviours that benefit the individual at the expense of the team. (259)

individualized consideration When the leader behaves in ways that help followers achieve their potential through coaching, development, and mentoring. (330)

inductive reasoning The ability to consider several pieces of information and then reach a more general conclusion regarding how those pieces are related. (232)

influence The use of behaviours to cause behavioural or attitudinal changes in others. (292)

informational justice The perceived fairness of the communications provided to employees from authorities. (171)

ingratiation The use of favours, compliments, or friendly behaviour to make the target feel better about the influencer. (293)

inimitable Incapable of being imitated or copied. (10)

initiating structure A pattern of behaviour where the leader defines and structures the roles of employees in pursuit of goal attainment. (321)

inspirational appeal An influence tactic designed to appeal to one's values and ideals, thereby creating an emotional or attitudinal reaction. (293)

inspirational motivation When the leader behaves in ways that foster an enthusiasm for and commitment to a shared vision of the future. (328)

instrumental support The help people receive from others that can be used to address a stressful demand directly. (117)

instrumentality The belief that successful performance will result in the attainment of some outcome(s). (135)

integrative bargaining A negotiation strategy that achieves an outcome that is satisfying for both parties. (304)

intellectual stimulation When the leader behaves in ways that challenge followers to be innovative and creative by questioning assumptions and reframing old situations in new ways. (330)

internal comparisons Comparing oneself to someone in your same company. (146)

interpersonal citizenship behaviour Going beyond normal job expectations to assist, support, and develop co-workers and colleagues. (34)

interpersonal justice The perceived fairness of the interpersonal treatment received by employees from authorities. (169)

interpersonal processes Teamwork processes, such as motivating and confidence building, that focus on the management of relationships among team members. (269)

intrinsic motivation Desire to put forth work effort due to the sense that task performance serves as its own reward. (136)

intuition An emotional judgment based on quick, unconscious, gut feelings. (198)

J

job analysis A process by which an organization determines requirements of specific jobs. (32)

job characteristics theory A theory that argues that five core characteristics (variety, identity, significance, autonomy, and feedback) combine to result in high levels of satisfaction with the work itself. (81)

Job Descriptive Index (JDI) A facet measure of job satisfaction that assesses an individual's satisfaction with pay, promotion opportunities, supervision, co-workers, and the work itself. (96)

job enrichment When job duties and responsibilities are expanded to provide increased levels of core job characteristics. (86)

job performance Employee behaviours that contribute either positively or negatively to the accomplishment of organizational goals. (29)

job satisfaction A pleasurable emotional state resulting from the appraisal of one's job or job experiences. It represents how a person feels and thinks about his or her job. (73)

job sharing When two people share the responsibilities of a single job. (122)

justice The perceived fairness of an authority's decision making. (161)

K

knowledge and skill The degree to which employees have the aptitude and competence needed to succeed on their job. (86)

knowledge of results A psychological state indicating the extent to which employees are aware of how well or how poorly they are doing. (81)

knowledge transfer The exchange of knowledge between employees. (210)

L

laissez-faire leadership When the leader avoids leadership duties altogether. (326)

language The jargon, slang, and slogans used within an organization. (370)

leader effectiveness The degree to which the leader's actions result in the achievement of the unit's goals, the continued commitment of the unit's employees, and the development of mutual trust, respect, and obligation in leader–member dyads. (315)

leader emergence The process of becoming a leader in the first place. (315)

leader-member exchange theory A theory describing how leader–member relationships develop over time on a dyadic basis. (313)

leadership The use of power and influence to direct the activities of followers toward goal achievement. (312)

leader-staff team A type of team that consists of members who make recommendations to the leader who is ultimately responsible for team decisions. (258)

learning A relatively permanent change in an employee's knowledge or skill that results from experience. (190)

learning orientation A predisposition or attitude according to which building competence is deemed more important by an employee than demonstrating competence. (197)

legitimate power A form of organizational power based on authority or position. (286)

life cycle theory of leadership A theory stating that the optimal combination of initiating structure and consideration depends on the readiness of the employees in the work unit. (322)

long breaks A form of physical withdrawal in which employees take longer-than-normal lunches or breaks to spend less time at work. (62)

looking busy A form of psychological withdrawal in which one attempts to appear consumed with work when not performing actual work tasks. (61)

loyalty A passive response to a negative work event in which one publicly supports the situation but privately hopes for improvement. (60)

M

management by objectives (MBO) A management philosophy that bases employee evaluations on whether specific performance goals have been met. (42)

management team A relatively permanent team that participates in managerial-level tasks that affect the entire organization. (252)

masculinity-femininity The degree to which a culture values stereotypically male traits (masculinity) or stereotypically female traits (femininity). (225)

mathematical reasoning The ability to choose and apply formulas to solve problems that involve numbers. (231)

matrix structure A complex form of organizational structure that combines a functional and multi-divisional grouping. (355)

maximum performance Performance in brief, special circumstances that demand a person's best effort. (240)

meaningfulness A psychological state reflecting one's feelings about work tasks, goals, and purposes, and the degree to which they contribute to society and fulfill one's ideals and passions. (149)

meaningfulness of work A psychological state indicating the degree to which work tasks are viewed as something that counts in the employee's system of philosophies and beliefs. (81)

meaning of money The idea that money can have symbolic value (e.g., achievement, respect, freedom) in addition to economic value. (137)

mechanistic organizations Efficient, rigid, predictable, and standardized organizations that thrive in stable environments. (347)

mental models The degree to which team members have a shared understanding of important aspects of the team and its task. (271)

mentoring The process by which a junior-level employee develops a deep and long-lasting relationship with a more senior-level employee within the organization. (387)

mercenary culture An organizational culture type in which employees think alike but are not friendly to one another. (372)

meta-analysis A method that combines the results of multiple scientific studies by essentially calculating a weighted average correlation across studies (with larger studies receiving more weight). (20)

missing meetings A form of physical withdrawal in which employees neglect important work functions while away from the office. (62)

moods States of feeling that are mild in intensity, last for an extended period of time, and are not directed at anything. (87)

moonlighting A form of psychological withdrawal in which employees use work time and resources to do non-work-related activities. (62)

moral awareness When an authority recognizes that a moral issue exists in a situation. (174)

moral identity The degree to which a person views himself or herself as a moral person. (178)

moral intensity The degree to which an issue has ethical urgency. (176)

moral intent An authority's degree of commitment to the moral course of action. (178)

moral judgment When an authority can accurately identify the "right" course of action. (176)

motivation A set of energetic forces that determine the direction, intensity, and persistence of an employee's work effort. (132)

motivational loss Process loss due to team members' tendency to put forth less effort on team tasks than they could. (265)

multi-divisional structure An organizational form in which employees are grouped by product, geography, or client. (353)

N

National Occupational Database (NOC) A national database of occupations in Canada, organizing over 30,000 job titles into 520 occupational group descriptions. (33)

near and far vision The ability to see things up close and at a distance. (238)

needs Groupings or clusters of outcomes viewed as having critical psychological or physiological consequences. (136)

negative affectivity A dispositional tendency to experience unpleasant moods such as hostility, nervousness, and annoyance. (223)

negative emotions Employees' feelings of fear, guilt, shame, sadness, envy, and disgust. (89)

negative life events Events such as a divorce or death of a family member that tend to be appraised as a hindrance. (110)

negative reinforcement An unwanted outcome is removed following a desired behaviour. (193)

neglect A passive, destructive response to a negative work event in which one's interest and effort in work decline. (60)

negotiation A process in which two or more interdependent individuals discuss and attempt to reach agreement about their differences. (303)

networked culture An organizational culture type in which employees are friendly to one another, but everyone thinks differently and does his or her own thing. (372)

neuroticism One of the Big Five dimensions of personality reflecting traits like being nervous, moody, emotional, insecure, jealous, and unstable. (219)

neutralizers Situational characteristics that reduce the importance of the leader and do not improve employee performance in any way. (333)

newcomer orientation The process of ensuring that a potential employee understands both the positive and negative aspects of the potential job. (386)

night vision The ability to see things in low light. (238)

non-programmed decisions Decisions made by employees when a problem is new, complex, or not recognized. (200)

normative commitment An employee's desire to remain a member of an organization due to a feeling of obligation. (51)

norming The third stage of team development, during which members realize that they need to work together to accomplish team goals and consequently begin to cooperate. (254)

number facility The capability to do simple math operations such as adding and subtracting. (231)

numerous small decisions People making many small decisions every day that are invisible to competitors. (11)

O

observable artifacts Aspects of an organization's culture that employees and outsiders can easily see or talk about. (369)

openness to experience One of the Big Five dimensions of personality reflecting traits like being curious, imaginative, creative, complex, refined, and sophisticated. (219)

oral comprehension The ability to understand spoken words and sentences. (231)

oral expression The ability to communicate ideas by speaking. (231)

organic organizations Flexible, adaptive, outward-focused organizations that thrive in dynamic environments. (348)

organizational behaviour (OB) Field of study devoted to understanding, explaining, and ultimately improving the attitudes and behaviours of individuals and groups in organizations. (4)

organizational chart A drawing that represents every job in the organization and the formal reporting relationships between those jobs. (343)

organizational citizenship behaviour Going beyond normal expectations to improve operations of the organization, as well as defending the organization and being loyal to it. (34)

organizational commitment An employee's desire to remain a member of an organization. (49)

organizational culture The shared social knowledge within an organization regarding the rules, norms, and values that shape the attitudes and behaviours of its employees. (368)

organizational design The process of creating, selecting, or changing the structure of an organization. (350)

organizational politics Individual actions directed toward the goal of furthering a person's own self-interests. (295)

organizational structure Formally dictates how jobs and tasks are divided and coordinated between individuals and groups within the company. (342)

originality The ability to develop clever and novel ways to solve problems. (232)

other awareness The ability to recognize and understand the emotions that other people are feeling. (235)

outcome interdependence The degree to which team members share equally in the feedback and rewards that result from the team achieving its goals. (258)

overreward inequity The ratio of outcomes to inputs is greater than some comparison other's ratio. (145)

P

parallel team A team composed of members from various jobs within the organization that meets to provide recommendations about important issues. (252)

participating When the leader shares ideas and tries to help the group conduct its affairs. (322)

passive management-by-exception When the leader waits around for mistakes and errors, then takes corrective action as necessary. (326)

past accomplishments The level of success or failure with similar job tasks in the past. (134)

pay satisfaction Employees' feelings about the compensation for their jobs. (76)

perceptual speed The ability to examine and compare numbers, letters, and objects quickly. (232)

performance-avoid orientation A predisposition or attitude by which employees focus on demonstrating their competence so that others will not think poorly of them. (197)

performance-prove orientation A predisposition or attitude by which employees focus on demonstrating their competence so that others think favourably of them. (197)

performing The final stage of team development, during which members are comfortable working within their roles, and the team makes progress toward goals. (255)

personal aggression Hostile verbal and physical actions directed toward other employees. (38)

personal appeals An influence tactic in which the requestor asks for something based on personal friendship or loyalty. (293)

personal development Participation in activities outside of work that foster growth and learning. (111)

personality The structures and propensities inside a person that explain his or her characteristic patterns of thought, emotion, and behaviour. Personality reflects what people are like and creates their social reputation. (218)

person-organization fit The degree to which a person's values and personality match the culture of the organization. (381)

physical structures The organization's buildings and internal office designs. (370)

physical withdrawal A physical escape from the work environment. (62)

physiological strains Reactions from stressors that harm the human body. (115)

pleasantness The degree to which an employee is in a good versus bad mood. (87)

political deviance Behaviours that intentionally disadvantage other individuals. (38)

political skill The ability to understand others and the use of that knowledge to influence them to further personal or organizational objectives. (296)

pooled interdependence A form of task interdependence in which group members complete their work assignments independently, and then their work is simply added together to represent the group's output. (257)

positive affectivity A dispositional tendency to experience pleasant, engaging moods such as enthusiasm, excitement, and elation. (221)

positive emotions Employees' feelings of joy, pride, relief, hope, love, and compassion. (89)

positive life events Events such as marriage or the birth of a child that tend to be appraised as a challenge. (111)

positive reinforcement When a positive outcome follows a desired behaviour. (192)

potency A team state reflecting the degree of confidence among team members that the team can be effective across situations and tasks. (271)

power The ability to influence the behaviour of others and resist unwanted influence in return. (285)

power distance The degree to which a culture prefers equal power distribution (low power distance) or an unequal power distribution (high power distance). (225)

pressure An influence tactic in which the requestor attempts to use coercive power through threats and demands. (294)

primary appraisal Evaluation of whether a demand is stressful and, if it is, the implications of the stressor in terms of personal goals and well-being. (105)

problem-focused coping Behaviours and cognitions of an individual intended to manage the stressful situation itself. (112)

problem sensitivity The ability to sense that there is or will be a problem. (231)

procedural justice The perceived fairness of decision-making processes. (168)

process gain When team outcomes are greater than expected based on the capabilities of the individual members. (263)

process loss When team outcomes are less than expected based on the capabilities of the individual members. (265)

production deviance Intentionally reducing organizational efficiency of work output. (38)

product structure An organizational form in which employees are grouped around different products that the company produces. (355)

programmed decisions Decisions that are somewhat automatic because the decision maker's knowledge allows him or her to recognize the situation and the course of action to be taken. (197)

projection bias The faulty perception by decision makers that others think, feel, and act the same way as they do. (203)

project team A team formed to take on one-time tasks, most of which tend to be complex and require input from members from different functional areas. (252)

promotion satisfaction Employees' feelings about how the company handles promotions. (78)

property deviance Behaviours that harm the organization's assets and possessions. (35)

psychological empowerment An energy rooted in the belief that tasks are contributing to some larger purpose. (148)

psychological strains Negative psychological reactions from stressors such as depression, anxiety, and anger. (116)

psychological withdrawal Mentally escaping the work environment. (61)

punctuated equilibrium A sequence of team development during which not much gets done until the halfway point of a project, after which teams make necessary changes to complete the project on time. (255)

punishment When an unwanted outcome follows an unwanted behaviour. (193)

Q

quitting A form of physical withdrawal in which employees voluntarily leave the organization. (63)

R

rare In short supply. (10)

rational decision-making model A step-by-step approach to making decisions that is designed to maximize outcomes by examining all available alternatives. (200)

rational persuasion The use of logical arguments and hard facts to show someone that a request is worthwhile. (292)

readiness The degree to which employees have the ability and the willingness to accomplish their specific tasks. (322)

realistic job previews The process of ensuring that a potential employee understands both the positive and negative aspects of the potential job. (386)

reality shock A mismatch of information that occurs when an employee finds that aspects of working at a company are not what the employee expected it to be. (377)

reciprocal interdependence A form of task interdependence in which group members interact with only a limited subset of other members to complete the team's work. (257)

referent power A form of organizational power based on the attractiveness and charisma of the leader. (289)

relationship conflict Disagreements among team members with regard to interpersonal relationships or incompatibilities in personal values or preferences. (269)

relativism The view that there are no universal moral rules. (178)

relaxation techniques Calming activities to reduce stress. (124)

resistance When a target refuses to perform a request and puts forth an effort to avoid having to do it. (295)

resource-based view A model that argues that rare and inimitable resources help firms maintain competitive advantage. (9)

response orientation The ability to choose the right action quickly in response to several different signals. (238)

response time The ability to respond to signalling information after it occurs. (238)

responsibility for outcomes A psychological state indicating the degree to which employees feel they are key drivers of the quality of work output. (81)

restructuring The process of changing an organization's structure. (359)

reward power A form of organizational power based on the control of resources or benefits. (288)

rituals The daily or weekly planned routines that occur in an organization. (371)

role The behaviour a person is generally expected to display in a given context. (258)

role ambiguity When an individual has a lack of direction and information about what needs to be done. (106)

role conflict When others have conflicting expectations of what an individual needs to do. (106)

role making The phase in a leader–follower relationship when a follower voices his or her own expectations for the relationship, resulting in a free-flowing exchange of opportunities and resources for activities and effort. (313)

role overload When an employee has too many demands to work effectively. (107)

role taking The phase in a leader–follower relationship when a leader provides an employee with job expectations and the follower tries to meet those expectations. (313)

routine task performance Well-known or habitual responses by employees to predictable task demands. (29)

rule of one-eighth The belief that at best one-eighth, or 12 percent, of organizations will actually do what is required to build profits by putting people first. (14)

S

sabotage Purposeful destruction of equipment, organizational processes, or company products. (35)

safety culture A specific culture type focused on the safety of employees. (373)

satisfaction with the work itself Employees' feelings about their actual work tasks. (78)

satisficing When a decision maker chooses the first acceptable alternative considered. (202)

schedules of reinforcement The timing of when contingencies are applied or removed. (194)

scientific management Using scientific methods to design optimal and efficient work processes and tasks. (4)

scout activities Boundary-spanning activities that are intended to obtain information about technology, competitors, or the broader marketplace. (268)

secondary appraisal When people determine how to cope with the various stressors they face. (111)

selective perception The tendency for people to see their environment only as it affects them and as it is consistent with their expectations. (202)

self-awareness The ability to recognize and understand the emotions in oneself. (235)

self-determination A sense of choice in the initiation and continuation of work tasks. (149)

self-efficacy The belief that a person has the capabilities needed to perform the behaviours required on some task. (134)

self-serving bias When one attributes one's own failures to external factors and success to internal factors. (205)

self-set goals The internalized goals that people use to monitor their own progress. (141)

selling When the leader explains key issues and provides opportunities for clarification. (322)

sequential interdependence A form of task interdependence in which group members perform different tasks in a prescribed sequence, and members only depend on the member who comes before them in the sequence. (257)

short-term vs. long-term orientation The degree to which a culture stresses values that are past- and present-oriented (short-term orientation) or future-oriented (long-term orientation). (225)

significance The degree to which a job really matters and impacts society as a whole. (84)

similarity-attraction approach A theory explaining that team diversity can be counterproductive because people tend to avoid interacting with others who are unlike them. (260)

simple structure An organizational form that features one person as the central decision-making figure. (351)

situational strength The degree to which situations have clear behavioural expectations, incentives, or instructions that make differences between individuals less important. (240)

S.M.A.R.T. goals Acronym that stands for specific, measurable, achievable, results-based, time-sensitive goals. (143)

social exchange Work relationships that are characterized by mutual investment, with employees willing to engage in "extra mile" sorts of behaviours because they trust that their efforts will eventually be rewarded. (181)

social identity theory A theory that people identify themselves based on the various groups to which they belong and judge others based on the groups they associate with. (203)

social influence model A model that suggests that employees with direct linkages to co-workers who leave the organization will themselves become more likely to leave. (55)

socialization The primary process by which employees learn the social knowledge that enables them to understand and adapt to the organization's culture. (376)

socializing A form of psychological withdrawal in which one verbally chats with co-workers about non-work topics. (61)

social learning theory Theory that argues that people in organizations learn by observing others. (196)

social loafing A type of motivational loss resulting from members feeling less accountable for team outcomes relative to independent work that results in individually identifiable outcomes. (265)

socially complex resources Resources created by people, such as culture, teamwork, trust, and reputation; the source of competitive advantage is known, but the method of replicating the advantage is unclear. (11)

social support The help people receive from others when they are confronted with stressful demands. (117)

span of control Represents how many employees each manager in the organization has responsibility for. (345)

spatial organization A good understanding of where one is relative to other things in the environment. (232)

specific and difficult goals Goals that stretch an employee to perform at his or her maximum level while still staying within the boundaries of his or her ability. (141)

speech recognition The ability to identify and understand the speech of another person. (239)

speed and flexibility of closure The ability to pick out a pattern of information quickly in the presence of distractions, even without all the information present. (232)

sportsmanship Maintaining a positive attitude with co-workers through good and bad times. (34)

staff validity The degree to which team members make good recommendations to the team leader. (266)

stamina The ability to work effectively while engaging in physical activity. (236)

static strength The ability to lift, push, or pull very heavy objects such as boxes or heavy equipment. (236)

status striving A strong desire to obtain power and influence within a social structure as a means of expressing one's personality. (221)

stereotype Assumptions made about others based on their social group membership. (203)

stories Anecdotes, accounts, legends, and myths passed down from cohort to cohort within an organization. (371)

storming The second stage of team development, during which conflict occurs due to members' ongoing commitment to ideas they bring with them to the team. (254)

strains Negative consequences of the stress response. (105)

strategic management Field of study devoted to exploring the product choices and industry characteristics that affect an organization's profitability. (4)

stress The psychological response to demands when there is something at stake for the individual, and where coping with these demands would tax or exceed the individual's capacity or resources. (105)

stress audit An assessment of the sources of stress in the workplace. (122)

stressors Demands that cause the stress response. (105)

subculture A culture created within a small subset of the organization's employees. (375)

substance abuse The abuse of drugs or alcohol before coming to work or while on the job. (38)

substitutability The degree to which people have alternatives in accessing the resources that a leader controls. (291)

substitutes Situational characteristics that reduce the importance of the leader while simultaneously providing a direct benefit to employee performance. (333)

substitutes for leadership model A model that suggests that characteristics of the situations can constrain the influence of the leader which makes it more difficult for the leader to influence employee performance. (333)

supervision satisfaction Employees' feelings about their boss, including his or her competency, communication, and personality. (78)

supportive practices Ways in which organizations help employees manage and balance their demands. (123)

surface-level diversity Diversity of observable attributes such as race, gender, ethnicity, and age. (261)

symbols The images an organization uses, which generally convey messages. (370)

T

tacit knowledge Knowledge that employees can only learn through experience. (191)

tardiness A form of physical withdrawal in which employees arrive late to work or leave work early. (62)

task complexity The degree to which the information and actions needed to complete a task are complicated. (142)

task conflict Disagreements among members about the team's task. (269)

task coordinator activities Boundary-spanning activities that are intended to coordinate task-related issues with people or groups in other functional areas. (267)

task interdependence The degree to which team members interact with and rely on other team members for information, materials, and resources needed to accomplish work for the team. (256)

task performance Employee behaviours that are directly involved in the transformation of organizational resources into the goods or services that the organization produces. (29)

task strategies Learning plans and problem-solving approaches used to achieve successful performance. (142)

taskwork processes The activities of team members that relate directly to the accomplishment of team tasks. (265)

team Two or more people who work interdependently over some time period to accomplish common goals related to some task-oriented purpose. (251)

team building roles Behaviours that influence the quality of the team's social climate. (259)

team composition The mix of the various characteristics that describe the individuals who work in the team. (258)

team diversity The degree to which team members are different from one another. (260)

team process The different types of activities and interactions that occur within a team as the team works toward its goals. (262)

team states Specific types of feelings and thoughts that coalesce in the minds of team members as a consequence of their experience working together. (270)

team task roles Behaviours that directly facilitate the accomplishment of team tasks. (259)

team viability Team commitment; the likelihood a team can work together effectively into the future. (272)

teamwork processes The interpersonal activities that promote the accomplishment of team tasks but do not involve task accomplishment itself. (268)

technology The method by which an organization transforms inputs to outputs. (351)

telling When the leader provides specific instructions and closely supervises performance. (322)

theft Stealing company products or equipment from the organization. (37)

theory A collection of verbal and symbolic assertions that specify how and why variables are related, as well as the conditions in which they should (and should not) be related. (16)

360-degree feedback A performance evaluation system that uses ratings provided by supervisors, co-workers, subordinates, customers, and the employees themselves. (42)

time-driven model of leadership A model that suggests that seven factors, including the importance of the decision, the expertise of the leader, and the competence of the followers, combine to make some decision-making styles more effective than others in a given situation. (318)

time pressure The sense that the amount of time allotted to do a job is not quite enough. (108)

training A systematic effort by organizations to facilitate the learning of job-related knowledge and behaviour. (209)

training interventions Practices that increase employees' competencies and skills. (123)

trait activation The degree to which situations provide cues that trigger the expression of a given personality trait. (240)

traits Recurring trends in people's responses to their environment. (218)

transactional leadership A pattern of behaviour where the leader rewards or disciplines the follower based on performance. (326)

transactive memory The degree to which team members' specialized knowledge is integrated into an effective system of memory for the team. (272)

transfer of training Occurs when employees retain and demonstrate the knowledge, skills, and behaviours required for their job after training ends. (210)

transformational leadership A pattern of behaviour where the leader inspires followers to commit to a shared vision that provides meaning to their work while also serving as a role model who helps followers develop their own potential and view problems from new perspectives. (326)

transition processes Teamwork processes, such as mission analysis and planning, that focus on preparation for future work in the team. (268)

trust The willingness to be vulnerable to an authority based on positive expectations about the authority's actions and intentions. (161)

trust propensity A general expectation that the words, promises, and statements of individuals can be relied upon. (162)

trustworthiness Characteristics or attributes of a person that inspire trust, including competence, character, and benevolence. (164)

Type A Behaviour Pattern People who tend to experience more stressors, to appraise more demands as stressful, and to be prone to experiencing more strains. (117)

typical performance Performance in the routine conditions that surround daily job tasks. (240)

U

uncertainty avoidance The degree to which a culture tolerates ambiguous situations (low uncertainty avoidance) or feels threatened by them (high uncertainty avoidance). (225)

underreward inequity The ratio of outcomes to inputs is lower than some comparison other's ratio. (145)

understanding and adaptation The final stage of socialization, during which newcomers come to learn the content areas of socialization and internalize the norms and expected behaviours of the organization. (377)

use of emotions The degree to which people can harness emotions and employ them to improve their chances of being successful in whatever they are seeking to do. (236)

utilitarianism The view that ethical actions are defined as those that achieve the most valuable ends. (178)

V

valence The anticipated value of the outcome(s) associated with successful performance. (136)

value in diversity problem-solving approach A theory that supports team diversity because it provides a larger pool of knowledge and perspectives. (260)

value-percept theory A theory that argues that job satisfaction depends on whether the employee perceives that his or her job supplies those things that he or she values. (74)

values Things that people consciously or unconsciously want to seek or attain. (74)

variable interval schedule Reinforcement occurs at random periods of time. (194)

variable ratio schedule Behaviours are reinforced after a varying number of them have been exhibited. (195)

variety The degree to which a job requires different activities and skills. (81)

verbal persuasion Pep talks that lead employees to believe that they can "get the job done." (135)

vicarious experiences Observations of and discussions with others who have performed some work task. (135)

virtual team A team in which the members are geographically dispersed, and interdependent activity occurs through e-mail, Web conferencing, and instant messaging. (253)

visibility How aware others are of a leader and the resources that leader can provide. (292)

visual colour discrimination The ability to perceive colours accurately. (238)

visualization The ability to imagine how separate things will look if they were put together in a particular way. (232)

voice When an employee speaks up to offer constructive suggestions for change, often in reaction to a negative work event. (35, 60)

W

wasting resources Using too many materials or too much time to do too little work. (38)

whistle-blowing When employees expose illegal actions by their employer. (174)

withdrawal behaviour Employee actions that are intended to avoid work situations. (50)

Wonderlic Personnel Test A 12-minute test of general cognitive ability used to hire job applicants. (243)

work complexity The degree to which job requirements tax or just exceed employee capabilities. (108)

work-family conflict A form of role conflict in which the demands of a work role hinder the fulfillment of the demands in a family role (or vice versa). (110)

work responsibility The number and importance of the obligations that an employee has to others. (108)

work specialization The degree to which tasks in an organization are divided into separate jobs. (344)

work team A relatively permanent team in which members work together to produce goods and/or provide services. (252)

written comprehension The ability to understand written words and sentences. (231)

written expression The ability to communicate ideas in writing. (231)

Z

zero acquaintance situations Situations in which two people have just met. (221)

Chapter Notes

Chapter 1

1. Canada's 10 Most Admired Corporate Cultures™ 2007. Marty Parker, Managing Director, Waterstone Human Capital Ltd., Toronto. Retrieved February 26, 2009, at www.waterstonehc.com/resources/Canada's_10_Most_Admired_Corporate_Cultures_2007_booklet(3).pdf.
2. Taylor, F.W. *The Principles of Scientific Management.* New York: Norton, 1974.
3. Weber, M. (1922). "Bureaucracy," in Gerth, H.H., and C. Wright Mills, *From Max Weber: Essays in Sociology.* London: Routledge and Kegan Paul, 1948; Weber, M. *The Protestant Ethic and the Spirit of Capitalism* (translated by Talcott Parsons). New York: Scribners, 1958.
4. Roethlisberger, F.J., and W.J. Dickson. *Management and the Worker.* Cambridge, MA: Harvard University, 1939; Wrege, C.D., and R.G. Greenwood. "The Hawthorne Studies," In D.A. Wren & J.A. Pearce II (Eds.), *Papers Dedicated to the Development of Modern Management.* Academy of Management, 1986.
5. Meyer, J.P., and N.J. Allen. *Commitment in the Workplace.* Thousand Oaks, CA: Sage, 1997.
6. Silke Carty, S. "Hyundai Lands in Top 3 for Quality." *USA Today,* June 8, 2006.
7. Ihlwan, M., and C. Dawson. "Building a 'Camry Fighter': Can Hyundai Transform Itself into One of the World's Top Auto Makers?" *BusinessWeek,* September 6, 2004, p. 62. Retrieved August 19, 2005, from the LexisNexis database.
8. Ihlwan, M., L. Armstrong, and M. Eldam. "Kissing Clunkers Goodbye." *BusinessWeek,* May 17, 2004, p. 45. Retrieved August 19, 2005, from the LexisNexis database.
9. Barney, J. "Firm Resources and Sustained Competitive Advantage." *Journal of Management* 17 (1991), pp. 99–120.
10. Aguinis, H., and C.A. Henle. "The Search for Universals in Cross-Cultural Organizational Behaviour." In *Organizational Behaviour: The State of the Science,* ed. J. Greenberg. Mahwah, NJ: Lawrence Erlbaum Associates, 2003, pp. 373–411.
11. "'No Frills' Airlines—Air Canada Discount Carriers," *Alberta Online Encyclopedia,* Heritage Community Foundation. Retrieved April 14, 2008, at www.abheritage.ca/aviation/history/frills_aircanada.html.
12. "Lime Coke Dashes to Launch." *The Grocer,* March 5, 2005, p. 76. Retrieved August 20, 2005, from the LexisNexis database.
13. Barney, J.B. "Looking Inside for Competitive Advantage. In *Strategic Human Resource Management,* ed. R. S. Schuler and S. E. Jackson. Malden, MA: Blackwell, 1999, pp. 128–41.
14. Huselid, M.A. "The Impact of Human Resource Management Practice on Turnover, Productivity, and Corporate Financial Performance." *Academy of Management Journal* 38 (1995), pp. 635–72.
15. Welbourne, T.M., and A.O. Andrews. "Predicting the Performance of Initial Public Offerings: Should Human Resource Management Be in the Equation?" *Academy of Management Journal* 39 (1996), pp. 891–919.
16. Canada's 10 Most Admired Corporate Cultures™ 2007. Marty Parker, Managing Director, Waterstone Human Capital Ltd., Toronto. Retrieved February 26, 2009, at www.waterstonehc.com/resources/Canada's_10_Most_Admired_Corporate_Cultures_2007_booklet(3).pdf.
17. Pfeffer, J., and J.F. Veiga. "Putting People First for Organizational Success." *Academy of Management Executive* 13 (1999), pp. 37–48.
18. Bacon, F., M. Silverthorne, and L. Jardine. *The New Organon.* Cambridge: Cambridge University Press, 2000.

19. Campbell, J P. "The Role of Theory in Industrial and Organizational Psychology." In *Handbook of Industrial and Organizational Psychology,* Vol. 1, eds. M.D. Dunnette and L. M. Hough. Palo Alto, CA: Consulting Psychologists Press, 1990, pp. 39–74.

20. Whetten, D.A. "What Constitutes a Theoretical Contribution?" *Academy of Management Review* 14 (1989), pp. 490–95.

21. Locke, K. "The Grounded Theory Approach to Qualitative Research." In *Measuring and Analyzing Behaviour in Organizations,* eds. F. Drasgow and N. Schmitt. San Francisco, CA: Jossey-Bass, 2002, pp. 17–43.

22. Locke, E.A., and G.P. Latham. "What Should We Do About Motivation Theory? Six Recommendations for the Twenty-First Century." *Academy of Management Review* 29 (2004), 388–403.

23. Herzberg, F., B. Mausner, and B.B. Snyderman. *The Motivation to Work.* New York: John Wiley & Sons, 1959; Taylor, F.W. *The Principles of Scientific Management.* New York: Harper & Row, 1911.

24. Peterson, S.J., and F. Luthans. "The Impact of Financial and Nonfinancial Incentives on Business-Unit Outcomes over Time." *Journal of Applied Psychology* 91 (2006), pp. 156–65.

25. Shadish, W.R., T.D. Cook, and D.T. Campbell. *Experimental and Quasi-Experimental Designs for Generalized Causal Inference.* Boston, MA: Houghton-Mifflin, 2002.

26. Ibid.

27. Stajkovic, A.D., and F. Luthans. "A Meta-Analysis of the Effects of Organizational Behaviour Modification on Task Performance, 1975–1995." *Academy of Management Journal* 40 (1997), pp. 1122–49.

Chapter 2

1. "Walkerton Marks Five Years since Water Tragedy." *Canadian Press,* May 22, 2005. Retrieved February 26, 2009, at www.ctv.ca/servlet/ArticleNews/story/CTVNews/1116787827492_24/?hub=Health.

2. "InDepth: Inside Walkerton: Canada's Worst-Ever *E. coli* Contamination." CBC News Online, December 20, 2004. Retrieved February 26, 2009, at www.cbc.ca/news/background/walkerton.

3. *R. v. Koebel and Koebel,* Ontario Superior Court of Justice (Central West Region), November 2004. Agreed Statement of Fact.

4. Ibid.

5. Ibid.

6. "InDepth: Inside Walkerton: Canada's Worst-Ever *E. coli* Contamination." CBC News Online.

7. "Walkerton Chronology." CTV News, December 20, 2004. Retrieved February 26, 2009, at www.ctv.ca/servlet/ArticleNews/story/CTVNews/1103559265883_98968465.

8. Ibid.

9. Ibid.

10. *R. v. Koebel and Koebel.*

11. Ibid.

12. "InDepth: Inside Walkerton: Canada's Worst-Ever *E. coli* Contamination." CBC News Online.

13. Campbell, J.P. "Modeling the Performance Prediction Problem in Industrial and Organizational Psychology." In *Handbook of Industrial and Organizational Psychology,* Vol. 1, 2nd ed., eds. M.D. Dunnette and L.M. Hough. Palo Alto, CA: Consulting Psychologists Press, 1990, pp. 687–732; Motowidlo, S.J., W.C. Borman, and M.J. Schmit. "A Theory of Individual Differences in Task and Contextual Performance." *Human Performance* 10 (1997), pp. 71–83.

14. Borman, W.C., and S.J. Motowidlo. "Expanding the Criterion Domain to Include Elements of Contextual Performance." In *Personnel Selection in Organizations,* eds. N. Schmitt and W.C. Borman. San Francisco: Jossey-Bass, 1993, pp. 71–98.

15. National Occupational Classification (NOC) online. Retrieved May 4, 2008 at www5.hrsdc.gc.ca/NOC-CNP.

16. LePine, J.A., J.A. Colquitt, and A. Erez. "Adaptability to Changing Task Contexts: Effects of General Cognitive Ability, Conscientiousness, and Openness to Experience." *Personnel Psychology* 53 (2000), pp. 563–93.

17. Anderson, D.K. (Producer), P. Docter, L. Unkrich, and D. Silverman (Directors). *Monsters, Inc.* Emeryville, CA: Disney Pixar Studios, 2001.

18. "InDepth: Plane Fire at Pearson Airport: Flight 358." CBC News Online, August 8, 2005. Retrieved August 17, 2005, at www.cbc.ca/news/background/plane_fire.

19. Ilgen, D.R., and E.D. Pulakos. "Employee Performance in Today's Organizations." In *The Changing Nature of Work Performance: Implications for Staffing, Motivation, and Development,* eds. D.R. Ilgen and E.D. Pulakos. San Francisco: Jossey-Bass, 1999, pp. 1–20.

20. Pulakos, E.D., S. Arad, M.A. Donovan, and K.E. Plamondon. "Adaptability in the Workplace: Development of a Taxonomy of Adaptive Performance." *Journal of Applied Psychology* 85 (2000), pp. 612–24.

21. National Occupational Classification (NOC) online. Retrieved May 4, 2008 at www5.hrsdc.gc.ca/NOC-CNP.

22. Ibid.

23. Weber, J., and C. Palmeri, "'Vertical Evacuation' at the Hilton," *BusinessWeek,* September 19, 2005. Retrieved March 14, 2007, at http://proquest.com.

24. Borman and Motowidlo, "Expanding the Criterion Domain."

25. Organ, D.W. *Organizational Citizenship Behaviour: The Good Soldier Syndrome.* Lexington, MA: Lexington Books, 1988.

26. Coleman, V. I., and W.C. Borman. "Investigating the Underlying Structure of the Citizenship Performance Domain." *Human Resource Management Review* 10 (2000), pp. 25–44.

27. Coleman and Borman, "Investigating the Underlying Structure."

28. MacMillan, P. *The Performance Factor: Unlocking the Secrets of Teamwork.* Nashville, TN: Broadman & Holman Publishers, 2001.

29. LePine, J.A., R.F. Piccolo, C.L. Jackson, J.E. Mathieu, and J.R. Saul. "A Meta-Analysis of Teamwork Process: Towards a Better Understanding of the Dimensional Structure and Relationships with Team Effectiveness Criteria." *Personnel Psychology* 61/2 (2008), pp. 273–307.

30. Coleman and Borman, "Investigating the Underlying Structure."

31. Van Dyne, L., and J.A. LePine. "Helping and Voice Extra-Role Behaviour: Evidence of Construct and Predictive Validity." *Academy of Management Journal* 41 (1998), pp. 108–19.

32. Motowidlo, S.J. "Some Basic Issues Related to Contextual Performance and Organizational Citizenship Behaviour in Human Resource Management." *Human Resource Management Review* 10 (2000), pp. 115–26.

33. Podsakoff, P.M., S.B. MacKenzie, J.B. Paine, and D.G. Bachrach. "Organizational Citizenship Behaviours: A Critical Review of the Theoretical and Empirical Literature and Suggestions for Future Research." *Journal of Management* 26 (2000), pp. 513–63.

34. Podsakoff, P.M., M. Ahearne, and S.B. MacKenzie. "Organizational Citizenship Behaviour and the Quantity and Quality of Work Group Performance." *Journal of Applied Psychology* 82 (1997), pp. 262–70.

35. Walz, S.M., and B.P. Neihoff. "Organizational Citizenship Behaviours and Their Effect on Organizational Effectiveness in Limited-Menu Restaurants." In *Academy of Management Best Papers Proceedings,* eds. J.B. Keys and L.N. Dosier. Statesboro, GA: College of Business Administration at Georgia Southern University (1996), pp. 307–11.

36. Allen, T.D., and M.C. Rush. "The Effects of Organizational Citizenship Behaviour on Performance Judgments: A Field Study and a Laboratory Experiment." *Journal of Applied Psychology* 83 (1998), pp. 247–60; Avila, R.A., E.F. Fern, and O.K. Mann. "Unraveling Criteria for Assessing the Performance of Sales People: A Causal Analysis." *Journal of Personal Selling and Sales Management* 8 (1988), pp. 45–54; Lowery, C.M., and T.J. Krilowicz. "Relationships Among Nontask Behaviours, Rated Performance, and Objective Performance Measures." *Psychological Reports* 74 (1994), pp. 571–78; MacKenzie, S.B., P.M. Podsakoff, and R. Fetter. "Organizational Citizenship Behaviour and Objective Productivity as Determinants of Managerial Evaluations of Salespersons' Performance." *Organizational Behaviour and Human Decision Processes* 50 (1991), pp. 123–50; MacKenzie, S.B., P.M. Podsakoff, and R.

Fetter. "The Impact of Organizational Citizenship Behaviour on Evaluation of Sales Performance." *Journal of Marketing* 57 (1993), pp. 70–80; MacKenzie, S.B., P.M. Podsakoff, and J.B. Paine. "Effects of Organizational Citizenship Behaviours and Productivity on Evaluation of Performance at Different Hierarchical Levels in Sales Organizations." *Journal of the Academy of Marketing Science* 27 (1999), pp. 396–410; Motowidlo, S.J., and J.R. Van Scotter. "Evidence That Task Performance Should Be Distinguished from Contextual Performance." *Journal of Applied Psychology* 79 (1994), pp. 475–80; Podsakoff, P.M., and S.B. MacKenzie. "Organizational Citizenship Behaviours and Sales Unit Effectiveness." *Journal of Marketing Research* 3 (February 1994), pp. 351–63; Van Scotter, J.R., and S.J. Motowidlo. "Interpersonal Facilitation and Job Dedication as Separate Facets of Contextual Performance." *Journal of Applied Psychology* 81 (1996), pp. 525–31.

37. Rotundo, M., and P.R. Sackett. "The Relative Importance of Task, Citizenship, and Counterproductive Performance to Global Ratings of Job Performance: A Policy Capturing Approach." *Journal of Applied Psychology* 87 (2002), pp. 66–80.
38. Allen and Rush, "The Effects of Organizational Citizenship Behaviour on Performance Judgments"; Kiker, D.S., and S.J. Motowidlo. "Main and Interaction Effects of Task and Contextual Performance on Supervisory Reward Decisions." *Journal of Applied Psychology* 84 (1999), pp. 602–609; Park, O.S., and H.P Sims Jr. "Beyond Cognition in Leadership: Prosocial Behaviour and Affect in Managerial Judgment." Working paper, Seoul National University and Pennsylvania State University, 1989.
39. Robinson, S.L., and R.J. Bennett. "A Typology of Deviant Workplace Behaviours: A Multidimensional Scaling Study." *Academy of Management Journal* 38 (1995), pp. 555–72.
40. Morrison, E.W. "Role Definitions and Organizational Citizenship Behaviour: The Importance of the Employee's Perspective." *Academy of Management Journal* 37 (1994), pp. 1543–67.
41. Hofstede, G. *Cultures and Organizations: Software of the Mind.* New York: McGraw-Hill, 1991.
42. Rotundo, M., and J.L. Xie. "Understanding the Domain of Counterproductive Work Behaviour in China." Working Paper, University of Toronto, 2007.
43. Cellitti, D.R., "MCA Disco-Vision: The Record That Plays Pictures," June 25, 2002. Retrieved August 16, 2005, at www.oz.net/blam/DiscoVision/RecordPlaysPictures.htm.
44. Hollweg, L. *Inside the Four Walls of the Restaurant: The Reality & Risk of Counter-Productive Behaviors,* 2003. Retrieved August 17, 2005, at / www.batrushollweg.com/files/Website.Inside_the_Four_Walls_of_the_Restaurant1.Reprint_9.pdf.
45. Harper, D. "Spotlight Abuse—Save Profits." *Industrial Distribution* 79 (1990), pp. 47–51.
46. Hollinger, R.C., and L. Langton. *2004 National Retail Security Survey.* Gainesville, FL: University of Florida, Security Research Project, Department of Criminology, Law and Society, 2005.
47. Andersson, L.M., and C.M. Pearson. "Tit for Tat? The Spiraling Effect of Incivility in the Workplace." *Academy of Management Review* 24 (1999), pp. 452–71.
48. Ibid.
49. Sackett, P.R. "The Structure of Counterproductive Work Behaviours: Dimensionality and Performance with Facets of Job Performance." *International Journal of Selection and Assessment* 10 (2002), pp. 5–11.
50. Sackett, P.R., and C.J. DeVore. "Counterproductive Behaviours at Work." In *Handbook of Industrial, Work, and Organizational Psychology,* Vol. 1, eds. N. Anderson, D.S. Ones, H.K. Sinangil, and C. Viswesvaran. Thousand Oaks, CA: Sage, 2001, pp. 145–51.
51. Drucker, P.F. *The Practice of Management.* New York: Harper and Brothers, 1954.

Chapter 3

1. Levering, R., and M. Moskowitz. "In Good Company." *Fortune,* January 22, 2007, pp. 94–114.
2. Greene, J. "Troubling Exits at Microsoft." *BusinessWeek,* September 26, 2005, pp. 99–108.
3. Ibid.

4. Elgin, B. "Revenge of the Nerds—Again." *BusinessWeek,* August 8, 2005, pp. 28–31.
5. Greene, "Troubling Exits."
6. Greene, "Troubling Exits"; Greene, J. "Less Could Be More at Microsoft." *Business-Week,* October 3, 2005, p. 40.
7. Greene, "Less Could Be More."
8. "Largest Ever Study of Global Workforce Finds Senior Management Holds Trigger to Unleash Talent Potential: Towers Perrin Study Demonstrates Connection between Employee Engagement and Financial Performance." Towers Perrin news release, October 22, 2007. Retrieved February 26, 2009, at www.towersperrin.com/tp/showdctmdoc.jsp?url=HR_Services/Canada/English/Press_Releases/2007/20071022/2007_10_22.htm&country=global.
9. McDougall, M. "50 Best Employers in Canada 2007." Hewitt Associates and *The Globe and Mail's Report on Business Magazine.* Retrieved at www.hewittassociates.com/Intl/NA/en-CA/AboutHewitt/Newsroom/PressReleaseDetail.aspx?cid=3631.
10. Clarke, S. "Compensation Planning Outlook 2008: The 'Alberta Effect' Puts Upward Pressure on Pay," Conference Board of Canada, October 2007, pp. 13–18.
11. "Estimating Turnover Costs." Retrieved October 20, 2005 at www.keepemployees.com/turnovercost.htm.
12. Ahlrichs, N.S. *Manager of Choice.* Mountain View, CA: Davies-Black Publishing, 2003.
13. Mowday, R.T., R.M. Steers, and L.W. Porter. "The Measurement of Organizational Commitment." *Journal of Vocational Behaviour* 14, (1979), pp. 224–47.
14. Hulin, C.L. "Adaptation, Persistence, and Commitment in Organizations." In *Handbook of Industrial and Organizational Psychology,* Vol. 2, ed. M.D. Dunnette and L.M. Hough. Palo Alto, CA: Consulting Psychologists Press, Inc., 1991, pp. 445–506.
15. Allen, N.J., and J.P. Meyer. "The Measurement and Antecedents of Affective, Continuance and Normative Commitment to the Organization." *Journal of Occupational Psychology* 63 (1990), pp. 1–18; Meyer, J.P., and N.J. Allen. "A Three-Component Conceptualization of Organizational Commitment." *Human Resource Management Review* 1 (1991), pp. 61–89.
16. Meyer and Allen, "A Three-Component Conceptualization of Organizational Commitment."
17. Ibid.
18. Meyer, J.P., and N.J. Allen. *Commitment in the Workplace.* Thousand Oaks, CA: Sage, 1997; Meyer, J.P., and L. Herscovitch. "Commitment in the Workplace: Toward a General Model." *Human Resource Management Review* 11 (2001), pp. 299–326; Allen and Meyer, "The Measurement and Antecedents of Affective, Continuance and Normative Commitment to the Organization."
19. Reade, C. "Antecedents of Organizational Identification in Multinational Corporations: Fostering Psychological Attachment to the Local Subsidiary and the Global Organization." *International Journal of Human Resource Management* 12 (2001), pp. 1269–91.
20. Shaffer, M.A., and D.A. Harrison. "Expatriates' Psychological Withdrawal from International Assignments: Work, Nonwork, and Family Influences." *Personnel Psychology* 51 (1998), pp. 87–118; Hechanova, R., T.A. Beehr, and N.D. Christiansen. "Antecedents and Consequences of Employees' Adjustment to Overseas Assignment: A Meta-Analytic Review." *Applied Psychology: An International Review* 52 (2003), pp. 213–36.
21. Black, J.S., M. Mendenhall, and G. Oddou. "Toward a Comprehensive Model of International Adjustment: An Integration of Multiple Theoretical Perspectives." *Academy of Management Review* 16 (1991), pp. 291–317.
22. Shaffer and Harrison, "Expatriates' Psychological Withdrawal."
23. Hechanova, Beehr, and Christiansen, "Antecedents and Consequences of Employees' Adjustment."
24. Mowday, Steers, and Porter, "The Measurement of Organizational Commitment."
25. Ibid.
26. Meyer, J.P., D.J. Stanley, L. Herscovitch, and L. Topolnytsky. "Affective, Continuance, and Normative Commitment to the Organization: A Meta-Analysis of Antecedents, Correlates, and Consequences." *Journal of Vocational Behaviour* 61 (2002), pp. 20–52.

27. Mathieu, J.E., and D.M. Zajac. "A Review and Meta-Analysis of the Antecedents, Correlates, and Consequences of Organizational Commitment." *Psychological Bulletin* 108 (1990), pp. 171–94.

28. Johns, G. "The Psychology of Lateness, Absenteeism, and Turnover." In *Handbook of Industrial, Work, and Organizational Psychology,* eds. N. Anderson, D.S. Ones, H.K. Sinangil, and C. Viswesvaran. Thousand Oaks, CA: Sage, 2001, pp. 232–52.

29. Ibid.

30. Yerema, R. "Canada's Top 100 Employers 2008." *Maclean's,* October 15, 2007, pp. 43–46.

31. McDougall, "50 Best Employers in Canada 2007."

32. Stebbins, R.A. "On Misunderstanding the Concept of Commitment: A Theoretical Clarification." *Social Forces* 48 (1970), pp. 526–29.

33. Becker, H.S. "Notes on the Concept of Commitment." *American Journal of Sociology* 66 (1960), pp. 32–42.

34. Rusbult, C.E., and D. Farrell. "A Longitudinal Test of the Investment Model: The Impact of Job Satisfaction, Job Commitment, and Turnover of Variations in Rewards, Costs, Alternatives, and Investments." *Journal of Applied Psychology* 68 (1983), pp. 429–38.

35. Meyer and Allen, *Commitment in the Workplace;* Meyer et al., "Affective, Continuance, and Normative Commitment to the Organization: A Meta-Analysis of Antecedents, Correlates, and Consequences."

36. Meyer et al., "Affective, Continuance, and Normative Commitment to the Organization: A Meta-Analysis of Antecedents, Correlates, and Consequences."

37. Meyer, J.P., S.V. Paunonen, I.R. Gellatly, R.D. Goffin, and D.N. Jackson. "Organizational Commitment and Job Performance: It's the Nature of the Commitment That Counts." *Journal of Applied Psychology* 74 (1989), pp. 152–156; Meyer and Allen, *Commitment in the Workplace;* Meyer et al., "Affective, Continuance, and Normative Commitment to the Organization: A Meta-Analysis of Antecedents, Correlates, and Consequences."

38. Levering, R., and M. Moskowitz. "The 100 Best Companies to Work For." *Fortune,* January 24, 2005, pp. 64–94.

39. Yerema, "Canada's Top 100 Employers 2008."

40. Meyer, J.P., N.J. Allen, and C.A. Smith. "Commitment to Organizations and Occupations: Extension and Test of a Three-Component Conceptualization." *Journal of Applied Psychology* 78 (1993), pp. 538–51.

41. Meyer and Allen, "A Three-Component Conceptualization."

42. Grow, B. "The Debate over Doing Good." *BusinessWeek,* August 15, 2005, pp. 76–78.

43. "Wardrop honoured as one of the top 20 Employers of New Canadians." Wardrop Engineering news release, March 25, 2008. Retrieved June 16, 2008, at www.wardrop.com/News/ArchivedNews/2008News Releases/Wardrophonouredasoneofthetop20Employersof/tabid/169/Default.aspx.

44. Eisenberger, R., S. Armeli, B. Rexwinkle, P.D. Lynch, and L. Rhoades. "Reciprocation of Perceived Organizational Support." *Journal of Applied Psychology* 86 (2001), pp. 42–51; Eisenberger, R., R. Huntington, S. Hutchison, and D. Sowa. "Perceived Organizational Support." *Journal of Applied Psychology* 71 (1986), pp. 500–507; Rhoades, L., and R. Eisenberger. "Perceived Organizational Support: A Review of the Literature." *Journal of Applied Psychology* 87 (2002), pp. 698–714.

45. Clarke, "Compensation Planning Outlook 2008."

46. Rusbult, C.E., D. Farrell, C. Rogers, and A.G. Mainous III. "Impact of Exchange Variables on Exit, Voice, Loyalty, and Neglect: An Integrating Model of Responses to Declining Job Satisfaction." *Academy of Management Journal* 31 (1988), pp. 599–627.

47. Farrell, D. "Exit, Voice, Loyalty, and Neglect as Responses to Job Dissatisfaction: A Multidimensional Scaling Study." *Academy of Management Journal* 26 (1983), pp. 596–607.

48. Hirschman, A.O. *Exit, Voice, and Loyalty: Responses to Decline in Firms, Organizations, and States.* Cambridge, MA: Harvard University Press, 1970.

49. Ibid.

50. Farrell, "Exit, Voice, Loyalty, and Neglect."

51. Rusbult, Farrell, Rogers, and Mainous, "Impact of Exchange Variables."

52. Ibid.

53. Griffeth, R.W., S. Gaertner, and J.K. Sager. "Taxonomic Model of Withdrawal Behaviours: The Adaptive Response Model." *Human Resource Management Review* 9 (1999), pp. 577–90.

54. Hulin, C.L., M. Roznowski, and D. Hachiya. "Alternative Opportunities and Withdrawal Decisions: Empirical and Theoretical Discrepancies and an Integration." *Psychological Bulletin* 97 (1985), pp. 233–50.

55. Fisher, A. "Turning Clock-Watchers into Stars." *Fortune,* March 22, 2004, p. 60.

56. Ibid.

57. McDougall, "50 Best Employers in Canada 2007"; Gibbons, J. "Employee Engagement: A Review of Current Research and Its Implications," *Conference Board of Canada,* November 2006, p. 7.

58. Hulin, C.L. "Adaptation, Persistence, and Commitment in Organizations." In *Handbook of Industrial and Organizational Psychology,* Vol. 2, ed. M.D. Dunnette and L.M. Hough. Palo Alto, CA: Consulting Psychologists Press, Inc., 1991, pp. 445–506.

59. Lim, V.K.G. "The IT Way of Loafing on the Job: Cyberloafing, Neutralizing, and Organizational Justice." *Journal of Organizational Behaviour* 23 (2002), pp. 675–94.

60. "Does Cyberloafing Undermine Productivity?" *Management Issues News,* 2005, retrieved October 24, 2005, at www.management-issues.com/display_page.asp?section=research&id=1417.

61. "Cyberslacking." *MacMillan English Dictionary,* 2005, retrieved October 25, 2005, at www.macmillandictionary.com/New-Words/040604-cyberslacking.htm.

62. Leger, K. "Stealing time at work on Net: Companies cracking down on cyberslacking." *The Gazette,* April 4, 2008.

63. Lim, "The IT Way."

64. Koslowsky, M., A. Sagie, M. Krausz, and A.D. Singer. "Correlates of Employee Lateness: Some Theoretical Considerations." *Journal of Applied Psychology* 82 (1997), pp. 79–88.

65. Blau, G. "Developing and Testing a Taxonomy of Lateness Behaviour." *Journal of Applied Psychology* 79 (1994), pp. 959–70.

66. Hamper, B. *Rivethead: Tales from the Assembly Line.* New York: Warner Books, 1991.

67. Muchinsky, P.M. "Employee Absenteeism: A Review of the Literature." *Journal of Vocational Behaviour* 10 (1977), pp. 316–40.

68. Fichman, M. "Motivational Consequences of Absence and Attendance: Proportional Hazard Estimation of a Dynamic Motivation Model." *Journal of Applied Psychology* 73 (1988), pp. 119–34.

69. Martocchio, J.J., and D.I. Jimeno. "Employee Absenteeism as an Affective Event." *Human Resource Management Review* 13 (2003), pp. 227–41.

70. Nicholson, N., and G. Johns. "The Absence Culture and the Psychological Contract: Who's in Control of Absence?" *Academy of Management Review* 10 (1985), pp. 397–407.

71. Van Blerkom, M.L. "Class Attendance in Undergraduate Courses." *Journal of Psychology* 126 (1992), pp. 487–94.

72. Ibid.

73. Devadoss, S., and J. Foltz. "Evaluation of Factors Influencing Student Class Attendance and Performance." *American Journal of Agricultural Economics* 78 (1996), pp. 499–507.

74. Shimoff, E., and A. Catania. "Effects of Recording Attendance on Grades in Introductory Psychology." *Teaching of Psychology* 28 (2001), pp. 192–95.

75. Devadoss and Foltz, "Evaluation of Factors."

76. Bamberger, P., and M. Biron. "Group Norms and Excessive Absenteeism: The Role of Peer Referent Others." *Organizational Behavior and Human Decision Processes* 103 (2007), pp. 179–96; Gellatly, I.R. "Individual and Group Determinants of Employee Absenteeism: Test of a Causal Model." *Journal of Organizational Behavior* 16 (1995), pp. 469–86; Harrison, D., G. Johns, and J. Martocchio. "Changes in Technology, Teamwork and Diversity: New Directions for a New Century of Absenteeism Research." *Research in Personnel and Human Resource Management* 18 (2000), pp. 43–91; Martocchio, J.J. "The Effects of Absence Culture on Individual Absence." *Human Relations* 47 (1994), pp. 243–62; Rentsch, J.R. and R.P. Steel. "What Does Unit-Level Absence Mean? Issues for Future Unit-Level Absence Research." *Human Resource Management Review* 13 (2003), pp. 185–202.

77. Lee, T.W., and T.R. Mitchell. "An Alternative Approach: The Unfolding Model of Voluntary Employee Turnover." *Academy of Management Review* 19 (1994), pp. 51–89; Mitchell, T.R., and T.W. Lee. "The Unfolding Model of Voluntary Turnover and Job Embeddedness: Foundations for a Comprehensive Theory of Attachment." *Research in Organizational Behavior* 23 (2001), pp. 189–246.

78. Mobley, W. "Intermediate Linkages in the Relationship Between Job Satisfaction and Employee Turnover." *Journal of Applied Psychology* 62 (1977), pp. 237–40; Hom, P.W., R. Griffeth, and C.L. Sellaro. "The Validity of Mobley's (1977) Model of Employee Turnover." *Organizational Behaviour and Human Performance* 34 (1984), pp. 141–74.

79. Lee and Mitchell, "An Alternative Approach."

80. Porter, L.W., and R.M. Steers. "Organizational, Work, and Personal Factors in Employee Turnover and Absenteeism." *Psychological Bulletin* 80 (1973), pp. 151–76.

81. Griffeth, R.W., P.W. Hom, and S. Gaertner. "A Meta-Analysis of Antecedents and Correlates of Employee Turnover: Update, Moderator Tests, and Research Implications for the Next Millennium." *Journal of Management* 26 (2000), pp. 463–88; Rosse, J.G., and H.E. Miller. "Relationship Between Absenteeism and Other Employee Behaviours." In *Absenteeism: New Approaches to Understanding, Measuring, and Managing Employee Absence,* eds. P.S. Goodman and R. S. Atkin. San Francisco: Jossey-Bass, 1984, pp. 194–228; Rosse, J.G. "Relations among Lateness, Absence, and Turnover: Is There a Progression of Withdrawal?" *Human Relations* 41 (1988), pp. 517–31.

82. Hulin, "Adaptation, Persistence, and Commitment."

83. Koslowsky, Sagie, Krausz, and Singer, "Correlates of Employee Lateness."

84. U.S. Bureau of Labor Statistics, 2005. Retrieved October 26, 2005, at www.wnjpin.net/OneStopCareerCenter/LaborMarketInformation/lmi03/uslfproj.htm.

85. Dessler, G. "How to Earn your Employees' Commitment." *Academy of Management Executive* 13 (1999), pp. 58–67.

86. Meyer, J.P., and N.J. Allen. *Commitment in the Workplace.* Thousand Oaks, CA: Sage, 1997

87. Levering and Moskowitz, "In Good Company."

88. Cappelli, P. "Managing without Commitment." *Organizational Dynamics* 28 (2000), pp. 11–24.

89. Byrnes, N., and A. Barrett. "Star Search: How to recruit, train, and hold on to great people. What works, what doesn't." *BusinessWeek,* October 10, 2005, p. 68.

90. Ibid.

Chapter 4

1. "About Performance Plants Inc." Performance Plants Web site. Retrieved June 20, 2008, at www.performanceplants.com/media.html.

2. "Performance Plants Receives Largest Private Investment in Canadian Ag-Biotech: Company to Increase Capacity, Advance Drought Resistance Technology to Market." Performance Plants news release, June 19, 2006. Retrieved June 20, 2008 at www.performanceplants.com/newsrelease190606.html.

3. "Technology without Borders: *Leading Canadian Biotechnology Company, Performance Plants Inc. (PPI) and Africa Harvest Biotech Foundation International (AHBFI) Agree to Use Drought Tolerance Biotechnology Developed in Canada to Help Ensure Sustainable Food Production in Africa."* Performance Plants news release, September 24, 2007. Retrieved June 20, 2008 at www.performanceplants.com/newsrelease240907.html.

4. Innovation Place Web site. www.innovationplace.com.

5. Locke, E.A. "The Nature and Causes of Job Satisfaction." In *Handbook of Industrial and Organizational Psychology,* ed. M. Dunnette. Chicago, IL: Rand McNally, 1976, pp. 1297–1350.

6. Maxwell, J. "How Canada Stacks Up on Work, Health and Well-being." Presentation to the Health Work and Wellness Conference, Vancouver. Canadian Policy Research Networks, October, 2004.
7. Chapman, D. "A New Look at Job Satisfaction in Canada: Workopolis Study: The Top 20 Jobs in Canada." March 2007. Retrieved March 25, 2009, at http://promotions2.workopolis.com/content/promotions/top20jobs/en/Top20JobsWhitepaper.pdf.
8. Ibid.
9. Locke, "The Nature and Causes."
10. Dawis, R.V. "Vocational Interests, Values, and Preferences." In *Handbook of Industrial and Organizational Psychology,* Vol. 2, eds. M.D. Dunnette and L.M. Hough Palo Alto, CA: Consulting Psychologists Press, 1991, pp. 834–71.
11. Locke, "The Nature and Causes."
12. Judge, T.A., and A.H. Church. "Job Satisfaction: Research and Practice." In *Industrial and Organizational Psychology: Linking Theory with Practice,* eds. C.L. Cooper and E.A. Locke. Oxford, UK: Blackwell, 2000, pp. 166–98.
13. Locke, "The Nature and Causes."
14. Smith, P.C., L.M. Kendall, and C.L. Hulin. *The Measurement of Satisfaction in Work and Retirement.* Chicago: Rand McNally, 1969.
15. Lawler, E.E. *Pay and Organizational Effectiveness: A Psychological View.* New York: McGraw-Hill, 1971.
16. Locke, "The Nature and Causes."
17. Chapman, "A New Look at Job Satisfaction in Canada."
18. Layard, R. *Happiness.* New York: Penguin Press, 2005, p. 41.
19. R. Layard, qtd. in Diener, E., and E. Suh. "National Differences in Subjective Well-Being." In *Well-Being: The Foundations of Hedonic Psychology,* eds. D. Kahneman, E. Diener, and N. Schwarz. New York: Russell Sage Foundation, 1999.
20. Layard, *Happiness.*
21. Smith, Kendall, and Hulin, "The Measurement of Satisfaction."
22. Locke, "The Nature and Causes."
23. Smith, Kendall, and Hulin, "The Measurement of Satisfaction."
24. Locke, "The Nature and Causes."
25. Smith, Kendall, and Hulin, "The Measurement of Satisfaction."
26. Ibid
27. Chapman, "A New Look at Job Satisfaction in Canada."
28. Ironson, G.H., P.C. Smith, M.T. Brannick, W.M. Gibson, and K.B. Paul. "Construction of a Job in General Scale: A Comparison of Global, Composite, and Specific Measures." *Journal of Applied Psychology* 74 (1989), pp. 193–200; Russell, S.S., C. Spitzmuller, L.F. Lin, J.M. Stanton, P.C. Smith, and G.H. Ironson. "Shorter Can Also Be Better: The Abridged Job in General Scale." *Educational and Psychological Measurement* 64 (2004), pp. 878–93.
29. Rode, J.C., M.L. Arthaud-Day, C.H. Mooney, J.P. Near, T.T. Baldwin, W.H. Bommer, and R.S. Rubin. "Life Satisfaction and Student Performance." *Academy of Management Learning and Education* 4 (2005), pp. 421–33.
30. Taylor, F.W. *The Principles of Scientific Management.* New York: Wiley, 1911; Gilbreth, F.B. *Motion Study: A Method for Increasing the Efficiency of the Workman.* New York: Van Nostrand, 1911.
31. Hackman, J.R., and E.E. Lawler III. "Employee Reactions to Job Characteristics." *Journal of Applied Psychology* 55 (1971), pp. 259–86.
32. Hackman, J.R., and G.R. Oldham. *Work Redesign.* Reading, MA: Addison-Wesley, 1980.
33. Ibid.
34. Ibid
35. Hackman, J.R., and G.R. Oldham. "Motivation through the Design of Work: Test of a Theory." *Organizational Behaviour and Human Decision Processes* 16 (1976), pp. 250–79.
36. Hackman and Oldham, *Work Redesign.*
37. Turner, A.N., and P.R. Lawrence. *Industrial Jobs and the Worker.* Boston: Harvard University Graduate School of Business Administration, 1965.
38. Hackman and Lawler, "Employee Reactions."
39. Terkel, S. *Working: People Talk About What They Do All Day and How They Feel About What They Do.* New York: Pantheon Books, 1974, pp. 159–60.

40. Ibid., pp. 318–21.

41. Berns, G. *Satisfaction: The Science of Finding True Fulfillment.* New York: Henry Holt and Company, 2005, p. xiv.

42. Hackman and Oldham, *Work Redesign.*

43. Turner and Lawrence, *Industrial Jobs.*

44. Terkel, *Working,* p. xxxii.

45. Ibid., pp. 213–14.

46. Hackman and Oldham, *Work Redesign.*

47. Terkel, *Working,* pp. 107–109.

48. Ibid., p. 589.

49. Hackman and Oldham, *Work Redesign.*

50. Turner and Lawrence, *Industrial Jobs.*

51. Breaugh, J.A. "The Measurement of Work Autonomy. *Human Relations* 38 (1985), pp. 551–70.

52. Terkel, *Working,* pp. 49–50.

53. Ibid., pp. 458–61.

54. Hackman and Oldham, *Work Redesign.*

55. Terkel, *Working,* p. 346.

56. Ibid., pp. 295–96.

57. Fried, Y., and G.R. Ferris. "The Validity of the Job Characteristics Model: A Review and Meta-Analysis." *Personnel Psychology* 40 (1987), pp. 287–322.

58. Hackman and Oldham, *Work Redesign.*

59. Loher, B.T., R.A. Noe, N.L. Moeller, and M.P. Fitzgerald. "A Meta-Analysis of the Relation of Job Characteristics to Job Satisfaction." *Journal of Applied Psychology* 70 (1985), pp. 280–89.

60. Campion, M.A., and C.L. McClelland. "Interdisciplinary Examination of the Costs and Benefits of Enlarged Jobs: A Job Design Quasi-Experiment." *Journal of Applied Psychology* 76 (1991), pp. 186–98.

61. Ibid.

62. Morris, W.N. *Mood: The Frame of Mind.* New York: Springer-Verlag, 1989.

63. Watson, D., and A. Tellegen. "Toward a Consensual Structure of Mood." *Psychological Bulletin* 98 (1985), pp. 219–35; Russell, J.A. "A Circumplex Model of Affect." *Journal of Personality and Social Psychology* 39 (1980), pp. 1161–78; Larsen, R.J., and E. Diener. "Promises and Problems with the Circumplex Model of Emotion." In *Review of Personality and Social Psychology: Emotion,* Vol. 13, ed. M.S. Clark. Newbury Park, CA: Sage, 1992, pp. 25–59.

64. Ibid.

65. Weiss, H.M., and K.E. Kurek. "Dispositional Influences on Affective Experiences at Work." In *Personality and Work: Reconsidering the Role of Personality in Organizations,* eds. M.R. Barrick and A.M. Ryan. San Francisco: Jossey-Bass, 2003, pp. 121–49.

66. Lazarus, R.S. *Emotion and Adaptation.* New York: Oxford University, 1991.

67. Hochschild, A.R. *The Managed Heart: Commercialization of Human Feeling.* Berkeley, CA: University of California Press, 1983; Rafaeli, A., and R.I. Sutton. "The Expression of Emotion in Organizational Life." *Research in Organizational Behaviour* 11 (1989), pp. 1–42.

68. Hatfield, E., J.T. Cacioppo, and R.L. Rapson. *Emotional Contagion.* New York: Cambridge University Press, 1994.

69. Ashkanasy, N.M., C.E.J. Hartel, and C.S. Daus. "Diversity and Emotion: The New Frontiers in Organizational Behaviour Research." *Journal of Management* 28 (2002), pp. 307–38.

70. Judge, T.A., C.J. Thoreson, J.E. Bono, and G.K Patton. "The Job Satisfaction–Job Performance Relationship: A Qualitative and Quantitative Review." *Psychological Bulletin* 127 (2001), pp. 376–407; Sy, T., S. Côté, and R. Saavedra. "The Contagious Leader: Impact of the Leader's Mood on the Mood of Group Members, Group Affective Tone, and Group Processes." *Journal of Applied Psychology* 90 (2005), pp. 295–305.

71. Brief, A.P., and H.M. Weiss. "Organizational Behaviour: Affect in the Workplace." *Annual Review of Psychology* 53 (2002), pp. 279–307.

72. Isen, A.M., and R.A. Baron. "Positive Affect as a Factor in Organizational Behaviour." *Research in Organizational Behaviour* 13 (1991), pp. 1–53.

73. Lucas, R.E., and E. Diener. "The Happy Worker: Hypotheses about the Role of Positive Affect in Worker Satisfaction." In *Personality and Work: Reconsidering the Role of Per-*

sonality in Organizations, eds. M.R. Barrick and A.M. Ryan. San Francisco: Jossey-Bass, 2003, pp. 30–59.

74. Beal, D.J., H.M. Weiss, E. Barros, and S.M. MacDermid. "An Episodic Process Model of Affective Influences on Performance." *Journal of Applied Psychology* 90 (2005), pp. 1054–68.

75. Locke, "The Nature and Causes."

76. LePine, J.A., A. Erez, and D.E. Johnson. "The Nature and Dimensionality of Organizational Citizenship Behaviour: A Critical Review and Meta-Analysis." *Journal of Applied Psychology* 87 (2002), pp. 52–65.

77. George, J.M. "Trait and State Affect." In *Individual Differences and Behaviour in Organizations,* ed. K.R. Murphy. San Francisco: Jossey-Bass, 1996, pp. 145–71.

78. Dalal, R.S. "A Meta-Analysis of the Relationship Between Organizational Citizenship Behaviour and Counterproductive Work Behaviour." *Journal of Applied Psychology* 90 (2005), pp. 1241–55.

79. Sackett, P.R., and C.J. DeVore. "Counterproductive Behaviours at Work." In *Handbook of Industrial, Work, and Organizational Psychology,* Vol. 1, eds. N. Anderson, D.S. Ones, H.K. Sinangil, and C. Viswesvaran. Thousand Oaks, CA: Sage, 2001, pp. 145–51.

80. Cooper-Hakim, A., and C. Viswesvaran. "The Construct of Work Commitment: Testing an Integrative Framework." *Psychological Bulletin* 131 (2005), pp. 241–59; Harrison, D.A., D. Newman, and P.L. Roth. "How Important Are Job Attitudes? Meta-Analytic Comparisons of Integrative Behavioural Outcomes and Time Sequences." *Academy of Management Journal* 49 (2006),pp. 305–25; Meyer, J.P., D.J. Stanley, L. Herscovitch, and L. Topolnytsky. "Affective, Continuance, and Normative Commitment to the Organization: A Meta-Analysis of Antecedents, Correlates, and Consequences." *Journal of Vocational Behaviour* 61 (2002), pp. 20–52.

81. Ibid.

82. Saari, L.M., and T.A. Judge. "Employee Attitudes and Job Satisfaction." *Human Resource Management* 43 (2004), pp. 395–407.

83. Kinicki, A.J., F.M. McKee-Ryan, C.A. Schriesheim, and K.P. Carson. "Assessing the Construct Validity of the Job Descriptive Index: A Review and Meta-Analysis." *Journal of Applied Psychology* 87 (2002), pp. 14–32; Hanisch, K.A. "The Job Descriptive Index Revisited: Questions about the Question Mark." *Journal of Applied Psychology* 77 (1992), pp. 377–82; Jung, K.G., A. Dalessio, and S.M. Johnson. "Stability of the Factor Structure of the Job Descriptive Index." *Academy of Management Journal* 29 (1986), pp. 609–16.

84. Ironson, Smith, Brannick, Gibson, and Paul, "Construction"; Russell, Spitzmuller, Lin, Stanton, Smith, and Ironson, "Shorter Can Also Be Better."

85. Balzer, W.K., J.A. Kihn, P.C. Smith, J.L. Irwin, P.D. Bachiochi, C. Robie, E.F. Sinar, and LF. Parra. "Users' Manual for the Job Descriptive Index (JDI; 1997 version) and the Job in General Scales." In *Electronic Resources for the JDI and JIG,* eds. J.M. Stanton and C.D. Crossley. Bowling Green, OH: Bowling Green State University, 2000.

86. Ibid.

87. Ibid.

88. Saari and Judge, "Employee Attitudes."

Chapter 5

1. *Canadian Idol* Web site. www.ctv.ca/idol/gen/Home.html.
2. Ibid.
3. Ibid.
4. Miller, J., and M. Miller. "Get a Life!" *Fortune* 152, no. 11 (November 28, 2005), pp. 109–124, www.ProQuest.com, (March 27, 2007).
5. Shields, M. "Unhappy on the Job." *Health Reports,* Vol. 17, No. 4 (October 2006), pp. 33–37. Statistics Canada Catalogue 82-003.
6. Lazarus, R.S., and S. Folkman. *Stress, Appraisal, and Coping* (New York: Springer Publishing Company, Inc., 1984).
7. Ibid.
8. LePine, J.A., M.A. LePine, and C.L. Jackson. "Challenge and Hindrance Stress: Relationships with Exhaustion, Motivation to Learn, and Learning Performance." *Journal of Applied Psychology* 89 (2004), pp. 883–91; LePine, J.A., N.P.

Podsakoff, and M.A. LePine. "A Meta-Analytic Test of the Challenge Stressor–Hindrance Stressor Framework: An Explanation for Inconsistent Relationships among Stressors and Performance." *Academy of Management Journal* 48 (2005), pp. 764–75; Podsakoff, N.P., J.A. LePine, M.A. LePine. "Differential Challenge Stressor–Hindrance Stressor Relationships with Job Attitudes, Turnover Intentions, Turnover, and Withdrawal Behaviour: A Meta-Analysis." *Journal of Applied Psychology* 92 (2007), pp. 438–54.

9. LePine, J.A., M.A. LePine, and J.R. Saul. "Relationships among Work and Non-Work Challenge and Hindrance Stressors and Non-Work and Work Criteria: A Theory of Cross-Domain Stressor Effects." In *Research in Occupational Stress and Well Being,* ed. P.L. Perrewé and D.C. Ganster (San Diego: JAI Press/Elsevier, 6) pp. 35–72.

10. Kahn, R., D. Wolfe, R. Quinn, J.. Snoek, and R.A. Rosenthal. *Organizational Stress: Studies in Role Conflict and Ambiguity* (New York: John Wiley, 1964); Pearce, J. "Bringing Some Clarity to Role Ambiguity Research." *Academy of Management Review* 6 (1981), pp. 665–74.

11. Miller and Miller, "Get a Life!"

12. Glazer, S., and T.A. Beehr. "Consistency of Implications of Three Role Stressors Across Four Countries." *Journal of Organizational Behavior* 26 (2005), pp. 467–87.

13. Wilkins, K. "Work Stress among Health Care Providers." *Health Reports,* Vol. 18, No. 4 (November 2007), pp. 33–36. Statistics Canada Catalogue 82-003.

14. Ibid.

15. Glazer and Beehr, "Consistency of Implications."

16. Mandel, M. "The Real Reasons You're Working So Hard . . . and What You Can Do about It." *BusinessWeek* 3953 (October 3, 2005), pp. 60–67, www.ProQuest.com (March 27, 2007).

17. Block, S. "Day in the Life of a Production Assistant." *Canadian Idol* Web site. Retrieved February 7, 2008, at www.ctv.ca/servlet/ArticleNews/story/CTVNews/20080428/CI6_Day_in_life_PA_080428/20080918?s_name=idol2008&no_ads=.

18. McCall, M.W., M.M. Lombardo, and A.M. Morrison. *The Lessons of Experience: How Successful Executives Develop on the Job* (Lexington, MA: Lexington Books, 1988).

19. Neufeld, S. *Work-Related Stress: What You Need to Know,* (n.d.) http://healthyplace.healthology.com/focus_article.asp?f=mentalhealth&c=work_related_stress (October 27, 2005); www.breastcancerfocus.com/focus_article.asp?b=healthology&f=mentalhealth&c=work_related_stress&pg=1 (March 27, 2007).

20. Crouter, A. "Spillover from Family to Work: The Neglected Side of the Work–Family Interface." *Human Relations* 37 (1984), pp. 425–42; Rice, R.W., M.R. Frone, and D.B. McFarlin. "Work and Nonwork Conflict and the Perceived Quality of Life." *Journal of Organizational Behaviour* 13 (1992), pp. 155–68.

21. Holmes, T.H., and R.H. Rahe. "The Social Readjustment Rating Scale." *Journal of Psychosomatic Research* 11 (1967), pp. 213–18; U.S. Department of Health and Human Services. *Mental Health: A Report of the Surgeon General* (Rockville, MD: U.S. Department of Health and Human Services, Substance Abuse and Mental Health Services, National Institutes of Health Services Administration, Center for Health, National Institute of Mental Health, 1999), Ch. 4.

22. Lazarus and Folkman, *Stress, Appraisal, and Coping.*

23. Folkman, S., R.S. Lazarus, C. Dunkel-Schetter, A. Delongis, and R.J. Gruen. "Dynamics of a Stressful Encounter: Cognitive Appraisal, Coping, and Encounter Outcomes." *Journal of Personality and Social Psychology* 50 (1986), pp. 992–1003.

24. Latack, J.C., and S.J. Havlovic. "Coping with Job Stress: A Conceptual Evaluation Framework for Coping Measures." *Journal of Organizational Behaviour* 13 (1992), pp. 479–508.

25. Kahn et al. *Organizational Stress;* Lazarus and Folkman, *Stress, Appraisal, and Coping.*

26. Lazarus, R.S. "Progress on a Cognitive–Motivational–Relational Theory of Emotion." *American Psychologist* 46 (1991), pp. 819–34.

27. Daniels, C. "The Last Taboo: It's Not Sex. It's Not Drinking. It's Stress—and It's Soaring." *Fortune* 146, no. 8 (2002), pp. 136–44, www.ProQuest.com (March 27, 2007).

28. Miller and Miller, "Get a Life!"

29. Selye, H. *The Stress of Life.* (New York: McGraw-Hill, 1976).

30. Ibid.

31. Goldstein, D.L. *Stress, Catecholamines, & Cardiovascular Disease.* (New York: Oxford University Press, 1995).

32. Cannon, W.B. "Stresses and Strains of Homeostasis." *American Journal of Medical Science* 189 (1935), pp. 1–14.

33. Kahn, R.L., and P. Byosiere. "Stress in Organizations." In *Handbook of Industrial and Organizational Psychology,* Vol. 4. ed. M.D. Dunette, J.M.R. Hough, and H.C. Triandis. Palo Alto, CA: Consulting Psychologists Press, 1992), pp. 517–650.

34. Defrank, R.S., and J.M. Ivancevich. "Stress on the Job: An Executive Update." *Academy of Management Executive* 12 (1998), pp. 55–66; Haran, C. "Do You Know Your Early Warning Stress Signals?," 2005, http://abcnews.go.com/Health/Healthology/story?id=421825 (October 27, 2005).

35. Stöppler, M.C. "High Pressure Work Deadlines Raise Heart Attack Risk," http://stress.about.com/od/heartdissease/a/deadline.htm (October 1, 2005).

36. Leitner, K., and M.G. Resch. "Do the Effects of Job Stressors on Health Persist over Time? A Longitudinal Study with Observational Stress Measures." *Journal of Occupational Health Psychology* 10 (2005), pp. 18–30.

37. Defrank and Ivancevich, "Stress on the Job"; Haran, *Do You Know?*

38. Pines, A., and D. Kafry. (1978), "Occupational Tedium in the Social Services." *Social Work* 23, no. 6 (1978), pp. 499–507.

39. Defrank and Ivancevich, "Stress on the Job."

40. Friedman, M., and R.H. Rosenman. *Type A Behaviour and Your Heart.* (New York: Knopf, 1974).

41. Ganster, D.C. "Type A Behaviour and Occupational Stress. Job Stress: From Theory to Suggestion. *Journal of Organizational Behaviour Management* 8 (Special issue, 1987), pp. 61–84.

42. Friedman and Rosenman, *Type A Behaviour;* Yarnold, P.R., and F.B. Bryant. "A Note on Measurement Issues in Type A Research: Let's Not Throw Out the Baby with the Bath Water." *Journal of Personality Assessment* 52 (1988), pp. 410–19.

43. Abush, R., and E.J. Burkhead. "Job Stress in Midlife Working Women: Relationships among Personality Type, Job Characteristics, and Job Tension." *Journal of Counseling Psychology* 31 (1984), pp. 36–44; Dearborn, M.J., and J.E. Hastings. "Type A Personality as a Mediator of Stress and Strain in Employed Women." *Journal of Human Stress* 13 (1987), pp. 53–60; Howard, J.H., D.A. Cunningham, and P.A. Rechnitzer. "Role Ambiguity, Type A Behaviour, and Job Satisfaction: Moderating Effects on Cardiovascular and Biochemical Responses Associated with Coronary Risk." *Journal of Applied Psychology* 71 (1986), pp. 95–101.

44. Cooper, C.L., P.J. Dewe, and M.P. O'Driscoll. *Organizational Stress.* Thousand Oaks, CA: Sage Publications, 2001.

45. Fusilier, M.R., D.C. Ganster, and B.T. Mayes. "Effects of Social Support, Role Stress, and Locus of Control on Health. *Journal of Management* 13 (1987), pp. 517–28.

46. Jayaratne, S., T. Tripodi, and W.A. Chess. "Perceptions of Emotional Support, Stress, and Strain by Male and Female Social Workers." *Social Work Research and Abstracts* 19 (1983), pp. 19–27; Kobasa, S. "Commitment and Coping in Stress among Lawyers." *Journal of Personality and Social Psychology* 42 (1982), pp. 707–17; LaRocco, J.M., and A.P. Jones. "Co-Worker and Leader Support as Moderators of Stress–Strain Relationships in Work Situations." *Journal of Applied Psychology* 63 (1978), pp. 629–34.

47. Kahn and Byosiere, "Stress in Organizations."

48. LePine et al., "A Meta-Analytic Test."

49. Cohen, S. "After Effects of Stress on Human Performance and Social Behaviour: A Review of Research and Theory." *Psychological Bulletin* 88 (1980), pp. 82–108.

50. Podsakoff et al., "Differential Challenge Stressor–Hindrance Stressor Relationships."

51. Bedeian, A.G., and A. Armenakis. "A Path-Analytic Study of the Consequences of Role Conflict and Ambiguity." *Academy of Management Journal* 24 (1981), pp. 417–24; Schaubroeck, J., J.L. Cotton, and K.R. Jennings. "Antecedents and Consequences of Role Stress: A Covariance Structure Analysis." *Journal of Organizational Behaviour* 10 (1989), pp. 35–58.

52. LePine et al., "A Meta-Analytic Test"; Podsakoff et al., "Differential Challenge Stressor–Hindrance Stressor Relationships."

53. Cavanaugh, M.A., W.R. Boswell, M.V. Roehling, and J.W. Boudreau. "An Empirical Examination of Self-Reported Work Stress among U.S. Managers." *Journal of Applied Psychology* 85 (2000), pp. 65–74.

54. Boswell, W.R., J.B. Olson-Buchanan, and M.A. LePine. "The Relationship Between Work-Related Stress and Work Outcomes: The Role of Felt-Challenge and Psychological Strain." *Journal of Vocational Behaviour* 64 (2004), pp. 165–81.

55. LePine et al., "Challenge and Hindrance Stress."

56. Ibid.

57. "Canadian Employers Rate Health Plans over Cash," *The Globe and Mail,* May 12, 2004.

58. Perkins, A. "Medical Costs: Saving Money by Reducing Stress." *Harvard Business Review* 72, no. 6 (1994), p. 12.

59. Sauter, S., L. Murphy, M. Colligan, N. Swanson, J. Hurrell Jr., F. Scharf Jr., R. Sinclair, P. Grubb, L. Goldenhar, T. Alterman, J. Johnston, A. Hamilton, and J. Tisdale. *Is Your Boss Making You Sick?* http://abcnews.go.com/GMA/Careers/story?id=1251346&gma=true (October 27, 2005).

60. Defrank and Ivancevich, "Stress on the Job"; Cooper, C.L. "The Costs of Stress at Work." *The Safety & Health Practitioner* 19 (2001), pp. 24–26.

61. Burke, M.E. *2005 Benefits Survey Report.* Alexandria, VA: Society of Human Resource Management Research Department, 2005.

62. Miller and Miller, "Get a Life!"

63. Noe, R., J.R. Hollenbeck, B. Gerhart, P.M. Wright, and S. Steen. (2006). *Fundamentals of Human Resource Management,* 1st Canadian Edition. Toronto: McGraw-Hill Ryerson, 2006, p. 89.

64. LePine et al., "A Meta-Analytic Test"; Podsakoff et al., "Differential Challenge Stressor–Hindrance Stress Relationships."

65. Sonnentag, S., and M. Frese. "Stress in Organizations." In *Comprehensive Handbook of Psychology: Vol. 12. Industrial and Organizational Psychology,* eds. W.C. Borman, D.R. Ilgen, and R.J. Klimoski. New York: Wiley, 2003, pp. 453–91.

66. Eisenberger, R., R. Huntington, S. Hutchison, and D. Sowa. "Perceived Organizational Support." *Journal of Applied Psychology* 71 (1986), pp. 500–07.; Rhoades, L., and R. Eisenberger. "Perceived Organizational Support: A Review of the Literature." *Journal of Applied Psychology* 87 (2002), pp. 698–714.

67. Murphy, L.R. "Stress Management in Work Settings: A Critical Review of Health Effects." *American Journal of Health Promotion* 11 (1996), pp. 112–35.

68. Neufeld, *Work-Related Stress.*

69. Haran, *Do You Know?*

70. Ibid.

71. Daniels, "The Last Taboo."

72. Sonnentag and Frese, "Stress in Organizations."

73. Neufeld, *Work-Related Stress.*

74. Bachmann, K. "Health Promotion Programs at Work: A Frivolous Cost or a Sound Investment?" The Conference Board of Canada. October 2002.

75. Ibid.

Chapter 6

1. "Backgrounder." WestJet Web site. Retrieved March 27, 2009, at www.westjet.com/pdffile/westjetBackgrounder.pdf.

2. Ibid.

3. Rigby, B., and D. Caney. "Southwest Plans Canada Pact with WestJet." Reuters, July 8, 2008. Retrieved March 27, 2009, at www2.canada.com/edmontonjournal/news/business/story.html?id=f6b50671-b275-4c82-8566-22c6b0a7777f.

4. "Annual Report 2007." WestJet Web site. Retrieved March 27, 2009, at www.westjet.com/pdffile/WestJet2007AR.pdf.

5. "Backgrounder." WestJet Web site. Retrieved March 27, 2009, at www.westjet.com/pdffile/westjetBackgrounder.pdf.

6. Ibid.

7. Ibid.

8. Ibid.

9. Steers, R.M., R.T. Mowday, and D. Shapiro. "The Future of Work Motivation." *Academy of Management Review* 29 (2004), pp. 379–87. See also Latham, G.P. *Work Motivation: History, Theory, Research, and Practice.* Thousand Oaks, CA: Sage, 2006.

10. Latham, G.P., and C.C. Pinder. "Work Motivation Theory and Research at the Dawn of the Twenty-First Century." *Annual Review of Psychology* 56 (2005), pp. 485–516.

11. Maier, N.R.F. *Psychology in Industry.* 2nd ed. Boston: Houghton-Mifflin, 1955.

12. Vroom, V.H. *Work and Motivation.* New York: Wiley, 1964.

13. Ibid.; see also Thorndike, E.L. "The Law of Effect." *American Journal of Psychology* 39 (1964), pp. 212–22; Hull, C.L. *Essentials of Behaviour.* New Haven: Yale University Press, 1951; Postman, L. "The History and Present Status of the Law of Effect." *Psychological Bulletin* 44 (1947), pp. 489–563.

14. Bandura, A. "Self-Efficacy: Toward a Unifying Theory of Behavioural Change." *Psychological Review* 84 (1977), pp. 191–215.

15. Brockner, J. *Self-Esteem at Work.* Lexington, MA: Lexington Books, 1988.

16. Bandura, "Self-Efficacy."

17. Ibid.

18. Ibid.

19. Gist, M.E., and T.R. Mitchell. "Self-Efficacy: A Theoretical Analysis of its Determinants and Malleability." *Academy of Management Review* 17 (1992), pp. 183–211.

20. Vroom, *Work and Motivation.*

21. Stillings, J., and L. Snyder. "Up Front: The Stat." *BusinessWeek,* July 4, 2005, p. 12.

22. Stead, D. "Up Front: The Big Picture." *BusinessWeek,* May 29, 2006, p. 11.

23. Vroom, *Work and Motivation.*

24. Pinder, C.C. *Work Motivation. Glenview, IL: Scott, Foresman, 1984.*

25. Landy, F.J., and W.S. Becker. "Motivation Theory Reconsidered." In *Research in Organizational Behavior,* Vol. 9, ed. B.M. Staw and L.L. Cummings. Greenwich, CT: JAI Press, 1987, pp. 1–38; Naylor, J.C., D.R. Pritchard, and D.R. Ilgen. *A Theory of Behavior in Organizations.* New York: Academic Press, 1980.

26. Maslow, A.H. "A Theory of Human Motivation." *Psychological Review* 50 (1943), pp. 370–96; Alderfer, C.P. "An Empirical Test of a New Theory of Human Needs." *Organizational Behavior and Human Performance* 4 (1969), pp. 142–75.

27. Ibid.; see also Deci, E.L., and R.M. Ryan. "The 'What' and 'Why' of Goal Pursuits: Human Needs and the Self-Determination of Behaviour." *Psychological Inquiry* 11 (2000), pp. 227–68; Cropanzano, R., Z.S. Byrne, D.R. Bobocel, and D.R. Rupp. "Moral Virtues, Fairness Heuristics, Social Entities, and Other Denizens of Organizational Justice." *Journal of Vocational Behaviour* 58 (2001), pp. 164–209; Williams, K.D. "Social Ostracism." In *Aversive Interpersonal Behaviors,* ed. R.M. Kowalski. New York: Plenum Press, 1997, pp. 133–70; Thomas, K.W., and B.A. Velthouse. "Cognitive Elements of Empowerment: An 'Interpretive' Model of Intrinsic Task Motivation." *Academy of Management Review* 15 (1990), pp. 666–81.

28. Deci and Ryan, "The 'What' and 'Why'"; Naylor, Pritchard, and Ilgen, *A Theory of Behavior in Organizations;* Gagné, M., and E.L. Deci. "Self-Determination Theory and Work Motivation." *Journal of Organizational Behavior* 26 (2005), pp. 331–62.

29. Ibid.

30. Speizer, I. "Incentives Catch on Overseas, but Value of Awards Can Too Easily Get Lost in Translation." *Workforce,* November 21, 2005, pp. 46–49.

31. Rynes, S.L., B. Gerhart, and K.A. Minette. "The Importance of Pay in Employee Motivation: Discrepancies Between What People Say and What They Do." *Human Resource Management* 43 (2004), pp. 381–394; Rynes, S.L., K.G. Brown, and A.E. Colbert. "Seven Common Misconceptions about Human Resource Practices: Research Findings Versus Practitioner Beliefs." *Academy of Management Executive* 16 (2002), pp. 92–102.

32. Rynes, Gerhart, and Minette, "The Importance of Pay."

33. Ibid.

34. Mitchell, T.R., and A.E. Mickel. "The Meaning of Money: An Individual Differences Perspective." *Academy of Management Review* 24 (1999), pp. 568–78.

35. Tang, T.L. "The Meaning of Money Revisited." *Journal of Organizational Behavior* 13 (1992), pp. 197–202.

36. Tang, T.L. "The Development of a Short Money Ethic Scale: Attitudes Toward Money and Pay Satisfaction Revisited." *Personality and Individual Differences* 19 (1995), pp. 809–16.

37. Tang, "The Meaning of Money Revisited."

38. Tang, "The Meaning of Money Revisited"; Tang, "The Development of a Short Money Ethic Scale."

39. Tang, "The Development of a Short Money Ethic Scale."

40. Vroom, *Work and Motivation;* Lawler E.E. III, and J.L. Suttle. "Expectancy Theory and Job Behavior." *Organizational Behavior and Human Performance* 9 (1973), pp. 482–503.

41. Locke, E.A. "Toward a Theory of Task Motivation and Incentives." *Organizational Behavior and Human Performance* 3 (1968), pp. 157–89.

42. Locke, E.A., K.N. Shaw, L.M. Saari, and G.P. Latham. "Goal Setting and Task Performance: 1969–1980." *Psychological Bulletin* 90 (1981), pp. 125–52.

43. Locke, E.A., and G.P. Latham. *A Theory of Goal Setting and Task Performance.* Englewood Cliffs, NJ: Prentice Hall, 1990.

44. Ibid.; see also Locke, E.A., and G.P. Latham. "Building a Practically Useful Theory of Goal Setting and Task Motivation: A 35-Year Odyssey." *American Psychologist* 57 (2002), pp. 705–17; Latham, G.P. "Motivate Employee Performance through Goal-Setting." In *Blackwell Handbook of Principles of Organizational Behavior,* ed. E.A. Locke. Malden, MA: Blackwell, 2000, pp. 107–19.

45. Locke and Latham, *A Theory of Goal Setting.*

46. Locke et al., "Goal Setting and Task Performance."

47. Ibid.; Locke and Latham, *A Theory of Goal Setting;* Locke and Latham, "Building a Practically Useful Theory."

48. Wood, R.E., A.J. Mento, and E.A. Locke. "Task Complexity as a Moderator of Goal Effects: A Meta-Analysis." *Journal of Applied Psychology* 72 (1987), pp. 416–25.

49. Ibid.

50. Hollenbeck, J.R., and H.J. Klein. "Goal Commitment and the Goal-Setting Process: Problems, Prospects, and Proposal for Future Research." *Journal of Applied Psychology* 72 (1987), pp. 212–20; see also Locke et al., "Goal Setting and Task Performance."

51. Klein, H.J., M.J. Wesson, J.R. Hollenbeck, and B.J. Alge. "Goal Commitment and the Goal-Setting Process: Conceptual Clarification and Empirical Synthesis." *Journal of Applied Psychology* 84 (1999), pp. 885–96; Donovan, J.J., and D.J. Radosevich. "The Moderating Role of Goal Commitment on the Goal Difficulty–Performance Relationship. A Meta-Analytic Review and Critical Reanalysis." *Journal of Applied Psychology* 83 (1998), pp. 308–15.

52. Hollenbeck and Klein, "Goal Commitment and the Goal-Setting Process"; Klein et al., "Goal Commitment"; Locke, E.A., G.P Latham, and M. Erez. "The Determinants of Goal Commitment." *Academy of Management Review* 13 (1988), pp. 23–29; Latham, G.P. "The Motivational Benefits of Goal-Setting." *Academy of Management Executive* 18 (2004), pp. 126–29.

53. Shaw, K.N. "Changing the Goal Setting Process at Microsoft." *Academy of Management Executive* (2004), 18, 139–142.

54. Ibid.

55. Aguinis, H., and C.A. Henle. "The Search for Universals in Cross-Cultural Organizational Behaviour." In *Organizational Behaviour: The State of the Science,* ed. J. Greenberg. Mahwah, NJ: Erlbaum, 2003, 373–411.

56. Earley, P.C., and C.B Gibson. "Taking Stock in our Progress on Individualism–Collectivism: 100 Years of Solidarity and Community." *Journal of Management* 24 (1998), pp. 265–304.

57. Erez, M. "A Culture-Based Model of Work Motivation." *New Perspectives on International Industrial/Organizational Psychology,* ed. P.C. Earley and M. Erez. , 1997, pp. 193–242. San Francisco: New Lexington Press.

58. Erez, M., and P.C. Earley. "Comparative Analysis of

Goal-Setting Strategies Across Cultures." *Journal of Applied Psychology* 72 (1987), pp. 658–65.

59. Audia, P.G., and S. Tams. "Goal Setting, Performance Appraisal, and Feedback Across Cultures." In *Blackwell Handbook of Cross-Cultural Management,* ed. M.J. Gannon and K.L. Newman. Malden, MA: Blackwell, 2002, pp. 142–54.

60. Adams, J.S., and W.B. Rosenbaum. "The Relationship of Worker Productivity to Cognitive Dissonance about Wage Inequities." *Journal of Applied Psychology* 46 (1962), pp. 161–64.

61. Adams, J.S. "Inequity in Social Exchange." In *Advances in Experimental Social Psychology,* Vol. 2, ed. L. Berkowitz. New York: Academic Press, 1965, pp. 267–99; see also Homans, G.C. *Social Behaviour: Its Elementary Forms.* London: Routledge & Kegan Paul, 1961.

62. Ibid.

63. Adams, "Inequity in Social Exchange."

64. Ibid.

65. Greenberg, J. "Employee Theft as a Reaction to Underpayment Inequity: The Hidden Cost of Paycuts." *Journal of Applied Psychology* 75 (1990), pp. 561–68; Greenberg, J. "Stealing in the Name of Justice: Informational and Interpersonal Moderators of Theft Reactions to Underpayment Inequity." *Organizational Behaviour and Human Decision Processes* 54 (1993), pp. 81–103.

66. Adams, "Inequity in Social Exchange."

67. Scholl, R.W., E.A. Cooper, and J.F. McKenna. "Referent Selection in Determining Equity Perceptions: Differential Effects on Behavioural and Attitudinal Outcomes." *Personnel Psychology* 40 (1987), pp. 113–24.

68. Ibid.

69. Ibid.; see also Finn, R.H., and S.M. Lee. "Salary Equity: Its Determination, Analysis, and Correlates." *Journal of Applied Psychology* 56 (1972), pp. 283–92.

70. Scholl, Cooper, and McKenna, "Referent Selection."

71. Colella, A., R.L. Paetzold, A. Zardkoohi, and M. Wesson. "Exposing Pay Secrecy." *Academy of Management Review* 32 (2007), pp. 55–71.

72. Ibid.

73. Thomas, K.W., and B.A. Velthouse. "Cognitive Elements of Empowerment: An 'Interpretive' Model of Intrinsic Task Motivation." *Academy of Management Review* 15 (1990), pp. 666–81.

74. Hackman, J.R., and G.R. Oldham. *Work Redesign.* Reading, MA: Addison-Wesley, 1980.

75. Thomas and Velthouse, "Cognitive Elements of Empowerment"; Spreitzer, G.M. "Psychological Empowerment in the Workplace: Dimensions, Measurement, and Validation." *Academy of Management Journal* 38 (1995), pp. 1442–65; Deci, E.L., and R.M. Ryan. *Intrinsic Motivation and Self-Determination in Human Behaviour.* New York: Plenum, 1985; Hackman and Oldham, *Work Redesign.*

76. Thomas, K.W. *Intrinsic Motivation at Work: Building Energy and Commitment.* San Francisco, CA: Berrett-Koehler Publishers, 2000.

77. Ibid.

78. Thomas and Velthouse, "Cognitive Elements of Empowerment"; Spreitzer, "Psychological Empowerment."

79. Thomas, *Intrinsic Motivation at Work.*

80. Thomas and Velthouse, "Cognitive Elements of Empowerment"; Spreitzer, "Psychological Empowerment."

81. Thomas, *Intrinsic Motivation at Work.*

82. Thomas and Velthouse, "Cognitive Elements of Empowerment."

83. Thomas, *Intrinsic Motivation at Work.*

84. Ibid.

85. Locke, E.A., and G.P. Latham. *A Theory of Goal Setting and Task Performance.* Englewood Cliffs, NJ: Prentice Hall, 1990.

86. Van Eerde, W., and H. Thierry. "Vroom's Expectancy Models and Work-Related Criteria: A Meta-Analysis." *Journal of Applied Psychology* 81 (1996), pp. 575–86.

87. Cohen-Charash, Y., and P.E. Spector. "The Role of Justice in Organizations: A Meta-Analysis." *Organizational Behaviour and Human Decision Processes* 86 (2001), pp. 287–321; Colquitt, J.A., D.E. Conlon, M.J. Wesson, C.O.L.H.

Porter, and K.Y. Ng. "Justice at the Millennium: A Meta-Analytic Review of 25 Years of Organizational Justice Research." *Journal of Applied Psychology* 86 (2001), pp. 425–45.

88. Ibid.

89. Ibid.

90. Ibid.

91. Lawler, E.E., III. *Rewarding Excellence: Pay Strategies for the New Economy.* San Francisco, CA: Jossey-Bass, 2000.

92. Hansen, F. "Pushing Performance Management." *Workforce,* November 21, 2005. p. 22.

93. Latham, G., and S. Latham. "Overlooking Theory and Research in Performance Appraisal at One's Peril: Much Done, More to Do." In *Industrial and Organizational Psychology: Linking Theory with Practice,* ed. C.L. Cooper and E.A. Locke. Oxford, UK: Blackwell, 2000, pp. 199–215.

94. Ibid.

95. McGregor, J. "The Struggle to Measure Performance." *BusinessWeek,* January 9, 2006, pp. 26–28.

96. Scullen, S.E., P.K. Bergey, and L. Aiman-Smith. "Forced Distribution Rating Systems and the Improvement of Workforce Potential: A Baseline Simulation." *Personnel Psychology* 58 (2005), pp. 1–32.

Chapter 7

1. Useem, J. "Should We Admire Wal-Mart?" *Fortune,* March 8, 2004, pp. 118–20.

2. Ibid.

3. Fishman, C. *The Wal-Mart Effect.* New York: Penguin Books, 2006.

4. Serwer, A. "Bruised in Bentonville." *Fortune,* April 18, 2005, pp. 84–89.

5. "Wal-Mart Looks to Canada for Growth." Associated Press, March 21, 2007.

6. "Company Profile." Wal-Mart Canada Web site. Retrieved March 27, 2009, at www.walmart.ca/wps-portal/storelocator/Canada-About_Walmart.jsp.

7. McDougall, M. "50 Best Employers in Canada 2007." Hewitt Associates and *The Globe and Mail's Report on Business Magazine.* Retrieved at www.hewittassociates.com/Intl/NA/en-CA/AboutHewitt/Newsroom/PressReleaseDetail.aspx?cid=3631.

8. Gunther, M. "The Green Machine." *Fortune,* August 7, 2006, pp. 42–57.

9. Useem, "Should We Admire Wal-Mart?"

10. Serwer, "Bruised in Bentonville."

11. Ibid.; Gunther, "The Green Machine."

12. "Wal-Mart to Appeal Union Decision in Saint-Hyacinthe," CBC News, February 14, 2005. Retrieved March 27, 2009, at www.cbc.ca/canada/story/2005/02/13/walmart-quebec050213.html.

13. Millan, L. "Wal-Mart Wins Appeal in Quebec Union Dispute." *The Lawyers Weekly,* February 29, 2008. Retrived March 27, 2009 at www.lawyersweekly.ca/index.php?section=article&articleid=626.

14. Birger, J. "The Unending Woes of Lee Scott." *Fortune,* January 22, 2007, pp. 118–22.

15. Bernstein, A. "Wal-Mart vs. Class Actions." *BusinessWeek,* March 21, 2005, pp. 73–74.

16. Daniels, C. "Wal-Mart's Women Problem." *Fortune,* July 12, 2004, p. 28.

17. Useem, "Should We Admire Wal-Mart?"

18. Marquez, J. "Wal-Mart Puts on a New Face." *Workforce,* August 14, 2006, pp. 29–34.

19. Schlender, B. "Wal-Mart's $288 Billion Meeting." *Fortune,* April 18, 2005, pp. 90–106.

20. Berner, R. "Can Wal-Mart Fit into a White Hat?" *BusinessWeek,* October 3, 2005, pp. 94–96.

21. Mayer, R.C., J.H. Davis, and F.D. Schoorman. "An Integrative Model of Organizational Trust." *Academy of Management Review* 20 (1995), pp. 709–34; Rousseau, D.M., S.B. Sitkin, R.S. Burt, and C. Camerer. "Not So Different After All: A Cross-Discipline View of Trust." *Academy of Management Review* 23 (1998), pp. 393–404.

22. McDougall, "50 Best Employers in Canada 2007."

23. Ibid.

24. Greenberg, J. "A Taxonomy of Organizational Justice Theories." *Academy of Management Review* 12 (1987), pp. 9–22.

25. Lind, E.A. "Fairness Heuristic Theory: Justice Judgments as Pivotal Cognitions in Organizational Relations." In *Advances in Organizational*

Justice, eds. J. Greenberg and R. Cropanzano. Stanford, CA: Stanford University Press, 2001, pp. 56–88; Van den Bos, K. "Fairness Heuristic Theory: Assessing the Information to Which People Are Reacting Has a Pivotal Role in Understanding Organizational Justice." In *Theoretical and Cultural Perspectives on Organizational Justice,* eds. S. Gilliland, D. Steiner, and D. Skarlicki. Greenwich, CT: Information Age Publishing, 2001, pp. 63–84; Van den Bos, K., E.A. Lind, and H.A.M. Wilke. "The Psychology of Procedural and Distributive Justice Viewed from the Perspective of Fairness Heuristic Theory." In *Justice in the Workplace,* Vol. 2, ed. R. Cropanzano. Mahwah, NJ: Erlbaum, 2001, pp. 49–66.

26. Trevino, L.K., G.R. Weaver, and S.J. Reynolds. "Behavioral Ethics in Organizations: A Review." *Journal of Management* 32 (2006), pp. 951–90.

27. Douglas, M.J. "What Are the Most-Trusted Occupations?" Monster.ca, March 27, 2006.

28. McAllister, D.J. "Affect- and Cognition-Based Trust as Foundations for Interpersonal Cooperation in Organizations." *Academy of Management Journal* 38 (1995), pp. 24–59.

29. Ibid.

30. Mayer et al., "An Integrative Model"; Rotter, J.B. "A New Scale for the Measurement of Interpersonal Trust." *Journal of Personality* 35 (1967), pp. 651–65; Rotter, J.B. "Generalized Expectancies for Interpersonal Trust." *American Psychologist* 26 (1971), pp. 443–52; Rotter, J.B. "Interpersonal Trust, Trustworthiness, and Gullibility." *American Psychologist* 35 (1980), pp. 1–7.

31. Rosenberg, M. "Misanthropy and Political Ideology." *American Sociological Review* 21 (1956), pp. 690–95; Wrightsman, L.S. Jr. "Measurement of Philosophies of Human Nature." *Psychological Reports* 14 (1964), pp. 743–51.

32. Mayer et al., "An Integrative Model."

33. Jones, W.H., L.L. Couch, and S. Scott. "Trust and Betrayal: The Psychology of Getting Along and Getting Ahead." In *Handbook of Personality Psychology,* eds. R. Hogan, J.S. Johnson, and S.R. Briggs. San Diego, CA: Academic Press, 1997, pp. 465–82.

34. Stack, L.C. "Trust." In *Dimensionality of Personality,* eds. H. London and J.E. Exner, Jr. New York: Wiley, 1978, pp. 561–99.

35. Webb, W.M., and P. Worchel. "Trust and Distrust." In *Psychology of Intergroup Relations,* eds. S. Worchel and W.G. Austin. Chicago: Nelson-Hall, 1986, pp. 213–28; Erickson, E.H. *Childhood and Society.* 2nd ed. New York: Norton, 1963.

36. Stack, "Trust."

37. Mayer et al., "An Integrative Model."

38. McAllister, D.J. "Affect- and Cognition-Based Trust"; Lewicki, R.J., and B.B. Bunker. "Developing and Maintaining Trust in Work Relationships." In *Trust in Organizations: Frontiers of Theory and Research,* eds. R.M. Kramer and T.R. Tyler. Thousand Oaks, CA: Sage, 1996, pp. 114–39.

39. Mayer et al., "An Integrative Model."

40. Ibid.; Gabarro, J.J. "The Development of Trust, Influence, and Expectations." In *Interpersonal Behavior: Communication and Understanding in Relationships,* eds. G. Athos and J.J. Gabarro. Englewood Cliffs, NJ: Prentice-Hall, 1978, pp. 290–303.

41. Gabarro, "The Development."

42. Mayer et al., "An Integrative Model"; Gabarro, "The Development."

43. Mayer et al., "An Integrative Model"; Simons, T. "Behavioral Integrity: The Perceived Alignment Between Managers' Words and Deeds as a Research Focus." *Organization Science* 13 (2002), pp. 18–35; Dineen, B.R., R.J. Lewicki, and E.C. Tomlinson. "Supervisory Guidance and Behavioral Integrity: Relationships with Employee Citizenship and Deviant Behaviour." *Journal of Applied Psychology* 91 (2006), pp. 622–35.

44. Dineen et al. "Supervisory Guidance"; Bates, S. "Poll: Employees Skeptical about Management Actions." *HR Magazine,* June 2002, p. 12.

45. Mayer et al., "An Integrative Model."

46. Ibid.

47. Lewis, J.D., and A. Weigert. "Trust as a Social Reality." *Social Forces* 63 (1985), pp. 967–85.

48. McAllister, "Affect- and Cognition-Based Trust"; Lewicki and Bunker, "Developing and Maintaining Trust"; Lewis and Weigert, "Trust as Noncognitive Security."

49. McAllister, "Affect- and Cognition-Based Trust."

50. Lind, "Fairness Heuristic Theory: Assessing"; Van den Bos, "Fairness Heuristic Theory: Justice"; Van den Bos et al., "The Psychology of Procedural and Distributive Justice."

51. Adams, J.S. "Inequity in Social Exchange." In *Advances in Experimental Social Psychology,* Vol. 2, ed. L. Berkowitz. New York: Academic Press, 1965, pp. 267–99; Leventhal, G.S. "The Distribution of Rewards and Resources in Groups and Organizations." In *Advances in Experimental Social Psychology,* Vol. 9, eds. L. Berkowitz and W. Walster. New York: Academic Press, 1976, pp. 91–131.

52. Leventhal, "The Distribution of Rewards."

53. Ibid.

54. Levering, R., and M. Moskowitz. "In Good Company." *Fortune,* January 22, 2007, pp. 94–114.

55. Leventhal, G.S. "What Should Be Done with Equity Theory? New Approaches to the Study of Fairness in Social Relationships." In *Social Exchange: Advances in Theory and Research,* eds. K. Gergen, M. Greenberg, and R. Willis. New York: Plenum Press, 1980, pp. 27–55. Thibaut, J., and L. Walker. *Procedural Justice: A Psychological Analysis.* Hillsdale, NJ: Erlbaum, 1975.

56. Folger, R. "Distributive and Procedural Justice: Combined Impact of 'Voice' and Improvement on Experienced Inequity." *Journal of Personality and Social Psychology* 35 (1977), pp. 108–19.

57. Colquitt, J.A., D.E. Conlon, M.J. Wesson, C.O.L.H. Porter, and K.Y. Ng. "Justice at the Millennium: A Meta-Analytic Review of 25 Years of Organizational Justice Research." *Journal of Applied Psychology* 86 (2001), pp. 425–45.

58. Tyler, T.R., K.A. Rasinski, and N. Spodick. "Influence of Voice on Satisfaction with Leaders: Exploring the Meaning of Process Control." *Journal of Personality and Social Psychology* 48 (1985), pp. 72–81; Earley, P.C., and E.A. Lind. "Procedural Justice and Participation in Task Selection: The Role of Control in Mediating Justice Judgments." *Journal of Personality and Social Psychology* 52 (1987), pp. 1148–60; Lind, E.A., R. Kanfer, and P.C. Earley. "Voice, Control, and Procedural Justice: Instrumental and Noninstrumental Concerns in Fairness Judgments." *Journal of Personality and Social Psychology* 59 (1990), pp. 952–59; Korsgaard, M.A., and L. Roberson. "Procedural Justice in Performance Evaluation: The Role of Instrumental and Non-Instrumental Voice in Performance Appraisal Discussions." *Journal of Management* 21 (1995), pp. 657–69.

59. Noe, R.A., J.R. Hollenbeck, B. Gerhart, P.M. Wright, and S. Steen. *Fundamentals of Human Resource Management,* Canadian Edition. McGraw-Hill Ryerson: Toronto, 2006, pp. 42–46.

60. Ibid.

61. "Canada's Best Diversity Employers." Mediacorp Canada Inc. Retrived March 27, 2009, ad www.canadastop100.com/diversity. Canada's Best Diversity Employers is a trademark of Mediacorp Canada Inc.

62. Signed letter to Mr. Tony Keller, Managing Editor, Special Projects, *Maclean's* magazine, August 14, 2006, from Dalhousie University, McMaster University, Simon Fraser University, University of Alberta, University of British Columbia, University of Calgary, University of Lethbridge, University of Manitoba, Université de Montréal, University of Ottawa, and University of Toronto.

63. Brockner, J., and B.M. Wiesenfeld. "An Integrative Framework for Explaining Reactions to Decisions: Interactive E8ffects of Outcomes and Procedures." *Psychological Bulletin* 120 (1996), pp. 189–208.

64. Ibid.

65. Colquitt et al., "Justice at the Millennium"; Cohen-Charash, Y. and P.E. Spector. "The Role of Justice in Organizations: A Meta-Analysis." *Organizational Behavior and Human Decision Processes* 86 (2001), pp. 278–321.

66. Bies, R.J., and J.F. Moag. "Interactional Justice: Communication Criteria of Fairness." In *Research on Negotiations in Organizations,* Vol. 1, eds. R.J. Lewicki, B.H. Sheppard, and M.H. Bazerman. Greenwich, CT: JAI Press, 1986, pp. 43–55; Greenberg, J. "The Social Side of Fairness: Interpersonal and Informational Classes of Organizational Justice." In *Justice in the Workplace: Approaching Fairness in Human Resource Management,* ed. R. Cropanzano. Hillsdale, NJ: Erlbaum, 1993, pp. 79–103.

67. Bies, R.J. "Interactional (In) justice: The Sacred and the Profane." In *Advances in Organizational Justice,* eds. J. Greenberg and R. Cropanzano. Stanford, CA: Stanford University Press, 2001, pp. 85–108.

68. Sutton, R.I. *The No Asshole Rule.* New York: Warner Business Books, 2007.

69. Miner, A.G., T.M. Glomb, and C. Hulin. "Experience Sampling Mode and Its Correlates at Work." *Journal of Occupational and Organizational Psychology* 78 (2005), pp. 171–93.

70. Gilliland, S.W., L. Benson, and D.H. Schepers. "A Rejection Threshold in Justice Evaluations: Effects on Judgment and Decision-Making." *Organizational Behavior and Human Decision Processes* 76 (1998), pp. 113–31.

71. Tepper, B.J. "Consequences of Abusive Supervision." *Academy of Management Journal* 43 (2000), pp. 178–90.

72. Bies and Moag, "Interactional Justice"; Greenberg, "The Social Side of Fairness."

73. "RadioShack Fires 400 Employees by Email," http://abcnews.go.com/Technology/wireStory?id= 2374917& CMPOTC-RSSFeeds0312 (May 28, 2007).

74. Folger, R., and D.P. Skarlicki. "Fairness as a Dependent Variable: Why Tough Times Can Lead to Bad Management." In *Justice in the Workplace: From Theory to Practice,* ed. R. Cropanzano. Mahwah, NJ: Erlbaum, 2001, pp. 97–118.

75. Shaw, J.C., R.E. Wild, and J.A. Colquitt. "To Justify or Excuse?: A Meta-Analysis of the Effects of Explanations." *Journal of Applied Psychology* 88 (2003), pp. 444–58.

76. Orey, M. "Fear of Firing." *BusinessWeek,* April 23, 2007, pp. 52–62.

77. Greenberg, J. "Employee Theft as a Reaction to Underpayment Inequity: The Hidden Cost of Paycuts." *Journal of Applied Psychology* 75 (1990), pp. 561–68.

78. Colquitt et al., "Justice at the Millennium"; Cohen-Charash and Spector, "The Role of Justice."

79. Trevino et al., "Behavioral Ethics."

80. Trevino et al., "Behavioral Ethics"; Rest, J.R. *Moral Development: Advances in Research and Theory.* New York: Praeger, 2006; Butterfield, K.D., L.K. Trevino, and G.R. Weaver. "Moral Awareness in Business Organizations: Influences of Issue-Related and Social Context Factors." *Human Relations* 53 (2000), pp. 981–1018.

81. Trevino et al., "Behavioral Ethics"; Rest, *Moral Development.*

82. Butterfield et al., "Moral Awareness."

83. Robertson, D.C. "Business Ethics Across Cultures." In *The Blackwell Handbook of Cross- Cultural Management,* eds. M.J. Gannon and K.L. Newman. Malden, MA: Blackwell, 2002, pp. 361–92.

84. Robertson, "Business Ethics Across Cultures."

85. McLean, B. "Sex, Lies, and Videogames." *Fortune,* August 22, 2005, pp. 66–70.

86. Sparks, J.R., and S.D. Hunt. "Marketing Research Ethical Sensitivity: Conceptualization, Measurement, and Exploratory Investigation." *Journal of Marketing* 62 (1998), pp. 92–109.

87. Jones, T.M. "Ethical Decision Making by Individuals in Organizations: An Issue-Contingent Model." *Academy of Management Review* 16 (1991), pp. 366–95; Butterfield et al., "Moral Awareness."

88. Trevino et al., "Behavioral Ethics"; Rest, *Moral Development.*

89. Kohlberg, L. "Stage and Sequence: The Cognitive Developmental Approach to Socialization." In *Handbook of Socialization Theory,* ed. D.A. Goslin. Chicago: Rand McNally, 1969, pp. 347–480; Kohlberg, L. "The Claim to Moral Adequacy of a Highest Stage of Moral Judgment." *Journal of Philosophy* 70 (1973), pp. 630–46.

90. Trevino et al., "Behavioral Ethics."

91. Ibid.; Rest, J., D. Narvaez, M.J. Bebeau, and S.J. Thoma. *Postconventional Moral Thinking: A Neo-Kohlbergian Approach.* Mahwah, NJ: Lawrence Erlbaum, 1999.

92. Forsyth, D.R. "A Taxonomy of Ethical Ideologies." *Journal of Personality and Social Psychology* 39 (1980), pp. 175–84.

93. Ibid.

94. Ibid.

95. Schminke, M., M.L. Ambrose, and T.W. Noel. "The Effect of Ethical Frameworks on Perceptions of Organizational Justice." *Academy of Management Journal* 40 (1997), pp. 1190–1207; Brady, F.N., and G.E. Wheeler. "An Empirical Study of Ethical Predispositions." *Journal of Business Ethics* 15 (1996), pp. 927–40.

96. Ibid.

97. Forsyth, "A Taxonomy of Ethical Ideologies."

98. Ibid.

99. Schminke et al., "The Effect of Ethical Frameworks"; Brady and Wheeler, "An Empirical Study of Ethical Predispositions."

100. Ibid.

101. Trevino et al., "Behavioral Ethics"; Rest, *Moral Development.*

102. Bergman, R. "Identity as Motivation: Toward a Theory of the Moral Self." In *Moral Development, Self and Identity,* eds. D.K. Lapsley and D. Narvaez. Mahwah, NJ: Lawrence Erlbaum, 2004, pp. 21–46.

103. Trevino et al., "Behavioral Ethics"; Schweitzer, M.E., L. Ordonez, and B. Douma. "Goal Setting as a Motivator of Unethical Behaviour." *Academy of Management Journal* 47 (2004), pp. 422–32.

104. Oh, H. "Biz Majors Get an F for Honesty." *BusinessWeek,* February 6, 2006, p. 14.

105. McCabe, D.L. "Academic Dishonesty in Graduate Business Programs: Prevalence, Causes, and Proposed Action." *Academy of Management Learning and Education* 5 (2006), pp. 294–305.

106. "Ryerson Student Fighting Cheating Charges for Facebook Study Group." CBC News, March 6, 2008. Retrieved January 4, 2009, at /www.cbc.ca/canada/toronto/story/ 2008/03/06/facebook-study.html?ref=rss.

107. Mayer, R.C., and M.B. Gavin. "Trust in Management and Performance: Who Minds the Shop While the Employees Watch the Boss?" *Academy of Management Journal* 48 (2005), pp. 874–88.

108. Blau, P. *Exchange and Power in Social Life.* New York: Wiley, 1964; Shore, L.M., L.E. Tetrick, P. Lynch, and K. Barksdale. "Social and Economic Exchange: Construct Development and Validation." *Journal of Applied Social Psychology* 36 (2006), pp. 837–67.

109. Ibid.

110. Dirks, K.T., and D.L. Ferrin. "Trust in Leadership: Meta-Analytic Findings and Implications for Research and Practice." *Journal of Applied Psychology* 87 (2002), pp. 611–28.

111. Ibid.

112. Carroll, A.B. "A Three-Dimensional Model of Corporate Social Performance." *Academy of Management Review* 4 (1979), pp. 497–505; Carroll, A.B. "The Pyramid of Corporate Social Responsibility: Toward the Moral Management of Organizational Stakeholders." *Business Horizons* 34 (1991), pp. 39–48; Carroll, A.B. "The Four Faces of Corporate Citizenship." *Business and Society Review* 100 (1998), pp. 1–7; Carroll, A.B. "Corporate Social Responsibility—Evolution of a Definitional Construct." *Business and Society* 38 (1999), pp. 268–95.

113. Carroll, "The Pyramid."

114. Noe et al., Fundamentals of Human Resource Management.

115. Ibid.

116. Carroll, "The Pyramid."

117. "TELUS Corporation's Ethics Policy." February 2008.

118. Ibid.

119. "2007 Corporate Social Responsibility Report." TELUS Corporation.

120. Carroll, "The Pyramid."

121. JumpStart Web site. Retrieved July 15, 2008, at www.canadiantire.ca/jumpstart/index.html.

122. "2007 Corporate Social Responsibility Report." TELUS Corporation.

123. Ibid.

Chapter 8

1. "Fact Sheet." Pricewaterhouse Coopers corporate Web site. Retrieved April 3, 2009, at www.pwc.com/extweb/aboutus.nsf/ docid/F818240917F5AD7785256EA90054D768/$file/fact_sheet.pdf; "Facts & Figures." Deloitte corporate Web site. Retrieved April 3, 2009, at www.deloitte.com/dtt/section_ node/0,1042, sid%253D147431, 00.html; "KPMG Says 2007 Revenue Rises," Reuters News Service, November 28, 2007. Retrieved April 3, 2009, at http://uk.reuters.com/article/hotStocksNews/idUKWNAS330920071128; "Ernst & Young Fiscal Year 2007 Global Revenues Rise 15% to US$21.1 Billion." Ernst & Young press release, November 1, 2007. Retrieved April 3, 2009, at www.ey.com/global/content.nsf/International/Media_-_Press_Release_-_Revenues_FY2007.

2. "KPMG Says 2007 Revenue Rises," Reuters News Service.
3. Ibid.
4. Weiss, H.M. "Learning Theory and Industrial and Organizational Psychology." In *Handbook of Industrial and Organizational Psychology,* eds. M.D. Dunnette and L.M. Hough. Palo Alto, CA: Consulting Psychologists Press, 1990, pp. 75–169.
5. Tai, B., and N.R. Lockwood. "Organizational Entry: Onboarding, Orientation, and Socialization." *SHRM Research Paper.* www.shrm.org. Accessed June 4, 2007.
6. Buford, B. *Heat.* New York: Knopf, 2006, pp. 49–50.
7. Ericsson, K.A. "An Introduction to *Cambridge Handbook of Expertise and Expert Performance:* Its Development, Organization, and Content." In *The Cambridge Handbook of Expertise and Expert Performance,* eds. K.A. Ericsson, N. Charness, P.J. Feltovich, and R.R. Hoffman. New York: Cambridge University Press, 2006, pp. 3–19.
8. Ericsson, K.A., and A.C. Lehmann. "Experts and Exceptional Performance: Evidence of Maximal Adaptation to Task Constraints." *Annual Review of Psychology* 47 (1996), pp. 273–305.
9. Brockmann, E.N., and W.P. Anthony. "Tacit Knowledge and Strategic Decision Making." *Group & Organizational Management* 27 (December 2002), pp. 436–55.
10. Wagner, R.K., and R.J. Sternberg. "Practical Intelligence in Real-World Pursuits: The Role of Tacit Knowledge." *Journal of Personality and Social Psychology* 4 (1985), pp. 436–58.
11. Wah, L. "Making Knowledge Stick." *Management Review* 88 (1999), pp. 24–33.
12. Eucker, T.R. "Understanding the Impact of Tacit Knowledge Loss." *Knowledge Management Review* March 2007, pp. 10–13.
13. McAdam, R., B. Mason, and J. McCrory. "Exploring the Dichotomies Within the Tacit Knowledge Literature: Towards a Process of Tacit Knowing in Organizations." *Journal of Knowledge Management* 11 (2007), pp. 43–59.
14. Lawson, C., and E. Lorenzi. "Collective Learning, Tacit Knowledge, and Regional Innovative Capacity." *Regional Studies* 21 (1999), pp. 487–513.
15. Nonaka, I. "The Knowledge-Creating Company." *Harvard Business Review* 69 (1991), pp. 96–104; Nonaka, I. "A Dynamic Theory of Organizational Knowledge Creation." *Organizational Science* 5 (1994), pp. 14–37.
16. Luthans, F., and R. Kreitner. *Organizational Behaviour Modification and Beyond.* Glenview, IL: Scott, Foresman, 1985.
17. Latham, G.P., and V.L. Huber. "Schedules of Reinforcement: Lessons from the Past and Issues for Future." *Journal of Organizational Behaviour Management* 13 (1992), pp. 125–49.
18. Luthans and Kreitner, *Organizational Behaviour Modification.*
19. Bandura, A. *Social Foundations of Thought and Action: A Social Cognitive Theory.* Englewood Cliffs, NJ: Prentice Hall, 1986.
20. Weiss, "Learning Theory."
21. Pescuric, A., and W.C. Byham. "The New Look of Behaviour Modeling." *Training & Development* 50 (July 1996), pp. 24–30.
22. Sims, R.R., and J. Brinkmann. "Leaders as Moral Role Models: The Case of John Gutfreund at Salomon Brothers." *Journal of Business Ethics* 35 (2002), pp. 327–40.
23. VandeWalle, D. "Development and Validation of a Work Domain Goal Orientation Instrument." *Educational and Psychological Measurement* 8 (1997), pp. 995–1015.

24. Payne, S.C., S. Youngcourt, and J.M. Beaubien. "A Meta-Analytic Examination of the Goal Orientation Nomological Net." *Journal of Applied Psychology* 92 (2007), pp. 128–50.

25. Ibid.

26. Dane, E., and M.G. Pratt. "Exploring Intuition and Its Role in Managerial Decision Making." *Academy of Management Review,* 32 (2007), pp. 33–54. Hayashi, A.M. "When to Trust Your Gut." *Harvard Business Review,* February 2001, pp. 59–65.

27. March, J.G. *A Primer on Decision Making.* New York: The Free Press, 1994.

28. www.quotationspage.com/quote/25953.html (April 2007).

29. Simon, H.A. "A Behavioural Model of Rational Choice." *Quarterly Journal of Economics* 69 (1955), pp. 99–118.

30. Simon, H.A. "Rational Decision Making in Organizations." *American Economic Review* 69 (1979), pp. 493–513.

31. March, J.G., and H.A. Simon. *Organizations.* New York: Wiley, 1958.

32. Hogg, M.A., and D.J. Terry. "Social Identity and Self-Categorization Process in Organizational Contexts." *Academy of Management Review* 25 (January 2000), pp. 121–40.

33. Judd, C.M., and B. Park. "Definition and Assessment of Accuracy in Social Stereotypes." *Psychological Review* 100 (January 1993), pp. 109–28.

34. Ashforth, B.E., and F. Mael. "Social Identity Theory and the Organization." *Academy of Management Review* 14 (1989), pp. 20–39; Howard, J.A. "Social Psychology of Identities." *Annual Review of Sociology* 26 (2000), pp. 367–93.

35. RBC Web site (www.rbc.com), accessed April 2008; Hirji, Z. "Growth and Innovation Rests on Diversity." *Canadian HR Reporter,* December 2006, p. 18; Shin, M. "Minority Report." *CorporateKnights: The Cleantech Issue* 2007, Volume 6.2, pp. 34–42.

36. Kahneman, D., and A. Tversky. "On the Psychology of Prediction." *Psychological Review* 80 (1973), pp. 237–51.

37. Ross, L. "The Intuitive Psychologist and His Shortcomings: Distortions in the Attribution Process." In *Advances in Experimental Social Psychology,* ed. L. Berkowitz. New York: Academic Press, 1977, pp. 173–220. See also Jones, E.E., and V.A. Harris. "The Attribution of Attitudes." *Journal of Experimental Social Psychology* 3 (1967), pp. 1–24.

38. Zemba, Y., M.I. Young, and M.W. Morris. "Blaming Leaders for Organizational Accidents: Proxy Logic in Collective versus Individual-Agency Cultures." *Organizational Behaviour and Human Decision Processes* 101 (2006), pp. 36–51.

39. Menon, T., M.W. Morris, C. Chiu, and Y. Hong. "Culture and the Construal of Agency: Attribution to Individual Versus Group Dispositions." *Journal of Personality and Social Psychology* 76 (1999), pp. 701–17.

40. Zemba et al., "Blaming Leaders."

41. Chiu, C., M.W. Morris, Y. Hong, and T. Menon. "Motivated Cultural Cognition: The Impact of Implicit Cultural Theories on Dispositional Attribution Varies as a Function of Need for Closure." *Journal of Personality and Social Psychology* 78 (2000), pp. 247–59.

42. Zemba et al., "Blaming Leaders."

43. Kelley, H.H. "The Processes of Casual Attribution." *American Psychologist* 28 (1973), pp. 107–28; Kelley, H.H. "Attribution in Social Interaction." In *Attribution: Perceiving the Causes of Behaviour,* ed. E. Jones . Morristown, NJ: General Learning Press, 1972.

44. Staw, B.M., and J. Ross. "Behaviour in Escalation Situations: Antecedents, Prototypes, and Solutions." In *Research in Organizational Behaviour,* Vol. 9, eds. L.L. Cummings and B.M. Staw. Greenwich, CT: JAI Press, 1987, pp. 39–78; Staw, B.M. "Knee-Deep in the Big Muddy: A Study of Escalating Commitment to a Chosen Course of Action." *Organizational Behaviour and Human Performance* 16 (1976), pp. 27–44.

45. Brockner, J. "The Escalation of Commitment to a Failing Course of Action: Toward Theoretical Progress." *Academy of Management Review* 17 (1992), pp. 39–61; Staw, B.M. "The Escalation of Commitment: An Update and Appraisal." In *Organizational Decision Making,* ed. Z. Shapira. New York: Cambridge University Press, 1997.

46. Ibid.

47. Conlon, D.E., and H. Garland. "The Role of Project Completion Information in Resource Allocation Decisions." *Academy of Management Journal* 36 (1993), pp. 402–13; Moon, H. "Looking Forward and Looking Back: Integrating Completion and Sunk-Cost Effects within an Escalation of Commitment Progress Decision." *Journal of Applied Psychology* 86 (2001), pp. 104–13.

48. Averbrook, J. "Connecting CLO's with the Recruiting Process." *Chief Learning Officer* 4 (2005), pp. 24–27.

49. "Spending on Learning and Training Is Increasing: ASTD Report." *HR Focus* 83 (2006), p. 9.

50. Carnevale, A.P. "The Learning Enterprise." *Training and Development Journal,* February 1989, pp. 26–37.

51. "$56 Billion Budgeted for Formal Training." *Training* 43 (2006), pp. 20–32.

52. Folkers, D. "Competing in the Marketspace: Incorporating Online Education into Higher Education–An Organizational Perspective." *Information Resources Management Journal* 18 (2005), pp. 61–77.

53. Golden, D. "Degrees@StateU: Online University Enrollment Soars as Quality Improves; Tuition Funds Other Projects." *The Wall Street Journal,* May 9, 2006, p. B1.

54. Ibid.

55. Arbaugh, J.B. "Is There an Optimal Design for On-Line MBA Courses?" *Academy of Management Learning and Education* 4 (2005), pp. 135–49.

56. Clark, R.C. "Harnessing the Virtual Classroom." *T + D* 59(2005), pp. 40–45.

57. Tyler, K. "Training Revs Up." *HRMagazine,* 50 (2005), pp. 58–63.

58. Stamps, D. "Communities of Practice." *Training,* February 1997, pp. 35–42.

59. Sauve, E. "Informal Knowledge Transfer." *T + D* 61 (2007), pp. 22–24.

60. Allan, B., and D. Lewis. "Virtual Learning Communities as a Vehicle for Workforce Development: A Case Study." *Journal of Workplace Learning* 18 (2006), pp. 367–83.

61. Noe, R.A. *Employee Training and Development.* Burr Ridge, IL: Irwin/McGraw-Hill, 1999.

62. Tracey, J.B., S.I. Tannenbaum, and M.J. Kavanaugh. "Applying Trained Skills on the Job: The Importance of the Work Environment." *Journal of Applied Psychology* 80 (1995), pp. 239–52.

63. Ibid.

Chapter 9

1. Ferguson, C.H. "What's Next for Google?" *Technology Review* 108, no. 1 (January 2005), pp. 38–46.

2. Elgin, B. "Google's Leap May Slow Rival's Growth." *BusinessWeek* 3943, no. 45 (July 18, 2005). ProQuest database (May 14, 2007).

3. "Brain Teasers Help Google Recruit Workers." *CNN.com Technology.* November 4, 2004, www.topcoder.com/pressroom/cnn_110404.pdf (June 2, 2006).

4. Eustace, A. "Pencils Down, People." *Google Blog.* September 30, 2004, http://googleblog.blogspot.com/soo4/09/pencils-down-people.html (May 12, 2006).

5. Kopytoff, V. "How Google Woos the Best and Brightest." *San Francisco Chronicle,* December 18, 2005, A1. Lexis Nexis Academic database (May 12, 2006).

6. Ibid.

7. Ibid.

8. Funder, D.C. "Personality." *Annual Review of Psychology* 52 (2001), pp. 197–221; Hogan, R.T. "Personality and Personality Measurement." *Handbook of Industrial and Organizational Psychology,* Vol. 2, eds. M.D. Dunnette and L.M. Hough. Palo Alto, CA: Consulting Psychologists Press, 1991, pp. 873–919.

9. Hogan, "Personality and Personality Measurement."

10. Ibid.

11. Rokeach, M. *The Nature of Human Values.* New York: Free Press, 1973; Steers, R.M., and C.J. Sanchez-Runde. "Culture, Motivation, and Work Behavior." In *Blackwell Handbook of Cross-Cultural Management,* eds. M.J. Gannon and K.L. Newman. Malden, MA: Blackwell, 2002, pp. 190–213.

12. Fleishman, E.A., D.P. Costanza, and J. Marshall-Mies. "Abilities." In *An Occupational Information System for the 21st Century: The Development of*

*O*NET,* eds. N.G. Peterson, M.D. Mumford, W.C. Borman, P.R. Jeanneret, and E.A. Fleishman. Washington, DC: American Psychological Association, 1999, pp. 175–95.

13. Goldberg, L.R. "From Ace to Zombie: Some Explorations in the Language of Personality." In *Advances in Personality Assessment,* Vol. 1, eds. C.D. Spielberger and J.N. Butcher. Hillsdale, NJ: Erlbaum, 1982, pp. 203–34. See also Allport, G.W., and H.S. Odbert. "Trait-Names: A Psycho-Lexical Study." *Psychological Monographs* 47, no. 1 (1936), Whole No. 211; Norman, W.T. *2800 Personality Trait Descriptors: Normative Operating Characteristics for a University Population.* Ann Arbor, MI: University of Michigan Department of Psychology, 1967.

14. Tupes, E.C., and R.E. Christal. *Recurrent Personality Factors Based on Trait Ratings.* USAF ASD Technical Report No. 61–97, Lackland Air Force Base, TX: United States Air Force, 1961; reprinted in *Journal of Personality* 60, pp. 225–51; Norman, W.T. "Toward an Adequate Taxonomy of Personality Attributes: Replicated Factor Structure in Peer Nomination Personality Ratings." *Journal of Abnormal and Social Psychology* 66 (1963), pp. 574–83; Digman, J.M., and N.K. Takemoto-Chock. "Factors in the Natural Language of Personality: Re-Analysis, Comparison, and Interpretation of Six Major Studies." *Multivariate Behavioral Research* 16 (1981), pp. 149–70; McCrae, R.R., and P.T. Costa Jr. "Updating Norman's 'Adequate Taxonomy': Intelligence and Personality Dimensions in Natural Language and in Questionnaires." *Journal of Personality and Social Psychology* 49 (1985), pp. 710–21; Goldberg, L.R. "An Alternative 'Description of Personality': The Big-Five Factor Structure." *Journal of Personality and Social Psychology* 59 (1990), pp. 1216–29.

15. Goldberg, L.R. "Language and Individual Differences: The Search for Universals in Personality Lexicons." In *Review of Personality and Social Psychology,* Vol. 2, ed. L. Wheeler. Beverly Hills, CA: Sage, 1981, pp. 141–65.

16. Saucier, G. "Mini-Markers: A Brief Version of Goldberg's Unipolar Big-Five Markers." *Journal of Personality Assessment* 63 (1994), pp. 506–16; Goldberg, L.R. "The Development of Markers for the Big-Five Factor Structure." *Psychological Assessment* 4 (1992), pp. 26–42; McCrae, R.R., and P.T. Costa Jr. "Validation of the Five-Factor Model of Personality Across Instruments and Observers." *Journal of Personality and Social Psychology* 52 (1987), pp. 81–90.

17. Barrick, M.R., and M.K. Mount. "The Big Five Personality Dimensions and Job Performance: A Meta-Analysis." *Personnel Psychology* 44 (1991), pp. 1–26.

18. Barrick, M.R., G.L. Stewart, and M. Piotrowski. "Personality and Job Performance: Test of the Mediating Effects of Motivation among Sales Representatives." *Journal of Applied Psychology* 87 (2002), pp. 43–51.

19. Barrick, M.R., M.K. Mount, and J.P. Strauss. "Conscientiousness and Performance of Sales Representatives: Test of the Mediating Effects of Goal Setting." *Journal of Applied Psychology* 78 (1993), pp. 715–22.

20. Stewart, G.L. "Trait Bandwidth and Stages of Job Performance: Assessing Differential Effects for Conscientiousness and its Subtraits." *Journal of Applied Psychology* 84 (1999), pp. 959–68.

21. Judge, T.A., C.A. Higgins, C.J. Thoreson, and M.R. Barrick. "The Big Five Personality Traits, General Mental Ability, and Career Success across the Life Span." *Personnel Psychology* 52 (1999), pp. 621–52.

22. Friedman, H.S., J.S. Tucker, J.E. Schwartz, L.R. Martin, C. Tomlinson-Keasey, D.L. Wingard, and M.H. Criqui. "Childhood Conscientiousness and Longevity: Health Behaviors and Cause of Death." *Journal of Personality and Social Psychology* 68 (1995), pp. 696–703.

23. Roberts, B.W., O.S. Chernyshenko, S. Stark, and L.R. Goldberg. "The Structure of Conscientiousness: An Empirical Investigation Based on Seven Major Personality Dimensions." *Personnel Psychology* 58 (2005), pp. 103–39.

24. Hogan, J., and B. Holland. "Using Theory to Evaluate Personality and Job-Performance Relations: A Socioanalytic Perspective." *Journal of Applied Psychology* 88 (2003), pp. 100–12.

25. Barrick and Mount, "The Big Five Personality Dimensions."

26. Frei, R.L., and M.A. McDaniel. "Validity of Customer Service Measures in Personnel Selection: A Review of Criterion and Construct Evidence." *Human Performance* 11 (1998), pp. 1–27.

27. Graziano, W.G., L.A. Jensen-Campbell, and E.C. Hair. "Perceiving Interpersonal Conflict and Reacting to It: The Case for Agreeableness." *Journal of Personality and Social Psychology* 70 (1996), pp. 820–35.

28. Mehl, M.R., S.D. Gosling, and J.W. Pennebaker. "Personality in Its Natural Habitat: Manifestations and Implicit Folk Theories of Personality in Daily Life." *Journal of Personality and Social Psychology* 90 (2006), pp. 862–77.

29. Albright, L., D.A. Kenny, and T.E. Malloy. "Consensus in Personality Judgments at Zero Acquaintance." *Journal of Personality and Social Psychology* 55 (1988), pp. 387–95; Levesque, M.J., and D.A. Kenny. "Accuracy of Behavioral Predictions at Zero Acquaintance: A Social Relations Analysis." *Journal of Personality and Social Psychology* 65 (1993), pp. 1178–87.

30. Barrick, M.R., G.L. Stewart, and M. Piotrowski. "Personality and Job Performance: Test of the Mediating Effects of Motivation among Sales Representatives." *Journal of Applied Psychology* 87 (2002), pp. 43–51.

31. Judge, T.A., J.E. Bono, R. Ilies, and M.W. Gerhardt. "Personality and Leadership: A Qualitative and Quantitative Review." *Journal of Applied Psychology* 87 (2002), pp. 765–80.

32. Ibid.

33. Thoreson, C.J., S.A. Kaplan, A.P. Barsky, C.R. Warren, and K. de Chermont. "The Affective Underpinnings of Job Perceptions and Attitudes: A Meta-Analytic Review and Integration." *Psychological Bulletin* 129 (2003), pp. 914–45.

34. Ibid.; Judge, T.A., D. Heller, and M.K. Mount. "Five-Factor Model of Personality and Job Satisfaction: A Meta-Analysis." *Journal of Applied Psychology* 87 (2003), pp. 530–41.

35. Magnus, K., E. Diener, F. Fujita, and W. Pavot. "Extraversion and Neuroticism as Predictors of Objective Life Events: A Longitudinal Analysis." *Journal of Personality and Social Psychology* 65 (1992), pp. 1046–53.

36. Palmeri, D. "Dr. Warren's Lonely Hearts Club." *BusinessWeek,* February 20, 2006, pp. 82–84.

37. "What Are the 29 Dimensions?" www.eharmony.com/singles/servlet/about/dimensions (January 6, 2007).

38. Paunonen, S.V. "Big Five Predictors of Personality and Replicated Predictions of Behavior." *Journal of Personality and Social Psychology* 84 (2003), pp. 411–24; Asendorpf, J.B., and S. Wilpers. "Personality Effects on Social Relationships." *Journal of Personality and Social Psychology* 74 (1998), pp. 1531–44.

39. Asendorpf and Wilpers, "Personality Effects on Social Relationships."

40. Barrick, M.R., and M.K. Mount. "Select on Conscientiousness and Emotional Stability." In *Blackwell Handbook of Principles of Organizational Behavior,* ed. E.A. Locke. Malden, MA: Blackwell, 2000, pp. 15–28.

41. Thoreson et al., "The Affective Underpinnings."

42. Ibid.

43. DeNeve, K.M., and H. Cooper. "The Happy Personality: A Meta-Analysis of 137 Personality Traits and Subjective Well-Being." *Psychological Bulletin* 124 (1998), pp. 197–229.

44. Bolger, N., and A. Zuckerman. "A Framework for Studying Personality in the Stress Process." *Journal of Personality and Social Psychology* 69 (1995), pp. 890–902.

45. Ibid.

46. Friedman, M., and R.H. Rosenman. *Type A Behavior and Your Heart.* New York: Knopf, 1974.

47. Barrick and Mount, "The Big Five Personality Dimensions"; Cellar, D.F., M.L. Miller, D.D. Doverspike, and J.D. Klawsky. "Comparison of Factor Structures and Criterion-Related Validity Coefficients for Two Measures of Personality Based on the Five Factor Model." *Journal of Applied Psychology* 81 (1996), pp. 694–704.

48. LePine, J.A., J.A. Colquitt, and A. Erez. "Adaptability to Changing Task Contexts: Effects of General Cognitive Ability, Conscientiousness, and Openness to Experience." *Personnel Psychology* 53 (2000), pp. 563–93; Thoreson,

C.J., J.C. Bradley, P.D. Bliese, and J.D. Thoreson. "The Big Five Personality Traits and Individual Job Performance Growth Trajectories in Maintenance and Transitional Job Stages." *Journal of Applied Psychology* 89 (2004), pp. 835–53.

49. Edmondson, G. "BMW's Dream Factory." *BusinessWeek,* October 16, 2006, pp. 70–80.

50. McAdams, D.P., and J.L. Pals, "A New Big Five: Fundamental Principles for an Integrative Science of Personality." *American Psychologist* 61 (2006), pp. 204–17.

51. McCrae, R.R., and A. Terracciano. "Personality Profiles of Cultures: Aggregate Personality Traits." *Journal of Personality and Social Psychology* 89 (2005), pp. 407–25.

52. Hofstede, G. *Culture's Consequences: International Differences in Work Related Values.* Beverly Hills, CA: Sage, 1980; Kirkman, B.L., K.B. Lowe, and C.B. Gibson. "A Quarter Century of *Culture's Consequences:* A Review of Empirical Research Incorporating Hofstede's Cultural Values Framework." *Journal of International Business Studies* 37 (2006), pp. 285–320.

53. Kirkman, Lowe, and Gibson, "A Quarter Century."

54. Black, J.S. "The Relationship of Personal Characteristics with the Adjustment of Japanese Expatriate Managers." *Management International Review* 30 (1990), pp. 119–34.

55. Oyserman, D., H.M. Coon, and M. Kemmelmeier. "Rethinking Individualism and Collectivism: Evaluation of Theoretical Assumptions and Meta-Analyses." *Psychological Bulletin* 128 (2002), pp. 3–72.

56. Jackson, C.L., J.A. Colquitt, M.J. Wesson, and C.P. Zapata-Phelan. "Psychological Collectivism: A Measurement Validation and Linkage to Group Member Performance." *Journal of Applied Psychology* 91 (2006), pp. 884–99.

57. Triandis, H.C., and E.M. Suh. "Cultural Influences on Personality." *Annual Review of Psychology* 53 (2002), pp. 133–60.

58. Jackson et al., "Psychological Collectivism."

59. Van der Zee, K.I., and J.P. Van Oudenhoven. "The Multicultural Personality Questionnaire: Reliability and Validity of Self- and Other Ratings of Multicultural Effectiveness." *Journal of Research in Personality* 35 (2001), pp. 278–88.

60. Van der Zee, K.I., and U. Brinkmann. "Construct Validity Evidence for the Intercultural Readiness Check Against the Multicultural Personality Questionnaire." *International Journal of Selection and Assessment* 12 (2004), pp. 285–90; Van Oudenhoven, J.P., and K.I. Van der Zee. "Predicting Multicultural Effectiveness of International Students: The Multicultural Personality Questionnaire." *International Journal of Intercultural Relations* 26 (2002), pp. 679–94; Van Oudenhoven, J.P., S. Mol, and K.I. Van der Zee. "Study of the Adjustment of Western Expatriates in Taiwan ROC with the Multicultural Personality Questionnaire." *Asian Journal of Social Psychology* 6 (2003), pp. 159–70.

61. Cox, T.H., S.A. Lobel, and P.L. McLeod. "Effects of Ethnic Group Cultural Differences on Cooperative and Competitive Behavior on a Group Task." *Academy of Management Journal* 34 (1991), pp. 827–47; Eby, L.T., and G.H. Dobbins. "Collectivistic Orientation in Teams: An Individual and Group-Level Analysis." *Journal of Organizational Behavior* 18 (1997), pp. 275–95; Ramamoorthy, N., and S.J. Carroll. "Individualism/Collectivism Orientations and Reactions Toward Alternative Human Resource Management Practices." *Human Relations* 51 (1998), pp. 571–88.

62. Jackson et al., "Psychological Collectivism."

63. O*Net Online, http://online.onetcenter.org/find/descriptor/browse/Abilities/#cur (June 5, 2006).

64. *Disability Fact Sheet Handbook* University of California, Irvine. www.disability.uci.edu/disability_handbook/famous_people.htm (June 9, 2006).

65. Vogelstein, F. "Google @ $165: Are These Guys for Real? *Fortune* 150, no. 12 (December 13, 2004), p. 98. ProQuest database (May 14, 2007).

66. Carroll, J.B. *Human Cognitive Abilities: A Survey of Factor-Analytic Studies.* New York: Cambridge University Press, 1993; Cattell, R.B. "The Measurement of Adult Intelligence. *Psychological Bulletin* 40 (1943), pp. 153–93; Galton,

F. *Inquire into Human Faculty and its Development.* London: Macmillan, 1883; Spearman, C. "General Intelligence, Objectively Determined and Measured." *American Journal of Psychology* 15 (1904), pp. 201–93; Thurstone, L.L. "Primary Mental Abilities." *Psychometric Monographs* (Whole No. 1, 1938); Vernon, P.E. *The Structure of Human Abilities.* London: Methuen, 1950.

67. Spearman, "General Intelligence"; Spearman, C. *The Abilities of Man: Their Nature and Measurement.* New York: MacMillan, 1927.

68. Bar-On, R. *Development of the Bar-On EQ-i: A Measure of Emotional Intelligence and Social Intelligence.* Toronto: Multi-Health Systems, 1997; Gardner, H., *The Shattered Mind.* New York: Knopf, 1975; Goleman, D. *Emotional Intelligence: Why It Can Matter More than IQ.* New York: Bantam Books, 1995; Thorndike, R.K. "Intelligence and Its Uses." *Harper's Magazine* 140 (1920), pp. 227–335.

69. Matthews, G., A.K. Emo, R.D. Roberts, and M. Zeidner. "What Is This Thing Called Emotional Intelligence?" In *A Critique of Emotional Intelligence: What Are the Problems and How Can They Be Fixed?* Ed. K.R. Murphy. Mahwah, NJ: Lawrence Erlbaum Associates, 2006, pp. 3–36.

70. Salovey, P., and J.D. Mayer. "Emotional Intelligence." *Imagination, Cognition, and Personality* 9 (1990), pp. 185–211.

71. Davies, M., L. Stankov, and R.D. Roberts. "Emotional Intelligence: In Search of an Elusive Construct." *Journal of Personality and Social Psychology* 75 (1998), pp. 989–1015.

72. Davies et al., "Emotional Intelligence"; Law, K.S., C.S. Wong, and L.J. Song. "The Construct and Criterion Validity of Emotional Intelligence and Its Potential Utility for Management Studies." *Journal of Applied Psychology* 89 (2004), pp. 483–96.

73. Ibid.

74. Ibid.

75. Ibid.

76. Fleishman, E.A. "Human Abilities and the Acquisition of Skill." In *Acquisition of Skill,* ed. E.A. Bilodeau. New York: Academic Press, 1966, pp. 147–67; Fleishman et al., "Abilities"; Fleishman, E.A., and M.E. Reilly. *Handbook of Human Abilities: Definitions, Measurements, and Job Task Requirements.* Palo Alto, CA: Consulting Psychologists Press, Inc., 1992.

77. Kazmi, S. "Firefighters Put Through Paces in One-Stop Testing." *Knight Ridder Tribune Business News,* August 18, 2005, p. 1. ProQuest database (May 13, 2006).

78. Barrick, M.R., M.K. Mount, and T.A. Judge. "Personality and Performance at the Beginning of the New Millennium: What Do We Know and Where Do We Go Next?" *International Journal of Selection and Assessment* 9 (2001), pp. 9–30; Hough, L.M., and A. Furnham. "Use of Personality Variables in Work Settings." In *Handbook of Psychology,* Vol. 12, eds. W.C. Borman, D.R. Ilgen, and R.J. Klimoski. Hoboken, NJ: Wiley, 2003, pp. 131–69.

79. Judge, T. A., and Ilies, R. "Relationship of Personality to Performance Motivation: A Meta-Analysis." *Journal of Applied Psychology,* 87 (2002), pp. 797–807.

80. Sackett, P.R., S. Zedeck, and L. Fogli. "Relations Between Measures of Typical and Maximum Job Performance." *Journal of Applied Psychology* 73 (1988), pp. 482–86.

81. Hough and Furnham, "Use of Personality Variables in Work Settings."

82. Mount, M. K., and Barrick, M. R. "The Big Five Personality Dimensions: Implications for Research and Practice in Human Resources Management." In G. R. Ferris, ed. *Research in Personnel and Human Resource Management* (1995), pp. 153–200. Greenwich, CT: JAI Press.

83. Salgado, J.F. "The Big Five Personality Dimensions and Counterproductive Behaviors." *International Journal of Selection and Assessment* 10 (2002), pp. 117–25.

84. Judge, Heller, and Mount, "Five-Factor Model."

85. Cullen, M.J., and P. Sackett. "Personality and Counterproductive Work Behavior." In *Personality and Work,* eds. M.A. Barrick and A.M. Ryan. San Francisco: Jossey-Bass, 2003, pp. 150–82.

86. Cooper-Hakim, A., and C. Viswesvaran. "The Construct of Work Commitment: Testing an Integrative Framework." *Psychological Bulletin* 131 (2005), pp. 241–59; Mathieu, J.E., and D.M. Zajac. "A Review and Meta-Analysis of the Antecedents, Correlates, and Consequences of Organizational Commitment." *Psychological Bulletin* 108 (1990), pp. 171–94.

87. Salgado, "The Big Five Personality Dimensions."

88. Cooper-Hakim and Viswesvaran, "The Construct of Work Commitment."

89. Grant, S., and J. Langan-Fox. "Personality and Occupational Stressor–Strain Relationships: The Role of the Big Five." *Journal of Occupational Health Psychology* 12 (2007), pp. 20–33.

90. Mischel, W. "The Interaction of Person and Situation." In *Personality at the Crossroads: Current Issues in Interactional Psychology,* eds. D. Magnusson and N.S. Endler. Hillsdale, NJ: Erlbaum, 1977, pp. 333–52; Weiss, H.M., and S. Adler. "Personality and Organizational Behavior." In *Research in Organizational Behavior,* Vol. 6, eds. B.M. Staw and L.L. Cummings. Greenwich, CT: JAI Press, 1984, pp. 1–50; Withey, M.J., I.R. Gellatly, and M. Annett. "The Moderating Effect of Situational Strength on the Relationship Between Personality and Provision of Effort." *Journal of Applied Social Psychology* 35 (2005), pp. 1587–608.

91. Barrick, M.R., and M.K. Mount. "Autonomy as a Moderator of the Relationship Between the Big Five Personality Dimensions and Job Performance." *Journal of Applied Psychology* 78 (1993), pp. 111–18; Gellatly, I.R., and P.G. Irving. "Personality, Autonomy, and Contextual Performance of Managers. *Human Performance* 14 (2001), pp. 229–43.

92. Tett, R.P., and D.D. Burnett. "A Personality Trait-Based Interactionist Model of Job Performance." *Journal of Applied Psychology* 88 (2003), pp. 500–17.

93. Lubinski, D. "Introduction to the Special Section on Cognitive Abilities: 100 years after Spearman's (1904) 'General Intelligence,' 'objectively determined and measured'." *Journal of Personality and Social Psychology* 86 (2004), pp. 96–111.

94. Frey, M.C., and D.K. Detterman. "Scholastic Assessment of *g*? The Relationship Between the Scholastic Assessment Test and General Cognitive Ability." *Psychological Science* 15 (2004), pp. 373–78.

95. Korbin, J.L., W.J. Camara, and G.B. Milewski. "The Utility of the SAT I and SAT II for Admissions Decisions in California and the Nation." *The College Board, Research Report No. 2002–6.* New York: College Entrance Examination Board, 2002.

96. Barrick, M.R., G.K. Patton, and S.N. Haugland. "Accuracy of Interviewer Judgments of Job Applicant Personality Traits." *Personnel Psychology* 53 (2000), pp. 925–51.

97. Wonderlic Web site, www.wonderlic.com/Products/product.asp?prod_id4 (July 12, 2006).

Chapter 10

1. www.pixar.com.

2. Lamonica, P.R. "Disney Buys Pixar," January 25, 2006, http://money.cnn.com/2006/01/24/news/companies/disney_pixar_deal/index.htm (December 12, 2006).

3. Schlender, B. "The Man Who Built Pixar's Incredible Innovation Machine." *Fortune* 150, no. 10 November 15, 2004), p. 206. ProQuest database (May 28, 2007).

4. Ibid.

5. Ibid.

6. Ilgen, D.R., D.A. Major, J.R. Hollenbeck, and D.J. Sego. "Team Research in the 1990s." In *Leadership Theory and Research: Perspectives and Directions,* ed. M.M. Chemers and R. Ayman. New York: Academic Press, Inc., 1993, pp. 245–270.

7. Morissette, R., and J.M. Rosa. Alternative Work Practices and Quit Rates: Methodological Issues and Empirical Evidence for Canada." Statistics Canada Catalogue no. 11F0019MiE-No. 199. March 2003.

8. Cohen, S.G., and D.E. Bailey. "What Makes Teams Work: Group Effectiveness Research from the Shop Floor to the Executive Suite." *Journal of Management* 23 (1997), pp. 239–90.

9. Ibid.

10. Sundstrom, E., M. McIntyre, T. Halfhill, and H. Richards. "Work Groups: From the Hawthorne Studies to Work Teams of the 1990s and Beyond." *Group Dynamics, Theory, Research, and Practice* 4 (2000), pp. 44–67.

11. Tuckman, B.W. "Developmental Sequence in Small Groups." *Psychological Bulletin* 63 (1965), pp. 384–99.

12. Treinen, J.J., and S.L. Miller-Frost. "Following the Sun: Case Studies in Global Software Development." *IBM Systems Journal* 45 (2006), pp. 773–83.

13. Schiff, D. "Global Teams Rock around the Clock." *Electronic Engineering Times* 1435 (August 7, 2006), pp. 12, 20.

14. Godinez, V. "Sunshine 24/7: As EDS' Work Stops in One Time Zone, It Picks Up in Another." *Knight Ridder Tribune Business News,* January 2, 2007. ProQuest database (February 12, 2007); Schiff, "Global Teams Rock"; Treinen and Miller-Frost, "Following the Sun."

15. Treinen and Miller-Frost, "Following the Sun."

16. Greenhouse, S. "IBM Explores Shift of White-Collar Jobs Overseas." *The New York Times,* July 22, 2003, pp. C1, 2. ProQuest Historical Newspapers database (February 12, 2007).

17. Gersick, C.J.G. "Time and Transition in Work Teams: Toward a New Model of Group Development." *Academy of Management Journal* 33 (1988), pp. 9–41; Gersick, C.J.G. "Marking Time: Predictable Transitions in Task Groups." *Academy of Management Journal* 32 (1989), pp. 274–309.

18. Thompson, J.D. *Organizations in Action.* New York: McGraw-Hill, 1967; Van de Ven, A.H., A.L. Delbeccq, and R. Koenig. "Determinants of Coordination Modes within Organizations." *American Sociological Review* 41 (1976), pp. 322–38.

19. Ibid.

20. Thompson, *Organizations in Action.*

21. Ibid.

22. Ibid.

23. Van de Ven et al., "Determinants of Coordination Modes."

24. Saavedra, R., P.C. Earley, and L. Van Dyne. "Complex Interdependence in Task Performing Groups." *Journal of Applied Psychology* 78 (1993), pp. 61–72.

25. Deutsch, M. *The Resolution of Conflict.* New Haven, CT: Yale University Press, 1973; Wong, A., D. Tjosvold, and Zi-you Yu. "Organizational Partnerships in China: Self-Interest, Goal Interdependence, and Opportunism." *Journal of Applied Psychology* 90 (2005), pp. 782–91.

26. MacMillan, P.S. *The Performance Factor: Unlocking the Secrets of Teamwork.* Nashville, TN: Broadman & Holman Publishers, 2001.

27. Ibid.

28. Shea, G.P., and R.A. Guzzo. "Groups as Human Resources." In *Research in Personnel and Human Resources Management,* Vol. 5, eds. K.M. Rowland and G.R. Ferris. Greenwich CT: JAI Press, 1987, pp. 323–56.

29. Brehmer, B., and R. Hagafors. "Use of Experts in Complex Decision Making: A Paradigm for the Study of Staff Work." *Organizational Behavior and Human Decision Processes* 38 (1986), pp. 181–95.

30. Benne, K., and P. Sheats. "Functional Roles of Group Members." *Journal of Social Issues* 4 (1948), pp. 41–49.

31. Devine, D.J., and J.L. Philips. "Do Smarter Teams Do Better: A Meta-Analysis of Cognitive Ability and Team Performance." *Small Group Research* 32 (2001), pp. 507–32; Stewart, G.L. "A Meta-Analytic Review of Relationships Between Team Design Features and Team Performance." *Journal of Management* 32 (2006), pp. 29–54.

32. LePine, J.A., J.R. Hollenbeck, D.R. Ilgen, and J. Hedlund. "Effects of Individual Differences on the Performance of Hierarchical Decision-Making Teams: Much More than *g*." *Journal of Applied Psychology* 82 (1997), pp. 803–11.

33. Steiner, I.D. *Group Process and Productivity.* New York: Academic Press, 1972.

34. Peeters, M.A.G., H.F.J.M. van Tuijl, C.G. Rutte, and I.M.M.J. Reymen. "Personality and Team Performance: A Meta-Analysis." *European Journal of Personality* 20 (2006), pp. 377–96.

35. Barrick, M.R., G.L. Stewart, M.J. Neubert, and M.K. Mount. "Relating Member

Ability and Personality to Work-Team Processes and Team Effectiveness." *Journal of Applied Psychology* 83 (1998), pp. 377–91; LePine et al., "Effects of Individual Differences"; Neuman, G.A., and J. Wright. "Team Effectiveness: Beyond Skills and Cognitive Ability." *Journal of Applied Psychology,* 84 (1999), pp. 376–89.

36. Peeters, M.A.G. et al., (2006).

37. LePine, J.A., and L. Van Dyne. "Voice and Cooperative Behavior as Contrasting Forms of Contextual Performance: Evidence of Differential Relationships with Personality Characteristics and Cognitive Ability." *Journal of Applied Psychology* 86 (2001), pp. 326–36.

38. McGrath, J.E. "The Influence of Positive Interpersonal Relations on Adjustment and Interpersonal Relations in Rifle Teams." *Journal of Abnormal and Social Psychology* 65 (1962), pp. 365–75.

39. Barrick, M.R., and M.K. Mount. "The Big Five Personality Dimensions and Job Performance: A Meta-Analysis." *Personnel Psychology* 44 (1991), pp. 1–26.

40. Barrick et al., "Relating Member Ability and Personality."

41. Barry, B., and G.L. Stewart. "Composition, Process, and Performance in Self-Managed Groups: The Role of Personality." *Journal of Applied Psychology* 82 (1997), pp. 62–78.

42. Williams, K., and C. O'Reilly. "The Complexity of Diversity: A Review of Forty Years of Research." In *Research in Organizational Behavior,* Vol. 21, eds. B. Staw and R. Sutton. Greenwich, CT: JAI Press, 1998, pp. 77–140.

43. Cox, T., S. Lobel, and P. McLeod. "Effects of Ethnic Group Cultural Differences on Cooperative and Competitive Behavior on a Group Task." *Academy of Management Journal* 34 (1991), pp. 827–47; Mannix, E., and M.A. Neal. "What Differences Make a Difference? The Promise and Reality of Diverse Teams in Organizations." *Psychological Science in the Public Interest* 6 (2005), pp. 31–55.

44. Gruenfeld, D.H., E.A. Mannix, K.Y. Williams, and M.A. Neale. "Group Composition and Decision Making: How Member Familiarity and Information Distribution Affect Processes and Performance." *Organizational Behavior and Human Decision Processes* 67 (1996), pp. 1–15; Hoffman, L. "Homogeneity and Member Personality and Its Effect on Group Problem Solving." *Journal of Abnormal and Social Psychology* 58 (1959), pp. 27–32; Hoffman, L., and N. Maier. "Quality and Acceptance of Problem Solutions by Members of Homogeneous and Heterogeneous Groups." *Journal of Abnormal and Social Psychology* 62 (1961), pp. 401–407; Nemeth, C.J. "Differential Contributions of Majority and Minority Influence." *Psychological Review* 93 (1986), pp. 22–32; Stasster, G., D. Steward, and G. Wittenbaum. "Expert Roles and Information Exchange During Discussion: The Importance of Knowing Who Knows What." *Journal of Experimental Social Psychology* 57 (1995), pp. 244–65; Triandis, H., E. Hall, and R. Ewen. "Member Heterogeneity and Dyadic Creativity." *Human Relations* 18 (1965), pp. 33–55; Watson, W., K. Kuman, and I. Michaelsen. "Cultural Diversity's Impact on Interaction Process and Performance: Comparing Homogeneous and Diverse Task Groups." *Academy of Management Journal* 36 (1993), pp. 590–602.

45. Byrne, D. *The Attraction Paradigm.* New York: Academic Press, 1971; Newcomb, T.M. *The Acquaintance Process.* New York: Holt, Rinehart, and Wilson, 1961.

46. Byrne, D., G. Clore, and P. Worchel. "The Effect of Economic Similarity-Dissimilarity as Determinants of Attraction." *Journal of Personality and Social Psychology* 4 (1996), pp. 220–24; Lincoln, J., and J. Miller. "Work and Friendship Ties in Organizations: A Comparative Analysis of Relational Networks." *Administrative Science Quarterly* 24 (1979), pp. 181–99; Triandis, H. "Cognitive Similarity and Interpersonal Communication in Industry." *Journal of Applied Psychology* 43 (1959), pp. 321–26; Triandis, H. "Cognitive Similarity and Communication in a Dyad." *Human Relations* 13 (1960), pp. 279–87.

47. Jackson, S.E., K.E. May, and K. Whitney. "Understanding the Dynamics of Diversity in Decision-Making Teams." In *Team Decision-Making*

Effectiveness in Organizations, eds. R.A. Guzzo and E. Salas. San Francisco: Jossey-Bass, 1995, pp. 204–61; Milliken, F.J., and L.L. Martins. "Searching for Common Threads: Understanding the Multiple Effects of Diversity in Organizational Groups." *Academy of Management Review* 21 (1996), pp. 402–33.

48. Harrison, D.A., K.H. Price, and M.P. Bell. "Beyond Relational Demography: Time and the Effects of Surface- and Deep-Level Diversity on Work Group Cohesion." *Academy of Management Journal* 41 (1998), pp. 96–107; Harrison, D.A., K.H. Price, J.H. Gavin, and A.T. Florey. "Time, Teams, and Task Performance: Changing Effects of Surface- and Deep-Level Diversity on Group Functioning." *Academy of Management Journal* 45 (2002), pp. 1029–45.

49. Ibid.

50. Ibid.

51. Ibid.

52. Stewart, "A Meta-Analytic Review."

53. Kozlowski, S.W.J., and B.S. Bell. "Work Groups and Teams in Organization." In *Comprehensive Handbook of Psychology: Industrial and Organizational Psychology,* Vol. 12, eds. W.C. Borman, D.R. Ilgen, and R.J. Klimoski. New York: John Wiley & Sons, 2003, pp. 333–75.

54. Gooding, R.Z., and J.A. Wagner III. "A Meta-Analytic Review of the Relationship Between Size and Performance: The Productivity and Efficiency of Organizations and Their Subunits." *Administrative Science Quarterly* 30 (1985), pp. 462–81; Markham, S.E., F. Dansereau, and J.A. Alutto. "Group Size and Absenteeism Rates: A Longitudinal Analysis." *Academy of Management Journal* 25 (1982), pp. 921–27.

55. Ilgen, D.R., D.A. Major, J.R. Hollenbeck, and D.J. Sego. "Team Research in the 1990s." In *Leadership Theory and Research: Perspectives and Directions,* eds. M.M. Chemers and R. Ayman. New York: Academic Press, Inc., 1993.

56. "Process." Merriam-Webster online dictionary, www.merriam-webster.com/dictionary/process (May 27, 2007).

57. Hackman, J.R. "The Design of Work Teams." In *Handbook of Organizational Behavior,* ed. J.W. Lorsch. Englewood Cliffs, NJ: Prentice Hall, 1987, pp. 315–42.

58. Steiner, *Group Processes and Productivity.*

59. Hackman, "The Design of Work Teams."

60. Hackman, "The Design of Work Teams."

61. Latane, B., K. Williams, and S. Harkins. "Many Hands Make Light the Work: The Causes and Consequences of Social Loafing." *Journal of Personality and Social Psychology* 37 (1979), pp. 822–32.

62. Latane et al., "Many Hands"; Jackson, C.L., and J.A. LePine. "Peer Responses to a Team's Weakest Link: A Test and Extension of LePine and Van Dyne's Model." *Journal of Applied Psychology* 88 (2003), pp. 459–75; Sheppard, A. "Productivity Loss in Performance Groups: A Motivation Analysis." *Psychological Bulletin* 113 (1993), pp. 67–81.

63. Shalley, C.E., J. Zhou, and G.R. Oldham. "The Effects of Personal and Contextual Characteristics on Creativity: Where Should We Go from Here?" *Journal of Management* 30 (2004), pp. 933–58.

64. Osborn, A F. *Applied Imagination* (Revised ed.). New York: Scribner, 1957.

65. Ibid.

66. Diehl, M., and W. Stroebe. "Productivity Loss in Brainstorming Groups: Toward a Solution of a Riddle." *Journal of Personality and Social Psychology* 53 (1987), pp. 497–509; Mullen, B., C. Johnson, and E. Salas. "Productivity Loss in Brainstorming Groups: A Meta-Analytic Investigation." *Basic and Applied Social Psychology* 12 (1991), pp. 3–23.

67. Diehl and Stroebe, "Productivity Loss."

68. Sutton, R.I., and A. Hargadon. "Brainstorming Groups in Context: Effectiveness in a Product Design Firm." *Administrative Science Quarterly* 41 (1996), pp. 685–718.

69. Brehmer and Hagafors, "Use of Experts in Complex Decision Making"; Ilgen, D.R., D. Major, J.R. Hollenbeck, and D. Sego. "Raising an Individual Decision Making Model to the Team Level: A New Research Model and Paradigm." In *Team Effectiveness and Decision Making in Organizations,* eds. R. Guzzo and E. Salas. San Francisco: Jossey-Bass, 1995, pp. 113–48.

70. Hollenbeck, J.R., J.A. Colquitt, D.R. Ilgen, J.A. LePine, and J. Hedlund. "Accuracy Decomposition and Team Decision Making: Testing Theoretical Boundary Conditions." *Journal of Applied Psychology* 83 (1998), pp. 494–500; Hollenbeck, J.R., D.R. Ilgen, D.J. Sego, J. Hedlund, D.A. Major, and J. Phillips. "Multilevel Theory of Team Decision Making: Decision Performance in Teams Incorporating Distributed Expertise." *Journal of Applied Psychology* 80 (1995), pp. 292–316.

71. Hollenbeck et al., "Multilevel Theory of Team Decision Making"; Hollenbeck, J.R., D.R. Ilgen, J.A. LePine, J.A. Colquitt, and J. Hedlund. "Extending the Multilevel Theory of Team Decision Making. Effects of Feedback and Experience in Hierarchical Teams." *Academy of Management Journal* 41 (1998), pp. 269–82.

72. Hollenbeck et al., "Extending the Multilevel Theory."

73. Hedlund, J., D.R. Ilgen, and J.R. Hollenbeck. "Decision Accuracy in Computer-Mediated vs. Face-to-Face Decision Making Teams." *Organizational Behavior and Human Decision Processes* 76 (1998), pp. 30–47.

74. Ancona, D.G. "Outward Bound: Strategies for Team Survival in an Organization." *Academy of Management Journal* 33 (1990), pp. 334–65.

75. LePine, J.A., R.F. Piccolo, C.L. Jackson, J.E. Mathieu, and J.R. Saul. "A Meta-Analysis of Team Process: Towards a Better Understanding of the Dimensional Structure and Relationships with Team Effectiveness Criteria." *Personnel Psychology* 61 (2008), pp. 273–307; Marks, M.A., J.E. Mathieu, and S.J. Zaccaro. "A Temporally Based Framework and Taxonomy of Team Processes." *Academy of Management Review* 26 (2001), pp. 356–76.

76. Marks et al., "A Temporally Based Framework." Please note that this entire section on teamwork processes is largely based on this body of work.

77. Kozlowski, S.W.J., and B.S. Bell. "Work Groups and Teams in Organizations." In *Handbook of Psychology,* Vol. 12: Industrial and Organizational Psychology, eds. W.C. Borman, D.R. Ilgen, and R.J. Klimoski. Hoboken, NJ: John Wiley & Sons, Inc., 2003, pp. 333–75.

78. De Dreu, C.K.W., and L.R. Weingart. "Task Versus Relationship Conflict, Team Performance, and Team Member Satisfaction: A Meta-Analysis." *Journal of Applied Psychology* 88 (2003), pp. 741–49.

79. Jehn, K. "A Multimethod Examination of the Benefits and Detriments of Intergroup Conflict." *Administrative Science Quarterly* 40 (1995), pp. 256–82.

80. De Dreu and Weingart, "Task Versus Relationship Conflict."

81. Thompson, L.L. *Making the Team: A Guide for Managers,* 2nd ed. Upper Saddle River, NJ: Pearson Prentice Hall, 2004.

82. De Church, L.A., and M.A. Marks. "Maximizing the Benefits of Task Conflict: The Role of Conflict Management." *The International Journal of Conflict Management* 12 (2001), pp. 4–22; De Dreu and Weingart, "Task Versus Relationship Conflict"; Van de Vliert, E., and M.C. Euwema. "Agreeableness and Activeness as Components of Conflict Behaviors." *Journal of Personality and Social Psychology* 66 (1994), pp. 674–87.

83. De Church and Marks, "Maximizing the Benefits"; Van de Vliert and Euwema, "Agreeableness and Activeness."

84. De Church and Marks, "Maximizing the Benefits."

85. Festinger, L. "Informal Social Communication." *Psychological Review* 57 (1950), pp. 271–82.

86. Beal, D.J., R.R. Cohen, M.J. Burke, and C.L. McLendon. "Cohesion and Performance in Groups: A Meta-Analytic Clarification of Construct Relations." *Journal of Applied Psychology* 88 (2003), pp. 989–1004; Mullen, B., and C. Copper. "The Relation Between Group Cohesiveness and Performance: An Integration." *Psychological Bulletin* 115 (1994), pp. 210–27.

87. Janis, I.L. *Victims of Groupthink: A Psychological Study of Foreign Policy Decisions and Fiascoes.* Boston, MA: Houghton Mifflin, 1972.

88. Hirokawa, R., Gouran, D., and Martz, A. "Understanding the Sources of Faulty Group Decision Making: A Lesson from the *Challenger* Disaster." *Small Group Behavior* 19 (1988), pp. 411–433; Esser, J., and Linoerfer, J. "Groupthink and the Space Shuttle *Challenger*

Accident: Toward a Quantitative Case Analysis." *Journal of Behavioral Decision Making* 2 (1989), pp. 167–177; Moorhead, G., Ference, R., and Neck, C. "Group Decision Fiascoes Continue: Space Shuttle *Challenger* and a Revised Groupthink Framework." *Human Relations* 44 (1991), pp. 539–550.

89. Stephens, J., and Behr, P. "Enron Culture Fed Its Demise." *Washington Post,* June 27, 2002, pp. A1–2.

90. Shea, G.P., and R.A. Guzzo. "Groups as Human Resources." In *Research in Personnel and Human Resource Management,* Vol. 5, eds. K.M. Rowland and G.R. Ferris. Greenwich, CT: JAI Press, 1987, pp. 323–56.

91. Gully, S.M., K.A. Incalcaterra, A. Joshi, and J.M. Beubien. "A Meta-Analysis of Team-Efficacy, Potency, and Performance: Interdependence and Level of Analysis as Moderators of Observed Relationships." *Journal of Applied Psychology* 87 (2002), pp. 819–32.

92. Klimoski, R.J., and S. Mohammed. "Team Mental Model: Construct or Metaphor?" *Journal of Management* 20 (1994), pp. 403–37.

93. Cannon-Bowers, J.A., E. Salas, and S.A. Converse. "Shared Mental Models in Expert Team Decision Making." *Individual and Group Decision Making,* ed. N.J. Castellan. Hillsdale, NJ: Erlbaum, 1993, pp. 221–46.

94. Wegner, D.M. "Transactive Memory: A Contemporary Analysis of the Group Mind." In *Theories of Group Behavior,* ed. B. Mullen and G.R. Goethals. New York: Springer-Verlag, 1986, pp. 185–208.

95. Hollingshead, A.B. "Communication, Learning, and Retrieval in Transactive Memory Systems." *Journal of Experimental Social Psychology* 34 (1998), pp. 423–42.

96. Wegner, "Transactive Memory."

97. Sundstrom, E., K.P. De Meuse, and D. Futrell. "Work Teams: Applications and Effectiveness." *American Psychologist* 45 (1990), pp. 120–33.

98. Stewart, G.L., C.C. Manz, and H.P. Sims Jr. *Team Work and Group Dynamics.* New York: John Wiley & Sons, 1999.

99. Stewart, "A Meta-Analytic Review."

100. Campion, M.A., G.J. Medsker, and A.C. Higgs. "Relations Between Work Group Characteristics and Effectiveness: Implications for Designing Effective Work Groups." *Personnel Psychology* 46 (1993), pp. 823–49; Campion, M.A., E.M. Papper, and G.J. Medsker. "Relations Between Work Team Characteristics and Effectiveness: A Replication and Extension." *Personnel Psychology* 49 (1996), pp. 429–52.

101. LePine et al., "A Meta-Analysis of Team Process."

102. Ibid.

103. DeMatteo, J.S., L.T. Eby, and E. Sundstrom. "Team-Based Rewards: Current Empirical Evidence and Directions for Future Research." *Research in Organizational Behavior* 20 (1998), pp. 141–83.

104. Deutsch, M.A. "A Theory of Cooperation and Competition." *Human Relations* 2 (1949), pp. 199–231.

105. Williams, K., S.G. Harkins, and B. Latane. "Identifiability as a Deterrent to Social Loafing: Two Cheering Experiments." *Journal of Personality and Social Psychology* 40 (1981), pp. 303–11.

106. Lawler, E.E. *Strategic Pay: Aligning Organizational Strategies and Pay Systems.* San Francisco: Jossey-Bass, 1990.

107. O'Dell, C. *People, Performance, Pay.* American Productivity Institute, 1987, cited in DeMatteo et al., "Team-Based Rewards."

108. Wageman, R. "Interdependence and Group Effectiveness." *Administrative Science Quarterly* 40 (1995), pp. 145–80.

109. Johnson, D.W., G. Maruyama, R. Johnson, D. Nelson, and L. Skon. "Effects of Cooperative, Competitive, and Individualistic Goal Structures on Achievement: A Meta-Analysis." *Psychological Bulletin* 89 (1981), pp. 47–62; Miller, L.K., and R.L. Hamblin. "Interdependence, Differential Rewarding and Productivity." *American Sociological Review* 28 (1963), pp. 768–78; Rosenbaum, M.E. "Cooperation and Competition." In *Psychology of Group Influence,* ed. P.B. Paulus. Hillsdale, NJ: Lawrence Erlbaum, 1980.

Chapter 11

1. Stewart, J. "The Kona Files: How an Obsession with Leaks Brought Scandal to Hewlett-Packard." *The New Yorker* 83, no. 1 (2007), pp. 152–67; Hardy, Q. "The UnCarly." *Forbes* 179, no. 5 (2007), pp. 82–90.
2. Murray, A. "H-P Lost Faith in Fiorina, but Not in Merger." *The Wall Street Journal,* May 24, 2006, p. A2.
3. Hardy, "The UnCarly."
4. Malone, M.S. "Hurd Instinct." *The Wall Street Journal,* September 14, 2006, p. A20.
5. Lashinsky, A. "The Hurd Way." *Fortune* 153 (2006), pp. 92–99; Hardy, "The UnCarly."
6. Lashinsky, A. "Mark Hurd Takes His First Swing at HP." *Fortune* 152 (2005), p. 24.
7. Tam, P. "Rewiring Hewlett-Packard." *The Wall Street Journal,* July 20, 2005, p. B1.
8. Burrows, P., and B. Elgin. "The Un-Carly Reveals his Game Plan." *BusinessWeek,* June 27, 2005, p. 36.
9. Burrows, P. "HP Says Goodbye to Drama." *BusinessWeek,* September 12, 2005, p. 83.
10. Lashinsky, "Mark Hurd."
11. McMurray, V.V. "Some Unanswered Questions on Organizational Conflict." *Organization and Administrative Sciences* 6 (1975), pp. 35–53; Pfeffer, J. *Managing with Power.* Boston: Harvard Business School Press, 1992.
12. Cotton, J.L. "Measurement of Power-Balancing Styles and Some of their Correlates." *Administrative Science Quarterly* 21 (1976), pp. 307–19; Emerson, R.M. "Power-Dependence Relationships." *American Sociological Review* 27 (1962), pp. 29–41.
13. Ashforth, B.E., and F.A. Mael. "The Power of Resistance." In *Power and Influence in Organizations,* eds. R.M. Kramer and M.E. Neal. Thousand Oaks, CA: Sage, 1998, pp. 89–120.
14. French, Jr., J.R.P., and B. Raven. "The Bases of Social Power." In *Studies in Social Power,* ed. D. Cartwright. Ann Arbor: University of Michigan, Institute for Social Research, 1959, pp. 150–67; Yukl, G., and C.M. Falbe. "The Importance of Different Power Sources in Downward and Lateral Relations." *Journal of Applied Psychology* 76 (1991), pp. 416–23.
15. Yukl, G. "Use Power Effectively." In *Handbook of Principles of Organizational Behavior,* ed. E.A. Locke. Madden, MA: Blackwell, 2004, pp. 242–47.
16. "WXN 2008 Canada's Most Powerful Women: Top 100 Winners." Women's Executive Network. Retrieved April 16, 2009, at www.wxnetwork.com/files/WXN-2008_Top100 Winners.pdf.
17. French and Raven, "The Bases of Social Power."
18. Hickson, D.J., C.R. Hinings, C.A. Lee, R.E. Schneck, and J.M. Pennings. "A Strategic Contingencies Theory of Intraorganizational Power." *Administrative Science Quarterly* 16 (1971), pp. 216–27; Hinings, C.R., D.J. Hickson, J.M. Pennings, and R.E. Schneck. "Structural Conditions of Intraorganizational Power." *Administrative Science Quarterly* 19 (1974), pp. 22–44; Salancik, G.R., and J. Pfeffer. "Who Gets Power and How They Hold on to It: A Strategic Contingency Model of Power." *Organizational Dynamics* 5 (1977), pp. 3–21.
19. McGregor, J. "The Office Chart That Really Counts." *BusinessWeek,* February 27, 2006, pp. 48–49.
20. Somech, A., and A. Drach-Zahavy. "Relative Power and Influence Strategy: The Effects of Agent/Target Organizational Power on Superiors' Choices of Influence Strategies." *Journal of Organizational Behavior* 23 (2002), pp. 167–79; Stahelski, A.J., and C.F. Paynton. "The Effects of Status Cues on Choices of Social Power and Influence Strategies." *Journal of Social Psychology* 135 (1995), pp. 553–60.
21. Yukl, G. *Leadership in Organizations. 4th ed. Englewood Cliffs, NJ: Prentice-Hall, 1998.*
22. Yukl, G., C. Chavez, and C.F. Seifert. "Assessing the Construct Validity and Utility of Two New Influence Tactics." *Journal of Organizational Behavior* 26 (2005), pp. 705–25; Yukl, G. *Leadership in Organizations,* 5th ed. (Upper Saddle River, NJ: Prentice Hall, 2002).
23. Yukl, G., H. Kim, and C. Chavez. "Task Importance, Feasibility, and Agent Influence Behavior as Determinants of Target Commitment." *Journal of Applied Psychology* 84 (1999), pp. 137–43.

24. Yukl, *Leadership in Organizations.*

25. Hardy, "The UnCarly"; Malone, "Hurd Instinct."

26. Yukl et al., "Task Importance."

27. Wayne, S.J., and G.R. Ferris. "Influence Tactics, Affect, and Exchange Quality in Supervisor–Subordinate Interactions: A Laboratory Experiment and Field Study." *Journal of Applied Psychology* 75 (1990), pp. 487–99.

28. Kelman, H.C. "Compliance, Identification, and Internalization: Three Processes of Attitude Change." *Journal of Conflict Resolution* 2 (1958), pp. 51–56.

29. Yukl et al., "Assessing the Construct Validity."

30. Buderi, R. "The Talent Magnet." *Fast Company* 106 (2006), pp. 80–84.

31. Chen, C.C., Y.R. Chen, and K. Xin. "Guanxi Practices and Trust in Management: A Procedural Justice Perspective." *Organization Science* 15 (2004), pp. 200–209.

32. Yang, M.M. *Gifts, Favors, and Banquets: The Art of Social Relationships in China.* Ithaca, NY: Cornell University Press, 1994.

33. Fu, P.P., T.K. Peng, J.C. Kennedy, and G. Yukl. "A Comparison of Chinese Managers in Hong Kong, Taiwan, and Mainland China." *Organizational Dynamics* 33 (2003), pp. 32–46.

34. Buderi, "The Talent Magnet."

35. Fu et al., "A Comparison."

36. Falbe, C.M., and G. Yukl. "Consequences for Managers of Using Single Influence Tactics and Combinations of Tactics." *Academy of Management Journal,* August 1992, pp. 638–52.

37. Yukl, G. *Leadership in Organizations.* 5th ed. Upper Saddle River, NJ: Prentice Hall, 2002.

38. Note: Engagement is more commonly referred to as "commitment" in this context. We have changed the original term to avoid any confusion with organizational commitment.

39. Somech and Drach-Zahavy, "Relative Power and Influence Strategy"; Yukl, *Leadership in Organizations,* 5th ed.; Yukl, "Use Power Effectively."

40. Mintzberg, H. "The Organization as Political Arena." *Journal of Management Studies* 22 (1985), pp. 133–54.

41. Kacmar, K.M., and R.A. Baron. "Organizational Politics: The State of the Field, Links to Related Processes, and an Agenda for Future Research." In *Research in Personnel and Human Resources Management,* Vol. 17, ed. G.R. Ferris. Greenwich, CT: JAI Press, 1999, pp. 1–39.

42. Ferris, G.R., D.C. Treadway, P.L. Perrewe, R.L. Brouer, C. Douglas, and S. Lux. "Political Skill in Organizations." *Journal of Management* 33 (2007), pp. 290–320; Treadway, D.C., G.R. Ferris, A.B. Duke, G.L. Adams, and J.B. Thatcher. "The Moderating Role of Subordinate Political Skill on Supervisors' Impressions of Subordinate Ingratiation and Ratings of Subordinate Interpersonal Facilitation." *Journal of Applied Psychology* 92 (2007), pp. 848–55.

43. Seldman, M., and E. Betof. "An Illuminated Path." *T + D* 58 (2004), pp. 34–39.

44. Ferris, G.R., D.C. Treadway, R.W. Kolokinsky, W.A. Hochwarter, C.J. Kacmar, and D.D. Frink. "Development and Validation of the Political Skill Inventory." *Journal of Management* 31 (2005), pp. 126–52.

45. Ferris et al., "Political Skill in Organizations"; Ferris et al., "Development and Validation."

46. Ibid.

47. Ibid.

48. Ferris, G.R., D.D. Frink, D.P.S. Bhawuk, J. Zhou, and D.C. Gilmore. "Reactions of Diverse Groups to Politics in the Workplace." *Journal of Management,* no. 1 (1996), pp. 23–44.

49. Kacmar and Baron, "Organizational Politics"; Hochwarter, W.A. "The Interactive Effects of Pro-Political Behavior and Politics Perceptions on Job Satisfaction and Commitment." *Journal of Applied Social Psychology* 33 (2003), pp. 1360–78; Randall, M.L., R. Cropanzano, C.A. Bormann, and A. Birjulin. "Organizational Politics and Organizational Support as Predictors of Work Attitudes, Job Performance, and Organizational Citizenship Behavior." *Journal of Organizational Behavior* 20 (1999), pp. 159–74; Witt, L.A. "Enhancing Organizational Goal Congruence: A Solution to Organizational Politics." *Journal of Applied Psychology* 83 (1998), pp. 666–74.

50. Eisenhardt, K.M., and L.J. Bourgeois. "Politics of Strategic Decision Making in High-Velocity Environments: Toward a Midrange Theory." *Academy of Management Journal* 31 (1988), pp. 737–70.

51. Biberman, G. "Personality and Characteristic Work Attitudes of Persons with High, Moderate, and Low Political Tendencies." *Psychological Reports* 60 (1985), pp. 1303–10; Ferris et al., "Reactions of Diverse Groups"; O'Connor, W.E., and T.G. Morrison. "A Comparison of Situational and Dispositional Predictors of Perceptions of Organizational Politics." *Journal of Psychology* 135 (2001), pp. 301–12.

52. Valle, M., and P.L. Perrewe. "Do Politics Perceptions Relate to Political Behaviors? Tests of an Implicit Assumption and Expanded Model." *Human Relations* 53 (2000), pp. 359–86.

53. Fandt, P.M., and G.R. Ferris. "The Management of Information and Impressions: When Employees Behave Opportunistically." *Organizational Behavior and Human Decision Processes* 45 (1990), pp. 140–58; O'Connor and Morrison, "A Comparison of Situational and Dispositional Predictors"; Poon, J.M.L. "Situational Antecedents and Outcomes of Organizational Politics Perceptions." *Journal of Managerial Psychology* 18 (2003), pp. 138–55.

54. Lewicki, R.J., and J.A. Litterer. *Negotiations.* Homewood, IL: Irwin, 1985; Thomas, K.W. "Conflict and Negotiation Processes in Organizations." In *Handbook of Industrial and Organizational Psychology,* 2nd ed., Vol. 3, eds. M.D. Dunnette and L.M. Hough. Palo Alto, CA: Consulting Psychologists Press, pp. 651–717.

55. Weingart, L., and K.A. Jehn. "Manage Intra-Team Conflict Through Collaboration." *Handbook of Principles of Organizational Behavior,* ed. E.A. Locke. Madden, MA: Blackwell, 2004, pp. 226–38.

56. Thomas, K.W. "Toward Multi-Dimensional Values in Teaching: The Example of Conflict Behaviors." *Academy of Management Review* 2 (1977), pp. 484–90; de Dreu, C.K.W., A. Evers, B. Beersma, E.S. Kluwer, and A. Nauta. "A Theory-Based Measure of Conflict Management Strategies in the Workplace." *Journal of Organizational Behavior* 22 (2001), pp. 645–68.

57. Fahey, J. "The Soul of a Laptop." *Forbes,* May 7, 2007, pp. 100–104.

58. Adapted from Neale, M.A., and M.H. Bazerman. "Negotiating Rationally: The Power and Impact of the Negotiator's Frame." *Academy of Management Executive* 2 (1992), pp. 42–51.

59. Bazerman, M.H., and M.A. Neale. *Negotiating Rationally.* New York: The Free Press, 1992; Pinkley, R.L., T.L. Griffeth, and G.B. Northcraft. "Fixed Pie a la Mode: Information Availability, Information Processing, and the Negotiation of Suboptimal Agreements." *Organizational Behavior and Human Decision Processes* 50 (1995), pp. 101–12.

60. Pinkley et al., "Fixed Pie a la Mode."

61. Kolb, D.M., and J. Williams. "Breakthrough Bargaining." *Harvard Business Review,* February 2001, pp. 88–97.

62. Donkin, R. "So What Do You Think You're Worth? The Evidence Seems to Support a New Book's Contention That If You Want a Good Salary, You Had Better Negotiate for It. But Recognize That It Takes Practice." *Financial Times,* November 18, 2004, p. 11.

63. Pinkley, R.L., and G.B. Northcraft. *Get Paid What You're Worth: The Expert Negotiators' Guide to Salary and Compensation.* New York: St. Martin's Griffin, 2003.

64. Gerhart, B., and S. Rynes. "Determinants and Consequences of Salary Negotiations by Male and Female MBA Graduates." *Journal of Applied Psychology* 76 (1991), pp. 256–62.

65. Adapted from Thompson, L.L. *The Mind and Heart of the Negotiator.* 3rd ed. Upper Saddle River, NJ: Prentice Hall, 2005; Pinkley and Northcraft, *Get Paid.*

66. Pinkley et al., "Fixed Pie a la Mode."

67. Thomas, "Conflict and Negotiation Processes."

Chapter 12

1. Young, J.S., and W.L. Simon. *iCon: Steve Jobs—The Greatest Second Act in the History of Business.* Hoboken, NJ: Wiley, 2005.

2. Ibid.

3. Ibid.

4. Ibid.

5. Ibid.

6. Schlender, B. "How Big Can Apple Get?" *Fortune,* February 21, 2005, pp. 66–76.

7. Burrows, P., and R. Grover. "Steve Jobs' Magic Kingdom." *BusinessWeek,* February 6, 2006, pp. 63–69.

8. Young and Simon, *iCon.*

9. Schlender, "How Big Can Apple Get?"

10. Yukl, G. *Leadership in Organizations,* 4th ed. Englewood Cliffs, NJ: Prentice-Hall, 1998.

11. Ibid.

12. Burrows, P. "The Teflon Factor: Is Steve Jobs Untouchable?" *BusinessWeek,* January 15, 2007, pp. 28–31.

13. Yukl, *Leadership in Organizations.*

14. Ibid.

15. Dansereau, F. Jr., G. Graen, and W.J. Haga. "A Vertical Dyad Linkage Approach to Leadership Within Formal Organizations: A Longitudinal Investigation of the Role Making Process." *Organizational Behaviour and Human Performance* 13 (1975), pp. 46–78; Graen, G., M. Novak, and P. Sommerkamp. "The Effects of Leader-Member Exchange and Job Design on Productivity and Satisfaction: Testing a Dual Attachment Model." *Organizational Behaviour and Human Performance* 30 (1982), pp. 109–31; Graen, G.B., and M. Uhl-Bien. "Relationship-Based Approach to Leadership: Development of Leader-Member Exchange (LMX) Theory of Leadership over 25 Years: Applying a Multi-Level Multi-Domain Perspective." *Leadership Quarterly* 6 (1995), pp. 219–47; Liden, R.C., R.T. Sparrowe, and S.J. Wayne. "Leader-Member Exchange Theory: The Past and Potential for the Future." In *Research in Personnel and Human Resources Management,* Vol. 15, ed. G.R. Ferris. Greenwich, CT: JAI Press, 1997, pp. 47–119.

16. Graen, G.B., and T. Scandura. "Toward a Psychology of Dyadic Organizing." In *Research in Organizational Behaviour,* Vol. 9, eds. L.L. Cummings and B.M. Staw. Greenwich, CT: JAI Press, 1987, pp. 175–208.

17. Ibid.

18. Graen and Uhl-Bien, "Relationship-Based Approach to Leadership."

19. Ibid.

20. Bauer, T.N., and S.G. Green. "Development of Leader-Member Exchange: A Longitudinal Test." *Academy of Management Journal* 39 (1996), pp. 1538–67; Gerstner, C.R., and D.V. Day. "Meta-Analytic Review of Leader-Member Exchange Theory: Correlates and Construct Issues." *Journal of Applied Psychology* 82 (1997), pp. 827–44; Liden, R.C., S.J. Wayne, and D. Stillwell. "A Longitudinal Study on the Early Development of Leader-Member Exchanges." *Journal of Applied Psychology* 78 (1993), pp. 662–74.

21. Graen and Uhl-Bien, "Relationship-Based Approach to Leadership."

22. Stogdill, R.M. "Personal Factors Associated with Leadership: A Survey of the Literature." *Journal of Applied Psychology* 54 (1948), pp. 259–69.

23. Den Hartog, D.N., and P.L. Koopman. "Leadership in Organizations." In *Handbook of Industrial, Work, and Organizational Psy chology,* Vol. 2, eds. N. Anderson, D.S. Ones, H.K. Sinangil, and C. Viswesvaran. Thousand Oaks, CA: Sage, 2002, pp. 166–87.

24. Yukl, *Leadership in Organizations;* Zaccaro, S.J. "Trait-Based Perspectives of Leadership." *American Psychologist* 62 (1998), pp. 6–16.

25. Vroom, V.H. "Leadership and the Decision-Making Process." *Organizational Dynamics* 28 (2000), pp. 82–94; Yukl, *Leadership in Organizations.*

26. Ibid.

27. Ibid.

28. Ibid.

29. Vroom, "Leadership and the Decision-Making Process."

30. Miller, K.I., and P.R. Monge. "Participation, Satisfaction, and Productivity: A Meta-Analytic Review." *Academy of Management Journal* 29 (1986), pp. 727–53; Wagner, J.A. III. "Participation's Effects on Performance and Satisfaction: A Reconsideration of Research Evidence." *Academy of Management Review* 19 (1994), pp. 312–30.

31. Vroom, "Leadership and the Decision-Making Process."

32. Rogelberg, S.G., D.J. Leach, P.B. Warr, and J.L. Burnfield. "'Not Another Meeting!' Are Meeting Time Demands Related

to Employee Well-Being?" *Journal of Applied Psychology* 91 (2006), pp. 86–96.

33. Lee, L. "Paul Pressler's Fall from The Gap." *BusinessWeek*, February 26, 2007, pp. 80–84.

34. Vroom, "Leadership and the Decision-Making Process"; Vroom, V.H., and A.G. Jago. *The New Leadership: Managing Participation in Organizations.* Englewood Cliffs, NJ: Prentice Hall, 1988; Vroom, V.H., and A.G. Jago. "Decision Making as a Social Process: Normative and Descriptive Models of Leader Behaviour." *Decision Sciences* 5 (1974), pp. 743–69; Vroom, V.H., and P.W. Yetton. *Leadership and Decision-Making.* Pittsburgh, PA: University of Pittsburgh Press, 1973.

35. Aditya, R.N., R.J. House, and S. Kerr. "Theory and Practice of Leadership: Into the New Millennium." In *Industrial and Organizational Psychology: Linking Theory with Practice,* eds. C.L. Cooper and E.A. Locke. Malden, MA: Blackwell, 2000, pp. 130–65; House, R.J., and R.N. Aditya. "The Social Scientific Study of Leadership: Quo Vadis?" *Journal of Management* 23 (1997), pp. 409–73; Yukl, *Leadership in Organizations.*

36. Vroom, V.H., and A.G. Jago. "On the Validity of the Vroom-Yetton Model." *Journal of Applied Psychology* 63 (1978), pp. 151–62. See also Vroom and Yetton, *Leadership and Decision Making;* Vroom and Jago, *The New Leadership;* Field, R.H.G. "A Test of the Vroom-Yetton Normative Model of Leadership." *Journal of Applied Psychology* 67 (1982), pp. 523–32.

37. Vroom and Yetton, *Leadership and Decision Making.*

38. Hemphill, J.K. *Leader Behaviour Description.* Columbus, OH: Ohio State University, 1950. Cited in Fleishman, E.A., E.F. Harris, and H.E. Burtt. *Leadership and Supervision in Industry: An Evaluation of a Supervisory Training Program.* Columbus, OH: Bureau of Educational Research, Ohio State University, 1955.

39. Hemphill, J.K., and A.E. Coons. "Development of the Leader Behaviour Description Questionnaire." In *Leader Behaviour: Its Description and Measurement,* eds. R.M. Stogdill and A.E. Coons. Columbus, OH: Bureau of Business Research, Ohio State University, 1957, pp. 6–38.

40. Fleishman, E.A. "The Description of Supervisory Behaviour." *Journal of Applied Psychology* 37 (1953), pp. 1–6; Fleishman et al., *Leadership and Supervision in Industry;* Hemphill and Coons, "Development of the Leader Behaviour Description Questionnaire"; Halpin, A.W., and B.J. Winer. *Studies in Aircrew Composition: The Leadership Behaviour of the Airplane Commander* (Technical Report No. 3). Columbus, OH: Personnel Research Board, Ohio State University, 1952. Cited in Fleishman et al.

41. Fleishman, "The Description of Supervisory Behaviour"; Fleishman et al., *Leadership and Supervision in Industry;* Fleishman, E.A., and D.R. Peters. "Interpersonal Values, Leadership Attitudes, and Managerial Success." *Personnel Psychology* 15 (1962), pp. 127–43.

42. Yukl, *Leadership in Organizations.*

43. Fleishman, "The Description of Supervisory Behaviour"; Fleishman et al., *Leadership and Supervision in Industry;* Fleishman and Peters, "Interpersonal Values."

44. Yukl, *Leadership in Organizations.*

45. Katz, D., N. Maccoby, and N. Morse. *Productivity, Supervision, and Morale in an Office Situation.* Ann Arbor, MI: Institute for Social Research, University of Michigan, 1950; Katz, D., N. Maccoby, G. Gurin, and L. Floor. *Productivity, Supervision, and Morale among Railroad Workers.* Ann Arbor, MI: Survey Research Center, University of Michigan, 1951; Katz, D., and R.L. Kahn. "Some Recent Findings in Human-Relations Research in Industry." In *Readings in Social Psychology,* eds. E. Swanson, T. Newcomb, and E. Hartley. New York: Holt, pp. 650–65; Likert, R. *New Patterns of Management.* New York: McGraw-Hill, 1961; Likert, R. *The Human Organization.* New York: McGraw-Hill, 1967.

46. Fleishman, E.A. "Twenty Years of Consideration and Structure." In *Current Developments in the Study of Leadership,* eds. E.A. Fleishman and J.G. Hunt. Carbondale, IL: Southern Illinois Press, 1973, pp. 1–37.

47. Judge, T.A., R.F. Piccolo, and R. Ilies. "The Forgotten Ones?

The Validity of Consideration and Initiating Structure in Leadership Research." *Journal of Applied Psychology* 89 (2004), pp. 36–51.

48. Aditya et al., "Theory and Practice of Leadership"; Den Hartog and Koopman, "Leadership in Organizations"; House and Aditya, "The Social Scientific Study of Leadership"; Korman, A.K. "'Consideration,' 'Initiating Structure,' and Organizational Criteria—A Review." *Personnel Psychology* 19 (1966), pp. 349–61; Yukl, *Leadership in Organizations;* Yukl, G., and D.D. Van Fleet. "Theory and Research on Leadership in Organizations." In *Handbook of Industrial and Organizational Psychology,* Vol. 3, eds. M.D. Dunnette and L.M. Hough. Palo Alto, CA: Consulting Psychologists Press, 1992, pp. 147–97.

49. Judge et al., "The Forgotten Ones?"

50. Hersey, P., and K.H. Blanchard. "Life Cycle Theory of Leadership." *Training and Development Journal,* May 1969, pp. 26–34; Hersey, P., and K.H. Blanchard. "So You Want to Know Your Leadership Style?" *Training and Development Journal,* February 1974, pp. 22–37; Hersey, P., and K.H. Blanchard. *Management of Organizational Behaviour,* 6th ed. Englewood Cliffs, NJ: Prentice Hall, 1993.

51. Hersey and Blanchard, *Management of Organizational Behaviour.*

52. Ibid.

53. Ibid.

54. Ibid.

55. Ibid.

56. Ibid.

57. Fernandez, C.F., and R.P. Vecchio. "Situational Leadership Revisited: A Test of an Across-Jobs Perspective." *Leadership Quarterly* 8 (1997), pp. 67–84.

58. Vecchio, R.P. "Situational Leadership Theory: An Examination of a Prescriptive Theory." *Journal of Applied Psychology* 72 (1987), pp. 444–51; Norris, W.R., and R.P. Vecchio. "Situational Leadership Theory: A Replication." *Group and Organization Management* 17 (1992), pp. 331–42.

59. Vecchio, "Situational Leadership Theory"; Norris and Vecchio, "Situational Leadership Theory: A Replication"; Blank, W., J.R. Weitzel, and S.G. Green. "A Test of Situational Leadership Theory." *Personnel Psychology* 43 (1990), pp. 579–97.

60. Fernandez and Vecchio, "Situational Leadership Theory Revisited."

61. Hersey and Blanchard, "Life Cycle Theory of Leadership"; Hersey and Blanchard, *Management of Organizational Behaviour.*

62. Strage, A., and T.S. Brandt. "Authoritative Parenting and College Students' Academic Adjustment and Success." *Journal of Educational Psychology* 91 (1999), pp. 146–56.

63. Grow, B. "Out at Home Depot." *BusinessWeek,* January 15, 2007, pp. 56–62.

64. Grow, B. "Renovating Home Depot." *BusinessWeek,* March 6, 2006, pp. 50–58.

65. Ibid.; Grow, "Out at Home Depot."

66. Sellers, P. "Six Sigma Man: Another GE Vet Atop Home Depot." *Fortune,* January 22, 2007, p. 30; Grow, "Renovating Home Depot."

67. Bass, B.M., and R.E. Riggio. *Transformational Leadership,* 2nd ed. Mahwah, NJ: Lawrence Erlbaum Associates, 2006; Bass, B.M. *Leadership and Performance Beyond Expectations.* New York: The Free Press, 1985; Burns, L.M. *Leadership.* New York: Harper & Row, 1978.

68. Bass, *Leadership and Performance Beyond Expectations.*

69. Ibid.

70. Bass and Riggio, *Transformational Leadership.*

71. Ibid.; Bass, B.M., and B.J. Avolio. *MLQ: Multifactor Leadership Questionnaire.* Redwood City, CA: Mind Garden, 2000.

72. Bass and Riggio, *Transformational Leadership;* Bass, *Leadership and Performance Beyond Expectations;* Burns, *Leadership.*

73. Bass and Riggio, *Transformational Leadership.*

74. Bass, *Leadership and Performance Beyond Expectations.*

75. Bass and Riggio, *Transformational Leadership;* Bass and Avolio, *MLQ.*

76. Bass and Riggio, *Transformational Leadership.*

77. Ibid; Bass and Avolio, *MLQ.*

78. Bass and Riggio, *Transformational Leadership.*

79. Ibid.; Bass and Avolio, *MLQ.*

80. Judge, T.A., and R.F. Piccolo. "Transformational and Transactional Leadership: A Meta-Analytic Test of their Relative Validity." *Journal of Applied Psychology* 89 (2004), pp. 755–68.

81. Ibid.

82. Bass and Riggio, *Transformational Leadership.*

83. Ibid.

84. Ibid.; Bass and Avolio, *MLQ.*

85. Conger, J.A. "Charismatic and Transformational Leadership in Organizations: An Insider's Perspective on these Developing Research Streams." *Leadership Quarterly* 10 (1999), pp. 145–79.

86. Young and Simon, *iCon.*

87. Johnson, A.M., P.A. Vernon, J.M. McCarthy, M. Molso, J.A. Harris, and K.J. Jang. "Nature vs. Nurture: Are Leaders Born or Made? A Behaviour Genetic Investigation of Leadership Style." *Twin Research* 1 (1998), pp. 216–23.

88. Judge, T.A., and J.E. Bono. "Five-Factor Model of Personality and Transformational Leadership." *Journal of Applied Psychology* 85 (2000), pp. 751–65.

89. Bass and Riggio, *Transformational Leadership.*

90. Conger, "Charismatic and Transformational Leadership in Organizations."

91. Bass and Riggio, *Transformational Leadership;* Bass and Avolio, *MLQ.*

92. Young and Simon, *iCon.*

93. Ibid.

94. House, R.J., P.J. Hanges, M. Javidan, P.W. Dorfman, and V. Gupta. *Culture, Leadership, and Organizations.* Thousand Oaks, CA: Sage, 2004.

95. Dorfman, P.W., P.J. Hanges, and F.C. Brodbeck. "Leadership and Cultural Variation: The Identification of Culturally Endorsed Leadership Profiles." In *Culture, Leadership, and Organizations,* eds. R.J. House, P.J. Hanges, M. Javidan, P.W. Dorfman, and V. Gupta. Thousand Oaks, CA: Sage, 2004, pp. 669–720.

96. Javidan, M., R.J. House, and P.W. Dorfman. "A Nontechnical Summary of GLOBE Findings." In *Culture, Leadership, and Organizations,* eds. R.J. House, P.J. Hanges, M. Javidan, P.W. Dorfman, and V. Gupta. Thousand Oaks, CA: Sage, 2004, pp. 29–48.

97. Dorfman et al., "Leadership and Cultural Variation."

98. Bass and Riggio, *Transformational Leadership.*

99. Ibid.; Bass and Avolio, *MLQ.*

100. Bass and Riggio, *Transformational Leadership.*

101. Ibid.; Bass and Avolio, *MLQ.*

102. Young and Simon, *iCon.*

103. Lowe, K.B., K.G. Kroeck, and N. Sivasubramaniam. "Effectiveness Correlates of Transformational and Transactional Leadership: A Meta-Analytic Review of the MLQ Literature." *Leadership Quarterly* 7 (1996), pp. 385–425.

104. Howell, J.M., and B.J. Avolio. "Transformational Leadership, Transactional Leadership, Locus of Control, and Support for Innovation: Key Predictors of Consolidated-Business-Unit Performance." *Journal of Applied Psychology* 78 (1993), pp. 891–902; Howell, J.M., D.J. Neufeld, and B.J. Avolio. "Examining the Relationship of Leadership and Physical Distance with Business Unit Performance." *Leadership Quarterly* 16 (2005), pp. 273–85; Keller, R.T. "Transformational Leadership, Initiating Structure, and Substitutes for Leadership: A Longitudinal Study of Research and Development Project Team Performance." *Journal of Applied Psychology* 91 (2006), pp. 202–10; Waldman, D.A., G.G. Ramirez, R.J. House, and P. Puranam. "Does Leadership Matter? CEO Leadership Attributes and Profitability under Conditions of Perceived Environmental Uncertainty." *Academy of Management Journal* 44 (2001), pp. 134–43.

105. Howell, J.M., and K.E. Hall-Merenda. "The Ties That Bind: The Impact of Leader-Member Exchange, Transformational and Transactional Leadership, and Distance on Predicting Follower Performance." *Journal of Applied Psychology* 84 (1999), pp. 680–94; Piccolo, R.F., and J.A. Colquitt. "Transformational Leadership and Job Behaviours: The Mediating Role of Core Job Characteristics." *Academy of Management Journal* 49 (2006), pp. 327–40; Wang, H., K.S. Law, R.D. Hackett, D. Wang, and Z.X. Chen. "Leader-

Member Exchange as a Mediator of the Relationship Between Transformational Leadership and Followers' Performance and Organizational Citizenship Behaviour." *Academy of Management Journal* 48 (2005), pp. 420–32.

106. Judge and Piccolo, "Transformational and Transactional Leadership"; Podsakoff, P.M., S.B. MacKenzie, J.B. Paine, and D.G. Bachrach. "Organizational Citizenship Behaviours: A Critical Review of the Theoretical and Empirical Literature and Suggestions for Future Research." *Journal of Management* 26 (2000), pp. 513–63.

107. Judge and Piccolo, "Transformational and Transactional Leadership."

108. Avolio, B.J., W. Zhu, W. Koh, and P. Bhatia. "Transformational Leadership and Organizational Commitment: Mediating Role of Psychological Empowerment and Moderating Role of Structural Distance." *Journal of Organizational Behaviour* 25 (2004), pp. 951–68; Kirkpatrick, S.A., and E.A. Locke. "Direct and Indirect Effects of Three Core Charismatic Leadership Components on Performance and Attitudes." *Journal of Applied Psychology* 81 (1996), pp. 36–51; Shamir, B., E. Zakay, E. Breinin, and M. Popper. "Correlates of Charismatic Leader Behaviours in Military Units: Subordinates' Attitudes, Unit Characteristics, and Superiors' Appraisals of Leader Performance." *Academy of Management Journal* 41 (1998), pp. 387–409.

109. Podsakoff, P.M., S.B. MacKenzie, and W.H. Bommer. "Transformational Leader Behaviours and Substitutes for Leadership as Determinants of Employee Satisfaction, Commitment, Trust, and Organizational Citizenship Behaviours." *Journal of Management* 22 (1996), pp. 259–98; Podsakoff, P.M., S.B. MacKenzie, R.H. Moorman, and R. Fetter. "Transformational Leader Behaviours and their Effects on Followers' Trust in Leader, Satisfaction, and Organizational Citizenship Behaviours." *Leadership Quarterly* 1 (1990), pp. 107–42; Shamir et al., "Correlates of Charismatic Leader Behaviours."

110. Meyer, J.P., D.J. Stanley, L. Herscovitch, and L. Topolnytsky. "Affective, Continuance, and Normative Commitment to the Organization: A Meta-Analysis of Antecedents, Correlates, and Consequences." *Journal of Vocational Behaviour* 61 (2002), pp. 20–52.

111. Judge and Piccolo, "Transformational and Transactional Leadership."

112. Piccolo and Colquitt, "Transformational Leadership and Job Behaviours." See also Bono, J.E., and T.A. Judge. "Self-Concordance at Work: Toward Understanding the Motivational Effects of Transformational Leaders." *Academy of Management Journal* 46 (2003), pp. 554–71; Shin, S.J., and J. Zhou. "Transformational Leadership, Conservation, and Creativity: Evidence from Korea." *Academy of Management Journal* 46 (2003), pp. 703–14.

113. Bono, J.E., and R. Ilies. "Charisma, Positive Emotions, and Mood Contagion." *Leadership Quarterly* 17 (2006), pp. 317–34; McColl-Kennedy, J.R., and R.D. Anderson. "Impact of Leadership Style and Emotions on Subordinate Performance." *Leadership Quarterly, 13* (2002), pp. 545–59.

114. Kerr, S., and J.M. Jermier. "Substitutes for Leadership: Their Meaning and Measurement." *Organizational Behaviour and Human Performance* 22 (1978), pp. 375–403.

115. Howell, J.P., P.W. Dorfman, and S. Kerr. "Moderator Variables in Leadership Research." *Academy of Management Review* 11 (1986), pp. 88–102.

116. Kerr and Jermier, "Substitutes for Leadership"; Jermier, J.M., and S. Kerr. "'Substitutes for Leadership: Their Meaning and Measurement': Contextual Recollections and Current Observations." *Leadership Quarterly* 8 (1997), pp. 95–101.

117. Howell, J.P., D.E. Bowen, P.W. Dorfman, S. Kerr, and P.M. Podsakoff. "Substitutes for Leadership: Effective Alternatives to Ineffective Leadership." *Organizational Dynamics* Summer 1990, pp. 21–38.

118. Podsakoff, P.M., and S.B. MacKenzie. "Kerr and Jermier's Substitutes for Leadership Model: Background, Empirical Assessment, and Suggestions for Future Research." *Leadership Quarterly* 8 (1997), pp. 117–25; Podsakoff, P.M., B.P. Niehoff, S.B. MacKenzie, and M.L. Williams. "Do Substitutes for Leadership Really Substitute for Leadership? An Empirical Examination of Kerr and Jermier's Situational Leadership Model." *Organizational Behaviour and Human Decision Processes* 54 (1993), pp. 1–44; Podsakoff et al., "Transformational Leadership Behaviours and Substitutes for Leadership"; Podsakoff, P.M., S.B. MacKenzie, M. Ahearne, and W.H. Bommer. "Searching for a Needle in a Haystack: Trying to Identify the Illusive Moderators of Leadership Behaviour." *Journal of Management* 21 (1995), pp. 422–70.

119. Howell et al., "Substitutes for Leadership: Effective Alternatives."

120. Gist, M.E., and D. McDonald-Mann. "Advances in Leadership Training and Development." In *Industrial and Organizational Psychology: Linking Theory with Practice,* ed. C.L. Cooper and E.A. Locke. Malden, MA: Blackwell, 2000, pp. 52–71.

121. Ibid; Dvir, T., D. Eden, B.J. Avolio, and B. Shamir. "Impact of Transformational Leadership on Follower Development and Performance: A Field Experiment." *Academy of Management Journal* 45 (2000), pp. 735–44; Barling, J., T. Weber, and E.K. Kelloway. "Effects of Transformational Leadership Training on Attitudinal and Financial Outcomes: A Field Experiment." *Journal of Applied Psychology* 81 (1996), pp. 827–32.

122. Barling, et al., "Effects of Transformational Leadership Training."

Chapter 13

1. Sony Canada corporate Web site (www.sony.ca/view/homepage.htm). Accessed April 16 2009

2. Singer, M. "Stringer's Way." *The New Yorker,* June 5, 2006, pp. 46–57.

3. Kane, Y.I., and P. Dvorak. "Howard Stringer, Japanese CEO." *The Wall Street Journal,* March 3, 2007, pp. A1, A6.

4. Singer, "Stringer's Way."

5. Hackman, J. R., and G. R. Oldham. *Work Redesign.* Reading, MA: Addison-Wesley, 1980.

6. Simon, H. *Administrative Behaviour.* New York: Macmillan, 1947.

7. Edwards, C. "Shaking Up Intel's Insides." *BusinessWeek,* January 31, 2005, p. 35.

8. Meier, K.J., and J. Bohte. "Ode to Luther Gulick: Span of Control and Organizational Performance." *Administration and Society* 32 (2000), pp. 115–37.

9. Theobald, N.A., and S. Nicholson-Crotty. "The Many Faces of Span of Control: Organizational Structure Across Multiple Goals." *Administration and Society* 36 (2005), pp. 648–60.

10. Child, J., and M. McGrath. "Organizations Unfettered: Organizational Forms in an Information-Intensive Economy." *Academy of Management Journal* 44 (2001), pp. 1135–48.

11. Hymowitz, C. "Today's Bosses Find Mentoring Isn't Worth the Time and Risks." *The Wall Street Journal,* March 13, 2006, p. B1.

12. Nuttal, C. "Intel Cuts 1,000 Management Jobs." *Financial Times,* July 14, 2006, p. 23.

13. Marquez, J. "Many Businesses, but One Mission." *Workforce Management,* June 12, 2006, pp. 32–36.

14. Scott, W.R., and G. F. Davis. *Organizations and Organizing: Rational, Natural, and Open System Perspectives.* New Jersey: Pearson Prentice Hall, 2007.

15. Porter, M. *Competitive Strategy.* New York: The Free Press, 1980.

16. Woodward, J. *Industrial Organization: Theory and Practice.* London: Oxford University Press, 1965.

17. Miller, C.C., W.H. Glick, Y. Wang, and G.P. Huber. "Understanding Technology–Structure Relationships: Theory Development and Meta-Analytic Theory Testing." *Academy of Management Journal* 34 (1991), pp. 370–99.

18. Gooding, J.Z., and J.A. Wagner III. "A Meta-Analytic Review of the Relationship Between Size and Performance: The Productivity and Efficiency of Organizations and their Subunits." *Administrative Science Quarterly* 30 (1985), pp. 462–81. See also Bluedorn, A.C. "Pilgrim's Progress: Trends and

Convergence in Research on Organizational Size and Environments." *Journal of Management* 21 (1993), pp. 163–92.

19. Lawler, E.E., III. "Rethinking Organizational Size." *Organizational Dynamics,* 26 (1997), pp. 24–35.
20. Scott and Davis, *Organizations and Organizing.*
21. Miles, R.E., and C.C. Snow. *Organizational Strategy, Structure, and Process.* New York: McGraw-Hill, 1978.
22. Turban, D.B., and T.L. Keon. "Organizational Attractiveness: An Interactionist Perspective." *Journal of Applied Psychology* 78 (1993), pp. 184–93.
23. Shaw, M. "Boxing It Up the Right Way." *Pulp & Paper,* September 2006, pp. 31–34.
24. Lashinsky, A. "The Hurd Way: How a Sales-Obsessed CEO Rebooted HP." *Fortune,* April 17, 2006, pp. 92–102.
25. Hosford, C. "Behind the Regus-HQ Merger: A Clash of Cultures that Wasn't." *Sales and Marketing Management,* March 2006, pp. 47–48.
26. Burns, L.R., and D.R. Wholey. "Adoption and Abandonment of Matrix Management Programs: Effects of Organizational Characteristics and Interorganizational Programs." *Academy of Management Journal* 36 (1993), pp. 106–38.
27. Hackman, J.R. "The Design of Work Teams." In *Handbook of Organizational Behaviour,* ed. J.W. Lorsch. New Jersey: Prentice Hall, 1987, pp. 315–42.
28. Hamm, S. "Big Blue Shift." *BusinessWeek,* June 5, 2006, pp. 108–10.
29. Larson, E.W., and D.H. Gobeli. "Matrix Management: Contradictions and Insight." *California Management Review* 29 (1987), pp. 126–38.
30. Rees, D.W., and C. Porter. "Matrix Structures and the Training Implications." *Industrial and Commercial Training* 36 (2004), pp. 189–93.
31. Areva NP corporate Web site (www.areva-np.com). Accessed April 26, 2007.
32. "One provincial board to govern Alberta's health system." Province of Alberta news release. May 15, 2008. Accessed April 20, 2009, at www.alberta.ca/acn/200805/23523ED9498C0- 0827-451C-E98A0B8430DC1879.html.
33. Noer, D.M. *Healing the Wounds.* San Francisco: Jossey-Bass, 1993; Mishra, K.; G.M. Spreitzer; and A. Mishra. "Preserving Employee Morale During Downsizing." *Sloan Management Review* 39 (1998), pp. 83–95.
34. Conlin, M. "The Big Squeeze on Workers; Is There a Risk to Wringing More from a Smaller Staff?" *BusinessWeek,* May 13, 2002, p. 96.
35. Brockner, J., G. Spreitzer, A. Mishra, W. Hockwarter, L. Pepper, and J. Weinberg. "Perceived Control as an Antidote to the Negative Effects of Layoffs on Survivors' Organizational Commitment and Job Performance." *Administrative Science Quarterly* 49 (2004), pp. 76–100.
36. Brockner, J. "The Effects of Work Layoffs on Survivors: Research, Theory and Practice." In *Research in Organizational Behaviour,* Vol. 10, eds. B.M. Staw and L.L. Cummings. Berkeley: University of California Press, 1988, pp. 213–55.

Chapter 14

1. Useem, J. "America's Most Admired Companies." *Fortune,* March 7, 2005, p. 67.
2. McLean, B., and P. Elkind. *Smartest Guys in the Room: The Amazing Rise and Scandalous Fall of Enron.* New York: Portfolio Publishing, 2003.
3. Useem, J. "Another Boss, Another Revolution." *Fortune,* April 5, 2004, pp. 112–17; Haasen, A., and G.F. Shea. *New Corporate Cultures that Motivate.* Westport, CT: Praeger, 2003.
4. Lear, R.W. "Jack Welch Speaks: Wisdom from the World's Greatest Business Leader." *Chief Executive,* July/August 1998, p. 64.
5. McLean and Elkind, *Smartest Guys.*
6. Haasen and Shea, *New Corporate Cultures.*
7. Fowler, T. "The Pride and Fall of Enron." *Houston Chronicle,* Oct. 20, 2002. Accessed on www.chron.com on January 29, 2007.
8. McLean and Elkind, *Smartest Guys.*
9. Verbeke, W., M. Volgering, and M. Hessels. "Exploring the Conceptual Expansion within the Field of Organizational Behaviour: Organizational Climate and Organizational Culture." *Journal of Management Studies* 35 (1998), pp. 303–29.

10. Deal, T.E., and A.A. Kennedy. *Corporate Cultures: The Rites and Rituals of Corporate Life.* Reading, MA: Addison-Wesley, 1982.

11. Adapted from O'Reilly, C.A., III, J. Chatman, and D.L. Caldwell. "People and Organizational Culture: A Profile Comparison Approach to Assessing Person–Organization Fit." *Academy of Management Journal* 34 (1991), pp. 487–516; Tsui, A.S., Z. Zhang, W. Hui, K.R. Xin, and J.B. Wu. "Unpacking the Relationship between CEO Leadership Behaviour and Organizational Culture." *The Leadership Quarterly* 17 (2006), pp. 113–37.

12. O'Reilly, C.A., and Jennifer A. Chatman. "Culture as Social Control: Corporations, Cults, and Commitment." In *Research in Organizational Behaviour,* Vol. 18, eds. Barry M. Staw and L.L. Cummings. Stamford, CT: JAI Press, 1996, pp. 157–200.

13. Chatman, J.A. "Matching People and Organizations: Selection and Socialization in Public Accounting Firms." *Administrative Science Quarterly* 36 (1991), pp. 459–84.

14. Trice, H.M., and J.M. Beyer. *The Cultures of Work Organizations.* Englewood Cliffs, NJ: Prentice Hall, 1993.

15. Shuit, D. P. "Yum Does a 360." *Workforce Management,* April 2005, pp. 59–60.

16. Kiger, P.J. "Corporate Crunch." *Workforce Management,* April 2005, pp. 32–38.

17. "2007 Corporate Social Responsibility Report." TELUS Corporation.

18. Higgins, J.M., and C. McAllaster. "If You Want Strategic Change, Don't Forget to Change Your Cultural Artifacts." *Journal of Change Management* 4 (2004), pp. 63–74.

19. "EnCana Corporate Constitution." July 2003. Accessed March 2008 at www.encana.com/aboutus/corporate constitution/index.htm.

20. Schein, E.H. "Organizational Culture." *American Psychologist* 45 (1990), pp. 109–19.

21. Schein, E. H. *Organization Culture and Leadership.* San Francisco, CA: Jossey-Bass, 2004.

22. Schein, E.H. "What Is Culture?" In *Reframing Organizational Culture,* ed. P.J. Frost, L.F. Moore, M.R. Louis, C.C. Lundberg, and J. Martin. Beverly Hills, CA: Sage, 1991, pp. 243–53.

23. Goffee, R., and G. Jones. *The Character of a Corporation.* New York: Harper Business, 1998.

24. Schneider, B., D.E. Bowen, M.G. Ehrhart, and K.M. Holcombe. "The Climate for Service: Evolution of a Construct." In *Handbook of Organizational Culture and Climate,* eds. N.M. Ashkanasy, C. Wilderom, and M.F. Peterson. Thousand Oaks, CA, Sage, 2000.

25. Schneider, B., M.G. Ehrhart, D.M. Mayer, J.L. Saltz, and K. Niles-Jolly. "Understanding Organization–Customer Links in Service Settings." *Academy of Management Journal* 48 (2005), pp. 1017–32.

26. "WestJet Culture." WestJet Corporate Web site. Accessed February 16, 2009, at http://c5dsp.westjet.com/guest/media/investorMedia.jsp?id=Facts.

27. Zohar, D., and G. Luria. "Climate as a Social-Cognitive Construction of Supervisory Safety Practices: Scripts as a Proxy of Behaviour Patterns." *Journal of Applied Psychology* 89 (2004), pp. 322–33.

28. Hofmann, D.A., F.P. Morgeson, and S.J. Gerras. "Climate as a Moderator of the Relationship Between Leader-Member Exchange and Content Specific Citizenship: Safety Climate as an Exemplar." *Journal of Applied Psychology* 88 (2003), pp. 170–78.

29. "2007 Sustainability Report (Health and Safety)." Syncrude Canada Ltd. Accessed February 16, 2009, at http://sustainability.syncrude.ca/sustainability2007/social/health.

30. Clarke, S. "Perceptions of Organizational Safety: Implications for the Development of Safety Culture." *Journal of Organizational Behaviour* 20 (1999), pp. 185–98.

31. RBC corporate Web site (www.rbc.com), accessed April 2008; Hirji, Z. "Growth and Innovation Rests on Diversity." *Canadian HR Reporter,* December 2006, p. 18; Shin, M. "Minority Report." *CorporateKnights: The Cleantech Issue 2007,* Volume 6.2, pp. 34–42.

32. Ibid.

33. McLean, L.D. "Organizational Culture's Influence on Creativity and Innovation: A Review of the Literature and Implications for Human Resource Development." *Advances in Developing Human Resources* 7 (2005), pp. 226–46.

34. Frauenheim, E. "On the Clock but Off on Their Own: Pet-Project Programs Set to Gain Wider Acceptance." *Workforce Management* April 24, 2006, pp. 40–41.

35. Poulton, T. "Got a Creative Creative Process? Fostering Creativity in an ROI-Focused Cubicle-Ridden Environment Ain't Easy. Here's How to Get your Team's Juices Flowing." *Strategy,* April 2006, p. 11.

36. O'Reilly, C.A. "Corporations, Culture, and Commitment: Motivation and Social Control in Organizations." *California Management Review* 31 (1989), pp. 9–25.

37. O'Reilly et al., "People and Organizational Culture."

38. Schein, E.H. "Three Cultures of Management: The Key to Organizational Learning." *Sloan Management Review* 38 (1996), pp. 9–20.

39. Boisner A., and J. Chatman. "The Role of Subcultures in Agile Organizations." In *Leading and Managing People in Dynamic Organizations,* eds. R. Petersen and E. Mannix. Mahwah, NJ: Lawrence Erlbaum Associates, 2003.

40. See Howard-Grenville, J.A. "Inside the 'BLACK BOX': How Organizational Culture and Subcultures Inform Interpretations and Actions on Environmental Issues." *Organization & Environment* 19 (2006) , pp. 46–73; Jermier, J., J. Slocum, L. Fry, and J. Gaines. "Organizational Subcultures in a Soft Bureaucracy: Resistance Behind the Myth and Façade of an Official Culture." *Organizational Science* 2 (1991), pp. 170–94.

41. Schneider, B., H.W. Goldstein, and D.B. Smith. "The ASA Framework: An Update." *Personnel Psychology* 48 (1995), pp. 747–73.

42. Graf, A.B. "Building Corporate Cultures." *Chief Executive,* March 2005, p. 18.

43. Ruiz, G. "Tall Order." *Workforce Management,* April 2006, pp. 22–29.

44. For good summaries of socialization, see Fisher, C.D. "Organizational Socialization: An Integrative View." *Research in Personnel and Human Resource Management* 4 (1986), pp. 101–45; Bauer, T. N., E.W. Morrison, and R.R. Callister. "Organizational Socialization: A Review and Directions for Future Research." In *Research in Personnel and Human Resource Management,* Vol. 16, ed. G.R. Ferris. Greenwich, CT: JAI Press, 1998, pp. 149–214.

45. Cable, D.M., L. Aiman-Smith, P.W. Mulvey, and J.R. Edwards. "The Sources and Accuracy of Job Applicants' Beliefs about Organizational Culture." *Academy of Management Journal* 43 (2000), pp. 1076–85; Louis, M.R. "Surprise and Sense-Making: What Newcomers Experience in Entering Unfamiliar Organizational Settings." *Administrative Science Quarterly* 25 (1980), pp. 226–51.

46. Chao, G.T., A. O'Leary-Kelly, S. Wolf, H.J. Klein, and P.D. Gardner. "Organizational Socialization: Its Content and Consequences." *Journal of Applied Psychology* 79 (1994), pp. 450–63.

47. Ibid.; Klein, H., and N. Weaver. "The Effectiveness of an Organizational-Level Orientation Training Program in the Socialization of New Hires." *Personnel Psychology,* Spring 2000, pp 47–66; Wesson, M. J., and C.I. Gogus. "Shaking Hands with a Computer: An Examination of Two Methods of Organizational Newcomer Orientation." *Journal of Applied Psychology* 90 (2005), pp. 1018–26.

48. Gravelle, M. "The Five Most Common Hiring Mistakes and How to Avoid Them." *The Canadian Manager* 29 (2004), pp. 11–13.

49. Van Maanen, J., and E.H. Schein. "Toward a Theory of Organizational Socialization." *Research in Organizational Behaviour* 1 (1979), pp. 209–64.

50. Ashford, S.J., and J.S. Black. "Proactivity During Organizational Entry: The Role of Desire for Control." *Journal of Applied Psychology,* 81 (1996), pp. 199–214; Kim, T., D.M. Cable, and S. Kim. "Socialization Tactics, Employee Proactivity, and Person–Organization Fit." *Journal of Applied Psychology* 90 (2005), pp. 232–41.

51. Mourier, P., and M. Smith. *Conquering Organizational Change: How to Succeed Where Most Companies Fail.* Atlanta: CEP Press, 2001.

52. McCracken, J. "'Way Forward' Requires Culture Shift at Ford." *The Wall Street Journal,* January 23, 2006, p. B1.

53. Schein, *Organization Culture and Leadership.*

54. Gubbins, E. "Nortel's New Execs Bring Cisco Experience." *Telephony,* April 11, 2005. pp. 14–15.

55. Weber, Y. "Measuring Cultural Fit in Mergers and Acquisitions." In *Handbook of Organizational Culture and Climate,* eds. N.M. Ashkanasy, C. Wilderom, and M.F. Peterson. Thousand Oaks, CA; Sage, pp. 309–20.

56. Brahy, S. "Six Solution Pillars for Successful Cultural Integration of International M&As." *Journal of Organizational Excellence,* Autumn 2006, pp. 53–63.

57. Platt, G. "Global Merger Activity Sets Record Pace." *Global Finance* 20 (2006), p. 60.

58. Edmondson, G. "Auf Wiedersehen, Mitsubishi." *BusinessWeek,* November 11, 2005, Accessed through www.businessweek.com on February 9, 2007; Bremmer, B. "A Tale of Two Auto Mergers." *BusinessWeek,* April 29, 2004, Accessed through www.businessweek.com on February 9, 2007.

59. Ewing, J. "Nokia and Siemens: Exciting the Market." *BusinessWeek,* June 19, 2006.

60. Stahl, G.K., and M.E. Mendenhall. *Mergers and Acquisitions: Managing Culture and Human Resources.* Stanford, CA: Stanford University Press, 2005.

61. Gibson, R. "Package Deal: UPS's Purchase of Mail Boxes Etc. Looked Great on Paper. Then Came the Culture Clash." *The Wall Street Journal,* May 8, 2006, p. R13.

62. Kristof-Brown, A.L., R.D. Zimmerman, and E.C. Johnson, "Consequences of Individuals' Fit at Work: A Meta-Analysis of Person–Job, Person–Organization, Person–Group, and Person–Supervisor Fit," *Personnel Psychology* 58 (2005), pp. 281–342.

63. Barber, A.E. *Recruiting Employees: Individual and Organizational Perspectives.* Thousand Oaks, CA: Sage, 1998.

64. Wanous, J.P. *Organizational Entry: Recruitment, Selection, Orientation and Socialization of Newcomers.* Reading, MA: Addison-Wesley, 1992.

65. Gravelle, "The Five Most Common Hiring Mistakes."

66. Anderson, N.R., N.A. Cunningham-Snell, and J. Haigh. "Induction Training as Socialization: Current Practice and Attitudes to Evaluation in British Organizations," *International Journal of Selection and Assessment* 4 (1996), pp. 169–83.

67. Wesson and Gogus, "Shaking Hands with a Computer."

68. Ibid.; Klein and Weaver, "The Effectiveness."

69. Marquez, J. "Despite Job Cuts, GM May Expand New-Hire Networking Program." *Workforce Management,* March 27, 2006, p. 16.

70. Wanberg, C.R., E.T. Welsh, and S.A. Hezlett. "Mentoring Research: A Review and Dynamic Process Model." *Research in Personnel and Human Resources Management* 22 (2003), pp. 39–124.

71. Allen, T.D., L.T. Eby, M.L. Poteet, E. Lentz, and L. Lima. "Outcomes Associated with Mentoring Protégés: A Meta-Analysis." *Journal of Applied Psychology* 89 (2004), pp. 127–36.

Photo Credits

Chapter 1

Page 2: Courtesy of Boston Pizza International Inc.
Page 9: Lethbridge Herald / Al Beeber
Page 16: © Corbis/SYGMA
Page 18: Chris Rank / Bloomberg News / Landov

Chapter 2

Page 27: John McPhee
Page 30: © Disney Enterprises, Inc. / Pixar Animation Studios / Photofest NYC
Page 37: © BananaStock / PunchStock
Page 39: Courtesy of Dr. Sandra L. Robinson

Chapter 3

Page 48: Dennis Van Tine / Landov
Page 52: Liquidlibrary / JupiterImages
Page 57: © François Duhamel / Sygma / Corbis
Page 59 (upper): Courtesy of Dr. John Meyer
Page 59 (lower): Courtesy of Dr. Natalie Allen
Page 62: © The New Yorker Collection 1994 Robert Mankoff from cartoonbank.com. All rights reserved.

Chapter 4

Page 72: Courtesy of Innovation Place, www.innovationplace.com
Page 73: Reprinted with permission of Peter Vey
Page 85: © TongRo Image Stock / Alamy
Page 91: © Warner Bros. / Photofest
Page 92: Courtesy of Dr. Stéphane Côté

Chapter 5

Page 103: CP / J.P. Moczulski
Page 106: © Image Source Pink / Alamy
Page 108: © The New Yorker Collection 2000 Gahan Wilson from cartoonbank.com. All rights reserved.
Page 109: © Photofest Inc.
Page 112: © RF / Corbis
Page 114: Courtesy of Dr. Julian Barling
Page 118: Ryan McVay / Getty Images

Chapter 6

Page 131: Toronto Star Collection
Page 133 (top left): Steve Mason / Getty Images
Page 133 (middle left): Ryan McVay / Getty Images
Page 133 (bottom left): Nick Koudis / Getty Images
Page 133 (top middle): © Daniel Goodchild / Alamy
Page 133 (top right): Ryan McVay / Getty Images
Page 139: Sony Pictures Entertainment / Photofest
Page 140: Courtesy of Dr. Latham
Page 149: © The New Yorker Collection 2000 Tom Cheney from cartoonbank.com. All rights reserved.
Page 150: The McGraw-Hill Companies, Inc. / Rick Brady, photographer

Chapter 7

Page 160: Dick Loek / Toronto Star
Page 164: © Brand X Pictures / PunchStock
Page 166: © Photofest Inc.
Page 173: Courtesy of Dr. Ramona Bobocel
Page 176: AP / Wide World Photos
Page 178: © The New Yorker Collection 1975 Dana Fradon from cartoonbank.com. All rights reserved.

Chapter 8

Page 189: Getty / Yellow Dog Productions RF
Page 191: Dynamic Graphics / JupiterImages
Page 193: © Digital Vision
Page 195: © The New Yorker Collection 1993 Tom Cheney from cartoonbank.com. All rights reserved.
Page 198: Courtesy of Sally Maitlis
Page 201: PARAMOUNT / THE KOBAL COLLECTION / MARKS, ELLIOTT

Chapter 9

Page 217: Norbert von der Groeben/The Image Works
Page 221: © The New Yorker Collection 1996 J.B. Handelsman from cartoonbank.com. All rights reserved.
Page 222: © Universal Studios / Photofest
Page 224: RF / Corbis
Page 225: AP / World Wide Photos
Page 231: © NBC Photographer: Paul Drinkwater / Photofest

Page 233: © The New Yorker Collection 2001 David Sipress from cartoonbank.com. All rights reserved.
Page 234: Courtesy of Dr. Kibeom Lee
Page 235: © Digital Vision

Chapter 10

Page 250: CP / Walt Disney
Page 260: © George Tiedemann / Corbis
Page 261: Courtesy Dr. Kevin Tasa
Page 262: © Ryan McVay / Getty Images
Page 264: © Warner Bros. / Photofest
Page 267: TRUMP PROD. / MARK BURNETT PROD. / THE KOBAL COLLECTION
Page 269: © SuperStock
Page 275: © The New York Times

Chapter 11

Page 284: © AP / Wide World Photos
Page 289: © The New Yorker Collection 1996 J.B. Handelsman from cartoonbank.com. All rights reserved.
Page 290: © Miramax / Photofest
Page 296: © The New Yorker Collection 2001 Alex Gregory from cartoonbank.com. All rights reserved.
Page 300: Courtesy of One Laptop Per Child
Page 303: Courtesy of Dr. Marylène Gagné

Chapter 12

Page 311 (left): © AP / Wide World Photos
Page 311 (right): © Krista Kennell / ZUMA / Corbis
Page 317: © The New Yorker Collection 2003 Alex Gregory from cartoonbank.com. All rights reserved.
Page 320: © New Line / Photofest
Page 325: Courtesy of Dr. Rick D. Hackett
Page 326: Tim Graham / Getty Images

Chapter 13

Page 341: AP / Wide World Photos
Page 343: © The New Yorker Collection 2003 Christopher Weyant from cartoonbank.com. All rights reserved.
Page 345: © Sunset Boulevard / Corbis
Page 348: LUCASFILM/20TH CENTURY FOX / THE KOBAL COLLECTION
Page 349: Courtesy of Dr. Michael Withey

Chapter 14

Page 545 (left): THOMAS LOHNES / AFP / Getty Images
Page 545 (right): © Richard Carson / Reuters / Corbis
Page 368: © The New Yorker Collection 1994 Mick Stevens from cartoonbank.com. All rights reserved.
Page 380: © Universal Studios / Photofest
Page 385: Courtesy of Dr. Jia Lin Xie

Name Index

Z

Company Index

L

M

N

O

P

Q

R

S

T

U

V

W

X

Y

Z

Subject Index

C

F

G

H

I

J

N

O

P

T

U

V

W

Z